Services in the International Economy

Keith E. Maskus, Peter M. Hooper, Edward E. Leamer, and
J. David Richardson, Editors
Quiet Pioneering: Robert M. Stern and His International Economic Legacy

Bjarne S. Jensen and Kar-yiu Wong, Editors
Dynamics, Economic Growth, and International Trade

Jagdish Bhagwati and Mathias Hirsch, Editors
The Uruguay Round and Beyond: Essays in Honor of Arthur Dunkel

Kala Marathe Krishna and Ling Hui Tan
Rags and Riches: Implementing Apparel Quotas under the Multi-Fibre Arrangement

Alan V. Deardorff and Robert M. Stern   *Measurement of Nontariff Barriers*

Thomas Cottier and Petros C. Mavroidis, Editors
The World Trade Forum, Volume I: State Trading in the Twenty-First Century

Rajesh Chadha, Sanjib Pohit, Alan V. Deardorff, and Robert M. Stern
The Impact of Trade and Domestic Policy Reforms in India: A CGE Modeling Approach

Alan V. Deardorff and Robert M. Stern, Editors
Constituent Interests and U.S. Trade Policies

Gary R. Saxonhouse and T. N. Srinivasan, Editors
Development, Duality, and the International Economic Regime: Essays in Honor of Gustav Ranis

Charles P. Kindleberger   *Essays in History: Financial, Economic, Personal*

Keith Acheson and Christopher Maule
Much Ado about Culture: North American Trade Disputes

Alan V. Deardorff and Robert M. Stern   *Social Dimensions of U.S. Trade Policies*

Thomas Cottier and Petros C. Mavroidis, Editors
Regulatory Barriers and the Principle of Non-Discrimination in World Trade Law

Bernard Hoekman and Jamel Zarrouk
Catching Up with the Competition: Trade Opportunities and Challenges for Arab Countries

Jun Fu
Institutions and Investments: Foreign Direct Investment in China during an Era of Reforms

Robert M. Stern, Editor   *Services in the International Economy*

Services in the International Economy

Robert M. Stern, Editor

Ann Arbor

THE UNIVERSITY OF MICHIGAN PRESS

Copyright © by the University of Michigan 2001
All rights reserved
Published in the United States of America by
The University of Michigan Press
Manufactured in the United States of America
♾ Printed on acid-free paper

2004   2003   2002   2001   4   3   2   1

A CIP catalog record for this book is available from the British Library.

Library of Congress Cataloging-in-Publication Data applied for
ISBN 0-472-11217-1 (cloth: alk. paper)

Contents

Part 2. Services and Economic Development

Part 3. Negotiating Options and Issues

Preface

This volume contains selected papers that were invited for presentation at the World Services Congress that was held in Atlanta, Georgia, on November 1-3, 1999. I served as Chair of the Academic Advisory Committee for the Congress and had the responsibility of soliciting a global Call for Papers and selecting those to be presented at the Congress. I was encouraged by Harry Freeman, President of The Mark Twain Foundation, to assemble a subset of what were considered to be the best of the invited papers and to publish them in the present volume. I am grateful to The Mark Twain Foundation and to the Capacity Building Project of the World Bank for financial support in preparing this volume.

I would like especially to thank Judith Jackson, now retired after 35 years of service in the University of Michigan School of Public Policy, for her superb and unflagging assistance in editing the papers and, in post-retirement, preparing the camera-ready copy for publication. We have worked together for many years on similar undertakings, and I owe her an enormous debt of gratitude.

I wish to dedicate this volume to Harry Freeman. He has worked tirelessly to call attention to the increasing importance of services in our economic lives. His efforts have been vital in encouraging research on the economic analysis and measurement of services activities. He has also personally played a central and active role in providing policy input that has been key in promoting the liberalization of services trade in the United States and globally. In all of these respects, he has been a genuine pioneer.

Robert M. Stern
Ann Arbor, Michigan
May 1, 2000

CHAPTER 1

An Overview of the First World Services Congress

Robert M. Stern

I. Introduction

The World Services Congress was held from November 1-3, 1999 in Atlanta, Georgia. The Congress was designed to enhance the level of awareness of the increasingly important role of services in the global economy as we enter a new century. It was an effort to reach out in this regard to governments, members of the business community, international organizations, academicians, and the media. A key objective of the Congress was to offer guidance to governments as they prepare for the Services 2000 negotiations to be carried out under the auspices of the World Trade Organization. A further objective was to provide a forum to members of the business community where they could share their know-how on obtaining and expanding their services operations in existing and new markets, including the provision of services to governments. Finally, the Congress served as a vehicle for the presentation and discussion of original research on the entire spectrum of services issues by business, government, and academic specialists.

J. Robert Vastine, President of the Coalition of Service Industries (CSI) Research and Education Foundation had the chief responsibility for the organization and fund raising for the Congress.[1] The Congress Chair was Dean R. O'Hare, Chairman and CEO, The Chubb Corporation. Three Advisory Committees were established to assist in organizing the Congress. The Business Advisory Committee was co-chaired by Gautam S. Kaji, Chairman, The Centennial Group, and former Managing Director, The World Bank, and Ken Whipple, former Chairman, Ford Financial Services Group, and Co-Chairman Emeritus, Financial Leaders Group. The Academic Advisory Group Chairman was Robert M. Stern, Professor of Economics and Public Policy in the Department of Economics and Gerald R. Ford School of Public Policy, University of Michigan, Ann Arbor. The Government Services Advisory Committee Chairman was Everett Ehrlich, President, ESC Incorporated, and former Undersecretary for Economic Affairs, U.S. Department of Commerce.

The Congress was organized in the form of plenary sessions that addressed issues of general interest for all participants. In addition, there were specialized breakout sessions in which issues of interest were presented and discussed by Congress participants. These included both panel discussions and the presentation of commissioned and invited papers. Details of the various sessions held over the three days of the Congress are given in Appendix 2 below. An important accomplishment of the Congress was the preparation of a series of recommendations on issues to be addressed in the Services 2000 negotiations. These recommendations were based on the discussions held in the Business Forums and Business Policy sessions at the Congress and were prepared by the chairmen and others involved in these sessions. The detailed recommendations are presented in Appendix 1 below.

Three preparatory conferences were held prior to and leading up to the World Services Congress. The first conference entitled, *GATS 2000: New Directions for Services Trade Liberalization*, was held in Washington, D.C. on June 1-2, 1999. This conference was organized by Pierre Sauvé, on leave from the OECD and a visiting faculty member at the Harvard University, Kennedy School of Government, and Research Associate at the Brookings Institution, together with Robert M. Stern of the University of Michigan. Commissioned papers were presented on cross-cutting and sectoral issues in the Services 2000 negotiations. The papers dealing with the cross-cutting issues were published by the Brookings Institution in early 2000 in a volume edited by Sauvé and Stern. The sectoral papers, which were commissioned by the American Enterprise Institute (AEI), dealt with: financial services; insurance; accounting; entertainment, video, culture; transportation; air freight, and electronic commerce. These sectoral papers are being edited by Claude Barfield and will be published by the AEI Press in the spring/summer of 2000. Most of the Brookings and AEI papers were also presented at the Atlanta Congress.

A second preparatory conference on "Global Services Trade and the Americas" was held in San Juan, Costa Rica, on July 8-9, 1999. It was sponsored by the Organization of American States (OAS), the Institute for the Integration of Latin America and the Caribbean of the Inter-American Development Bank, and the Minister of Foreign Trade of Costa Rica. The conference proceedings, *Services in the Western Hemisphere: Liberalization, Integration, and Reform*, edited by Sherry Stephenson of the OAS, are to be published in summer 2000 jointly by the Brookings Institution/OAS.

A third preparatory conference was held in Hong Kong in late August 1999 under the sponsorship of the Hong Kong Coalition of Service Industries. This conference focused mainly on services issues of interest to countries in Asia. The proceedings were not published.

Papers that were presented in the Business and Academic sessions at the World Services Congress consisted of many that had been prepared especially for the June 1-2 Washington conference noted above. In addition, a Call for Papers for the Congress academic sessions was widely circulated, and selections were made for the papers to be invited for presentation at the Congress. It was decided subsequently to select what were considered to be the best of these invited papers and to publish them in the present volume. The exceptions are the papers in Chapters 13 and 14, which are case studies of services issues in Senegal and Kenya and were commissioned as part of the Capacity Building Project at the World Bank.[2] They have been included in this volume to complement the other country studies in Part 2 of the volume.

To inform the reader about what each of the papers in the volume covers, chapter summaries are provided in Section II following. Section III discusses the implications for further research and policy.

II. Chapter Summaries

In **Chapter 2, Productivity in the Services Sector,** Jack E. Triplett and Barry P. Bosworth note that in some services industries, the concept of real output is unclear. They ask: what is the output of an insurance company? Of an economics or statistics consulting firm? In what units would those outputs be measured? When the economic concepts that statistical agencies measure are unclear, it is hardly surprising that their output measures and price indexes are problematic. And if it is difficult to measure the output of an industry, it must also be difficult to measure its productivity.

The importance of this topic is indicated by two facts. First, as Zvi Griliches has pointed out, the post-1973 slowdown in U.S. productivity growth is concentrated in precisely those industries in which output-measurement problems exist. For example, productivity growth in finance and insurance has been negative. Do measurement errors in output and price deflators contribute to the negative productivity trend? Second, those hard-to-measure services sectors are also accounting for a growing proportion of the economy. Their measurement problems are accordingly making an increasing impact on the nation's overall measures of economic performance.

Triplett and Bosworth are in charge of the Brookings Institution Program on Output and Productivity Measurement in the Services Sector, which is designed to address conceptual and measurement problems in the difficult-to-measure services industries. This chapter presents a progress report. It reviews measurement issues and recent research on a group of industries, including banking, insurance, retail and wholesale trade (including e-commerce), medical care, and business and professional services. In the case of medical care, it makes a preliminary assessment of the impact of measurement errors on productivity growth.

In **Chapter 3, Forecasting U.S. Trade in Services,** Alan V. Deardorff, Saul H. Hymans, Robert M. Stern, and Chong Xiang provide a set of forecasts of U.S. international trade in services, both at the aggregate level and for four subcategories. These subcategories are: travel, which is mostly tourist expenditures; passenger fares, which is mostly passenger air transportation; transportation, other than passenger transportation; and other private services, including education, financial services, insurance, telecommunications, and business, professional and technical services. A forecasting model is constructed and estimated, based on conventional economic forces of supply and demand and dependent on cost variables and income variables as well as relative prices. For forecasting purposes, these variables are taken from the Michigan Quarterly Econometric Model of the U.S. Economy, a macroeconometric forecasting model with forecasts provided regularly by the University of Michigan Research Seminar in Quantitative Economics.

The equations of the services trade model are reported and discussed, and the performance of the estimated equations is evaluated. The quarterly forecast paths are provided for both aggregate and sectoral services trade, including exports and imports, through the end of 2001. Results indicate that imports will continue to rise over the forecast period, while exports, after remaining nearly stationary for several quarters in some sectors in 1999, will resume their rise thereafter. This forecasting work is to be continued, and it is suggested, in addition, that future research would be useful to explore the determinants of the production and sales of foreign services affiliates of U.S. parent companies.

In **Chapter 4, Measurement and Classification of Service Sector Activity: Data Needs for GATS 2000**, Obie G. Whichard examines needs for statistics on trade in services, indicates in general terms what data are now available, describes the existing international body of methodological guidance for statistical compilation, discusses strategies for improving trade-in-services statistics, and identifies some of the data needs that remain unmet and some of the difficulties and special situations involved in data collection. Because it is likely that many of its readers are most interested in services statistics as a tool for supporting negotiations, Whichard devotes special attention to identifying areas where negotiators have adopted definitions that differ from those found in guidelines for statistical compilation.

Whichard investigates the availability of data on trade in services by tabulating numbers of countries reporting various types of services to the IMF and the OECD. This exercise indicates widespread coverage of services, such as travel and transportation, which have a lengthy history in international trade, but significantly less thorough (though improving) coverage of services, such as computer services and financial services, which have only recently become subject to significant trade. For services supplied through locally established foreign affiliates, statistical coverage is just getting underway in most countries. Often, it is limited to information on the activities of foreign-owned firms located in the compiling economy, which can be produced simply by identifying the foreign-owned subset of firms covered by existing domestic enterprise statistics. As might be expected, for both types of data, coverage appears best among the higher income developed countries.

A review of international guidelines for statistical compilation—that is, the "international methodological infrastructure for trade-in-services statistics"—focuses on the activities of the IMF, the OECD, and the UN, all of which have major statistical functions as integral parts of their work programs. The most detailed review is of the IMF *Balance of Payments Manual*, 5th edition, which is widely followed by balance-of-payments compilers and which provides guidance on both the definition and the classification of trade in services between residents of different countries. Particular attention is given to relationships between the guidelines for compilation and the definitions contained in or implied by the General Agreement on Trade in Services (GATS). In addition to reviewing the activities of the individual international organizations, Whichard describes the work of the Task Force on Statistics of International Trade in Services, through which these organizations are working together to prepare a statistical manual on trade-in-services that will specifically address needs posed by the GATS.

The process of improving data on trade in services is a multidimensional one, more likely to involve a number of small steps than a few large ones. Typically, the initial tasks must be preparatory ones that set the stage for actual improvements later on. These might include such tasks as securing or strengthening legal authority for data collection, identifying gaps in existing data, and developing a plan for sequencing improvements. The improvements themselves are discussed under three headings—methodological realignment, expanded surveying activity, and preparation of indirect estimates.

Whichard concludes by discussing four somewhat problematic issues in data collection—services sold to individuals, price data, mode-of-supply information, and data on affiliate activities related to outward direct investment.

In **Chapter 5, Multilateral Liberalization of Services Trade**, Philippa Dee and Kevin Hanslow compare the gains from eliminating barriers to trade in services with those from eliminating post-Uruguay Round barriers remaining in the traditional areas of agriculture and manufacturing. They use a computable general equilibrium (CGE) model that incorporates a bilateral treatment of foreign direct investment (FDI), one of the key vehicles by which services are traded internationally. This allows examination of the comprehensive removal of restrictions on all modes of service delivery, including restrictions on services delivered via FDI (though not on FDI more generally).

The modeling framework distinguishes barriers to commercial presence (primarily through FDI) from those affecting other modes of service delivery (cross-border supply, consumption abroad, and the presence of natural persons). It also distinguishes non-discriminatory barriers to market access from discriminatory restrictions on national treatment. It makes use of the first of a comprehensive new set of estimates of barriers to services trade.

Dee and Hanslow find that the world as a whole is projected to be better off by more than US$260 billion annually as a result of eliminating all post-Uruguay Round trade barriers. About US$50 billion of this would come from agricultural liberalization, and a further US$80 billion from liberalization of manufactures. This shows that there are still considerable gains to be had from liberalization in traditional areas, even if no progress is made in services. But an additional US$130 billion would come from liberalizing services trade.

And about US$100 billion of the gains from services liberalization would accrue in China alone.

The results highlight that services-trade liberalization could lead to a significant loss of rents generated by existing services-trade restrictions. This is especially the case for the United States and the European Union, economies that are important sources of current outward FDI. Their loss of rents would be partially offset by increased flows of FDI into other liberalizing economies, with associated gains in repatriated income.

Dee and Hanslow also note that because the structure of trade barriers in the services area is relatively complex, there is a real question as to the best way to approach partial (as opposed to full) liberalization in that sector. It is important to determine paths of partial liberalization of services trade that avoid worsening disparities in protection, moving resources further away from their pattern in a world free of distortions, and worsening real income.

The detailed results show that it is difficult of find a Pareto improvement (an outcome where at least some economies gain and none lose) from partial liberalization, when it involves removing only one type of barrier (to market access, national treatment, commercial presence or other modes of service delivery). This suggests that a better strategy may be to negotiate gradual reductions in *all* types of barriers simultaneously.

In **Chapter 6, Imperfect Competition and Trade Liberalization under the GATS**, Joseph F. Francois and Ian Wooton consider the impact of improved domestic market access for a foreign service provider. They emphasize the interaction between the different modes of market access commitments in services (cross-border and establishment) market structure, and regulation. They work with an analytical model in which the domestic industry is assumed to imperfectly competitive and, as a result of domestic regulation, able to act as a cartel. They also examine the incentives for the domestic firms to accommodate the entry of the foreign firm by inviting it to join the cartel.

The analytical results point to linkages between the degree of competition, the mode and degree of market access, and the pro-competitive effects of liberalization. When establishment abroad is introduced in conjunction with low cross-border barriers, they find that the foreign service provider takes on the domestic cartel, which is a pro-competitive result. With higher cross-border trade barriers, the foreign provider may be co-opted into the domestic cartel, with resulting negative consequences for profit shifting.

In **Chapter 7, International Trade in Services, Free Trade Agreements, and the WTO**, Scott L. Baier and Jeffrey H. Bergstrand note that, beginning with Krugman's works in 1991, a resurgence in the study of free trade agreements (FTAs) has occurred over the last decade. This literature has largely followed two tracks. Krugman dichotomized these tracks, with the first addressing the "economics" of FTAs and the second the "politics" of FTAs. A main impact of Krugman's analyses was to clarify the economics of trading blocs, in particular, the relative importance of *proximity* in determining the relative benefits of an FTA, using a model of monopolistic competition with increasing returns to scale. Krugman showed that, with zero intercontinental transportation costs on goods, continental FTAs decrease welfare unambiguously. However, with prohibitive intercontinental transport costs, such FTAs increase welfare unambiguously, leaving the results contingent upon the degree of transportability of goods.

This contrasting result—termed by Frankel, Stein, and Wei (FSW) as the "Krugman vs. Krugman debate"—led FSW to evaluate the net welfare gains or losses of continental FTAs under intercontinental transport costs varying from zero to prohibitive. However, a potentially serious omission in this literature is the role of *services trade*. On average, services comprise about 61 (47) percent of national output in developed (developing) economies. Moreover, in the policy arena, the most prominent FTAs in the world have liberalized services trade much more extensively than the WTO has services multilaterally.

Baier and Bergstrand seek to re-evaluate the implications of the Krugman and FSW studies to argue that—in the presence of services—the increasing regionalization of world trade, using continental FTAs, is not excessive. Their analysis concerns the relative welfare benefits of an FTA in a setting with international trade in goods and services, and where multilateral liberalization of services trade is limited compared with that in goods.

First, by taking into account the lower relative tradability of most services—the primary distinction between trade in goods and services—they argue that the degree of regionalization being witnessed is not excessive. Second, noting that the other major difference between trade in goods and services is that governments impose more severe restrictions on services trade than on goods trade, owing to the intangible nature of services and associated problems of asymmetric information, they show how the relative merits of a regional FTA are altered after accounting for greater government restrictions on services trade. Third, as fairly widely acknowledged, liberalization of services trade under the GATS has been modest at best. However, the EEA, NAFTA, and MERCOSUR are all continental FTAs that have liberalized international trade in services as well as goods. They show, in the context of the Krugman-FSW model framework, how the benefits of a regional FTA in goods and services *relative to* multilateral WTO liberalization in goods alone are related to the lower relative transportability of services internationally and the greater relative government barriers to services trade. This result may help explain the proliferation of FTAs in the 1990s compared with the stagnation of multilateral liberalization under the WTO.

In **Chapter 8, The Economic Performance of the Service Sector in Brazil, Mexico, and the United States,** Nanno Mulder analyzes the development and performance of the service sectors in Brazil, Mexico and the United States in the period from 1950 to 1996. These are the three biggest economies in the Western hemisphere, representing 25 percent of world output and 9 percent of world population in 1997. In all three countries, services are the biggest and most rapidly growing sector. In the United States, the service sector domination dates from the late 1920s. Moreover, the United States has developed into the international productivity leader, major locus of innovation, and largest exporter of services. In Brazil and Mexico, the large expansion of the service sector only started in the post-war period and occurred simultaneously with rapid GDP per capita growth.

Several factors are important in explaining the acceleration of the development of services in Brazil and Mexico after 1950. They include: the high elasticity of consumer demand linked to rising incomes; expanding demands for government services; increased participation of women in the labor market; more leisure time; the fast pace of urbanization; and replacement of what were previously household activities. Another influence was the growing proportion of services in intermediate demand due to outsourcing and the increasing demand for services due to more complicated production processes that continuously adjust to consumer demand. The relatively slow growth of productivity in services caused service employment to rise faster than the service share of GDP. Finally, several forces are discussed that affected the development of particular services, such as foreign direct investment, government policies, hyperinflation and unequal income distribution.

Mulder asks: what impact did increased service-orientation have on the performance of the Brazilian and Mexican economies? To answer this question a detailed comparison is made of the performance, as proxied by labor productivity, of the commodity producing and service sectors. The comparison shows that labor productivity grew more slowly in services than elsewhere. However, slower productivity growth in services than in the commodity producing sector does not necessarily mean a worse performance if productivity levels in the former were higher than in the latter. To check this, the performance of the individual sectors in Brazil and Mexico is compared to the United States, using the methodology of the International Comparisons of Output and Productivity (ICOP) project. International comparisons of output and productivity require the construction of sector-specific purchasing power converters (PPPs), as nominal exchange rates are unsuitable for this purpose. PPPs are based on prices that are mostly obtained implicitly by the ratio of revenues to produced quantities. Volume measurement in services is complex due to their intangible character. A survey is made of output indicators currently in use, and a number of new yardsticks are proposed. Mulder concludes that, when compared to the United States, Brazilian and Mexican services performance from 1950 to 1996 was better than the performance in their primary and secondary sectors. Public utilities, transport and communications, and finance performed relatively better than wholesale and retail trade, health care, and education.

In **Chapter 9, Globalization, Producer Services, and the City: Is Asia a Special Case?**, Peter W. Daniels notes that research in Europe and in North America suggests that there is a strong relationship between the expanding global reach of service and manufacturing transnationals and the rise of advanced producer services. The latter reveal a preference for locating in the major corporate complexes near their competitors and many of their multinational clients. It is less certain whether this model is applicable to economic development in the major cities of Asia. Interviews with major service and manufacturing transnationals in Singapore and Hong Kong are used to identify some of the key factors determining the transition of Asian cities to 'full service' urban complexes based on indigenous rather than overseas advanced producer service suppliers. The most obvious factor is the ability of service transnationals that follow their clients also to attract local clients.

In **Chapter 10, Electronic Commerce in Developing Countries: Issues for Domestic Policy and WTO Negotiations,** Catherine L. Mann notes that electronic commerce and its related activities over the Internet can be the engines that improve domestic economic well-being through liberalization of domestic services, more rapid integration into globalization of production, and leap-frogging of available technology. Electronic commerce integrates the domestic and global markets from its very inception. Negotiating on trade issues related to electronic commerce will demand self-inspection of key domestic policies, particularly in telecommunications, financial services, and distribution and delivery.

Technical aspects of electronic commerce, its complexity and the characteristic of network externalities should change the way that developing countries approach the external negotiating process to depend more on cooperative effort through such regional forums as Asia-Pacific Economic Cooperation (APEC) and the Free Trade Area for the Americas (FTAA). Further, since electronic commerce is characterized by "network externalities," developing countries should take advantage of the technical leadership coming out of the private sector in the most advanced countries (and their own private sector, even if nascent) and "draft" in behind.

E-commerce is neither a service, nor a good, but something that is comprised of both. In the context of WTO commitments, embracing this idea could lead to a liberalizing bias in favor of electronic delivery of goods and services as compared to delivery by a scheduled mode. Rather than view this outcome with alarm, Mann concludes that developing countries should encourage it as a positive force that furthers the development of electronic commerce and engenders deeper liberalization and deregulation throughout the economy.

In **Chapter 11, GATS and Developing Countries: A Case Study of India,** Rajesh Chadha notes that the General Agreement on Trade in Services (GATS) is the first multilateral agreement, under the auspices of Uruguay Round, to provide legally enforceable rights to trade in a wide range of services along with their progressive liberalization. Though very little liberalization was actually achieved, the negotiations on trade in services established the institutional structure for negotiating liberalization in the future. Many of the developing countries have not been very receptive to the conception of GATS mainly due to non-existence of such rules in the past and also because many of the service sectors had always enjoyed heavy protection. He argues that GATS provides developing countries with an opportunity to integrate into the global economy through adopting more liberal policies with regard to trade in services. Both the developing as well as the developed countries would gain through liberalization of various service sectors. Inefficiencies in the service sectors of a developing economy impact negatively on the export competitiveness of its agriculture and manufacturing sectors, through forward linkages, thus becoming one of the contributory factors leading to an unfavorable balance on current account.

Chadha employs a multi-country computable general equilibrium (CGE) model to demonstrate potential gains in welfare for the developing countries from their liberalization of trade in services. The gains get enhanced further when developed countries undertake similar liberalization. He also examines salient features of India's commitments under GATS along with a case study of India's brilliant success in software services. Unilateral moves by the Indian government towards liberalizing imports of computer software and hardware along with facilitating inflow of foreign direct investment into these sectors during the 1990s have been the major contributory factors in this success story.

In **Chapter 12, Egypt's Service Liberalization, Service Barriers, and Implementation of the GATS Agreement,** Sahar Tohamy discusses Egypt's service sector, openness in service trade, GATS commitments, and main service-liberalization policies. Using two openness indicators—share of imports and exports relative to Gross Domestic Product (GDP) and a country's share in world trade relative to its share in world output—Egypt does not appear more closed than a typical developing country.

In a cross-country comparison of Egypt's GATS commitments, Tohamy finds that Egypt has made commitments in construction, financial and banking services, tourism, and transport services. Its choice of these four sectors is generally consistent with the willingness of both developed and developing countries to offer commitments in these sectors. Business services and communication services are sectors in which Egypt has not made commitments, in comparison to over 50 percent of both developed and developing countries. These two sectors may therefore be candidates for commitments in the Services 2000 negotiations.

Tohamy surveys the main developments in Egypt's liberalization and privatization policies in five main service sectors: telecommunications; banking and insurance; tourism; maritime services; and air transport. Two issues appear to have retarded service liberalization in Egypt. First, government monopolies have dominated many service sectors for the past four decades. There is, therefore, legitimate concern that eliminating barriers to allow private-sector participation will require strong antitrust laws and regulatory bodies to govern the newly-privatized sectors. Second, the government's approach appears to view liberalization as a means to achieve other goals, such as providing lower prices of services to exporters of commodities, raising saving and investment levels, and achieving progress in privatizing public-sector firms. This emphasis on service liberalization as a means of promoting other sectors in the economy overlooks liberalization in service sectors that have higher growth potential and a smaller risk of enhancing market power.

Input/output analysis is used to show that demand and employment creation potentials for some types of services are significantly higher than those for industry. Especially with regard to employment creation, services with the potential to compete in international markets such as hotels and restaurants (tourism), insurance, and transportation may have greater benefits within the economy when compared to other export-oriented sectors, such as chemicals, food production, or furniture. It is stressed, finally, that service liberalization should be a goal in its own right, and that emphasis should be placed on more competitive sectors where the risk of market power is limited.

In **Chapter 13, GATS 2000: As Seen from Senegal,** Abdoulaye Ndiaye notes that participation of African countries to GATT negotiations had always been very weak and marginal over the years. Among the main reasons why they were not proactive are: lack of capacity; weakness of financial means to attend to the rounds regularly; and especially the lack of motivation due to the fact that there were few African manufactured products that could compete favorably with products made in developed countries. With the extension of negotiations to services through GATS, some African countries such as Senegal started perceiving their participation in the WTO as an opportunity to attract direct foreign investments.

Senegal is a West African country geographically well located between Europe, Latin America, and Africa. This led the Government to adopt a strategy positioning Senegal as a service-providing country on an international scale. As a result, Senegal developed services in areas such as communications, distribution, tourism and travel, recreation, culture, sports, transportation, and finance. Nonetheless, Senegal's commitments in the GATS did not reflect the full potential of this country in the services sectors. Following other African countries, Senegal defined its strategy of negotiation cautiously. Its commitments could thus be perceived as a first step in the negotiation process where the country reserves the possibility later to undertake more bold commitments.

Regarding services sectors with export potential, Senegal can consolidate a series of commitments in maritime and land transportation, education, and certain professional services, and relax its restrictions on audiovisual, basic telecommunication, and telecommunication services.

Ndiaye concludes that, in order to better negotiate in the WTO, African countries must constitute a critical mass by joining their forces and adopting a common strategy in services sectors where they share the same problems. In the sub-region of West Africa, this policy can be adopted in services such as insurance, banking, maritime, and air transport. The West African Economic and Monetary Union that covers eight countries is a suitable institutional framework for the members to prepare carefully a common position for the next negotiations in the WTO.

In **Chapter 14, Kenya's Trade in Services: Should the Country Fully Liberalize?**, Gerrishon K. Ikiara, Moses I. Muriira, and Wilfred N. Nyangena consider Kenya's service sector with a specific focus on growth and trade performance, constraints to trade, service areas of particular interest to the country, levels of commitments made under GATS, and service areas in which the country can profitably make bindings. It also makes recommendations on the way forward for Kenya's service trade.

The most important service sectors for Kenya today, in terms of external trade, are tourism and transport. These two service sectors play an important role in the country's current-account balance, with net surpluses in most years. Communication, computer, information, and other services are emerging as important new export sectors for Kenya. The most important service imports for Kenya are shipping and insurance services.

In the context of the ongoing GATS negotiations, Kenya's interests in international trade in services will be largely in foreign travel (tourism), transport, insurance, professional services, communication services, and information technology. Some of the specific issues that the country could pursue in order to maximize its interests in international trade in services include: (1) binding those services that already enjoy little or no protection and pushing for reciprocal actions from other WTO members; (2) liberalizing and making commitments on those sectors (such as telecommunications and information technology) where the country stands to benefit from transfer of technology; and (3) placing restrictions on foreign suppliers and investors in those sectors (such as financial, insurance, and transport services) where there is a considerable number of domestic firms already involved in the supply of services.

There are a number of areas in which Kenya could request more market access, both at the regional and international levels. These include increased mobility of professional, skilled, semi-skilled, and unskilled workers across national boundaries, and recognition of local qualifications in areas such as accounting, auditing, and other professional fields. For negotiations to be effective, there is a need for a co-ordinated regional approach. Member states belonging to regional groups will need to consider joint provision of some services and granting preferential market access and national treatment in services to each other for capacity development.

In **Chapter 15, Examining the Potential Benefits of Services Liberalization in a Developing Country: The Case of South Africa**, James W. Hodge notes that in the lead-up to the next round of multilateral negotiations, some commentators have argued that developing countries should liberalize their service industries for their own benefit and not just in response to industrial country demands. Hodge critically explores this position for the case of South Africa, drawing on the results of a number of studies recently conducted within the country on services liberalization.

Hodge begins with a general discussion of the theoretical benefits and adjustment costs associated with liberalization of trade in services for any country. The objective is to set out the benefits and costs of pro-competitive regulatory reform separately from those associated with opening of market access to foreign providers (trade liberalization). He argues that service-market reforms in themselves bring major benefits to countries even if trade is not liberalized. These benefits include: lower price-cost margins; greater efficiency; and higher innovation rates. The trickle-down impact on other industries and consumers of these lower prices and improved product quality and variety are also highly significant and may well offset any negative adjustment costs in the reforming sector.

Hodge further notes that the additional step of liberalizing trade in services can bring about a sharpening of competitive forces, and by expanding the market allow greater scale efficiency and product variety, and enhance the transfer of technology. But it may also raise adjustment costs. Exploring each mode of supply individually, he finds that opening to commercial presence only limits the adjustment costs faced by a country as all market expansion takes place within the liberalizing country. However, it may also limit the benefits associated with a larger market size. The extent to which a country is affected by the opening of cross-border trade depends crucially on the degree of substitutability between cross-border and other modes of supply, the relative competitiveness of the domestic sector, and the extent to which the local market size restricts competition, scale and specialization. Opening trade through the movement of natural persons provides an effect that constitutes a combination of both commercial presence and cross-border transactions. Foreign labor may displace local labor, but a portion of the gains to foreign labor will be spent in the host country and technology transfer will be more significant. Finally, opening access in the consumption abroad mode is only likely to benefit a country insofar as it provides foreign consumers access to the local market.

Hodge considers some developing country characteristics that may impact on the degree to which certain benefits and adjustment costs are realized. The most important of these are: narrow markets in services dominated by the commercial-presence mode of supply; poor regulatory and competition policy capacity; high demand leakages; and human-capital constraints. However, liberalization may actually remove some of the other growth constraints that a developing country faces, including removing shortages of investment capital, human capital, and foreign exchange.

Although South Africa has a relatively modern and efficient producer services sector, Hodge notes that it has still benefited greatly from both pro-competitive market reforms and limited trade liberalization. But it has also suffered many of the pitfalls faced by developing countries. Poor regulatory and competition-policy capacity and enforcement have left incumbents pursuing anti-competitive practices to retain market power by forcing out new entrants. Rapid market growth in some sectors has seen skilled labor capture many of the gains as human-capital shortages are exacerbated by a restrictive regime around the presence of natural persons mode of supply.

Hodge concludes that developing countries like South Africa will gain from further market reform and trade liberalization of services. But they should be aware of the potential adjustment costs involved and attempt to shape the process so as to minimize these costs.

In **Chapter 16, Implementing Telecommunications Liberalization in Developing Countries after the WTO Agreement on Basic Telecommunications Services,** Peter F. Cowhey and Mikhail M. Klimenko discuss the main consequences and lessons of the WTO Agreement on Basic Telecommunications Services for economic reforms in developing countries. They emphasize that the Agreement changed market and policy expectations (the "international regime") about the supply, pricing, and demand growth of communications services that eventually reduce the incentives for protecting monopolistic incumbents. In particular, they note that the Agreement will have a significant impact on the pricing of cross-border services (such as international phone services), and this will induce general rate rebalancing and the promotion of new services. They also show that the WTO-enforced regulatory code in telecommunications (the Reference Paper) strengthens the hand of domestic advocates of competition by enhancing the bargaining position of foreign companies. Reliance on general provisions of the WTO would not have the same impact. This has consequent implications for the general direction of trade policy.

In **Chapter 17, Domestic/International Regulation and Trade in Insurance Services: Implications for the Services 2000 Negotiations,** R. Brian Woodrow argues that international as well as domestic regulation—and particularly the roles and functions it plays within an important financial services sector like insurance—is currently changing and will come under serious scrutiny, possibly resulting in additional disciplines in the upcoming services negotiations. Woodrow draws upon a typology of the evolution of insurance regulation/supervision that relates domestic/international activities to specific regulation/supervision and broader public policy purposes.

In insurance as in other financial services, the role and functions of regulation remain both extensive and rather diverse, particularly as between OECD members and many developing countries. Domestic regulation of insurance services varies from country to country but distinct patterns and trends can be identified: enhanced foreign competition in domestic markets; continued reliance on the policing function of regulation; more integrated regulation/supervision; "financial convergence" in the insurance marketplace; regulatory capacity-building especially among developing countries; and increasing linkages between domestic regulation and international trade. One notable recent feature of domestic regulation in insurance has been increasing activity at the international level through the coordination and standards-setting activities of the International Association of Insurance Supervisors, other Bank for International Settlements (BIS) agencies, the OECD and UNCTAD. International insurance concerns are now very much part of ongoing efforts at reforming the "international financial architecture" and influencing the development of global public policies.

With regard to the Services 2000 services negotiations, governments and the insurance industry worldwide find themselves operating very much on that "domestic/international interface," engaged in a "two-level game" of international negotiation and the domestic political process and where additional disciplines on insurance regulation are likely to become the subject of future services-trade negotiations. Woodrow notes that it is important to remember that negotiation of domestic regulation disciplines under GATS, including its international dimensions, should be directed at transparent and equitable treatment of foreign and domestic services suppliers within each member state, rather than the pursuit of an illusory harmonization of policy and regulation among all member states.

In **Chapter 18, Canadian Magazine Policy: International Conflict and Domestic Stagnation**, Keith Acheson and Christopher Maule note that the process of producing and distributing a magazine combines commerce in a good and the provision of a service. Foreign distribution may involve a split-run or regional edition of a magazine with some additional content and advertising aimed at the particular market. For the past 40 years, Canada has introduced a series of policies aimed at diverting advertising from foreign to Canadian magazines. These policies have led to frictions with publishers in the United States. The policies include: discriminatory postal subsidies; screening of foreign investment; taxation of advertising expenditures so as to discourage the publication of foreign split-runs in Canada; and tariff measures and excise or service taxes to deter split-runs of non-Canadian magazines.

These pillars of domestic magazine policy have all been recently modified or removed as a result of conflicts with Canada's international obligations. Decisions of a WTO dispute and a subsequent appeals panel, responding to a complaint by the United States, played a significant role in shaping a recent agreement between the governments of Canada and the United States that provided at least a temporary resolution of the dispute. Before this accommodation, each pillar of Canadian magazine policy illustrated the vagueness and emotionalism of the underlying policy imperative, a lack of policy transparency, and erratic enforcement. Acheson and Maule argue accordingly that the domestic policy structure after the Canada-U.S. agreement begs for further rationalization and a parallel development of an international governance structure for cultural issues. The latter must address the overlapping and sometimes conflicting obligations of the GATT and the GATS when both goods and services are involved while expanding access to foreign markets for content providers and distributors. Whether cultural trade can be governed within a more integrated WTO structure or requires the negotiation of a sectoral agreement is moot.

In **Chapter 19, Chile and Australia GATS 2000: Towards Effective Liberalization of Trade in Services—Proposals for Action**, Francisco Javier Prieto and Alison Burrows identify ten significant weaknesses in the implementation of the General Agreement on Trade in Services (GATS). These include: the limitations of Members' commitments; some aspects of sectoral classification and the definition of modes of supply; MFN exemptions; the weak provisions on increasing participation of developing countries; and the lack of clarity on the treatment of regional trading agreements.

They propose six urgent priorities to address these weaknesses:

1. Promoting expanded commitments in *all* service sectors and modes of supply.
2. Developing a negotiating modality based on the adoption of commitments organized, *wherever possible* around *clusters*, and allowing for reservations on non-conforming measures regarding the Market Access and National Treatment obligations.
3. Developing a methodology to enhance greater transparency of the commercial significance of reservations that affect Market Access and National Treatment, and selecting and weighting the protection effect of measures on specific *clusters*.
4. Developing a domestic regulation necessity test to prevent qualification requirements and procedures, technical standards and licensing requirements from turning into unnecessary barriers to trade in services.
5. Facilitating, by means of special disciplines, the temporary entry of service suppliers to the markets of member countries.
6. Improving foreign and domestic institutional schemes to ensure the adequate functioning of the markets. The existence of natural monopolies, asymmetries in the size of competitors, and the need to protect the interests and well being of users call for developing standards that permit simulating highly competitive conditions in markets where these do not occur spontaneously.

In **Chapter 20, Inter-State Bargaining Coalitions in Services Negotiations: Interests of Developing Countries**, Amrita Narlikar begins by noting that: "united we stand, divided we fall." The reasoning behind the approach of the weak in their dealings with the strong is simple and direct. Since the mid-1980s, the collapse of the Informal Group in the GATT, has left developing countries adrift, in search of new coalition patterns that would allow them greater bargaining power in international trade. In precipitating the collapse of the Informal Group, and in providing the venue for subsequent experiments with alternative coalition types, the services sector has been critical.

Narlikar describes, classifies, and analyzes coalition formations attempted by developing countries in the GATT and the WTO. She notes four coalition types and specifies the conditions and countries for which each of these types is likely to yield lesser or greater success. Accompanying the analytical content of this chapter is a prescriptive, policy-oriented one. From the analysis of previous and ongoing successes and failures, lessons may be drawn for coalition construction and maintenance in the future. These lessons and derivative policy prescriptions are important, given the high stakes of both developed and developing countries in services, and the role that coalitions play in promoting agreement or deadlock in multilateral negotiations. They are critical, in light of the high costs that uncertainty of coalition partners has entailed for developing countries.

III. Implications for Further Research and Policy

This book brings together a collection of papers that deal with the role of services in national economies, how to measure services output and productivity, trade, and foreign direct investment (FDI), and how to approach the Services 2000 negotiations to be conducted under WTO auspices. The chapters cover a broad spectrum of topics that are central to understanding the economic forces affecting services and the national and international policies in both advanced and developing countries that are key in facilitating the liberalization of services domestically and globally. There are many important issues raised in the individual chapters. Rather than reviewing these issues here, readers are encouraged to consult those chapters that may be of particular interest and concern to them. I wish nonetheless to discuss what appear to me to be a number of research and policy implications that are suggested by the chapters.

Data and Measurement Issues

While several of the chapters in Part 1 of the volume address data and measurement issues, one important element that was not covered in any detail was the measurement of barriers to services trade and foreign direct investment (FDI). The measurement of barriers is at the heart of the ongoing efforts to liberalize services-related activities since it is necessary to identify what these barriers are and the economic effects of their reduction or elimination. In this connection, there are two noteworthy research programs worthy of mention. These are the work programs on services being conducted by the World Bank's Development Research Group and by the Australian Government's Productivity Commission in collaboration with the Australian National University.

The World Bank program was launched in 1999. It aims to generate and draw together data and research, with the objective of improving services-trade-policy formulation and facilitating the services negotiations at the WTO. Particular attention is being given to issues of interest to developing countries. The program supplements the sector-specific work already taking place at the World Bank on telecommunications, finance, transport, and other services sectors. One central component of the program is creation of a database on measures affecting cross-border trade and FDI in services. Once completed, the database is expected to serve as an informational tool for policy makers, regulators, researchers, and the private sector. It may also facilitate work on the quantification of the economic effects of barriers to services trade and FDI by providing scholars with the necessary inputs for estimation purposes in modeling analyses. Additional information on this program, summaries of current research projects, and links to service-related studies and data are available at the following web address: http://www.worldbank.org/trade/ services.html.

In a collaborative project, the Australian Government Productivity Commission and the Australian National University have been measuring and modeling the effect of restrictions on trade in services for a number of economies in Europe, Asia, and North and South America. The methodology involves:

- developing an index to measure restrictions on services, based on coverage and some initial judgment about the relative restrictiveness of the different sorts of restrictions;
- applying the index and calculating restrictiveness index scores for economies;
- developing an econometric model to measure the determinants of economic performance (e.g., price, profit margin, cost or quantity) of service firms in different countries, taking account of all the factors that economic theory would suggest are relevant, including the index measurement of trade restrictiveness;
- estimating the determinants of the performance of services firms, wherever possible entering the components of the trade restrictiveness index separately so that the econometrics can reveal something about the relative weights attached to the different components;
- and using the results of the econometrics to calculate the effect of trade restrictions on performance, where necessary converting a quantity or a profit effect into a comparable price or cost effect.

The Australian research team has calculated restrictiveness indexes in banking services for 35 economies, education services for 29 economies, telecommunications services for 136 economies, and maritime services for 38 economies. Work is in progress on restrictiveness indexes in distribution (wholesale and retail trade) for 38 economies and professional services (accountants, engineers, architects, and lawyers) for up to 34 countries. An index is being calculated for services sectors in 15 Asia Pacific Economic Cooperation (APEC) member economies. The research team has also estimated the effect of restrictions on the economic performance of service firms in such sectors as banking, telecommunications, and maritime services and is currently assessing the impact of restrictions on price-cost margins for such sectors as distribution, engineering, and international air services. Finally, the research team has commenced a project characterizing domestic regulatory regimes across countries for selected industries, including aviation, electricity, and telecommunications. The objective will be to trace the effects of domestic regulation on the economic performance of the selected industries.

An example of the Australian group's modeling research on the economic effects of reducing barriers to trade and FDI in services is to be found in Chapter 5 by Dee and Hanslow. This chapter also contains references to the ongoing and completed work by the project members. Additional information is available on the Productivity Commission web site: http://www.pc.gov.au.

The foregoing brief descriptions of the World Bank and Productivity Commission work programs offer great promise to expand the knowledge base of the barriers that affect services trade and FDI and the economic consequences associated with the maintenance or removal of these barriers. There are of course a number of other ongoing efforts on the part of governments, international organizations, institutes, and individual researchers that are designed to improve and expand the knowledge of services-related activities. We can expect accordingly that research on services will move forward significantly as existing data are improved and new data generated.

Interactions of Modes of Supply of Services

There are four modes of supplying services: cross-border trade; foreign direct investment; movement of consumers across borders (e.g., tourism, etc.); and movement of natural persons across borders (e.g., temporary immigration of skilled and unskilled workers). A facet of services that is not explored to any great extent in the chapters of this book is the interaction of the different modes of supply. That is, it is important to know more about how providers of the different modes of services respond to existing market conditions and associated policies and technological changes such as those prominent in the development of information technology and the spread of electronic commerce and communications made possible by the Internet and innovations in telecommunications. Casual observation suggests that there may well be significant interactions among and between the different modes of supply. It would be interesting accordingly if research were addressed to identifying and measuring the degrees of substitution and complementarity involving the different modes. This would improve our knowledge and understanding of the determinants of economic performance within and between services sectors. It would also help in the formulation of changes in regulatory policies and in negotiations for services liberalization.

Developing Country Interests in Services Reform

Part 2 of this volume contains several case studies of the role of services and the potential benefits of liberalization of domestic regulatory and trade policies for services in developing countries. It is not always realized that services are provided both for final consumption and as inputs into other sectors in an economy. Thus, policies that have the effect of increasing the costs and prices of services will have a detrimental impact on agriculture and manufacturing. More research needs to be done therefore in developing countries to further the understanding of how the different sectors are related to each other and what kinds of responses there may be within and between sectors when policies are changed.

We need to know more also about the role of interest groups in developing countries, including the stakes that different groups have in the status quo and how they may be affected by changes in policies. Such knowledge is essential for designing policies for services reforms in order to provide the political consensus for any changes to be made. In particular, winners and losers should be identified and provisions made to minimize costs of adjustment to changes in policies.

Finally, policy officials in developing countries engaged in international services negotiations need to take measures to improve their understanding of the role that trade agreements can play in improving their economic welfare. WTO member countries that are party to the WTO Services 2000 negotiations have to understand how requests for and offers of services liberalization will impact on their economies and affect their national welfare. To accomplish this requires more and better data on services for developing countries especially and analytical methodologies that are capable of providing empirical measurement of the economic consequences of changes in policies within and between countries. Very little in-depth research on these issues is being done presently in most developing countries. The need for more research is abundantly clear.

Notes

[1] Much of the detailed work involved in setting up the structure and overseeing the actual implementation of the Congress was ably handled especially by Bonnie Jessup and Jaime Niño, with the assistance of other staff members of the CSI Research and Education Foundation.

[2] Other papers prepared as part of the World Bank's Capacity Building Project include: Chapter 4 by Whichard; Chapter 11 by Chadha; Chapter 12 by Tohamy; Chapter 16 by Cowhey and Klimenko; Drusilla K. Brown and Robert M. Stern, "Measurement and Modeling of the Economic Effects of Trade and Investment Barriers in Services;" and Alan V. Deardorff, "Fragmentation and Outsourcing: Implications for the Location of Services Activities." These latter two papers, which were presented at the Atlanta Congress, are to be published in the *Review of International Economics* in late 2000. The World Bank's Capacity Building Project is supported by: the governments of the United Kingdom (Department for International Development), Italy, and the Netherlands; Societe Generale de Surveillance (SGS), Geneva; the World Bank Institute; and the World Bank's Research Support Budget.

Part 1. Measurement, Modeling, and Analytical Issues

CHAPTER 2

Productivity in the Services Sector

Jack E. Triplett and Barry P. Bosworth

I. Overview and Introduction

From 1949 to 1973, the Bureau of Labor Statistics (BLS) estimates that U.S. non-farm multifactor productivity grew at 1.9% per year. After 1973, multifactor productivity grew only 0.2% per year (table 1). Despite a 20-year intensive research effort to find the cause, no convincing explanation of the post-1973 productivity slowdown exists.

Whatever the ultimate cause, circumstantial evidence suggests that services industries play some important role in the slowdown. In the first place, the aggregate numbers indicate that the productivity slowdown is greater in the non-goods producing portions of the economy. While no official estimate of productivity in services is published by the BLS, non-farm multifactor productivity slowed by 1.7 percentage points (from 1.9% per year to 0.2%), and manufacturing productivity fell by 0.6 percentage points (from 1.5% per year to 0.9%). Because manufacturing accounts for about 22% of non-farm business, this implies a 2 percentage point slowdown in the non-manufacturing sector.[1]

If the data are right, one might infer, as did Baumol (1967) many years ago, that productivity improvements in services are harder to achieve than in goods-producing industries. If so, the shift of the economy toward a larger share of services implies a reduction in the national rate of productivity improvement.

But this view of manufacturing and services is undoubtedly too simple. Substantial disparities exist among productivity growth rates within the manufacturing sector and also within the non-manufacturing sector. It simply is not true that all individual services industries have productivity growth rates that are lower than all individual manufacturing industries, or even below the average for manufacturing industries.

But more importantly, perhaps, the data may not be right. One popular hypothesis about the productivity slowdown is that it is a product of mismea-

Table 1. U.S. Labor and Multifactor Productivity, Average Annual Rates of Change, 1949-96 and Selected Subperiods

	Non-Farm Business	Manufacturing	Estimated Non-Manufacturing
Output per Hour			
1949-73	2.8	2.6	3.0
1973-96	1.5^r	2.7	1.0^r
1973-79	1.3^r	2.1	1.0^r
1979-96	1.5^r	2.9	1.1^r
Multifactor Productivity			
1949-73	1.9	1.5	2.1
1973-96	0.2	0.8	0.0
1973-79	0.4	- 0.6	0.8
1979-96	0.1	1.3	- 0.3

^{r} indicates that numbers incorporate the revised October 1999 GDP data.
Sources: output per hour: U.S. Department of Labor, Bureau of Labor Statistics, 1999a; multifactor productivity: U.S. Department of Labor, Bureau of Labor Statistics, 1999b

surement. According to this hypothesis, the mismeasurement of output contributes to the productivity slowdown because an increasing portion of output is not captured in the basic statistics.

Again, circumstantial evidence points to the services industries. Griliches (1994) pointed out that some of the services industries whose productivity growth rates in the 1947-1973 era were as high or higher than productivity growth in manufacturing industries had, since 1973, much lower productivity improvements. Additionally, the productivity slowdown has been particularly intense in services industries where output is hard to measure—health services, for example, have the greatest labor productivity slowdown of any industry in table 2, and both banking and health services have large multifactor productivity slowdowns (see table 3). This points again to possible mismeasurement.

Another puzzle involves computers. The 1992 capital-flow table shows the purchases, by industry, of computer equipment (Bonds and Aylor, 1998). The five industries that are the largest purchases of computers are all services—in order, financial services, wholesale trade, business services, insurance, and communications. Those five services industries account for more than 50% of US investment in computers. Within these industries computers have created new forms of service output that may not be fully captured in the statistics. An example is the growth of ATM machines in banks that reduce the time spent waiting in line for teller transactions, make the transactions available on weekends, and have, with computer-assisted verification systems for credit card purchases, virtually eliminated the need to carry traveler's checks on foreign travel to many countries. Prior to the 1999 revisions to GDP, ATM usage was not reflected in the measure of banking output in the national accounts.

In all of these services industries, conceptual and empirical problems in measuring output and prices are notorious. For example, an economic consulting firm is part of the business services industry. How do we measure the output of an economic consulting firm? How would we construct a price index for economic consulting? And how would we compute the productivity of economists? The science of economics is no closer to developing methods for measuring the output of economists' own activities than it is for measuring the output of banks, law firms, and insurance agents. All of these services pose difficult problems for constructing price indexes and real output measures and therefore for measuring productivity.

This paper gives a progress report of a project we are conducting, with collaborators, on service sector output and productivity. Its major message is that there is no central theme to the problem of services measurement. Each industry we have examined contains unique problems. If quality change is, as Shapiro and Wilcox (1996) put it, the "house-to-house fighting" of price indexes, measuring service output requires, at least, a hedgerow-by-hedgerow assault.

In the next section, we present some measures of the growth in labor and multifactor productivity within the services industries in a form that is consistent with the published measures for the aggregate economy. This allows us to document the wide dispersion of productivity growth rates across industries and the pervasiveness of the post-1973 slowdown. Section III summarizes recent research on individual sectors that have been subjects of Brookings Institution workshops on measurement issues in services industries.

II. Available Data

Reviewing trends in service-sector productivity and measurement issues requires a decision between two alternative databases that can be used for productivity analysis. Other researchers in this field face the same choice.

On the one hand are the aggregate, sector, and industry estimates published by BLS, which cover both labor productivity and multifactor productivity. As a general statement, we believe that the BLS productivity figures, where available, are the best current sources of U.S. productivity trend information. However, the BLS industry labor-productivity estimates do not cover all industries at present, although an expansion is underway that will eliminate most of the lacunae. An aggregate services sector productivity number—which we need for this review—is not available from BLS, though it is possible to infer one (see table 1). It is difficult to combine published manufacturing and non-manufacturing-industry productivity estimates to reach the

Table 2. Labor Productivity by Industry, 1960-97 Annual Percentage Rate of Change

Industry	Percentage Share (1992) (1)	1992 Level (2)	Growth Rate 1960-73 (3) Thousands	1973-97 (4)	1987-97 (5)	Change (4)-(2) (6)
Nonfarm business – hours	87		3.0	1.1	1.0	-2.0
Nonfarm business – persons	87		2.6	0.9	1.1	-1.5
Total Private - A (Aggregates)	100.0		2.7	0.9	1.1	-1.7
Total Private Sector	100.0	56	2.5	0.9	1.1	-1.4
Agriculture	2.1	37	3.9	3.8	2.2	-1.7
Mining	1.7	142	3.6	1.2	4.4	0.7
Construction	4.3	39	-2.1	-0.7	-0.1	2.0
Manufacturing	19.8	59	3.3	2.7	2.9	-0.4
Durables (ex elect.)	7.8	53	3.7	2.4	2.5	-1.2
Electronics	2.8	63	0.2	5.8	8.7	8.6
Nondurables	9.1	64	3.6	2.1	1.3	-2.2
Services	71.3	57	2.2	0.4	0.7	-1.5
Transportation	3.6	54	3.2	0.9	0.8	-2.4
Communications	3.0	138	5.0	3.9	2.9	-2.1
Public Utilities	3.3	184	4.8	1.5	3.8	-0.9
Wholesale Trade	7.6	65	3.2	2.9	4.0	0.7
Retail Trade	10.1	31	2.0	0.8	1.6	-0.3
Finance	21.4	164	1.3	0.5	1.6	0.4
Other Services	22.4	39	1.3	-0.5	-0.7	-2.0

Finance, Insurance and Real Estate	21.4	164	1.3	0.5	1.6	0.4
Depository and Nondepository Inst.	4.3	95	0.2	-0.3	-0.3	-0.4
Security and Commodity Brokers	0.9	97	0.0	4.0	8.8	8.9
Insurance Carriers	1.6	57	1.9	-0.1	4.6	2.6
Insurance Agents	0.7	48	0.2	-0.8	-0.3	-0.5
Real estate	13.7					
Nonfarm housing	10.3					
Other	3.4	116	1.0	0.5	1.5	0.5
Holding and Investment Offices	0.2	53	0.1	-0.3	0.0	-0.1
Finance less nonfarm housing	*11.1*	85	1.0	0.5	1.9	0.9
Other Services	22.4	39	1.3	-0.5	-0.7	-2.0
Hotels and other lodging	0.9	34	0.7	0.0	2.9	2.2
Personal services	0.2	24	1.7	-0.9	-0.3	-2.0
Business and professional	0.8	44	-0.2	-0.4	0.0	0.2
Auto repair	1.0	40	2.9	-0.8	0.1	-2.8
Miscellaneous repair	0.3	32	0.0	-1.6	-3.0	-3.0
Motion pictures	0.4	43	0.7	1.0	-1.0	-1.7
Amusement and recreation	0.9	44	-0.8	0.2	-0.8	0.0
Health services	6.9	45	0.6	-1.5	-2.2	-2.8
Legal services	1.7	79	0.9	-2.5	-0.8	-1.7
Educational services	0.9	26	0.0	-0.5	-0.9	-0.8
Social services and membership org.	1.4	19	0.1	-0.3	-0.5	-0.6
Private Households	0.2	12	..	..	..	..

Source: Bureau of Economic Analysis data. Pre-1977 output data are estimated using the 1982-base industry data as extrapolators, except for those sectors whose output can be derived from other tables of the revised national accounts.

Gross product is gross output minus intermediate inputs, and the aggregates are constructed as Fisher aggregates of component industries.

Persons engaged in production are defined as full-time equivalents plus the self-employed (Table 6.8).

The productivity slowdown is measured as the difference in the growth rate between 1987-97 and 1960-73.

Table 3. Multifactor Productivity by Industry, 1960-97 Annual Percentage Rate of Change

Industry	Percentage Share (1992) (1)	Growth Rate 1960-73 (2)	Growth Rate 1973-97 (3)	Growth Rate 1987-97 (4)	Change (4)-(2) (5)
TOTAL PRIVATE SECTOR	100.0	1.7	0.5	0.9	-0.8
Agriculture	2.1	0.4	3.5	2.7	2.2
Mining	1.7	1.4	-0.2	4.0	2.5
Construction	4.3	-2.4	-0.5	0.1	2.5
Manufacturing	19.8	2.5	2.0	2.4	-0.1
Durables (ex elect.)	7.8	3.1	2.0	2.4	-0.6
Electronics	2.8	-0.9	4.6	7.3	8.2
Nondurables	9.1	2.6	1.2	0.5	-2.0
Services	71.3	1.6	0.2	0.5	-1.1
Transportation	3.6	3.3	1.3	1.4	-1.9
Communications	3.0	2.7	1.8	1.4	-1.3
Public Utilities	3.3	3.1	0.4	2.4	-0.7
Wholesale Trade	7.6	0.4	1.0	2.7	2.3
Retail Trade	10.1	1.2	0.4	1.0	-0.2
Finance	21.4	-0.6	-0.9	-0.5	0.1
Other Services	22.4	0.3	-0.6	-0.8	-1.2
Finance, Insurance and Real Estate	21.4	-0.6	-0.9	-0.5	0.1
Depository and Nondepository Inst.	4.3	-1.4	-3.2	-3.7	-2.3
Security and Commodity Brokers	0.9	-0.6	3.6	9.0	9.5
Insurance Carriers	1.6	0.6	-2.3	2.1	1.5
Insurance Agents	0.7	-0.9	-0.7	0.0	0.9
Real estate	13.7	..	..	..	..
Nonfarm housing	10.3	..	..	..	..
Other	3.4	-0.7	0.1	0.4	1.1
Holding and Investment Offices	0.2	-3.5	-0.9	2.2	5.6
Finance less non-farm housing	*11.1*	-0.9	-0.9	-0.3	0.6
Other Services	22.4	0.3	-0.6	-0.8	-1.2
Hotels and other lodging	0.9	0.3	-0.1	2.6	2.3
Personal services	0.2	0.7	-0.8	-0.4	-1.1
Business and professional	0.8	-1.3	0.0	-0.2	1.1
Auto repair	1.0	1.5	-1.3	-1.0	-2.6
Miscellaneous repair	0.3	-0.1	-1.7	-3.2	-3.1
Motion pictures	0.4	-0.2	0.5	-1.6	-1.4
Amusement and recreation	0.9	-0.7	0.9	0.0	0.7
Health services	6.9	-0.3	-1.8	-2.6	-2.3
Legal services	1.7	0.5	-2.6	-1.0	-1.5
Educational services	0.9	0.0	-0.4	-0.9	-0.9
Social services and membership org.	1.4	0.1	-0.3	-0.6	-0.8
Private Households	0.2	..	..	..	..

Source: table 2 plus capital stock data of the Bureau of Economic Analysis and authors' estimates as described in the text published aggregates, such as the non-farm-business, labor-productivity number (Gullickson and Harper, 1999, show aggregation with "Domar" weights). These are liabilities if one's objective is to compare industry labor and multifactor productivity trends with aggregate and sector labor and multifactor productivity trends.

A second alternative is to make use of the data on gross product originating (GPO) by industry published by the Bureau of Economic Analysis (BEA). The GPO data are consistent with national accounts and with the estimate of non-farm business output. Using BEA gross product data to compute productivity yields estimates that are consistent across industries, can be aggregated to sector and economywide totals, and are consistent between labor productivity and multifactor productivity concepts.

Set against these advantages, however, is the fact that GPO and other BEA data are not exactly what we want for computing industry productivity measures.[2] For its productivity measures, BLS starts from gross output per industry and adjusts for intraindustry sales. GPO is value added and value added deducts, additionally, inputs purchased from other industries. (Value added is used in national accounts in order to obtain an unduplicated total for GDP.) The BLS output measure is preferable for industry-productivity purposes. The BEA series on full-time equivalent employees by industry, which we use, is converted into employment hours by BLS, and nonemployee hours are added; then, an adjustment is made for labor quality. Because these adjustments are larger for the earlier post-war period than for the last decade, our measure of labor input produces a larger productivity slowdown than the BLS labor-input measure (see the first two lines of table 2). Finally, the BLS produces capital input by industry by following the Jorgenson (1989) principles for producing capital services and capital rental prices. The BLS capital-input measure is conceptually superior to the use of BEA net capital stock by industry, which we employ in the calculations for table 3.

In table 4 we calculate the effect of the alternative output concepts, which turns out to matter more for some of the services industries we discuss than for manufacturing. In subsequent work, we will carry out similar comparisons for labor-input and capital-input choices.

Thus, the choice is between comprehensive and consistently compiled industry data from BEA or data that are more fragmentary and less consistent, but more appropriate for productivity analysis, from BLS. Ultimately, our decision to use GPO data and BEA capital and labor measures was motivated by the desire to have a comprehensive data set for all industries, one for which consistent labor and multifactor productivity measures could be derived. We also needed a dataset from which we could split trends at the 1973 onset of the productivity slowdown. A complimentary study of the productivity slowdown that begins with BLS data is Gullickson and Harper (1999). Their study covers

Table 4. Output Versus Product and the Proportion of Output Directed to Final Demand

Industry	Gross Product Percentage Share (1992) (1)	Output/Product Ratio Annual Percentage Change (2)	Final Demand Share (percent) (3)	Methodology (4)
Total Private Sector	100.0	..	..	..
Agriculture	2.1	-2.1	21.0	dd
Mining	1.7	-1.5	4.2	dd
Construction	4.3	-0.6	76.5	dd
Manufacturing	19.8	-0.4	51.4	dd
Durables (ex elect.)	7.8	-0.2	51.6	dd
Electronics	2.8	0.0	58.9	dd
Nondurables	9.1	-0.5	49.2	dd
Services	71.3	..	63.9	..
Transportation	3.6	..	43.9	dd
Communications	3.0	..	54.0	dd
Public Utilities	3.3	0.6	45.2	dd
Wholesale Trade	7.6	-2.8	49.0	dd
Retail Trade	10.1	-1.0	89.9	dd
Finance	21.4	0.0	64.4	..
Other Services	22.4	..	64.7	..
Finance, Insurance and Real Estate	21.4	..	64.4	
Depository and Nondepository Inst.	4.3	..	63.0	x
Security and Commodity Brokers	0.9	2.3	41.7	dd
Insurance Carriers	1.6	1.4	83.7	dd
Insurance Agents	0.7	-0.5	0.4	dd
Real estate	13.7	..	..	
Nonfarm housing	10.3	..	..	
Other	3.4	..	41.0	dd
Holding and Investment Offices	0.2	..	41.7	x
Finance less non-farm housing	*11.1*	..	50.6	
Other Services	22.4	..	64.7	
Hotels and other lodging	0.9	0.9	53.7	dd
Personal services	0.2	0.9	74.4	dd

Industry	Gross Product Percentage Share (1992)	Output/Product Ratio Annual Percentage Change	Final Demand Share (percent)	Methodology
	(1)	(2)	(3)	(4)
Business and professional	0.8	..	20.7	x
Auto repair	1.0	1.0	57.4	dd
Miscellaneous repair	0.3	3.0	74.4	dd
Motion pictures	0.4	1.5	66.0	dd
Amusement and recreation	0.9	..	66.0	dd
Health services	6.9	1.9	97.6	dd
Legal services	1.7	1.1	29.3	dd
Educational services	0.9	..	92.8	dd
Social services and membership org.	1.4	..	92.8	x
Private Households	0.2	..	92.4	dd

Note: For the methodology, dd represents double-deflation, and x represents extrapolation with employment or wage deflation

1947-77, and 1977-92. These are not optimal years for analyzing the productivity slowdown, which began in 1973, not 1977.

Data on Gross Product Originating (GPO) by industry as published by the BEA provide a means of examining the role of the service industries within a framework that is in principle consistent with the aggregate economy-wide productivity estimates for non-farm business. The data are published at the level of 65 private-sector industries; and with the 1996 revisions (Yuskavage, 1996), estimates are available for gross output (shipments), gross product (value-added) and its components, and intermediate inputs beginning in 1977.[3] Because the estimates are tied into the 5-year benchmark input-output tables, they are consistent with the national accounts aggregates. The measures of real gross output and real gross product (value added) incorporate the chain Fisher indexes used for the national accounts. For most industries, real product is derived by separately deflating inputs and outputs, 'double deflation'.

However, the GPO series have not yet incorporated the revisions to GDP that were released by BEA in October 1999. Some of these revisions are substantial. For example, when BLS incorporated them into revised estimates of non-farm labor productivity, the post-1973 growth rate was raised by 0.4 percentage points per year (from 1.1 percent to 1.5 percent—see table 2). When these GDP revisions are eventually incorporated into the GPO series, they will also cause revisions to the industry multifactor productivity rates. The data in this paper reflect pre-October data for GDP, except where noted.

We have used an older data set to extend the estimates for the real value of gross product back to 1960 in order to have a rough perspective on the contribution of the service industries to the post-1973 productivity slowdown.

Labor Productivity

Estimates of gross product per worker are constructed using BEA data on persons engaged in production.[4] We did not incorporate hours worked into the analysis, but variations in hours appear to be significant only in the 1960s. The resulting measures of labor productivity are summarized in table 2.

The level of output per worker, shown in column 2, varies widely by industry, but the average for the broad definition of services is nearly identical to that for manufacturing ($57,000 and $59,000, respectively). Labor productivity is particularly high in the capital-intensive sectors of communications, public utilities and FIRE (finance, insurance, and real estate—but the real estate number is affected by the inclusion of owner-occupied housing, which has no labor input). The notion of low productivity service-sector jobs is accurate only for retail trade and the miscellaneous collection of other services.

Growth rates of labor productivity are reported in columns (3)-(6), where we distinguish between the pre- and post-1973 experiences. We also show the average growth of the last decade. For a number of industries, post-1987 productivity growth is considerably faster than shown in the 1973-97 data.

For comparison purposes, the first two rows of table 2 show the aggregate series for the non-farm business sector. The first row shows the non-farm productivity rate previously published by the Bureau of Labor Statistics (BLS).[5] For the pre-1977 period, the rates are the published version, from the major sector detail of the national accounts (version A) and Fisher indexes of gross product for the private-sector aggregate from our constructed estimates of the underlying industry detail (version B). The discrepancy of 0.2 percentage points over the 1960-73 period is indicative of the error introduced by our use of the old data to extend the output estimates back before 1977.

The industry detail reveals a very pervasive pattern of slowing productivity growth after 1973 (column 3 versus column 4). Within the goods-producing industries, the rate of growth in labor productivity continues to be quite rapid for agriculture and there has been a strong recovery in mining over the 1987-97 period. Although labor-productivity change in construction is negative over the full 37 years, the post-1973 experience actually represents an improvement over the prior period. While the slowdown is often said to have come to an end for manufacturing, the recovery is largely the result of a rapidly expanding electronics industry.[6] Excluding electronics, durable and nondurable manufacturing both still show a deceleration of productivity gains.

It is particularly large for nondurables and it has continued to deteriorate in the most recent period.

The productivity slowdown is more pronounced in the broadly-defined service sector which includes a very heterogeneous mix of industries. For the service sector as a whole, the post-1973 labor slowdown is 1.8 percentage points, measured from the whole period (2.2 minus 0.4), and 1.5 percentage points, using only the last decade's data.[7]

Within the transportation industries, deregulation was followed by substantial productivity gains for railroads, as was anticipated; but the gains from deregulation seem small or nonexistent for trucking and airlines. The high reported rate of productivity improvement for communications (2.9% for 1987-97) actually represents a slowing relative to the 1960-73 period; but there are questions about the extent to which the price indexes incorporate new technologies.

Wholesale trade is an exception in showing an acceleration of productivity growth in the last decade. It is also one of those industries that has made an extensive investment in computers. However, the quality of the data is affected by a blurring of the distinction between manufacturer's distribution activities and wholesalers and the backward integration of retailers into wholesaling. Moreover, the old U.S. SIC system contained a definition of wholesale trade that caused many retailing establishments in office supplies, hardware, and other retailing activities to be classified as wholesalers, which complicates the interpretation of the wholesale trade productivity numbers.

The retail trade sector is reported to have a modest slowdown. But the statistical methodology may not fully capture the effects of continuing changes in store formats. and, as noted, the old SIC system caused many of the most technically dynamic retailers incorrectly to be included in the data for wholesale trade.

Finance, insurance and real estate (FIRE) and the category "other services" include many of the industries where the problems of defining and measuring real output are most severe. For several of these industries, annual rates of change in labor productivity are actually negative.[8] In industries representing about 13 percent of GDP, the estimates of real output growth are based on changes in employment. Recent research also has suggested that there are major problems with the price indexes used to derive output of medical care.[9] Productivity growth has accelerated substantially within finance, but that is primarily due to the large output gains recorded for security brokers during the recent stock market boom. The conceptual basis of the output measures for banking and insurance continues to be an area of substantial debate. Labor productivity is recorded as declining in large portions of other services, including health services.

In summary, the distribution of labor-productivity gains by industry and the pattern of the post-1973 slowdown is consistent only in broad terms with a focus on mismeasurement of output in the service industries. The slowdown has not disappeared in the manufacturing sector, though that sector is of sharply diminished importance in a service-dominated economy. The decline in productivity growth in the early 1970s also seems too abrupt to attribute to a deterioration in the quality of the data.

Within services, the patterns of change are quite disparate and different industries raise different types of potential problems. Furthermore, evidence of a slowdown in productivity growth is quite pervasive across industries, rather than being focused exclusively on industries with difficult measurement problems. For example, it is not clear why auto repair, with negative post-1973 productivity, should be mismeasured (Levy, 1999). Yet, while some of the negative values for productivity change might be explained as the consequence of shifts in the composition of output, their frequency in the service sectors is suggestive of an understatement of real output growth.

Multifactor Productivity

BEA publishes estimates of the stock of plant and equipment by industry which we have used to compute crude measures of multifactor productivity (MFP) at the level of individual industries.[10] Those estimates are shown in table 3.

Since the capital inputs generally grow faster than employment, the growth of MFP is usually less than that for labor productivity. Further, because the growth of capital slowed sharply relative to labor inputs after 1973, the post-1973 slowdown in private-sector MFP is only about half as large as that for labor productivity. At the level of the total private sector, the MFP growth rate slowed by 0.8 percentage points between 1987-97 and 1960-73, compared to 1.5 points for labor productivity. The contribution of increased capital per worker is particularly large in communications, wholesale trade, and financial institutions. After deducting the contribution of increased capital per worker, nearly half of the industries had negative rates of change in MFP over the 1973-97 period, and most of those are in finance and other services. The gains in labor productivity are larger than those for MFP only in transportation, business services, entertainment, and social services.

The estimates of MFP shown in table 3 use gross product (equivalent to value added) as the measure of output. The BLS studies of productivity generally focus on gross output at the industry level, and define multi-factor productivity within a framework that allows for three inputs: capital, labor and inputs purchased from other industries. A recent study by Gullickson and Harper (1999) used that framework to examine the trends in industry productivity over the 1947-92 period.[11] While they use a more refined methodology and focus on different subperiods, the results are broadly similar in finding negative productivity trends for construction, finance and many of the industries included in other services.

The BEA data set includes measures of gross output only for the 1977-97 period; as shown in column 2 of table 4, the distinction between gross output and gross product is important for several industries—particularly public utilities, insurance, and health services. While the choice of the output concept has a large effect on labor productivity, it is less significant for MFP because purchased materials are included as an input in the calculation. If the analysis is limited to those industries for which both output concepts are available, the aggregate growth of gross output exceeds that of gross product by about 0.1 percentage points. But reliance on the gross output concept would significantly raise the growth of labor productivity in the service sector and lower it for the goods-producing industries.

Our use of BEA net capital stocks by industry introduces potential problems among services-industry productivity estimates, especially those industries that are heavy users of computers (which have short service lives). We will explore the implications of this step in later research.

Intermediate Products and Aggregate Productivity

Finally, it is important to note that conclusions about potential bias in the estimates of industry productivity may not carry through to the aggregate economy. The output of some industries is largely consumed as an input by others. Thus, an understatement of productivity growth in one industry may be offset by an overstatement for those industries that use its output.

For example, the real output of business and other services is extrapolated on the basis of employment, producing an assumed zero rate of growth in labor productivity. Yet, as shown in column (3) of table 4, 80 percent of the industry's output is delivered to other industries. Thus, any errors in measuring business services output lead to compensating effects on the inputs and productivity of industries that use business services. Improved measures of real output for business services would have only a minor impact on the estimates of economy-wide productivity growth.

On the other hand, employment is also used to project the output of the banking industry, but nearly two-thirds of its output goes to final demand. The recent revision to the measure of banking in GDP will have an effect on economy-wide GDP. An even more extreme example is provided by medical-care services where nearly all of the output is directed to final demand.

Gullickson and Harper used input-output analysis to adjust for the proportion of an industry's output that is an input to others for those industries with negative productivity trends.[12] They concluded that the inter-industry effects would reduce the economy-wide impact of a change in the industry productivity by about one-third.

III. Individual Services Sectors

As noted in the introduction, there is no overall theme to measurement problems in services industries. Each appears to be a special case, with specific measurement problems unique to the characteristics of services industry output. Each industry problem requires a specific solution, an attack designed uniquely for the special problems posed by the nature of the industry's output. This section reviews some of the problems and the state of the statistics in topics that have been addressed in the series of Brookings Institution Workshops on Measuring Prices and Output of Services Industries.[13]

Business Services

Business services include a diverse set of activities, such as professional and consulting services (other than legal and financial), advertising, data processing and building maintenance. As noted above, about 80 percent of the output of the business services industry is purchased by other domestic firms. The 20 percent that goes to final demand is sold to government and overseas.

The gross product originating (GPO) of the business services sector has more than doubled as a share of GDP over the past quarter century to about 5 percent. It is also one of the fastest-growing export sectors. Yet until recently we had no measures of real output of the industry, or of real exports, and GPO is projected on the basis of employment data (Yuskavage, 1996).

In many cases, measuring the output of business services involves an effort to determine who should receive credit for the productivity gains recorded by the users of business services. When the output of business services is projected on the basis of employment or the use of other inputs, all productivity gains are assigned to the purchaser of the service. If the provider of the service is credited with some productivity gain, it comes at the expense of measured productivity gains in the purchasing industry. Thus, to the extent that business services are intermediate products, they have no implication for the measurement of economy-wide productivity, only its distribution. On the other hand, understanding why the economy is making more use of business services, and why they contribute so strongly to U.S. export performance, demands better measures of output, so improving the measurement of business services is important for other reasons, even if not for measuring aggregate productivity growth.

Since 1995, the BLS has expanded the Producer Price Index to measure the prices or fees for some components of business services. It now publishes indexes for accounting, legal, advertising agency, and engineering services. In each of these cases, the BLS asks respondents to re-price at periodic intervals a bundle of services that was observed in the period where pricing was initiated. This is an application of what is known, internationally, as "model" pricing, a methodology that was first developed by Statistics Canada for pricing construction. The BLS methods and results were described in Gerduk (1999) and Swick (1999).

Model pricing amounts to collecting a hypothetical price for a defined bundle of services. The BLS does ask respondents to take account of market conditions, and they make some adjustments for quality change. However, respondents may simply mark up the individual inputs that go into the bundle of services. The new PPI indexes appear similar to the pattern of change in average hourly earnings.

The problems are even more severe in other areas of business services, such as business consultants, because it is difficult to define the firms' activities in a way that leads to clear measures of their output. A few attempts have been made to collect from business services providers information about what they contribute to the output of their customers. Examples are Nachum (1999), who surveyed a group of European management consulting firms, and Gordon (1999b), who collected information from U.S. consultants. The results are interesting, but have not so far yielded any breakthroughs on the most difficult of the problems. In some cases, management consultants are used to validate decisions already made by management, as a tool to assure broader employee cooperation in a major corporate change, for example; even if this use of the consultant improves the productivity of the purchasing firm, extracting an estimate of the consultant's effect from surveys—either of the seller or the buyer of the service—is not a promising approach.

Because business services are so diverse, measuring them requires an industry-by-industry approach, and painstaking resolutions of unique problems that are found in individual industries.

Retail Trade

For effective measurement of real output and thus productivity in the retail trade sector, several conceptual problems must be resolved. Much of the industry's innovation is reflected in shifts in the distribution of sales among stores with different formats and changes among product lines within stores. Yet, these shifts are explicitly ruled out in the construction of the major price indexes that focus on a specific product in a specific store. The shift of sales from department stores to lower-priced discount outlets, for example, is treated as a reduction in quality (and therefore output), not a reduction in price. Nor is there any estimate of the value of increased product variety. Additionally, the old SIC system may be one of the mismeasurement culprits, because some retail establishments with high productivity may be incorrectly classified in the wholesale trade industry, as noted in a previous section.

At present, two statistical agency programs provide measures of real output in retailing. The BLS produces indexes of output and output per labor hour at the level of three and four-digit SIC codes. BEA publishes a measure of Gross Product Originating (GPO) at the level of total retail trade and measures of gross output for more detailed sub-groups within the retail category. The BLS employs a consistent methodology for all of its industry productivity work of using a concept of *gross output* that is equivalent to shipments or sales, not value added; and the indexes are Tornqvist aggregations of output at the lowest available level of detail.[14] The BEA, on the other hand, uses a measure of the gross margin—sales minus cost of goods sold—as its basic concept of gross output in the retail sector. The two estimates are more nearly similar than might be expected, however, because BEA assumes that the margin is a fixed percentage of sales at the lowest level of detail.

Generally, the output measure for an industry is what the industry sells. A shoe store sells shoes, which is the way the BLS measures retail output. The problems with the BLS approach are well represented by the example of computers. Because of manufacturers' improvements in computational speed and capacity, the real value of computer-store sales has grown spectacularly, over 25 percent per year since the mid 1980s. Much of that growth is in the increased quality per machine. The computer stores, however, are basically selling boxes; and while the number sold has increased, it has not grown at anywhere near the increase in the output of computer manufactures. An index that combines the increase in computer quality with growth in the number of machines bears little relationship to the actual activities of the computer store (even though it is the appropriate way to measure the output of the computer producer).

There are several suggested lines of research to deal with these problems. One option would involve the construction of input price indexes, as for manufacturing, so that a measure of the real value of the gross margin could be obtained by double deflation. However, many analysts doubt that indexes of sufficient accuracy could be developed to obtain, in effect, the real value of the margin as the residual of changes in two large numbers.

Alternatively, it might be possible to develop price indexes that could be used to deflate the gross margin directly. For example, one approach would identify characteristics of stores that account for variation in the gross margins, and construct an hedonic index based on changes in those characteristics or their prices. The BLS is currently conducting a research program that asks individual retailers for the replacement cost of goods sold as well as the retail price. At the same time, they propose to obtain information on the store characteristics, such as number of SKUs, square footage, storage area, and whether the store is a discount, gourmet, warehouse, or combination outlet. This will provide a data set that will allow for the exploration of the sources of variation in retail margins.

Output and productivity in retail trade have been greatly affected in the past by cost-shifting from the store to the customer—self-service retail trade, for example. The evidence is overwhelming that the changes are positively perceived by consumers. But part of the cost shifting ought to be deducted from retail productivity, and increasing services to customers should be added (Oi, 1992; 1998).

E-commerce

One widely cited estimate (Whinston et al, 1999) puts the volume of e-commerce at $301 billion, with a growth rate of 173% per year. What are the issues for measuring productivity that come out of the growth of e-commerce?

First, it helps to understand what are not issues for measuring productivity. The estimate of $301 billion cannot be interpreted as the net contribution of e-commerce to GDP. Only about $101 billion of the total represents final e-commerce sales (Whinston et al, 1999). The other two-thirds represent high-tech investment by e-commerce firms and purchases of other inputs, such as software and web site hosting services. These inputs would be netted out of any GDP estimate, so the $301 billion double counts in the traditional national accounting sense. Although it is of some use to know the total volume of transactions that is associated with e-commerce, the total volume of transactions does not give a measure of unduplicated output, which traditionally is calculated by value added.

Even some of the $101 billion of e-commerce sales are not net additions to GDP. In the case of computers and software (by far the largest category of e-commerce sales at present), only the e-commerce *margin* properly is included in GDP, not the total e-commerce transaction, because manufacturers' sales of computers and software are counted in the manufacturing industries.

Although the growth rates of e-commerce are impressive, its size is still miniscule, even compared to catalog sales. There is no evidence that GDP or aggregate productivity is currently missing very much because of e-commerce. Moreover, unlike the situation with service sector statistics in the past, the Census Bureau has already mounted survey activity to determine how many retail sales take place over the Internet (Mesenbourg, 1999). It appears likely that e-commerce sales will be smoothly integrated into existing retail sales information before they get very large. Accordingly, the macro implications of e-commerce are not very important, and, actually, not very interesting.

The more important questions are: What does e-commerce do to the productivity of firms that adopt it? How does it affect internal business processes, and therefore productivity? What are the effects of displacement on other, competing, industries? And what does it do to competition and the structure of existing industries? Unfortunately, data to study those questions will be harder to obtain.

Some of those questions concern inputs to production. The U.S. statistical system has historically been weak in providing information about detailed input usage, and this is especially true for inputs of high-tech equipment, software, and services. That means there is little benchmark information to determine the changes that will be wrought by e-commerce. Essentially, there is no good picture of business processes and input usage in U.S. statistics before the advent of e-commerce.

Many final sales over the Internet, and many business-to-business Internet sales as well, are substitutions for more traditional kinds of retailing, not only against traditional "brick and mortar" stores, but more specifically mail-order catalogs. How readily do people substitute Internet transactions for older types of transactions?

Papers by Brynjolfsson, Smith, and Bailey (1999) and by Goolsbee (1999) suggest that Internet buyers are, first, quite sensitive to price differences, but quite sensitive as well to various nonprice elements, such as advertising, trust, delivery times, and so forth. Indeed, there seem to be two competing forces, which have been described as an "arms war" between business and consumers. On the one hand, it has often been suggested that the Internet makes it easier for consumers to search for prices, which should reduce the amount of price dispersion in markets. On the other hand, businesses use the Internet to increase product differentiation and tailor products to individual buyers, thereby increasing the amount of price dispersion. Studies (Brynjolfsson et al, 1999) have found that when consumers learn about nonprice aspects of the transaction, they turn out to be more sensitive to the nonprice aspects than to the price dispersion. The studies also find a large amount of price dispersion on the Internet, which is consistent with the finding that nonprice aspects of the transaction, including advertising, are very important to Internet sales. The widely-publicized notion of a frictionless Internet economy, with no advantages with respect to seller's size, is not supported by current research.

As another issue, some of the changes wrought by e-commerce cross the traditional "production boundary" used in national accounts. For example, a book bought from a conventional bookstore implies that the consumer incurs travel costs and time costs to go to the bookstore to make the purchase. Those costs are not now counted in the acquisition price of the book. A book purchased over the Internet, however, incurs handling and shipping costs that are included in the price of the book. Conversely, some people like shopping or like to browse in bookstores, which cannot be done over the Internet. Looked at this way, these services are part of the value created by traditional retailing, and the Internet provides fewer retailing services. If our statistics simply compare the price of the book in the two settings we will omit the value of retailing services (which are not explicitly priced) to the ultimate buyer, and miscount as well costs to the buyer that are non-market in the one case (travel costs to the store) but are explicit and charged for in the other (shipping and handling for e-commerce sales).

These problems are no different from other kinds of retailing shifts. There is serious concern that we already mismeasure output in the retailing sector because implicitly-priced store services are not directly accounted for (see the section on retail trade). So in this sense, e-commerce does not raise new issues, but it may raise them in new and particularly intractable forms.

Finally, there are interactions between e-commerce and other economic changes. Declines in communication costs, and perhaps to a lesser degree, in transportation costs, are a major force behind the growth in e-commerce. We may not be measuring the decline in the costs of communication well. The growth of e-commerce may just be a response to other economic innovations that are more fundamental, and e-commerce may not be the major technological change in itself.

A closely related matter is the decline in prices for Internet service providers. Work is underway on this in both the United States (in a Brookings sponsored project) and Canada. But because Internet service contracts are increasingly being bundled into the purchase price for computers, or else Internet service is being paid for by advertising, obtaining price indexes and real output measures for Internet service providers is likely to pose difficulties that have not yet been addressed.

Insurance

Labor productivity for insurance carriers dropped precipitously after 1973, and turned negative, as did multifactor productivity. (The 1973-97 productivity growth rates are −0.1 for labor productivity and −2.3 for multifactor productivity—see tables 1 and 2). Negative productivity growth rates are always suspect, but they are especially so in the case of insurance, because this industry is among the largest purchasers of computer equipment. The use of computers for claims and premium processing is obvious.

After 1987, however, the insurance-carriers industry shows very rapid rates of productivity growth, 4.6% for labor productivity and 2.1% for multifactor productivity, perhaps because investment in IT equipment has borne fruit. As a result, recent productivity growth in the insurance carriers industry exceed its pre-1973 rates.[15]

Despite the insurance industry's recent impressive productivity growth, there are reasons to believe that its output may still be mismeasured, and that the industry's true productivity growth may be stronger than the available current data show. We conclude that a major unresolved problem in measuring the output of insurance is the measurement and valuation of risk. The management of risk is what insurance companies sell. Anecdotal evidence suggests that insurance companies have greatly improved their ability to manage and control for risk. Because there is no explicit adjustment for risk in present price and real output measures, we suspect that output levels and output growth are both understated.

A major difficulty in focusing on what seems to us the real question—that is, measuring and valuing risk—is that insurance has been the topic of one of those long-standing national accounts disputes that seemingly are never resolved. There are a number of interlocking issues, partly real issues and partly, we feel, confusions, which were discussed extensively in the April, 1998 Brookings workshop on measuring insurance.

Two major issues are: (1) Should the current price measure of insurance output be the insurance company's revenue from premiums or, instead, its premiums minus claims paid out? (2) However the first question is resolved, should the insurance company be treated as operating in two lines of business, namely, (a) selling insurance and (b) investing reserves? 16

(1) *The current price (nominal) output measure—premiums versus premiums minus claims.* This output definition controversy corresponds to two different conceptual models about the insurance company's production process. The premiums minus claims view is equivalent to a risk-pooling model where the insurance company is merely a facilitator and administrator. The policyholders create a pool for sharing risk, essentially operating as a cooperative, and the members of the cooperative pay a service fee to the insurance company for administering the pooling scheme. The price of insurance in this model is the service fee for administering the plan. The rationale for this approach to insurance is presented by Hill (1998), and it is the view that is incorporated into the Systems of National Accounts, or SNA (Commission of the European Communities et al, 1993).

In the risk-pooling model of insurance, the insurance company's productivity could rise if it becomes more efficient at processing premiums and claims. But if the premium falls because the insurance company finds ways to identify more risky business (and either rejects it, or prices it to match its greater risk) or if it finds ways to eliminate inflated or fraudulent claims, the effects would be eliminated from the insurance margin, and hence from the insurance industry productivity measure.

In the alternative view, the insurance company assumes the risk. The policyholder buys the service of protection of assets or income from loss. The output is the insurance premium times the quantity of risk assumed. The price charged for assuming risk is $p = P/R$, where p is the price of insurance, P is the premium charged, and R is a measure of risk assumed (Bradford and Logue, 1998). Under this model, the price of insurance reflects both efficiencies in processing premiums and claims and efficiencies in matching and administering risk, so both sets of factors influence insurance industry productivity.

A major implementation problem with the risk-pooling insurance model (the national accounts convention for insurance) arises out of the fact that the insurance business does not function the way this model suggests. Although there are insurance companies with the word mutual in their names, there is very little evidence that they act as cooperatives on behalf of the policyholders. In the April 1998 Brookings workshop, one participant remarked that he had sat on the board of directors for a major insurance company, but nothing he ever heard there suggested that the company thought it was acting on behalf of the policyholders. One of us had a similar conversation with an executive in a large European insurance company. Because insurance companies do not operate as if they were providing administrative services to policyholders, no price or fee corresponding to the risk-pooling model of insurance can be found. Eurostat, in work leading up to its Harmonized Indexes of Consumer Prices (HICP), found that insurance companies could not provide a price that corresponded to the risk-pooling concept (Astin, 1999). Thus, even if a risk-pooling model of insurance were the only one that was compatible with national accounting conventions, it cannot be implemented, in terms of estimating real output from consistently defined measures of current-price output and of prices.

The risk-assuming model of insurance, which yields the gross insurance premium as a measure of current dollar output of insurance, yields a much larger gross output for the insurance industry than does the premiums minus claims view. Sherwood (1999) in his table 2, shows that the smaller definition runs from one-third to one-fifth of the larger one (data are for casualty insurance). This must have implications for international comparisons of productivity. However, it is not exactly clear whether the two concepts of insurance yield different rates of productivity growth in the U.S. economy. Although Sherwood (1999) calculates that the effect of the alternatives on total non-farm business sector output is small, he does not explicitly calculate the effect on insurance industry productivity and does not reach definitive conclusions.

(2) *Insurance company investment earnings.* There is a growing consensus that the investment earnings of insurance companies should be added into their industry output. Because of moral hazard, insurance companies collect premiums in advance of claims liabilities. The surpluses are invested. Evidence strongly suggests that competition among insurance companies leads to the distribution of insurance industry investment earnings back to the policyholders in the form of reduced premiums, and it is commonly observed that casualty insurance companies do not cover the full cost of their claims from their premiums earnings. Treating an insurance company as producing a joint product (insurance policies and investment activity) is not a conceptual step very far beyond the current treatment of other industries that have jointly-produced products. Whether national accountants should also treat the insurance policyholder as earning the insurance company's investment income in the form of more insurance (the treatment prescribed in the SNA) is not central to the question of computing industry productivity measures. (For the record, we do not think this national accounts approach yields a sensible measure of real consumption or of the price of insurance in the CPI.)

If the insurance industry has used computers merely to process premiums, premium notices, and claims services more efficiently, the effects are probably captured in the existing productivity numbers. This use of computers implies substitution of capital for labor and the existing insurance-productivity numbers (4.6% increase in labor productivity and 2.1% increase in multifactor productivity since 1987) are consistent with substantial capital-labor substitution in this industry. On the other hand, if computers combined with innovations in risk management make it possible for insurance companies to be more efficient in assessing and valuing risk, then it is not at all certain that these technological improvements are incorporated into existing statistics.

The BLS, in its producer-price index and productivity-measurement programs, has begun to measure the output of the insurance industry with a gross-premiums-plus-investment-income approach (Sherwood, 1999; Dohm and Eggleston, 1998). This is a step forward. Incorporating more explicit measures of risk, and valuation of improvements in insurance companies' ability to manage risk, is the next step toward improving the output measurement of insurance. [17]

Banking

Like insurance, the measurement of banking output in national accounts has been the subject of a long-standing controversy that impedes progress. In the NIPA, as in the SNA, current-price banking output is defined as the spread between borrowers' and depositors' interest rates, plus fees for services that are explicitly priced. The issues in measuring banking output were the subject of a Brookings workshop in November 1998.

Subsequently, BEA introduced a change in its extrapolator for real banking output in the October 1999 GDP revisions. This extrapolator is effectively the measure of banking output that has long been used by the BLS for its banking labor-productivity measures. It includes counts of various banking processes, such as checks cashed and number of ATM transactions. Because we have not yet been able to examine the effects of the BEA change on banking industry output growth, we will address discussion of banking productivity at a later time.

For the record, we think the BEA change is an improvement, but that more work on banking output measurement, both conceptual and empirical, is needed.

Medical Care

It has become commonplace that medical care inflation outstrips the overall inflation rate. For example, between 1985 and 1995, the medical care component of the CPI rose 6.5% per year, when the overall CPI rose only 3.6%.

Until fairly recently, deflators for medical-care output have been based almost exclusively on the medical-care components of the CPI. Many economists believe that the CPI medical-price indexes overstated inflation in medical care.[18] If so, productivity growth in medical care is understated. Significantly, measured productivity in the health-care industry has been negative. From 1973-97, health-care industry productivity declined by 2.6 % per year, and from 1987-97 by 1.8 % per year.

In 1992, BLS introduced new price indexes for health care in its Producer Price Index (PPI) program. These new indexes introduced a new methodology for measuring the price of medical care. Rather than pricing the cost of a day in the hospital, as did the historical CPI, the BLS now draws a probability sample of treatments for medical conditions. For example, for the PPI price index for mental-health-care treatment in a hospital, the probability selection might be "major depression." The BLS then collects the monthly change in costs for treating that identical medical condition (see Berndt et al., 1998, and Catron and Murphy, 1996, for more information on BLS procedures). The new medical-care PPI indexes are great improvements on the previously-available CPI medical-price information (see the assessment in Berndt et al., 1998). Overall, the new PPI indexes present a picture of lower medical care inflation, compared to CPI measures, for the period where the two overlap (Catron and Murphy, 1996).

BLS subsequently introduced similar methodology into the CPI (Cardenas, 1996). However, even with the new PPI methodology, it has been difficult for BLS to find data to adjust for changes in the efficacy of treatment. Although there is some controversy on how far statistical agencies should go in building measures of treatment efficacy into price and output measures, we doubt if anyone seriously disagrees that the price index should be "adjusted" or corrected *in some fashion* for improvements in medical efficacy. Because medical economists generally believe that progress has been made in medical technology—better prognoses, less time spent in the hospital for any given condition, less painful and onerous conditions during treatment, and so forth— they believe that inadequate adjustment for changes in medical technology creates upward biases in price indexes for medical care.

There is less universal agreement, however, on the basis for adjustment. In the PPI, the BLS looks for information on the change in costs that are associated with improvements in medical efficacy. Some economists would go considerably further and ask for information about the medical outcome and the value to the patient of changes in medical outcomes. Research on cataract surgery by Shapiro and Wilcox (1996) serves to illustrate the issues.

At one time, cataract surgery involved a lengthy hospital stay, a week or ten days in intensive care. Now, it is mostly an outpatient procedure, often performed in a doctor's office or clinic. Put another way, the number of days in the hospital has dropped from 10 or more to zero. If one were to ask, in the usual "cost-based" formulation, how much more costly was the improved procedure, the answer is negative. If the price index were based, as the CPI was formerly, on the cost of a day in the hospital, there is no reasonable way to "adjust" the price index for the value of an improvement that reduced the number of days to zero.

But from the patient's point of view, the modern operation is surely better. The operation once required that the patient be immobilized for a lengthy period. Given the choice between immobilization and the far less unpleasant recovery period associated with the modern operation, patients would undoubtedly be willing to pay more for the modern operation. Not only is it less costly *in terms of what is paid for* (hospital care, for example), it is also far less unpleasant for the patient. The operation also has fewer adverse side-effects, does not require wearing thick corrective lenses, and is in many other ways improved from the patient's point of view.

A medical outcome measure would take into account all the ways in which the improvement in cataract surgery was beneficial to the patient. But some of those improvements discussed in the previous paragraph go outside the traditional "market boundary" of national accounts. The patient might well be *willing* to pay for the improved technology, but in fact the technology comes to him (or to his insurance company) for less monetary cost or expenditure of market resources than the old treatment cost.

But should these improvements be credited to the productivity of the medical care industry, or to its output in national accounts? Or should improvements that are not explicitly paid for, and for which the value of a transaction cannot be directly inferred, be ruled out of national accounts (or out of national health accounts) on the grounds that they fall outside the market boundary that has been traditional for measuring GDP?

For example, the time spent in recovery from cataract surgery is part of the cost to the patient—even leaving aside the disutility of immobilization— but this time cost is not traditionally considered in national accounts, nor is the value of the reduction in time in recovery from surgery, or the reduced disutility of reduced time spent immobilized, directly valued. The time cost of the patient, the greater utility to the patient of less unpleasant treatments, and the value to the patient of reductions in unwanted side effects are all elements that would go into a measure of medical outcomes (see Gold et al., 1996). But should they go into an economic accounting for medical care? That remains somewhat controversial among economists.[19] Many of these issues were discussed in the conference papers contained in Triplett (1999a).

Stating the problem this way underscores the difficulties that statistical agencies face in producing price indexes for medical care. Calculating the change in costs for treating an episode of an illness requires not only the traditional statistical agency skills in gathering prices, but also a great deal of medical knowledge about changes in the efficacy of medical treatments (knowledge which, in many cases, is scientifically uncertain, or in contention). It also requires knowledge about patient valuations of changes in treatments, particularly when treatments change in dimensions that involve the patient's time, tolerance for pain, and valuation of the disutility of side effects, or of the onerous implications of treatments (such as, for example, a frequent treatment regimen for a pharmaceutical).

Additionally, some changes in medical treatment cause shifts in expenditures among PPI index categories; the PPI methodology contains no obvious way to take these cost savings into account. As an example, consider increased use of drugs that permit treatment of mental conditions on an outpatient basis, rather than in a mental hospital. Substitution of drugs (and clinical visits) for hospital care will reduce the cost of treatment, but this cost reduction will be reflected inadequately in the PPI because the PPI holds the weights for the various expenditure categories (hospitals, doctors offices, pharmaceuticals, and so forth) constant.

New research price indexes for medical treatments that adjust for changes in the effectiveness of medical treatments include: Cutler et al. (1996, 1999); Frank, Berndt and Busch (1998; forthcoming); and, as already noted, Shapiro and Wilcox (1996). These new price indexes confirm that the historical CPI medical care component was upward biased as a deflator for medical-care-industry output, as does comparison of the new PPI indexes with movements of the CPI. How much do medical care productivity measures that use the historical CPI as output deflators understate the amount of productivity growth in medical care?

To provide an evaluation of the bias in existing measures, Triplett (1999b) "backcasts" an estimate for a mental-health-care-price index. One part of the backcast is an estimate formed by matching, for the period following 1992, PPI and CPI components and using the differences in trends as an adjustment factor for the CPI for the earlier period. He weights these indexes according to costs for treatment of mental health and makes an additional correction based on the research of Frank, Berndt, and Busch (forthcoming). The adjusted mental-health-care-price index shows essentially no medical inflation during the 1985-95 interval (table 5).

He then uses the adjusted price index to estimate the growth in the quantity of per capita mental-health-care services (or real expenditure growth).[20] For the 1985-95 period, the unadjusted real output growth rate is negative, at about -1.5% per year, which is very roughly consistent with the negative 1987-97 productivity trend for health care, shown in table 3, of -2.6% annually. Adjusted, real output growth is substantially positive, at about 6.6% for 1985-95, or nearly 8 percentage points higher than the unadjusted estimates (table 5). The implications for medical care productivity are obvious.

Table 5. Growth Rates, Expenditures and Prices, Mental Health Treatments, 1972-95

	Annual Expenditure Growth Rates	Price Indexes (percent increase)		Real Expenditure Growth	
		Unadjusted	Adjusted	Unadjusted	Adjusted
1985-90	7.06	8.78	-1.11	-1.54	8.31
1990-95	4.94	6.47	-0.04	-1.37	5.02
1985-95	6.00	7.62	-0.58	-1.46	6.66

Source: Triplett, 1999b

Mental health may not be representative of the rest of medical care. Improved price indexes for other diseases might not make so much difference to output trends as in the case of mental health. However, the heart-attack price index of Cutler et al. (1996), or the cataract surgery price index in Shapiro and Wilcox (1996) suggest that revisions to real expenditure trends for these disease categories might be similar to the revisions for mental health.

As an exercise, however, Triplett (1999b) assumes that the correction applied to the mental-health price and output measures applies to the entire medical care sector. This would raise medical care productivity from -2.6% per year in table 3 to 5.6% per year. This is clearly a major impact.

It is important to emphasize limitations of this backcast. It is unlikely that the backcast is exactly valid, but neither is the historical CPI. Improvement of productivity in medical care seems more likely than the deterioration that present measures of medical care output show.

Notes

[1] The non-farm multifactor productivity numbers are due for revision in the near future, to incorporate the revisions to GDP that were released in October 1999. This will undoubtedly raise the non-goods estimate but not the manufacturing productivity estimate, because the productivity numbers published by the BLS for the non-farm and manufacturing sectors are based on different data and underlying output concepts.

[2] We should note that BEA does not explicitly produce productivity data, and so the following remarks are not meant as criticism of BEA statistics for their own purposes.

[3] The data on gross product and its components in current prices extend back to 1947.

[4] Person engaged in production are defined as full-time equivalent employees plus the self-employed. Employees on part-time schedules are included as a fraction of a full-time employee on the basis of weekly hours. Unpaid family workers are excluded.

[5] As shown in table 1, the 1.1 previously published BLS labor productivity rate in table 2 has now been revised to 1.5. Additionally, the estimate of 0.9 in table 2 shows the effect of using employment, instead of hours.

[6] The importance of computer manufacture in the post-1994 improvement in productivity growth is emphasized by Gordon (1999a). Because of data limitations, his definition of electronics is a broad one that includes all of SIC 36 and 38 machinery manufacturing industries. This aggregate's productivity growth for the pre-1973 period is not properly interpreted as electronics productivity, partly because much more of it was non-electronic in those days, and partly because the part that was electronic was not as well measured.

[7] This 1.8 point slowdown, calculated directly from the industry data, can be compared with the estimated slowdown (by backing off the manufacturing estimate from the total) of 2.0 percentage points, in table 1.

[8] Banking, insurance agents (and carriers before 1987), personal services, business services (before 1987), and repair, health, legal, and educational services. The negative

rates of growth in labor productivity for many service industries were emphasized in Sliffman and Corrado (1996).

[9] The methodology used to compute gross output and product by industry is reported in Yuskavage (1996), and an overview of the problems with medical care prices is provided in Berndt et al. (1998).

[10] Thus, we are using the net stock of fixed capital as a proxy for the index of capital inputs. The theoretically appropriate measure is the productive stock, which yields the flow of capital services, as emphasized by Jorgenson (1989). The distinction between the net, or wealth, capital stock and the productive capital stock is discussed in Triplett (1996). Capital and labor are combined with a Tornqvist index using the share of labor compensation in GDP after adjusting for the self-employed.

[11] The BLS definition of gross output differs from that of the BEA by excluding intra-industry shipments. In addition, the Gullickson-Harper estimates of multi-factor productivity use a more elaborate measure of capital input that includes land and inventories, and the labor input is based on hours worked, with an adjustment for labor quality.

[12] Gullickson and Harper (1999), pp. 58-59.

[13] Agendas for the workshops, and some of the papers, are accessible at: www.brook.edu\es\research\rs7.htm.

[14] Kunze and Jablonski (1998).

[15] The gains are not shared by the insurance agents industry. This industry will not be considered further in the present discussion.

[16] A third issue is also debated: If the answer to question (2) is positive, should the investment part of the insurance company's output be imputed back to insurance purchasers in the form of imputed increases in the quantity of insurance? The latter question amounts to asking whether there is a difference between insurance *company* output in industry productivity measures and insurance *product* information in, for example, the consumer price index. Because this last issue is important for measuring CPIs and for measuring real consumption, but not for industry productivity measures, it is not included in the present discussion.

[17] Some additional national accounting concerns are present. First, problems arise because the BEA does not have a separate capital account. The insurance premium, and not premiums minus claims, is the cost to current production for keeping the capital stock whole against unforeseen losses. Second, double-counting is of concern to BEA because it wants to use the output of the car repair industry, minus a more or less arbitrary adjustment for repairs to business cars, as a measure in Personal Consumption Expenditures. Finally, insurance claims are not always spent to replace the item of capital equipment that was lost (emphasized by Hill, 1998).

[18] A comprehensive discussion of price indexes for medical care is Berndt et al. (1998). See also Triplett and Berndt, 1999.

[19] We leave aside here problems with measuring medical outcomes, which are formidable. The question is what one wants to do with medical-outcomes measures, if perfected or improved.

[20] Treatments for mental disorders account for over eight per cent of total U.S. health care expenditures, about a tenth (9.5%) of all allocable U.S. personal health care expenditures and just over one per cent of gross domestic product (GDP).

References

Astin, John. 1999. Presentation to the Brookings Workshop on Measuring the Price and Output of Insurance, April, 1998.

Baumol, William J. 1967. "Macroeconomics of Unbalanced Growth: The Anatomy of Urban Crises." *American Economic Review* 57: 415-26, June.

Berndt, Ernst R., David M. Cutler, Richard G. Frank, Zvi Griliches, Joseph P. Newhouse, and Jack E. Triplett. 1998. "Price Indexes for Medical Care Goods and Services: An Overview of Measurement Issues." *National Bureau of Economics Working Paper* W6817, November.

Bonds, Belinda and Tim Aylor. 1998. "Investment in New Structures and Equipment in 1992 by Using Industries." *Survey of Current Business* 78 (12), December.

Bradford, David F. and Kyle D. Logue. 1998. "The Effects of Tax Changes on Property-Casualty Insurance Prices." In David F. Bradford (ed.), *The Economics of Property-Casualty Insurance*. Chicago: University of Chicago Press.

Brynjolfsson, Eric, Michael D. Smith, and Joseph Bailey. 1999. "Understanding Digital Markets: Review and Assessment." Paper presented at the Brookings Workshop on E-Commerce, September 24.

Cardenas, Elaine M. 1996. "Revision of the CPI Hospital Services Component." *Monthly Labor Review* 119(12): 40-48, December.

Catron, Brian and Bonnie Murphy. 1996. "Hospital Price Inflation: What Does the New PPI Tell Us?" *Monthly Labor Review* 120(7): 24-31, July.

Commission of the European Communities, International Monetary Fund, Organisation for Economic Co-operation and Development, United Nations, and World Bank. 1993. *System of National Accounts 1993*. Office for Official Publications of the European Communities Catalogue number CA-81-93-002-EN-C, International Monetary Fund Publication Stock No. SNA-EA, Organisation for Economic Co-operation and Development OECD Code 30 94 01 1, United Nations publication Sales No. E.94.XVII.4, World Bank Stock Number 31512.

Cutler, David M., Mark B. McClellan, Joseph P. Newhouse, and Dahlia Remler. 1996. "Are Medical Prices Declining? Evidence from Heart Attack Treatments." *Quarterly Journal of Economics* 113(4): 991-1024, November.

Cutler, David M., Mark B. McClellan, and Joseph P. Newhouse. 1999. "The Costs and Benefits of Intensive Treatment for Cardiovascular Disease." In Jack E. Triplett (ed.), *Measuring the Prices of Medical Treatments*. Washington D.C.: The Brookings Institution Press.

Dohm, Arlene, and Deanna Eggleston. 1998. "Producer Price Indexes for Property/Casualty and Life Insurance." Paper presented to the Brookings Workshop on Measuring the Price and Output of Insurance, April.

Frank, Richard G., Ernst Berndt, and Susan H. Busch. 1998. "Price Indexes for Acute Phase Treatment of Depression." *National Bureau of Economic Research Working Paper* 6799 (November).

Frank, Richard G., Ernst R. Berndt, and Susan Busch. Forthcoming. "Price Indexes for the Treatment of Depression." In Ernst Berndt and David Cutler (eds.), *Medical Care Output and Productivity.* National Bureau of Economic Research, Studies in Income and Wealth 59: Chicago: University of Chicago Press.

Gerduk, Irwin. 1999. "New PPI Indexes for Accounting, Legal, and Advertising Services." Paper presented at Brookings Workshop on Measuring the Output of Business Services, May 14.

Gold, Marthe R., Joanna E. Siegel, Louise B. Russell, and Milton C. Weinstein. 1996. *Cost-Effectiveness in Health and Medicine.* New York: Oxford University Press.

Goolsbee, Austan. 1999. "In a World without Borders: The Impact of Taxes on Internet Commerce." Paper presented at the Brookings Workshop on Measuring the Output of Business Services, May 14.

Gordon, Robert. 1999a. "Has the New Economy Rendered the Productivity Slowdown Obsolete?" Presentation at CBO Panel of Economic Advisors, June 2, 1992 (revised, 14/6/99)

Gordon, Robert. 1999b. "Management Consulting Firms: Some Approaches to Output Measurement." Paper presented at the Brookings Workshop on Measuring the Output of Business Services, May 14.

Griliches, Zvi. 1994. "Productivity, R&D, and the Data Constraint." *American Economic Review* 84(1): 1-23, March.

Gullickson, William and Michael Harper. 1999. "Possible Measurement Bias in Aggregate Productivity Growth," *Monthly Labor Review* (February), pp. 47-67.

Hill, Peter. 1998. "Insurance in the SNA." Paper presented at the Brookings Workshop on Measuring the Price and Output of Insurance, April.

Jorgenson, Dale W. 1989. "Capital as a Factor of Production." In Dale W. Jorgenson and Ralph Landau (eds.), *Technology and Capital Formation.* Cambridge, Mass. The MIT Press.

Kunze, Kent and Mary Jablonski. 1998. "Productivity in Service-Producing Industries." Paper presented at the Brookings Workshop on New Government Datasets, June.

Levy, Frank. 1999. "Some Initial Results on Productivity in Car Dealerships and Auto Repair." Paper presented at the Brookings Workshop on Measuring the Output of Business Services, May 14.

Mesenbourg, Thomas. 1999. "Measuring Electronic Business." Paper presented at the Brookings Workshop on Measuring the Output of Business Services, May 14.

Nachum, Lilac. 1999. "Measurement of Productivity in Swedish Management Consulting Firms." Paper presented at the Brookings Workshop on Measuring the Output of Business Services, May 14.

Oi, Walter. 1992. "Productivity in the Distributive Trades: The Shopper and the Economies of Massed Reserves." In Zvi Griliches (ed.), *Output Measurement in the Service Sectors.* University of Chicago Press for the National Bureau of Economic Research.

Oi, Walter. 1998. "Adapting the Retail Format to a Changing Economy." Paper presented at the Brookings Workshop on Measuring the Output of Retail Trade, September 18.

Shapiro, Matthew P. and David W. Wilcox. 1996. "Mismeasurement in the Consumer Price Index: An Evaluation." *NBER Macroeconomics Annual* 11: 93-142.

Sherwood, Mark K. 1999. "Output of the Property and Casualty Insurance Industry." Paper presented at the Brookings Workshop on Measuring the Price and Output of Insurance, April 1998. Now published in: *Canadian Journal of Economics* 32(2), April.

Sliffman, Larry and Carol Corrado. 1996. "Decomposition of Productivity and Unit Costs," Occasional Staff Studies, OSS-1, Washington DC: Board of Governors of the Federal Reserve.

Swick, Roslyn. 1999. Paper presented at the Brookings Workshop on Measuring the Output of Business Services, May 14.

Triplett, Jack E. (ed.) 1999a. *Measuring the Prices of Medical Treatments.* Washington D.C.: The Brookings Institution Press.

Triplett, Jack E. 1999b. "What's Different about Health: Human Repair and Car Repair in National Accounts and in National Health Accounts." The Brookings Institution. Forthcoming in Ernst Berndt and David Cutler (eds.), *Medical Care Output and Productivity.* National Bureau of Economic Research, Studies in Income and Wealth 59. Chicago: University of Chicago Press.

Triplett, Jack E. 1996. "Depreciation in Production Analysis and in Income and Wealth Accounts: Resolution of an Old Debate." *Economic Inquiry* 34: 93-115.

U.S. Department of Labor, Bureau of Labor Statistics. 1999a. Major sector productivity and costs index, http://146.142.4.24/cgi-bin/dsrv?pr. Accessed November 23, 1999.

U.S. Department of Labor, Bureau of Labor Statistics. 1999b. Major sector multifactor productivity index, http://146.142.4.24/cgi-bin/dsrv?mp. Accessed November 23, 1999.

Whinston, Andrew, Anitesh Barua, Jon Pinnell, and Jay Shutter. 1999. "Measuring the Internet Economy." Paper presented at the Brookings Workshop on Measuring the Output of Business Services, May 14.

Yuskavage, Robert E. 1996. "Improved Estimates of Gross Product by Industry, 1959-94," *Survey of Current Business* (August) pp. 133-55.

CHAPTER 3

Forecasting U.S. Trade in Services[*]

Alan V. Deardorff, Saul H. Hymans, Robert M. Stern, and Chong Xiang

I. Introduction

Trade in services[1] is a major part of U.S. participation in the global economy. Since the mid-1980s, the dollar value of service imports has, on average, equaled more than 21 percent of the value of goods imports, while service exports have, on average, been 40 percent as large as goods exports. In calendar 1998, U.S. service exports, as measured in the balance-of-payments accounts, totaled $260.4 billion compared with $181.5 of service imports, yielding a U.S. trade surplus in services of $78.9 billion.[2]

The United States has been running a positive balance in service trade since 1974. In the late 1970s, the service balance was in the range of $4-$5 billion per year; during the 1980s, the annual service surplus was generally in the $12-$15 billion range; and by the late 1980s, service trade was producing $20-$30 billion surpluses. The 1990s have seen a marked growth in service trade, with export growth outpacing import growth to generate service trade surpluses rising until 1998, as follows (annually, in billions of $s, transaction-based):

1990	1991	1992	1993	1994	1995	1996	1997	1998
$27.9	43.1	57.4	60.7	65.3	73.8	82.8	87.7	78.9

The economic and financial problems in the Asia-Pacific region have taken a toll on U.S. exports. This is especially true for goods exports, but service exports have been impacted as well. By mid-1997, service exports had grown to $263 billion at an annual rate, up from $232 billion a year earlier. Thereafter, service exports stalled, and they have remained essentially flat in the range of $255-$263 billion from the second quarter of 1997 (1997.2) to 1998.4. Only in 1999.1 does it appear that the upward movement may have resumed, reaching $266 billion. Service imports, on the other hand continued to rise throughout 1998, with the result that the balance of trade in services declined to an annual rate of under $74 billion in 1998.3. The balance picked up after that, reaching just over $79 billion as of the latest quarter (1999.1) for which we had data at the time that we initially drafted this study.

In what follows, we report on the construction of a forecasting model for U.S. international trade in services. The model builds upon the data and forecasts of the U.S. economy done by the Research Seminar in Quantitative Economics (RSQE) at the University of Michigan, from which we take our estimates of the paths that will be followed by the explanatory variables in our model. The effects of these variables on prices and quantities of trade in services are estimated here using a standard theoretical framework of supply and demand that is described below in Section III, after first providing a brief review of the literature in Section II. Section IV discusses the data and our procedures for estimation, leading to discussion of the estimated equations themselves in Section V. The forecast is in Section VI, to which the reader may turn immediately if not interested in the details of the model. Section VI describes the inputs to the forecast as well as several perspectives on the paths that we forecast for both aggregate services trade and the four disaggregated categories of services that our model treats separately.

II. Literature Review

In the past two decades, there have been a number of econometric forecasting efforts for the United States that have dealt to some extent with services. Some of these studies have treated services in the aggregate or with limited disaggregation while others have combined goods and services for forecasting purposes.

Thus for example, Helkie and Hooper (1988) discuss the forecasting properties of the partial equilibrium model of the U.S. current account, known as USIT, which has been maintained at the Federal Reserve Board. The USIT model has provided input into the Federal Reserve Multi-Country Model (MCM) and the later version of the MCM model now known as FRB/Global. Hooper and Helkie (pp. 27-29) distinguished "other services receipts and payments," with the explanatory variables being income and relative prices and real merchandise trade volumes as a proxy for transportation services. The FRB/Global model was instituted in 1996 and is laid out in Levin et al. (1997). Other service receipts and payments are still treated in the aggregate, with separate equations for the volumes and price deflators.

Other forecasting work on U.S. services trade includes Helkie and Stekler (1996), Dunnaway (1988), and Nedde (1992). Helkie and Stekler seek to allow for improvements in the data for aggregate services exports and imports by including dummy variables in the context of the FRB-USIT model noted above. Dunnaway's partial equilibrium model of the U.S. current account distinguishes three categories of services receipts and payments, including travel and passenger fares, transportation, and other services. His model is designed to analyze the sources of changes in the U.S. trade balance, sensitivity to changes in key exogenous determinants, and the impact of the post-1985 real depreciation of the U.S. dollar. Nedde's quarterly model of the U.S. current account was designed for use in IMF projections associated with the World Economic Outlook. She used an error-correction methodology to identify the lag structure and capture longer-run supply effects more fully. Equations for services receipts and payments in the aggregate and their implicit deflators are estimated and included in the analysis and evaluation of the forecasting properties of the current-account model.

The models mentioned above relate either to the U.S. current account as such or to the current account as embodied in a more comprehensive model of the U.S. macro-economy. There are of course many existing macro-econometric forecasting models of the U.S. economy and other economies as well as a number of multi-country models. As far as we can tell from an examination of several of these models, it appears that exports and imports of goods and services are typically combined for estimating and forecasting purposes. Since our interest in this chapter is to develop a disaggregated forecasting structure for the four main categories of U.S. services exports and imports, the aggregate research is not altogether helpful. We have had accordingly to tailor our research to capture the main determinants of the volume and prices of each of the U.S. disaggregated services trade categories and to assess the forecast properties of the individual equations involved.

III. Theory

Our estimation and forecasting are based upon a simple and standard theoretical model of trade in services. We assume that services are supplied and demanded perfectly competitively in each country of the world, and that the services provided by different countries are to some extent differentiated (the Armington Assumption), so that services in the same industrial category may be both exported and imported by a country. This could reflect true product differentiation based on country of origin (national differences in airline service, for example), but it could just as easily reflect the necessary aggregation of different services into single data categories, within which the mix is different across countries.

On the supply side, we assume that services are provided at constant cost. This cost in turn depends on general cost conditions in the exporting country and, for some categories of services, on additional cost variables that may be appropriate such as the price of oil. The elasticity of supply, as implicit in the assumption of constant cost, is assumed to be infinite, so that the supply price does not rise or fall with the quantity supplied.

On the demand side, we assume that demands for services parallel demands for goods, responding positively to an aggregate income or output variable of the demanding (importing) country, and negatively to the price of the imported service relative to alternative services and goods. Income and price elasticities of demand are assumed finite and are estimated from the data. For most of the service categories, which are in the nature of final services, the driving income variable is real GDP—U.S. or the "rest-of-world"—depending on whether the service is being imported or exported, respectively.

For both supply and demand, we also allow for additional sector-specific determinants as appropriate, letting the data dictate whether such variables actually do play a significant empirical role. For example, because transportation services are largely traded as a means to trading goods, demand in this sector is permitted to depend on exports and imports of goods.

Because we assume supplies to be perfectly elastic, the supply equations specify price rather than quantity. Demand equations then determine quantity as a function of this price and other variables. Since we are modeling international trade in services, not domestic transactions, suppliers' prices are naturally specified in their own currency, and these must be translated using exchange rates in order to enter demand functions.

In sum, then, our model of trade in any service sector, i, consists of the following two equations for U.S. exports:

$$p_i^X = S_i^X (c_i^U) \quad (1)$$

$$q_i^X = D_i^X (I_i^W, e^\$ p_i^X / p_i^W) \quad (2)$$

Here, (1) is the export price equation representing domestic supply. p_i^X is the U.S. dollar price of exports in sector i, c_i^U includes one or more U.S.-based cost variables appropriate to the sector and measured in dollars, and S_i^X is the supply-price function, positively dependent on costs. Equation (2) is the export quantity equation based on foreign demand. q_i^X is the quantity demanded. I_i^W is an income variable measured in world currency (see below). $e^\$ p_i^X$ is the export price from (1) converted to world currency with the exchange value of the dollar $e^\$$. This is entered relative to p_i^W, which is the world-currency price either of competing services or of broader substitute goods and services. D_i^X is the demand function, depending positively on the first argument and negatively on the second. Additional variables are occasionally included in both of these function as needed for particular sectors, but (1) and (2) show the major economic effects that are included in the model.

For U.S. imports in service sector i, similar equations are used, the main difference being the source and currency denomination of the explanatory variables:

$$p_i^M = S_i^M (c_i^W) \quad (3)$$

$$q_i^M = D_i^M (I_i^U, p_i^M / e^\$ p_i^U) \quad (4)$$

In the import price equation (3), the foreign-currency price of U.S. imports, p_i^M, depends on c_i^W, a measure of world costs relevant to sector i. In the import quantity equation (4), I_i^U and p_i^U are U.S. income and substitute price variables measured in dollars.

Functional Form and Lags

All of our equations are estimated in logarithms, thus imposing constant elasticities on the functions above. We also choose an error-correction formulation to capture the dynamic behavior that is omitted above. That is, we assume that each underlying functional relationship determines a target value of the variable, and that the actual variable moves a constant fraction θ of the distance toward that target each time period (quarter). Thus, for any variable y specified in logs as a function of explanatory variable x also in logs, $y=f(x)=a_0+a_1x$ such as any of those above, we assume that

$$y(t) = y(t-1) + a_2 \Delta f(x(t)) + \theta \big[f(x(t-1)) - y(t-1) \big], \ with \ 0 < \theta < 1$$

or

$$\Delta y(t) = \theta a_0 + a_2 a_1 \Delta x(t) + \theta a_1 x(t-1) - \theta y(t-1) \qquad (5)$$

In the standard theory of error-correction models, the coefficient a_2 should be unity, but we allow for a looser formulation which permits the instantaneous response to a variable to differ from the long-run, or equilibrium, response. The latter is given by a_1, which we measure by the ratio of the coefficient of $x(t-1)$ to the absolute value of the coefficient of $y(t-1)$, as estimated in equation (5). In the estimation of equation (5), the data can always choose a_2 to be essentially unity. That rarely happens, however, which indicates that the looser formulation of the error-correction model is generally preferred empirically.

IV. Data and Estimation

Most of the data for the model were already available in the RSQE database. These data, which extend on a quarterly basis from as early as 1976 to the present, are available from the authors on request.

Since the quality of the foreign data was suspect prior to 1980, we used the earlier data for those equations that required only U.S. explanatory variables. Equations for export prices (which depend on U.S. costs) and import quantities (which depend on U.S. incomes and prices) were therefore estimated on data from 1976 to 1996. Export quantities and import prices, both of which depend on foreign variables, were estimated on data from 1980 to 1996. All estimates were done using ordinary least squares.

Our procedure was to perform the estimation in two stages. We first estimated price and quantity equations for aggregated services trade. Then, after that was successful, we repeated the process with the four disaggregated categories of services reported here. In the disaggregated estimates, we were better able to tailor the explanatory variables to the trade being estimated, using GDP for example as the income variable for travel and passenger fares, but an index of industrial production for transportation services. This is entirely reasonable since transportation services are used to move finished and semi-finished goods and raw materials, which is better measured by industrial production than by GDP.

In each stage, we began with a number of time series tests on the data to establish that they were co-integrated as expected. We then estimated the equations in the form suggested above by theory, but also with several lags of the explanatory variables to let the data determine the timing of their effects. We did a good deal of experimenting with different selections of the explanatory variables, including several that we thought might enter the equations but that, in most cases, failed to do so significantly. Once we had settled on the variables that seemed to provide the most explanatory power, we adjusted the lag structure to eliminate lagged variables that were not making a useful contribution. The end result is the set of equations reported in the Appendix, each of which we feel does at least an adequate job of fitting the data, and many of which perform extremely well. Before accepting the final form of each equation, we also tested its residuals to confirm, as a maintained hypothesis, that they were white noise.

V. Estimated Equations

The estimated equations are reported in detail in the Appendix, together with various measures of statistical performance. Table 1 collects the most important of the estimated coefficients for ease of comparison and to give an overview of the results.

With the exception of the price of other private services, we succeeded in each category of services in finding a cost variable with significant explanatory power for prices. On the export side, where costs originate in the U.S., the long-run elasticities except for the price of transportation are close to unity, suggesting that we have a good handle on costs. For transportation, the cost variable reported in Table 1 is the price of oil, and our equation also includes U.S. unit labor costs as an additional variable that plays a major role. The cost variables are mostly no less significant on the import side, but their long-run elasticities are smaller, suggesting that we were less successful in identifying foreign costs completely.

Our quantity equations show strong effects from the various income variables that we selected, not only statistically significant but also with long-run elasticities always above one. This is important, since it means that the demands for these traded services tend to grow as a fraction of the economy as incomes rise, accounting in part for the growth of services and services trade that has been observed over time.

Table 1. Estimated Elasticities of Cost, Income, and Relative Price Variables in Equations for Exports and Imports of Services

| | Price Equations | | Quantity Equations | | | |
| | Cost | | Income | | Relative Price | |
	Short-Run	Long-Run	Short-Run	Long-Run	Short-Run	Long-Run
Exports						
Travel	0.64***	1.04	0.48**	2.18	-0.27***	-1.20
Pass. Fare	3.02***	1.21	0.63**	3.11	-1.79***	-1.28
Transport.	0.09***	0.35	1.38***	1.11	-0.34***	-0.22
Other	0.07	0.92	0.80***	2.13	-0.31**	-0.33
Imports						
Travel	0.09***	0.40	1.40***	1.22	-1.02***	-1.04
Pass. Fare	0.12***	0.51	0.85	2.09	-0.82***	-0.53
Transport.	0.08***	0.56	0.17**	1.06	-0.43***	-1.29
Other	n.a.		0.82***	3.59	-0.16	-0.68

Stars indicate level of statistical significance of the short-run coefficients: ***=1%, **=5%, *=10%

The estimated effects of relative prices on demands for traded services are all significant on the export side but less so on the import side, where the data, coming from the United States, are arguably better. The estimated elasticities suggest that import demands for services are often inelastic, especially in the short run, and that they are seldom very elastic even in the long run. This is largely similar to what has been found for trade in goods.

VI. Forecasts

Inputs

The outlook for service trade over the next several years will depend most heavily on three key factors: the strength of the U.S. economy, as measured by the growth of U.S. real GDP; the growth rate of America's major trading partners; and the international value of the U.S. dollar. The first two of these drive the income variables in the demands for service imports and exports respectively. The exchange rate contributes to the relative prices that matter for both. These and other needed inputs are processed through our econometric model to produce the forecast.

The model uses a trade-weighted average of real GDP in five countries to represent economic activity among U.S. major trading partners. The five countries defining the "rest-of-world" for this purpose are Canada, Mexico, Japan, U.K., and Germany. The exchange rate, or value of the U.S. dollar, that is used in the model is the Major Currencies Index published by the Federal Reserve

Board. It is calculated as a trade-weighted average of the value of the U.S. dollar against the currencies of Canada, the Euro-11, Japan, the U.K., Switzerland, Australia, and Sweden.

For purposes of this forecast, we used input values generated in the May 1999 economic forecast published by the RSQE. Table 2 contains annual data on the three variables just discussed, taken from the RSQE forecast.

To characterize these and other inputs:

- The U.S. economy is expected to produce its third straight year of just about 4 percent real growth in 1999, followed by continued expansion at more sustainable rates close to 2 1/2 percent during 2000 and 2001. The U.S. inflation rate is expected to remain moderate over the next few years, but to be increasing from the unsustainably low levels of the past two years during which U.S. inflation benefited from generally sluggish economic conditions abroad accompanied by declining commodity and finished goods import prices.

- The Japanese economy declined at an average annual rate of 3.1 percent from 1997.1 through 1998.4, and the near-term economic outlook for Japan remains highly uncertain. There is, however, growing evidence that the worst is over, and that the combination of financial reforms and fiscal stimulus policies put in place in late 1998 will be followed by an economic turnaround before the end of 1999. We project that Japanese output growth will reach a 2 percent pace during the second half of year 2000 and accelerate further to a pace above 2.5 percent by the second half of 2001.

- The U.S. four major, non-Asian trading partners—Canada, Mexico, the U.K., and Germany—grew at an average rate of nearly 2 1/2 percent during 1998, down from more than 4 1/2 percent during 1997. We expect a moderate further slowdown to about 2 1/4 percent for 1999, followed by a pick-up to more than 2 3/4 percent for 2000 and 2001.

- For our five-country aggregate, therefore, we expect only 1.5 percent growth in 1999, down from 2 percent in 1998, followed by an acceleration to 2.2 and 2.8 percent for years 2000 and 2001, respectively. One of the implications of this growth path is that the economies of U.S. major trading partners are not likely to contribute much to a real recovery in the U.S. export growth rate until well into the year 2000.

- The U.S. dollar has appreciated for three straight years, 1996 through 1998, as other countries ran into economic and financial difficulties and international investors turned increasingly to the U.S. economy in a "flight to quality" for their short term financial investment. In the context of sustained economic recovery abroad, generally calmer non-crisis conditions in financial markets, and the expectation of a continuing deterioration in the overall U.S. current account deficit, the trade-weighted value of the U.S. dollar is forecast to edge down during the second half of 1999 and to depreciate at 2-3 percent rates during the 2000-2001 period.

Table 2. Inputs to the Forecast Exchange Rates, U.S. and Foreign GDP Actual and Forecast by RSQE Model, 1995-2001

	Actual					Forecast			Percent Changes						
	1995	1996	1997	1998	1999	2000	2001	1995-96	1996-97	1997-98	1998-99	1999-2000	2000-01
Trade-wtd. Value of Dollar 3/73=100	81.4	85.2	91.9	96.5	94.4	92.6	89.7	4.7	7.8	5.1	-2.2	-1.9	-3.1
U.S. Real GDP	6761.8	6994.8	7269.8	7551.9	7851.9	8035.7	8237.0	3.4	3.9	3.9	4.0	2.3	2.5
Five-country real GDP 1992=100	105.7	108.7	112.8	115.1	116.9	119.5	122.8	2.9	3.8	2.0	1.5	2.2	2.8

Forecast of Trade in Total Services

Table 3 contains the forecast of total service trade for calendar years 1999-2001, showing transactions-based service exports, service imports, and the balance of trade in services. The table shows the data both as levels in billions of (current) dollars, and as year-to-year percent changes. For perspective, the table contains data for 1995-1998 as well.

The quarterly forecasts of total service trade are graphed in Figure 1, starting with actual first-quarter-1999 values of net exports, exports, and imports of services. Like the annual values in Table 3, these are in current dollars and include some slight upward trend due to inflation, but most of the increase shown is in fact real.

As noted above, for calendar 1998 service exports were reduced to less than a 1 percent growth rate, compared with the more than 8 percent growth rates in the two previous years. The recovery of economies abroad produced a partial recovery in service exports starting already in the first quarter of 1999. Service exports are forecast to expand by about 3½ percent in 1999 and 2000, and then to resume their almost 9 percent growth in 2001.

U.S. service import growth slowed somewhat to 6.4 percent for 1998, picking up a bit in the fourth quarter but slowing again in the first quarter of 1999. Unlike service exports, service imports are forecast to continue growing in excess of 6 percent in 1999, and then to grow much faster in 2000 and 2001.

As a result, the balance of trade in total services is expected to drop continuously throughout 1999, and to reach a low of just over $62 billion annual rate in the last half of 2000. This is down about 30 percent from 1997's level, but it turns around slightly in 2001.

In summary, our forecast of total service trade suggests that the reduced growth in total service trade, both gross and net, that was observed in 1998 was only temporary, although it will take some time for previous high rates of growth to resume. Growth of service imports will recover sooner than service exports, causing a decline in the U.S. service trade surplus through the year 2000. By 2001, however, service exports will be growing significantly again, and the service trade surplus will begin then to increase.

Forecast of Trade in Services Sectors

Our model includes separate forecasting equations for four subcategories of service trade:

- Travel—mostly tourist expenditures
- Passenger Fares—mostly passenger air transportation
- Transportation—other than passenger transportation
- Other Private Services—includes education, financial services, insurance, telecommunications, and business, professional and technical services

Table 3. Total Services Trade Actual and Forecast, 1995-2001 Transactions Based[a] (Billions of Current Dollars)

| | Actual | | | | Forecast | | | Percent Changes | | | | |
	1995	1996	1997	1998	1999	2000	2001	1995 -96	1996 -97	1997 -98	1998 -99	1999- 2000	2000 -01
Services Trade Balance	73.8	82.8	87.7	78.9	75.7	63.1	66.4	12.1	6.0	-10.1	-4.0	-16.7	5.3
Exports	219.8	238.8	258.3	260.4	269.4	278.7	302.9	8.6	8.2	0.8	3.5	3.4	8.7
Imports	146.0	156.0	170.5	181.5	193.6	215.6	236.5	6.9	9.3	6.4	6.6	11.3	9.7

[a]Forecasts were done using NIPA data, then converted for this table to transactions basis by assuming that the ratio of transactions-based exports to NIPA-based exports remains constant over time at the level of 1998.

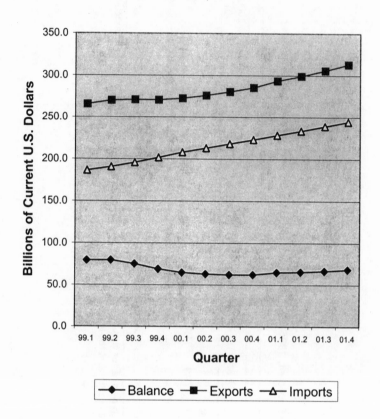

Figure 1
Quarterly Forecast of Total Trade in Services

Prices and quantities of service exports and imports were forecast for each of these service categories separately, the results then summed and scaled to obtain the forecast for total services reported above. Thus, the forecasts for total trade in services that we have just discussed were built up from our forecasts of trade in these four sectors, to which we now turn.

Tables 4-7 contain the forecasts on an annual basis for each of these categories, using the same format as Table 3. Figures 2-5 present graphs of the quarterly forecasts for each category.

As shown in Table 4 and Figure 2, the United States is a net exporter of travel services, which consists mostly of expenditures by foreign tourists in the U.S. (exports) and by U.S. tourists abroad (imports). The slowdown abroad reduced U.S. exports in 1998, while U.S. imports continued to grow, albeit at a slower rate. Our forecast shows both of these growing faster in 1999 and after, with imports of travel services recovering faster than exports, just as we noted above for trade in total services.

Trade in passenger fares, in Table 5 and Figure 3, slowed in both directions in 1998. That is, both exports and imports of passenger fares declined slightly. Exports in this category are forecast to hold essentially constant in 1999, then to resume substantial growth in 2000 and 2001. Imports of passenger fares pick up sooner than exports, growing already by more than 4 percent in 1999 and by over 10 percent in 2000. As a result, the trade balance in passenger fares—which is a small positive number throughout this period—declines by small amounts absolutely (and by large amounts percentage-wise) in 1999 and 2000, before rising in 2001.

Trade in transportation services (Table 6 and Figure 4) was already growing only rather slowly (compared to other categories of services) in 1996-97. Exports of transportation services then fell absolutely in 1998 due to the Asian crisis. Interestingly, our forecast shows both exports and imports increasing already in 1999 and growing steadily thereafter at rates above what were seen in the last few years.

Our last category of services, other private services, is reported in Table 7 and Figure 5. Here both exports and imports have grown very rapidly in recent years, and the problems of 1998 only reduced those annual rates of growth from double-digit to single-digit levels. Our forecast shows imports resuming rapid growth after the middle of 1999, while exports actually decline in late 1999 and grow hardly at all in 2000. By 2001, export growth will have picked up, but it will remain below the double-digit rates of a few years ago.

Together, these results for categories of services all show patterns that are similar to what we saw for total services, the differences across categories being primarily of timing and of degree. In particular, three of the four categories—all but transportation—show imports recovering sooner than exports from the decline that was seen in 1998, so that net exports decline at least into the year 2000. Our disaggregated results do not suggest that any one sector is primarily responsible for what is observed at the aggregate level.

Table 4. Trade in Travel (Tourist Services) Actual and Forecast, 1995-2001 (Billions of Current Dollars)

	Actual				Forecast			Percent Changes					
	1995	1996	1997	1998	1999	2000	2001	1995 -96	1996 -97	1997 -98	1998 -99	1999- 2000	2000 -01
Services Trade Balance	18.5	21.7	22.1	19.5	18.3	16.5	19.1	17.3	1.6	-11.5	-6.0	-9.9	15.6
Exports	63.4	69.8	73.3	72.0	74.2	76.8	82.9	10.1	5.0	-1.7	3.0	3.6	7.9
Imports	44.9	48.1	51.2	52.5	55.8	60.3	63.8	7.1	6.6	2.5	6.4	8.0	5.8

Table 5. Trade in Passenger Fares Actual and Forecast, 1995-2001 (Billions of Current Dollars)

	Actual				Forecast			Percent Changes					
	1995	1996	1997	1998	1999	2000	2001	1995 -96	1996 -97	1997 -98	1998 -99	1999- 2000	2000 -01
Services Trade Balance	4.3	4.6	2.7	2.6	1.9	1.3	1.5	7.6	-41.8	-2.1	-29.0	-28.8	16.0
Exports	18.9	20.4	20.9	20.8	20.8	22.3	24.9	7.9	2.3	-0.6	0.0	7.3	11.6
Imports	14.7	15.8	18.2	18.1	18.9	21.0	23.3	8.0	15.2	-0.4	4.2	10.9	11.3

Table 6. Trade in Transportation Services Actual and Forecast, 1995-2001 (Billions of Current Dollars)

	Actual				Forecast			Percent Changes					
	1995	1996	1997	1998	1999	2000	2001	1995 -96	1996 -97	1997 -98	1998 -99	1999- 2000	2000 -01
Services Trade Balance	-0.7	-0.7	-1.4	-2.6	-2.8	-3.4	-3.4	7.7	92.9	93.7	6.8	23.6	-2.1
Exports	26.8	27.0	27.9	27.6	29.3	31.5	33.8	0.8	3.3	-1.2	6.2	7.6	7.3
Imports	27.5	27.7	29.3	30.2	32.1	35.0	37.2	1.0	5.6	3.1	6.2	9.0	6.4

Table 7. Trade in Other Private Services Actual and Forecast, 1995-2001 (Billions of Current Dollars)

	Actual					Forecast		Percent Changes					
	1995	1996	1997	1998	1999	2000	2001	1995 -96	1996 -97	1997 -98	1998 -99	1999- 2000	2000 -01
Services Trade Balance	28.1	32.1	38.4	38.9	38.4	30.9	30.3	14.1	19.7	1.2	-1.1	-19.4	-2.1
Exports	63.6	70.9	82.2	85.8	88.6	89.6	97.7	11.5	15.9	4.4	3.3	1.0	9.1
Imports	35.5	38.8	43.8	47.0	50.2	58.6	67.5	9.4	12.8	7.3	7.0	16.7	15.1

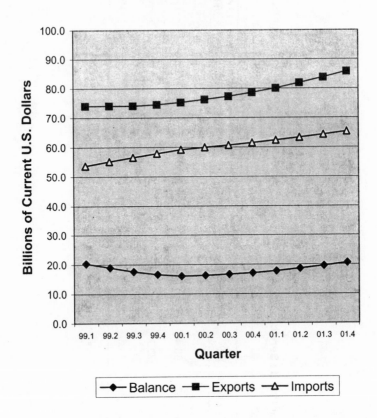

Figure 2
Quarterly Forecast of Trade in
Travel Services

Figure 3
Quarterly Forecast of Trade in Passenger Fares

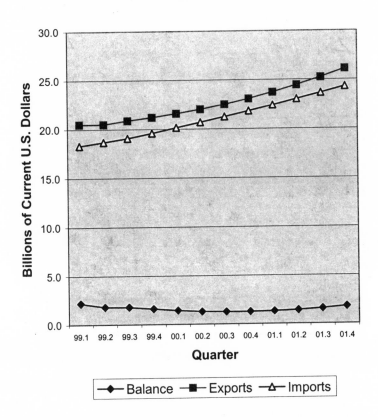

Figure 4
Quarterly Forecast of Trade in
Transportation

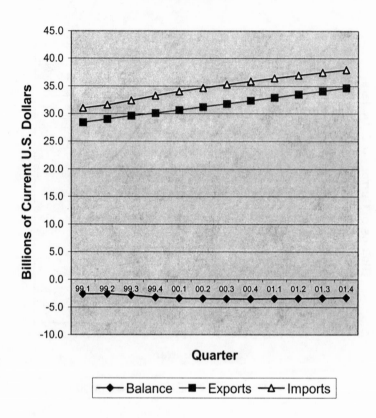

Figure 5
Quarterly Forecast of Trade in Other Private Services

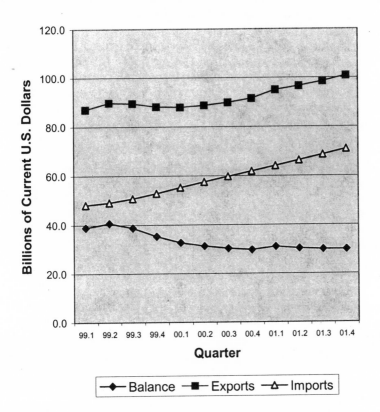

VII. Conclusion

Trade in services between the United States and the world has grown rapidly over the last decade and more, with both imports and exports expanding steadily. The Asian crisis cut into this growth to varying degrees in all of the sectors of services that we are able to distinguish in the data. Our forecasts consistently predict, however, that growth of services trade will resume, though in some cases after a delay of a year or two. In particular, we expect U.S. service imports to recover more rapidly than service exports, so that the large U.S. trade surplus in services will decline over 1999-2000 before beginning to rise again in the year 2001. Even with this decline, however, we do not expect U.S. net exports of services to fall below the more than $60 billion reached earlier in this decade.

Our effort to provide a forecasting structure for U.S. service trade will hopefully set an example for others to follow, both in the United States and in other major trading countries in which service trade is important. There is no doubt that more work needs to be done to improve the equations that we have constructed and estimated. We plan to continue our forecasting effort on a semi-annual basis for the next two years.

It should also be noted that we have concentrated on so-called cross-border service trade, leaving aside the very substantial magnitudes of international service transactions that are generated by the activities of the foreign affiliates of U.S. multinational corporations. Indeed, the level of U.S. service sales through foreign affiliates (establishment trade) amounted to $258 billion in 1997. It would be of interest accordingly to develop a framework that could be used to identify the major determinants of the location and sales activities of these U.S.-owned services affiliates operating abroad and their foreign-owned counterparts operating in the United States and elsewhere.

Notes

* We wish to thank Janet Wolfe for advice on econometric estimation issues, Yuan Xiao for assistance with the data, and Harry Freeman for helpful comments on the forecasts. The research was funded by a grant from The Mark Twain Institute.

[1] We use the term *services* to refer exclusively to the services portion of what is reported as trade in goods and services. It does not include factor income, interest income, and the like that are part of the current account.

[2] Balance-of-payments figures are transaction-based and represent actual international payments for services. NIPA-based figures, used for National Income and Product Accounting purposes, differ from actual transactions primarily by including imputed values for financial services rendered in kind and gross two-way parent-affiliate transactions. NIPA figures are conceptually more compatible with other variables of the forecasting model and have therefore been used here for that purpose. We report transaction figures, however, and an adjusted transactions-based forecast, for ease of comparison with the more familiar numbers that are reported in the press.

References

Dunnaway, Steven V. 1988. "A Model of the U.S. Current Account," International Monetary Fund, Working Paper, WP/88/27 (March 22).

Helkie, William L. and Lois E. Stekler. 1996. "Forecasting U.S. Exports and Imports of Services," presented at the International Symposium of Forecasting, Istanbul, Turkey (June).

Helkie, William L. and Peter Hooper. 1988. "An Empirical Analysis of the External Deficit, 1980-86," in Ralph C. Bryant, Gerald Holtham, and Peter Hooper (eds.), *External Deficits and the Dollar: The Pit and the Pendulum*. Washington, D.C.: The Brookings Institution.

Levin, Andrew, John H. Rogers, and Ralph W. Tryon. 1997. "A Guide to FRB/Global," Board of Governors of the Federal Reserve System, International Finance Discussion Papers, Number 588 (August).

Nedde, Ellen M. 1992. "A Dynamic Error-Correction Model of the U.S. Current Account," in International Monetary Fund, *The United States Economy: Performance and Issues*. Washington, D.C.: IMF.

Appendix

Equations of the Model

All export quantity and import price equations are estimated from 1980.2 to 1996.4, and all export price (except the passenger fare equation) and import quantity equations are estimated from 1976.2 to 1996.4. All estimates are obtained using ordinary least squares. Notation is defined at the end.

Numbers in parentheses are the standard errors of the estimated coefficients above them. Each equation is followed by the following diagnostic statistics

R^2:   This measures the fraction of the variance in the data that the equation is able to account for, or "explain," over the sample period. An R^2 of 1.00 would be perfect. In time series equations like these, an R^2 above .9 is considered quite normal when the dependent variable is the level of a price or quantity. However, when the dependent variable is a quarterly *change* in price or quantity, as in our model, a considerably smaller R^2, in the range of .4 to .6, would be expected.

s.e.:   This is the "standard error" of the equation, a measure of the "average" error (regardless of sign) in the fit of the equation to the observed values of the dependent variable. Its quantitative interpretation, however, depends on the units of measurement of the variable being explained. In all of our equations, which have the change in a logarithm (of price or quantity) as their dependent variable, the standard error is interpreted as the average or expected error (regardless of sign) that the equation makes in explaining the quarterly rate of change of price or quantity. Thus, a standard error of 0.03 indicates that the equation has an expected (or normal, or average) error of about 3 percentage points in explaining the quarterly percent changes in the price or quantity variable. In econometric work of this kind, standard errors in the range of 0.03 to 0.06 are quite common.

DW(0):   This is the most relevant of several "Durbin-Watson Statistics" that can be calculated. It measures the extent to which the equation's residuals (errors) can be considered random over time. If the residuals exhibit a pattern (i.e., lack of randomness), this usually indicates that something systematic is not being accounted for in the equation. A DW(0) value that is not "close" to 2.0 usually indicates lack of randomness. In econometric work of this kind, DW(0) values between 1.5 and 2.5 are, from a practical perspective, "close" to 2.0.

Travel Services

Export Quantity: xstrav92 = real exports of travel services

$\Delta\log(xstrav92) = -0.2036 + 0.4803 \log(gdprow4)_{-1} - 0.2674 \log(pxstrav^*jexrm/pcrow4)_{-1}$
$\qquad\qquad\quad (1.0280) \quad (0.2535) \qquad\qquad\qquad (0.0815)$

$\qquad\qquad -0.2236 \log(xstrav92)_{-1} - 0.1583\ d91q1 + 0.0795\ d84q1on + 0.2651\ d84q1$
$\qquad\qquad\quad (0.0723) \qquad\qquad\qquad (0.0526) \qquad (0.0294) \qquad\qquad (0.0578)$

$\qquad\qquad R^2 = 0.56 \qquad$ s.e. $= 0.051 \qquad DW(0) = 2.46$

Export Price: **pxstrav** = price deflator of travel exports

$\Delta\log(pxstrav) = -0.0506 + 0.0984 \log(pcpi)_{-1} + 0.6395\ \Delta\log(pcpi) - 0.0943 \log(pxstrav)_{-1}$
$\qquad\qquad\quad (0.0323) \ (0.0394) \qquad\qquad (0.1056) \qquad\qquad (0.0361)$

$\qquad\qquad R^2 = 0.55 \qquad$ s.e. $= 0.006 \qquad DW(0) = 1.88$

Import Quantity: **mstrav92** = real imports of travel services

$\Delta\log(mstrav92) = -6.1320 + 1.0034 \log(gdp92)_{-1} + 1.3989\ \Delta\log(gdp92)$
$\qquad\qquad\quad (0.9671) \ (0.1494) \qquad\qquad (0.4966)$

$\qquad\qquad -0.8513 \log(pmstrav/ppnf)_{-1} - 1.0210\ \Delta\log(pmstrav/ppnf)$
$\qquad\qquad\quad (0.1351) \qquad\qquad\qquad (0.1634)$

$\qquad\qquad -0.8217 \log(mstrav92)_{-1} - 0.0689\ d91q1$
$\qquad\qquad\quad (0.1130) \qquad\qquad\qquad (0.0374)$

$\qquad\qquad +0.3639\ d84q1on + 0.0536\ d84q1$
$\qquad\qquad\quad (0.0547) \qquad\quad (0.0644)$

$\qquad\qquad R^2 = 0.77 \qquad$ s.e. $= 0.036 \qquad DW(0) = 2.06$

Import Price: **pmstrav** = price deflator of travel imports

$\Delta\log(pmstrav^*jexrm) = +1.0889 + 0.0905 \log(pcrow5)_{-1} + 0.0647 \log(pmgoil^*jexrm)_{-2}$
$\qquad\qquad\quad (0.4463) \ (0.0272) \qquad\qquad (0.0217)$

$\qquad\qquad +0.0215\ [\log(pmgoil^*jexrm) - \log(pmgoil^*jexrm)_{-2}]$
$\qquad\qquad\quad (0.0205)$

$\qquad\qquad -0.2273 \log(pmstrav^*jexrm)_{-1} - 0.0285\ d84q1on$
$\qquad\qquad\quad (0.0646) \qquad\qquad\qquad (0.0128)$

$\qquad\qquad R^2 = 0.22 \qquad$ s.e. $= 0.029 \qquad DW(0) = 1.89$

Transportation Services

Export Quantity: **xstrans92** = real exports of transportation services

$$\Delta\log(xstrans92) = -0.3010 + 0.3356 \log(jiprow5)_{-1} + 1.3756 \Delta\log(jiprow5)$$
$$\quad (0.5851) \ (0.1660) \qquad\qquad (0.2680)$$

$$-0.0661 \log(pxstrans*jexrm/pcrow5)_{-1}$$
$$(0.0309)$$

$$-0.3371 \Delta\log(pxstrans*jexrm/pcrow5)$$
$$(0.0898)$$

$$-0.3028 \log(xstrans92)_{-1}$$
$$(0.0978)$$

$$R^2 = 0.49 \qquad s.e. = 0.024 \qquad DW(0) = 2.19$$

Export Price: **pxstrans** = price deflator of transportation exports

$$\Delta\log(pxstrans) = +0.2408 + 0.0289 \log(pmgoil)_{-1} + 0.0922 \Delta\log(pmgoil) + 0.2597$$
$$\log(julc)_{-1}$$
$$\qquad\qquad (0.0682) \qquad (0.0087) \qquad\qquad (0.0181) \qquad\qquad (0.0641)$$

$$-0.3403 \log(pxstrans)_{-2} - 0.0818 [\log(pxstrans)_{-1} - \log(pxstrans)_{-2}]$$
$$(0.0793) \qquad\qquad (0.1049)$$

$$R^2 = 0.43 \qquad s.e. = 0.019 \qquad DW(0) = 1.96$$

Import Quantity: **mstrans92** = real imports of transportation services

$$\Delta\log(mstrans92) = -0.9557 + 0.1693 \log(gdp92-x92) + 0.3056 \Delta\log(xg92)$$
$$(0.4664) \ (0.0733) \qquad\qquad (0.1242)$$

$$-0.2064 \log(pmstrans/ppnf)_{-1} - 0.4271 \Delta\log(pmstrans/ppnf)$$
$$(0.0838) \qquad\qquad (0.1619)$$

$$-0.1604 \log(mstrans92)_{-1} + 0.2919 \Delta\log(mg92)$$
$$(0.0558) \qquad\qquad (0.1310)$$

$$R^2 = 0.38 \qquad s.e. = 0.030 \qquad DW(0) = 2.20$$

Import Price: **pmstrans** = price deflator of transportation imports

$$\Delta\log(pmstrans*jexrm) = +0.2303 + 0.0766 \log(pcrow5)_{-1} + 0.0739 \log(pmgoil*jexrm)_{-1}$$
$$(0.2934) \ (0.0221) \qquad\qquad (0.0148)$$

$$+0.0799 \Delta\log(pmgoil*jexrm) - 0.1379 \log(pmstrans*jexrm)_{-1}$$
$$(0.0277) \qquad\qquad (0.0350)$$

$$R^2 = 0.40 \qquad s.e. = 0.028 \qquad DW(0) = 2.10$$

Passenger Fare Services

Export Quantity: **xspf92** = real exports of passenger fare services

$$\Delta\log(xspf92) = -\ 1.1795 + 0.6325\ \log(gdprow4)_{-1} + 1.1724\ \Delta\log(jexrm)$$
$$\qquad\qquad(1.2867)\ (0.3038)\qquad\qquad(0.4308)$$

$$-\ 0.2595\ \log(pxspf*jexrm/pcrow4)_{-1} - 1.7922\ \Delta\log(pxspf*jexrm/pcrow4)$$
$$\qquad(0.1022)\qquad\qquad\qquad\qquad(0.5052)$$

$$-\ 0.2034\ \log(xspf92)_{-1} - 0.2466\ d91q1 + 0.1535\ d91q1_{-1}$$
$$\qquad(0.0769)\qquad\qquad(0.0586)\qquad\qquad(0.0566)$$

$$R^2 = 0.50\qquad \text{s.e.} = 0.054\qquad DW(0) = 2.33$$

Export Price: **pxspf** = price deflator of passenger fare exports

$$\Delta\log(pxspf) = -\ 0.1772 + 0.1985\ \log(pcs)_{-2} + 3.0227\ [\log(pcs)_{-1}$$
$$\qquad\qquad(0.0706)\ (0.0451)\qquad\qquad(0.8622)$$

$$-\log(pcs)_{-2}] - 0.1644\ \log(pxspf)_{-1}$$
$$\qquad\qquad\qquad(0.0470)$$

$$R^2 = 0.36\qquad \text{s.e.} = 0.014\qquad DW(0) = 1.62$$

Import Quantity: **mspf92** = real imports of passenger fare services

$$\Delta\log(mspf92) = -\ 3.0778 + 0.4075\ \log(gdp92)_{-1} + 0.8548\ \Delta\log(gdp92)$$
$$\qquad\qquad(1.3418)\ (0.1743)\qquad\qquad(0.6915)$$

$$-\ 0.1039\ \log(pmspf/ppnf)_{-1} - 0.8161\ \Delta\log(pmspf/ppnf)$$
$$\qquad(0.1023)\qquad\qquad\qquad(0.2555)$$

$$-\ 0.1952\ \log(mspf92)_{-1} - 0.1494\ d91q1 - 0.1859\ d84q1$$
$$\qquad(0.0796)\qquad\qquad(0.0526)\qquad\qquad(0.0535)$$

$$R^2 = 0.41\qquad \text{s.e.} = 0.050\qquad DW(0) = 2.19$$

Import Price: **pmspf** = price deflator of passenger fare imports

$$\Delta\log(pmspf*jexrm) = +\ 0.6637 + 0.1170\ \log(pcrow5)_{-1} + 0.0952\ \log(pmgoil*jexrm)_{-2}$$
$$\qquad\qquad\qquad(0.2678)\ (0.0283)\qquad\qquad(0.0197)$$

$$+\ 0.0387\ [\log(pmgoil*jexrm)_{-1} - \log(pmgoil*jexrm)_{-2}]$$
$$\qquad(0.0262)$$

$$+\ 0.0848\ \Delta\log(pmgoil*jexrm) - 0.2284\ \log(pmspf*jexrm)_{-1}$$
$$\qquad(0.263)\qquad\qquad\qquad(0.0478)$$

$$+\ 0.0572\ d91q1$$
$$\qquad(0.0286)$$

$$R^2 = 0.42\qquad \text{s.e.} = 0.024\qquad DW(0) = 1.70$$

Other Private Services

Export Quantity: xsopriv92 = real exports of other private services

$\Delta\log(xsopriv92) = -1.6608 + 0.7966 \log(gdprow5)_{-1}$
         (0.9104) (0.2090)

$-0.1231 \log(pxsopriv*jexrm/pcrow5)_{-4}$
  (0.0527)

$-0.2324 [\log(pxsopriv*jexrm/pcrow5)_{-2}$
  (0.1071)

$-\log(pxsopriv*jexrm/pcrow5)_{-4}]$

$-0.3061 [\log(pxsopriv*jexrm/pcrow5)_{-1}$
  (0.1671)

$-\log(pxsopriv*jexrm/pcrow5)_{-2}]$

$+0.2741 \max(jus.row - jus.row_{-1}, 0) - 0.3743 \log(xsopriv92)$
  (0.1447)   (0.0631)

$R^2 = 0.43$ s.e. = 0.041 $DW(0) = 1.56$

Export Price: pxsopriv = price deflator of other private service exports

$\Delta\log(pxsopriv) = +0.0435 + 0.0873 \log(julc)_{-3} + 0.1976 [\log(julc)_{-1} - \log(julc)_{-3}]$
         (0.0178) (0.0270)   (0.0544)

$+0.0707 \Delta\log(julc) - 0.3391 [\log(pxsopriv)_{-1} - \log(pxsopriv)_{-2}]$
  (0.0835)   (0.1102)

$-0.0954 \log(pxsopriv)_{-2}$
  (0.0266)

$R^2 = 0.44$ s.e. = 0.006 $DW(0) = 1.87$

Import Quantity: msopriv92 = real imports of other private services

$\Delta\log(msopriv92) = -6.3956 + 0.8190 \log(gdp92)_{-1} - 0.1564 \log(pmsopriv/ppnf)_{-1}$
         (1.8146) (0.2280)   (0.1662)

$-0.5480 [\log(msopriv92)_{-1} - \log(msopriv92)_{-2}]$
  (0.1058)

$-0.2280 \log(msopriv92)_{-2} + 0.0705\ d91q1$
  (0.0611)   (0.0539)

$R^2 = 0.29$ s.e. = 0.053 $DW(0) = 1.99$

Import Price: **pmsopri** = price deflator of other private service imports

$$\Delta\log(pmsopriv) = + 0.2367 + 0.0942\ \Delta\log(pcrow5/jexrm)$$
$$(0.0526)\ (0.0338)$$

$$- 0.2666\ [\log(pmsopriv)_{-1} - \log(pmsopriv)_{-2}] - 0.0515\ \log(pmsopriv)_{-2}$$
$$(0.1153) \qquad\qquad\qquad\qquad (0.0116)$$

$$R^2 = 0.28 \qquad \text{s.e.} = 0.009 \qquad DW(0) = 2.14$$

Notation:

Variable	Definition
gdp92	US real GDP, in billions of 1992 dollars
gdprow4	average real gdp of 4 countries (UK, Germany, Canada, Japan)
gdprow5	average real gdp of 5 countries (4 plus Mexico)
jexrm	average real exchange rate of developed countries
jiprow5	index of average industrial production of 5 countries (UK, Germany, Canada, Japan, Mexico)
julc	index of US unit labor costs
jus.row	the ratio of the 3-month T-bill rate to the trade-weighted 3-month foreign interest rate
mg92	real imports of goods, billions of 1992 dollars
msopriv92	real imports of other private services
mspf92	real imports of passenger fare services
mstrans92	real imports of transportation services
mstrav92	real imports of travel services
pcpi	US consumer price index
pcrow4	average consumer price index of 4 countries (UK, Germany, Canada, Japan)
pcrow5	average consumer price index of 5 countries (4 plus Mexico)
pcs	price deflator for personal service consumption
pmgoil	price index of oil measured in US $
pmsopriv	price deflator of other private service imports
pmspf	price deflator of passenger fare imports
pmstrans	price deflator of transportation imports
pmstrav	price deflator of travel imports
ppnf	price index of US non-farm business
pxsopriv	price deflator of other private service exports
pxspf	price deflator of passenger fare exports
pxstrans	price deflator of transportation exports
pxstrav	price deflator of travel exports
x92	real export of goods and services, billions of 1992 dollars
xg92	real export of goods, billions of 1992 dollars
xsopriv92	real exports of private services
xspf92	real exports of passenger fare services
xstrans92	real exports of transportation services
xstrav92	real exports of travel services

Dummy Variables

d84q1	1 for 84q1, 0 otherwise
d84q1on	1 for 84q1 and after, 0 otherwise
d91q1	1 for 91q1, and 0 otherwise

CHAPTER 4

Measurement and Classification of Service Sector Activity: Data Needs for GATS 2000

*Obie G. Whichard**

I. Introduction

Over roughly the last 15 years, growth in trade in services and the advent of trade negotiations and agreements covering services have made it increasingly important that measurement of services trade be as comprehensive, detailed, accurate, and internationally comparable as possible. International organizations and national statistical offices have responded by issuing new methodological guidelines and classifications, improving the coverage of transactions, and reporting services trade in greater detail. In addition, a number of countries have begun to develop data on services delivered to international markets through locally established foreign affiliates. Overall, a remarkable amount of progress has been achieved. Yet the area still is not one most people would consider highly developed. Available data tend to be highly aggregated, particularly in comparison with those on trade in goods, often do not separately identify prices and quantities for specific services, do not indicate the mode through which the service was supplied, and may classify cross-border trade and (if data on them are available at all) sales by foreign affiliates on fundamentally different bases—all limitations that help to define the wish lists of data users.

This paper will examine needs for statistics on trade in services, indicate in general terms what data are now available, describe the existing international body of methodological guidance for statistical compilation, attempt to provide some insight into what is involved in improving trade-in-services statistics (using as an illustration the efforts of the United States, with which the author has been involved), and identify some of the needs that remain unmet and some of the difficulties and special situations involved in data collection.

Because it is likely that many of its readers are most interested in services statistics as a tool for supporting trade negotiations, the paper devotes special attention to identifying areas where negotiators have adopted definitions that differ from those found in guidelines for statistical compilation. For these readers, it may help motivate the discussion that follows to point out a reason why statistics on the trade subject to negotiation may be even more critical for services than for goods—namely, the greater need for indirect tools for gauging impediments. Barriers to services trade are almost exclusively non-tariff barriers and thus difficult to quantify, and impossible to quantify precisely.[1] However, sufficiently detailed and accurate trade statistics might allow levels of protection to be gauged indirectly, through comparisons between actual trade flows and flows predicted by economic models.

II. Data Needs

Data on trade in services are used for a variety of purposes, and it is with these purposes in mind that needs must be considered. The most longstanding purpose is for general economic measurement and accounting. Trade in services is recorded in balance of payments accounts, which provide a statistical record of economic transactions between the residents of a nation and those of other countries; these accounts, in turn, feed into the national income and product accounts used for gauging overall economic activity. Another purpose—and one that has provided much of the impetus for data improvement—is for use in connection with trade policy, including the support of negotiations and the resulting agreements. Finally, the data may be used by businesses in assessing market opportunities and by researchers in conducting economic analysis.

Needs for data on trade in services may be approached from different perspectives. The one that comes most readily to mind is that of the *types* of information needed, and this is the principal concern addressed below. However, no less important are issues related to the *quality* and the *comparability* of the data. For users to feel they can depend upon them, the data must be accurate and timely. For the data to be as useful as possible analytically, it must be possible to compare them from country to country and to relate them to statistics on the domestic economy.

The types of information required to meet the needs of economic accountants, negotiators and policy officials, business analysts, and researchers can be stated rather straightforwardly. Putting aside for the time being questions of what is feasible or cost effective, four basic types of needs can be identified; these are discussed below under the headings of *values*, *prices*, *modes of supply*, and *foreign-affiliate activities*.

Values.—The most basic need is simply for data on the values of services exports and imports, both in the aggregate and for specific services. These should be available in some degree of detail, preferably classified according to an internationally agreed system that allows comparisons among countries and, for a given country, with data on domestic production and consumption of those same services.

Prices.—Information on the prices governing the transactions is needed to allow estimates of trade flows in real terms to be developed, to address terms-

of-trade issues, and to assist in efforts to estimate and analyze supply and demand for traded services.

Modes of supply.—A relatively new need is for a breakdown of statistics
on the basis of the "modes of supply" through which services are delivered.
While analysts had for some time recognized that services transactions may be
differentiated based on the location of the producer and consumer of the service at the time of the transaction, the discussion was mostly couched in theoretical terms.[2] It was only with the General Agreement on Trade in Services
(GATS), under which commitments may be restricted to services supplied via
particular modes, that mode of supply became identified as a significant statistical need.[3]

Foreign-affiliate activities.—Related to the need for mode-of-supply information is the need for data on the sales and other activities of foreign affiliates. Though important for both goods and services, supply through foreign affiliates may be particularly important for services, due to the need for close
and continuing contact between producers and consumers and, in many cases,
the impracticality—or even impossibility—of supplying the market through
any other mode. Although given impetus by trade agreements, data on foreign
affiliates' activities also are needed in connection with the study of globalization phenomena and, in particular, of the ways multinational firms organize
their international operations and of the effects of these operations on home-
and host-country economies.

III. Data Availability

A good overall impression of the availability of data on trade in services may
be obtained by examining publications of international organizations that re-
compile data supplied by their member countries. Data for the largest number
of countries are those found in the International Monetary Fund's *Balance of
Payments Statistics Yearbook* (IMF, 1998). In it, data on services trade (and
other international transactions) are broken down according to the standard
components recommended by the Fund's *Balance of Payments Manual* (5th
edition, often referred to as "BPM5"), which provides guidelines for balance of
payments compilers (IMF, 1993). (These guidelines will be discussed in the
next section.) The 1998 edition of the *Yearbook* contains data for 159 countries and covers the years 1990-97. Of the 159 countries, data on total services
trade are provided for both 1990 and either 1996 or 1997 for 110 countries.[4]
Table 1 shows how many of these countries reported data for each of the various services components for 1990 and for the latest year reported (1997, in all
but a few cases).

Table 1. Number of IMF Member Countries Providing Services Data

	Exports		Imports	
	1990	1996 or 1997	1990	1996 or 1997
Total services	110	110	110	110
Transportation	105	106	108	109
Travel	105	106	104	107
Other services	109	109	109	109
Communications	30	66	32	67
Construction	16	34	16	40
Insurance	83	86	97	98
Financial services	16	41	17	43
Computer and information services	8	34	8	33
Royalties and license fees	34	46	52	66
Other business services	102	102	105	108
Personal, cultural, and recreational services	11	31	20	36
Government, n.i.e.	95	102	99	104

Note—This table covers the 110 countries for which data on total services are shown for both 1990 and either 1996 or 1997 in the 1998 edition of the *Balance of Payments Yearbook*.

As can be seen, almost all of the countries reported data for the three major categories—transportation, travel, and "other" Within "other," however, a category encompassing a very wide variety of services, the picture is not so bright. Most countries reported on insurance, "other business services," and government services, but for several other services, only a minority of countries reported. For construction, financial services, computer and information services, and personal, cultural and recreational services, a minority—generally around 30-40 percent in the latest year—reported for both exports and imports. For royalties and license fees—basically, transactions related to intellectual property—a minority reported exports (receipts), perhaps reflecting to some extent a genuine absence of such exports by a number of mainly less-developed countries, but around 60 percent of the countries reported imports (payments). Considering that this is a highly aggregated list to begin with—only 11 categories altogether, excluding subtotals—these results probably are not very encouraging to trade negotiators. (The Services Sectoral Classification List (often referred to as the "W120 list") used in connection with the GATS, for example, lists about 150 separate services.[5])

Despite the rather low numbers of countries reporting on several of the services, it is encouraging that these numbers are growing. For construction, financial services, computer and information services, and personal, cultural and recreational services, the numbers of countries reporting more than doubled from 1990 to 1996-97 for both exports and imports. This would seem to indicate that countries are beginning to devote increased attention and resources to providing more detailed and comprehensive data on services trade, even if the available detail remains rather limited. Of course, during this developmental period, the changing number of countries reporting various services itself greatly complicates the analysis of global trends in services trade, and this factor must be kept in mind in interpreting the available data. A related complication stems from the fact that newly reported services may in some cases have been included previously in higher-level groupings, making it difficult to know the extent to which discontinuities for individual services carry over to groups of services or services as a whole.

While the IMF data are the most comprehensive in terms of country coverage, the aggregated nature of the standard components does not allow analysis of data availability for very many specific types of services. However, it is likely that most of the countries that have more detail are developed countries (one would expect this *a priori*, and their reporting of the IMF standard components tends to be the most complete), and many of these countries report detailed data on services trade to the Organization for Economic Co-Operation and Development. Table 2 indicates the number of countries, from among the 27 covered by a recent OECD statistical publication on trade in services, reporting data for different types of services, including several that are not broken out separately in the IMF *Yearbook*.

The general impression obtained from the table is one of good coverage of the major broad categories, with lesser but still significant coverage of most individual services. Several countries do not provide separate information on most or all of the services within the "business, professional, and technical" group, but a significant number do. Reporting for exports and imports is very similar, with there being just a few instances of trade reported in only one direction.

All the data described above show values only and do not distinguish between movements attributable to price change and movements attributable to changes in quantities. Nor do they distinguish among the different modes of supply. To the best of the author's knowledge, comparable cross-country estimates breaking down values for specific services into price and quantity components or allocating those values on the basis of mode of supply simply do not exist.[6]

Concerning sales of services by foreign affiliates and other related information on the operations of direct investment enterprises that might relate to the commercial presence mode of supply, the data availability situation is difficult to assess. For most countries, this is a relatively new area of data collection; only a few have actually begun it. International guidelines are still evolving, and systematic recompilation by international organizations has not yet

Table 2. Number of OECD Countries Providing Statistics on Trade in Different Types of Services, 1996

	Exports	Imports
Total services	27	27
Transportation	27	27
Travel	27	27
Communications	25	24
Construction	23	23
Insurance	27	27
Financial services	25	26
Computer and information services	22	22
Royalties and license fees	25	25
Other business services	27	27
Merchanting and other trade-related	23	22
Operational leasing	23	24
Misc. business, professional and technical services	26	26
Legal, accounting, management, and public relations services	20	20
Advertising, market research, and public opinion polling	20	20
Research and development services	20	19
Architectural, engineering, and other technical consultancy	17	17
Agricultural, mining, and on-site processing	16	16
Other business, professional and technical services	20	20
Services between affiliated enterprises, n.i.e.	14	14
Personal, cultural, and recreational services	26	26
Audio-visual and related services	18	18
Other personal, cultural, and recreational services	18	17
Government services, n.i.e.	27	27
Other services	25	25

Source: OECD, 1999; derived from tables B.1 - B.28

begun. Among the countries that have collected data on sales by foreign affiliates for some time are the United States, Japan, and Sweden. These data are classified by the primary industry of the affiliate rather than by type of service, and only the United States data break down sales by affiliates in each industry as between sales of goods and sales of services.

In 1997, the Statistical Office of the European Communities (Eurostat) issued a *FATS Task Force Report*, reporting on the work of a task force established to investigate statistical issues related to activities by foreign affiliates—which the report termed "foreign affiliates' trade."[7] Included in the report was a prototype survey, later implemented jointly with the OECD, requesting information disaggregated by industry of affiliate on five key operating statistics— turnover (sales), employment, value added, exports, and imports. About a dozen responses were received, most of them providing information on only some of the items requested and only for foreign-owned firms in the domestic economy (inward direct investment). Additional countries can be expected to make progress in this area in the coming years, at least with respect to inward investment, though there is no indication that the availability of data is likely to become truly widespread any time soon.[8]

IV. The International Methodological Infrastructure for Trade-in-Services Statistics

International organizations have influenced the available statistics on trade in services not only by republishing member-country data, but also by providing definitions and methodological guidelines for compilation, generally through internationally coordinated consultative processes involving member-country statistical offices. The organizations most directly involved in these activities have been the IMF, the OECD, and the UN, all of which have major statistical functions as integral parts of their work programs. These organizations, together with the World Trade Organization and Eurostat, are jointly endeavoring to integrate and expand the body of international guidance on trade-in-services statistics through a Task Force on Statistics of International Trade in Services, whose activities are described below along with those of the primary statistical organizations.

International Monetary Fund (IMF)

Of the numerous steps international organizations have taken to promote better data on services trade, perhaps the most fundamental ones are those reflected in the 5th edition of the IMF's *Balance of Payments Manual*. Published in 1993, BPM5 was the first edition of the *Manual* to provide a statistical definition of trade in services, together with a single heading within the current account under which services trade would be separately recorded. It gave definitions of what to include under this heading and what to exclude, and it specifically addressed a number of borderline cases. In recommending that the total be distributed among a number of "standard components," it provided a broad international classification for trade in services.

Because of its centrality in determining how trade in services is statistically recorded and because agreements such as the GATS may use definitions that differ from the statistical definitions, it will be useful to review some of BPM5's main features relating to trade in services, to describe how it handles certain borderline cases, and to call attention to its treatment of a few services that present unique definitional issues.

Residency.—BPM5 defines international transactions in terms of residency. Specifically, a transaction is considered "international" if it is between residents and nonresidents of the compiling economy. In most cases, an individual must remain in a country for a period of a year or more to be considered a resident of that country. Exceptions are provided for students, medical patients, and government employees, such as diplomats and military personnel, all of whom are considered residents of their country of origin even if they remain in another country for a year or more. For a business enterprise, a foreign operation is considered to constitute a foreign affiliate, resident in its country of location, if it maintains a production establishment in that country and plans to do so "indefinitely or over a long period of time" (para. 73). In addition, it must qualify as a bona fide business enterprise in the host country, such as by maintaining its own accounts, receiving funds for its own account for work that it does, having a physical presence in the country of location (e.g., plant and equipment and employees), and paying local income taxes.

To give a concrete example of how these definitions would work in the context of services, if an individual stayed abroad as a service provider for a period of six months, then the fees charged by the individual to residents of the foreign country for performing the service would be recorded as an international transaction—specifically, as an export by the individual's permanent country of residence and as an import by the country in which the services were performed. However, if the individual remained in the latter country for, say, 18 months, then for statistical purposes the individual would be deemed a resident of that country and the fees would be regarded, not as international transactions, but as transactions occurring wholly within the country where the services were performed.

Trade negotiations and agreements might not differentiate between these two cases, or they might do so in a way different from that adopted for statistical purposes. In the GATS, for example, a natural person (i.e., an individual) is regarded as a "natural person of another Member" if the person is, under the law of that Member, a "national" (or the equivalent, in certain special cases).[9] This is more of a legal definition than one geared to economic measurement and accounting, and it could result in situations where service providers working outside their country of nationality are considered for statistical purposes as resident in the country where they work, but for purposes of the GATS remain persons of their country of nationality. Their fees for providing services would be relevant to the agreement, yet they would not be recorded statistically as international transactions. While the practical importance of the variance from the statistical definition may not be great in most cases, the potential for differences exists, and users of the data need to be aware of how definitions differ, to have reflected upon how the differences may affect the usefulness of the data for their particular purposes, and possibly to determine whether any supplemental information may be required.

Similar definitional issues may arise with respect to enterprises. For example, a construction project abroad may be accounted for statistically either as a services export by the home country of the construction firm that carries it out or as an operation of that firm's foreign affiliate in the country of the project, depending on its duration and other characteristics, following the guidelines outlined above. In the former case, the transaction would be included in the balance of payments accounts as an international transaction, whereas in the latter, the transaction would be wholly within the country of the project and thus would (apart from the related capital and income flows) be excluded. (However, it *would* be included in statistics covering the activities of foreign affiliates, provided the countries involved maintained them.)

It is worth noting that these statistical definitions differentiate only between transactions that are between residents of the same country and transactions that are between residents of different countries. No distinctions are drawn based on the location of the provider and the consumer of the service at the time the service is performed—the key criteria for determining the mode of supply. However, the treatment of foreign affiliates as residents of their countries of location (rather than of their owners' countries) does—by resulting in the exclusion of sales by these entities from the balance of payments accounts—help to isolate transactions effected through commercial presence from transactions effected through the other modes of supply.

Definition of services.—BPM5 does not provide a conceptual definition of services, but it is, with only a few noted exceptions, harmonized with the *System of National Accounts 1993* (SNA), which states that "services are heterogeneous outputs produced to order and typically consist of changes in the conditions of the consuming units realized by the activities of producers at the demand of the consumers."[10] In any event, there are relatively few economic outputs that might be treated as services by some definitions but not by others, and BPM5 takes note of some of these and provides conventions for treating them statistically. However, because some of the conventions are at variance with the way outputs have been categorized by negotiators, it is useful to highlight these cases.

Among the borderline cases specifically addressed by BPM5 are transactions involving repair, processing, goods procured in ports by transportation carriers, merchanting, and intellectual property. These will be discussed in turn below, both to illustrate the issues involved and to indicate their resolution. It is not, strictly speaking, possible to say how closely these definitions are aligned with the GATS, because the GATS does not itself define "services" for purposes of the agreement (other than to exclude services supplied in exercise of governmental authority). However, sectoral classification lists or other information can sometimes be used as the basis for inferences.

BPM5 calls for transactions in *repair* to be recorded under trade in goods. Although often thought of as a service in a domestic context, repair in an international context often involves such activities as major overhauls of vessels or aircraft—activities that may take place in factory-type settings and may have more in common with manufacturing activities than with services operations. In meetings of balance of payments compilers held in connection with

BPM5, consideration was given to drawing a distinction between repairs to investment goods and repairs to other goods, and including the latter in services (a treatment followed in the SNA), but a decision not to attempt this was made on practical grounds, taking into consideration the apparent predominance of repair to investment goods in international transactions. Although recorded statistically as trade in goods, for purposes trade agreements, repair may be among the activities considered as services. For example, the W120 list includes an entry for "maintenance and repair of equipment."

Processing presents another borderline case. Processing occurs when goods are imported, have value added to them, and then are re-exported without a change in ownership having occurred. In the fourth edition of the *Balance of Payments Manual*, processing was recorded on a net basis as a service; that is, the goods themselves were excluded from exports and imports of goods and the processor's fee recorded as a service. In BPM5, in contrast, the goods before and after processing are to be recorded on a gross basis, as separately identifiable components of exports and imports of goods. This treatment presumably is more closely aligned with the needs of negotiators than the treatment of the fourth *Manual*, inasmuch as the activities involved, such as petroleum refining or factory-type assembly work done under contract, are seldom discussed in connection with services.[11]

In another change from the fourth *Manual*, *goods procured in ports by transportation carriers* is included by BPM5 in trade in goods, rather than as a part of transportation services. While this helps sharpen the distinction between services and goods, this item may be considered to provide additional information pertinent to agreements on air and maritime transport, and special note of this treatment is therefore taken here.

Merchanting refers to cases where goods are bought and subsequently resold by a resident of a country, without the goods physically entering or leaving that country. If both the purchase and sale occur in the same period, the difference between the acquisition cost and sale proceeds is to be recorded as a service in the balance of payments of the country of the merchant.[12] However, from the standpoint of trade agreements, the transaction presumably would be governed by provisions applicable to trade in goods between the country where the goods were acquired and (if different) the country where they were resold.

As a final illustration of borderline cases, *royalties and license fees*—payments for use of such items of intellectual property as patents, trademarks, copyrights, and proprietary industrial processes—are included by BPM5 in trade in services, even though, as returns on existing assets, consideration had been given to regarding them as payments of income, to be grouped with investment income and compensation of employees. Here, the issue for negotiators relates to the way negotiations have been structured and, in particular, to the fact that multilateral negotiations and agreements related to intellectual property rights have been handled separately, outside the GATS.

Special definitions.—By and large, trade in tangible goods is measured the same way for all goods. Trade in most services is likewise measured uniformly, in terms of the total values of the receipts and payments that flow between buyer and seller. There are a few instances, however, in which special definitions have been adopted to provide an economically more meaningful measure of the trade, or in which special definitions might have been appropriate conceptually but have not been implemented for practical reasons. These concern transportation, insurance, financial services, travel, and government services. The issues involved and the treatment recommended by BPM5 are outlined below.

For *transportation* services, the value of the actual payments between residents and nonresidents for transportation of freight is not the measure recorded as international transactions. Were it to be, an inconsistency in the valuation of merchandise would exist, inasmuch as merchandise values would sometimes include and sometimes exclude transportation charges, depending on whether the buyer or the seller was responsible for paying the freight. To provide for uniform valuation of merchandise, as well as to simplify data collection and reporting, a convention has been adopted under which all freight charges are deemed to be paid by the importer. Thus, for a given country, freight exports are defined as domestic carriers' receipts for carriage of the country's exports (as well as any receipts for carrying freight between foreign countries), and freight imports are defined as domestic residents' payments to foreign carriers for carriage of the country's imports. Figures computed on this basis provide the information needed for compiling the balance of payments. However, because confusion may arise if information from industry sources gives a different picture (perhaps because of the inclusion of data covering transportation that is "international" in the sense of involving movement of freight from one country to another but that does not fall within the scope of the above definitions), it is important that data users be familiar with the definitions underlying the published statistics.

For *insurance* services, the value of trade is measured in BPM5, not by total premiums, but by "service charges included in total premiums" (para. 257). Different methods of estimating the insurance service charge are given for different types of insurance, but the basic concept underlying all of them is that of intermediation, in which a portion—ordinarily a large one—of premiums simply represents transfers between all policyholders and those policyholders to whom claims are paid, with a smaller amount representing the value of the services provided by insurance companies.[13] For other purposes, however, knowledge of the gross financial flows involving insurance is needed, and in this regard it can be noted that the OECD and Eurostat have developed an expanded list of components, consistent with the BPM5 components but with added detail, in which gross premiums and claims are requested as memorandum items. (This list is described below.)

Financial services are sometimes provided without an explicit charge, with the cost of services being implicitly covered by the difference between the rates of interest financial institutions charge to borrowers and the rates they pay to depositors, or by bid-asked spreads on traded financial assets. For this reason, an imputed amount—"financial intermediation services indirectly measured" (FISIM)—is provided in the SNA as a measure of such services. For practical reasons, BPM5 does not require the estimation of FISIM in the measurement of international transactions in financial services. However, negotiators and other users of the data should be aware of this omission, and of the fact that it tends to result in an understatement of the relative importance of financial services in international trade. They may wish to examine data on international income flows in conjunction with data on explicit charges for financial services, to obtain an idea of the international borrowing and lending activity that might have been subject to FISIM, and thus to gauge the order of magnitude of the understatement.

Travel is regarded by BPM5 as a service, and in fact is one of the largest services in international trade. Strictly speaking, however, travel is not a *type* of service, but rather a category for recording all of the expenditures of non-resident individuals, including expenditures for goods as well as for services. *Government services, n.i.e.* likewise is a transactor-based category and may include expenditures for goods as well as services.

Organization for Economic Cooperation and Development (OECD)

Some of the earliest international discussions on services statistics were those held in the OECD. In the early 1980's, statistical issues began to arise from time to time in the Trade Committee, a group normally concerned with trade policy. In 1983, the Working Party of the Committee met for the first time in a "statistical mode" to discuss services statistics, with representatives of statistical offices joining the trade policy officials that usually attended these meetings. Subsequently, regular meetings dealing solely with statistics began to be held, and a work program was developed, housed within the regular statistical part of the organization. The major elements of the program have been the development of a classification of trade in services and the compilation of member country data on services trade.

Recognizing that the need for data was immediate, whereas it would take considerable time to agree to a classification and even longer for widespread implementation to occur, work on both elements was pursued in tandem, rather than postponing the compilation efforts until a classification had been agreed upon and reflected in data collection. The initial compilations followed the then-current (i.e., the fourth) edition of the IMF *Manual* as far as the major categories were concerned, but with whatever additional detail countries could provide within those categories. Because there was then no agreed international classification for trade in services, there was considerable heterogeneity among countries in both the amount of detail and how it was grouped and presented. While the compilation was a unique resource, analysis of the data was hampered by the country-to-country inconsistencies in classification.

The OECD-Eurostat Trade in Services Classification was designed with a view to promoting international consistency in classification, at least among OECD members. Preliminary versions of this classification were available during the period when BPM5 was being developed, and as the result of close cooperation between the organizations involved and efforts to avoid inconsistencies, the OECD-Eurostat Classification can be characterized as an "extended subsystem" of the BPM5 standard components for services. That is, it contains all of the standard components, but with further breakdowns provided for a number of services. While the OECD-Eurostat classification provides for more detail by type of service than BPM5, its extensions are relatively modest. Its aim was for a level of detail that most OECD member countries could be expected to provide, not for separate enumeration of every possible traded service.

The OECD-Eurostat Classification is given in the annex at the end of this paper. In it, BPM5 standard components and "services sub-items" (items suggested to be provided as supplementary information) are labeled with an asterisk (*), so that the table can be used to display the BPM5 classification as well. This classification, or one very much like it, is likely to be the primary basis for compilation of data on services trade (except via commercial presence) worldwide for some time to come. It is, with minor modifications (mainly involving additional memorandum items needed in connection with the GATS), to be the basis recommended in an international manual on trade-in-services statistics that is currently being prepared. In 1998, for the first time, the OECD and Eurostat requested that submissions of trade-in-services data be reported on the basis of this classification, and the data were presented in this format in the data publication released in 1999 (OECD, 1999).

In a separate exercise conducted within a working group of the Industry Committee, the OECD also has also done work that should help in the development of international guidelines for compilation of data on the activities of foreign affiliates. It is through this group that a manual of globalization indicators is being prepared, and this manual and the above mentioned manual on trade-in-services statistics are to be harmonized, insofar as possible. This work is still in progress, and the details of the statistical recommendations are still in flux. However, it appears likely that the recommendations will be for these statistics to be applied to foreign affiliates that are majority-owned by direct investors, for the principal basis of attribution to be an industry classification rather than a product (i.e., type of good or service) classification, and for a variety of indicators of affiliate activity—such as sales, value added, employment, exports, and imports—to be covered.

Finally, although its recommendations have now been incorporated in the SNA and in BPM5, the OECD is the originator of the currently accepted international guidelines for compiling statistics on foreign direct investment (OECD, 1996). While the relationship of this to trade in services may seem tangential, its significance becomes more apparent in light of the fact that relatively few countries (and hardly any developing countries) now maintain the kinds of statistics on foreign-affiliate activities that are needed for monitoring the commercial presence mode of supply. Though they are not exactly what is needed, statistics on foreign direct investment do provide an alternative indicator of commercial presence. In addition, they may contribute to the development of the statistics that *are* needed, by providing a readily available register of firms that are foreign-owned.

United Nations (UN)

The United Nations has influenced statistics on trade in services in a number of ways. The UN is of course among the international organizations responsible for the SNA, whose external account for goods and services is almost completely harmonized with BPM5 and which therefore provides a somewhat parallel source of guidance with respect to trade in services, but without some of the details covered by BPM5 and presented in the larger context of the overall national accounts. However, it is perhaps with respect to classification that the UN has had the largest effect on trade-in-services statistics, for it is both the originator and the custodian of the major international systems for classifying economic outputs by product and by industrial activity.[14]

The Central Product Classification (CPC) is the only international product classification covering both goods and services. It began to be developed during the mid-to-late 1970s and was published as a provisional classification in 1991. In 1997, the UN Statistical Commission approved a revised version to be released as version 1.0, which was published the following year (United Nations, 1998). Inasmuch as an international product classification already existed for goods (the Harmonized System, with which the goods portion of the CPC corresponds very closely), the principal contribution of the CPC can be said to lie in its classification of services. While the CPC was not designed specifically as a trade classification, it has played a prominent role in such classifications. For example, the CPC was used in drawing up the above mentioned W120 list used in connection with the GATS. In addition, BPM5 contains an appendix (Appendix III) that relates its classification of services to the CPC, and the OECD/Eurostat classification also has been concorded to the CPC.[15] The forthcoming international statistical manual on trade-in-services statistics likewise will relate its classification of services trade to the CPC. Because concordance with the CPC is a common element in each of these trade-related classifications, the CPC thus provides a tool through which the classifications can be related to one another.[16]

While the CPC has thus played a significant role in international classifications of trade in services, it has served more as a dictionary, used to describe the content of the various services categories, than as a guide to aggregation structure or even as a guide to the boundary between goods and services. As would be expected, the trade classifications are designed to show the greatest detail for the services that figure most prominently in international trade. In addition, the trade classifications include two categories—travel and government services—that are transactor-based rather than product-based.[17] Finally, while the CPC has not been represented as a guide to distinguishing goods from services, its groupings and nomenclature suggest different dividing lines in some cases from those reflected in the classifications for international trade. Among the more significant differences are the classifications for repair and processing, both of which are among the borderline cases discussed above. Repair, treated by BPM5 as a part of trade in goods, is included in the CPC division for "maintenance and repair services." Processing, called for by BPM5 to be recorded on a gross basis in exports and imports of goods, is covered by the CPC division for "production services, on a fee or contract basis."

With respect to industry classification, the UN is responsible for the International Standard Industrial Classification of All Economic Activities (ISIC), which promises to figure prominently in statistics on the activities of foreign affiliates (United Nations, 1990). Now in its third revision, the ISIC is recommended as a basis for industry classification in the SNA and in the *OECD Benchmark Definition of Foreign Direct Investment*. Pilot surveys on foreign-affiliate activities conducted by the OECD have requested reporting on the basis of a selected subset of ISIC categories, and a similar ISIC-based classification is being proposed for the forthcoming statistical manual on trade-in-services statistics. Many national and regional industry classification systems follow the ISIC, in whole or in part. For example, the NACE system used within the European Union is very closely related to the ISIC, and the recently introduced North American Industry Classification System used by Canada, Mexico, and the United States is designed to be consistent with the ISIC at the 2-digit level.

Task Force on Statistics of International Trade in Services

In 1994, the UN Statistical Commission established the Interagency Task Force on Services Statistics. In recognition of the fact that all of its work involved *trade* statistics, it was subsequently redesignated as the Task Force on Statistics of International Trade in Services. Apart from facilitating communication among the international organizations represented and thus helping to rationalize work on trade-in-services statistics and avoid duplication of effort, the main project of the Task Force has been the preparation of a manual on trade-in-services statistics. This manual—the *Manual on Statistics of International Trade in Services*—will take account of a broad spectrum of statistical needs, specifically including those of the GATS. It will do this by building upon, rather than by attempting to replace, existing standards for compilation.

The manual will be consistent with existing international guidelines for statistical compilation—specifically including BPM5—but it will provide for the added dimensions called for by needs such as those of the GATS. Thus, for example, in addition to the core BPM5 rules for recording trade between residents and nonresidents will be recommendations for disaggregating this trade on the basis of mode of supply or as between intrafirm trade and trade between unrelated parties. Also provided will be guidelines for compiling data on the activities of foreign affiliates—to be termed "foreign affiliates trade in services," or FATS (a usage which has been adopted for the remaining sections of this paper). Recognizing that the totality of the recommendations to be provided generally lies beyond the capability of most, if not all, countries to implement in the short term, the manual will also indicate priorities for implementation. The priorities should be particularly useful for developing countries, which will tend to have the most work ahead of them and the least resources available for doing it.

V. The Step-by-Step Approach to Data Improvement

From the standpoint of developing statistics, one of the key distinctions between trade in services and trade in goods is the fact that services lack a central registration point that can be exploited as a data collection vehicle. While there may be numerous and varied impediments to services trade, customs declarations, specifying the type of service and its value, are not required for services. Add to this lack of administrative records the above-discussed special definitions and conventions and the requirement for data on commercial presence, and it becomes obvious that improving trade-in-services statistics is a multidimensional exercise, more likely to involve many small steps than a few large ones. Whether this makes statistics *harder* to improve for trade in services than for trade in goods is difficult to say. On the one hand, the sheer number of steps that must be taken can be daunting. On the other hand, there are likely to be many opportunities, varied in terms of difficulty of implementation, to make improvements, and at any given time there usually will be at least *some* opportunity that is within reach. Furthermore, the improvements do not have to be made all at once, but may be implemented incrementally over time.

While the steps taken to improve data on trade in services in any given country will depend on the particulars of the needs, the available resources, and the institutional framework for data collection, in many cases the improvements will involve one or more of three broad elements—methodological realignment, new or expanded surveys, and indirect estimation. Each of these may, in turn, involve multiple steps. What each of these may involve will be discussed momentarily, illustrated by the experience of the United States, with whose statistics the author has been involved.[18] Before any significant improvements can be made, however, a country must know the dimensions of the task and also must have a sense of priorities—what is most important. In addition, the responsible statistical office must have the legal authority to collect the necessary data. This preparatory work, though not a data improvement in itself, is nonetheless essential and can be considered as a fourth typical element in a data improvement program. It is termed here "setting the stage" and is discussed first.

Setting the stage.—Because of the lack of a central registration point and the diverse sources of information and methodologies that typically must be used in developing estimates, data on trade in services cannot be collected through a single all-inclusive instrument, such as a survey. For example, travel transactions, which involve individuals, require a different instrument from transactions between businesses, such as those in advertising, accounting, or legal services. Furthermore, the specific categories for which data are desired generally must be enumerated in surveys, inasmuch as residual, "all other" categories can be confusing to respondents in a system based on multiple instruments. (It is difficult to enforce exclusion from a given residual of those items for which data are collected using other instruments.) To sort out these issues, actual collection of additional data may need to be preceded by a period of study, in which the national statistical office attempts to make a precise determination of the largest or most important data gaps, and to develop a strategy for filling them.

In the United States, a number of studies were conducted to review and evaluate data on trade in services and to recommend improvements. As early as 1984, the Bureau of Economic Analysis, which compiles the balance of payments accounts and also provides statistics describing the operations of multinational companies, issued a staff paper that described the then available data on U.S. trade and investment in services, identified gaps in the data, and made a number of suggestions for improvement (Whichard, 1984). Two years later, a report by the Congressional Office of Technology Assessment addressed some of these same issues (U.S. Congress, 1986). In 1992, after a number of data improvements had already been made, a study panel organized by the National Research Council issued a report in which the improvement efforts were evaluated and a number of suggestions for further improvements were made (National Research Council, 1992). Finally, although it did not issue any comprehensive reports, an important part of the process of sorting out data needs and of reaching a consensus within the U.S. Government on the approach to data improvement was through the work of an Interagency Task Force on Services Trade Data. Established in 1982, it was chaired by the Office of the U.S. Trade Representative and was charged with reviewing existing statistics, examining the specific needs of data users, recommending data improvements, and generally coordinating the interagency aspects of work in this area.

An outcome of the study phase of an improvement program should be not only the identification of gaps and other data inadequacies, but also the setting of priorities for improvements. In the not unlikely event that more needs are identified than can be met in the near term, plans for sequencing improvements must be developed. Although not formally structured as such, this exercise is akin in spirit to a cost-benefit analysis, in which answers are sought to the questions "What improvements are most important?" and "How do the improvements rank from the standpoint of cost and feasibility of implementation?" This process of sorting out priorities could be particularly important for developing countries, which, as mentioned, are likely to have numerous needs, but only limited resources that can be devoted to meeting them.

Because the initial U.S. studies predated the publication of BPM5, methodological issues did not play a major role in their recommendations. Rather, the recommendations dealt for the most part with the identification of gaps in coverage. One major need for improvement that was identified was in the areas of business, professional, and technical services—services that may not have been important in international trade in the past but that appeared to be increasing in significance as cheaper and better means of international travel and communication made them more tradable and as increasingly globalized markets for goods and capital stimulated their demand.[19] Needs also were identified for information on services delivered through foreign affiliates. As described later, major improvements were made in both of these areas.

Judging from the information on data availability presented earlier, these same types of needs seem likely to be the ones most often identified in other countries as well. A typical pattern for many countries is to provide data on travel and transportation, but to have at least some gaps—often major ones—in the area of business services. Data on services supplied through foreign affiliates tend to be even more fragmentary. Thus, as a working hypothesis, it is not unrealistic to suppose that the needs most often identified will be in these two areas—conventional resident/nonresident trade in business services and services sold through foreign affiliates. In any event, this pattern is probably sufficiently prevalent that it is a useful stereotype for illustrating approaches to developing priorities.

For a country that has major gaps in both areas—as is likely to be true of many developing countries—top priority probably should be given to improving the data on trade in business services, for these are needed not only to support trade policy, but also for entry in the basic economic accounts needed in the conduct of monetary and fiscal policy. Furthermore, in the absence of direct measures of services supplied through foreign affiliates, data on stocks and flows of direct investment may provide acceptable, if somewhat indirect, interim indicators of commercial presence.

For a country with some data on business services—perhaps limited in detail—but no data on foreign-affiliate activities—a pattern still prevalent among many middle-to-high-income countries—the choice is less clear-cut. A strategy observed in a number of OECD countries has been to attempt to make some progress on both fronts, while limiting resource commitments by relying on least-cost approaches to developing the information on affiliate activities. Typically this has meant developing information on affiliate activities only with respect to inward investment, using links between statistics on inward direct investment and domestic enterprise statistics, which may allow statistics to be derived for the foreign-owned subset of enterprises with little or no new data collection.

To promote international co-ordination in the sequencing of improvements, the forthcoming *Manual on Statistics of International Trade in Services* will—as mentioned earlier—suggest priorities for implementing its recommendations. As reflected in the draft circulating at the time of this writing, a very high priority will be assigned to providing the basic statistics on resident/nonresident trade recommended by BPM5, with intermediate priority given to providing additional details on the specific types of services traded and to providing basic measures of services supplied through foreign affiliates, and lower priority given to nuances such as disaggregating trade flows by mode of supply or on the basis of whether the trade is within multinational firms or between unrelated parties.[20]

Not only study, but also legal authority and financial resources are essential precursors of a data improvement program for trade in services. To the extent that surveys are involved in the improvements, mandatory authority is generally necessary to ensure complete reporting. Businesses on the whole benefit from statistical improvements, particularly in a case such as trade in services, where the data may be used in support of efforts to create a more open and liberalized trading environment. However, responding to surveys is not without cost, and it may be difficult to connect the benefits to one's own individual response. Thus, it is better if reporting is mandatory, both from the standpoint of the resulting statistics and from that of the individual respondent, who can devote efforts to recordkeeping and responding in the knowledge that competitors are having to do the same. In the United States, new survey work for trade in services did not begin until legal authority was secured for collecting the data on a mandatory basis. At about the same time, additional funding was obtained to finance increased survey work and other data improvements.

Methodological realignment.—What is meant here by "methodological realignment" is simply the reconfiguration of definitions and classifications to conform to current international standards. Countries cannot, of course, be compelled to follow these standards, but they generally see the benefits from conformity, the chief one being that it facilitates comparisons with statistics compiled by other countries. Because the standards themselves have recently changed or, in the case of statistics on the activities of foreign affiliates, are still evolving, realignment is likely to be a part of the data improvement program of almost every country.

For the United States, a fairly large number of steps toward realignment have been taken. Given the magnitude of the task, as well as the fact that some steps had to await the development of new source data or were not identified as needs until some time after the initial studies were conducted, the steps have tended to be spread out over time rather than being implemented all at once. While an all-at-once approach might have been better from the standpoint of minimizing the number of disruptions imposed on data users, the incremental approach was, realistically, the only option feasible. The steps taken have ranged from very broad changes in the structure of the accounts—perhaps the broadest being the creation of a separate subtotal for services within the current account—to very specific issues involving classification of individual types of transactions.

Expanded surveying activity.—While there may be some countries that have no need for additional data collection on trade in services, they are likely to be few and far between. Trade in services has only recently become a central concern of balance of payments compilers, and relatively few countries maintain statistics on the services activities of foreign affiliates in their countries of location. Furthermore, trade in services not only is growing, but it also is coming to encompass new and different types of services. Finally, information on mode of supply has been identified as a new need, but little or no data are now being collected on that basis.

In the United States, two new "families" of surveys have proved necessary to achieve satisfactory coverage of trade in services, along with a number of improvements to pre-existing surveys. One family—consisting of a benchmark survey conducted every 5 years and a more limited annual survey conducted in nonbenchmark years—currently collects data on about 30 different types of mainly business, professional, and technical services.[21] The second family— also consisting of benchmark and annual surveys—collects data on financial services. In addition to these new surveys, existing surveys have been expanded, both to improve coverage and to increase the possibilities for subdividing the data by type of service. One of the more important changes to existing surveys involved the surveys on the operations of multinational companies. In those surveys, questions on the sales of foreign affiliates of U.S. companies and of U.S. affiliates of foreign companies were expanded to require reporting of sales of services separately from sales of goods. In this way, an economical means was found for measuring services delivered to foreign markets by U.S. firms, and in the U.S. market by foreign firms, through affiliates, thus providing information relevant to the GATS commercial presence mode of supply.

Indirect estimates.—While surveys may provide the most obvious source of information on services trade, they can be costly for governments to conduct, and they impose burdens on the respondents who must complete them. Fortunately, it is sometimes possible to develop information without surveying the universe of transactors. One example of this is when benchmark and annual surveys are conducted. An effort is made to capture essentially the entire universe of transactions only in the benchmark survey. Higher reporting thresholds are used in the annual surveys, with the unreported part of the universe being extrapolated forward from the benchmark year, based on movements in the transactions reported by firms that report in both types of surveys. This is done in the United States, for example, for the services covered by the two new surveys discussed above.

Estimation may also be used where a price or unit value is available from a sample of transactions and a universe measure or indicator of the volume of transactions is available from another source. For example, average expenditures of travelers to foreign countries may be estimated based on surveys given to a sample of travelers; this average may then be multiplied by the total number of travelers, obtained from the immigration authorities, to obtain an estimate of total expenditures by all travelers. As another example, transportation charges per unit of freight hauled may be estimated using a sample; this average can then be multiplied by the total volume of freight, obtained from customs documents, to produce an estimate of the total value of transportation charges. Similarly, expenditures of students studying abroad may be estimated by multiplying average charges for tuition and other expenses, which may be obtained from educational institutions or associations, by the numbers of students, which may be obtained either from these same sources or from visa information.

In the United States, a number of data improvements have taken the form of such indirect estimates, which not only help to minimize reporting burdens on the businesses or individuals involved in the transactions, but also do a great deal to economize on scarce statistical agency resources. These have involved the services mentioned above, as well as a few others.

VI. Issues in Data Collection

While considerable progress in improving data on trade in services has been made already, and while further improvements are underway, there are a number of difficult issues in data collection and estimation that should be acknowledged, with the aim of informing the data user, stimulating thinking about possible solutions, and—to face a hard fact—recognizing the existence of a few difficulties that simply tend to defy resolution. What follows is a discussion of what the author views as some of the more difficult or important problem areas. Four areas are discussed—services sold to individuals, price data, mode-of-supply information, and data on affiliate activities related to outward direct investment (sometimes termed "outward FATS statistics").

Services sold to individuals.—Except for questionnaires distributed to travelers, surveys of international trade in services are almost exclusively surveys of businesses, not of individuals. While international travelers are not hard to identify—they can be found at airports and customs checkpoints—the same cannot be said of individuals in general. The percentage of individuals involved in international trade in services other than as travelers is very small, yet collectively their transactions could be significant—becoming more so as developments in electronic commerce and the international use of credit cards make it increasingly easy and convenient for individuals to purchase services directly from abroad.[22] In almost all cases, the individuals in question are dealing, not with other individuals, but with businesses. Thus, problems in capturing services sold to individuals tend mainly to be those of compilers in the importing country. How can these transactions be identified? The answers, it must be said, are far from obvious.

As a concrete example, consider telecommunications callback services. These services may lower the cost of international calls by shifting their origin to a country that has lower rates than the country of the customer. Traditionally, telecommunications services are tracked statistically through the use of data on settlements payments between telecommunications common carriers. With callback services, however, funds also flow between individual customers and the callback service providers, typically through charges to credit cards. While data can be collected from the providers, the country of the customer would have only the individual customers from whom to collect data. However, it would have little way of identifying them, and—inasmuch as it may be illegal, or at least a gray area of the law, to bypass the national telephone monopoly in this way—the customers, even if aware of the need for reporting, might be reluctant to reveal themselves. Faced with such a situation, how is the importing country to obtain these data? In some cases, data exchanges with exporting countries might offer a solution, though the exporting countries typically would have no reason to track callback receipts as a separate item. In others, information obtained from credit card companies might be explored, though privacy concerns might preclude this alternative in many countries. A final possibility is for compilers simply to make their own rough estimates, based on industry sources or other information. Such estimates can be useful in eliminating downward biases in broad aggregates, but they cannot be regarded as providing precise information on trade in particular types of services.

Prices.—Almost all discussions of statistics on trade in services are about statistics on the values of the trade. Perhaps this is simply out of a sense of realism as to what is, or could be expected to become, available. It could not be for a lack of need for separate information on prices and quantities, for these are among the most basic variables in all of economics; indeed, supply and demand are defined in terms of them. Nor could it be because the information is altogether lacking. After all, exports and imports enter into the computation of GDP, an aggregate for which almost all countries provide estimates in real terms as well as in terms of current-period prices. Rather, what tends to be missing is service-by-service deflators, developed on the basis of a sampling of prices applicable to traded services alone.

One might think the law of one price would allow domestic prices to proxy for international prices. However, the validity of this method for purposes of analyzing trade in specific services tends to be limited by the aggregated nature of the categories for which value data are collected, together with the likelihood that the composition of international transactions within these categories differs significantly from that of domestic transactions and the fact that there may be added costs (which would be reflected in prices) of conducting business across national boundaries. Furthermore, in some cases the output itself—consulting or legal services provided in connection with a large international merger, for example—is almost uniquely defined, with the result that it is difficult even to state the units of output to which the prices apply. While hedonic techniques—through which what might be called "virtual products" are constructed in terms of their underlying characteristics—have been used to good effect to estimate prices of goods that have varied and rapidly changing characteristics (e.g., computers), it stretches the imagination to suppose that data on traded services will be collected in sufficient detail to permit an analogous approach to be used for services anytime soon.

Probably the best that can be expected is for price indexes specific to international transactions to be developed for selected services for which prices can be related to outputs readily and in a manner that can be followed consistently over time. In the United States, for example, the International Price Program of the Bureau of Labor Statistics provides price indexes for international transportation, including passenger transportation. Before expansion of the program was limited due to resource constraints, communication was being considered as an area for future work.

Modes of supply.—Many statisticians must have wondered why it was necessary for the GATS to add such a requirement as mode of supply to a data improvement agenda that was already rather formidable. However, it would have been hard for the GATS to ignore this dimension of services trade, for it is not simply a basis for making commitments under the agreement, but a factor that was reflected in existing barriers. To take medical services as an example, access to a country's local market through movement of natural persons or commercial presence might be effectively restricted through board-certification requirements or the existence of a national health care system, yet the country's own nationals might be free to seek care abroad (consumption abroad mode of supply), and local practitioners might be free to utilize remote diagnostic services (cross-border supply). With policies differentiated in this manner, it was almost a necessity that a mode-of-supply perspective be reflected in the agreement, calling in turn for the establishment of a new statistical domain.

While the need is thus clear, the means of supplying it is not. Although data on transactions between residents and nonresidents will naturally be separated from data on services supplied through foreign affiliates, and mode of supply will occasionally be identifiable as a result of differences in the types of transactors involved (see the next paragraph), the author knows of no data on resident/nonresident trade that are actually collected with a particular view to allocating the transactions by mode of supply. The prospects for this dimension to be reflected in collection efforts are clouded by both practical and conceptual difficulties. Not only would statistical agencies require added resources to collect data by mode of supply, but the companies that must supply the data would face an increase in reporting burden; considering that mode-of-supply is not a dimension ordinarily tracked by corporate accounting systems, the increase could be significant. A further difficulty stems from the fact that transactions involving multiple modes of supply probably are not uncommon.[23]

Considerations such as these suggest that the straightforward addition of a mode-of-supply dimension to statistical questionnaires on trade in services probably is not going to happen in the near or medium term, and perhaps not even in the long term. A more likely, and promising, course is that through study and analysis, the range of uncertainty concerning mode of supply can be narrowed. First steps in this direction are reflected in the above-cited work of Karsenty (2000). Case studies of particular service industries might provide further insights. Finally, a few services may be naturally differentiated along mode-of-supply lines, because of differences in the identity of the participants to the transactions. For example, with respect to educational or medical services, there should be no problem in determining the portion of the total that represents consumption-abroad transactions, inasmuch as these reflect the activities of readily identifiable classes of individuals.

Outward FATS statistics.—As mentioned earlier, a number of countries are beginning to develop statistics on the activities of foreign-owned enterprises in the domestic economy (inward FATS), but only a very small number have collected data on the activities of their own residents' foreign affiliates (outward FATS). Why is this? I believe it is for two basic reasons, both of which may be rooted as much in perceptions as in reality. The first is related to the difficulty in collecting the data; the second, to relative differences in the need for the data. While these factors, individually or in combination, may reasonably lead a country to compile FATS statistics only with respect to inward investment, a case can be made for greater efforts to cover outward investment as well.

First, the issue of difficulty. Unlike statistics on inward FATS, which can often be tabulated simply by identifying the foreign-owned portion of the universe of firms covered by domestic enterprise statistics, developing statistics on outward FATS will invariably entail additional data collection, with attendant increases in the resource requirements of statistical agencies and in the reporting burdens imposed on companies. An added obstacle to data collection that is often cited is the fact that the firms covered by the statistics are located, not in the compiling economy, but abroad. While this should be recognized as an obstacle, regarding it as an overwhelming one probably is not justified. As generally implemented, only majority-owned affiliates are covered by FATS statistics, and basic information on the operations of such affiliates would be needed by the parent company, both to prepare consolidated financial statements for the worldwide enterprise and to manage that enterprise effectively. In addition, a few countries have actually collected outward FATS statistics, thus providing an empirical demonstration of feasibility.

Even if it can be accepted that the development of outward FATS statistics is within the realm of possibility, a country must ask itself if the effort is justified. Here, a reasonable case can be made that inward FATS statistics should be given the higher priority. Under the GATS, countries make commitments with respect to the supply of services in their own economies, not services they supply abroad. Thus, for services supplied via the commercial presence mode, the most directly related data may be those on the activities of foreign-owned firms in the domestic economy. Nonetheless, the reason countries make commitments presumably is to improve their ability to supply services abroad.[24] For commercial presence, this supply is tracked by data on outward FATS, which therefore also must be considered to be relevant.

Whatever the arguments related to needs or practicalities, the reality is that in the near to medium term, far more countries are likely to develop FATS statistics for inward investment than for outward investment. However, because one country's inward FATS statistics are another country's outward FATS statistics, there is the potential for data exchanges to provide countries with information on the overseas activities of their multinational corporations, even if it is through data compiled by partner countries rather than by themselves.[25] The importance of standardized definitions and methodologies in assembling such data is obvious, and in this regard the international organizations can play an important role. In addition, by republishing member-country data, these organizations can, in effect, serve as clearinghouses for the information. The value of such clearinghouses can be considerable, inasmuch as they can help to achieve a kind of consistency in presentation and can reduce the number of contacts required to assemble the data.

VII. Conclusion

As this paper has attempted to demonstrate, considerable progress has been made in improving data on trade in services, yet unmet needs remain. While further progress can be expected, the new requirements for data flowing from the GATS are considerable, and some of them are likely to be met only over an extended period of time or will have to be satisfied through such expediencies as indirect indicators, proxy measures, or data exchanges among partner countries. There is work to do both for national statistical offices, which must collect and compile additional data, and for international organizations, which must assist in developing internationally agreed standards for compilation and which can play an important role in facilitating data exchanges and in disseminating member country data in consistent formats.

Notes

[*] Bureau of Economic Analysis, U.S. Department of Commerce. I would like to thank Bernard Hoekman for providing useful comments on an earlier draft. The views expressed in this paper are those of the author and do not necessarily represent those of the U.S. Department of Commerce.

[1] Despite the difficulties, some efforts to quantify these barriers have been made. For a discussion of the work in this area, see Warren and Findlay, 2000.

[2] See, for example, Stern and Hoekman, 1987.

[3] As many readers are no doubt already aware, the GATS identifies four modes of supply. Three of them subdivide the bulk of the services transactions between residents and nonresidents that are recorded in balance of payments accounts: Cross-border supply (service is transmitted from a producer in one country to a consumer in another country), consumption abroad (purchaser consumes the service in the country of the producer), and presence of natural persons (producer performs the service in the country of the consumer). A fourth mode—commercial presence—covers services supplied

through foreign affiliates or through short-term commercial operations that do not qualify as direct investment (e.g., some construction projects).

[4] Most of the remaining countries did not exist in the same form throughout the period (e.g., Soviet republics that became separate countries) or began reporting during the period.

[5] The IMF Yearbook contains additional detail that is not shown in table 4.1, but all of it is within travel and transportation, many countries did not supply some or all of it, and its addition would in any event still leave the list far more aggregated than the W120 list. The W120 list was originally published in GATT, 1991; a more generally accessible source is United Nations Conference on Trade and Development and the World Bank, 1994, pp. 169-72. For a discussion of linkages between the W120 list and the statistical classifications used by balance of payments compilers, see Henderson, 1997.

[6] Notwithstanding the statement in the text, Karsenty has found it possible to make order-of-magnitude assessments of the relative importance of the different modes of supply, by making assumptions about the various categories of transactions recorded in balance of payments accounts and by examining the available data on activities of foreign affiliates (Karsenty, 2000).

[7] Statistical Office of the European Communities, 1997. In this publication, "FATS" stands for "foreign affiliates trade statistics." In the draft Manual of Statistics of International Trade in Services—described in the next section—the same acronym is used to represent "foreign affiliates trade in services." These terms have largely replaced the term "establishment trade," which for many years was used in trade policy circles as a shorthand way of referring to activities falling under the commercial presence mode of supply.

[8] The greater availability of data for inward investment than for outward investment is likely to be a continuing feature of data on foreign-affiliate operations. For inward investment, it may be possible to develop estimates by linking data on direct investment, which can help to identify the firms in the domestic economy that are foreign-owned, with domestic enterprise statistics. In this way, estimates can often be developed without any actual new data collection being required. For outward investment, in contrast, no such linking opportunities are available, and so new surveys or expansion of existing surveys generally would be required to develop the data. Some of the implications of this situation are considered in the last section of the paper.

[9] See GATS, Article XVIII, Section k.

[10] Commission of the European Communities, International Monetary Fund, Organisation for Economic Co-operation and Development, United Nations, and World Bank, 1993, paragraph 6.3. This definition derives from Hill, 1977, p. 318.

[11] It has been argued, however, that a services aspect may be present in some such cases. Feketekuty has put forth the view that "[t]he globalization of production, which results in the unbundling and distribution of different steps in the production process to different countries gives manufacturing many of the same characteristics as the production of services. . . [I]t can be argued that partial processing of manufactured goods is more effectively treated as the production of a value-added service rather than as the manufacturing of a good" (Feketekuty, 2000).

[12] If the purchase and resale occur in different periods, the purchase is recorded as an import of goods, and the subsequent resale is recorded as a deduction from such imports (i.e., as a negative goods import).

[13] In the SNA, an additional element, represented by income on technical reserves, is included in the insurance service charge for domestic transactions. However, both the SNA and BPM5 indicate that, for practical reasons, this element is to be ignored in the measurement of international trade in insurance. This omission may result in some understatement (similar to the case of "financial intermediation services indirectly measured," discussed below with respect to financial services), though the types of insurance for which income on technical reserves is most important probably are not the ones most important in international trade.

[14] The assistance provided to the UN by the group of country experts known as the Voorburg Group in connection with these classification systems should be acknowledged. This group met for the first time in 1986 (in Voorburg, the site of the Statistics Netherlands headquarters offices), primarily to provide a means through which representatives of national statistical offices could assist the UN Statistical Office with the parts of the classifications dealing with services. Over time, it has evolved into an annual forum for the exchange of views and information on a wide variety of statistical issues pertaining to services.

[15] The existing concordances are with the provisional CPC. Work is underway to create concordances with CPC ver. 1.0.

[16] The CPC is used in this way in the previously cited work of Henderson, relating the W120 list to balance of payments classifications (Henderson, 1997).

[17] It is true, as some have pointed out, that what is recorded under these categories consists of specific goods and services, all of which have a place in the CPC. However, for practical reasons the trade classifications do not call for these to be separately enumerated, either by CPC category or by any other product classification.

[18] For a more detailed account of the U.S. data improvements than will be provided here, see Ascher and Whichard, 1991. Improvements subsequent to this paper are described in various issues of the *Survey of Current Business*, where both the U.S. balance of payments accounts and the U.S. data on foreign affiliate activities are published.

[19] As is well known, a significant share of the demand for traded services is a derived demand, stemming from international trade in goods and flows of capital. For example, a firm in one country may engage an accounting or consulting firm in another country for help in connection with an acquisition of a firm in that other country, or a firm may provide after-sale service and support abroad for its products that are sold in foreign countries.

[20] For more information on the draft manual, see Arkell (1999).

[21] When this survey was instituted in 1986, it collected data for 18 types of services; new services have been added in connection with each subsequent benchmark survey.

[22] Consonant with the topic of this paper, services alone are mentioned in the text; however, these developments obviously also create new potentials for gaps in statistics on trade in goods.

[23] As an illustration of a multi-mode transaction, a consultant might go abroad to study a situation on behalf of the client (presence of natural persons mode of supply), then return home to prepare a report, which is then transmitted to the client via a postal or telecommunications link (cross-border supply).

[24] There may be efficiency gains from having more services supplied from abroad, but these could be achieved through unilateral liberalization.

[25] While this approach offers promise as a means of overcoming resource constraints or concerns about reporting burden, one drawback is that it may tend to leave countries, such as many developing countries, that cannot compile statistics for inward investment out in the cold, inasmuch as it deprives them of what might otherwise be a promising source of information on the operations of foreign-owned firms in their own economies (namely, partner countries' statistics for outward investment).

References

Arkell, Julian. 1999. "Manual on Statistics of International Trade in Services," paper prepared for World Services Congress, Atlanta, GA, November.

Ascher, Bernard, and Obie G. Whichard. 1991. Developing a Data System for International Sales of Services: Progress, Problems, and Prospects. In Peter Hooper and J. David Richardson (eds.), *International Economic Transactions: Issues in Measurement and Empirical Research*. Chicago: University of Chicago Press: 203-34.

Commission of the European Communities, International Monetary Fund, Organisation for Economic Co-operation and Development, United Nations, and World Bank. 1993. *System of National Accounts, 1993*. Brussels/Luxembourg, New York, Paris, Washington.

Feketekuty, Geza. 2000. "Assessing the WTO General Agreement on Trade in Services and Improving the GATS Architecture," in Pierre Sauvé and Robert M. Stern (eds.), *Services 2000: New Directions in Services Trade Liberalization*. Washington, D.C.: Brookings Institution.

GATT Secretariat. 1991. *Services Sectoral Classification List*. Document MTN.GNS/W/120. Geneva.

Henderson, Hugh. 1997. "On Building Bridges: A Canadian Perspective on Linking Services Categories of the World Trade Organization and Balance of Payments Compilers," paper presented at Tenth Meeting of IMF Committee on Balance of Payments Statistics. Washington, DC, October.

Hill, T.P. 1977. "On Goods and Services," *Review of Income and Wealth* 23 (December): 315-38.

International Monetary Fund. 1993. *Balance of Payments Manual*, 5th ed. Washington, DC.

International Monetary Fund. 1998. *Balance of Payments Statistics Yearbook*. Washington, DC.

Karsenty, Guy. 2000. "Just How Big Are the Stakes? An Assessment of Trade in Services by Mode of Supply," In Pierre Sauvé and Robert M. Stern (eds.), *Ser-

vices 2000—New Directions in Services Trade Liberalization. Washington, D.C.: Brookings Institution.

National Research Council, Panel on Foreign Trade Statistics. 1992. *Behind the Numbers*, Anne Y. Kester, ed. Washington, DC: National Academy Press.

Organisation for Economic Co-Operation and Development. 1996. *OECD Benchmark Definition of Foreign Direct Investment*, 3rd edition. Paris.

Organisation for Economic Co-Operation and Development. 1999. *Services: Statistics on International Transactions, 1987-96.* Paris.

Statistical Office of the European Communities (Directorate B, Unit B-5). 1997. *Fats Task Force Report*, January.

Stern, Robert M., and Bernard M. Hoekman. 1987. "Issues and Data Needs for GATT Negotiations on Services," *World Economy* 10 (March): 39-60.

United Nations Conference on Trade and Development and the World Bank. 1994. *Liberalizing International Transactions in Services: A Handbook.* New York and Geneva.

United Nations, Department of Economic and Social Affairs, Statistics Division. 1998. *Central Product Classification (CPC)*, version 1.0 (United Nations, Statistical Papers, Series M, No. 77, Ver. 1.0).

United Nations. 1990. *International Standard Industrial Classification of All Economic Activities*, Statistical Papers, Series M, No. 4, Rev. 3. New York.

U.S. Congress, Office of Technology Assessment. 1986. *Trade in Services: Exports and Foreign Revenues—Special Report*, OTA-ITE-316. Washington, DC: U.S. Government Printing Office, September.

Warren, Tony, and Christopher Findlay. 2000. "How Significant are the Barriers? Measuring Impediments to Trade in Services," in Pierre Sauvé and Robert M. Stern (eds.), *Services 2000: New Directions in Services Trade Liberalization.* Washington, D.C.: Brookings Institution.

Whichard, Obie G. 1984. "U.S. International Trade and Investment in Services: Data Needs and Availability," U.S. Department of Commerce, Bureau of Economic Analysis, Staff Paper 41.

Annex—Joint OECD-Eurostat Trade In Services Classification

*1. Transportation

    *1.1 Sea transport
       *1.1.1 Passenger
       *1.1.2 Freight
       *1.1.3 Other

    *1.2 Air transport
       *1.2.1 Passenger
       *1.2.2 Freight
       *1.2.3 Other

    1.3 Other transport
       1.3.1 Passenger
       1.3.2 Freight
       1.3.3 Other

    Extended classification of other transport (1.3)
    1.4 Space transport
    1.5 Rail transport
       1.5.1 Passenger
       1.5.2 Freight
       1.5.3 Other

    1.6 Road transport
       1.6.1 Passenger
       1.6.2 Freight
       1.6.3 Other

    1.7 Internal waterway transport
       1.7.1 Passenger
       1.7.2 Freight
       1.7.3 Other

    1.8 Pipeline transport

    1.9 Other supporting and auxiliary transport services

Memorandum items
Freight transportation on the basis of an ex works valuation of mer

chandise:
Sea freight
Air freight
Road freight
Other freight

*2. Travel*2.1 Business
    2.1.1 Expenditure by seasonal and border workers
    2.1.2 Other

    *2.2 Personal
        *2.2.1 Health-related
        *2.2.2 Education-related
        *2.2.3 Other

  Memorandum items:
    Tourists
    Goods purchased in the frontier area by travelers
    Hotel and restaurant services

*3. Communications services
    3.1 Postal and courier services
    3.2 Telecommunication services

    Memorandum items
    Postal services
    Courier services

    *4. Construction services
        4.1 Construction abroad
        4.2 Construction in the compiling economy

    *5. Insurance services
        5.1 Life insurance and pension funding
        5.2 Freight insurance
        5.3 Other direct insurance
        5.4 Reinsurance
        5.5 Auxiliary services

        Memorandum item
        Gross insurance premiums
        Gross insurance claims

*6. Financial services

*7. Computer and information services
    7.1 Computer services
    7.2 Information services

*8. Royalties and license fees

*9. Other business services

    *9.1 Merchanting and other trade-related services
        9.1.1 Merchanting
        9.1.2 Other
    *9.2 Operational leasing services

    *9.3 Miscellaneous business, professional, and technical services
        *9.3.1 Legal, accounting, management consulting, and public relations
            9.3.1.1 Legal services
            9.3.1.2 Accounting, auditing, book-keeping and tax consulting services
            9.3.1.3 Business and management consultancy and public relations services
        *9.3.2 Advertising, market research, and public opinion polling
        *9.3.3 Research and development
        *9.3.4 Architectural, engineering and other technical services
        *9.3.5 Agricultural, mining and on-site processing services
            9.3.5.1 Waste treatment and depollution
            9.3.5.2 Other
        9.3.6 Other
        9.3.7 Services between affiliated enterprises, n.i.e.

        Memorandum items
            Merchanting gross flows
            Agricultural services
            Mining services

*10. Personal, cultural, and recreational services
    *10.1 Audiovisual and related services
    *10.2 Other personal, cultural and recreational services

*11. Government services, n.i.e.
    11.1 Embassies and consulates
    11.2 Military units and agencies
    11.3 Other

Note.—Items marked with an asterisk (*) are listed in BPM5 as standard components or "services sub-items" (items suggested to be provided as supplementary information).

Source: OECD. 1999.

CHAPTER 5

Multilateral Liberalization of Services Trade

Philippa Dee and Kevin Hanslow[*]

Introduction

This chapter uses comprehensive new measures of barriers to services trade in a multi-region, multi-sectoral CGE model of world trade and investment. The model is used to examine the impact of multilateral liberalization of services trade. Barriers to commercial presence are distinguished from those affecting other modes of service delivery (cross border supply, consumption abroad, and the presence of natural persons), and barriers to national treatment are distinguished from barriers to market access. The effects of liberalization are examined using version 4.1 of the GTAP model of world trade, modified to handle services delivered via commercial presence through the inclusion of bilateral FDI flows. This treatment follows the work of Petri (1997). GTAP's welfare decomposition is also modified to allow for income earned from abroad. The model is used to demonstrate the importance of multilateral liberalization of services trade, relative to liberalization of trade in agricultural and manufactured products.

As the world faces a possible new round of multilateral trade negotiations, it is timely to examine what is at stake. This chapter provides preliminary estimates of the benefits to individual economies, and to the world as a whole, from eliminating the barriers to trade that will remain after full implementation of the Uruguay Round.

The analysis compares the gains from eliminating remaining barriers in the traditional areas of agriculture and manufacturing, with those from eliminating barriers to trade in services. To do so, it uses a model that incorporates a treatment of foreign direct investment (FDI), one of the key vehicles by which services are traded internationally. This allows examination of the comprehensive removal of restrictions on all modes of service delivery, including restrictions on services delivered via FDI (though not on FDI more generally).

The structure of the chapter is as follows. It first describes the model used—a multi-sector, multi-regional computable general equilibrium model of world trade and investment. The theoretical structure of the model covers both FDI and portfolio investment. The model's database contains estimates of FDI stocks and the activities of FDI firms, each on a bilateral basis. These estimates allow a comparison of the extent to which goods and services are delivered via FDI or via conventional trade. The chapter then looks at the size of the trade barriers that will remain after full implementation of the Uruguay Round. These estimates include comprehensive new measures of existing barriers to services trade. Next, the chapter looks at the implications of eliminating those trade barriers entirely. Since any new trade round is likely to lead to partial rather than full liberalization, the chapter then evaluates some options for partial liberalization of services trade. Finally, it outlines directions for further research.

The FTAP Model

The model is a version of GTAP (Hertel 1997) with foreign direct investment, known as FTAP. The treatment of FDI follows closely the pioneering work of Petri (1997). FTAP also incorporates increasing returns to scale and large-group monopolistic competition in all sectors. This follows Francois, McDonald and Nordstrom (1995), among others, who adopted this treatment for manufacturing and resource sectors, and Brown et al. (1995) and Markusen, Rutherford and Tarr (1999), who used similar treatments for services. Finally, FTAP makes provision for capital accumulation and international borrowing and lending. This uses a treatment of international (portfolio) capital mobility developed by McDougall (1993), and recently incorporated into GTAP by Verikios and Hanslow (1999). FTAP is implemented using the GEMPACK software suite (Harrison and Pearson 1996). Its structure is documented fully in Hanslow, Phamduc and Verikios (1999). The model and its documentation are available at http://www.pc.gov.au.

Theoretical Structure

FTAP takes the standard GTAP framework as a description of the *location* of economic activity, and then disaggregates this by *ownership*. For example, each industry located in Australia comprises Australian owned firms, along with U.S., European, and Japanese multinationals. Each of these firm-ownership *types* is modeled as making its own independent choice of inputs to production, according to standard GTAP theory. And each firm type has its own sales structure.

On the purchasing side, agents in each economy make choices among the products or services of each firm type, distinguished by both ownership and location, and then among the individual (and symmetric) firms of a given type. Thus, the model recognizes the firm-level product differentiation associated with monopolistic competition. Firms choose among intermediate inputs and investment goods, while households and governments choose among final goods and services.

Agents are assumed to choose first among products or services from domestic or foreign locations, with a CES elasticity of substitution of 5. They then choose among particular foreign locations, and among ownership categories in a particular location, both with a CES elasticity of substitution of 10. Finally, they choose among the individual firms of a particular ownership and location, with a CES elasticity of substitution of 15. With firm-level product differentiation, agents benefit from having more firms to choose among, because it is more likely that they can find a product or service suited to their particular needs. Capitalizing on this, Francois, McDonald and Nordstrom (1995) show that the choice among individual firms can be modeled in a conventional model of firm types (not firms) by allowing a productivity improvement whenever the output of a particular firm type (and hence the number of individual firms in it) expands. But because the substitutability among individual firms is assumed here to be very high, the incremental gain from greater variety is not very great and this productivity enhancing effect is not particularly strong (the elasticity of productivity with respect to output[1] is $1/15 = 0.0667$).

The first two choices, among domestic and foreign locations, are identical to the choices in the original GTAP model. They have been parameterized using values, 5 and 10, that are roughly twice the standard GTAP Armington elasticities. Two reasons can be given for doubling the standard elasticities. One is that only with such elasticities can GTAP successfully reproduce historical changes in trade patterns (Gehlhar 1997). The other is that higher elasticities accord better with notions of firm-level product differentiation.

The order of the first three choices, among locations and then among ownership categories, is the opposite of the order adopted by Petri (1997). The current treatment assumes that from an Australian perspective, for example, a U.S. multinational located in Australia is a closer substitute for an Australian owned firm than it is for a U.S. firm located in the United States. Petri's treatment assumes that U.S.-owned firms are closer substitutes for each other than for Australian firms, irrespective of location.

There are two reasons for preferring the current treatment.

The first is that Petri's treatment produces a model in which multilateral liberalization of tariffs on manufactured goods produces large economic welfare losses, for most individual economies and for the world as a whole—an uncomfortable result at odds with conventional trade theory. The reason for the result can be seen by considering the choices that Australians would make at the top of Petri's decision tree in the face of a tariff cut. They would choose between an aggregate of the output of Australian firms (irrespective of location) and an aggregate of the output of U.S. firms (irrespective of location). The first aggregate would be overwhelmingly dominated by the output of domestically located Australian firms, since 'boomerang' imports from Australian firms located offshore would be minimal. Thus the first aggregate would have a very small proportion of goods attracting a tariff. The second aggregate would include both goods produced by U.S. multinationals located in Australia, and imports from U.S. firms located in the United States. Only the latter would initially attract a tariff. Depending on relative shares, there is no guarantee that the price of the U.S. aggregate would be dominated by the removal of the tariff on imports, rather than by endogenous changes in the cost structure of U.S. multinationals in Australia. Simulations with a model of this structure showed that the price of the U.S. aggregate *rose* relative to the price of the Australian aggregate in the face of a tariff cut, encouraging resources in Australia to move *into* the domestic protected sector as its protection was removed. This led to a deterioration in allocative efficiency and an overall economic welfare loss. The story was repeated in many other regions.

The second reason for preferring the current treatment is that, in many instances, it accords better with reality. Some Australian examples help to illustrate. Many Australian consumers prefer roomy cars with large capacity, 6-cylinder engines. Holden, originally locally owned but bought out by General Motors, has produced such cars for some time. Ford Australia has invested in significant local design capacity in order to produce a close rival. Now Mitsubishi and Toyota in Australia also produce 6-cylinder versions of 4-cylinder cars for the local market. Similarly, Hungry Jacks, the local version of Burger King, has had some success with a hamburger reminiscent of those popular in Australia before the arrival of international franchises—one with no pickle, but with a rasher of bacon, a fried egg, and above all, a slice of beetroot. Recently, McDonalds in Australia announced that it had delayed introducing a burger with beetroot because it had been unable to secure adequate supplies.

Thus U.S. firms are often not the same, irrespective of location, even when their foreign direct investment is 'horizontal' rather than 'vertical'. Indeed, one of the distinguishing characteristics of services is that they are tailored each time to meet the needs of the individual consumer. Another characteristic is that they are often delivered face to face, sometimes making commercial presence (through FDI) the only viable means of trade. These taken together mean that service firms in a given location, irrespective of ownership, will tailor their services to meet local tastes and requirements, and thus appear to be close substitutes, as in the current treatment.

While the demand for the output of firms distinguished by ownership and location is determined as above, the supply of FDI is determined by the same imperfect transformation among types of wealth as in Petri (1997). Investors in each economy first divide their wealth between 'bonds' (which can be thought of as any instrument of portfolio investment), real physical capital, and land and natural resources in their country of residence. This choice is governed by a CET semi-elasticity of 1, meaning that a one percentage point increase in the rate of return on real physical capital, for example, would increase the ratio of real physical capital to bond holdings by one per cent. A bond is a bond, irrespective of who issues it, implying perfect international arbitrage of rates of return on bonds. However, capital in different locations is seen as different things. Investors next choose the industry sector in which they invest (with a CET semi-elasticity of 1.2). They next choose whether to invest at home or overseas in their chosen sector (with a CET semi-elasticity of 1.3). Finally, they choose a particular overseas region in which to invest (with a CET semi-elasticity of 1.4).

The less than perfect transformation among different forms of wealth can be justified as reflecting some combination of risk aversion and less than perfect information. It is important to note, however, that while the measure of economic welfare in FTAP currently recognizes the positive income contribution that FDI can make, it does not discount that for any costs associated with risk taking, given risk aversion. This is an important qualification to the current results, and will be the subject of further research.

While the chosen CET parameters at each 'node' of the nesting structure may appear low, the number of nests means that choices at the final level (across destinations of FDI) are actually very flexible. For example, it can be shown that, holding total wealth fixed but allowing all other adjustments across asset types and locations to take place, the implied semi-elasticity of transformation between foreign destinations can easily reach 20, and be as high as 60. The variation across regions in these implied elasticities comes about because of the different initial shares of assets in various regional portfolios.

The choice of CET parameters at each 'node' was determined partly by this consideration of what they implied for the final elasticities, holding only total wealth constant. They were also chosen so that this version of FTAP gave results that were broadly comparable to an earlier version of GTAP with imperfect international (portfolio) capital mobility, for experiments involving the complete liberalization of agricultural and manufacturing protection. That earlier version of GTAP was developed by Verikios and Hanslow (1999). Imperfect capital mobility was also a feature of the GTAP-based examination of APEC liberalization by Dee, Geisler and Watts (1996) and Dee, Hardin and Schuele (1998). These parameters thus provide a familiar starting point, from which variations could be made in the future.

In one respect, however, the current version of FTAP does differ from previous versions of GTAP with imperfect capital mobility. The GTAP variants assumed that capital was perfectly mobile across sectors, whereas FTAP has less than perfect sectoral mobility. Furthermore, the choice of sector is relatively early in the nesting structure, so that the implied elasticities guiding choice of sector, holding only total wealth constant, are relatively low (e.g., 1.2 in the United States). As a result, FTAP tends to exhibit behavior where resources move less readily between sectors in a given region, but more readily across regions in a given sector, although the differences are not dramatic. The current treatment is consistent with the idea that the knowledge capital often required to succeed in foreign direct investment, despite the difficulties of language and distance, is likely to be sector-specific.

Petri's model assumed that total wealth in each region was fixed. In FTAP, while regional endowments of land and natural resources are fixed (and held solely by each region's residents), regional capital stocks can accumulate over time, and net bond holdings of each region can adjust to help finance the accumulation of domestic and foreign capital by each region's investors. The treatment of capital accumulation follows the original treatment of McDougall (1993), and was also used by Verikios and Hanslow (1999), Dee, Geisler and Watts (1996) and Dee, Hardin and Schuele (1998).

With this treatment of capital accumulation, FTAP provides a long-run snapshot view of the impact of trade liberalization, ten years after it has occurred. To the extent that liberalization leads to changes in regional incomes and savings, this will be reflected in changes to the capital stocks that investors in each region will have been able to accumulate. As noted, investors in each region are not restricted to their own savings pool in order to finance capital investment. They may also issue bonds to help with that investment, but only according to their own preferences about capital versus bond holding, and only according to the willingness of others to accept the additional bonds.

Model Database

The starting point for FTAP's database was not the standard GTAP database, since this includes measures of trade and investment barriers that are still to be eliminated under the Uruguay Round agreement. Instead, the starting point was an updated version of the GTAP database, following a simulation in which the barriers yet to be eliminated under the Uruguay Round had been removed. Such a database was provided by the work of Verikios and Hanslow (1999), under their assumption of less than perfect capital mobility.

The Petri treatment of FDI requires the addition of data on bilateral FDI stocks, and on the activity levels and cost and sales structures of FDI firms. The methods used to estimate such data were similar to those of Petri. APEC (1995) and United Nations (1994) provided limited data on FDI stocks by source, destination and sector. These data were fleshed out to provide a full bilateral matrix of FDI stocks by source, destination and sector, using RAS methods (Stone, Strzelecki and Welsh 2000). The results are summarized in table 1. Unlike Petri, the FDI stocks have not been 'grossed up' to account for the contributions of local joint venture partners, for reasons to be explained shortly. Thus the estimates given here are lower than his, but the pattern is similar. Europe and the United States are the main sources of and destinations for FDI. Japan is much more important as a source than as a destination. The OECD provides 87 per cent of outward FDI and receives 73 per cent of inward FDI. The detailed data show that 80 per cent of FDI from Asia (excluding Japan) remains in Asia, and that there are strong bilateral, bi-directional ties between neighboring countries (Australia-New Zealand, United States-Canada). Finally, about 20 per cent of FDI is in the primary sector, with about 40 per cent each in the secondary and tertiary sectors.

Table 1. FDI stock estimates (U.S.$ billion)

	Inward FDI Stocks				Outward FDI Stocks			
	Pri	Sec	Ter	Total	Pri	Sec	Ter	Total
Australia	17.7	14.8	42.1	74.6	4.8	7.3	16.3	28.4
NZ	1.6	4.0	4.2	9.8	0.9	2.0	1.3	4.2
Japan	0.5	16.3	9.5	26.3	29.3	91.0	251.1	371.5
Korea	0.4	5.1	3.3	8.8	2.5	1.7	1.2	5.4
Indonesia	54.3	9.2	1.9	65.4	0.5	1.1	0.7	2.3
Malaysia	7.4	8.9	7.1	23.4	0.4	1.0	0.6	2.0
Philippines	1.6	1.6	1.0	4.2	0.0	0.2	0.7	0.8
Singapore	0.6	14.7	20.5	35.7	2.2	4.9	3.2	10.4
Thailand	1.7	5.1	6.2	12.9	0.0	0.1	0.6	0.7
China	7.3	15.6	16.7	39.6	0.4	0.2	0.4	1.0
Hong Kong	0.0	7.0	22.5	29.6	8.8	19.4	12.7	40.9
Taiwan	0.3	14.8	2.0	17.1	0.3	3.3	1.8	5.4
Canada	15.9	60.4	37.1	113.4	8.8	39.5	32.6	80.9
USA	36.7	185.4	219.5	441.6	57.3	196.0	228.3	481.6
Mexico	3.9	14.4	20.6	38.9	0.3	0.6	0.4	1.3
Chile	7.4	1.3	3.8	12.4	0.1	0.2	0.2	0.5
R. Cairns	10.1	47.1	20.5	77.8	1.0	2.2	1.5	4.7
EU	121.9	310.0	319.4	751.2	166.6	366.3	238.5	771.5
R. World	34.3	87.4	90.0	211.7	39.0	85.8	55.9	180.7
World	323.5	823.0	847.9	1,994.3	323.5	822.9	847.9	1,994.3

Source: Based on APEC (1995) and United Nations (1994).

As shown in table 1, the data were collected (and the model implemented) for 19 regions (where R. Cairns stands for the rest of the Cairns group—Brazil, Argentina, Colombia and Uruguay) and three broad sectors. The three sectors—primary (agriculture, resources and processed food), secondary (other manufacturing), and tertiary (services)—correspond broadly to the three areas of potential trade negotiation in a new round. The intention is to use similar methods to produce a model with greater sectoral detail in the future.

The FDI stock data were used in turn to generate estimates of the output levels of FDI firms. Capital-income flows were estimated by multiplying the FDI stocks by rates of return. The GTAP database does not contain rate of return estimates by sector, so these were calculated (using averages over 5 years where available) from the accounting information in the Worldscope Global Equity Database (Disclosure 1999).

Using the idea that there could be a premium earned on the firm-specific assets embodied in FDI, the rate of return taken to be relevant for a given FDI stock was the greater of the average rate in the home and host region. Thus the model allows rates of return to differ between locally owned and foreign firms. For this reason, it was considered unwise to allow for some fixed proportion of local equity in joint ventures, as in Petri (1997), since welfare results would then be tainted by the relatively arbitrary reallocation of locally owned capital between domestically owned firms and joint ventures. Furthermore, many of the barriers to trade in services directly affect that proportion!

Capital rentals were then grossed up to get an output estimate for FDI firms, using capital rental to output ratios from the GTAP database. Thus FDI firms were assumed to have the same capital-rental-to-output ratios as domestically owned firms, although those rentals may imply a higher rate of return on the underlying capital stock. These output estimates for FDI firms were then compared with GTAP's output estimates, and adjusted downwards (along with the underlying FDI stock) in instances where they implied negative values for the residual output of locally owned firms. The resulting output estimates are summarized in tables 2 and 3, which compare the output of outward FDI firms with conventional exports (post-Uruguay), and the output of inward FDI firms with conventional imports (post-Uruguay). The tables confirm the impression that, in many regions, goods and services delivered via FDI are as important as conventional trade.

The detailed cost and sales structures of FDI firms were assumed to be the same as for locally owned firms, and were obtained by pro-rating the GTAP database. A subject for future research will be to make use of available information on the true cost and sales structures of FDI firms.

In a final step, estimates of existing barriers to services trade were injected into the model's database, using the techniques of Malcolm (1998). The process is documented in Hanslow, Phamduc, Verikios and Welsh (2000). The GTAP model already contains estimates of the barriers to trade in agricultural and manufactured goods, and the updated version of this database obtained from Verikios and Hanslow (1999) has these at their post-Uruguay levels. However, GTAP does not contain estimates of barriers to services trade. Instead, estimates of barriers to trade in banking services were taken from Kaleeswaran et al. (2000), and estimates of barriers to trade in telecommunications services were taken from Warren (2000). These are the first of a comprehensive new set of estimates of barriers to services trade, to be documented in Findlay and Warren (2000). The rates can be taken as indicative of post-Uruguay rates, since while the Uruguay Round established the architecture for services trade negotiations, it did not achieve much in the way of services trade liberalization (Hoekman 1995).

A simple average of the estimates for banking and telecommunications was taken as being typical of most services—all of the GTAP service categories of trade and transport and finance, business and recreational services, and half of public administration and defense, education and health. The remainder of public administration and defense, education and health, along with electricity, water and gas, construction, and ownership of dwellings were assumed to be strictly non-traded (note that engineering services are part of business services, not construction). The resulting average estimates of barriers to trade in the tertiary sector would have been about 50 to 100 per cent bigger, had

Table 2. FTAP's Exports and Outward FDI Output (U.S.$ billion)

	Conventional Exports			Outward FDI Output		
	Pri	Sec	Ter	Pri	Sec	Ter
Australia	42.5	16.1	11.1	19.1	14.4	8.8
NZ	9.4	5.3	3.4	0.8	3.0	1.7
Japan	4.4	417.4	56.7	57.1	159.3	134.3
Korea	3.8	113.9	22.2	3.4	2.4	0.5
Indonesia	20.2	28.5	4.7	0.2	1.6	1.2
Malaysia	15.0	64.2	6.1	0.2	1.2	0.8
Philippines	3.7	15.2	8.1	0.0	0.4	0.6
Singapore	6.5	90.8	24.3	1.2	5.5	3.6
Thailand	16.5	38.2	12.2	0.0	0.2	0.6
China	18.5	189.3	16.4	0.9	0.2	0.3
Hong Kong	1.1	33.4	41.2	5.2	18.1	25.6
Taiwan	4.8	117.6	8.8	0.1	6.5	2.3
Canada	33.1	145.3	19.4	22.2	64.5	17.5
USA	84.9	472.8	179.5	167.2	417.5	126.9
Mexico	13.6	60.2	9.2	0.3	0.8	0.4
Chile	7.2	8.2	2.6	0.0	0.2	0.2
R. Cairns	43.4	40.9	11.2	1.1	2.8	1.7
EU	224.3	1577.6	422.7	299.1	538.2	196.3
R. World	296.9	379.6	152.3	108.9	213.9	75.8
World	849.7	3,814.7	1,012.2	686.8	1,450.8	599.3

Table 3. FTAP's Imports and Inward FDI Output (U.S.$ Billion)

	Conventional Imports			Inward FDI Output		
	Pri	Sec	Ter	Pri	Sec	Ter
Australia	7.0	54.8	18.1	19.9	25.9	28.2
NZ	1.7	11.3	4.4	3.2	5.2	3.2
Japan	122.0	201.7	108.5	0.0	27.6	6.6
Korea	30.9	98.2	24.7	0.0	6.9	1.5
Indonesia	7.0	34.8	8.1	85.7	4.9	2.1
Malaysia	6.1	64.6	9.0	7.7	9.3	5.1
Philippines	6.8	24.7	6.4	4.8	1.9	1.0
Singapore	15.0	101.1	15.7	0.0	20.2	18.7
Thailand	9.2	60.0	14.9	2.0	1.8	2.8
China	19.8	141.0	16.3	7.3	19.7	32.5
Hong Kong	12.8	82.1	18.9	11.3	9.8	9.6
Taiwan	11.3	81.6	17.0	0.0	28.1	1.5
Canada	16.3	136.7	26.0	9.0	115.4	21.4
USA	117.9	657.2	128.3	45.0	247.0	167.6
Mexico	6.5	55.8	7.8	5.5	12.5	5.5
Chile	2.7	12.7	3.1	15.0	1.1	2.0
R. Cairns	16.6	74.9	20.2	9.7	44.7	11.5
EU	348.6	1512.6	409.8	377.0	678.5	187.2
R. World	151.2	582.7	154.8	83.8	190.3	91.3
World	909.4	3,988.3	1,012.2	686.8	1,450.8	599.3

the banking and telecommunications estimates been taken as indicative of the whole of the services sector. A topic of future research is to use the next version of the GTAP database, which will have more services sector detail, to model barriers to each service separately, thus overcoming the extreme arbitrariness of these assumptions.

The resulting structure of post-Uruguay Round barriers to trade in services is summarized in table 4. Barriers to trade in agricultural and food products are represented via a combination of taxes on imports, and subsidies (shown in table 4 as negative taxes) on exports and output. Unfortunately, at FTAP's three sector level of aggregation, the actual taxes on primary exports and output are a combination of subsidies used for protective purposes, and taxes (e.g. excises on alcohol and tobacco) used for revenue raising. (While the average taxes on primary output are not shown in table 4, they are all relatively small and mostly positive.) In modeling the liberalization of post-Uruguay Round trade barriers, the greater sectoral detail of Verikios and Hanslow's database was used to calculate what would happen to the average tax rates on primary exports and output, were the subsidies (where they occur) to be removed but the taxes (where they occur) to remain. In this way, the problem of averaging could be partially overcome when modeling liberalization. A remaining problem is that GTAP's database aggregation facility implicitly uses import weights to aggregate import taxes, and the work of Anderson and Neary (e.g. 1994, 1996) shows that these give insufficient weight to very high (and therefore very distortionary) import taxes, leading to incorrect welfare results from trade liberalization. In the future, this 'aggregation bias' will be reduced by using a database with greater sectoral detail.

Once the Uruguay Round is fully implemented, the remaining trade barriers on manufacturing will comprise mainly tariffs on imports, since the export tax equivalents of the Multifibre Arrangement will have been eliminated. These average tariff levels are shown in the second column of table 4.

The structure of barriers to services trade in the last five columns of table 4 requires some explanation. The General Agreement on Trade in Services (GATS) framework distinguishes four modes of service delivery—via commercial presence, cross border supply, consumption abroad, and the presence of natural persons. Accordingly, the FTAP model distinguishes barriers to establishment from barriers to ongoing operation. This is similar to the distinction between commercial presence and other modes of delivery, since barriers to establishment are a component of the barriers to commercial presence.

In table 4, barriers to establishment have been modeled as taxes on capital. Barriers to ongoing operation may affect either FDI firms or those supplying via the other modes, and have been modeled as taxes on the output of locally-based firms (either domestic or foreign owned), and taxes of the same size on the exports of firms supplying via the other modes, respectively. The estimates of export taxes on services in the fourth column of table 4 are trade-weighted averages of the taxes on exports to particular destinations, where these are

Table 4. Tax Equivalents of Post-Uruguay Round Barriers to Trade and Investment (Per Cent)

	Imports		Exports		Domestic output	Foreign affiliates' output	Domestic capital	Foreign affiliates' capital
	Pri	Sec	Pri	Ter	Ter	Ter	Ter	Ter
	(1)	(2)	(3)	(4)	(5)	(6)	(7)	(8)
Australia	1.69	7.30	0.65	4.81	0.00	0.69	0.62	14.79
NZ	1.16	4.51	-3.25	3.78	0.00	0.67	0.41	4.18
Japan	16.19	1.81	-8.12	4.41	3.59	4.75	0.33	3.01
Korea	12.95	6.61	-1.22	4.57	5.11	6.78	1.91	22.01
Indonesia	4.40	6.71	0.00	4.68	13.23	28.11	22.69	68.06
Malaysia	21.18	5.97	6.68	4.50	3.58	10.20	15.35	37.58
Philippines	16.16	18.51	-0.10	4.80	8.38	22.65	7.40	54.28
Singapore	3.22	0.56	0.01	4.70	3.40	8.32	2.42	24.50
Thailand	12.12	14.81	-16.98	4.14	4.69	13.36	12.16	36.49
China	8.92	28.45	5.13	4.08	18.75	36.40	123.46	250.66
Hong Kong	0.00	0.00	0.00	9.91	1.39	2.36	1.35	5.41
Taiwan	27.31	5.63	-1.82	4.35	2.88	4.90	1.90	19.19
Canada	3.57	1.40	-0.43	3.54	0.25	1.67	0.53	6.11
USA	1.29	2.24	-0.02	4.26	0.07	1.08	0.00	3.83
Mexico	-1.50	2.99	1.89	5.23	2.17	5.59	0.68	12.99
Chile	6.76	10.26	0.02	4.36	2.97	4.11	14.15	20.36
R. Cairns	3.82	13.39	6.30	4.49	0.98	5.55	7.19	19.45
EU	3.17	1.13	-2.33	4.72	0.10	1.31	1.33	6.49
R. World	15.94	13.67	0.59	4.95	4.89	13.92	39.07	86.97

Source: FTAP model database.

equal in turn to the taxes on foreign affiliates' output in the destination region, shown in the sixth column. The reason for modeling these as taxes in the exporting region, rather than as tariffs in the importing region, is that it allows the rents created by the barriers to be retained in the exporting region. The issue of rents is addressed in more detail shortly.

The GATS framework also distinguishes restrictions on market access from restrictions on national treatment. The former are restrictions on entry, be it by locally owned or foreign owned firms. In this sense, they are non-discriminatory. Restrictions on national treatment mean that foreign owned firms are treated less favorably than domestic firms. These restrictions are discriminatory. Thus the taxes on domestic capital and domestic output in table 4 represent the effects of restrictions on market access (affecting establishment and ongoing operation, respectively). The taxes on the capital and output of foreign affiliates are higher than the corresponding taxes on domestic firms, because they represent the effects of restrictions on both market access and national treatment. The estimation of barriers to trade in banking and telecom-

munications services by Kaleeswaran et al. (2000) and Warren (2000) allowed
the price effects to be split up according to this two-by-two classification.

The estimates in table 4 indicate that barriers to trade in services are generally at least as large as those on agricultural and manufactured products. In
addition, the ad valorem equivalent of barriers to establishment are generally
much higher than those on ongoing operation. This is significant, since taxes
on capital can distort input decisions in ways that taxes on output do not.

Most economies have at least some significant barriers to trade in services. The only regions where barriers are low across the board are New Zealand, Japan, Hong Kong, Canada, the United States and the European Union.
But this statement should be heavily qualified, because it is based only on estimates of barriers to banking and telecommunications.

Barriers to trade in services have been modeled as tax equivalents that
generate rents—a mark-up of price over cost—rather than as things that raise
costs above what they might otherwise have been (e.g., Hertel 1999). This decision was based on the way in which the price impacts of barriers to trade in
banking and telecommunications services were measured. Kaleeswaran et al.
(2000) measured the effects of trade restrictions on the net interest margins of
banks, a direct measure of banks' mark-up of price over cost. Warren (2000)
measured the effects of trade restrictions on the quantities of telecommunications services delivered, and these were converted to price impacts using an
estimate of the elasticity of demand for telecommunications services. Thus,
Warren's estimates did not provide direct evidence of a mark-up of price over
cost, but the relative profitability of telecommunications companies in many
countries suggests that some element of rent may exist. By contrast, there is
evidence that trade restrictions in sectors such as aviation raise costs (Johnson
et al. 2000). As estimates of the effects of trade barriers in these sectors are incorporated into the model, it will be appropriate to treat some restrictions as
cost-raising rather than as rent-creating.

One important implication of the current treatment is that welfare gains
from liberalizing trade in services are likely to be understated, perhaps significantly. If trade restrictions create rents, then the allocative efficiency gains
from trade liberalization are the 'triangle' gains associated with putting a given
quantum of resources to more efficient use. By contrast, if trade restrictions
raise costs, then the allocative efficiency gains from trade liberalization include 'rectangle' gains (qualified by general equilibrium effects) from lower
costs, equivalent to a larger effective quantum of resources for productive use.

Because barriers to services trade appear to be significant, and because
they have been modeled as taxes, the rents they generate will be significant. A
key issue is whether those rents should be modeled as being retained by incumbent firms, appropriated by governments via taxation, or passed from one
country to another by transfer pricing or other mechanisms. In FTAP, the rents
on outputs have been modeled as accruing to the selling region, and those on
capital have been modeled as accruing to the region of ownership, once the
government in the region of location has taxed them at its general property in-

come tax rate. Despite this, the asset choices of investors are modeled as being driven by pre-tax rates of return. This is because many economies, in the developed world at least, have primarily destination-based tax systems. For example, if tax credits are granted for taxes paid overseas, investors are ultimately taxed on *all* income at the owning region's tax rate. Although such tax credits have not been modeled explicitly, their effect has been captured by having investors respond to relative pre-tax rates of return. Nevertheless, investor choices are also assumed to be determined by rates of return excluding any abnormal rent component. Investors would like to supply an amount of capital consistent with rates of return including abnormal rents, but are prevented from doing so by barriers to investment. The amount of capital actually supplied is, therefore, the amount that investors would like to supply at rates of return excluding abnormal rents.

Thus a portion of the rent associated with barriers to services trade is assumed to remain in the region of location in the form of property income tax revenue, while the remainder accrues to the region of ownership. Thus liberalization of services trade could have significant income effects in both home and host regions as these rents are gradually eliminated. The next section shows how significant these effects are, relative to the allocative efficiency effects and other effects normally associated with trade liberalization.

A final point to note is that the model's database does not contain estimates of barriers to investment in agriculture and manufacturing, even though they are likely to be significant. It is unlikely that a new trade round would include negotiations on them. Nevertheless, their omission will affect the model's estimates of the effects of liberalization elsewhere, and the results need to be qualified accordingly.

The Effects of Eliminating Post-Uruguay Round Barriers to Trade

The FTAP model has been used to examine the effects of eliminating the post-Uruguay Round barriers to trade summarized in table 4. The results are comparative static, showing only the impact of trade liberalization. During the ten year adjustment period, many other changes will affect each economy, but they are not taken into account in the current analysis. For this reason, the results should not be interpreted as indicating the likely changes that would occur over time in each economy—such results would require *all* changes, not just changes in trade barriers, to be taken into account. The model results should instead be seen as providing an indication, at some point in time ten years after liberalization, of how different each economy would be, compared with the alternative situation at the same point in time, had the liberalization not taken place.

The distinction is important to keep in mind. Sometimes, to aid fluency, the results are couched as if key indicators 'rise' or 'fall'. This should not be interpreted to mean that the indicators would be higher or lower than they are now. It means that they would, at some future time, be higher or lower than they otherwise would have been had the liberalization not occurred. In both cases, in a growing economy, these indicators could be higher than they are now.

Table 5 shows first the projected effect on resource allocation, by showing the percentage changes in sectoral outputs. As expected, liberalization of trade in agricultural and manufactured products is projected to encourage resources to shift out of the relatively highly protected agricultural sectors in Japan, Korea, Malaysia, Philippines, Thailand, China, Taiwan, the European Union and the rest of the world region. According to table 4, the agricultural sector in the European Union does not look to be particularly highly protected post-Uruguay Round. However, this is an artifact of the averaging of subsidy assistance and revenue-raising taxes, mentioned earlier. As noted, liberalization has been modeled by eliminating the subsidies but keeping the revenue-raising taxes.

It is harder to generalize about the effects on manufacturing sectors of liberalizing trade in agricultural and manufactured products. Some of the Asian economies, such as the Philippines, Thailand and China, have the highest levels of manufacturing assistance post-Uruguay Round. But eliminating this protection also means they have much to gain by way of improvements in allocative efficiency. Thus, the manufacturing sectors in these economies are projected to expand, despite facing the biggest reductions in protection. On the other hand, the manufacturing sectors in the United States and Canada are projected to be smaller than otherwise, despite experiencing the loss of relatively modest protection. This is partly because resources are reallocated into the primary and tertiary sectors in those regions.

The sectoral effects of liberalizing barriers to trade in services are relatively straightforward. The services sectors in most Asian economies are projected to expand as their relatively large barriers to entry are removed. The services sector in China is projected to be fully 33 per cent bigger than otherwise, because its barriers to entry had been particularly high. Services sectors in economies with low barriers to entry, such as Australia, New Zealand, Canada, the United States, and the European Union are expected to be slightly smaller than otherwise. In part, this is because of increased competition via cross-border trade from the newly expanded Asian service sectors. But if the size of barriers to services trade in these economies has been underestimated, then the reductions in their service sector output will be overstated.

Table 6 shows the effects of these sectoral resource shifts on regional activity levels (as measured by changes in real GDP) and on economic wellbeing (as measured by the equivalent variation, a measure of the change in net national product, or real income accruing to the residents in each economy). It shows that all economies except Singapore are projected to be bigger than otherwise as a result of full trade liberalization. But the Singaporean economy being smaller than otherwise does not make Singaporeans poorer than otherwise. They may simply have substituted FDI for investment at home, and earning

Table 5. Projected Effects on Sectoral Output of Eliminating Post-Uruguay Trade Barriers

	Primary and Secondary Liberalization			Tertiary Liberalization		
	Primary	Secondary	Tertiary	Primary	Secondary	Tertiary
	%	%	%	%	%	%
Australia	3.6	-8.1	0.6	1.2	1.0	-0.3
NZ	27.4	-22.1	-1.2	1.8	1.0	-0.7
Japan	-9.3	2.0	0.1	-0.4	-0.3	0.1
Korea	-4.2	5.6	-0.8	-0.8	-1.6	1.1
Indonesia	1.0	2.0	-0.2	0.3	2.6	9.2
Malaysia	-0.4	3.6	-0.6	0.1	0.1	1.5
Philippines	-4.4	36.8	-2.4	-1.9	-3.6	2.5
Singapore	54.2	-0.1	-6.5	-3.9	-6.6	1.0
Thailand	-3.9	2.7	1.4	-0.1	-0.8	1.3
China	-0.8	3.1	1.1	-0.2	2.4	32.5
Hong Kong	26.5	27.2	-6.9	0.2	-2.2	0.6
Taiwan	-1.0	6.2	-1.5	0.1	1.0	-0.2
Canada	1.3	-3.6	0.8	0.7	1.0	-0.6
USA	6.0	-2.4	0.3	0.6	0.6	-0.4
Mexico	0.5	-2.2	0.7	-0.1	0.1	0.1
Chile	2.1	-2.7	0.6	0.1	-1.0	0.9
R. Cairns	3.7	-4.1	0.9	0.3	0.4	-0.1
EU	-5.5	-0.5	0.7	1.0	1.3	-0.6
R. World	-0.6	-0.7	0.8	-0.2	-0.4	1.5

Source: FTAP model projections.

significantly higher incomes from these foreign investments. This is examined in more detail shortly.

In terms of real income, the world as a whole is projected to be better off by more than U.S.$260 billion as a result of eliminating all post-Uruguay Round trade barriers. About U.S.$50 billion of this would come from agricultural liberalization, and a further U.S.$80 billion from liberalization of manufactures. This shows that there are still considerable gains to be had in traditional areas, even if no progress is made in services.[2] But an additional U.S.$130 billion would come from liberalizing services trade. And about U.S.$100 billion of this would accrue in China alone.[3]

Australia would gain as much from global liberalization of services trade as it would from global liberalization of trade in agriculture and manufacturing. Each would make Australia's real income about U.S.$2 billion higher than otherwise, for an overall gain of about U.S.$4 billion a year. This is the projected gain in annual income, about ten years after the liberalization has occurred and the associated resource adjustments have taken place.

Table 6. Projected Effects on Real GDP and Welfare of Eliminating Post-Uruguay Round Trade Barriers

	Real GDP			Equivalent Variation (EV)		
	Primary and Secondary	Tertiary	Total	Primary and Secondary	Tertiary	Total
	%	%	%	$USm	$USm	$USm
Australia	0.2	0.0	0.2	1,994	2,098	4,092
NZ	1.2	-0.1	1.1	4,400	257	4,657
Japan	0.3	0.0	0.3	20,964	4,130	25,094
Korea	1.5	0.1	1.6	8,784	1,886	10,670
Indonesia	0.7	5.1	5.9	1,451	2,470	3,921
Malaysia	3.7	0.7	4.5	3,532	1,015	4,547
Philippines	5.1	0.4	5.5	1,601	1,236	2,837
Singapore	-0.3	-1.3	-1.5	7,421	-247	7,174
Thailand	2.6	0.2	2.8	4,063	1,698	5,762
China	3.4	14.6	18.0	14,088	90,869	104,957
Hong Kong	-0.2	1.0	0.9	916	5,896	6,812
Taiwan	2.7	0.2	3.0	11,659	-142	11,517
Canada	0.1	-0.1	0.0	-539	-499	-1,038
USA	0.2	-0.1	0.1	22,734	-1,809	20,925
Mexico	0.3	0.1	0.4	-83	357	274
Chile	0.7	0.4	1.1	45	330	375
R. Cairns	1.2	0.1	1.3	12,766	6,970	19,736
EU	0.1	0.0	0.1	6,394	-6,169	225
R. World	1.1	0.8	1.9	11,324	23,039	34,363
World				133,515	133,386	266,901

Source: FTAP model projections.

Most other economies are also projected to gain individually from these reforms. Only Canada is projected to be slightly poorer than otherwise as a result of complete trade liberalization.

For some economies—the European Union, the United States, Canada, Singapore and Taiwan—the contribution of multilateral services trade liberalization is projected to be negative. For the European Union, the projected loss of $6 billion would almost completely outweigh its gains from multilateral liberalization of agriculture and manufacturing. The United States is projected to lose almost $2 billion from services trade liberalization, though it would still gain significantly overall. The following discussion tries to uncover the reasons for these projected income losses.

The measure of real income used here is similar to that in the GTAP model—a measure of national income, deflated by an index of the prices of household consumption, government consumption, and national saving. But for FTAP, as noted, the relevant measure of national income is net national product—the income accruing to the residents of a region—rather than net domestic product—the income generated within the borders of a region. Thus, net domestic product must be adjusted for the income earned on outward FDI, net of the income repatriated overseas from inward FDI, plus the income from net bond holdings.

As in the GTAP model, the measure of welfare can be decomposed into a number of influences. For agricultural and manufacturing liberalization, the welfare results are dominated by two things—the contribution of improvements in allocative efficiency, and the contribution of changes in the terms of trade (which can be positive or negative). As shown above, the model's regions are projected to experience positive income gains, or in a few cases small losses, as a result of these effects.

For services liberalization, however, changes in foreign direct investment patterns contribute two additional effects. Firstly, FDI can lead to an expansion or contraction in the capital stock located within a region, leading to a positive or negative contribution to income from this change in national endowments. Secondly, the changes in rents earned on foreign direct investments can also affect national incomes.

The first column of table 7 shows the contribution to real income from changes in real capital endowments. Generally, if capital endowments improve, real GDP is higher than otherwise. However, sometimes real GDP can rise, even if endowments fall, because those endowments are used more efficiently. The benefit of having additional varieties as output expands is another source of productivity improvement.

Some of the change in endowments comes from foreign direct investment, and some comes from investment by domestic residents. The second column of table 7 shows the contribution to real income from changes in real FDI stocks. The third column shows the contribution to real income from changes in real bond holdings. Both help to indicate the way in which changes in capital endowments are financed.

For example, Japan's capital stock shrinks, partly because it has a big increase in outward FDI. In fact, it also borrows (a negative change on bond holding) in order to finance its outward FDI. By contrast, China's increase in capital endowments comes partly from a large increase in inward FDI, and partly from additional foreign borrowing. The United States is .projected to have a smaller capital endowment than otherwise, offset by an increase in outward FDI and increased lending to other regions. The pattern for the European Union is the same as for the United States.

Table 7. Contributions to Real Income Changes from Liberalizing Services Trade

	Contribution of Endow-ment Change to EV (1)	Contribution of Change in Real FDI Stocks to EV (2)	Contribution of Change in Real Bond Holding to EV (3)	Contribution of Change in Rents on FDI Capital (4)	Contribution of Change in Rents on FDI Output (5)
	$USm	$USm	$USm	$USm	$USm
Australia	58	0	4	534	-39
NZ	-43	5	52	-10	6
Japan	-1,030	3,120	-2,978	-3,629	-5,101
Korea	438	-5	39	51	72
Indonesia	7,158	-541	-4,519	162	368
Malaysia	367	-103	-168	253	332
Philippines	164	-91	47	70	144
Singapore	-1,071	-198	-108	401	1,049
Thailand	305	-24	-393	227	259
China	52,164	-12,649	-5,776	4,163	8,686
Hong Kong	102	7,829	-621	-2,638	-5,573
Taiwan	312	378	-583	-137	-286
Canada	-747	34	1,086	27	-52
USA	-5,713	2,665	1,708	-3,057	-3,659
Mexico	131	-67	332	247	266
Chile	202	-39	-54	101	56
R. Cairns	401	-137	1,800	450	486
EU	-3,672	1,441	6,327	-2,265	-3,110
R. World	15,002	-2,337	3,285	5,427	6,581

Source: FTAP model projections.

The last two columns of table 7 show the income contributions to recipient countries of changes in the rents from barriers to services trade, as these barriers are eliminated. What is striking is the loss of rents to the main providers of outward FDI—Japan, Hong Kong, the United States and the European Union. In fact, the loss of rents to the United States is more than sufficient to explain its projected real income loss from services trade liberalization in table 6, and the loss of rents in the European Union would explain most of its projected loss from services trade liberalization. Given the uncertainty about the allocation of existing rents, it is not at all clear that the true impact on the United States and European Union would be as great as shown in table 7. And if barriers to services trade in these economies have been understated, then so too will their gains in allocative efficiency. Thus, their projected net income losses from services trade liberalization in table 6 should be heavily qualified. Similarly, Canada's overall income loss, which comes primarily from adverse terms of trade effects, should also be qualified, given uncertainty about many key features of the model.

The Effects of Partial Liberalization of Services Trade

While the preceding section examined the effects of complete liberalization, a new trade round is likely to deliver only partial liberalization. Because the structure of trade barriers in the services area is relatively complex, there is a real question as to the best way to approach partial liberalization in that sector. It is well known that some approaches to partial liberalization can worsen disparities in protection, moving resources further away from their pattern in a world free of distortions, and worsening real income. Thus, it is important to determine paths of partial liberalization of services trade that avoid such outcomes.

It is hard to identify such paths a priori. In liberalization of goods trade, 'tops-down' and 'across-the-board' strategies to lowering tariffs are known to generally avoid second-best economic welfare losses. A 'tops-down' approach to services trade liberalization might suggest that restrictions on national treatment be tackled first, since these cause barriers to be higher for foreign than for domestic service providers. It might also suggest that barriers to commercial presence be tackled ahead of barriers to other modes of service delivery, since their ad valorem equivalents tend to be higher (see table 4). Putting these two propositions together, does this mean that the best strategy is to remove restrictions on national treatment for firms seeking to deliver via commercial presence? The problem is that, given the pervasiveness of restrictions elsewhere, there is a real danger that resources will move in the 'wrong' direction, a result demonstrated in a partial equilibrium framework in Dee, Hardin and Holmes (2000).

Table 8 gives a breakdown of the effects on world real income of various partial approaches to services liberalization, comparing the removal of restrictions on market access and national treatment, as well as the removal of barriers on establishment versus ongoing operation. The first thing to note is that, because of interaction effects, the effects of various types of partial liberalization are not strictly additive. Instead, the effects of combining two types of liberalization generally exceed the sum of the effects of doing each separately. One reason is that the more widespread the liberalization, the less the chance of a second-best deterioration in allocative efficiency.

Table 8 shows that the best *single* type of liberalization for world economic welfare is the removal of those barriers to establishment that affect domestic and foreign firms equally (i.e., affect market access). Removing *all* barriers to establishment would be better than removing *all* barriers to ongoing operation. This reflects the particularly distortionary effects of taxes on capital. Removing *all* restrictions on market access would be much better than removing *all* restrictions on national treatment. This is more like an 'across-the-board' than a 'tops-down' approach, and it avoids the second-best welfare losses identified in Dee, Hardin and Holmes (2000).

Of course, the pattern shown in table 8 need not hold for individual economies. Detailed results show, however, that the global removal of those barriers to establishment affecting domestic and foreign firms equally (i.e., affecting market access) remains a winning outcome for 14 of the 19 regions in the model (including Australia), leading to significant real income gains in those economies. The exceptions include Japan, Hong Kong and Canada, all significant sources of outward FDI. However, the United States and the European Union are not exceptions. Thus, the exceptions do not seem to arise because of a loss of rents—this tends to occur no matter what the type of liberalization. Instead, it seems to reflect differences in the pattern of allocative efficiency and terms of trade effects.

The detailed results therefore show that it is difficult of find a Pareto improvement (an outcome where at least some economies gain and none lose) from partial liberalization when it involves a particular *type* of barrier. This suggests that a better strategy may be to negotiate gradual reductions in *all* types of barriers simultaneously.

Table 8. Effects of Partial Services Liberalization on World Real Income (U.S.$Billion)

	Remove Restrictions on Market Access	Remove Restrictions on National Treatment	Both
Remove Barriers to Establishment	56.8	3.7	64.2
Remove Barriers to Ongoing Operation	25.6	12.9	39.3
Both	98.8	19.3	133.4

Source: FTAP model projections.

Agenda for Further Research

Much of the development agenda has been outlined already. It involves continuing to obtain estimates of the price impacts of barriers to services trade, along the lines outlined in Findlay and Warren (2000). Such methods could also be used to estimate the price impact of barriers to foreign direct investment in agriculture and manufacturing. More sectoral detail needs to be incorporated into FTAP, so as to be able to model the barriers to each service separately. More research is required to obtain more realistic cost and sales structures for FDI firms and, if possible, a realistic initial allocation of rents.

And the welfare measure in FTAP needs to be amended to take account of the costs of risk taking, given risk aversion.

Notes

* The views expressed in this chapter are those of the authors and do not necessarily reflect those of the Productivity Commission. This chapter is the culmination of a large team effort and we thank our colleagues, Patrick Jomini, Tien Phamduc, Susan Stone, Alexandra Strzelecki, George Verikios and Andrew Welsh.

[1] The equivalent elasticity of productivity with respect to *inputs* is $0.0667/(1 - 0.0667)$ = 0.0714, where this latter concept is used by Francois, McDonald and Nordstrom (1995). The elasticities of productivity with respect to output and inputs are not equal because of the assumption of increasing returns to scale.

[2] It might seem a possible source of second-best welfare problems to reduce trade barriers in agriculture and manufacturing, while leaving even higher restrictions in services untouched. But because services are a general equilibrium complement (rather than substitute) to agriculture and manufacturing, reducing trade restrictions in the traditional areas would mitigate the restrictions in services.

[3] In a recent similar exercise, Hertel's (1999) world welfare gains from eliminating barriers to services trade were smaller than those projected here. Although his income base was 2005 rather than 1995, and although he treated services trade barriers as being cost-raising rather than rent-creating, his exercise was limited to barriers in construction and business services (using estimated price impacts from Francois (1999), and did not include liberalization of FDI. Hertel's estimated gains from full liberalization of agriculture and manufacturing were larger than those presented here. But correcting for the difference in income base by applying FTAP's results to Hertel's income base (we are grateful to Tom Hertel for making this available), FTAP's gain from liberalizing manufactures is $120 billion, very close to Hertel's estimate of $129 billion. FTAP's gains from liberalizing agriculture are still about half of Hertel's estimate of $160 billion. This is largely because Hertel assumed no effective Uruguay Round liberalization post-1995, leaving much more to be done in a post-Uruguay Round environment. Reconciling FTAP's results with DFAT (1999) is more difficult because of a lack of detail in the DFAT study.

References

Anderson, J. E. and Neary, P .J. 1994. "Measuring the Restrictiveness of Trade Policy," *World Bank Economic Review* 8(2):151–69.

Anderson, J. E. and Neary, P. J. 1996. "A New Approach to Evaluating Trade Policy," *Review of Economic Studies* 3(2):107–25.

APEC (Asia-Pacific Economic Cooperation). 1995. *Foreign Direct Investment and APEC Economic Integration*. APEC Economic Committee, Singapore.

Brown, D. K., Deardorff, A. V., Fox, A. K. and Stern, R. M. 1995. "Computational Analysis of Goods and Services Liberalization in the Uruguay Round," in Martin, W. and Winters, L.A. (eds.), *The Uruguay Round and the Developing Economies*, Discussion Paper No. 307. World Bank, Washington, D.C.

Dee, P., Geisler, C. and Watts, G. 1996. *The Impact of APEC's Free Trade Commitment*, Industry Commission Staff Information Paper. AGPS, Canberra.

Dee, P., Hardin, A. and Holmes, L. 2000. "Issues in the Application of CGE Models to Services Trade Liberalization," in Findlay, C. and Warren, T. (eds.), *Impediments to Trade in Services: Measurement and Policy Implications*. Routledge, London and New York (forthcoming).

Dee, P., Hardin, A. and Schuele, M. 1998. *APEC Early Voluntary Sectoral Liberalization*. Productivity Commission Staff Research Paper. Ausinfo, Canberra.

Department of Foreign Affairs and Trade (DFAT). 1999. *Global Trade Reform: Maintaining Momentum*. Ausinfo, Canberra.

Disclosure. 1999. *Global Researcher—Worldscope Database*. Disclosure, United States, January.

Findlay, C. and Warren, T. (eds.). 2000. *Impediments to Trade in Services: Measurement and Policy Implications*. Routledge, London and New York (forthcoming).

Francois, J. F. 1999. "A Gravity Approach to Measuring Services Protection," unpublished manuscript, Erasmus University, Rotterdam.

Francois, J. F., McDonald, B. and Nordstrom, H. 1995. "Assessing the Uruguay Round," in Martin, W. and Winters, L.A. (eds.), *The Uruguay Round and the Developing Economies*, Discussion Paper No. 307, World Bank. Washington D.C.

Gehlhar, M. 1997. "Historical Analysis of Growth and Trade Patterns in the Pacific Rim: An Evaluation of the GTAP Framework," in Hertel, T. (ed.), *Global Trade Analysis: Modeling and Applications*. Cambridge University Press, Cambridge.

Hanslow, K., Phamduc, T., Verikios, G. and Welsh, A. 2000. "Incorporating Barriers to FDI into the FTAP Database," Research Memorandum, Productivity Commission, Canberra.

Hanslow, K., Phamduc, T. and Verikios, G. 1999. "The Structure of the FTAP Model," Research Memorandum, Productivity Commission, Canberra, December.

Harrison, J. W. and Pearson, K. R. 1996. "Computing Solutions for Large General Equilibrium Models Using GEMPACK," *Computational Economics* 9(2):83–127.

Hertel, T. 1997. *Global Trade Analysis: Modeling and Applications*. Cambridge University Press, Cambridge.

Hertel, T. 1999. "Potential Gains from Reducing Trade Barriers in Manufacturing, Services and Agriculture," paper presented at the 24th Annual Economic Policy Conference, Federal Reserve Bank of St. Louis, 21–22 October.

Hoekman, B. 1995. "Assessing the General Agreement on Trade in Services," in Martin, W. and Winters, L.A. (eds.), *The Uruguay Round and the Developing Economies*, Discussion Paper No. 307, World Bank, Washington, D.C.

Johnson, M., Gregan, T., Belin, P. and Gentle, G. 2000. "Modeling the Impact of Regulatory Reform," in Findlay, C. and Warren, T. (eds.), *Impediments to Trade in Services: Measurement and Policy Implications*. Routledge, London and New York (forthcoming).

Kaleeswaran, K., McGuire, G., Nguyen-Hong, D. and Schuele, M. 2000. "The Price Impact of Restrictions on Banking Services," in Findlay, C. and Warren, T. (eds.) 2000, *Impediments to Trade in Services: Measurement and Policy Implications*. Routledge, London and New York (forthcoming).

Malcolm, G. 1998. "Adjusting Tax Rates in the GTAP Data Base," GTAP Technical Paper No. 12, Center for Global Trade Analysis, Purdue University.

Markusen, J., Rutherford, T. F. and Tarr, D. 1999. "Foreign Direct Investment in Services and the Domestic Market for Expertise," paper presented at Second Annual Conference on Global Economic Analysis, Denmark, 20-22 June.

McDougall, R. 1993. "Incorporating International Capital Mobility into SALTER," SALTER Working Paper No. 21, Industry Commission, Canberra,

Petri, P.A. 1997. "Foreign Direct Investment in a Computable General Equilibrium Framework," paper prepared for the conference, "Making APEC work: Economic Challenges and Policy Alternatives," 13-14 March, Keio University, Tokyo.

Stone, S., Strzelecki, A. and Welsh, A. 2000, "Estimating Foreign Returns to Capital for the FTAP Model," Research Memorandum, Productivity Commission, Melbourne (forthcoming).

United Nations. 1994. *World Investment Directory Latin America and the Caribbean.* New York: UN.

Verikios, G. and Hanslow, K. 1999. "Modeling the Effects of Implementing the Uruguay Round: A Comparison Using the GTAP Model under Alternative Treatments of International Capital Mobility," paper presented at Second Annual Conference on Global Economic Analysis, Denmark, 20-22 June.

Warren, T. 2000, "The Impact on Output of Impediments to Trade and Investment in Telecommunications Services," in Findlay, C. and Warren, T. (eds.), *Impediments to Trade in Services: Measurement and Policy Implications.* Routledge, London and New York (forthcoming).

CHAPTER 6

Imperfect Competition and Trade Liberalization under the GATS

Joseph F. Francois and Ian Wooton

I. Introduction

From its inception, the multilateral trading system has been focused on trade in goods. Hence, from 1947 through the Tokyo Round, services were not covered in successive rounds of trade negotiations. The Uruguay Round and the subsequent launch of the WTO changed this. They brought an incorporation of services into the multilateral trading system under the General Agreement on Trade in Services (GATS). However, the actual degree of liberalization has been relatively limited, with many of the GATS schedules involving simple stand-still commitments (or less). It is generally recognized that there remains significant scope for liberalization in the service sectors.

This chapter is concerned with the analytical implications of service-sector liberalization, and in particular the role of market structure. The trade theory literature has traditionally focused on trade in goods, with the literature on international trade in services being a relatively limited and recent addition. [See, for example, Francois (1990a), Hoekman (1994), Markusen (1988,1989), Sampson and Snape (1985), Stern and Hoekman, (1988), Francois and Schuknecht (1999).] In addition, while there is a sizable empirical literature on service sector policy and deregulation, this is largely focused on domestic deregulation.[1] In contrast, we focus here explicitly on trade in services, and the interaction of international trade with market structure and public regulation.[2]

Of course, in many ways the insights from the theoretical literature on international trade apply equally to goods and services. This is particularly true for cross-border trade. There are, however, some important differences. One is the role of proximity (see Francois, 1990b; Sampson and Snape, 1985), which has important analytical implications. The significance of proximity for service transactions means that "trade" in the case of services often requires a mix of cross-border transactions and local establishment (i.e., FDI). The importance of trade through affiliates is illustrated, for the case of the United

Table 1. United States Cross-Border and Affiliate Trade in Services

Year	U.S. cross-border exports	U.S. cross-border imports	U.S. foreign sales through affiliates	Foreign sales in U.S. through affiliates
	billions of dollars			
1987	86.0	73.9	72.3	62.6
1988	100.1	81.0	83.8	73.2
1989	117.1	85.3	99.2	94.2
1990	136.2	98.2	121.3	109.2
1991	151.2	99.9	131.6	119.5
1992	162.3	100.4	140.6	128.0
1993	170.6	107.9	142.6	134.7
1994	186.0	119.1	159.1	145.4
1995	202.2	128.2	190.1	149.7
1996	221.1	137.1	223.2	168.4
1997	240.4	152.4	258.3	205.0
1998	245.7	165.3		

Source: Bureau of Economic Analysis, 1999.

States, in Table 1. The United States is the leading service exporter, with $245.7 billion in 1998. The level of U.S. service sales through affiliates (establishment trade) is comparable. Establishment sales amounted to $258 billion in 1997, which compares to $240 billion in direct exports.

The empirical and operational importance of establishment leads to a second important difference between goods and services. This is an institutional difference. While the GATT emphasizes barriers at the border (tariffs, quotas, etc.), the GATS has a different focus. From the outset, it has emphasized both cross-border barriers and barriers to local establishment. Consequently, the GATS blurs trade and investment restrictions, and covers both trade and investment rules to the extent that they limit market access in service sectors.

Given the structure of the GATS, negotiations involve parallel commitments on cross-border trade and local establishment by foreign service providers. We argue in this chapter that these two modes (a simplification of the four modes actually listed in the GATS) can carry different implications for national welfare, market structure, profits, and related metrics tied to trade liberalization. In particular, given imperfect competition in services (often in conjunction with domestic regulation), realization of gains from trade liberalization is tied closely to issues of market regulation and market structure.[3] This in turn means that assessment of services commitments should take into account market structure and regulatory issues that affect the degree of competition.

The remainder of the chapter is organized as follows. In Section II we provide some background and motivation. In Section III we develop a stylized model of trade in services, involving alternatively establishment or cross-border trade. In Section IV we then examine liberalization of trade and establishment restrictions. Finally, our results are summarized in Section V.

II. Services Trade and the WTO

As noted by Hill (1977), a critical distinction between goods and services is that services are consumed as they are produced. As a result of the flow nature of the transaction, service transactions involve an interaction between user and provider. Based on this element of interaction between user and provider, Sampson and Snape (1985) draw a distinction between services that require physical proximity, and those that do not. The GATS also recognizes this distinction, in that it covers trade that requires no direct proximity (the cross-border mode) and trade that involves proximity (the modes of movement of providers, movement of consumers, and foreign establishment). The most important distinction across the four types is *cross-border* versus *local* supply of services.

While GATS commitments relate to these four modes, there are also overlapping commitments in other areas under the WTO umbrella. For example, the code on government procurement provides scope for government commitments on market access to domestic service markets, to the extent that they supply the procurement market. In addition, the rules on trade-related investment measures (TRIMs), to the extent that they touch on service operations, also provide scope for overlapping commitments.

Critically, while competition policy is not formally a part of the WTO structure, competition also has an important role to play in market access. WTO members have recognized that competition policy can be relevant to the extent that it impinges on commitments made within the WTO. Hence, the recent U.S.-Japan dispute over photographic film hinged on the degree of competition in the distribution sector, while threatened U.S. action on Japanese auto imports has also emphasized competition in the domestic distribution and sales network. Though these touch indirectly on market access in services, there are also more direct links between competition and market access in services.

Traditionally, many of the service sectors—like banking, telecommunications, air transport, and insurance—have been heavily regulated. This regulation has sometimes, as in the case of PTTs, been undertaken in conjunction with state-sanctioned monopoly or outright ownership. More recently, there has been a move toward deregulation and divestment of state ownership. While the most visible example may be telecommunications, similar moves are occurring in banking and other sectors. For this reason, GATS-related negotiations on services have taken and will take place in the context of domestic regulatory changes, and in a climate of imperfect competition.

III. A Simple Model

We start with a simple model of a domestic service sector that is imperfectly competitive. The domestic oligopoly faces competition from a cross-border firm. The domestic industry is protected from foreign competition. We will then examine the implications of lowering these barriers and giving the foreign firm open access to consumers through granting the firm the right of establishment in the domestic country.

Basic Structure

Formally, consider the market for a homogeneous service S in the home (h) country. This service is provided by n identical domestic firms within a regulated industry, as well as by a single foreign (f) firm based overseas and facing barriers to serving the domestic consumers. The inverse demand for the service relates the market price to the total quantity supplied to the market (the sum of the outputs of the home firms and the foreign firm):

$$p = x - y\left(nq_h + q_f\right) \tag{1}$$

The revenues of the two types of firm are derived directly from the demand-curve (1):

$$R_i = \left[x - y\left(nq_h + q_f\right)\right]q_i, \quad \text{for } i = h, f \tag{2}$$

Home firms face a constant marginal cost c, while the foreign firm additionally has to pay t to provide the service to home consumers.[4] Consequently, total costs and marginal costs of the two types of firms are, respectively,

$$
\begin{aligned}
C_h &= cq_h & MC_h &= c \\
C_f &= \left(c + t\right)q_f & MC_f &= c + t
\end{aligned}
\tag{3}
$$

The marginal revenue of the foreign firm is determined by the partial differentiation of (1), imposing the Cournot assumption that firms set quantity strategically, while assuming no subsequent reaction by competing forms (that is, $\partial q_h / \partial q_f = 0$). The firm's perceived marginal revenue is:

$$MR_f = x - y\left(nq_h + 2q_f\right) \tag{4}$$

Equating marginal revenue to marginal cost for the foreign firm yields the reaction function:

$$q_f\left(q_h\right) = \frac{x - \left(c + t\right) - ynq_h}{2y} \tag{5}$$

The marginal revenues of the home firms will depend on the assumed structure of the home market. Home firms are assumed to be regulated and the nature of this regulation is crucial to the firms' behavior. To bound the range of effects, we adopt two polar assumptions about regulation. The first is that the regulator ensures that the home firms behave independently, engaging in pure Cournot competition with both their domestic and foreign rivals. The other extreme is to assume that the domestic regulator promotes collusion on the part of home firms, such that they act as a cartel. In either situation, the foreign firm is at first assumed to be a Cournot competitor.[5] We shall consider, below, the implications of the foreign firm being welcomed as a new member in the cartel.

Consider firstly the perceived marginal revenue for a representative, non-cooperative home firm (labeled *hn*), whose Cournot assumption is that its domestic and foreign rivals will not change their outputs in response to its output change ($\partial q_{hk} / \partial q_{hj} = \partial q_f / \partial q_{hj} = 0$, for $k \neq j$):

$$MR_{hn} = x - y\left[(n+1)q_h + q_f\right] \tag{6}$$

where, using symmetry, it is assumed that all home firms choose the same level of output. The corresponding reaction function for an individual home firm is:

$$q_{hn}(q_f) = \frac{x - c - yq_f}{(n+1)y} \tag{7}$$

This can be contrasted with the behavior of the representative firm (labeled *hc*) that is part of a regulated cartel. This firm acts in collaboration with the other home firms, each adjusting output by the same anticipated amount. Consequently the perceived marginal revenue of a representative home firm is:

$$MR_{hc} = x - \left(2nq_h + q_f\right) \tag{8}$$

The corresponding reaction function is:

$$q_{hc}(q_f) = \frac{x - c - yq_f}{2ny} \tag{9}$$

Output Equilibria

The foreign firm's reaction function (5) can be interacted with each of the home country's two possible reaction functions, (7) and (9), to solve for the market equilibrium in the non-cooperative and cartel cases, respectively.

When the home firms compete with both domestic and foreign firms, the equilibrium output levels are:

$$q_{hn}* = \frac{x - c + t}{(n + 2)y}$$

$$q_{fn}* = \frac{x - c - (n + 1)t}{(n + 2)y}$$

(10)

In the case of cartel behavior on the part of the home firms, the firms' equilibrium levels of output are:

$$q_{hc}* = \frac{x - c + t}{3ny}$$

$$q_{fc}* = \frac{x - c - 2t}{3y}$$

(11)

The reaction functions and the corresponding production equilibria are illustrated in Figure 1. As should be expected, home firms supply more when they act non-cooperatively. The foreign firm is able to free ride on the restrictive behavior of the cartel, selling a greater equilibrium quantity than when the home firms behave non-cooperatively.

IV. Industry Structure, Barriers to Entry, and Improved Market Access

We now consider the implications for consumer welfare and the profitability of firms when the competitive structure of the service industry is changed as a result of commitments to liberalize market-access conditions. This change can arise either through giving the foreign firm better market access or through forcing home firms to act more competitively.

Improving Cross-border Access

Market access for the foreign firm is improved by reducing t, the impediment the firm faces in servicing the home market from abroad. The foreign firm would be accorded national treatment if $t = 0$, equivalent to the firm having the right of establishment in the home market where it would compete on an equal footing with the domestic firms. We shall, later, discuss the potential for the foreign firm being admitted to the domestic cartel.

We can solve for the price of the service when the domestic firms in the home country behave non-cooperatively by substituting the equilibrium outputs (10) into the inverse demand function (1), yielding:

Figure 1. Equilibrium Output Levels

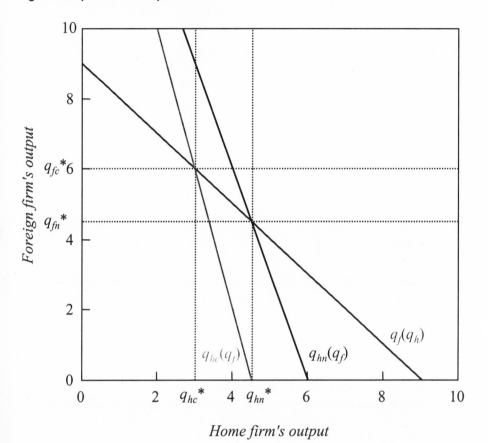

Home firm's output

$$p_n{}^* = \frac{x-(n+1)c+t}{n+2}$$ (12)

Profits of a firm are the difference between its revenues (2) and its costs (3):

$$\pi_i = R_i - C_i, \quad \text{for } i = h, f$$ (13)

Thus, equilibrium profits are calculated by substituting (10) into (13):

$$\pi_{hn}{}^* = \frac{(x-c+t)^2}{(n+2)^2 y}$$

$$\pi_{fn}{}^* = \frac{\left[x-c-(n+1)t\right]^2}{(n+2)^2 y}$$ (14)

Figure 2a illustrates the effects of reducing the trade barrier t on price $p_n{}^*$, profits of the foreign firm $\pi_{fn}{}^*$, and profits of the home industry $\Pi_{hn}{}^*$ (n times the profits of an individual firm $\pi_{hn}{}^*$, where $n = 2$ in these simulations). The higher the barrier to the foreign firm, the smaller its market share and its profits, while the domestic firms enjoy a higher level of profitability. The market price rises with the barrier—home firms face less competition from abroad resulting in a less competitive price. When the trade barrier is eliminated, all firms compete on an equal basis and receive the same level of profits (so that the profits of the home industry is n times that of the foreign firm).

Similar calculations can be made for the equilibrium price and profit levels when the regulated home firms behave as a cartel by substituting the equilibrium output levels (11) into (1) for the price:

$$p_c{}^* = \frac{x+2c+t}{3}$$ (15)

and into (13) for firms' profit levels:

$$\pi_{hc}{}^* = \frac{(x-c+t)^2}{9ny}$$

$$\pi_{fc}{}^* = \frac{(x-c-2t)^2}{9y}$$ (16)

Figure 2a. Improving Cross-border Access (non-cooperative home firms)

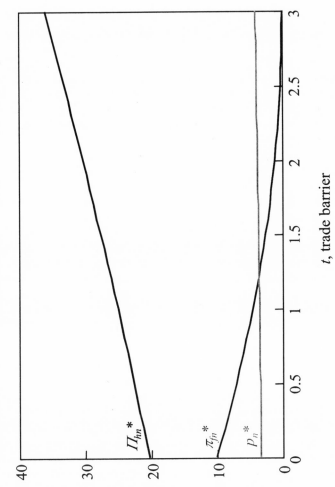

Π_{hn}^*

π_{fn}^*

p_n^*

t, trade barrier

Figure 2b shows the impact of trade-barrier reduction on the price p_c*, foreign firm's profits π_{fc}*, and the profits of the cartelized home industry Π_{hc}* = $n\pi_{hc}$* (where n is again assumed to be equal to 2). In large respect, the lines are the same as those for the non-cooperative home industry, illustrated in Figure 2a. The principal difference is that, when all barriers are eliminated (giving the foreign firm equal access to the market) the foreign *firm* and the home *industry* have equal market shares. This is because the domestic firms behave as if they were a single firm.

Encouraging Domestic Competition

A simple instrument to simulate the effects of domestic regulation is n, the number of home firms. If we calculate the equilibria for a cartel and for a competitive *single* home firm (that is $n = 1$), we get the same outcome. Consequently, we can determine the impact of forcing a cartelized home industry to behave more competitively by calculating the non-cooperative equilibrium outcome for increasing values of n, between 1 and the actual number of firms in the industry.[6]

We illustrate the results of this exercise in Figure 3. In the figure, the equilibrium price p_n* and the profits of the foreign firm π_{fn}* and the home industry Π_{hn}* are shown as a function of n, the number of firms in the home industry. The foreign firm faces a barrier to trade and hence will always have a lower level of profitability than its home counterpart in the domestic market. However, it will have higher profits, the fewer home firms that it has to compete with. Profits of the home industry are not monotonic in the number of home firms. Two home firms obtain a larger share of the market than does a cartel so that, even though the overall market is more competitive, the home industry in total is better off with the increased competition. Larger numbers of non-cooperative home firms will, however, drive down overall profits in the market and lower the total profits of the home firms, despite their increased share of sales.

Establishment—Admitting the Foreigner into the Cartel

We now consider market access liberalization through establishment. Given the domestic cartel, establishment poses the immediate question—should the foreign firm be admitted into the cartel? This is the solution adopted by the Korean insurance industry in the face of U.S. pressure (Cho 1988). The interest of the foreign firm in agreeing to such an arrangement proves to hinge on the size of trading costs.

Figure 2b. Improving Cross-border Access (home cartel)

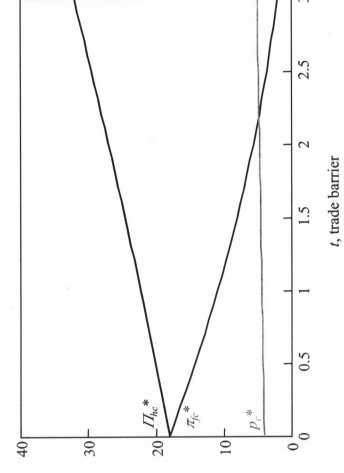

Figure 3. Encouraging Domestic Competition

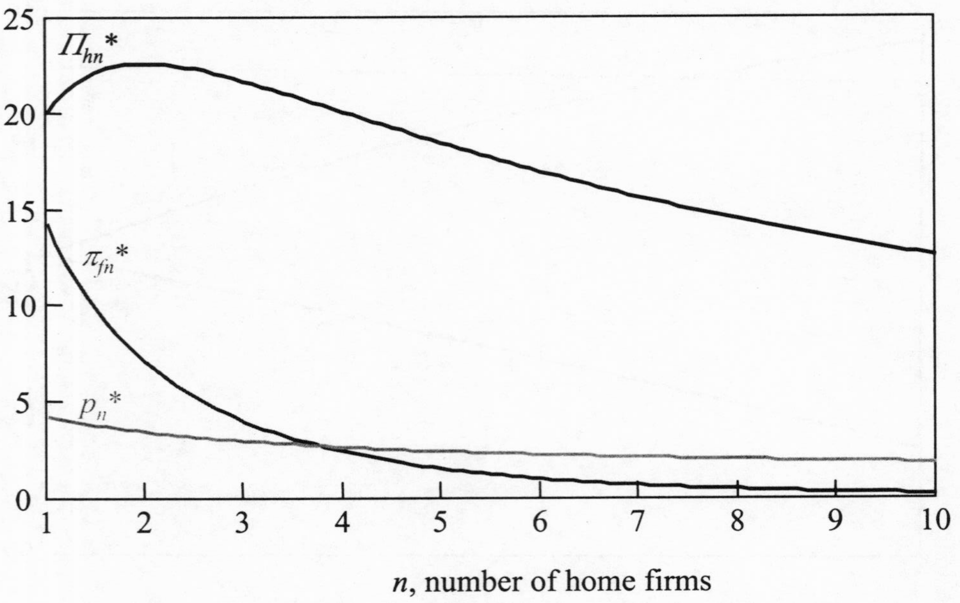

Π_{hn}^*

π_{fn}^*

p_n^*

n, number of home firms

Given establishment, when is it in the interests of any of the parties for the foreign firm to be admitted into the domestic cartel? We consider the earnings of firms at various trade costs, both when the foreign firm is in competition with the cartel (subscripted, as before, by c) and when it has been admitted as a full participant in the restrictive agreement (subscripted by a). The results are illustrated in Figure 4, where the number of home firms is again set at 2.

It is clear that, in the case illustrated, when the trade costs ($t > t_2$) are high the cartel wants to keep the foreign firm out, while the foreign firm would like to have the right of establishment, even as part of the cartel. At middle trade costs ($t_1 < t < t_2$), the home cartel is feeling increased pressure on its profits from the increasingly competitive foreign firm. The cartel would therefore like to admit the foreign firm to the cartel, an option that the foreign firm also prefers. At low trade costs ($t < t_1$), the foreign firm would rather compete with the home cartel than be a part of it. The consumer *always* appears to lose from the formation of the cartel, even if it avoids trade costs in the process of admitting the foreign firm.

V. Summary

The GATS places emphasis on two broad modes of trade—cross-border (i.e., international) trade and trade through local establishments. Cross-border trade includes movement of service providers, movement of consumers, and cross-border sales. Hence, in contrast to trade in goods, GATS-based negotiations take place on the dual margins of trade and investment concessions.

Our approach in this chapter has been to work with a formal model of oligopoly to examine the effects of market-access concessions for domestic and foreign firms and for domestic consumers. We have argued that the relative benefits of cross-border and establishment-related market-access concessions hinge critically on underlying issues of regulation and market structure. In particular, the interests of the domestic and foreign industry will depend, in part, on the impact that trade has on the market power of domestic firms.

We can summarize our analytical results as follows. Given an imperfectly competitive industry (alternatively Cournot or perfect collusion), less market access (i.e., greater restrictions) implies the following:

1. The foreign service provider will have a smaller market share and profits.
2. Domestic service providers will have higher profitability.
3. Home firms face less competition from abroad resulting in a higher home market price.

When we consider the effect of a regulatory environment that tolerates collusion among a small number of domestic firms, we find that less competition has the following implications:

Figure 4. Choice of Regime

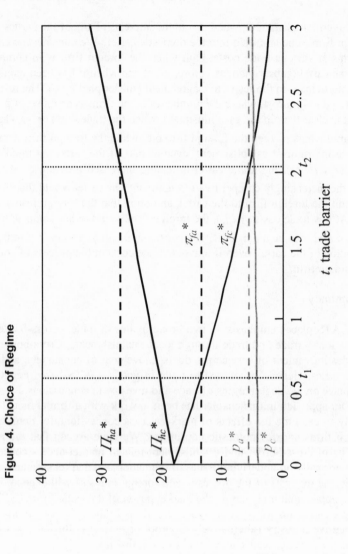

4. The foreign firm will have higher profits, the less competitive the domestic industry.
5. Profits of the home industry are not monotonic in the number of home firms. Initial moves away from monopoly can actually boost the market share and profits of the total domestic industry.

Consider next the incentive for bringing a foreign firm into a dometic cartel. This involves establishment and yields the following conclusions:

1. When the trade costs are high, a domestic cartel wants to keep the foreign firm out (it opposes establishment), while the foreign firm would like to have the right of establishment, even as part of the cartel.
2. At more moderate trade costs, both the home and foreign firms favor bringing the foreign firm into the domestic cartel.
3. At low trade costs, the foreign firm would rather compete with the home cartel than be a part of it.

These results tell us that the interest of a domestic industry, in terms of favoring or opposing a foreign right of establishment, will depend on the conditions for cross-border access. In fact, the industry's position can be reversed as cross-border restrictions are negotiated down. This is because, given erosion of market power through trade, the domestic industry may find it advantageous to co-opt the foreign sector by inviting them into the cartel and sharing rents. Once cross-border barriers are sufficiently low, however, the foreign view of establishment is that they prefer to play against, rather than with, the cartel.

Collectively, these results point to linkages between the degree of competition, the mode and degree of market access, and the pro-competitive effects of liberalization. When we introduce establishment in conjunction with low cross-border barriers, we find that the foreign service provider takes on the domestic cartel. This is clearly a pro-competitive result. At higher levels of cross-border trade barriers, establishment may instead lead to an equilibrium where the foreign provider is simply co-opted into the domestic cartel. This has well known negative consequences related to profit shifting. The impact of establishment on the degree of competition, and on potential gains or losses from liberalization, hinge on the underlying degree of competition (a regulatory issue), but also on barriers to cross-border trade.

Notes

[1] A thorough overview is provided by WTO (1998).

[2] An exception is Cho (1988), who discusses Korean-U.S. negotiations on insurance and the implications of the Korean insurance cartel for the gains from trade in insurance services

[3] Competition in service sectors can also have important implications for trade in goods. For example, cartels in the international transportation sector can pose a significant barrier to trade in goods (Francois and Wooton, 1999). In addition, the presence of transport costs typically means prices are not fully transmitted across markets (i.e.,

markets are segmented).   This has important implications for trade and competition linkages.

[4] The foreign firm may, of course, also sell services in a third market.   We are effectively assuming market segmentation here, which combined with the constant marginal cost assumption lets us proceed with the model developed in this section.

[5] We assume Cournot competition rather than Bertrand, as the latter would result in the competition between the foreign and home firms driving the price to the competitive level.

[6] This technique was used by the authors in Francois and Wooton (1999) in their discussion of shipping conferences and maritime trade.

References

Cho, Yoon Je, "Some policy lessons from the opening of the Korean insurance market." *The World Bank Economic Review*, [May 1988], 241-54.

Deardorff, A.V., "Comparative advantage and international trade and investment in services." In R.M. Stern ed., *Trade and Investment in Services: Canada/U.S. Perspectives*. [1985] Toronto: Ontario Economic Council.

Francois, J.F., "Increasing returns due to specialization, monopolistic competition, and trade in producer services." *Canadian Journal of Economics*, [1990a] vol. XXIII: 109-24.

Francois, J.F., "Trade in nontradables: proximity requirements and the pattern of trade in services." *Journal of International Economic Integration* (now the *Journal of Economic Integration*) [Spring 1990b] 5(1): 31-46.

Francois, J.F. and L. Schuknecht, "International trade in financial services, competition, and growth performance." [1999] CEPR discussion paper.

Francois, J.F. and I. Wooton, "Trade in international transport services: the role of competition." [1999].

Hill, T.P., "On goods and services." *The Review of Income and Wealth.* [1977] 23(4) December: 315-38.

Hoekman, Bernard, "Conceptual and political economy issues in liberalizing international transactions in services." In Deardorff, A.V., and Stern, R.M., eds., *Analytical and negotiating issues in the global trading system.*, Studies in International Trade Policy, Ann Arbor: University of Michigan Press, pages 501-38 [1994].

Markusen, J.R., "Production, trade, and migration with differentiated, skilled workers." *Canadian Journal of Economics*, 21:3, [August 1988], 492-506.

Markusen, J.R., "Trade in producer services and in other specialized intermediate inputs." *American-Economic-Review*; 79:1 [March 1989], 85-95.

Sampson, G.P. and R.H. Snape, "Identifying the issues in trade in services." *The World Economy* 8(2) [June 1985]: 171-81.

Stern, Robert M. and Bernard M. Hoekman, "Conceptual issues relating to services in the international economy." In Chung-H. Lee and Seiji Naja (eds), *Trade and Investment in Services in the Asia-Pacific Region*. Pacific and World Studies series, no. 1, Inchon, Korea: Inha University, 7-25, [1988].

CHAPTER 7

International Trade in Services, Free Trade Agreements, and the WTO

Scott L. Baier and Jeffrey H. Bergstrand

> Trade and investment in services presumably are determined by the same influences that shape comparative advantage in goods. (Stern, 1985, p. 155)

> A central question that arises in the context of trade in services is whether services are economically similar to goods and, hence, whether traditional trade theories apply equally to goods and services. At first sight, the answer to this question would seem to be "yes." After all, on the supply side, goods and services use similar factors of production; equally, on the demand side, both goods and services compete for the consumer's income. Although a common approach to both goods and services seems therefore warranted, it cannot be denied that services exhibit certain characteristics with specific consequences for international transactions. The major one is, undoubtedly, that services tend to be less traded than goods both in absolute value terms and relative to domestic output. This situation has generally been ascribed to two factors: the inherent non-tradability of some services, and government restrictions that impose barriers to trade in services. (Sapir and Winter, 1994, p. 274)

I. Introduction

According to Frankel (1997), one-third of the roughly 100 free trade agreements (FTAs) created in the last 50 years were created in the first half of the 1990s. This explosion in the number of free trade agreements has been matched by an explosion in the number of *studies* of FTAs. Beginning with Krugman (1991a,b), a resurgence in the study of free trade agreements (FTAs) has occurred over the last decade. This literature has largely followed two tracks. Krugman (1991b) dichotomized these tracks neatly with the first addressing the "economics" of FTAs and the second on the "politics" of free trade agreements. In the newest volume of the *Handbook of International Economics*, this bifurcation of the literature is revealed by Baldwin and Venables' (1995) chapter on the relative economic merits of an FTA in a competitive setting (perfectly or monopolistically) and Rodrik's chapter addressing the political economy of trade agreements in a non-competitive setting. Baldwin and Venables categorized the "economic approaches" to an FTA into first-generation (static perfect competition with constant returns to scale), second-generation (static monopolistic competition with increasing returns), and third-generation (dynamic competitive factor-accumulation) models.

A main impact of Krugman (1991a,b) was on clarifying the economics of trading blocs, in particular, the relative importance of proximity in determining the relative benefits of an FTA, using a (second-generation) monopolistic competition with increasing returns model. In Krugman, with zero intercontinental transportation costs on goods, continental FTAs decrease welfare unambiguously. However, with prohibitive intercontinental transport costs, such FTAs increase welfare unambiguously, leaving the results contingent upon the degree of transportability of goods.

This contrasting result—termed in Frankel, Stein, and Wei (1995) the "Krugman vs. Krugman debate"—led Frankel, Stein, and Wei (henceforth, FSW) to evaluate the net welfare gains or losses of continental FTAs under intercontinental transport costs varying from zero to prohibitive. In the context of Krugman's model, FSW found that continental FTAs were welfare-reducing for c.i.f.-f.o.b. factors less than 18 percent. With c.i.f.-f.o.b. factors averaging about 8 percent, the FSW results suggest that nations' governments have been enacting continental FTAs that are welfare reducing. This led FSW (1998) to conclude that—if continents followed the European examples of *complete* free trade areas (as opposed to partial liberalization)—the "regionalization of world trade would be excessive" (pp. 111-112).

However, a potentially serious omission in this literature is the role of *services*. Krugman (1991a,b) and FSW (1995, 1996, 1998) have used one-sector, one-factor models aimed at exploring FTAs in the context of trade in goods, in particular, manufactures. Yet, on average, services comprise about 61 (47) percent of national output in developed (developing) economies. Although trade in services is less than that in goods, services trade worldwide is currently at least one-third of the value of goods trade and the former is growing faster than the latter. Moreover, in the policy arena, the most prominent FTAs in the world (such as the European Economic Area or EEA, North American Free Trade Agreement or NAFTA, and MERCOSUR) have liberalized services trade much more extensively than the WTO has liberalized trade in services multilaterally.

This chapter is aimed at re-evaluating the implications of the Krugman and FSW studies to argue that—in the presence of services—the increasing regionalization of world trade, using continental FTAs, is not excessive. Our analysis concerns the relative welfare benefits of a free trade agreement (FTA) in a setting with international trade in goods and services and where multilateral liberalization of services trade is limited compared with that in goods. With this goal in mind, an overview of the chapter is as follows. First, we extend the simple one-factor, one-industry model in Krugman and FSW to a world with two factors and two industries. This extension allows us to re-evaluate the conclusions of Krugman and FSW about the net gains from continental FTAs in goods and services. Taking into account the lower relative tradability of most services—the primary distinction between trade in goods and services, as noted by Sapir and Winter in the introduction—we argue that the degree of regionalization being witnessed is not excessive.

Second, Sapir and Winter (1994) note that the other major difference between trade in goods and services is that governments impose more severe restrictions on services trade than on goods trade, owing to the intangible nature of services and associated problems of asymmetric information. We show how the relative merits of a regional FTA are altered after accounting for greater government restrictions on services trade.

Third, as fairly widely acknowledged, liberalization of services trade under the WTO (in particular, the General Agreement on Trade in Services, or GATS) has been modest at best. Lawrence (1996) noted that GATT agreements have enjoyed "spectacular success in lowering trade barriers on industrial products" (p. 5). However, as the focus shifts from the "relatively easy task of reducing barriers protecting industrial products, achieving agreement has become more difficult. . . . In many important areas, such as services and agriculture, liberalization has remained fairly limited" (p. 5). Hoekman (1999) is even stronger in his dismissal of liberalization under the GATS:

> Its provisions, let alone its existence, remain relatively unknown or understood even among those who have an interest in the functioning of the trading system (multinational business). No major disputes regarding the implementation of the agreement have been brought forward, no doubt reflecting in part that *no liberalization* was achieved" (pp. 1-2; italics added).

However, the EEA, NAFTA, and MERCOSUR are all continental FTAs that have liberalized international trade in services as well as goods. We show, in the context of the Krugman-FSW model, how the benefits of a regional FTA in goods and services *relative to* multilateral WTO liberalization in goods alone are related to the lower relative transportability of services internationally and the greater relative government barriers to services trade. This result may help explain the proliferation of FTAs in the 1990s compared with the stagnation of multilateral liberalization under the WTO.

The remainder of the chapter is as follows. Section II presents some background information. Section III presents the theoretical model, an extension of the Krugman and FSW models to reflect goods and services. Section IV discusses the relative welfare benefits of a regional FTA in goods and services. Section V discusses the welfare benefits and costs of a regional FTA in goods and services relative to a WTO multilateral liberalization of trade in goods alone. Section VI concludes.

II. Background Information

This section provides some analytical and empirical background for the distinctions between goods and services raised in the introduction. First, we address the overall importance of the service sector in developed and developing economies. With approximately half of the typical country's national output in services, the distinction between goods and services in economies commands attention. Second, we provide background information and arguments on the primary distinction between goods and services: the relatively lower transportability of services. Third, we provide background details and arguments on the second notable distinction between goods and services: the greater relative protection internationally of services.

Services Role in Aggregate Economic Activity

In most developed and many developing economies, services comprise more than half of gross domestic product (GDP). Table 1 from UNCTAD (1994) presents a decomposition of nominal GDP by sectors: agriculture, (raw materials) industry, manufacturing, and services. As the table indicates for 1990, 61 percent of nominal GDP in OECD economies was comprised of services and 47 percent of nominal GDP in developing economies was comprised of services.

Partly related to this observation, it is commonly believed that the share of services in (real) economic activity—that is, the share of services in *real GDP*—has also been increasing, associated with rising standards of living (measured by real per capita incomes). However, this has not necessarily been the case. Baumol, Blackman, and Wolff (1989, Ch. 6) show that the real share of services tends to fall moderately with real per capita incomes, even though the share of services in nominal GDP rises with per capita income. This argument is consistent with the data in Table 2 from UNCTAD (1994), which show that services output is not necessarily growing faster than national output. For instance, among OECD countries, the services share of real GDP grew between 1965 and 1980; however, this share was constant between 1980 and 1990. Moreover, for lower middle-income developing economies, the services share of real GDP grew between 1965 and 1980, but fell between 1980 and 1990.

Table 1. Percentage Breakdown of Gross Domestic Product by Sector and by Country Group, 1965 and 1990 (at Current Prices)

Country group[a]	Agriculture 1965	Agriculture 1990	Industry 1965	Industry 1990	Manufacturing[b] 1965	Manufacturing[b] 1990	Services[c] 1965	Services[c] 1990
Developing economies	29	17	30	37	20	25	40	47
Low-income	41	31	26	36	19	27	32	35
Lower middle-income	22	17	32	31	20	23[d]	44	50
Upper middle-income	16	9	36	40	19	25	47	51
High-income economies	5	--	43	--	32	--	54	--
OECD members	5	3[e]	43	35[e]	32	23[f]	54	61[e]
Others[g]	8	4[d]	45	41[d]	14	--	46	54[d]

Source: UNCTAD (1994)
Primary Source: World Bank, World Development Report data base

[a]Low-income economies are those with a 1990 GNP per capita of $610 or less. Lower middle-income economies are those with a 1990 GNP per capita of more than $610 but less than $2,465. Upper middle-income countries have a 1990 GNP per capita of more than $2,465 but less than $7,620, High-income economies are those with a 1990 GNP per capita greater than $7,620.

[b]Because manufacturing is generally the most dynamic part of the industry sector, its share of GDP is shown separately.

[c]In the World Development Report data used here, services encompass value added in transport and communications, trade, banking, dwelling, public administration, other services, imputed bank-service charges, import duties as well as any statistical discrepancies noted by national compilers.

[d]1989 figure used.

[e]1986 figure used

[f]1985 figure used.

[g]Israel, Singapore, Hong Kong, United Arab Emirates, and Kuwait.

Table 2. Average Annual Rates of Growth in Output, by Country Group and Sector, 1965-1980 and 1980-1990[a] (at Constant Prices)

Country group[a]	GDP 1965-1980	GDP 1980-1990	Agriculture 1965-1980	Agriculture 1980-1990	Industry 1965-1980	Industry 1980-1990	Manufacturing[b] 1965-1980	Manufacturing[b] 1980-1900	Services[c] 1965-1980	Services[c] 1980-1990
Developing economies	5.9	3.2	2.9	3.2	6.8	3.8	8.0	6.0	7.1	3.6
Low-income	4.9	6.1	2.6	3.9	7.3	8.2	6.7	11.1	6.2	6.5
Lower middle-income	5.5	2.6	3.6	2.5	5.0	2.8	6.1	2.5[d]	7.7	2.5
Upper middle-income	7.0	2.4	3.2	2.3	7.8	2.0	8.9	3.5	7.4	2.7
High-income economies	3.7	3.1	--	1.7	2.7	2.1[d]	3.2	3.4[d]	4.5	3.1[d]
OECD members	3.7	3.1	1.2	1.7	2.8	2.2[d]	3.1	3.3[d]	4.5	3.1[d]
Others[e]	8.2	2.4[d]	--	6.4[d]	--	-0.7[d]	--	7.7[d]	--	5.3[d]

Source: UNCTAD (1994)

Primary Source: World Development Report data base

[a]For a definition of the country groups, see Table 1

[b]Because manufacturing is generally the most dynamic part of the industrial sector, its share of GDP is shown separately

[c]Services are defined in note c to Table 1

[d]Based on the period 1980-1989

[e]Israel, Singapore, Hong Kong, United Arab Emirates, and Kuwait

One reason for the secular increase in the services share of nominal GDP is the role of relative prices. Prices of services relative to goods rise with per capita income, tending to increase the share of services in nominal GDP. Three reasons are offered typically for this effect. First, productivity growth historically has been faster in goods than in services. This reduction in the relative output of services over time pushes up the relative price of services, raising the share of services in nominal GDP as the elasticity between goods and services tends to be low (cf., Balassa, 1964; Samuelson, 1964). Second, services (goods) have tended historically to be labor-intensive (capital-intensive) in production. Per capita income grows over time partly due to growth in capital per worker. As an economy develops, the increase in the relative abundance of capital to labor shifts production toward relatively capital-intensive goods. This reduces the relative output of services, increasing services' relative price and the share of services in nominal GDP (cf., Bhagwati, 1984). Third, as an economy develops, the demand for services rises relative to that for goods, if services (goods) are luxuries (necessities) in consumption. This pushes up both the relative demand and relative price of services, tending to increase the share of services in nominal GDP (cf., Bergstrand, 1991).

Nevertheless, while mixed evidence exists of a growing share of services in real GDP, it is reasonable to estimate that on average about half of countries' GDPs are composed of services. Consequently, there is little doubt that services play a major role, and possibly an increasing one, in economic activity.

Services Relative Nontradability

As Sapir and Winter (1994) note, one of the primary distinctions between goods and services is "the inherent *non-tradability* of some services" (p. 274; italics added). In an earlier survey, McCulloch (1988) notes that "In most empirical research on international trade, services are simply ignored or are treated as nontradable goods" (p. 369). Many researchers return to Hill (1977) to note that the issue of "nontradability" of services is inextricably tied to the notion that their production and consumption usually takes place simultaneously. Sapir and Winter (1994, p. 275) identified concisely four categories of supplying trade in services, summarized in Figure 1 from Sapir and Winter:

> Four types of international transactions in services can be distinguished:
>
> 1. Immobile users in one nation obtain services produced by immobile providers located in another nation. This occurs, for instance, in financial services and professional services, where transactions flow via telecommunications networks.

Figure 1. Types of Services

	Provider does not move	Provider moves
User does not move	Commodity Trade (type 1)	**Temporary movement** Factor trade (type 3) **Permanent movement** FDI/migration (type 4)
User moves	**Temporary movement** Commodity trade (type 2) **Permanent movement** migration	

Source: Sapir and Winter (1994)

2. Mobile users from one nation travel to another nation to have services performed. This situation is most frequent in tourism, education, health care, ship repair and airport services.

3. Mobile providers from one nation travel to another nation in order to perform services. This situation occurs in certain business services, such as engineering, where frequent or close interaction is not [*sic*] required.

4. Providers from one nation establish a branch in another nation in order to perform services. This is the most common pattern of international service competition, involving frequent and close interaction between buyers and sellers. It is the dominant type in most services, including accounting, advertising, banking, consulting services and distribution.

Trade in services is restricted typically to types 1, 2 and 3; type 4 is considered foreign direct investment and conventionally deemed outside of the scope of "trade" in services. These categories are broadly consistent with the four "modes" of supply of services under the GATS (although the numbering system differs). Of the first three classifications, types 2 and 3 are generally considered to have very high transportation and transaction costs, owing largely to the cost of either laborers being transported to the consumer (type 3) or consumers being transported to the producer (type 2). Moreover, the "costs of doing business" are not restricted to simply "transportation" costs. Frankel (1997) organized the costs of doing business internationally into three categories. The first category is transportation costs. The second is the time elapsed in transporting, which could be a substantial additional burden for type 2 and 3 service transactions. The third is, what Frankel terms, the cost of "cultural unfamiliarity," which includes language. Certainly in services transactions, such a transaction cost is substantial.

Since type 1 transactions typically are done via telecommunications networks, this trade may be virtually costless in terms of "transportation" and "time elapsed." However, as in type 2 and 3 services transactions, the costs of cultural unfamiliarity are still nontrivial to type 1 transactions internationally.

How much of international services transactions might be physically "costless"? There is, at present, very little research that might measure this with any degree of accuracy. Data on the costs of trading services internationally are essentially nonexistent. However, an interesting study by Schuknecht (1999) suggests that the share of world trade in services that is physically "costless," i.e., transmitted electronically, is about $370 billion annually, or roughly 30 percent of current world trade in services. Thus, about 70 percent of world trade in services appears to require costly physical movement of persons. Hence, it is reasonable to conclude—as revealed by the relative size of economies' service sectors and the considerably lower share of services in international trade—that services on average are inherently much more costly to trade internationally than goods.

Greater Relative Governmental Restrictions on Services

Sapir and Winter (1994) note that the other key distinction between services trade and goods trade is that services are prone to much more governmental restrictions than goods trade. McCulloch (1988) draws attention to this also, noting "the extensive role of domestic regulation in service activities" (p. 369).

Unlike goods trade, services trade is protected almost exclusively by nontariff barriers. Protection of services takes a wide array of nontariff barrier forms, and has been surveyed comprehensively in McCulloch (1988), Sapir and Winter (1994), UNCTAD (1994), Fieleke (1995), Hoekman and Primo Braga (1997), and Hoekman (1999). As Fieleke (1995) writes:

> Examples of these barriers are rife. By way of illustration, suppliers are impeded from traveling to receivers by limits on the inflow of temporary workers for construction projects, or by limits on domestic practicing by foreign professionals, such as physicians. Receivers are hindered from going to suppliers by measures that obstruct their traveling abroad for purposes such as tourism or education. Cross-border movement of services themselves is restricted by limitations on foreign content in radio and television broadcasting and in the cinema. As for the provision of services through affiliates, many governments have strictly controlled direct investment by foreigners in sensitive domestic industries such as transportation, telecommunications, banking, and advertising (p. 33).

Quantitative estimates of the degree of protection in services relative to goods are difficult to come by. One approach has been to calculate tariff-equivalents of services trade protection. A second approach has been to use price-cost margins as estimates of the degree of protection. Using this method, Hoekman (1999) estimates that services margins are higher than manufacturing margins (indicating relatively greater protection) by 10 to 100 percent. A third, and the most formalized, method "backs out" estimates of the greater relative protection of services using a gravity model (Francois, 1999). According to Francois' estimates, services protection is about *twice* that of goods.

III. The Model

As already mentioned, we shall re-evaluate the conclusions in Krugman (1991a,b) and Frankel, Stein, and Wei (1995, 1996, 1998) about the impact of regional FTAs on the welfare of consumers by taking into account the role of *services*. For ease of comparison, we benchmark our results to those papers. We now outline the model, a straightforward extension of the Krugman-FSW model to account for two factors and two industries, where the industries are potentially asymmetric in terms of the "transportability" of the good or service and in terms of the degree of "government protection" on the good or service.[1]

In the spirit of the Krugman-FSW frameworks, international trade within each of two monopolistically-competitive sectors and among four countries on two continents is generated by the interaction of consumers having tastes for diversity and production being characterized by economies of scale. This framework is standard in modeling international trade in goods (e.g., manufactures) in the context of the new trade theory. Such a framework is a reasonable starting point for services also.[2] Within each sector, a taste for diversity exists, captured formally by Dixit-Stiglitz preferences. Increasing returns to scale internal to the firm are captured with fixed costs and linear cost functions. We assume two factors of production, capital and labor, each perfectly mobile between sectors within a country, but immobile internationally. We label the two sectors goods and services; initially, these labels are arbitrary. However, we will differentiate the two sectors later along lines of transportability and protection; goods (services) will have lower (higher) transportation costs and lower (higher) degrees of protection.[3] Goods (services) can be allowed to be capital (labor) intensive in production, as often assumed theoretically and estimated empirically. However, for the purposes at hand, we omit this distinction.[4]

Consumers

Each country has a representative consumer who derives utility from consuming goods and services (g and s, respectively) based upon Cobb-Douglas preferences. Within each sector, the consumer has a taste for diversity captured formally by Dixit-Stiglitz preferences. Continents are denoted by 1 and 2; countries on each continent by A and B. Thus, representative consumer i in each of the four countries (i = 1A, 1B, 2A, 2B) has a nested utility function:

$$U_i = \left[\left(\Sigma_{k=1}^{n_i^g} g_{iik}^{\theta^g} + \Sigma_{k=1}^{n_{i'}^g} g_{ii'k}^{\theta^g} + \Sigma_{j \neq i,i'} \Sigma_{k=1}^{n_{j \neq i,i'}^g} g_{ijk}^{\theta^g} \right)^{1/\theta^g} \right]^{\gamma}$$

$$\left[\left(\Sigma_{k=1}^{n_i^s} s_{iik}^{\theta^s} + \Sigma_{k=1}^{n_{i'}^s} s_{ii'k}^{\theta^s} + \Sigma_{j \neq i,i'} \Sigma_{k=1}^{n_{j \neq i,i'}^s} s_{ijk}^{\theta^s} \right)^{1/\theta^s} \right]^{1-\gamma} \tag{1}$$

where U_i denotes the utility of the representative household in country i (i = 1A, 1B, 2A, 2B). Let g_{iik} be consumption in country i of (differentiated) firm k's good produced in the home country (i), $g_{ii'k}$ is consumption in country i of good k produced in the foreign country on the same continent (i'), and g_{ijk} is consumption in country i of good k produced in each of the two foreign countries on the other continent (j). Similarly, s_{iik} is consumption of (differentiated) firm k's service produced in the home country, $s_{ii'k}$ is consumption of service k produced in the foreign country on the same continent, and s_{ijk} is consumption of service k produced in each of the two foreign countries on the other continent. Let 2^g (2^s) denote the parameter determining the elasticity of substitution in consumption in goods (services) with $0 < 2^g, 2^s < 1$. Let ((1-() be the Cobb-Douglas preference parameter for goods (services). Finally, let n_i^g (n_i^s) be the number of varieties of goods (services) produced in the home country, $n_{i_\square}{}^g$ ($n_{i_\square}{}^s$) the number of varieties of goods (services) produced in the foreign country on the same continent, and n_j^g (n_j^s) the number of varieties of goods (services) produced by a foreign country on the other continent.

Within any country, households and firms are assumed symmetric, so that we may replace $\Sigma_{k=1}^{n_i^g}$ ($\Sigma_{k=1}^{n_i^s}$) by n_i^g and n_i^s, respectively. Consequently, the budget constraint for the representative consumer in country i is

$$w_i + r_i(K_i/L_i) + T_i = n_i^g p_i^g g_{ii} + n_i^g p_{ii'}^g g_{ii'} + \Sigma_{j \neq i,i} \, n_j^g \, p_{ij}^g g_{ij} + n_i^s p_i^s s_{ii}$$
$$+ \, n_i^s p_{ii'}^s s_{ii'} + \Sigma_{j \neq i,i} \, n_j^s \, p_{ij}^s g_{ij} \, . \tag{2}$$

where w_i is the wage rate of the representative consumer-worker (or household) in country i, r_i is the rental rate on capital per household, K_i/L_i is the amount of capital supplied (or endowed) per household, T_i is tariff revenue redistributed back to households in a lump sum, p_i^g (p_i^s) is the price of the good (service) produced in the home country, $p_{ii'}^g$ ($p_{ii'}^s$) is the c.i.f. price of the good (service) produced in the foreign country on the same continent, and p_{ij}^g (p_{ij}^s) is the c.i.f. price of the good (service) produced in a foreign country on the other continent. Under symmetry within a country, subscript k can be eliminated.

Following FSW, c.i.f. prices differ from home prices due to Samuelson-type "iceberg" transportation costs and *ad valorem* tariffs. Let a (b) represent the fraction of output exported by a country that is "consumed" (or lost) due to intra- (inter-) continental transport.[5] Let $t_{ii'}$ and t_{ij} denote the *ad valorem* tariff rates in country i (that can potentially differ by trading partner). In the presence of positive tariffs and transport costs, the price level of the good (service) of the foreign country on the same continent, $p_{ii'}^g$ ($p_{ii'}^s$), is:

$$p_{ii'}^g = p_i^g \, [1/(1-a^g)] + p_i^g \, t_{ii'}^g \tag{3a}$$

$$p_{ii'}^s = p_i^s \, [1/(1-a^s)] + p_i^s \, t_{ii'}^s \tag{3b}$$

The price level of the good (service) of a foreign country on the other continent, p_{ij}^g (p_{ij}^s), is:

$$p_{ij}^g = p_i^g\{1/[(1-a^g)(1-b^g)]\}+p_i^g \, t_{ij}^g \tag{4a}$$

$$p_{ij}^s = p_i^s\{1/[(1-a^s)(1-b^s)]\}+p_i^s \, t_{ij}^s \tag{4b}$$

Tariff rates and transport costs are allowed to differ between sectors. For each country's consumer, maximizing (1) subject to equations (2), (3), and (4) yields a set of demand equations which, for brevity, are omitted here.

Firms

Each firm in the goods industry is assumed to produce output subject to the technology:

$$g_i = z_i^g (k_i^g)^{\alpha^g} (l_i^g)^{1-\alpha^g} - \varphi^g \tag{5}$$

where g_i denotes output of the representative firm, z_i^g is an exogenous productivity term for goods producers, k_i^g is the amount of capital used by the representative firm in country i, l_i^g is the amount of labor used by the representative firm in i, and φ^g represents a fixed cost facing each firm (e.g., marketing costs), the latter assumed identical across countries for simplicity. Similarly each firm in the services industry is assumed to produce output subject to the technology:

$$s_i = z_i^s (k_i^s)^{\alpha^s} (l_i^s)^{1-\alpha^s} - \varphi^s \tag{6}$$

where s_i denotes output of the representative firm, z_i^s, k_i^s, l_i^s, and φ^s are defined analogously for services, and factor intensities α^g and α^s need not be the same.

Firms in each industry in each country maximize profits subject to the technology defined in equations (5) and (6), given the demand schedules implied above. Equilibrium in these types of models is characterized by two conditions. First, profit maximization ensures that prices are a markup over marginal production costs:

$$p_i^g = (\theta^g)^{-1} [(C / z_i^g) r_i^{\alpha^g} w_i^{1-\alpha^g}] \tag{7}$$

$$p_i^s = (\theta^s)^{-1} [(D / z_i^s) r_i^{\alpha^s} w_i^{1-\alpha^s}] \tag{8}$$

where $C = (\alpha^g)^{-\alpha^g} (1 - \alpha^g)^{-(1-\alpha^g)}$ and $D = (\alpha^s)^{-\alpha^s} (1-\alpha^s)^{-(1-\alpha^s)}$. Second, under monopolistic competition firms earn zero profits which implies:

$$g_i = g = \frac{\theta^g \varphi^g}{1 - \theta^g}. \tag{9}$$

$$s_i = s = \frac{\theta^s \varphi^s}{1 - \theta^s}. \tag{10}$$

As common to this class of models, output of the representative firm in each industry is determined parametrically. Output of each goods-producing (service-producing) firm is identical across countries.

Factor Endowment Constraints

As is standard, we assume that endowments of capital (K_i) and labor (L_i) are exogenous, with both factors internationally immobile. Assuming full employment:

$$K_i = K_i^g + K_i^s = n_i^g k_i^g + n_i^s k_i^s \tag{11}$$

$$L_i = L_i^g + L_i^s = n_i^g l_i^g + n_i^s l_i^s \tag{12}$$

Equilibrium

The number of firms and product varieties in each industry and country, factor employments and prices in each industry and country, consumptions of each good, and goods prices can be determined uniquely given parameters of the model. Consistent with Krugman and FSW, we consider here only the case of symmetric economies in terms of absolute and relative factor endowments.[6] The key endogenous equations summarizing the model are available from the authors on request.

IV. The Gains from Continental FTAs in Goods and Services

A cursory examination of regional FTAs suggests that such agreements have pursued more extensive sectoral coverage of liberalization than multilateral negotiations. Reviews of such agreements in Lawrence (1996) and Frankel (1997) suggest that liberalization has been extended to services as well as to goods sectors.

In this section, we first replicate the results of FSW to show that, under certain further assumptions, our model simplifies to the FSW model. Second, we examine the effect of an intersectoral asymmetry in transport costs on the gains from trade from a continental FTA in goods and services. Third, we examine the effect of intersectoral asymmetries in transport costs *and* trade protection on the gains from trade from a continental FTA.

Perfect Symmetry between Sectors

As a benchmark, we compare the case of perfect symmetry in goods and services in our model with the single-industry case in FSW. With perfect symmetry, tariff rates between sectors and countries (t_{ii}^g, t_{ij}^g, t_{ii}^s, t_{ij}^s) are identical, transport costs between continents (b^g, b^s) and between countries on the same continent (a^g, a^s) are identical between sectors, factor intensities (α^g, α^s) are identical, elasticities of substitution in consumption in goods and services (determined by θ^g and θ^s) are identical, and the preferences for goods and services are identical ($\gamma = 1-\gamma = \frac{1}{2}$). For simplicity at this point, transport costs between countries on the same continent (a^g, a^s) are assumed zero, fixed costs in each sector (φ^g, φ^s) are unity, tariff rates are 0.30 initially, and there are no productivity shocks ($z_i^g = z_i^s = 1$), as in FSW.

If we consider the case in FSW where $2 = 0.75$ (implying an elasticity of substitution in consumption in each sector of 4), the relative welfare benefits from regional FTAs are identical to those in FSW, as shown in Figure 2. The top dashed line represents the gains from multilateral free trade in goods and services and the solid line represents the welfare benefits from regional FTAs in goods and services. Not surprisingly, multilateral free trade in goods and services is welfare superior to regional free trade in goods and services at any level of inter-continental transport costs. As in FSW, at high intercontinental transportation costs, net benefits from a regional FTA are positive. Yet, as in FSW, regional FTAs reduce welfare for a transport-cost factor, b, between 0 and 15 percent; a value of b of 15 percent suggests a c.i.f.-f.o.b. factor of 18 percent (b/[1-b]). This result from FSW has led many researchers to argue that regional FTAs may be welfare diminishing, and led to the FSW (1998) conclusion that the degree of "regionalization of world trade" observed has been "excessive" (pp. 111-112).

Intersectoral Asymmetry in Transport Costs

As discussed above, one of two fundamental distinguishing factors between services and goods trade is that services have typically been considered nonstorable. Historically, services must have been consumed as they were produced. The nonstorability of most services has typically led researchers to characterize services as *nontradable* internationally, although many argue that recent technological advances are creating services which are storable and thus increasingly less costly to trade (i.e., the growing importance of type 1 transactions). However, as discussed earlier, these electronic advances still may have left 70 percent of world services trade as less tradable than goods.

Many estimates of transport costs for goods support the interpretation of Figure 2 that "natural" FTAs are, in the language of FSW, "super-natural"; that is, at present transport-cost-factor estimates, regional FTAs reduce welfare. A cursory examination of c.i.f.-f.o.b. factors for merchandise trade from the IMF's *International Financial Statistics* between 1965 and 1995 suggests values ranging between 6.5 and 9 percent, with an average of 8 percent; these figures imply values of b^g ranging between 0.07 and 0.10. FSW, following Linnemann (1966) and others, argue that the costs of transporting goods exceeds simply insurance and freight costs. FSW (1996, 1998) calculated an approximate value of b^g using estimated elasticities from a gravity equation for merchandise trade. These estimates suggest a value of b^g around 0.16 to 0.18, with which they argue that "continental FTAs would put us firmly over the line into the supernatural zone" (1998, p. 111).

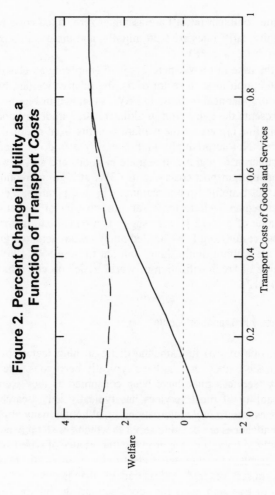

Figure 2. Percent Change in Utility as a Function of Transport Costs

Transport Costs of Goods and Services

Welfare

Solid line: Continental Free Trade Agreement
Dashed line: Multilateral Free Trade Agreement

Yet the results in Figure 2 assume that b^g and b^s are *identical*. Since many economists have argued until recently that most services are inherently non storable, consider the case where services are "nontradable" intercontinentally ($b^s = 1$). Figure 3 illustrates that regional FTAs are welfare improving on net at any level of transport costs for goods. The intuition is that—with prohibitive intercontinental transport costs on services—a continental FTA on goods and services creates extensive trade creation intracontinentally of services that more than offsets the trade diversion intercontinentally of goods.

Alternatively, consider the case where the intercontinental transport-cost factor on goods is set at 10 percent ($b^g = 0.1$), consistent with a c.i.f.-f.o.b. factor for goods of approximately 11 percent ($b^g /[1- b^g]$), and the share of goods (services) in the economy is still 50 percent ($\gamma=0.5$). Figure 4 illustrates that the intercontinental transport-cost factor on services need only exceed 20 percent to benefit from a regional FTA. Thus, it may be the case that the results of Krugman and FSW, suggesting that most regional FTAs may be "supernatural," may be misleading by not distinguishing between the transport costs of goods and services.

Intersectoral Asymmetry in Trade Liberalization Costs

As Sapir and Winter (1994) note, the other of the two distinguishing characteristics that has likely led to the smaller share of services trade in world trade compared with goods is the greater relative national protection of service industries. As discussed in section II, estimates of the degree of protection in services relative to goods are scant and must be interpreted cautiously. However, as Hoekman (1999) notes, one of the few studies to date that have attempted to estimate the degree of protection of services relative to manufactures is Francois (1999). Francois' empirical analysis suggests that the degree of protection of services is on average *about twice* that of goods.

In the previous simulations, tariffs were set at 30 percent, consistent with those used in Krugman and FSW. We now consider doubling the initial tariff rate on services to 60 percent. Figure 5 illustrates the gains from regional FTAs on both continents, allowing transport costs on goods and services to be identical. Comparison of figures 2 and 5 reveals that the (identical) level of transport costs on goods and services at which a continental FTA becomes welfare-reducing is reduced dramatically when services are protected at twice the level of goods. In the context of the parameters chosen, a continental FTA is welfare reducing only at c.i.f.-f.o.b. factors below 5 percent.

Figure 6 considers the same scenario, but now sets the c.i.f.-f.o.b. factor for goods at 11 percent ($b^g = 0.1$). In this case, regional FTAs in goods and services are welfare improving at almost any transaction cost level for services; a continental FTA reduces welfare only if b^s is less than 3 percent.

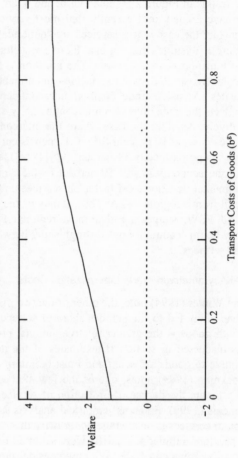

Figure 3. Percent Change in Utility as a Function of Transport Costs of Goods

Transport Costs of Goods (b^g)

Welfare

Assume b^s=1.0.

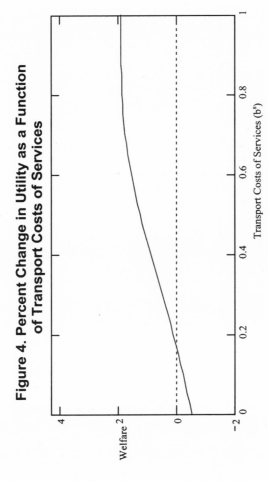

Figure 4. Percent Change in Utility as a Function of Transport Costs of Services

Welfare

Transport Costs of Services (b^s)

Assume $b^g = 0.1$.

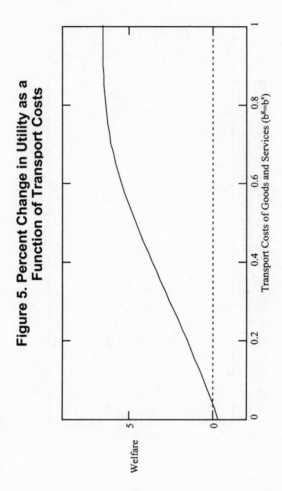

Figure 5. Percent Change in Utility as a Function of Transport Costs

Figure 6. Percent Change in Utility as a Function of Transport Costs of Services

Welfare

Transport Costs of Services (b^s)

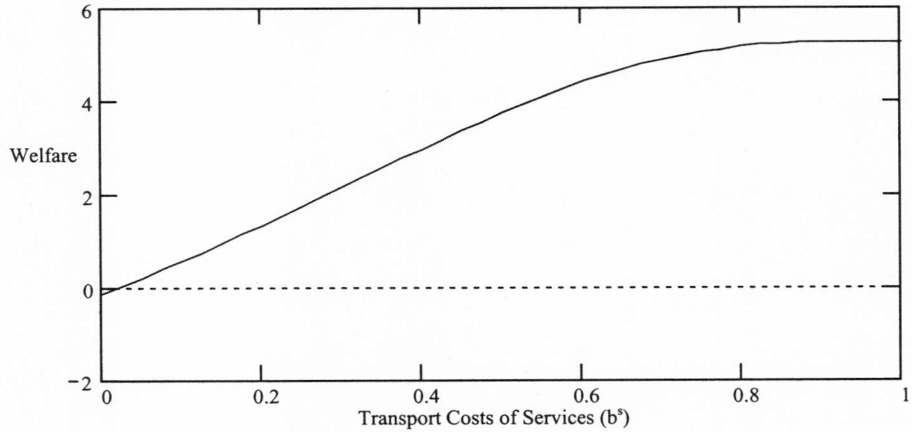

Assume b^g=0.1.

V. Regional FTAs and the WTO

> No liberalization of trade in services occurred during the Uruguay
> Round. (Hoekman, 1999, p. 1.)

The Uruguay Round was touted as the first major round of trade liberalization
to address protection in services. The GATS agreement negotiated during the
Uruguay Round created a framework under which liberalization could occur.
As noted above in Hoekman (1999), there have been no major disputes
brought forward under the GATS because many economists argue that in part
there has actually been no liberalization. The first major liberalization under
this framework has been the financial services agreement, and Sorsa (1997)
notes that this start was modest at best.

By contrast, regional FTAs have been successful in actually liberalizing
trade in services. A focal point of the 1992 European Economic Area (EEA)
initiative was the "free movement of goods, persons, services, and capital
within the EEA," embracing the establishment of "common rules and equal
conditions of competition and adequate means of enforcement (including the
judicial level)" (Lawrence, 1996, p. 127). NAFTA was implemented in 1994
designed to phase in free trade in goods and services. MERCOSUR is aimed
also at free movement of goods, services, capital, and labor.[7]Hoekman and
Primo Braga (1997) speculate on possible reasons behind the inability of the
WTO to liberalize trade in services *multilaterally* relative to the ability of regional FTAs to liberalize trade in services *bilaterally*. First, governments may
be more willing to negotiate liberalization of service sectors with other governments at similar stages of development on the same continent, owing to potentially greater mutual objectives. Second, standards for qualifications may be
easier to impose regionally. Third, geographical proximity may reduce the
costs associated with monitoring liberalization of services regionally than multilaterally.

Whatever the rationale, it is clearly the case that services trade liberalization multilaterally has been "limited," and clearly less than what has been attained at the continental level. The most supportive evidence of this is that the
GATS uses a "positive-list" approach; service sectors where liberalization has
occurred are listed, but omitted sectors retain barriers and new service sectors
are protected. By contrast, NAFTA employs a "negative-list" approach; liberalization covers all services *unless explicitly excluded*. The negative-list approach is generally considered to liberalize trade more aggressively than the
positive-list approach.

While the results in the previous section help to explain the proliferation
of regional FTAs and the associated welfare benefits, these results do not explain a proliferation of regional FTAs *as a substitute for* multilateral liberalization under the WTO. Given the lack of liberalization of services trade under
previous GATT rounds, but the success of multilateral liberalization of goods
trade, the framework at hand may be helpful. In the following we consider two

second-best scenarios. On one hand, a regional FTA in goods and services is a second-best policy because it lacks completeness in countries. On the other hand, multilateral liberalization of goods trade is a second-best policy because it lacks completeness in industries. There is a tradeoff. Given the lower level of tradability of services relative to goods and the higher level of protection of services relative to goods, we show for plausible transport cost values that regional FTAs may be *welfare-superior* to multilateral trade liberalization in goods alone.

Figure 7 illustrates the relative welfare gains from regional FTAs on goods and services versus multilateral free trade on goods alone as the transport costs on services vary (assuming $b^g = 0.1$, $t^g = 0.3$ initially, and $t^s = 0.6$ initially). At low services transport costs, multilateral liberalization on goods alone is welfare superior to regional FTAs on goods and services. But if services are costly to transport intercontinentally (in Figure 7, $b^s > 0.18$), regional FTAs on goods and services are welfare superior to multilateral liberalization of goods alone.

The intuition is the following. At high services transport costs, there is little intercontinental trade in services. Consequently, a regional liberalization of goods and services trade leads to considerably more trade creation than trade diversion for services. Moreover, the welfare-improving net trade creation from services more than offsets the welfare—diminishing trade diversion for goods from regional (versus multilateral) liberalization. Combined these effects more than offset the minimal trade creation from multilateral tariff eliminations on goods since, in this symmetric case, goods contribute only half to national output.

Recent arguments on the relative merits of FTAs have portrayed such FTAs as second-best policies. While FTAs in goods and services are second best relative to multilateral liberalization of goods and services, it is not apparent a priori that FTAs in goods and services are welfare-superior or inferior to another second-best policy, multilateral liberalization in goods alone. The analysis in this section suggests that relative transaction costs and relative barriers in the two sectors play a potentially influential role in this debate.

VI. Conclusions

Krugman (1991a,b) argued that, in a one-sector world with zero transportation costs, continental FTAs are unambiguously welfare decreasing. Frankel, Stein, and Wei (1995, 1996, 1998) responded that the net benefits from continental FTAs are sensitive to the *degree* of transportability of goods. Frankel (1997) estimated the degree of costs associated with international goods trade. Using estimates from a gravity equation, Frankel calculated that the transport cost factor, b, ranged between 0.1 and 0.2, which "suggests that continental FTAs would put us firmly over the line into the supernatural zone" (p. 111).

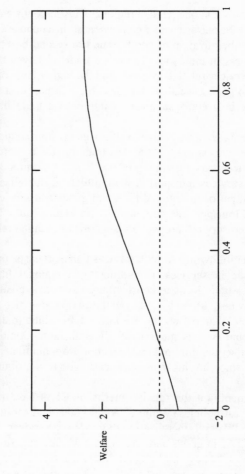

Figure 7. Percent Change in Utility from a Regional FTA in Goods and Services Versus a Multilateral FTA in Goods

Assume b^g=0.1, t^g=0.3 initially, and t^s=0.6 initially.

We have argued that the relative benefits of a continental FTA should take into account three important aspects of the present world economy. First, for many services, transportation costs are considerably higher than for goods. Second, government protection from foreign competition is considerably higher for most services than for goods. Third, multilateral liberalization of services trade has been modest at best and, according to many, non-existent. By contrast, many continental FTAs have liberalized services regionally.

We show in an extension of the Krugman and Frankel-Stein-Wei models that the net benefits from a regional FTA are higher after accounting for the lower relative tradability of services. Second, the relative benefits of a regional FTA are higher after accounting for the higher relative protection in services industries. Third, in the absence of multilateral liberalization of services trade, a regional FTA in goods and services may be welfare superior to the alternative second-best policy, multilateral trade liberalization in goods alone. We show for a plausible range of costs of transporting services that the net benefits of a regional FTA in goods and services may exceed such benefits from multilateral liberalization of trade in goods alone.

Notes

[1]This is not, of course, the first attempt to model goods and services. Deardorff (1985), for instance, discussed international trade in services, in the context of the potential relevance of the notion of comparative advantage. This, and other papers, are useful complements to ours. As Deardorff noted, economists traditionally have "lumped together" goods and services, with little distinction. Like Deardorff, we start from a simple model where goods and services are not distinguished, and proceed to differentiate the sectors "piecemeal." As he noted, "Select, one at a time, various characteristics that distinguish services from goods, characteristics that intuition suggests *may* have a bearing on trade . . . . (p. 41). Goods and services, of course, differ also in terms of their capital-labor intensity in production; however, this issue is beyond the scope of our analysis.

[2]Sapir and Winter (1994) note that "Most service sectors operate under conditions of imperfect competition resulting from various degrees of market power on the part of producers" (p. 277).

[3]At this time, we have not fully explored subtler distinctions between trade in final services from trade in intermediate, or producer, services; we are sensitive though to such issues and intend to explore them. Our aim here is to start from the case *most symmetric* to FSW and Krugman (i.e., trade in final goods and final services), and then consider marginal departures from that symmetry. The model is flexible enough to consider in the future trade in intermediate services.

[4]We explore the roles of relative factor intensities and abundances in another study, cf., Baier and Bergstrand (2000).

[5]Note these transport costs are of the hub-and-spoke variety discussed in Frankel, Stein, and Wei (1995) where each continent represents a hub. For intercontinental shipments, the costs are broken down into two components. The cost of transporting a good (ser-

vice) from one hub to another is given by b^g (b^s), and the cost to distribute the good (service) to each spoke is a^g (a^s). Transportation costs of shipping goods (services) intra-continentally only consist of the cost of shipping the good from spoke-to-spoke. Note that we are ignoring at this time an important consideration for the trade of many services, namely, that the provision of some services requires factor mobility. In our model, at present, factors are internationally immobile. We are sensitive to this constraint and intend to address this in subsequent research. To contrast our model with Krugman and FSW, we consider for now services representable by iceberg transport costs.

[6]We address asymmetries in absolute and relative factor endowments in Baier and Bergstrand (2000).

[7]See Lawrence (1996), Appendix.

References

Baier, Scott L. and Jeffrey H. Bergstrand. 2000. "Is Bilateralism Good? On the Economics of Free Trade Agreements," manuscript.

Balassa, Bela. 1964. "The Purchasing–Power–Parity Doctrine: A Reappraisal," *Journal of Political Economy* 72:584–96.

Baldwin, R.E. and Anthony Venables. 1995. "Regional Economic Integration," in Gene M. Grossman and Kenneth Rogoff (eds.), *Handbook of International Economics, Volume 3*. Amsterdam: Elsevier Science.

Baumol, William J., Sue Anne Batey Blackman, and Edward N. Wolff, (eds.). 1989. *Productivity and American Leadership: The Long View*. Cambridge, MA: MIT Press.

Bergstrand, Jeffrey H. 1991. "Structural Determinants of Real Exchange Rates and National Price Levels: Some Empirical Evidence," *American Economic Review* 82:325–34.

Bhagwati, Jagdish. 1984. "Why are Services Cheaper in the Poor Countries?" *Economic Journal* 94:279–86.

Deardorff, Alan. 1985. "Comparative Advantage and International Trade and Investment in Services," in Robert M. Stern (ed.), *Trade and Investment in Services*. Toronto: Ontario Economic Council.

Fieleke, Norman. 1995. "The Soaring Trade in 'Nontradables'," *New England Economic Review*, November/December: 25–36.

Francois, Joseph. 1999. "Estimates of Barriers to Trade in Services," manuscript.

Frankel, Jeffrey A. 1997. *Regional Trading Blocs*. Washington, DC: Institute for International Economics.

Frankel, Jeffrey A. (ed.). 1998. *The Regionalization of the World Economy*. Chicago: The University of Chicago Press.

Frankel, Jeffrey A., Ernesto Stein, and Shang–Jin Wei. 1995. "Trading Blocs and the Americas: The Natural, the Unnatural, and the Super–Natural," *Journal of Development Economics* 47:61–95.

Frankel, Jeffrey A., Ernesto Stein, and Shang–Jin Wei. 1996. "Regional Trading Arrangements: Natural or Supernatural?", *American Economic Review, Papers and Proceedings* 86:52–56.

Frankel, Jeffrey A., Ernesto Stein, and Shang–Jin Wei. 1998. "Continental Trading Blocs: Are They Natural or Supernatural?" in J. A. Frankel (ed.), *The Regionalization of the World Economy*. Chicago: The University of Chicago Press.

Hill, T.P. 1977. "On Goods and Services," *Review of Income and Wealth*, Vol. 23, No. 4, December.

Hoekman, Bernard. 1999. "Services Liberalization and the Millennium Round," paper presented at the Federal Reserve Bank of St. Louis conference, "Multilateral Trade Negotiations: Issues for the Millenium Round."

Hoekman, Bernard and Carlos A. Primo Braga. 1997. "Protection and Trade in Services: A Survey," *Open Economies Review* 8:285–308.

Krugman, Paul. 1991a. "Is Bilateralism Bad?" in E. Helpman and A. Razin (eds.), *International Trade and Trade Policy*. Cambridge, MA: MIT Press.

Krugman, Paul. 1991b. "The Move Toward Free Trade Zones," in *Policy Implications of Trade and Currency Zones*, proceedings of a symposium sponsored by the Federal Reserve Bank of Kansas City.

Lawrence, Robert Z. 1996. *Regionalism, Multilateralism, and Deeper Integration*. Washington, D.C.: The Brookings Institution.

Linnemann, Hans. 1966. *An Econometric Study of International Trade Flows*. Amsterdam: North–Holland.

McCulloch, Rachel. 1988. "International Competition in Services," in Martin Feldstein (ed.), *The United States in the World Economy*. Chicago: The University of Chicago Press.

Rodrik, Dani. 1995. "Political Economy of Trade Policy," in Gene M. Grossman and Kenneth Rogoff (eds.), *Handbook of International Economics, Volume 3*. Amsterdam: Elsevier Science.

Samuelson, Paul A. 1964. "Theoretical Notes on Trade Problems," *Review of Economics and Statistics* 46:145–64.

Sapir, Andre, and Chantal Winter. 1994. "Services Trade," in David Greenaway and L. Alan Winters (eds.), *Surveys in International Trade*. Oxford, UK: Blackwell.

Schuknecht, Ludger. 1999. "A Quantitative Assessment of Electronic Commerce," World Trade Organization Staff Working Paper ERAD–99–01, September.

Sorsa, Piritta. 1997. "The GATS Agreement on Financial Services: A Modest Start to Multilateral Liberalization," World Trade Organization Working Paper No. WP/97/55–EA.

Stern, Robert M. 1985. "Global Dimensions and Determinants of International Trade and Investment in Services," in Robert M. Stern (ed.), *Trade and Investment in Services*. Toronto: Ontario Economic Council.

United Nations Conference on Trade and Development (UNCTAD). 1994. *Liberalizing International Transactions in Services: A Handbook*. New York: United Nations.

CHAPTER 8

The Economic Performance of the Service Sector in Brazil, Mexico, and the United States

Nanno Mulder

I. Introduction

This chapter compares the productivity performance of the service sectors in Brazil, Mexico and the United States in the period from 1950 to 1996.[1] To evaluate the performance of these economies, the focus is on labor productivity, leaving aside capital and total factor productivity. Labor productivity is measured by value added per person engaged. The emphasis on this partial indicator was inevitable due to lack of data on capital inputs by sector in Brazil and Mexico, but in most services labor is in any case the main production factor.

In the twentieth century, Brazil, Mexico, and the United States experienced a large transformation of the sectoral composition of their economies. This is illustrated in figure 1 by changes in the sectoral shares in employment. In the course of time the shares of the service sector increased, while those of the primary sector fell. In the United States, this process was already well under way at the beginning of this century, whereas in Brazil and Mexico these shifts only started in the 1930s. From 1950 to 1996, the shares of services doubled from 25 to over 50 percent in the two Latin countries and increased from 57 to 78 percent in the United States. In the same period, the shares of the primary sector fell from 60 to less than 25 percent in Brazil and Mexico, compared to a drop from 12 to 3 percent in the United States. Trends in the shares of the manufacturing/construction sector over the post-war period moved in the opposite direction, increasing by 10 percentage points in Brazil and Mexico and falling from 30 to 15 percent in the USA.

In the first half of this century, the service sector represented a much higher share of GDP than of employment. After 1950, its share further increased. However, due to the lower rate of labor productivity growth in services compared to the rest of the economy, the growth of the service sector share of GDP was much smaller than in employment. From 1950 to 1996, the largest increase of the service sector share was in the United States (57 to 76 percent), followed by an increase of 10 percentage points to 65 percent in Mexico and a rise of 8 percentage points to 61 percent in Brazil. In the Latin countries, the share of the primary sector in total GDP dropped from over 20 percent in 1950 to roughly 8 percent in 1996, whereas the United States experienced a fall from 10 to 3 percent. Opposite trends were observed for the secondary sector shares in the post-war period, which increased in both Brazil and Mexico, but fell in the United States.

II. Why Did the Service Share Increase?

The growing share of services in employment is one of the main features of structural change in Brazil, Mexico and the United States. The speed at which the share of services in employment increases depends on: the rate of growth of income per head; changes in the structure of final and intermediate demand; differential rates of labor productivity growth by sector; and miscellaneous factors. Changes in the composition of final and intermediate demand could be estimated only from 1970 onwards due to data restrictions,[2] whereas productivity growth rates could be compared across sectors from 1950 onwards.

Rising Incomes and Demand Elasticity

The increase in the share of services in employment is partly driven by the substitution of primary and manufactured goods by services when per capita income rises, which is also referred to as Engel's law. The hierarchy of consumer preferences explains the dominant position of agricultural products in the consumption of people with low incomes. As per capita income increases, the need for basic commodities becomes saturated and demand shifts to manufactured products, which accelerates the growth of manufacturing. After a certain income level has been reached, consumers acquire a stock of durable goods, such as televisions and washing machines, and will spend a smaller fraction of their income on these products for replacement purposes. In turn, they will increase the share of their budgets spent on services. Changes in demand structure can be measured by income elasticities: the demand for a product is elastic when its share in spending increases with income and inelastic when its share decreases.

The experiences of Brazil and the United States, and to a lesser extent that of Mexico, confirm Engel's law. From the 1970s to the mid 1990s, per capita income rose 60 percent in Brazil, 28 percent in Mexico, and 36 percent in the United States. The shares of services in final demand rose from 28 to 43 percent in Brazil and from 57 to 62 percent in the United States, whereas in Mexico the share only rose from 32 to 34 percent during the same period (see figure 2). Education and health care were the fastest growing categories of final demand in Brazil and Mexico, corresponding to the large increase in the supply of these services for the poor. In the United States, health care and transport showed the highest increase as far as their share in final demand is con-

Figure 1. Structure of Employment by Sector of the Economy, Brazil, Mexico and the United States, 1900-96

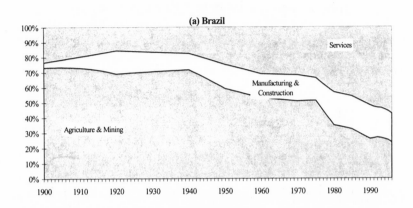

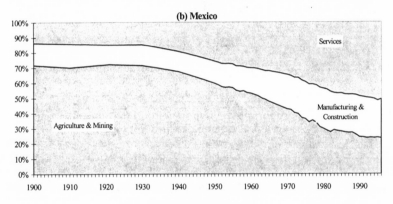

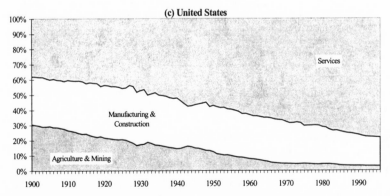

Source: Mulder (2000)

**Figure 2. Share of Services and Goods in Final Demand,
Brazil, Mexico, and the United States, 1970-96**

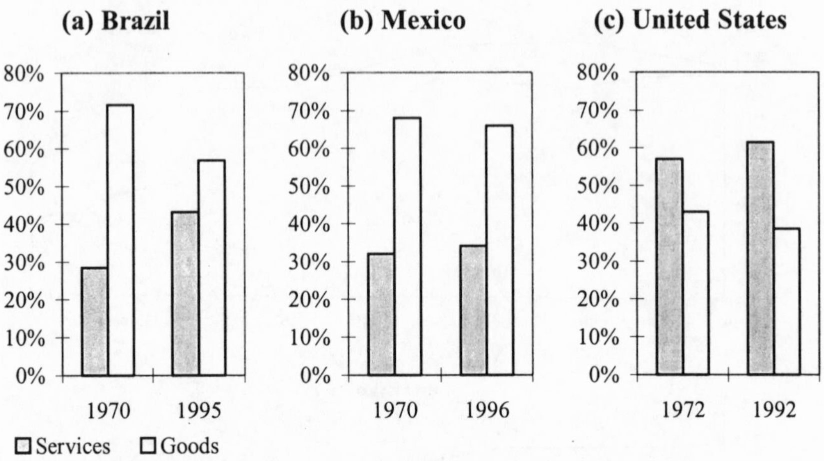

| (a) Brazil | (b) Mexico | (c) United States |

□ Services   □ Goods

Sources: Input-output tables as described in Mulder (2000)

cerned. In the United States, services account for the major share of final expenditure.

The larger proportionate demand for services also stems from the increased desire for leisure as income rises. In Brazil, Mexico and the United States, working hours have been reduced since 1950. In the United States, this process had already started in 1860. The largest part of the money spent during leisure time goes to services such as education, museums, restaurants and tourism. Consumer demand patterns have also been influenced by the rate of investment, pressure from advertising, access to foreign goods, and technological possibilities which, for example, boosted expenditure on health care in these countries.

The service share in final demand depends on per capita incomes, but also on the distribution of income, age composition of the population, the participation rate of women in the labor market, urbanization and on the role of governments. These will be discussed in more detail below.

Per Capita Incomes and Income Distribution

From 1950 to 1982, per capita incomes in Brazil and Mexico were converging to U.S. levels, after which they diverged. Aggregate per capita income data need to be supplemented by evidence on the distribution of income. Low-income groups have different spending patterns than high-income groups, and as such the income distribution has important consequences for the overall rate of substitution of agricultural products and manufactures for services in consumption. The Gini coefficients in Table 1 illustrate that, from 1950 to 1989, income distribution in Brazil and Mexico was more unequal than in the United

Table 1. Income Distribution: Gini Coefficients and Ratio of Fifth to First Quintile Brazil, Mexico, United States, 1950-91

	Brazil			Mexico			United States	
	Gini Coeffi- cient	Ratio of Fifth to First Quintile		Gini Coeffi- cient	Ratio of Fifth to First Quintile		Gini Coeffi- cient	Ratio of Fifth to First Quintile
1960	0.53	18.7	1950	0.60	35.4	1950	0.36	9.5
1976	0.60	23.7	1963	0.56	17.8	1960	0.35	8.6
1985	0.62	22.2	1975	0.58	25.4	1975	0.34	7.5
1989	0.60	26.3	1984	0.51	13.6	1985	0.37	9.3
			1989	0.55	18.5	1989	0.38	9.7
						1991	0.38	9.8

Source: Squire and Deininger (1996)

States. In the course of time, the distribution of income has become more unequal in Brazil, while in Mexico and the United States it has become slightly more equal. However, after the 1970s this distribution became more unequal in the United States, a pattern that was followed by Mexico in the 1980s.

Gini-coefficients do not indicate the shares of income earned by particular groups of households. This is illustrated by the ratio of the income share earned by the quintile of richest households to that of the quintile of poorest ones (see Table 1). The higher the ratio, the larger the share of income earned by the wealthiest. Although the Gini coefficient in 1950 in Mexico was the same as the 1976 and 1989 coefficients in Brazil, the share of income earned by the richest as compared to the poorest was much larger in Mexico than in Brazil.

Gini coefficients and income distribution by quintiles do not show what proportion of the population lives below the poverty line. International comparisons are very difficult, as each country adopts its own definition of poverty. An alternative, internationally comparable, poverty indicator is the number of children per 1,000 newborn that die before age of five: 69 in Brazil, 38 in Mexico and 11 in the United States in 1990. The information on per capita revenues, income distribution and infant mortality suggests that in 1990 more people lived in poverty in Brazil than in Mexico.

High income inequality increases the consumption of luxury services, such as domestic servants and expensive leisure activities. However, the demand for more basic types of services such as education, health care and telecommunications was constrained, as the middle and low-income groups received smaller fractions of income. Both countries had similar income levels, but services accounted for a larger share of final spending in Brazil than Mexico in 1970 and 1995/96. This suggests that an uneven income distribution favored the substitution of goods for services in these countries. However, as other forces were also at work, one cannot draw firm conclusions.

Changes in Demographics and Labor Force Participation

Population growth and age structure have important consequences for the relative demand for education and health care. The necessity for schooling largely depends on the share of the young in the total population, which is determined by birth and infant mortality rates. The demand for health care is to a large degree affected by the share of the elderly in the total population. The need for other services, such as proximity shopping, specialized transport and tourism, also depends on the age structure of the population. The high share of the young as shown in table 2 in combination with an increased public commitment to schooling explain the boom in expenditure on education from 0.5 and 0.6 percent of GDP in 1955 to 3.7 and 3.5 percent in 1990 in Brazil and Mexico, respectively. Since the 1970s the proportion of people under fifteen has been falling in both countries.[3] Nevertheless, the relative expenditure has continued to increase, due to rising enrollment levels in the different types of education. In the United States, the aging of the population[4] is a major cause of the rapid growth of health care spending from 4 percent of GDP in 1950 to 14 percent in 1994.

Table 2. Population Structure (Percentage of Total Population), Brazil, Mexico and the United States, 1950-1990

	Brazil		Mexico		United States	
	14 years and below	60 years and over	14 years and below	60 years and over	14 years and below	60 years and over
1950	42	4	43	4	31	10
1975	40	6	46	3	25	11
1990	34	8	38	4	22	17

Sources: World Bank (1999)

The volume of housing and retail services grew in line with the number of households, which, in the postwar period, was above the growth of the population due to higher divorce rates, fewer children per family and a growing proportion of one-person homes. Another socio-economic development that caused the demand for services to rise faster than population was the increasing participation of women in the labor market. This boosted the necessity of laundry services, nursery schools, prepared food and restaurant services that were previously produced at home. Home provision is not considered as a market activity. From 1950 to 1990 the proportion of women in the work force doubled from 15 to 30 percent in Brazil, and increased from 13 percent to 23 percent in Mexico (Hofman, 1999). U.S. female participation rates were much higher throughout the whole period. The higher share of working women boosted the demand for these formerly domestic services.

Urbanization

The final demand for services also depends on whether people live in rural areas or cities. City dwellers buy relatively more products in stores, while rural citizens grow part of their own food consumption themselves. Rural people also engage more in barter trade. Urban households have a higher demand for communication and recreational services. Even though per capita incomes in Brazil and Mexico were much lower than in the United States in 1990, the share of the population living in cities of more than 100,000 inhabitants was about the same: 42 percent in Brazil, 43 in Mexico, and 41 in the United States (World Bank, 1999). Since the 1970s, Mexico City and São Paolo are among the largest cities in the world.

Another difference between cities and rural areas lies in the alternative sources of subsistence income available, in the absence of job opportunities in the formal sector. In cities, most people enter the informal service sector, whereas in rural areas surplus labor is concentrated in agriculture. Within the informal sector, most people are engaged in services. In Brazil and Mexico, the informal workforce represented about 60 percent of the total in 1993. In Brazil, 41 percent of this informal workforce were employed in retailing, followed by food stands (19 percent), and other services (13 percent) in 1985. In Mexico, retailing accounted for 46 percent of informal employment, followed by repair services (12 percent) and food stands (11 percent) in 1988 (Mulder 2000).

The much higher share of services in employment in Brazil and Mexico in 1996 when compared to similar income levels in the United States in 1915 partly stems from the much higher rate of urbanization of the Latin countries.

The Expanding Role of Government

After 1950, public education and health care belonged to the fastest growing categories of final demand. In Brazil and Mexico, government expenditure as a share of GDP increased from one percent in 1950 to seven percent in 1990. In the United States it rose from five to eleven percent. The increased expenditure share stems largely from the public commitment to provide these services for the largest possible range of the population, including the poor. In these countries, the increase of educational and health standards is considered indispensable for improving people's well-being and productivity, and as such forms a precondition for economic development.

In the 1950-96 period, the demand for other government services (including the armed forces) also rose significantly in Brazil and Mexico. The implementation of import substitution policies in these countries required a large government, controlling extensive parts of the economy. From 1950 to 1996, the share of the government (excluding education and health care) in total employment rose from 3.0 to 10.2 percent in Brazil and from 4.5 to 16.9 percent in Mexico. In contrast, in the United States, the role attributed to the government first increased, but later contracted, as is illustrated by the rising share of employment from 11.5 percent in 1950 to 14.3 percent in 1967, after which it fell to 9.7 percent in 1996.

Growing Share of Services in Intermediate Demand

When per capita income rises, the share of services in intermediate demand increases, which in turn raises the proportion of the service sector in employment. Figure 3 shows that from the 1970s until the early 1990s, in all three countries the share of services in intermediate demand increased compared to goods. The largest increase of services in intermediate demand occurred in the United States: from 39 to 52 percent of intermediate demand. Smaller increases occurred in Brazil (from 21 to 25 percent) and in Mexico (from 18 to 25 percent).

The changes in the shares of individual services in intermediate demand differed from country to country (not shown in figure 3). In Brazil, the share of transport in total intermediate demand fell from 1970 to 1995. In contrast, the demand for financial services and business services increased. In Mexico, the intermediate demand for transport rose most rapidly, while that for distributive services and real estate decreased from 1970 to 1996. In the United States, the intermediate demand for transport fell, while the demand for distributive and financial services increased from 1972 to 1992.

The growing share of services in intermediate demand is explained by two simultaneous processes: outsourcing and innovation. The former refers to purchases of service inputs from outside firms, which were previously produced internally. In recent decades, rapid improvements in information and communication technologies have made outsourcing much more feasible, as these permit the rapid exchange of information between the contractor and the service producer. As such, firms tend to focus on their core business and contract other firms for catering, cleaning, financial services, marketing, and other services.

Innovation relates to the increased complexity of production and the corresponding increased use of intermediate services. The output of firms has become more differentiated and the life-cycle of their products has shortened, in order to respond to rapidly changing consumer preferences ("customizing"). Manufacturing and services have become more integrated, and the latter especially represent a growing share of the sales value of products. In high-income countries, innovation has been a far more important source of the growth of intermediate services then outsourcing.

**Figure 3. Share of Services and Goods in Intermediate Demand,
Brazil, Mexico and the United States, 1970-96**

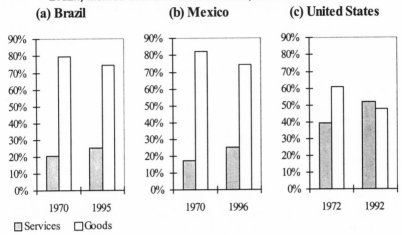

Source: Mulder (2000)

Below Average Labor Productivity Growth in Services

Lower labor productivity growth in services, as compared to the goods-producing sectors in all three countries, causes the share of services in employment to rise faster than its share in GDP. Growth rates of labor productivity are presented in Table 3. From 1950 to 1996, labor productivity growth in services was the lowest of all sectors in all three countries. In Brazil and the United States, labor productivity in the primary sector grew three-fold, and productivity in the secondary sector twice as fast as productivity in services. In Mexico, the differences between sectors are even larger, e.g., productivity in agriculture increased four-fold, and that of the secondary sector twice as fast as in services. Within the service sector, public utilities and transport and communications performed better relative to distribution and "other services" in all three countries.

The impact of lagging labor productivity growth in services on the tertiary sector employment share is estimated by the growth of the service employment share minus the increase in the service share of GDP at constant prices. When the percentage points increase in the service share of employment equals that of GDP, productivity growth in the tertiary sector is the same as the advances in the rest of the economy. However, in Brazil and Mexico and to a much lesser extent in the United States, the percentage points increase in the service share of GDP was smaller than that of employment during the 1950-96 period. For example, in Brazil the service employment share increased 32 points while the service share of GDP grew only 9 points. The difference, 23 points, may be attributed to lagging productivity growth. As such, sluggish

Table 3. Labor Productivity Growth by Sector, Brazil, Mexico and the United States, 1950-96 (Average Annual Compound Growth Rates)

	Brazil	Mexico	United States	Brazil Minus U.S.	Mexico Minus U.S.
Primary Sector	3.2	2.7	2.8	0.4	-0.1
Secondary Sector	2.4	1.4	2.2	0.2	-0.8
Tertiary Sector	1.2	1.0	1.0	0.2	0.0
TOTAL (All branches)	2.6	2.2	1.3	1.3	0.9

Source: Mulder (2000)

productivity growth "explains" about three quarters of the increase of the service employment share during the 1950-96 period in Brazil, 60 percent in Mexico, and 11 percent in the United States.

The view that services have little potential for labor productivity growth is too pessimistic and simplistic, as productivity gains have been achieved in several service industries. In many of these services, such as communications, banking and insurance, direct interaction between producer and consumer is not absolutely necessary. Although many of these so-called disembodied services are still produced during direct contact with the client, the progress in telecommunications and information technology allows for their distribution over large distances. This offers many possibilities for realizing economies of scale and productivity improvements.

Productivity gains were more limited in embodied services, which require a direct interaction between producer and consumer. In cultural activities, education, health care, and wholesale and retail trade, there are fewer options to automate activities, as labor is indispensable for the production of the service itself. The possibilities for productivity increases in the service sector depend on the relative importance of embodied and disembodied services in the total. In Brazil and Mexico, the low rates of labor productivity growth in services originate mainly from the expansion of embodied services, such as distribution, education and health care.

Other Factors Affecting the Development of the Service Sector

Inflation has had a negative impact on the development of many service industries. In Brazil, high inflation in the early 1960s, 1980s and 1990s, sharply reduced real incomes, especially of the poor, whose earnings were not protected against inflation. Spending on durables and most services fell and concentrated increasingly on food. Nevertheless, some services benefited from high inflation, such as hypermarkets, where consumers immediately spent their income after having received their salaries. Banks also benefited from hyperinflation, as financial intermediation became an increasingly profitable activity, on account of the large spread between the real debit and credit interest rates. Moreover, a variety of profitable monetary and non-monetary assets were introduced to protect depositors and banks against inflation. In Brazil, the share of the financial sector in GDP reached 25 percent in 1993, but the stabilization of prices afterwards reduced this to 6 percent in 1996. The share of finance in employment reached 2 percent in the late 1980s, but dropped later to 1.4 percent. Mexico also experienced substantial inflation in the 1980s, which, in contrast to Brazil, had a negative impact on the share of finance in GDP and employment. This was because deposits were not indexed, which induced many people to transfer their money abroad.

Regulatory legal environments in Brazil and Mexico. In the two Latin countries, many industries, such as public utilities, transport and communications, were controlled by public enterprises. Despite some productivity gains, public transport and communication enterprises were very inefficient, as is demonstrated by their low productivity levels. Other branches were strongly regulated. In wholesale and retail trade, the government imposed opening hours, regulated the location of stores, and requested high social contributions from formal employees. Furthermore, store owners required an operation permit that often took up to a year to obtain. The long and costly procedures induced many distributors to operate on an informal basis. Informal distributors had no access to credit or other facilities, and therefore most of them were not able to increase the size of their business, nor were they able to operate from a fixed location.

In all three countries, the governments imposed interest-rate ceilings in banking, which were intended to control the cost of credit and reserve requirements. In Brazil and Mexico, reserve requirements were increasingly used to finance the growing budget deficit in the 1970s and 1980s. As a result, banks intermediated fewer funds to the private sector. In all countries, the sphere of operations of each type of financial institution was limited until the late 1980s and 1990s. In Brazil and Mexico, universal banks—offering banking, insurance, and stock exchange services—were forbidden until the 1980s. In the United States, the government prohibited the opening of bank branches in other states, and as a result the banking sector remained highly fragmented, with thousands of small banks. The U.S. government also forced banks and other financial institutions to insure their deposits. This arrangement induced moral hazard behavior by fund managers and contributed to the Savings and Loans Crisis in the second half of the 1980s.

Limited international trade and foreign direct investment in services. In Brazil and Mexico, most service industries were protected against foreign competition until the late 1980s, or in some cases (banking, telecommunications) even until the mid-1990s. This delayed technological progress and productivity improvement, as many firms had few incentives to increase the efficiency and quality of their products. This was especially the case in communications, finance and transport.

In Brazil and Mexico, some transfer of technology, however, occurred through foreign direct investment, especially in wholesale and retail trade. Foreigners set up stores in Mexico in the 1970s and in Brazil in the 1980s. They introduced new store formats, such as hypermarkets, and new forms of inventory management. Foreign retailers offered a larger choice of goods at often lower prices, and demanded a wider range of products of better quality and in larger quantities from domestic manufacturers. In Brazil, the largest wholesale and retail chains were foreign-owned in the early 1990s. Since the 1980s, the efficiency gains of the larger stores were more than compensated by low or negative productivity growth of the small stores and street vendors, which dominated employment in distribution in both Brazil and Mexico.

The service sector as a refuge for the self-employed. In Brazil and Mexico, the downturn of the 1980s had little effect on the growth of the share of the service sector in employment for several reasons. Firstly, there were only a small number of benefit schemes for the unemployed in these countries. Therefore, working in the informal sector was their only alternative source of income. Most informal activity is concentrated in services, as it requires little human and physical capital. Secondly, as the share of self-employed in services is higher than in manufacturing, there is more disguised unemployment in this part of the economy. Thirdly, labor compensation is much more flexible in services, due to the higher share of self-employment and the smaller role of labor unions especially when compared to the commodity sector. Finally, many types of services are consumed in every part of the economic cycle. This in contrast to commodities, of which the consumption may be delayed.

III. The Impact of Service Expansion on Economic Performance

Comparisons of growth rates of productivity give only partial information on how countries performed, as they fail to indicate the relative efficiency at which resources are used. Comparisons of productivity levels are therefore an important complement to comparisons of productivity growth rates. Countries with high productivity growth may be less efficient in their use of resources than those with low productivity growth. In practice, an inverse relationship between productivity growth and levels is often observed, and results from the gains of backwardness for countries with low productivity levels. These gains result from the large available stock of technology in the world that a country can adopt. This "catch-up" bonus is much smaller for countries at the frontier of technological progress, such as the United States. The comparison with the United States indicates how large the gap of Brazil and Mexico is with the "best practice," and the bonus for catch-up growth.

Methodology for International Comparisons by Industry of Origin

International comparison of productivity levels is more complicated than intertemporal comparison of growth rates. Suitable converters are required to express values of two or more countries in a common currency. Exchange rates are unsuitable for this purpose, as they represent at best the relative price of tradables, and not that of non-tradable sectors. Moreover, they are often not representative for relative prices of tradables, as the exchange rates tend to be affected by capital movements, monetary policy and speculation.

Purchasing power parity (PPP) is an alternative conversion factor. There are two approaches to estimate PPPs: (a) use of prices by category of final expenditure, and (b) comparison of producer prices by sector of the economy. The former approach was followed in the International Comparisons Project (ICP) of the United Nations, and was also adopted by EUROSTAT and the OECD. Benchmark expenditure PPPs are available for 1970, 1975, 1980, 1985, 1990 and 1993. The ICP approach is unsuitable for sectoral comparisons because: (1) ICP includes prices of imported commodities and excludes prices of exports; and (2) ICP excludes intermediate sectors like mining, freight transport, trade and business services that are "disguised" and embodied in final expenditure. Expenditure PPPs are based on retail prices including trade and transport margins and not on factor cost.

The origins of the production approach to international comparison stem from the work of Rostas (1948) and Paige and Bombach (1959). It was further developed by the International Comparison of Output and Productivity (ICOP) project of the University of Groningen, which compares value added by branch of the economy. It derives purchasing power parities from values of output and quantities produced. Using labor and other inputs, it compiles measures of labor, capital and total factor productivity. Most ICOP comparisons have been bilateral, with the United States as the numéraire country. ICOP has focused on manufacturing (see van Ark, 1993), though there are some studies on agriculture and mining. Pilat (1994) was the first ICOP author to include some rough comparisons of output and productivity in services for Korea/U.S. and Japan/U.S. The present study is the first to apply the ICOP approach to services in a systematic and detailed way

I have made two binary comparisons, comparing Brazil/U.S. and Mexico/U.S. separately. To convert value added to a common currency, binary PPPs were calculated based on ratios of prices per unit of output. PPPs for specific services were aggregated to the industry level using quantity weights of either Brazil or Mexico, which are referred to as country X:

$$ppp_j^{XU(X)} = \frac{\sum\limits_{i=1}^{s} P_{ij}^X * Q_{ij}^X}{\sum\limits_{i=1}^{s} P_{ij}^U * Q_{ij}^X} \tag{1}$$

or quantity weights of the United States, country U:

$$ppp_j^{XU(U)} = \frac{\sum\limits_{i=1}^{s} P_{ij}^X * Q_{ij}^U}{\sum\limits_{i=1}^{s} P_{ij}^U * Q_{ij}^U} \tag{2}$$

i=1...s is the sample of matched services in industry j, Q is quantity, P is unit value or price. A PPP of the Paasche type is derived when quantity weights of country X are used, and a PPP is of the Laspeyres type when US weights (the numéraire country) are used. I subsequently calculated a Fisher PPP, which is the average of the Paasche and Laspeyres estimates.

For most services, prices are not available in censuses, but can be derived implicitly by using quantity indicators. The quantity ratios of output in industry j were weighted by the corresponding gross value of output (GVO) as shown in formulae (3) and (4):

$$PPP_j^{XU(U)} = \frac{\sum\limits_{i=1}^{r} [GVO_{ij}^{X(X)} / \dfrac{Q_{ij}^X}{Q_{ij}^U}]}{GVO_j^{U(U)}} \tag{3}$$

applying output weights of country X and:

$$PPP_j^{XU(X)} = \frac{GVO_j^{X(X)}}{\sum\limits_{i=1}^{r} [\dfrac{Q_{ij}^X}{Q_{ij}^U} * GVO_{ij}^{U(U)}]} \tag{4}$$

using the output weights of country U. Formulae (3) and (4) yield the same results as formulae (1) and (2) if the value of output weights in the quantity approach, formulae (3) and (4), are the same as the product of P and Q in formulae (1) and (2).

The measurement of the quantity produced is often difficult, especially in the so-called "comparison-resistant resistant" services. The latter include education, health care, and government. For example, at the macro level, it is almost impossible to assess the impact of physician services on the health status of a population. As an alternative, proxy indicators of the production process are used, like the number of patient visits. Neither is the unit of output for many non-comparison-resistant services clear-cut. For example, passenger kilometers, a commonly used output measure of passenger transport by rail fails to account for differences in the proportionate importance of terminal services across countries, and quality in terms of speed, reliability, and safety. Table 4 gives an overview of the proxies used in this study to measure output in the different service industries.

Table 4. Classification of Activity and Nature of Output Indicators

ISIC Code	Sector	Output Indicator	Quality Adjust-ment
6	Distribution		
61	- Wholesale trade}	Double deflation: deflation of sales using expenditure PPPs and defla-	No
62	- Retail trade }	tion of purchases destined for re-sale and inputs using ICOP PPPs	No
71	Transport:		
	- Rail goods transport	Weighted index of ton-km (trans-port services) tons (terminal services)	No
	- Rail passenger trans-port	Weighted index of pass.-km and passengers	Yes
	- Road goods transport	Weighted index of ton-km and tons	Yes
	- Road passenger trans-port	Passengers	Yes
	- Maritime goods trans-port	Tons	No
	- Air goods transport	Weighted index of ton-km and tons	No
	- Air passenger transport	Weighted index of pass.-km and passengers	Yes
72	Communications:		
	- Postal services	Pieces of mail sent	Yes
	- Telecommunications	Weighted index of network and calls	Yes
8	Finance, Insurance & Real Estate:		
81	- Banking services	Weighted index of transactions,, deposit savings accounts, and loans	No
82	- Insurance services	Health insurance and life insurance policies	No
83	- Real estate	Number of houses, adjusted for size	Yes
9	Services and govern-ment:		
931	- Education	Students numbers adjusted for level of education	Yes
933	- Hospital services	Patients-days, adjusted for case-mix differences	Yes
933	- Physician services	Patient visits	Yes
91	- Government	ICP PPP for government services	No
(a)	- Other Services	Reweighted ICOP PPPs for ser-vices	No

(a)   Business services, lodging places and miscellaneous services
Source: Mulder (2000)

The physical output of many services cannot be captured by a single indicator. When possible, a combination of proxies representing the various dimensions of a service is used. For example, transport output is measured by a weighted average of moving, loading, and unloading services. Banking includes maintenance of deposits, cashing checks and issuing loans. Many output indicators also fail to reflect quality differences. I relied often on rough proxy adjustments for quality as illustrated by four examples. In bus transport, the number of passengers per bus kilometer was taken as a proxy measure. On average Brazilian and Mexican buses carried almost twice the number of passengers per vehicle km as their U.S. counterparts. Other indicators of quality are frequency of service, number of accidents, respect of announced schedules, and speed. Our measure is supposed to reflect these quality differences. In postal services, the number of post-offices per 100,000 population, an indicator of access to postal services, was used as a proxy. In education, a double quality adjustment was made. Firstly, the enrollment data were adjusted by the dropout ratio, i.e. the share of the pupils not completing an educational cycle. These were much higher in the Latin countries compared to the United States. Secondly, test scores were used to adjust for the lower quality of Brazilian and Mexican education.

IV. In Comparative Perspective, Services Performed Better Than Other Sectors

Relative productivity levels are summarized in Table 5. In Brazil and Mexico, labor productivity varied strongly between different service activities. Brazilian communications and public utilities were characterized by very low productivity levels. Telecommunications were of very poor quality, as illustrated by the high share of local calls that could not be completed and the long delays (often for several years) in having a telephone line installed. Inefficiency was also found in state enterprises distributing electricity, gas, and drinking water as they often did not charge customers. Mexico showed a somewhat better performance, particularly in telecommunications.

In Brazil and Mexico, years of public neglect turned railways and water transport into the poorest productivity performers. Intensive use of bus transport contributed to relatively high productivity levels in road-passenger transport. The predominant position of road-passenger transport in both countries partly compensated the low performance in the other transport branches, resulting in a total performance of a third of the U.S. level in Brazil and 42 percent of the U.S. performance in Mexico.

Wholesale and retail trade was the predominant branch of the tertiary sector, accounting for about one third of total employment in all three countries. Food retailing in Brazil and Mexico performed poorly due to the predominance of small (informal) retail outlets in the total. The productivity gap between the countries in wholesale trade was smaller. Banking and insurance were among the most productive services in Brazil and Mexico. In Brazil,

Table 5. PPPs, Productivity Levels and Relative Prices, Brazil/U.S. and Mexico/U.S., 1975

Sector	Brazil/U.S.			Mexico/U.S.		
	Purchasing Power Parity (Fisher, /cruzeiros US$)	Value Added per Person Engaged, Brazil (US=100)	Relative Price Level Brazil (US=100)	Purchasing Power Parity (Fisher, pesos/US$)	Value Added per Person Engaged, Mexico (US=100)	Relative Price Level Mexico (US=100)
Agriculture	7.56	5.6	93	14.67	9.7	117
Mining	4.80	45.0	59	9.43	39.1	75
Total Primary Sector	7.14	4.3	88	12.71	9.5	102
Manufacturing	7.78	46.4	96	13.66	25.2	109
Construction	4.89	53.6	60	6.48	73.1	52
Total Secondary Sector	7.03	45.4	86	11.78	31.4	94
Public utilities	11.11	14.3	137	12.15	18.3	97
Transport	5.53	35.4	68	9.42	41.5	75
Communications	17.23	12.5	212	16.59	24.5	133
Distribution	8.78	42.8	108	11.36	33.5	91
Financial Services	11.05	51.3	136	14.78	58.7	118
Real Estate	7.39	33.5	91	13.08	33.4	105
Health Care	3.25	52.4	40	14.26	53.7	114
Education	7.15	52.4	88	6.52	73.6	52
Government	3.35	96.4	41	6.31	59.6	50
Other Services	6.66	41.8	82	10.29	47.5	82
Total Tertiary Sector	6.66	47.8	82	10.29	42.9	82
TOTAL (All sectors)	6.89	23.3	85	11.02	29.0	88

Source: Mulder (2000)

banks developed many profitable instruments to protect clients against high inflation. Moreover, they invested in computer technology to accelerate the processing of transactions.

In Brazil, health care was poorly adapted to the needs of the population. Expensive and inefficient hospital care for the rich and middle income class dominated, and resources to fight maternal, infant, and infectious diseases of the poor were relatively scarce. In Mexico, inefficient public hospitals mainly catered to the urban and insured people. Free care for the poor was rather scarce. In Brazil and Mexico, the quality of the educational system was also poor, as demonstrated by high repetition rates, high drop-out rates, and low scores on international tests. Surprisingly the relatively high productivity in 1975 resulted from the very low price of education in both countries, even after we adjusted for quality differences.

Productivity performance in Brazilian services was below that of the secondary sector, whereas Mexican services performed somewhat better than the secondary sector. Total economy performance was much lower than that of the secondary and tertiary sector, at 21 percent of the U.S. level in Brazil and 27 percent in Mexico. This is mainly due to the large weight that agriculture has in Brazil and Mexico.

Brazil showed very low productivity in agriculture, which stems from the dualistic nature of this sector. Most of the land is owned by a small elite and is cultivated with relatively modern machinery. The majority of farmers, however, owns only small plots of land and have little or no machinery. As a consequence their productivity is low. The huge expansion of the agricultural area has not improved the distribution of land very much. Although productivity is substantially higher in mining, the overall performance in the primary sector remained very low, as mining accounted for only 0.3 percent of employment in the primary sector in Brazil, as opposed to 18 percent in the United States. Mexico performed relatively better than Brazil in agriculture, which may be related to its more equal distribution of land.

V. Comparative Labor Productivity Performance, 1950-96

The labor productivity results for 1975 were extrapolated to 1950-96 (see figures 4 and 5). This was done by using time series of GDP at constant prices and employment (Mulder 2000). The low productivity levels of Brazilian and Mexican services, when compared to the United States in 1950, reflect their slow development in the previous century. The development of transport infrastructure was retarded in the two Latin countries when considered in relation to the United States. In 1870 there were already 85,000 km of railways in the United States as opposed to just a few hundred in Brazil and Mexico. The United States built extensive canal and road networks in the nineteenth century, whereas road building on a large scale did not start until the 1930s in Brazil and Mexico. Aviation developed rapidly in Brazil and Mexico. Compared to the United States, the Latin countries showed only a relatively small delay in development, partly on account of the poor situation of other modes of transport. In both Latin countries, the telegraph and telephone were introduced only a decade later than in the United States, but the spread of these mediums was rather slow.

In the United States, department stores and supermarkets were introduced at the end of the nineteenth and early twentieth centuries. In Brazil and Mexico, these formats were uncommon until after the 1950s. Heavy regulation in Brazil and political chaos in Mexico in the nineteenth century delayed the development of the financial system to the end of the nineteenth century, whereas the United States already had a banking network in the early nineteenth century. In Mexico, the Revolution retarded the development of the financial system by at least twenty years.

Health care and education in Brazil and Mexico also developed at a very slow pace in the nineteenth century. In Brazil, this was mainly due to the lack of interest of the imperial government, whereas in Mexico political turmoil was the major cause. At the turn of the century, the governments of both countries showed increased activities both in fighting infectious diseases and the improvement of public health. It was not until the 1930s that a public health system was established in the two Latin countries, which had already been developed in the United States in the nineteenth century. The development of education occurred at a very low pace in Brazil and Mexico. By 1890, less than 15 percent of the Brazilian and Mexican population could write, as compared to 85 percent in the United States. From the 1930s onwards, major efforts in both Latin countries improved schooling levels a little. In 1950, half of the population was still illiterate.

In Brazil, the relative productivity of services rose from 25 to 35 percent of the U.S. level in the 1950-82 period. Transport and communications was the branch with the lowest productivity level in 1950. Its relative performance doubled from 1950 to 1982. Initially the labor productivity performance in wholesale and retail trade was above that of most other services. Its performance remained constant until the early 1980s, after which it decreased due to the large expansion of informal employment with low productivity levels. In finance a catch-up process with the U.S. levels occurred in the 1950s, 1970s, and the second half of the 1980s. During these periods, banks earned high profits, which was due to the large spread between loan and deposit rates. In the course of time, productivity gains were also achieved by a large-scale merger process of the banking sector, resulting in a few dozen large banks, and large investments in computer technology. After 1990, productivity decreased. This was caused by the sharp fall in output and profits, which was only partly compensated by a reduction of employment. In the absence of value added trends for health care and education, these services were included in the category "other services." Until the 1982 crisis, this sector showed a small upward trend.

Figure 4. Value Added per Person Engaged, Brazil/U.S., 1950-96

U.S.=100

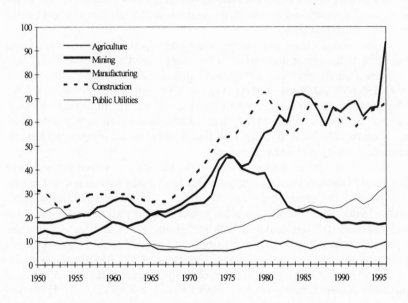

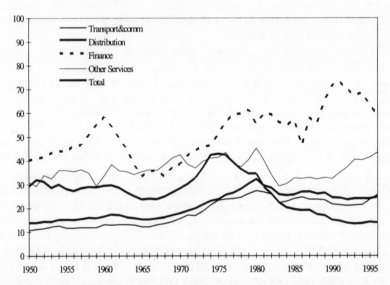

Sources: 1975 benchmark from Table 4 extrapolated with time series from Mulder (2000)

Figure 5. Value Added per Person Engaged, Mexico/U.S., 1950-96

U.S.=100

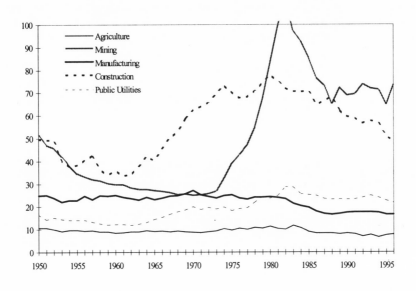

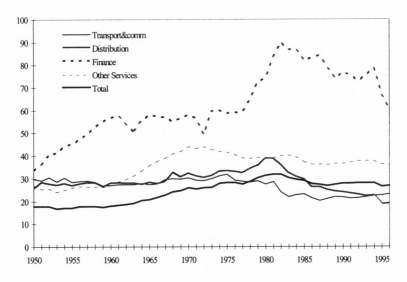

Sources: 1975 benchmark from Table 4 extrapolated with time series of Mulder (2000).

V. What Was the Impact of Differences in Production Structure?

The productivity performance of the total economy depends not only on the performance in the individual sectors, but also on differences between countries in the sectoral composition of GDP and employment. In 1950, the relatively low productivity levels of Brazil and Mexico were primarily due to the large share of agriculture in employment in both countries and their poor performance in this sector. In the course of time, employment shifted from agriculture to sectors with higher productivity levels. Employment shifts improved the overall productivity performance of Brazil and Mexico vis-à-vis the United States. International productivity differences are decomposed as follows (Mulder 2000):

$$\frac{P_m^X - P_m^U}{P_m^U} = \frac{\sum_{k=1}^{n} (P_k^X - P_k^U) * S_k^U}{\sum_{k=1}^{n} P_k^U} + \frac{\sum_{k=1}^{n} P_k^X * (S_k^X - S_k^U)}{\sum_{k=1}^{n} P_k^U} \tag{5}$$

with Y and L representing output and employment by sector (k=1..n) and the total economy (m), P representing productivity (Y/L), and S representing the sectoral employment share (Lk/Lm); X refers to Brazil or Mexico and U to the United States. The productivity gap between two countries consists of two parts: the first indicates the part due to labor productivity differences within sectors; and the second the part due to differences in structure. The ratio of each part to the total productivity gap indicates how much of the total gap it "explains."

Table 6 shows that these intrabranch productivity differentials accounted for more than 90 percent of the total productivity gaps. The part ascribed to structural differences was small, despite the distinct sectoral composition of the Latin and U.S. economies. The limited role of structural differences mainly resulted from the rather similar relative productivity levels between sectors, especially in the 1950s and after the 1980s. From 1950 to 1975, the size of the catch-up potential for structural-change productivity increased a little due to the growing productivity differentials between sectors. Nevertheless, the part ascribed to structural differences always remained below 10 percent of the total productivity gap between countries. From this, the conclusion may be drawn that the elimination of structural differences between the three countries would have only marginally reduced the productivity gap with the United States.

Table 6. Decomposition of Labor Productivity Differences: Brazil/U.S. and Mexico/U.S., 1950-96

	Brazil/U.S., contribution of:			Mexico/U.S., contribution of:		
	Intra-branch productivity differences	Structural differences	Total	Intra-branch productivity differences	Structural differences	Total
1950	97.8	2.2	100.0	94.5	5.5	100.0
1975	91.4	8.6	100.0	93.5	6.5	100.0
1982	94.8	5.2	100.0	94.2	5.8	100.0
1989	97.0	3.0	100.0	96.5	3.5	100.0
1996	97.3	2.7	100.0	97.2	2.8	100.0

Sources: 1975 from Table 5, other years obtained by extrapolating the 1975 benchmark with time series of GDP at constant prices and employment; see Mulder (2000).

VI. Conclusion

This chapter has aimed to compare Brazilian and Mexican productivity performance in services with that in other sectors of the economy, as well as in relation to the United States. In this way we may come to see how far the Latin American countries lagged behind the "best practice" and their potential for catch-up. Until 1982, the two Latin countries showed a modest catch-up with U.S. productivity levels, but their relative performance worsened later. When compared to the United States, performance in services in Brazil and Mexico after 1950 was slightly better than their relative performance in their secondary sectors. In both Latin countries, performance in the tertiary sectors was much better than in the primary sectors. In Brazil, productivity levels in the secondary and tertiary sectors rose approximately 10 percentage points from 1950 to 1982, reaching 35 percent of the U.S. level. In Mexico, the comparative performance in both sectors remained stable. From 1982 to 1996, the secondary sectors experienced a larger fall in productivity than in services in both countries,[5] despite the faster rate of employment growth in services. Productivity growth was most rapid in agriculture in Brazil and Mexico, but did not advance faster than in the United States.

From 1950 to 1982, the growth of output and labor productivity in services was stimulated by increasing per capita incomes, industrialization and urbanization, which raised the demand for final and intermediate services. Governments in both Latin countries promoted the development of public utilities, transport, communications, finance, education and health care by state ownership and subsidies. Productivity growth in services was somewhat higher in Brazil than Mexico. Brazil started from a lower level in 1950 and was able to achieve higher growth rates. In Brazil, inflation was an important stimulus to the expansion of the banking sector. At the same time this lowered demand for other services due to its negative impact on real incomes of the poor.

More research needs to be done to explain the tendency of faster catch-up (and smaller divergence after 1982) of productivity levels in the service sector, relative to the manufacturing sector, in Brazil and Mexico vis-à-vis the United States. Some argue that service production is much more homogeneous than goods production. Catch-up in services may be more rapid as similar types of technology are used in different countries and therefore technical diffusion is easier. In manufacturing, countries tend to specialize in the production of goods in which they have a comparative advantage. As countries produce a greater variety of goods, there are no a priori reasons why production tech-nologies should be the same or why they should converge in the course of time. Some catch-up does however occur in manufacturing, as there are spill-overs across goods (Bernard and Jones, 1996).

For the translation of productivity levels of each country into a common currency, PPPs based on sectoral comparisons have been used, with 1975 as the benchmark year. Prices in services often cannot be determined clearly, on account of intercountry variations in the quality of output, and therefore PPPs have to be derived implicitly. Quantities are relatively easy to measure in ser-vices like transport and communications, but measurements are extremely dif-ficult for comparison-resistant services such as education and health care. These difficulties arise from the intangible characteristics of services and the large quality differences between countries. In several Brazilian and Mexican services, quality adjustments were made, which increased their relative price and reduced their relative productivity levels.

In Brazil and Mexico, relative prices in services were below those of the commodity sector in 1975. In Mexico, lower relative prices in services partly resulted from smaller productivity differentials in this sector, when compared to the secondary sector in the United States. In Brazil, relative productivity in services was below that of the secondary sector despite the lower relative prices in the service sector. The PPPs for total GDP in both countries were be-low the exchange rate. Nevertheless, there are large differences in the price and productivity levels between service industries. In Brazil and Mexico, communications, financial services and public utilities were relatively expen-sive, while education and government services were less so in 1975. In turn, relative labor productivity levels were closely linked to prices, except for fi-nancial services which showed quite high productivity in Brazil and Mexico in 1975.

The measurement of output and prices in services still needs to be refined to improve its reliability. Conceptual and measurement problems still con-taminate our results. A lack of consensus on how to measure output leads to the use of various proxy indicators that may distort comparisons. Moreover, in Brazil and Mexico, the statistical apparatus for services is often inadequately developed, which limits the range of output indicators available.

Notes

[1] This paper is based on a larger study carried out mostly at the University of Groningen and published by Edward Elgar, see Mulder (2000).

[2] The impact of increased final and intermediate demand for services on the service share in employment and GDP is estimated on the basis of input-output tables. The first year for which these are available for both Brazil and Mexico is 1970. For the United States, I used the 1972 I/O table, which is closest to 1970. The most recent tables were for 1995 in Brazil, 1996 in Mexico and 1992 in the United States. Imported goods and services were excluded. The production structure based on the I/O table differs somewhat from that of GDP, as the demarcation of sectors is based on functional criteria in the former compared to institutional ones in the latter. According to the functional criteria, different types of output of a firm are allocated to the corresponding product or services categories in the I/O table, while according to institutional criteria, all the output of the firm is allocated to one sector based on its main activity. As such, an intertemporal analysis based on I/O data underestimates the growth of the service sector in institutional terms, as its breakdown is based on homogeneous types of goods and services, and not on the main activity of a firm or an establishment. On the contrary, an analysis based on of GDP trends overstates the growth of service output in functional terms, as many were previously produced within the firm, but outsourced later.

The intertemporal analysis of the I/O tables shows that the share of the service sector in total production increased from 29 to 36 percent in Brazil from 1970-95, from 24 to 30 percent in Mexico from 1970-96, and from 49 to 60 percent in the United States from 1972-92. Correspondingly, the shares of the commodity producing sector decreased.

[3] In 1970 the share of people under fifteen in the total population was 42, 46 and 28 percent in Brazil, Mexico and the United States, respectively. In 1995, the share had fallen to 32, 36 and 22 percent (World Bank, 1999).

[4] The share of people sixty years and older in total population increased from 10 percent in 1950 to 17 in 1990 in the United States, from 4 to 8 percent in Brazil, and remained stable at 4 percent in Mexico.

[5] From 1982 to 1996, the relative productivity level of services fell 9 points in Brazil compared to 5 points in Mexico. The performance of the secondary sector fell 12 points in Brazil and 9 points in Mexico.

References

Ark, B. van. 1993. "International Comparisons of Output and Productivity: Manufacturing Performance of Ten Countries from 1950 to 1990," *Monograph Series, No. 1*, Groningen Growth and Development Centre.

Baumol, W. J. 1967. "Macroeconomics of Unbalanced Growth: The Anatomy of Urban Crisis," *The American Economic Review* 57:415-26.

Bernard,-A.B. and C.I. Jones. 1996. "Comparing Apples to Oranges: Productivity Convergence and Measurement across Industries and Countries," *American Economic Review* 86:1216-38.

Gordon, R. J. 1996. "Problems in the measurement and performance of service-sector productivity in the United States," NBER Working Paper, No. 5519, Cambridge MA.

Hofman, A. 1999. *The Economic Development of Latin America in the Twentieth Century*. Edward Elgar, Aldershot.

Mulder, N. 2000. *The Economic Performance in the Americas: The Role of the Service Sector in Brazil, Mexico and the USA*, Edward Elgar, Cheltenham, forthcoming.

Paige, D. and G. Bombach. 1959. *A Comparison of National Output and Productivity of the United Kingdom and the United States*, OEEC and the University of Cambridge, Paris.

Pilat, Dirk. 1994. *The Economics of Rapid Growth, The Experience of Japan and Korea*. Edward Elgar, Aldershot.

Rostas, L. 1948. *Comparative Productivity in British and American Industries*, NIESR, Occasional Papers, No. 13, Cambridge University Press, Cambridge.

Squire, L. and K. Deininger. 1996. "A New Data Set Measuring Income Inequality," *World Bank Economic Review* 10:565-91.

World Bank. 1999. *World Development Indicators,* Washington DC.

Part 2. Services and Economic Development

CHAPTER 9

Globalization, Producer Services, and the City: Is Asia a Special Case?[*]

Peter W. Daniels

I. Introduction

The broad context for this chapter is the global dimension of the modern economy (Dicken, 1992; Dunning, 1993). Service industries' $18 trillion output is
the bulk of world production (Coalition of Service Industries, 1998). They account for close to 70 per cent of GDP in industrialized nations, and close to 50
per cent in developing ones. Trade in services now exceeds $2 trillion annu-
ally. It has grown faster than trade in goods and now accounts for at least 20
per cent of world trade (probably an underestimate because the most dynamic
trade in services, telecommunications, is not being properly measured, see
Hoekman and Braga, 1997). Services also now account for close to 60 per cent
of the world's foreign direct investment (FDI) (Landesmann and Petit, 1995;
UNCTAD, 1998). This growing visibility of services in the global economy is
largely a result of the integration of *producer services* into flows of FDI and
trade, especially amongst the leading players from the advanced economies such
as the United States (Daniels, 1993, 1999).

   This increased activity is being driven by powerful forces, including the
inexorable shift to knowledge-rich goods production that draws on producer
services, the impact of electronic commerce on trade in services, the deregulation and privatization of service industries, and the reliance of global multinational corporations on advanced services. Producer-service research has only
recently begun to incorporate the global dimension in analyses of growth and
change in the sector. Interest in the international dimension has emerged from
concern with balance-of-payments impacts as outlined by Howe and Markusen
(1993), and whether large or small communities are involved in the activity
(Beyers and Lindahl, 1996). Other approaches to the internationalization of
services have focused on specific sectors such as advertising (Cho, Choi and
Yi, 1994; Daniels, 1995b; Kim, 1995), banking (Grubel, 1977; Fujita, M,
1989; Laulajainen, 1998), engineering consultants (Rimmer, 1988), R&D
(Howells, 1990; Angel and Savage, 1996) and property services (Thrift, 1986).

One of the outcomes from these studies is the identification of a global hierarchy of cities of the kind illustrated by Sassen (1994) and for the Asia-Pacific region by Edgington and Haga (1998). Advanced producer services reveal a preference for locating in the world's major corporate complexes near to their competitors and many of their multinational clients. These cities are also well connected by transport and advanced telecommunications services both within their regional markets and globally. There is no reason to believe that Asian cities are not sharing in this process, but there is evidence to suggest that they are lagging behind their competitors in North America and Western Europe (Daniels, 1998). More research is undoubtedly required in order to understand what is going on, but the preliminary evidence suggests that while Asia has certainly become a major player in global manufacturing, this has not been matched by the performance of its services, especially advanced producer services. This is reflected in smaller shares of employment in these services in many Asian cities and, perhaps more important, a more limited presence of Asian producer-service firms in other global markets. One reason for this is the competitive advantage exerted by North American and European professional and business firms that, during the last 15-20 years, have been expanding vigorously into international markets through mergers and take-overs or the establishment of new local/regional offices. Most of the target markets are served from major cities with the extent of the overseas presence determined by local fiscal and regulatory requirements for service firms from outside the country.

After briefly examining some general data that attempts to put Asia's position in global service transactions in context, the remainder of this chapter reports some interviews with transnational service and manufacturing firms with offices and plants in Singapore and Hong Kong. These are used to identify some of the issues confronting international producer-service firms located in two key regional cities. The chapter is concluded with an outline for some further research on services trade and producer-service companies in the region.

II. Asian Services in the Global Economy

There are a number of indicators that can be used to assess the participation of Asian services in the global economy. Most of these are based on data for national economies rather than individual cities although it is safe to assume that many of the service functions involved are located in the major cities of each country.

Asian Service Corporations

The annual listings of the global top 500 service and manufacturing corporations show that Asian manufacturers are more prominent than service corporations, although the latter generated a larger share of the total revenues of the top 500 than manufacturing (Fig. 1). Over half (278) of the global 500 in 1996 were service corporations, but only 28 per cent (78) had their headquarters in Asia. On the other hand, the corporate revenues of Asia's service corporations (more than $2bn) amounted to approximately 35 per cent of the total for all service corporations. This compared with just over 28 per cent for Asian manufacturing corporations. The Asian service corporations in the top 500 were also much leaner (mean size = 32,600 employees) than their manufacturing counterparts (mean size = 53,016 employees) in 1996. Service firms with headquarters in Asia are most prominent in trading, where they account for 82 per cent of the 22 companies, and in insurance (life, health [mutual]) with 12 of the 19 in the global 500 in 1996 (see Appendix 1). The revenues of these two service types are also a major component of the global total for their categories; for most other categories of services the share of Asian corporate revenues is much more modest. There are also several types of services where Asia is not represented in the top 500. These include wholesalers, diversified financials, specialist retailers, insurance (property, casualty), food services, and healthcare. These data only refer to mutual and joint stock corporations; the growing number of professional and business-service firms that operate as partnerships or are not large enough to make the top 500 would also reveal modest representation of firms from Asia amongst the leading players. Most of the leading management consultants, accountants, advertising firms or corporate lawyers, for example, are based in North America or in parts of Europe such as the United Kingdom and France.

Balance of Trade, 1985-96

One of the consequences of the relatively weak representation of services, especially producer services, in a profile of Asian economies, is its impact on trade flows (Table 1). While the balance of trade in merchandise has fluctuated between positive and negative between 1985 and 1996, there has been a steady deterioration in the services balance of payments. This is the converse of the pattern for Europe which has consistently been in surplus on services trade and even more so for North America which has seen a strong increase in the positive balance for services as its merchandise deficit has continued to grow. Looked at another way, however, services exports from Asia and the Far East increased by 114 per cent between 1985-90 and 1991-96, ahead of merchandise that had equivalent figures of 90.3 per cent and 84.5 per cent respectively. These rates were just above the equivalent world figure for the first period and about twice the world rate for the second period. However, by comparison with the value of merchandise exports from the region (almost $US 1.5 trillion in 1996) the exports of services ($US 284 bn) is relatively insignificant. One final trade-related indication of the weak position of the Asian economies is their share of total world exports and total imports of merchandise and services (Fig. 2).

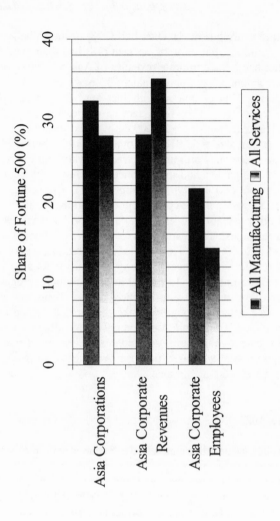

Figure 1. Asian Share of Fortune Top 500 Corporations, 1996

Figure 2. Share of World Exports and Imports, Merchandise (M) and Commercial Services (S), Asia, 1985-96

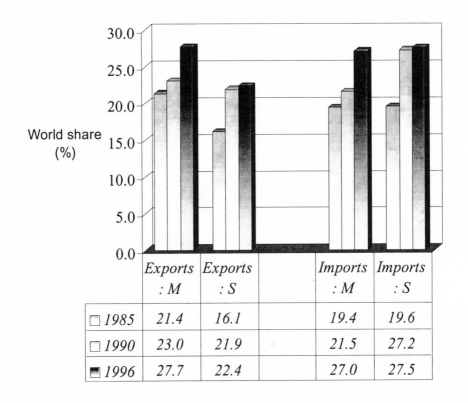

	Exports : M	Exports : S		Imports : M	Imports : S
☐ 1985	21.4	16.1		19.4	19.6
☐ 1990	23.0	21.9	.	21.5	27.2
■ 1996	27.7	22.4		27.0	27.5

Table 1. Balance of Trade in Merchandise and Commercial Services, by Value ($US Bn), World Regions, 1985-1996

	1985		1990		1996	
	Merchan-dise	Ser-vices	Merchan-dise	Ser-vices	Merchan-dise	Ser-vices
Asia and Far East	27	-16.1	30.2	-47.1	-9.5	-64.2
Africa	11.2	-9.6	7.3	-8.3	-4.6	-10.8
Latin America	25.6	-4.3	19.6	-5.2	-19.3	-8.8
Western Europe	-19.07	28.6	-63.22	21.9	36.49	31.4
North America	-123.86	2.5	-119.58	29.4	-171.21	67.3
Central and East-ern Europe/Baltic States/CIS	8	...	-8.3	...	-6.45	...
Middle East	13.4	...	34.6	...	20.8	...

Source: IMF, Balance-of-Payments Statistics; National Statistics and WTO
         Secretariat estimates

Although the region has consistently increased its share of total world trade between 1985 and 1996 for imports and exports, its share of service exports has always been 4-5 per percentage points behind its share of merchandise trade. On the other hand, its share of service imports has been higher than for manufacturing and significantly higher than the equivalent proportions for exports. While the world share of the region's commercial service exports increased from 16 per cent in 1985 to more than 22 per cent in 1996, its share of world commercial service imports also increased from almost 20 percent in 1985 to more than 27 per cent in 1996. Thus, while the region's share of merchandise imports and exports more or less balanced, the commercial services 'gap' was much larger. Data recently published by the EU (Commission of the European Communities, 1998) provide details of trade flows by sector between Japan and the EU-15, the United States and the rest of the world (Table 2) in 1996. This confirms the expected deficit in services trade, but perhaps more important in the context of this chapter, is the very large share of the deficit attributable to other services (including business and professional services). Well over half of the services trade deficit with the United States is in other services and almost 32 per cent in the case of the EU.

The dependence of Asian economies such as those of Japan, Singapore, Hong Kong or Malaysia on imports of high level services is often manifest, especially where the local regulatory environment permits, in the form of direct representation of U.S. and European service transnationals. The international expansion of leading firms in advertising, accountancy, management consulting, legal and computer services, for example, has been proceeding apace since the mid-1980s. This expansion has been driven in part by the demands of their clients and by new market opportunities in circumstances where local-producer-service provision has been inadequate for the needs of inward investors or for the requirements of indigenous enterprises looking to engage with international markets. This raises questions about how the emerging Asian economies, and especially the cities where the majority of advanced producer services are concentrated, move towards a situation in which domestic producer services work alongside or compete with overseas firms. Some of the issues that need to be addressed have been identified via a small number of face-to-face interviews with representatives of some major transnational service firms with offices in Singapore and Hong Kong (undertaken during November 1998 and May 1999).

Table 2. Balance of Trade (mill. ECU) in Merchandise and Services, Japan, 1996

Partner	Merchandise	Services	Other services %
Intra EU-15	12,882	-13,126	31.7
United States	29,353	-17,247	55.5
Rest of the world	52,995	-35,969	26.4

Source: European Communities, 1998, extracted from Table 22

III. Case Studies in Singapore and Hong Kong

Case 1: International Property Consultant, Singapore

Singapore is the economic hub for Southeast Asia. Its policies are designed to fend off efforts by Hong Kong, in particular, to exert a wider hegemony than at present. It is consciously trying to shift away from its dependence on manufacturing as a major contributor to GDP as it strives to become a global financial center. The Singapore financial markets are now more open, but there remains a need for further deregulation (even more so across the region). The majority of its service firms are not large enough to have international ambitions, but bank mergers, for example, will make DBS Bank better able to establish in markets outside the region. Over time it is expected that some other sectors may do the same, and this will encourage local firms to think globally rather than locally or regionally. The smaller size and limited diversity of advanced services in Singapore can be attributed to a lag effect between the core economies and the newly emerging economies of Asia. The process of 'catch-up' will be facilitated by an increasing trend towards deregulation of financial and other markets, freeing up the flow of capital and making the region more attractive for transnationals looking for alternative locations or new market opportunities. An example is the decision by Caltex to move its world HQ from Denver to Singapore. The skills gap between Asia and the core economies is also a problem, and rectification of this will also improve the competitiveness of service firms in the region. The National University of Singapore, for example, has been actively recruiting foreign staff and providing funds for overseas students undertaking Ph.D.s in Singapore as part of a strategy for encouraging more rapid knowledge transfer. Singapore more generally is actively encouraging firms to recruit foreign staff with high level skills for the same reason.

Their experience of decisions (including other transnational firms in Singapore) about sourcing advanced services that they use is that *consistency* and *quality* are key factors in supplier choice. At present, this tends to favor core economy suppliers, partly because local suppliers cannot match them and partly because the ambitions of local suppliers have been regional rather than international or global. It was noted that manufacturing transnationals based in the region that have expanded to other world locations have pulled indigenous service suppliers within them – these tend to serve Japanese or Korean clients, for example, rather than host region companies.

Case 2: International Legal Services Firm, Singapore and Hong Kong

This U.K.-based international legal firm opened its Singapore office in 1981, based largely on the intuition and enthusiasm of one particular partner. Much the same could be said of the Hong Kong office which was established in 1983. In both cases the initial reason for opening offices was to follow their clients. The current rationale is based on anticipated expansion of GDP (despite the recent setbacks) to a world share of about 27 per cent (about the same as the United States and Europe, respectively). The firm plans to be represented in all the major global cities and has recently taken a major step towards that goal. Thus, the Chinese market was largely serviced from the Hong Kong office until 1993. Since then the firm has opened offices in Shanghai (1993), Vietnam (1993), Ho Chi Minh City (1994), and Bangkok (1998) as part of its commitment to improving client services across Asia. This has again been partly dictated by clients, but is also based on the recognition of opportunities for new work.

The Singapore office has subsequently grown much more slowly than the Hong Kong office. The former has some 20 partners and 25 support staff and has contracted by more than 10 per cent following the recent crises in the region. The latter has 130+ staff and has experienced a more limited slowdown since early 1998. It is considered impractical to service the Singapore region (Indonesia especially) from Hong Kong or even further afield. Face-face-contact continues to be necessary for some legal negotiations and transactions.

The slower growth of fee income for the Singapore office was attributed to cultural and social factors. The firm experiences a reluctance by Singapore clients to pay appropriate fees for work similar to that undertaken in Hong Kong, and, as a result, it is sometimes difficult to collect fees. It was suggested that lawyers are held in low esteem in Singapore – even more so than is the case in most cities! For example, much of the work done for banking clients is delegated by them to the most junior staff who, in turn, treat the lawyers in a cavalier way. Local clients have a habit of calling in at 18.15 on a Friday with requests to get things off their desks 'by Monday,' i.e., 'on Monday.' There is no hesitation about listening to the advice provided by one of the firm's lawyers and then telling one partner in a deal one thing and another something else. If thus queried by the lawyer, they are told that they are there to do what they are told. Therefore, from this particular firm's perspective, the social and cultural milieu for conducting business is not helpful. The insularity of the Singaporeans is regarded as a real problem; young, enthusiastic lawyers seconded by the firm from London, for example, soon become deflated. Even relationships with local partners of the firm can give rise to difficulties.

Therefore, over the years the proportion of work for Singapore-based clients has fallen. The firm tends to act much more for clients in other jurisdictions, and these tend to be the same financial institutions and manufacturing multinationals that appear in the top ten or twenty list of clients by fee income for each of their offices around the world. Last year only three Singapore-based enterprises appeared in the top ten clients of that office. All were negotiating atypical business that is unlikely to be repeated (bearing in mind that the office specializes in advice, etc. regarding loans). This situation partly reflects the fact that the firm cannot practice Singapore law and is not allowed to recruit staff to train them in European law or in Singaporean law. This is very different from Hong Kong where the environment for legal practices is more open. There are only three 'local partners.' Most of the others are seconded primarily from London, although they have varied national backgrounds (Indian, Malaysian, Australian etc). The firm is desperate to find a lawyer specializing in mergers and acquisitions, but with no success so far. It was thought ironic that Singapore sends so many students to graduate in the United Kingdom and elsewhere, but will not allow legal firms to recruit individuals trained in Anglo-Saxon law.

Indeed, it is important not to understate the hegemony of U.S. and English law for the legal aspects of all international cross-border transactions. This means that the established U.S. and European legal firms (providing banking or corporate legal services for example) have deep-rooted and long-established comparative advantage over local legal firms. In China, for example, until very recently legal or banking advice was provided by state-run firms, often without the protection provided by insurance in the event of the client suing the adviser. This regularly happens to international legal firms, but their clients know that they will have proper redress because the necessary professional indemnity cover has been deployed. It is therefore not surprising that overseas firms making inward investments use well established professional service firms to assist with the process.

The Hong Kong office was more upbeat about its client relations. The banking side of the business is very much concerned with servicing international (rather than local) clients. The corporate side depends on new clients from the region rather than long-established international clients. This has made it more vulnerable to local economic fluctuations. Prior to the 1997 financial crisis, the Chinese family networks were seeking new sources of finance, etc., and turned to international legal firms to give their plans the legitimacy afforded by using them as advisers. This activity collapsed after 1997 when few lenders were prepared to look at such opportunities, and the family networks themselves faced financial difficulties and became more inward looking again. Because of this, during the last few years the corporate side of the firm has returned to acting on behalf of North American and West European clients, exploring acquisitions and other opportunities in Asia.

Over the years decisions on the consumption of services have become more centralized and controlled from London. There is a regional sub-group for services acquisition in Hong Kong, but it does what it is told by London. The firm may buy IT equipment locally, for example, but the advice and expertise behind this is purchased from elsewhere, usually Europe. Anything to do with promoting a coherent image for the firm is done centrally; auditors are chosen centrally rather than by the branch offices as in the past. Even the business cards handed out by individual staff are printed in London! Smaller tasks such as invitations to functions in Singapore or Hong Kong will be sourced locally. There is clearly considerable leakage of expenditures back to London. It was also observed that if the firm wants new office space, for example, it is much more likely to seek assistance from core-economy international property consultants with offices in each city, thus reinforcing the 'external' orientation of service multinationals in the region.

Case 3: Asian Service Multinationals: Major International Bank, Singapore

It may be equally instructive to examine the experience of service multinationals that derive the majority of their business from Asia. This bank has a regional headquarters in Singapore responsible for an area extending from Japan to Burma, with 70 per cent of profits derived from business in the region. With European and North American banks downsizing or leaving the region altogether in the wake of the recent financial crises, this bank is maintaining or even extending its presence. It called in many loans (1,000 a year in 1997 and 1998) in anticipation of the crisis. As the region's major conglomerates are offloading all but their core activities in an effort to remain solvent, the bank has begun to target small and medium enterprises, which will become even more important as this process continues. It recognizes, however, that advanced services (including the financial services sector) lag behind the core economies. This contributed in part to the recent financial crisis (i.e., bank lending practices have not matched the more rigorous standards applied by core-economy financial services).

Government protection has also delayed the growth of advanced services; there has been a more open attitude to manufacturing growth. Domestic Japanese, Korean and Taiwanese financial services have not been strong enough to match the expansion of manufacturing, hence the tendency for leakage of consumption of these services to the core economies. The expansion of the Asian economies has been much more compressed in time. Advanced services need soft and hard infrastructure at a much higher level than manufacturing. Rules and regulations can be changed overnight, but factors such as human resources and skills grow at their own pace. There is certainly a skills gap, and this will take time to rectify. It is not clear whether government involvement with producers/markets (as in Japan or Korea in particular) is really an impediment to services expansion.

Critical mass is crucial to the provision of diverse and high quality advanced services. They need brainpower, experience and infrastructure. Because this is not yet in place in Singapore, there is undoubtedly leakage of demand to the core economies. The bank therefore regularly uses international management consultants such as McKinsey or the leading international computer services firms. Only services that require local knowledge, such as marketing or advertising for example, are purchased from Singapore. Its policy for executive transport within the region is to use Singapore Airlines because it has the best network, high standards, etc. In this respect, the service relationship works two ways. Nevertheless, it is likely that the bank and other transnationals in Singapore will continue to suffer leakage of demand to suppliers in the core economies. As to the future of Singapore as an advanced service center, it is perhaps fortunate not to be as focused as Hong Kong, which is highly dependent on China for a good part of its services trade. Singapore is still primarily oriented to Southeast Asia (Indonesia, Malaysia, Thailand), but these relatively diverse connections spread the risk. There is scope for Singapore to expand into Hong Kong territory because of the latter's heavy dependence on China. Singapore needs to grow in stages, and it is moving away from hinterland-led growth.

Case 4: Asian-based Trading Company, Hong Kong

This trading company employs 250,000 worldwide and is centrally managed by 25 executives and staff from an office in central Hong Kong. Almost all its business is in services, ranging from security services, to vehicle dealerships, to investment banking. Some 86 per cent of turnover is generated from its business within the Asia. Nevertheless the company's primary listing is on the London Stock Exchange with a secondary listing on the Singapore Exchange, to which it was moved from Hong Kong in anticipation of the uncertainties that might follow the handover to China in 1997. The company sees itself as a multinational at the heart of Asia, but 60 per cent of its business is in Hong Kong and China. It therefore needs to expand within the region, in addition to adopting more global aspirations. Most of the offices of companies in the group are based in Hong Kong, with the most recent established in Shanghai, Beijing and Guangzhou. The group has more joint ventures (70+) in China than any other major service transnational. Most of these, in common with similar activities by other transnationals are not very profitable at present (following the financial crisis). Because it has its roots, as well as knowledge and experience, that are partly linked with London and Europe, it may find it easier to fulfil this ambition than some other Asian service companies with global ambitions (all of whose roots lie in the region). The success of the strategy will depend upon the performance of the various individual groups within the company. It was suggested that each group should not be waiting for global competitors to come to Asia, rather they should be looking to increase their profile in Europe and elsewhere.

However, this is easier said than done because one of the disadvantages of being a transnational embedded in Asia is that many of the human resources are not at the leading edge of international business practice. Young staff are given responsibility early for larger groups of staff than their opposite number in Europe, at the expense of gaining the knowledge and experience that proves advantageous later. This observation emerged from a discussion about the recruitment of high quality, highly qualified staff from within Asia. It was acknowledged that it is difficult to find appointees of a suitable caliber for senior positions; they must be imported and/or responsibility given to individuals earlier in their career than is optimal. Once good staff are recruited, especially Hong Kong residents, they tend to stay with the company. Young European and North American recruits have to think about whether their limited exposure to leading-edge knowledge and business techniques in Hong Kong will make it difficult for them to return to work in Europe.

Apart from public relations, which is sourced locally for most parts of the group, it produces services internally, such as training, corporate communications, payroll and personnel management, routine legal work, internal management audits (non-mandatory) and routine legal work, because there is no suitable provision locally. Higher-level producer services are either imported from Europe and North America or acquired from the local offices of international professional and business-service providers. Reputation, brand, reliability, trust and the quality of the advice available all determine the choices. There are no indigenous providers that can really match the services offered by service transnationals from outside the region. The company purchases substantial quantities of computer software from computer-service firms in India. It costs much less than equivalent quality work provided by U.K. consultants, for example. A third type of outsourcing by the company, some of which is for services, is based on price rather than reputation. There is a group-wide agreement with United Parcel Services, for example, or with Shell for oil and oil products. Most indigenous firms cannot compete on price either, simply because they are not large enough to command the scale economies achievable by large transnationals. In view of this, the company thought it unlikely that there would be a dramatic shift to local sourcing, especially of higher order services.

Case 5: Manufacturing Transnational (ASEAN Regional HQ), Singapore

Singapore makes sense for this major manufacturing firm because it is considered easy to fly in and out and is at the center of one of the largest single concentrations of population in the world (mostly within 4 hours flying time). The stable government control, strong but not intrusive, is seen as an advantage. Asia is regarded as offering significant growth potential for the kinds of consumer goods produced by the company. However, it was suggested that growth has been forced upon Asia when it was not ready. People and countries are going with the flow, but they do not really know why. Even governments and state regulators do not understand the rapidity of the adjustments needed or expected. Even if suitable advanced services are available locally (and this is not often the case), it takes longer for them to understand the needs of transnationals because most local service firms are only just starting out. They simply do not possess the depth or breadth of expertise that will satisfy the expectation of indigenous or overseas transnationals.

It is more difficult to build a service mentality than a manufacturing mentality. Asia is very culturally and ethnically diverse, and this makes it a difficult for services. Knowledge based on management recipes transferred from elsewhere does not work. Perhaps one of the reasons why indigenous advanced services have found it difficult to become competitive is the preference (both in Singapore and elsewhere) for individuals to want to work for themselves. There is family pressure to do so – thus graduates will start working with a large international firm to gain experience and knowledge and may make several moves between such firms over a short period before setting up their own consultancies, etc. Certainly, staff turnover in recent years amongst Singapore's large firms has been high (although this has slowed in the present economic climate). Once these small businesses are set up, they lose the scope of their much larger competitors and find it difficult to grow and to expand market share in any meaningful way. This suggests that external suppliers of advanced services will continue to hold sway. It may take ten or more years for the necessary adjustments to allow local service firms to be genuine alternatives. Indeed, the producer services gap in Asia could widen before it narrows (if it ever does so). In this regard, Singapore is a very special (almost atypical place) in the region. Nowhere else comes anywhere near it for infrastructure, environment, or economic and political stability.

This transnational's preference for internal production of advanced services is now beginning to shift. It is currently undergoing a major restructuring that will include a critical assessment of the value of obtaining externally purchased services that are only needed infrequently or that can offer superior advice in areas such as information technology policy and implementation or advertising. Initially, external purchases will be controlled from the U.S. world headquarters, and it is estimated that it will be at least ten years before there is substantial dependence on local suppliers of advanced services.

IV. Further Research and Conclusion

These and other interviews (not discussed here) suggest a number of factors that help to explain the relative absence of advanced producer services, especially indigenous suppliers in major Asian cities. The most obvious factor is the recent expansion into Asia of service transnationals that have followed clients but also captured local clients. This results in transactions that are service imports. Several respondents agreed that there is significant repatriation of fee and other income to the core economies. The scope for import substitution through the supply of advanced services by local firms to national and international firms in the local economy is held back because of the significant competitive edge held by overseas service transnationals. The future role of indigenous service firms will depend on their ability to acquire the knowledge, expertise and standards of service expected by their local and/or national market clients. Some of these may be service and manufacturing transnationals that are looking for opportunities to purchase services locally or, as noted above, are exploring the scope for higher levels of outsourcing than has been the case in the past. This could benefit local advanced service suppliers. But they, and their clients, are faced with a variety of human resource and cultural issues that, at least in the medium term, suggest that it will be difficult for them to provide the level and quality of service expected. In the meantime, demand will continue to 'leak' to suppliers in the core economies.

Many of these problems revolve around the dynamics of the relationship between clients, service suppliers and their markets.. These can be represented as a simple model (Table 3). There are three stages: Stage 1, a bi-polar market structure comprising (1a), foreign service providers meeting the needs of foreign clients, and (1b), national service providers meeting the needs of national clients; Stage 2, foreign service providers meet the needs of national clients; and Stage 3, national service providers meet the needs of foreign clients. Examples of Stage 1 include instances where foreign clients always insist on foreign service providers, or foreign service firms may be barred by regulation from servicing national market clients. This will limit the demand for national providers to national clients who may engage transnational service providers to gain access to better international contacts and skills (Stage 2). It is also possible that foreign clients will seek out national service providers to take advantage of specific local knowledge or in response to Government pressure (Stage 3). Different types of producer services will have different attitudes to the linkages implied by the above framework and to the stages outlined. The relative importance of each stage may vary between markets (countries). Thus, the growth of advanced producer services will be shaped by the mix and attitude of foreign firms, the regulatory environment and the capacity of national service providers to adapt and respond to the competition from transnational service companies.

Table 3. Simple Stage Model of the Relationship between National/Foreign Service Firms and Their Clients

Clients	National Service Firms	Foreign Service Firms
National	Stage 1a	Stage 2
Foreign	Stage 3	Stage 1b

This is important because the way that accounting and advertising firms, for example, organize and restructure in response to opportunities (in North America, Japan and Europe) shapes the local outcome for service-sector growth (Bagchi-Sen and Sen, 1997). A strong theme, reiterated by Dicken (1994) and by Fujita (1998), is *follow-the-leader* behavior. However, this perspective may be rather limited in that it relegates producer services to a secondary role and overlooks the way in which they can create opportunities that encourage or enable production to take place in other sectors. Ho's (1998) work on regional headquarter location in the Asia-Pacific region recognizes this broader scope. The business environment at the destination location will influence firm behavior and how it changes over time as it becomes more embedded in the host city/economy.

The emerging markets in Asia therefore provide a very different context for exploring the development of producer services. Research to date (Daniels, 1998) and the information outlined earlier in this chapter suggest that service-sector development, especially producer services, has lagged behind the region's success in manufacturing growth and trade. Notwithstanding the apparently slower growth, the organization and production of services in the region is also probably more diverse than elsewhere. The activity of North American and European transnational service corporations takes place alongside the considerable service activity embedded in Japanese *keiretsus* and Korean *chaebol*. In addition, Chinese family networks provide yet another organizational structure for the production of services, as outlined by Yueng and Olds (1999). This diversity presents a formidable challenge to researchers trying to understand how advanced services produced by Asian firms will emerge to compete at the national and international levels with the established players (O'Connor and Hutton, 1998).

Note

* I would like to acknowledge the invaluable discussions about some of the ideas and issues outlined in this paper with Kevin O'Connor, Department of Geography and Environmental Science, Monash University during a short visit to Melbourne as Faculty of Arts Visiting Scholar during November/December 1998.

References

Angel, D. P. and L. A. Savage. 1996. "Global localisation? Japanese research and development laboratories in the USA," *Environment and Planning A* 28:819-33.

Baghi-Sen, S. and J. Sen. 1997. "The current state of knowledge in international business in producer services," *Environment and Planning A* 29:1153-74.

Beyers, W. B. and D. Lindahl. 1996. "Explaining the demand for producer services: is cost driven externalisation the major factor?" *Papers of the Regional Science Association* 75:351-74.

Cho, D-S, J. Choi, and Y. Yi. 1994. "International advertising strategies by NIC multinationals: the case of a Korean firm," *International Journal of Advertising* 13:77-92.

Coalition of Service Industries. 1998. *CSI Reports: The Service Economy*. Washington, D.C.: CSI.

Daniels, P. W. 1993. *Service Industries in the World Economy*. Oxford: Blackwell.

Daniels, P. W. 1995. "The internationalization of advertising services in a changing regulatory environment," *The Service Industries Journal* 15:276-94.

Daniels, P. W. 1998. "Economic development and producer services growth: the APEC experience," *Asia Pacific Viewpoint* 39:145-59.

Daniels, P. W. 1999. "Overseas investment by US service enterprises," in Taylor, P and Slater, D (eds.), *The American Century: Consensus and coercion in the projection of American power*. Oxford: Blackwell.

Dicken, P. 1992. *Global Shift: The internationalization of economic activity*, 2nd Ed. London: Paul Chapman.

Dicken, P. 1994. "Global-local tensions: firms and states in the global space-economy," *Economic Geography* 70:101-28.

Dunning, J. H. 1993. *Multinational Enterprises and the Global Economy*. Berkshire: Addison-Wesley.

Edgington, D. W. and H. Haga. 1998. "Japanese service sector multinationals and the hierarchy of Pacific Rim cities," *Asia Pacific Viewpoint* 39: 161-78.

European Communities. 1998. *International Trade in Services, EU, 1987-96*. Luxembourg: Office des publications officielles des Communautés européennes.

Fujita, K. 1998. "Financial crisis and development in Asian global cities," paper presented at a Workshop on Globalising Asian Cities, Nordic Institute for Asian Studies, University of Helsinki, 22-23 May.

Fujita, M. 1989. "Internationalization of Japanese commercial banking and the yen: the recent experience of city banks," in R. Sato and T. Negishi (eds.), *Developments in Japanese Economics*. Tokyo: Academic Press.

Grubel, H. 1977. "A theory of multinational banking," *Banca Nazionale del Lavoro Quarterly Review* 123:349-64.

Ho, K. C. 1998. "Corporate regional functions in the Asia Pacific," *Asia Pacific Viewpoint* 39:179-191.

Hoekman, B. and C.A.P. Braga. 1997. "Protection and trade in services: a survey." *Open Economies Review* 8:285-308.

Howells J.R.L. 1990. "The internationalization of R & D and the development of global research networks," *Regional Studies* 24:495-512.

Kim, K. K. 1995. "Spreading the net: the consolidation process of large transnational advertising agencies in the 1980s and early 1990s," *International Journal of Advertising* 14:195-217.

Landesmann, M. A. and P. Petit. 1995. "International trade in producer services - alternative explanations," *The Service Industries Journal* 15:123-61.

Laulajainen, R. 1998. *Financial Geography: a Banker's View.* Gothenburg: Gothenburg School of Economics and Commercial Law.

O'Connor, K. and T. Hutton. 1998. "Producer services in the Asia Pacific region: an overview of research issues," *Asia Pacific Viewpoint* 39:139-44.

Rimmer, P. J. 1988. "The internationalization of engineering consultancies: problems of breaking into the club," *Environment and Planning A* 20:761-88.

Thrift, N. 1986. "The internationalization of producer services and the integration of the Pacific Basin property market," in M. J. Taylor and N. J. Thrift (eds.), *Multinationals and the Restructuring of the World Economy, The Geography of Multinationals,* Vol. 2, London: Croom Helm.

UNCTAD. 1998. *World Investment Report 1998: Trends and Determinants.* Geneva: UNCTAD.

Yueng, H. W-C. and K. Olds. (eds.) 1999. *The Globalisation of Chinese Business Firms.* London: Macmillan.

Appendix 1

Table A1. Service Corporations in the *Fortune* Top 500, 1996: Asia and World

Sector	Companies (No.)			Revenues ($mill)		Employees (No.)	
	A	B	A%B	C	%World	D	%World
Trading	18	22	81.8	1011875	90.3	301576	46.8
Miscellaneous	4	6	66.7	44492	67.5	65135	35.0
Insurance (Life, Health (Mutual)	2	19	63.2	327220	72.7	440220	77.5
Publishing, Printing	1	4	50.0	22945	46.7	65780	38.5
Hotels, Casinos, Resorts	3	2	50.0	14061	58.0	10240	5.1
Railroads	4	7	42.9	44416	44.2	153110	20.0
General Merchandisers	1	14	28.6	64941	18.0	78995	3.7
Securities	17	4	25.0	22694	30.2	1790	2.5
Banks: Commercial And Savings	6	69	24.6	235784	18.8	337140	12.7
Food and Drug Stores	3	27	22.2	95808	21.1	604655	24.4
Insurance: Life, Health (Stock)	1	16	18.8	37930	13.2	36710	9.2
Entertainment	3	6	16.7	9936	14.3	26513	8.4
Insurance: Property, Casualty (Stock)	1	20	15.0	40412	8.7	35672	5.5
Airlines	1	7	14.3	13913	14.3	19046	4.3
Mail, Package and Freight Delivery	1	8	12.5	23689	13.7	142538	6.2
Telecommunications	1	22	4.5	78321	14.7	230300	10.7
Wholesalers	0	9	0.0	0	0.0	0	0.0
Diversified Financials	0	5	0.0	0	0.0	0	0.0
Specialist Retailers	0	5	0.0	0	0.0	0	0.0
Insurance: Property, Casualty (Mutual)	0	2	0.0	0	0.0	0	0.0
Food Services	0	2	0.0	0	0.0	0	0.0
Health Care	0	2	0.0	0	0.0	0	0.0
All Services	78	278	28.1	2088437	35.2	2549420	14.3

Notes: A = Asia; B = World; C = Asia; D = Asia
Source: Compiled from data in *Fortune*, 4 August 1997

CHAPTER 10

Electronic Commerce in Developing Countries: Issues for Domestic Policy and WTO Negotiations[*]

Catherine L. Mann

I. Introduction

Electronic commerce and its related activities over the Internet can be the engines that improve domestic economic well-being through liberalization of domestic services, more rapid integration into globalization of production, and leap-frogging of available technology. Since electronic commerce integrates the domestic and global markets from its very inception, negotiating on trade issues related to electronic commerce will, even more than trade negotiations have in the past, demand self-inspection of key domestic policies, particularly in telecommunications, financial services, and distribution and delivery. Because these sectors are fundamental to the workings of a modern economy, liberalization here will rebound to greater economic well-being than comparable liberalization in more narrowly focussed sectors. Thus, the desire to be part of the e-commerce wave can be a powerful force to erode domestic vested interests that have slowed the liberalization of these sectors.

Technical aspects of electronic commerce, its complexity and the characteristic of network externalities should change the way that developing countries approach the external negotiating process. Specifically, the complexity of negotiations will require more cooperative effort among countries through their regional forums such as APEC and FTAA, which heretofore have operated at the periphery of the WTO process. Second, since electronic commerce is characterized by network externalities, developing countries should take advantage of the technical leadership coming out of the private sector in the most advanced countries (and their own private sector, even if nascent) and "draft" in behind. Standing on the shoulders of giants makes sense when network externalities and interoperable standards are key to maximizing the benefits of e-commerce. Trying to develop domestic standards or following the old tech-

---

nique of import substitution to develop a domestic industry is even more economically wasteful in the context of the Internet and electronic commerce than
it was in more traditional sectors.

Trade negotiations are often the tool used to liberalize domestic sectors.
But the complementarity between domestic policy and trade strategy is tighter
in the case of e-commerce and the Internet. Moreover, this complementarity
emphasizes that e-commerce is neither a service, nor a good, but something
that is comprised of both. In the context of the WTO commitments, embracing
this idea could lead to a liberalizing bias in favor of electronic delivery of
goods and services as compared to delivery by another scheduled mode. For
example, insurance products could be sold over the Internet even if the physical presence of a foreign insurance firm was not scheduled for liberalization
under GATS. Rather than view this outcome with alarm, developing countries
should embrace it as a positive force that furthers the development both of
electronic commerce, as well as encourages deeper liberalization and deregulation throughout the economy.

II. Electronic Commerce Merges Domestic and International Marketplaces

"Electronic commerce" is a shorthand term that embraces a complex amalgam
of technologies, infrastructures, processes, and products. It brings together
whole industries and narrow applications, producers and users, information
exchange and economic activity into a global marketplace called "the Internet." There is no universal definition of electronic commerce because the
Internet marketplace and its participants are so numerous and their intricate relationships are evolving so rapidly.[1] Nonetheless, one of the best ways of understanding electronic commerce is to consider the elements of its infrastructure, its impact on the traditional marketplace, and the continuum of ways in
which electronic commerce is manifested. This approach shows clearly how
electronic commerce is intricately woven into the fabric of domestic economic
activity and international trade.

Electronic commerce as it has evolved today requires three types of infrastructure:

- *Technological infrastructure to create an Internet marketplace.* Electronic
  commerce relies on a variety of technologies, the development of which is
  proceeding at breakneck speeds (e.g., interconnectivity among telecommunications, cable, satellite, or other Internet 'backbone'; Internet service
  providers (ISPs) to connect market participants to that backbone; and end-
  user devices such as PCs, TVs, or mobile telephones).
- *Process infrastructure to connect the Internet marketplace to the traditional marketplace.* This infrastructure makes payment over the Internet
  possible (through credit, debit, or Smart cards, or through online currencies). It also makes possible the distribution and delivery (whether online

or physical) of those products purchased over the Internet to the consumer.

- *"Infrastructure" of protocols, laws, and regulations.* This infrastructure affects the conduct of those businesses engaging in and impacted by electronic commerce, as well as the relationships between businesses, consumers, and government. Examples include: technical communications and interconnectivity standards; the legality and modality of digital signatures, certification, and encryption; and disclosure, privacy, and content regulations.

Together, these infrastructures enable electronic commerce to innovate the traditional marketplace in three ways:

- *Process innovations:* Electronic commerce simplifies, makes more efficient, reduces costs, or otherwise alters the process by which an existing transaction takes place. For example, Cisco Systems replaced its phone and fax ordering process with an online ordering process and saved more than one-half billion dollars and reduced error rates from 25 percent to 2 percent.[2] Boeing used computer-aided design and electronic communication to coordinate 238 design teams in the globalized production of the 777 aircraft, a process never before attempted in this way, and which cut error rates by 50 percent, and reduced both costs and time to market.[3]

- *Product innovations:* Electronic commerce creates or facilitates new industries and products not previously available. For example, MP3 both enables consumers to play music downloaded from a computer and enables musicians to upload music directly to the Internet, thereby creating a new medium to produce and consume music; WebMD repackages existing health information in an easy-to-use online format, offers opportunities to "chat" with people with similar health concerns, and provides "real-time" responses to health questions.

- *Market innovations*: Electronic commerce also creates new markets in time, space, and in information that heretofore did not exist because transaction and coordination costs were prohibitively high. For example, the online bank Wingspan offers 24-hour bill payment features; PeopleLink is a global advertising location for artisans in remote parts of Latin America and Africa; reverse auctions through Priceline inform businesses of the exact price a consumer is willing to pay for the products, as well as reduce the consumer's purchase cost.

In reviewing the infrastructures that make electronic commerce possible, as well as the impact electronic commerce has on the traditional marketplace, we can see how electronic commerce is intricately woven into the fabric of domestic economic activity and international trade.

- *The infrastructures on which e-commerce depends also are key to domestic activity.* The three service-sector infrastructures of telecoms, financial services, and distribution and delivery are critical components for overall economic activity. Comprehensive liberalization of services could raise global GDP by 4 to 6 percentage points—twice that credited to the Uruguay Round—as well as raise the long-run global growth rate from 3.2 to 5.0 percent.[4] While the transition to liberalization is almost never without cost, liberalizing services promises more comprehensive benefits since services are an input to production in virtually all sectors of the economy. In contrast, liberalization of selected goods sectors has a narrower conduit through which it affects the overall economy.

- *Electronic commerce is global from the very start.* While traditional borders still matter in the world of international trade, electronic commerce diminishes their importance. No longer do customers need to be physically present to see or hear what they are buying. As a result, companies on the Internet instantly become international: Amazon was selling books to customers in over 40 countries in its first *month* of existence; the company now sells a variety of products to customers in over 160 countries. The electronic marketplace is currently free from explicit trade barriers. The absence of international tariffs or other barriers on electronic commerce encourages more people to try and to continue using the Internet marketplace, creating a greater level of efficiency and economic benefit for its participants.

- *Electronic commerce is integral to existing WTO commitments.* While there are currently no explicit trade barriers on electronic commerce, the infrastructures that make electronic commerce possible are still burdened by a myriad of trade and investment barriers. The growth of electronic commerce depends on continued liberalization of these infrastructures, many of which are already part of WTO commitments. Most important are computers and other information technology products (covered by ITA I and under consideration for ITA II), telecommunications (covered by the Basic Telecommunications Agreement), financial services (addressed in the Financial Services Agreement), distribution (relevant under TRIMS), and delivery services (under consideration for GATS 2000), among others. Exploiting the synergies among these service sectors allows electronic commerce to flourish and maximizes economic benefits.

III. Electronic Commerce is Gaining as an Economic Activity

Estimates of the growth of Internet usage and electronic commerce both within domestic markets and worldwide are notorious for their hyperbole. Even so, each year the actual growth has surpassed the estimate rather than falling short of it. Respected sources such as Forrester Research expect worldwide electronic commerce revenues to surpass $300 billion by 2002 and accelerate to $1.3 trillion in 2003. Currently an overwhelming (close to 85%) share of electronic commerce is concentrated in the United States, but diffusion into Europe and Asia, followed by Latin America and Africa will be rapid.

In developing countries Internet use and its economic potential are growing exponentially. The share of active Internet users in the Asia/Pacific Rim, Latin America, and "rest of world" could increase from 23 percent in 1999 to 35 percent in 2002.[5] In India, for example, the number of Internet users nearly doubled in the last year to 270,000, and could rise to over 2 million by the end of 2000.[6] E-commerce revenues could jump from $2.8 million in 1998 to $575 million in 2002. In China, a reported 60 percent of businesses are using the Internet, and e-commerce revenues could rise from $11.7 million in 1998 to $1.9 billion in 2002.[7] In Latin America, Internet usage rose nearly eight-fold between 1995 and 1997 with revenues estimated to be $167 million in 1998 and projected to be $8 billion by 2003.[8] Africa is fully wired now that Somalia recently added its first ISP; in South Africa, electronic commerce is expected to generate US $1.1 billion in 1999.[9]

Two important facts about e-commerce are often overlooked. First, the vast bulk of the actual and to an even greater extent the expected growth in revenues from e-commerce comes from business-to-business transactions. In 1998, the ratio of B-to-B over B-to-C was 5.5 to 1; but by 2003 the ratio is expected to be 12 to 1. Second, in virtually all countries other than the United States, electronic commerce is export oriented. In the United States, the share of export sales in total e-commerce revenues is only 10 percent, but in Canada it is 83 percent, in Latin America it averages 79 percent, and in Asia/Pacific it is 38 percent.[10]

Moreover, the nature of the production process (comprising both manufacturing and services) is becoming increasingly fragmented and globalized.[11] Multinational firms and strategic business alliances communicate, get price quotes, submit bids, transfer data, produce product designs, and basically *do business* in an international arena. Countries that do not have an environment conducive to Internet usage and electronic commerce will be marginalized from the globalized production process and global economy, at increasingly great cost to their citizens.

These observations have important implications for both domestic policy and international negotiations. First, business-to-business transactions often build on existing legal and regulatory foundations from physical trade so that issues of content, liability, and encryption are more easily surmounted. On the other hand, the importance of B-to-B and the desire to create a level playing field for all size businesses highlight the need for the international arena to offer a transparent and codified approach to these issues.

IV. Domestic Reforms Will Speed the Uptake of Electronic Commerce

Developing countries need to address a number of socioeconomic and regulatory barriers before their electronic commerce and Internet use matches that of the United States or Europe. While the socioeconomic challenges are difficult to surmount and will be slower to achieve, the path to reducing regulatory barriers is clearer and the benefits quicker to observe. High Internet access rates, low penetration of electronic means of payment (such as credit, debit, or Smart cards), and cumbersome delivery systems are primary obstacles to the growth of electronic commerce in developing countries.

One area that is most easily quantified and compared is *Internet monthly access fees*. ITU data show that these fees vary substantially across countries and that the share of the fees accounted for by ISP charges versus accounted for by local telephone charges also varies substantially. For example, in the United States, the approximately $20 per month Internet access charge is all an ISP charge. In Korea, the $25 charge is about 1/3 ISP charge and 2/3 local call charges. In Brazil, the $37 charge is nearly all a local ISP charge. In China, the $65 charge is about half ISP charge and about half a local phone charge.[12] More importantly, when adjusted by the level of per capita GDP, the difference in charges is tremendous. For example, U.S. and Australian fees are about $25 per month, accounting for less than 2 percent of monthly GDP per capita. In contrast, in Mexico, the fee at about $27 per month accounts for about 5 percent of monthly income and in Mozambique, that $27 per month accounts for about 70 percent of monthly GDP per capita.[13]

Because the Internet creates new electronic business environments, "surfing" is a key way for users to see what businesses are now doing, and what market niches remain to be exploited. Consequently, large "entry" and ongoing costs are a great disincentive to Internet usage and therefore to the development of e-commerce business both within a country and for international trade. Competition, both for telephone access as well as among ISPs, is a key area where government policy can make a difference in access and uptake of the Internet.

Further, a supportive *electronic payments infrastructure* is crucial to promote electronic commerce, which exposes a key link between electronic commerce and the financial foundation of the economy. The efficiency of the payments system itself can help or hinder the development of electronic commerce. Issues of security for transactions, types of electronic media or techniques for making transactions, as well authorization and clearing functions are key aspects of the problem.

Electronic payments require an easy-to-use and secure payment vehicle. Although a number of countries are focussing on "cash on delivery" for tangible products, the future will require a payment method that is on-line so as to accommodate products (both goods and services) delivered digitally. For business-to-business transactions, an easy-to-use electronic payments mechanism is crucial to achieve the cost reductions promised by Internet-based commerce. In addition, security for financial transactions is the sine qua non; electronic payment must be secure and legal, with liability clearly identified, limited, and prosecuted.

Eighty percent of e-commerce transactions use credit cards, even as debit, Smart cards or digital cash are being viewed as alternatives. Credit-card penetration by countries varies widely and for various reasons. In some countries, including China, the preference for cash to avoid audit trails undermines the use of credit cards as the basis for electronic commerce transactions, even as other forms of Internet usage (such as e-mail) have risen. In other countries, such as Taiwan, people are unwilling to use credit cards for Internet transactions because there is unlimited liability in the case of fraudulent use of the credit card number. Finally, the additional charge to businesses (which in some cases is transferred in full to the customer) for the use of an internationally recognized credit card can be as high as 5 to 7 percent of the transaction (for example in Bulgaria), much too high to be acceptable to business or consumer. [14]

Beyond individual transactions, full efficiency and realization of the benefits of e-commerce depend on rapid authorization, payments, and settlement of accounts through the "financial plumbing" of the economy. At a minimum, authorization for transactions between Internet businesses and payment institutions (such as credit card companies or banks) needs to be in real time, so as to allow immediate delivery of digital products. Moreover, the shorter the time between authorization and actual payment, the more efficient the transaction and the lower the institutional risk. Many developing countries do not have financial institutions or central bank payments mechanisms that are up to this task.

When countries maintain controls on foreign exchange usage, full participation in e-commerce for international trade is problematical. Some countries allow exporters greater access to international exchange than other businesses (as in Morocco, for example). This strategy could limit the development of electronic commerce by indigenous small businesses who need to import in order to produce for a market niche in the external or even for the domestic market; Saffron producers, for example, may achieve greater global sales by importing marketing expertise over the Internet. The desire to maintain a closed capital account but an open current account (as in Sri Lanka for example) is more difficult when the nature of the Internet transactions is not transparent to the authorities; who can tell whether the cross-border credit-card payment was for a U.S. Treasury bond rather than for a Dell computer? [15]

Finally, *distribution and delivery systems* round out the set of service infrastructures that are key components to developing e-commerce. Speed is one of the most important manifestations of electronic commerce. Overnight delivery, just-in-time processing, 24 by 7 operations all are examples of how much faster and more precisely timed economic activities are in the e-commerce world. A country with inefficient distribution and delivery systems and without multi-modal transport for international participation will be left behind in e-commerce.

Moreover, there is a very important link between the effectiveness of the distribution and delivery systems and the incentives for the private sector to innovate and invest in new technology. Suppose the private sector spends money on Internet technologies, but cannot get products to customers because of distribution and delivery barriers, as was the case for apparel producers in Sri Lanka attempting to break into the upscale international fashion market.

When the economic benefits that might accrue to the private company are eroded by inefficiencies elsewhere in the chain-to-market, it reduces the incentives for further private investment in known technologies as well as creates a barrier to innovating new ideas for the local market. [16]

How should policymakers respond to these needs for domestic reforms? First, clear synergies exist between the elements of policy reform. Making substantial progress on only one element (such as telephone charges) will reap smaller rewards than expected because of the tight relationship between the three foundations for e-commerce readiness. Second, exploiting existing technology available worldwide has great advantages of interoperability and can jump-start the globalization of domestic producers. Finally, the greatest innovation, profit, and increase in economic well-being will be generated by private sector entrepreneurs serving market niches unique to the home country, since only domestic entrepreneurs are truly able to understand their own market. Domestic policy might favor international infrastructures and overseas innovation when network externalities and interoperability are important to create the needed foundation for domestic initiatives. But the ones who benefit will be domestic entrepreneurs.

V. Electronic Commerce and International Negotiations in the WTO

The WTO has done a substantial amount of work with regard to electronic commerce, but the cross-cutting and rapidly evolving environment of electronic commerce poses a true challenge both to the organizing structure of the WTO (GATT and GATS, and role of subcommittees), as well as to the operational method of its members (request-offer negotiations and negative vs. positive commitments).[17] One the other hand, traditional WTO principles of nondiscrimination, transparency, neutrality, and market openness remain valid and should be applied to electronic commerce. New rules are not necessary if liberalizing commitments embodied in GATT, GATS, TRIPs, and other WTO agreements are honored.

Probably the key issue is whether electronic commerce and digitized products should be classified into *GATT, GATS, both, or neither*. The European Union strongly asserts that "all electronic transmissions consist of services;" and, therefore, these products should fall under the purview of GATS.[18] Most countries, including the United States, agree that services delivered over the Internet are covered by GATS, but other products are more like a good or are a hybrid between a good and a service (electronic books are a popular example). Thus the United States is arguing that more time is needed to monitor the development of electronic commerce before any final classification takes place. A key point is that classifying these products under GATS could make their treatment under the WTO less liberal, because market access in GATS exists only in sectors where members have made specific commitments (software downloaded from the Internet, for example, is not covered by

GATS). Moreover, whether existing commitments include electronic transmissions as a mode of delivery is itself under contention.[19]

A compromise that would yield the greatest liberalization sidesteps the classification issue and requires that WTO members follow the course of most liberal treatment of these products, either under GATT or GATS, particularly when a specific product does not fit neatly within a negotiated service sector commitment. In some cases, this could mean that electronic delivery of goods and services would be treated more favorably than other forms of delivery. For example, financial products or architectural services could be sold over the Internet even as the physical presence of a foreign bank or licensing of foreign architects had not yet been scheduled for liberalization under GATS. This liberalization bias engendered by electronic commerce can act as a positive force, stimulating further the development of electronic commerce, as well as encouraging deeper liberalization and deregulation throughout the economy.[20]

Governments do have a legitimate concern that their standards and regulations (e.g., pharmaceutical prescriptions, gambling restrictions, and the prudential regulation of banks) might be undermined by the more favorable treatment afforded by electronic commerce. Now is a good time for governments to review how electronic commerce puts stress on existing standards and regulations, and to decide what combination of private-sector response and public legislation will ensure the greatest benefits of electronic commerce for their citizens.

Moreover, societies do differ in their preferences toward certain aspects of privacy and levels of security (among other things), and governments are elected to represent those views. Diversity in the level of government intervention into some areas of governance of the electronic commerce environment could be appropriate, and appears to be inevitable in any case.

Given the global nature of electronic commerce, *governments should try to coordinate (which need not mean harmonize) new regulations* with other countries on a bilateral and multilateral basis. What does this mean? An example in the area of privacy regulation illustrates the idea. As background and in simple terms, the U.S. approach to privacy is to let the private sector offer different levels of privacy, whereas the European Union Privacy Directive mandates a particular level of privacy.[21] Do these different approaches become a barrier to cross-border trade, or can a "trusted third party", a private firm, bridge these two approaches to privacy? Such a firm would investigate the privacy policies and methods of the U.S. firm and guarantee that it was abiding by the EU Directive; the EU would give the firm its seal of approval that its methods met the standards of the EU.[22] This represents a market-oriented solution to the need to mediate between firms who wish to trade data across borders and societies (or at least governments) who wish to have different approaches to privacy.

A second issue relevant for developing countries and the WTO is *negotiating method*. This issue grows out of the synergies between the elements of e-commerce readiness. Because of these synergies, country delegations will begin emphasizing the "horizontal" approach to negotiations on electronic commerce. The initial U.S. proposal on services in mid-summer 1999 argued for the "use of all appropriate negotiating modalities, including request-offer, horizontal, and sectoral approaches."[23] In the horizontal approach, negotiators seek to apply liberalizing measures, such as transparency and good governance in regulations as well as consistency of ownership across sectors, to a broad range of services. For example, negotiators would seek to eliminate any discrimination across a particular mode of delivery—like electronic commerce or rights of establishment—across a range of services, such as financial services and small package delivery.[24] This horizontal approach in negotiations is consistent with and formally extends the liberalization bias engendered by electronic commerce.

A final question of particular relevance for the developing countries is the *WTO work program on electronic commerce*. WTO members also need to decide how, or whether, to continue the WTO's work program on electronic commerce. The different country positions on this issue mirror the debate over how to classify e-commerce trade. The EU asserts that because all electronic deliveries are services, the work program must proceed under the auspices of the Services Council. Before the Seattle Ministerial, the developing countries were finding it difficult to staff all the meetings taking place in the various councils and thus preferred to have electronic commerce addressed only in the General Council. To promote the cross-cutting nature of electronic commerce, the United States is proposing that a "non-negotiating working group" be set up in the WTO's General Council. This proposal would satisfy the needs of the developing countries, but would not presuppose the outcome of the classification issue.

A future WTO work program on electronic commerce should have the following features: First, it should be reconstituted under the General Council rather than fragmented throughout the WTO. While input from the different councils and committees is important, the cross-cutting nature of electronic commerce means that leadership from the General Council is key. Moreover, close coordination of the work program under the General Council will help developing countries, which have smaller negotiating staffs, participate more fully.

Second, private-sector participation has been the hallmark of all the regional trade forums' discussions of electronic commerce (including those proceeding under APEC and FTAA). The private sector is leading the way in setting global technological standards for electronic commerce; it can also help resolve policymaking concerns such as tax administration and privacy protection. Private-sector participation and contribution to the WTO work program is therefore vital.

WTO members face an important watershed: to establish a predictable environment in which electronic commerce can thrive, allowing the benefits of this new form of international trade to be realized by all consumers in all countries. In accomplishing these objectives, the WTO can work to ensure that electronic commerce remains free from international trade barriers and continues to drive domestic and global growth.

VI. How Should Developing Countries Approach Negotiations in the WTO?

The issues involved with electronic commerce are extremely complex, not only within a country but perhaps even more so between countries in the international arena. Leveraging human and administrative capital resources, both in negotiation and non-negotiating bodies is a must, to keep up with e-commerce knowledge and to gain more traction in international negotiations. But the WTO negotiations obviously address more than just e-commerce; developing countries may be able to leverage their greater participation in e-commerce into greater openness in sectors of their traditional interest.

Many developing countries are already members of *regional groups*, such as APEC, FTAA, and SADC (Southern Africa Development Community). Some of these groups have forums for private sector interaction, such as through the FTAA's Joint Private Sector Committee of Exports and APEC's Pacific Basin Economic Council. Such venues could increase the potential for public-private-investment partnerships in key infrastructures. In addition, such interaction can help ensure that governmental initiatives are interoperable with the global private sector, as in standards setting for example.

WTO negotiations involve political as well as economic considerations and therefore, inevitably involve *trading-off of one sector for another*. Electronic commerce offers particular promise to developing countries. Market innovations and improved market efficiencies gained through electronic commerce and its prerequisite infrastructures will have the greatest impact in those sectors and countries where coordination and transactions costs are highest. By the same token, U.S. businesses and workers, especially in the high-tech and service sectors, stand to benefit from the liberalization of electronic commerce and its infrastructures. Other countries also stand to benefit through the new opportunities created by electronic commerce, as well as through the increased efficiencies electronic commerce is making to traditional sectors. This is a clear win-win proposition for both the industrial and developing countries.

The overall benefits will be reduced, however, if markets are not open for the goods and services that developing countries will come to produce more efficiently than they do now. Developing countries, for example, face U.S. barriers in textiles and apparel and some elements of data processing, communications and software programming, precisely those areas in which electronic commerce (and the related improvements in domestic infrastructures) can enhance the competitiveness of developing country producers. If U.S. negotiators fail to acknowledge the need to lower these barriers, developing countries may limit their commitments to liberalize key areas of electronic commerce, which would reduce benefits to all participants: the United States and other industrial countries, as well as the developing countries themselves.

The choices are clear and the stakes are enormous. WTO members can establish a predictable environment in which electronic commerce can thrive, allowing the benefits of this new form of international trade to be realized by all consumers in all countries. In the United States, where electronic commerce has its strongest hold, the information-technology sector contributes to approximately eight percent of the economy. The remarkable growth in IT-related industries, especially those directly linked to electronic commerce, has helped to create the longest period of economic growth with low inflation in U.S. history.[25] Such gains are available to all countries, not just first-users like the United States and Europe; liberalization via electronic commerce is not a "zero-sum game."

VII. Final Remarks

Electronic commerce and the Internet integrate both services and goods sectors, across domestic and international boundaries. Key synergies exist between telecommunications, financial infrastructure, distribution and delivery, and governance. The Internet and electronic commerce both depend on and facilitate liberalization in these areas. The WTO process can help prod domestic liberalization and open markets abroad. In addition, it can be a forum where developing countries use their existing regional relationships to convey information to the individual countries to raise knowledge levels and work with private sector partners. Electronic commerce and the Internet represent the opportunity to leap forward to the next stage of economic development, where value is created not just by resource endowments or manufacturing might, but also by knowledge, information, and the use of technology.

Notes

[1] For more elaborate discussion of definitions see www.oecd.org/dsti/sti/it/ec/act/ SACHER.HTM and Box 1.1, page 28-29 in *The Economic and Social Impact of Electronic Commerce*, OECD, 1999.

[2] OECD (1999, pp. 60-61).

[3] See www.boeing.com/news/1995/news.release.950614-a.html

[4] See "The Globalization of Services: What Has Happened? What Are the Implications?," by Gary Clyde Hufbauer and Tony Warren, Working Paper no.99-12, Institute for International Economics, October 1999 and OECD, *The World in 2020: Towards a New Global Age*, Paris: OECD, 1997.

[5] www.Estats.com, October 1999

[6] See http://www.emarketer.com/estats/102599_india.html

[7] See International Telecommunication Union, *Challenges to the Network: Internet for Development*, October 1999 (updated), page 47, using data from International Data Corp.

[8] Ibid.

[9] See http://www.nua.ie/surveys/

[10] ITU (1999, Figure 3.2, p. 45).

[11] For a discussion of the fragmentation and globalization of production in the context of U.S. trade, see Catherine L. Mann, *Is the US Trade Deficit Sustainable?*, Institute for International Economics, 1999, pp. 39-40.

[12] ITU (1999, Table 9, p. A-30).

[13] ITU (1999, Figure 2.8, p. 31 and table 9, p. A-29) using data for 1998 from the OECD.

[14] Examples from field research by the author and colleagues, as independent consultants to ARD, Inc.

[15] Ibid.

[16] Ibid.

[17] The issues on electronic commerce and the WTO are developed more fully in Catherine L. Mann and Sarah Cleeland Knight, "Electronic Commerce in the World Trade Organization," in Jeffrey, Schott, ed. *The WTO After Seattle,* Institute for International Economics, July 2000.

[18] World Trade Organization, "Communication from the European Communities and their Member States on the WTO Work Programme on Electronic Commerce," 9 August 1999.

[19] Ibid.

[20] William Drake and Kalypso Nicolaides, "The Information Revolution and Services Trade Liberalization After 2000," in Pierre Sauvé and Robert M. Stern (eds.), *GATS 2000: New Directions in Services Trade Liberalization*, Brookings Institution 2000, argue that this approach in effect changes the outcome of the negotiations agreed to in the Uruguay Round. As negotiators, they are correct. However, from the standpoint of economic well-being, the liberalizing bias is to be welcomed, not avoided.

[21] The privacy issue is quite complex and evolving and cannot be fully developed here. See Peter Swire and Robert Litan, *None of Your Business*, Brookings Institution, 1998, as well as pp. 37-41 and pp.. 122-135 in *Global Electronic Commerce: A Policy Primer*, by Catherine L. Mann, Sue E. Eckert, and Sarah Cleeland Knight, Institute for International Economics, July 2000.

[22] The firm, Privacy Council, is one company attempting to meet this market need.

[23] Preparations for the 1999 Ministerial conference; communication from the United States, "Further Negotiations As Mandated by the General Agreement on Trade in Services (GATS)," as replicated in *Inside US Trade*, July 30, 1999.

[24] Susan Esserman, "Testimony on "Approaching the New Round: American Goals in Services Trade," before the Senate Finance Subcommittee on Trade, October 21, 1999.

[25] See the Department of Commerce's "The Emerging Digital Economy II" (1999) at www.ecommerce.gov/ede for a comprehensive study of the impact of information technologies on the U.S. economy. Chapter 6 of Mann, *Is the US Trade Deficit Sustainable?*, discusses the role of IT in raising U.S. productivity growth and the "new paradigm" of rapid macroeconomic growth with low inflation.

CHAPTER 11

GATS and Developing Countries: A Case Study of India*

Rajesh Chadha

I. Introduction

The preamble to the General Agreement on Trade in Services (GATS) states that the general goal of participants is to establish a multilateral framework of principles and rules for trade in services with a view to expanding such trade under conditions of transparency and progressive liberalization. This would promote the economic growth of all trading partners and the development of developing countries. The agreement expresses the desire "to facilitate the increasing participation of developing countries in trade in services and the expansion of their service exports including, *inter alia*, through the strengthening of their domestic services capacity and its efficiency and competitiveness." The preamble clearly recognizes the right of all parties to regulate the supply of services within their territories. It takes "particular account of the serious difficulty of the least-developed countries in view of their special economic situation and their development, trade and financial needs."

The objective of this chapter is to analyze the growing importance of the service sectors in the developing countries and identify the developing-country specific features implicit in the GATS. The relative comparative advantage of the developing and the developed countries is also examined for various types of services through calculating their revealed comparative advantage. India's commitments in GATS are highlighted along with a discussion of how protected and inefficient service sectors reduce the competitiveness of India's manufacturing sectors. The success story of the software sector in India's economy and trade is also discussed. The potential gains to some of the developed countries/regions of the world as well as the Asian developing countries/regions, which are expected to accrue as a result of successful implementation of the Uruguay Round's trade liberalization commitments in goods and service sectors, are highlighted. This is done through using a multi-country, multi-sector computable general equilibrium (CGE) model of world production and trade. Particular attention is paid to analysis of the impact on India's economy.

II. GATS: Implications For Developing Countries

Growing Importance of Services in Developing Countries

World exports of goods and commercial services averaged $6.6 trillion annually during the triennium ending 1997, including $1.3 trillion worth of exports of services accounting for 20 per cent of total world exports (IMF, 1998).[1] While the export of services accounts for 17 per cent of developing-country exports, the corresponding share is higher at 21 per cent for industrial countries. The share of developing countries in the world export of services increased from 22.3 per cent in 1991 to 29.3 per cent in 1997. The share of Asian developing countries in total world exports increased from 9.9 per cent to 15.2 per cent during this period.

The share of value added by services has been rapidly increasing in the GDP of low and middle-income economies as compared with high-income economies since 1980 (World Bank, 1998/99).

While the share of value added by services in GDP increased from 38 per cent in 1980 to 42 per cent in 1997 for the low-income economies, the corresponding figures were 40 and 50 per cent for the middle-income economies and above 60 per cent for the high-income economies. The services sector has been growing at a rate faster than that of GDP for the low and middle-income economies but not for high-income economies.

In the case of India, the share of value-added by services in GDP increased from 36 per cent in 1980 to 43 per cent in 1997. While GDP grew at an average annual rate of 5.8 per cent during the period 1980-90 and by 5.9 per cent during 1990-97, the corresponding growth rates for value-added by services were 6.7 and 7.5 per cent, respectively (WDR, 1998/99). India's share in world exports of services increased from 0.55 to 0.65 per cent during this period.

In order to estimate the index of comparative advantage of the export of major services by the developing-country groups, I have computed their revealed comparative advantage in such exports. The revealed comparative advantage (RCA) of a "service" for a country/region is the ratio of share of export of this "service" in a country's/region's services exports to the share of world exports of this "service" to total world services exports. The value of RCA indicates whether the country/region has relative comparative advantage in such exports compared with the world average. Thus, a RCA value above one is indicative of relative comparative advantage. It can be seen in Table 1 that the developing countries have revealed comparative advantage (RCA) in "freight" and "travel" while the industrialized countries have RCA in "passenger services," "other transport" and "other services."[2]

Table 1. Revealed Comparative Advantage in Service Exports (three year moving average)

	Passenger services	Freight	Other Transporta- tion	Travel	Other Services
Developing countries					
1992	0.83	1.14	0.99	1.13	0.91
1993	0.81	1.14	0.95	1.14	0.92
1994	0.77	1.12	0.96	1.13	0.94
1995	0.72	1.12	0.95	1.13	0.95
1996	0.68	1.10	0.95	1.12	0.97
Developed/Industrialized countries					
1992	1.05	0.96	1.01	0.96	1.03
1993	1.07	0.96	1.02	0.96	1.03
1994	1.09	0.96	1.02	0.96	1.02
1995	1.11	0.96	1.02	0.95	1.02
1996	1.13	0.96	1.02	0.95	1.01

Developing countries: region-wise

	Year	Africa	Asia	Europe	Middle East	Western Hem.
Passenger services						
	1992	1.55	0.64	0.79	0.80	1.12
	1993	1.58	0.61	0.78	0.76	1.14
	1994	1.62	0.57	0.80	0.72	1.12
	1995	1.62	0.50	0.71	0.74	1.16
	1996	1.64	0.48	0.61	0.74	1.14
Freight						
	1992	0.85	1.24	1.80	0.55	0.65
	1993	0.80	1.22	1.75	0.72	0.66
	1994	0.75	1.20	1.62	0.80	0.60
	1995	0.68	1.20	1.55	0.84	0.58
	1996	0.67	1.18	1.52	0.78	0.56
Other transportation						
	1992	1.25	0.64	0.84	1.89	1.40
	1993	1.22	0.65	0.76	1.76	1.43
	1994	1.17	0.67	0.87	1.59	1.52
	1995	1.14	0.65	0.98	1.51	1.55
	1996	1.16	0.62	1.10	1.48	1.57

Travel

	1992	1.24	1.15	0.96	0.68	1.57
	1993	1.29	1.12	1.07	0.72	1.52
	1994	1.34	1.08	1.10	0.75	1.50
	1995	1.40	1.04	1.20	0.80	1.48
	1996	1.41	1.00	1.23	0.83	1.50
Other services						
	1992	0.54	1.03	0.93	1.23	0.51
	1993	0.52	1.04	0.89	1.20	0.55
	1994	0.52	1.07	0.87	1.19	0.59
	1995	0.50	1.10	0.80	1.17	0.63
	1996	0.51	1.13	0.79	1.16	0.63

Source: IMF (1998)

Relevance of GATS to the Developing Economies[3]

The GATS is the first multilateral agreement under the auspices of the Uruguay Round to provide legally enforceable rights to trade in a wide range of services along with their progressive liberalization. The main objectives of the GATS are the expansion of trade in services, progressive liberalization of such trade through negotiations, transparency of rules and regulations, and increasing participation of developing countries. Though very little liberalization was actually achieved, the Uruguay Round negotiations on trade in service sectors established the institutional structure for negotiating liberalization in the future.[4]

The core principles of the GATT, namely Most-Favored Nation (MFN) and National Treatment (NT), apply generally to the GATS. However, these are highly qualified (Srinivasan, 1998). First, a member can exempt any service from the application of MFN and seek further exemptions within sixty days beginning four months after entry into force of the Uruguay Round agreement. Second, a member can improve, modify or withdraw all or part of its specific commitments on financial services during this period. Third, NT applies only to sectors and sub-sectors listed in the member's schedule.

The GATS imposes few limitations on national policy, with the only requirement that there should be no discrimination across alternative sources of supply (Hoekman, 1995). The participating countries are not required to alter regulatory structures or to pursue an active antitrust or competition policy. The positive-list approach enabled many developing countries to accede to GATS with minimal commitments. Accordingly, the GATS may affect developing countries only in a limited way since its rules apply only if specific commitments are made.

There are certain Articles in the GATS that deal with specific provisions relating to developing countries (UNCTAD-World Bank, 1994). These include: Article III (transparency); IV (increasing participation of developing countries); V (economic integration); XII (measures to safeguard the balance of payments); XV (subsidies); XIX (negotiation of commitments); and XXV (technical collaboration). Articles IV and XXV deal exclusively with developing countries. The Annex on telecommunications contains a special article on technical cooperation in the telecommunications industry.[5]

GATS Article IV seeks increasing participation of the developing countries in world trade in services through negotiated specific commitments for access to technology on a commercial basis, improved access to distribution channels and information networks, and the liberalization of market access in sectors of export interest to developing countries. With regard to transparency, the industrialized nations were asked to establish contact points within two years of the entry into force of the agreement. These points would facilitate the access of developing country services suppliers to information relating to the commercial and technical aspects of specific services, requirements for registration, recognition and obtaining of professional qualifications, and the availability of services technology. The final provision of Article IV states that special priority shall be given to least developed countries in the implementation of provisions of Article IV.

GATS Article XXV on technical cooperation reaffirms the access of developing country services suppliers to contact points to be established in developed countries (Article IV). It further states that technical assistance to developing countries shall be provided at the multilateral level by the competent Secretariat and shall be decided upon by the Council for Trade in Services. Apart from the Secretariat, other multilateral organizations, such as the United Nations and the World Bank, could also be involved in providing such assistance.

Although the developing countries are accorded limited special and differential treatment under GATS, this agreement contains no provisions similar to Part IV of the GATT on more favorable treatment of developing countries. GATS Article XIX allows developing countries to make fewer specific commitments than industrialized nations. The developing countries have limited flexibility to offer less liberalization of services than developed countries, but they are not allowed a free ride. The GATS is based on the argument that if the national governments have concern for economic efficiency, the optimal policies would be the same both for developed and developing countries.

III. Trade in Services: India's Case Study

Efficient services are crucial to an economy's global competitiveness. We have seen in the previous section that the benefits to a developing economy are greatly enhanced when service sectors are liberalized. Yet another way of exploring the inefficiencies in the service sectors is to calculate how protection in services affects effective rates of protection (ERPs).[6] It has been pointed out that the actual effective protection to manufacturing sectors may turn out to be lower if adjustment for high protection to service sectors, due to regulatory policies, is also taken into account (Hoekman and Djankov, 1997).[7] I have computed such ERPs for the manufacturing sectors of India for the year 1997-98, using Hoekman's "guesstimates" of tariff equivalents of implicit protection on India's service sectors. The results for the 30 input-output sectors, which account for more than 20 per cent share of services in total intermediate inputs, are reported in Table 2. Note that in 25 out of 30 sectors, the inefficient-services adjusted ERP is less than the normal ERP with the difference becoming large in some sectors. In the case of electrical machinery, the adjusted ERP is negative at –6.6 per cent compared with original value at 26.2 per cent. The difference is substantial also for coal tar products, steel and ferrous alloys, fertilizers and woolen textiles. The upshot is that the inefficient service sectors may thus act as a tax on manufacturing and thereby reduce effective protection.

The Indian government is aware of the need to improve the provision of services, and that the investment requirement is beyond the means available to the government. Hence, the government is looking forward to private support (Mohan, 1996). India has liberalized its FDI regime during the 1990s.[8] Foreign equity up to 51 per cent is now automatically allowed in: restaurants and hotels; support services for land and water transport; parts of renting and leasing; business services including software; and health and medical services. The automatic approval provision for foreign equity is 74 per cent in the case of mining services, non-conventional energy generation and distribution, land and water transport, and storage and warehousing. The limit is 100 per cent in the case of electricity generation, transmission and distribution. However, foreign equity is limited to 49 per cent in telecommunications, 40 per cent in domestic airlines and to 20 per cent in banking services. Railway transport continues to remain among four industries reserved for the public sector. The insurance sector has only recently been opened to the private sector.

India's schedule under the GATS provides for specific commitments covering: business services; communications; construction work for civil engineering; financial services; health-related and social services; and tourism services (WTO, 1998, p.152). The extent of commitments varies across sectors, with certain restrictions on market access and national treatment under the four modes of supply of services. India has not made any commitments on services relating to: distribution; education; environment; recreation, culture and sporting; transport; and other services not included elsewhere. In all, India has made commitments in 33 activities, compared with an average of 23 for developing countries (GATT, 1994). These commitments generally bind India's existing policy framework, although in some cases, the applied policy may be more liberal than the binding commitments.[9] India has listed some MFN exemptions under Article II of the GATS and reserves the right to offer more favorable treatment to some WTO members in communication. recreational and

Table 2: Protection in India 1997-98 (Per cent)

Sectors	Nominal Rate of Protection (NRP)	Share of Services in Total Inputs	Effective Rate of Protection (ERP)	Adjusted ERP*
1 Cement	43.7	35.1	57.9	36.0
2 Coal tar products	30.6	31.5	43.4	7.1
3 Inorganic heavy chemicals	34.3	29.3	36.0	16.4
4 Other non-metallic mineral prods.	42.1	28.5	48.3	37.9
5 Non-ferrous basic metals	31.6	28.3	34.4	17.6
6 Electrical industrial machinery	29.1	27.8	26.2	-6.6
7 Organic heavy chemicals	33.8	26.6	34.8	17.7
8 Other transport equipment	45.0	26.4	49.5	51.9
9 Iron steel & ferro-alloys	28.4	25.8	28.4	6.0
10 Paper, paper prods. & newsprint	33.4	25.6	35.3	22.2
11 Structural clay products	39.4	24.8	47.9	39.5
12 Iron & steel casting & forging	35.0	24.3	43.1	29.8
13 Cotton Textiles & Khadi	41.1	23.9	59.0	59.1
14 Watches & clocks	39.2	23.7	39.6	39.8
15 Ships & boats	32.9	23.3	32.7	28.6
16 Communication equipment	36.3	23.3	36.7	31.1
17 Jute, Hemp, mesta, textiles	45.0	22.9	52.9	49.3
18 Industrial machinery (others)	26.6	22.7	23.1	13.8
19 Paints, varnishes & lacquers	35.0	22.6	35.1	26.7
20 Fertilizers	25.7	22.5	19.9	2.6

21 Iron & steel foundries	35.0	22.2	41.0	27.6
22 Electronic equipment (incl. TV)	29.7	22.1	27.3	18.2
23 Leather footwear	45.0	21.8	52.3	53.6
24 Leather & leather products	32.1	21.7	32.2	27.1
25 Art silk, synthetic fiber textiles	43.3	21.3	50.0	47.9
26 Industrial machinery	31.7	20.9	24.3	16.2
27 Readymade garments	45.0	20.6	48.1	49.2
28 Motor cycles & scooters	45.0	20.5	51.1	51.0
29 Synthetic fibers, resins	40.0	20.4	44.7	39.3
30 Woolen textiles	23.2	20.3	12.8	3.9

* Adjustment made for tariff equivalents for services.
Sources: NCAER (1998), Hoekman (1995), and Chadha (1998)

transport services.[10] India further liberalized its commitments in basic telecommunication services in early 1998. It is among 43 countries participating in the Information Technology Agreement covering: computers; telecommunication equipment; semiconductors; manufacturing equipment for semiconductors; software and scientific instruments. India has offered zero duty on 217 information-technology-related tariff lines at the Harmonized System (HS) 6-digit level by 2005.[11]

India's Success Story: Software

The GATS Services Sectoral Classification List (GNS List) includes "computer and related services" as a component of "business services" (GNS code 1B). Computer and related services include: (1) consultancy services related to the installation of computer hardware; (2) software implementation services; (3) data processing services; (4) database services; and (5) others.[12] However, uncertainty prevails with respect to computer software concerning where to draw the line between "software" and "services."[13] In the case of India's commitments under "computer and related services," *cross-border supply* (Mode 1) and *consumption abroad* (Mode 2) are unbound both under market access and national treatment. *Commercial presence* (Mode 3) gets national treatment, but *market access* is possible only through incorporation with foreign equity. The *presence of natural persons* (Mode 4) is unbound except as indicated in horizontal section.

India possesses the world's second largest pool of scientific manpower that is also English speaking. Moreover, Indian software is of high quality and with relatively low cost. The software industry has emerged as one of the fastest-growing and most vibrant segments of India's economy during the 1990s. The domestic software market increased from US$160 million in 1992-93 to US$944 million in 1997-98, thus registering an average growth rate of 43 per cent per annum (NASSCOM, 1999). The exports of software increased from US$225 million in 1992-93 to US$1,750 million in 1997-98, which is an average annual growth rate of 51 per cent.[14] A National Task Force on Information Technology and Software Development was set up in May 1998, consisting of ministers, bureaucrats, scientists, academicians and industry representatives.[15]

India has already acquired a substantial market share in the global cross-country, customized-software development market. Its share in the global market has increased from 11.9 per cent in 1991 to 18.5 per cent in 1998. India has been recognized as an important base for software development. In 1997-98, more than 158 of Fortune 500 companies outsourced their software requirements to India. Quality has become the hallmark of the industry with more than 109 Indian software companies having acquired international quality certification. Two out of six companies in the world, which have acquired SEI (level 5) are in India, namely Motorola and Wipro. After a major success in servicing the Y2K issue in the international market, India has already set its eyes on servicing Euro currency solutions, with 82 Indian software companies already participating in this effort. The strategic "12-hour" time difference with the United States provides India with a unique opportunity to facilitate a 24-hour working day for many of the United States companies who would prefer to "follow the sun."

The cost competitiveness of India is here to stay for at least another decade. The relaxed U.S. H1-B visa numbers from 65,000 in 1998 to 115,000 for 1999 and 2000 may revert back to the original figure in 2001 with the demise of Y2K. But given the continued shortage of software-skilled U.S. manpower, U.S. companies should increasingly outsource their work to India. However, I do not see a major disadvantage to the software-trained Indian workforce in view of the continued H1-B visa restrictions as work would "reach" India due to its reputation as one of the best outsourcing destinations. The often quoted lower wages of Indian software development and support manpower in comparison with their U.S. counterparts should not discourage the Indian workforce since the myth of these figures should be clearly understood. That is, assume that Indian wages are about 10 per cent of the corresponding U.S. wages (Mattoo, 1999). Firstly, for an Indian, this figure should be read as 40 per cent, instead of 10 per cent, under the 'purchasing power parity' paradigm (World Bank, 1998). This figure gets enhanced to about 60 per cent if one accounts for 'implicit' wage discrimination against the 'alien' H1-B visa holders by about 30 per cent.[16] This may further increase over the next ten years with the United States and some other developed countries outsourcing their software-related work to India.

IV. Service Sector Liberalization and Developing Countries

Brown et al. (1996) have analyzed the potential impacts of the liberalization of trade in services. In view of there being no actual liberalization of trade in services during the Uruguay Round negotiations, their focus was on examining what the effects of service-sector liberalization might be when such liberalization finally occurs. Using Hoekman's (1995) "guesstimates" of the size of trade barriers in services, the effects were calculated of an assumed 25 per cent reduction in these barriers, which was assumed as the plausible magnitude that may eventually be achieved.[17] To provide a benchmark for comparison, Brown et al. also calculated the effects of the liberalization of tariffs on industrial products that were actually negotiated. They concluded that the world's major trading countries/regions could expect to gain from liberalization of trade in services, with gains increasing further when tariffs on industrial goods are reduced simultaneously.

I make a similar attempt in this chapter to compare gains in welfare, trade, resource allocation, and real returns to factors of production from liberalization of trade in services for the developed as well as the developing countries/regions. To estimate the potential results of liberalization in trade in services as well as in industrial products, I use a specially constructed version of the Michigan Brown-Deardorff-Stern (BDS) computable general equilibrium (CGE) Model of World Production and Trade (Brown et al., 2000, and Chadha et al., 2000).[18] The developing countries/regions included are: India (IND), Rest of South Asia (RSA), ASEAN-4 (ASN) and NIE-4 (NIE).[19] The developed countries/regions include: the European Union (EUN); Japan (JPN); and the United States (USA). The closure of the model is achieved by assigning the remaining countries to a residual rest-of-world (ROW). In each country or region, the model covers 25 sectors, all of which are "tradable." These include one sector of agriculture, sixteen of manufacturing, and eight of services and government. Thus, there are eight regions in all including ROW. However, the ROW is a residual and only the remaining seven countries/regions are modeled.

Most of the assumptions made are similar to the ones made by Brown et al. (1996, 2000). The model relies on some basic assumptions of the new trade theory, namely, imperfect competition, increasing returns to scale and product heterogeneity. It is assumed that the agricultural sector is perfectly competitive, and the manufacturing and services sectors are monopolistically competitive with free entry. Under perfect competition, goods/services are differentiated by country of production. Under monopolistic competition, goods/services are differentiated by producing firm. The reference year for the database of the model is 1995, and most of it is based on Global Trade Analysis Package (GTAP) Release-4 (McDougall et al., 1998). The details of database and documentation as well as a full statement and description of the model are available on request.

Model Simulations

Two experiments are conducted. The liberalization of goods trade is taken as the benchmark in the first experiment. In the second experiment, I examine the welfare gains for various developing and developed countries/regions when there is comparable liberalization of trade in services as well. The assumed bilateral reduction of 25 per cent of the "hypothetical" tariff equivalents of service barriers is accompanied here by an equal bilateral reduction in average import tariff rates, taken from the GTAP database, on agricultural and industrial products. The following experiments are performed:

Simulation 1 Bilateral reduction of 25 per cent in average import tariffs rates from 1995 on the agricultural, mining, and manufactured goods sectors. Agriculture is assumed to be under perfect competition with all manufactured goods and service sectors under monopolistic competition (this excludes the effects of the elimination of the Multi-Fibre Arrangement).

Simulation 2 Simulation 1 plus reduction of 25 per cent in *ad valorem* tariff-equivalents on service sectors.

Aggregate Impacts of Trade Liberalization Scenarios

Economic Welfare

The aggregate results measure impacts of liberalization on the terms of trade, welfare, trade and factor payments for the seven countries/regions (Table 3). The impact on economic welfare, the "equivalent variation," is of special interest. It may be observed that the gain in economic welfare is positive for all participating countries/regions under both experiments. The liberalization of goods trade enhances economic welfare, with the Asian developing countries gaining more in proportional terms (Simulation 1). The welfare gains are higher when services trade is also liberalized simultaneously (Simulation 2). The developed countries/regions gain more in proportional terms under the services liberalization compared to the goods liberalization. The overall proportional gains are substantial for the Asian developing countries. Under simulation 2, the economic welfare of the Rest of South Asia (RSA) increases by 3.0 per cent followed by 2.9 per cent in ASEAN-4, 2.5 per cent in NIE-4 and 1.4 per cent in India. The developed countries/regions also gain in welfare. The United States and Japan gain by 1.2 per cent each and the European Union (EU) by 1.0 per cent. In terms of U.S. dollars, the absolute gains are $84 billion for the United States, $79 billion for the EU, $60 billion for Japan, $22 billion for NIE, $14 billion for ASN, $3 billion for RSA and $ 4.8 billion for India. Our results for the gain in economic welfare in dollar terms are somewhat larger than Brown et al. (1996a). This may be due to use of a different database (GTAP), and an assumed 25 per cent bilateral reduction in tariffs on agricultural and manufactured products.

Table 3: Summary Results of Trade Liberalization: Changes in Trade, Welfare, and Real Return to Labor and Capital

Country	Trade		Equivalent Variation		Factor Returns	
	Imports (Millions dollars)	Exports (Millions dollars)	(Percent change)	(Millions of dollars)	Real Wage Rate (Percent change)	Real Return to Capital (Percent change)
Simulation 1:						
IND	1723	2211	0.7	2327	0.2	0.4
RSA	1445	1710	2.1	2229	0.5	1.0
ASN	5993	7081	0.9	4427	0.8	0.8
NIE	8514	8678	0.8	7093	0.5	0.6
USA	11663	10569	0.2	11516	0.0	0.1
JPN	9544	8672	0.4	17858	0.1	0.2
EUN	8958	8931	0.2	13090	0.0	0.1
Simulation 2:						
IND	2718	3274	1.4	4759	0.4	0.6
RSA	2028	2364	3.0	3153	0.8	1.4
ASN	13618	14984	2.7	13869	1.6	1.7
NIE	24744	24238	2.5	22343	1.4	1.5
USA	38910	35690	1.2	83713	0.3	0.4
JPN	25126	25517	1.2	59678	0.3	0.4
EUN	34009	36290	1.0	78919	0.2	0.2
Additional gain from service liberalization (Simulation 2 minus Simulation 1):						
IND	995	1063	0.7	2432	0.2	0.2
RSA	583	654	0.9	924	0.3	0.4
ASN	7625	7903	1.8	9442	0.8	0.9
NIE	16230	15560	1.7	15250	0.9	0.9
USA	27247	25121	1.0	72197	0.3	0.3
JPN	15582	16845	0.8	41820	0.2	0.2
EUN	25051	27359	0.8	65829	0.2	0.1

Real Wages and Return to Capital

It may be observed from Table 3 that the real returns to the factors of production also increase for all the countries for both labor and capital. The returns increase as one moves from Simulation 1 to Simulation 2. The gains to capital are higher than the gains to labor in all the countries/regions except in the case of EU where they are equal. Increases in returns to both labor and capital may seem inconsistent with the Stolper-Samuelson theorem, which suggests that trade liberalization will increase the return to the more abundant factor in each country while making the other factor worse off. But in the context of the differentiated-products model with increasing returns to scale, Brown et al. (1993) show that other forces at work may undermine the impact of the Stolper-Samuelson theorem.

Sector Specific Impacts of Trade Liberalization Scenarios

Sector-specific results for changes in employment in the seven countries/regions are reported in Table 4 for Simulation 2. In each country/region, employment increases in some sectors and decreases in others. In the case of India, employment increases in both experiments in such labor-intensive sectors as: mining; food, beverages and tobacco; textiles; wearing apparel; and leather products. In the case of the United States and the EU, there is a decline in employment in textiles and wearing apparel sectors.

The sector-specific results for India under Simulation 2 are reported in Table 5. It may be observed that there are large increases in services trade, although from a small initial base. The output gains are substantial in: mining; food beverages and tobacco; textiles; wearing apparel; and leather products. Labor and capital tend to shift into these sectors. The change in output per firm (scale effect) is also positive in all these sectors. Output and employment decline in such manufacturing sectors as non-ferrous metals, machinery and equipment, and iron and steel.

V. Concluding Remarks

The main objectives of GATS are the expansion of trade in services, progressive liberalization of such trade through negotiations, transparency of rules and regulations, and increasing participation of developing countries. The developing countries have revealed comparative advantage (RCA) in "freight" and "travel" while the industrialized countries have RCA in "passenger services," "other transport" and "other services." Efficient services are crucial to an economy's global competitiveness. High protection granted to the service sectors by an economy through its regulatory policies creates inefficient service sectors, thus reducing the effective protection to various sectors of production in the economy.

India's schedule under GATS provides for specific commitments covering: business services; communications; construction work for civil engineering; financial services; health-related and social services; and tourism services. The extent of commitments varies across sectors with certain restrictions on market access and national treatment under the four modes of supply of services. India has not made any commitments on services relating to: distribution; education; environment; recreation, culture and sporting; transport; and other services not included elsewhere. In all, India has made commitments in

**Table 4: Sectoral Employment Effects of Trade Liberalization
(Simulation 2) (Percent)**

Sectors	IND	RSA	ASN	NIE	USA	JPN	EUN
Agriculture	-0.06	-0.04	-0.09	-1.77	2.05	-0.93	0.14
Mining	3.08	0.03	0.04	-2.17	-0.32	0.53	0.50
Food	0.39	-0.35	0.13	-0.56	0.39	-0.36	0.13
Textiles	0.89	3.20	1.51	1.28	-0.76	0.12	-0.06
Wearing Apparel	5.65	16.34	4.35	3.54	-1.85	-0.24	-0.55
Leather Products	5.41	8.38	4.12	0.11	-1.79	-0.89	0.23
Wood Products	-0.15	-0.73	-0.44	-1.23	-0.17	-0.04	-0.04
Paper, Printing, Publishing	-0.36	-2.47	-0.65	-0.20	0.05	0.06	0.02
Petroleum Products	-0.14	-0.16	0.30	0.32	0.14	0.33	0.06
Chemicals, Rubber, Plastic	-0.57	-1.91	-1.15	-0.69	-0.17	0.39	0.25
Nonmetal. min. prod.	-0.38	-2.07	-1.40	-0.86	-0.26	0.16	0.08
Iron, Steel	-1.24	-5.83	-2.44	-1.55	-0.56	0.70	0.36
Non-Ferrous Metal	-2.30	-6.91	0.10	-1.66	-0.33	0.86	0.49
Ferrous Metal Products	3.40	-2.75	-2.26	-0.69	-0.14	0.19	0.01
Transport Equipment	-1.05	-6.39	-4.63	-0.96	-0.33	1.43	0.05
Manufactures; Including Electronic	-1.02	-1.94	2.00	-0.56	-0.42	0.32	-0.17
Machinery & Equipment	-3.65	-6.90	1.79	-1.40	-0.61	0.89	0.19
Electricity	0.24	0.99	0.54	0.30	0.14	0.22	0.01
Gas	0.24	0.91	0.28	0.16	0.12	0.22	-0.01
Water	0.24	0.95	0.52	0.24	0.14	0.17	-0.02
Construction	0.00	0.14	-0.29	-0.04	0.12	0.07	-0.02
Trade & Transport	-0.47	-0.94	0.64	2.41	0.15	-0.21	-0.33
Financial, Business, Recreation	-0.04	1.64	-0.57	-1.09	0.22	0.09	0.01
Public Admn., Defense, Education, Health	0.53	0.58	-1.98	-0.89	0.07	-0.04	-0.02
Dwellings	-0.12	-0.04	0.01	-0.17	0.02	0.15	-0.12

33 activities, compared with an average of 23 for developing countries. India has demonstrated a success story in the export of software services. The CGE model used in this study clearly demonstrates the additional benefits that the liberalization of trade in services can bring about for developing as well as developed countries/regions.

The main message for the developing countries is that they stand to gain through the liberalization of trade in services. The liberalization of trade in services is at a stage similar to where the liberalization of trade in goods sectors began more than 50 years ago. There should be no doubt that reduced barriers on trade in services in the future would bring benefits to both the developed as well as the developing economies, depending upon their respective degrees of comparative advantage in different service sectors in a liberalized world economy.

Table 5: Sectoral Effects on India of Trade Liberalization (Simulation 2) (Percent)

Sectors	Exports	Imports	Output	No. of firms	Scale Effect	Labor	Capital
Agriculture	6.40	1.09	-0.09	0.00	-0.09	-0.06	-0.10
Mining	6.27	-3.40	3.62	2.76	0.86	3.08	3.04
Food	6.47	9.80	0.41	0.13	0.28	0.39	0.18
Textiles	7.05	10.50	1.02	0.59	0.43	0.89	0.66
Wearing Apparel	10.76	11.31	5.73	5.26	0.47	5.65	5.42
Leather Products	8.37	8.54	5.69	4.89	0.79	5.41	5.18
Wood Products	4.13	13.50	-0.14	-0.28	0.13	-0.15	-0.39
Paper, Printing, Publishing	5.49	4.32	-0.26	-0.64	0.37	-0.36	-0.59
Petroleum Products	5.07	4.38	-0.13	-0.54	0.41	-0.14	-0.37
Chemicals, Rubber, Plastic	4.87	6.60	-0.44	-0.95	0.51	-0.57	-0.80
Nonmetal. min. prod.	6.27	13.96	-0.05	-0.50	0.44	-0.38	-0.61
Iron, Steel	5.20	7.51	-1.15	-1.54	0.39	-1.24	-1.47
Non-Ferrous Metal	4.32	3.19	-2.24	-2.64	0.41	-2.30	-2.53
Ferrous Metal Products	6.76	5.83	3.92	3.23	0.69	3.40	3.16
Transport Equipment	5.36	11.09	-0.60	-1.17	0.56	-1.05	-1.28
Manufactures, Including Electronic	4.38	12.87	-0.69	-1.24	0.55	-1.02	-1.25
Machinery & Equipment	3.73	9.55	-2.99	-3.77	0.78	-3.65	-3.88
Electricity	41.89	28.40	0.27	0.00	0.27	0.24	0.01
Gas	00.00	00.00	0.27	0.00	0.27	0.24	0.00
Water	00.00	00.00	0.27	0.00	0.27	0.24	0.01
Construction	8.39	6.68	-0.21	0.00	-0.21	0.00	-0.25
Trade & Transport	29.77	24.79	-0.38	-0.74	0.36	-0.47	-0.78
Financial, Business, Recreation	16.44	15.97	-0.08	-0.21	0.13	-0.04	-0.27
Public Admn., Defense, Education, Health	16.77	7.65	1.04	-0.19	1.23	0.53	0.30
Dwellings	00.00	00.00	-0.45	0.00	-0.45	-0.12	-0.35

Stiglitz (1999) has asked the WTO members to have well balanced trade negotiations in the next round, which should reflect the interests and concerns of the developing world. The two key principles of the next round should be "fairness," especially to the developing countries, and "comprehensiveness" such that sectors like construction and maritime services, which are of interest to the developing countries, must also get greater attention.

The next round of service negotiations requires a change in negotiating strategies (Mattoo, 1999). The developing countries need to push for liberalization of domestic service markets laying more emphasis on competition than a change of ownership. These countries should undertake domestic deregulation to encourage economic efficiency in remedying market failures and pushing social goals. Further, external service markets need to be effectively liberalized by the elimination of both explicit restrictions and implicit regulatory barriers. The developed countries should play a responsible role by eliminating their barriers against imports from the developing countries. These efforts would lead GATS negotiations into a "virtuous cycle of mutually beneficial liberalization." India's dynamic and growing software sector would transform India into a global software powerhouse even if the developed countries continue to impose restrictions on the movement of foreign workers.

The developing countries should look forward to more active participation during the next round of trade negotiations, and in particular to furthering the cause of GATS. The developing countries need to take great initiative in the process of GATS negotiations to put forward their points of view lest they should have to accept sectoral agreements in which they did not fully participate. No doubt, the developed countries must listen to the needs and aspirations of the developing countries and themselves also adhere to the basic lessons of comparative advantage. The gains are going to be shared by both, the developed as well as the developing countries, and both these groups should participate actively to ensure more equitable distribution of the resulting gains. Keeping in view specific provisions for freer movement of capital under GATS commitments, similar provisions must also address freer movement of labor. The future negotiations under GATS must focus on a 'comprehensive' approach rather than a 'case-by-case' approach to discussions. The negotiations during the last five years have been focussed on financial services, insurance and maritime transport. Simultaneous negotiations on all services must proceed in parallel so as to keep the interests of the developing countries fully involved. The developing countries would have great interest especially in various segments of transport other than maritime, construction and related services, and other sectors for which they may have a comparative advantage.

Notes

* The author expresses sincere thanks to Alan V. Deardorff and Robert M. Stern for continued guidance and support on issues relating to trade and CGE modeling. Special thanks to Rakesh Mohan for providing enduring encouragement and useful comments

during the course of this study. Thanks are also due to Sanjib Pohit who worked with the author on the NCAER's initiative on CGE trade models. Devender Pratap, Bikram Prakas Ghosh and Praveen Sachdeva provided excellent research support.

[1] See Tables B-2 and B-3 in the *Balance of Payments Statistics - Yearbook*, Parts 2 and 3, pp. 20-23 (IMF, 1998). "Services" include "transportation" (sea; air; and other), "travel" (business and personal), and "other services" (communications; construction; insurance; financial, computer and information; royalties and license fees; other business services; personal, cultural and recreational services; and government n.i.e).

[2] Within developing countries, Africa and Western Hemisphere have RCA in passenger services. The developing countries of Asia and Europe have RCA in freight services, which has been declining during the 1990s. The developing countries of Africa, the Middle East and Western Hemisphere have RCA in other transportation. While this has been declining in Africa and Middle East during the 1990s, it has been increasing in the Western Hemisphere. The developing countries of Europe achieved RCA in other transportation after the mid-1990s. In the case of travel, the developing countries of Africa, Asia and Western Hemisphere have RCA. While RCA has been increasing in the case of Africa, it has been declining for Asia and the Western Hemisphere. In the case of other services, Asia and Middle East have RCA. While it has been increasing in the case of Asia, it has been declining in the case of Middle East.

[3] Various theoretical aspects relating to trade in services have been discussed in detail in Bhagwati (1984), Grubel (1987) and UNCTAD-World Bank (1994). Issues relating to trade in services have been identified and discussed in Hindley (1988), Sampson and Snape (1985), and Sauvant (1990). Discussions of the implications and analysis of the GATS are provided in Brown, Deardorff, Fox and Stern (1996), Feketekuty (1998), Hoekman (1995, 1996), Hoekman and Braga (1997), Low (1995), Mattoo (1999) and Snape and Bosworth (1996).

[4] The structure of the GATS reflects both the special characteristics of services and services trade and the scope and coverage of the agreement itself. It includes the scope and definition of trade in services, general obligations and disciplines, specific (negotiated) commitments, progressive liberalization (through successive rounds of negotiations), and institutional and final provisions. The GATS thus consists of two major components, namely: (1) the framework agreement including the Articles of the Agreement and its Annexes; and (2) the schedules of specific commitments on national treatment and market access along with lists of exemptions from MFN treatment submitted by member governments. (See WTO, 1995: *The Results of the Uruguay Round of Multilateral Trade Negotiations: The Legal Texts* for details of GATS.)

[5] The developed countries are required to abstain from imposing conditions on the access to and use of public telecommunications transport networks and services. The conditions may, however, be imposed by the developed countries if necessary to ensure the availability of services to the general public, protect the technical integrity of networks or prevent the supply of services by countries that have not made specific commitments in the area of telecommunications. On the other hand, the developing countries may impose reasonable conditions on the access to and use of telecommunications networks that they consider necessary to strengthen domestic telecommunications infrastructure and capacity and to increase their participation in international trade in telecommunications services. The GATS members are expected to make available to developing countries information on international telecommunications services and de-

velopments in telecommunications and information technology in order to assist in the strengthening of their domestic telecommunications industries.

[6] The effective rate of protection (ERP) is a measure of the extent to which trade barriers protect domestic value added in production. The effective protection coefficient (EPC) is computed by dividing the value added at domestic prices by value added at world prices. The ERP = EPC – 1.

[7] Analogous to tariffs on traded inputs, the higher the tariff-equivalent of regulatory policies for services, the lower the effective protection for industries that use the service inputs involved (Hoekman and Braga, 1997).

[8] See Industrial Policy Statement, Ministry of Commerce, Government of India.

[9] India's commitments under GATS can be downloaded from the WTO website. These commitments are summarized in Tables AIV.3 and AIV.4 in WTO (1998).

[10] India had originally declared some MFN exemption in financial services (banking and insurance), which were later withdrawn during negotiations on financial services. India also increased the annual limit on foreign bank branches from eight to twelve.

[11] A detailed and very informative discussion of India's existing regulatory policies and commitments under GATS in financial, transportation, telecommunication, tourism and software services is provided in WTO (1998).

[12] Telecommunication services under GATS constitute a sector, which is very closely related to computer services. Telecommunication services constitute a component of "communication services" (GNS code 2C). With regard to telecommunications, there appears to be considerable overlap, particularly for the activities such as database and data processing services to be performed and/or supplied on line. Given the interplay between the two sectors' listed activities, it may not be clear when telecommunication-services, computer-services or both are supplied. While GATS directly addresses the progressive liberalization of computer and telecommunication services, the WTO agreements to eliminate tariff and non-tariff barriers on information and communication technology products are of great importance to both these services (1B and 2C).

[13] "Software" appears not covered under the existing GATS classification (GNS 1B). The provisional United Nations Central Product Classification (UNCPC) code 842 refers only to "consultancy" services related to "development and implementation" of software. The packaged or standardized software may be treated as a good, but consultants or other professionals, hired by a firm producing packaged software, may get covered by GATS' Mode-4 commitments. Moreover, it is not clear whether the online supply of packaged or even customized software should be classified as a good or a service. The provisional UNCPC code 842 refers only to "consultancy" services related to "development and implementation" of software.

[14] The share of on-site development, which was about 90 per cent in 1998-99, was 59 per cent in 1997-98. The offshore project development has been increasing since 1995 due to proliferation of Software Technology Parks, service of high speed data transfer provided by VSNL, liberalized economic policy, and visa restrictions by U.S. and some Western European countries. While the share of products and packages in the domestic market was 52 per cent in 1997-98, it is only 8.8 per cent in the export market. Major components of software export activity include professional services (48.4 per cent) and projects (31.5 per cent). The United States accounted for 58 per cent of India's software exports and Europe, 21 per cent.

[15] The Government of India has been supporting the development of the software and hardware sectors during the 1990s. Electronic Hardware Technology Parks (EHTPs) and Software Technology Parks (STPs) have been established since 1992 so as to attract foreign investment. Compulsory industrial licensing for the electronic-related industries was abolished in 1996. Investment in the electronics industry is unrestricted in terms of foreign share holdings or repatriation of profits. For export industries, there have been additional incentives such as a five-year tax holiday, tax exemption for income from exports, duty free imports of inputs and access to some imports through Special Import Licenses (SILs). There is no ceiling on the amount of foreign equity participation in EHTPs and STPs and export-processing zones (EPZs), or in 100 per cent export-oriented units. There is almost a computer revolution in the country, and both government and industry are getting more and more determined to strengthen the brand equity of Indian software industry and make the country an IT superpower.

[16] An Indian H1-B visa holder may get only $70 instead of $100 paid to a native for similar work. See Batuk Vora (1999) at www.indiatimes.com

[17] It is not possible to provide quantitative measures of commitments to liberalize trade in services in the same way as for goods since there are no comprehensive international data for trade in services by the four different modes of supply. Further, there is no equivalent of customs duties in services. The barriers to trade in services are camouflaged under quantitative restrictions, prohibition and the framework of government regulation with regard to the supply of services. The analysis of the economic impact of such measures or the effect of their removal thus does not lend itself readily to quantitative measurement. Hoekman (1996) provides "guesstimates" of the size of trade barriers in services. More recently, however, Dee and Hanslow (Chapter 5 above) provided estimates of services barriers based on sectoral studies of the banking and telecommunications sectors. Also, Brown and Stern (1999) have used estimates of services barriers derived from measures of price-cost margins.

[18] Also, the reader may consult the website, www.spp.umich.edu/rsie/ for more details on the Michigan Model.

[19] Rest of South Asia (RSA) includes Bangladesh, Bhutan, Maldives, Nepal, Pakistan and Sri Lanka. ASN includes Indonesia, Malaysia, the Philippines and Thailand. NIE includes Hong Kong, Singapore, South Korea and Taiwan Province of China.

References

Bhagwati, Jagdish N. 1984. "Splintering and Disembodiment of Services and Developing Nations," *World Economy* 7:133-44.

Brown, Drusilla, Alan V. Deardorff and Robert M. Stern. 1993. "Protection and Real Wages: Old and New Trade Theories and their Empirical Counterparts," Discussion Paper 331, Research Forum for International Economics, Institute of Public Policy Studies, University of Michigan.

Brown, Drusilla K., Alan V. Deardorff, Alan Fox and Robert M. Stern. 1996. "The Liberalization of Services Trade: Potential Impacts in the Aftermath of the Uruguay Round," in Will Martin and L. Alan Winters (eds.), *The Uruguay Round and the Developing Countries*. Cambridge: Cambridge University Press.

Brown, Drusilla K. and Robert M. Stern. 1999. "Measurement and Modeling of the Economic Effects of Trade and Investment Barriers in Services," presented at World Services Congress, Atlanta, GA, November 1-3.

Brown, Drusilla K, Alan V. Deardorff and Robert M. Stern. 2000. "Computational Analysis of the Accession of Chile to NAFTA and Western Hemisphere Integration," *The World Economy* 23:145-74.

Chadha, Rajesh and Sanjib Pohit. 1998. "Rationalising Tariff and Non-Tariff Barriers on Trade: Sectoral Impact on Indian Economy," paper prepared for *Tariff Commission*, Government of India.

Chadha, Rajesh, Sanjib Pohit, Robert M. Stern and Alan V. Deardorff. 1998. *The Impact of Trade and Domestic Policy Reforms in India: A CGE Modeling Approach.* Ann Arbor: University of Michigan Press.

Chadha, Rajesh, Drusilla K. Brown, Alan V. Deardorff, and Robert M. Stern. 2000. "Computational Analysis of India's Post-1991 Economic Reforms and the Impact of the Uruguay Round and Forthcoming WTO-2000 Trade Negotiations," presented at NCAER-World Bank, "WTO 2000 South Asia Workshop," New Delhi, December 20-21, 1999.

Feketekuty, Geza 1998. "Trade in Services-Bringing Services into the Multilateral Trading System," in Jagdish Bhagwati and Mathias Hirsch (eds.) *The Uruguay Round and Beyond.* New York: Springer.

Grubel, Herbert G. 1987. "All Trade Services Are Embodied in Material or People," *World Economy* 10(3): 319-30.

Hill, T.P. 1977. "On Goods and Services," *Review of Income and Wealth* 23, December.

Hindley, Brian. 1977. "Service Sector Protection: Considerations for Developing Countries," *World Bank Economic Review*, 2(2).

Hindley, B. and A. Smith. 1984. "Comparative Advantage and Trade in Services," *World Economy* 7(4): 369-90.

Hoekman, Bernard. 1995. "Tentative First Steps: An Assessment of the Uruguay Round Agreement on Services," *Centre for Economic Policy Research*, Working Paper.

Hoekman, Bernard 1996. "Assessing the General Agreement on Trade in Services," in Will Martin and L. Alan Winters (eds.), *The Uruguay Round and the Developing Countries.* Cambridge: Cambridge University Press.

Hoekman, Bernard and Carlos A. Primo Braga. 1997. "Protection and Trade in Services A Survey," *Open Economies Review* 8:285-308.

Hoekman, Bernard and Simeon Djankov 1997. "Towards A Free Trade Agreement with the European Union: Issues and Policy Options for Egypt," in A. Galal and Bernard Hoekman (eds.), *Regional Partners in Global Markets.* London: CEPR.

International Monetary Fund 1998. *Balance of Payments Statistics Year Book.* Washington, D.C

Low, Patrick 1995. "Impact of the Uruguay Round on Asia: Trade in Services and Trade-Related Investment Measures," unpublished manuscript.

Mattoo, Aaditya 1999. "Developing Countries in the New Round of GATS Negotiations: From a Defensive to a Pro-Active Role," *The WTO/World Bank Conference on Developing Countries and the Millennium Round*, Geneva, September.

McDougall, Robert et al. 1998. *Global Trade, Assistance and Protection: GTAP-4 Database.* Purdue University.

Mohan, Rakesh. 1996. Expert Group on Infrastructure, *India Infrastructure Report*. NCAER, New Delhi.

NCAER 1998. *Protection in Indian Industry*, Mimeograph.

NASSCOM 1999. *The Software Industry in India: A Strategic Review*, NASSCOM, New Delhi (www.nasscom.org)

Sampson, P. Gary and Richard H. Snape. 1985. "Identifying the Issues in Trade in Services" *World Economy* 8(2): 171-82.

Sauvant, Karl P. 1990. "The Tradability of Services" *Services in the World Economy*, The World Bank.

Snape, Richard H. and Malcolm Bosworth. 1996. "Advancing Services Negotiations," in Jeffrey J. Schott (ed.), *The World Trading System: Challenges Ahead*. Washington, DC: Institute for International Economics

Srinivasan, T. N. 1998. *Developing Countries and the Multilateral Trading System*. Westview.

Stiglitz, E. Joseph. 1999. "Two Principles for the Next Round: How to Bring Developing Countries in from the Cold," Keynote Address at the *WTO/World Bank Conference on Developing Countries and the Millennium Round*, Geneva, September.

UNCTAD-World Bank. 1994. *Liberalizing International Transactions in Services: A Handbook*, United Nations.

World Bank. 1998. *World Development Report, 1998/99*. Washington, D.C.

WTO. 1995. *The Results of the Uruguay Round of Multilateral Trade Negotiations: The Legal Texts*. Geneva.

WTO. 1998. *Trade Policy Review: India*. Bernan Associates, Geneva.

CHAPTER 12

Egypt's Service Liberalization, Service Barriers, and Implementation of the GATS Agreement[*]

Sahar Tohamy

I. Introduction

Given the upcoming WTO negotiations, countries and groups of countries are assessing further liberalization of their service sectors and are preparing nego-tiation strategies to maximize their benefits from the next round of WTO nego-tiations. The decision to liberalize services, however, may be made independ-ent of binding any policies with a WTO multilateral commitment. Many countries have decided to unilaterally liberalize and enhance competition in their economies without locking-in these policies in a multilateral agreement. Others capitalized on, what is known in the literature as, 'anchoring' policies. What this means, especially for developing countries, is that a commitment within the framework of a bilateral or multilateral legally binding agreement increases the expected impact of any change in policy.

This chapter focuses on Egypt. It attempts to summarize recent develop-ments in its services sectors, service trade patterns, and policy options regard-ing liberalization of services. The following questions are addressed:
1.   How important is the service sector in the Egyptian economy?
2.   What is the level of openness in Egypt's trade in services?
3.   What are the main features of Egypt's GATS commitments?
4.   What are the main service liberalization policies? Can they serve as a pre-condition to Egypt's next round of more extensive GATS commitments?

I first discuss the contribution of services to the Egyptian economy and thereafter the openness of Egypt's service sector relative to other countries, Egypt's GATS commitments, and the main features of Egypt's recent liberali-zation and privatization policies. Some policy recommendations are presented in the conclusion.

II. Contribution of Services to the Egyptian Economy

While there are many differences in economic structures among countries reflecting development levels, geographic location or resource endowment, variance in the size of services to GDP appears limited. Thus, for example, while the service sector's share in GDP amounts to 80 percent for a developed economy such as the United States, it only falls to 53 percent for a typical middle income country and to 37 for an average low-income economy. This means that irrespective of the level of development or income, services represent a large share in any economy, and what is even more important is that the share of services in economic activity grows with development. Any country pursuing economic development policies can therefore count on an increasing share of services in its GDP. Egypt's share of services in GDP appears to be generally consistent with other developing countries (Table 1).

Table 1. Contribution of Services to GDP in 1996, Selected Countries (%)

Country	Agriculture	Industry	Services
Algeria	13	48	38
Egypt	**17**	**32**	**51**
Indonesia	16	43	41
Jordan	5	30	64
Kuwait	0	53	46
Malaysia	13	46	41
Morocco	20	31	49
Pakistan	26	25	50
Turkey	17	28	55
Low Income	27	35	37
Middle Income	11	36	53
Low & Middle Income	15	34	51

Source: World Development Indicators, World Bank 1998

In contrast to the significant role that services play relative to commodity sectors within countries' economic activity, the contribution of services in international trade is significantly smaller. The share of services in foreign trade, while rising over the years, has been consistently smaller than the share of goods in international trade.[1] That share has stabilized over the last few years at around 20 percent of total trade in goods and commercial services.[2] The limited contribution that services play in international trade compared to their role in output can be a function of the existing patterns of trade liberalization in goods and the diminished attention that countries have paid to service liberalization.[3]

The contribution of services to Egypt's balance of payments shows a significant share for service receipts of Egypt's earnings of foreign currency. Similar to Egypt's pattern of export concentration in general, service exports are also concentrated in the traditional sources of service exports: tourism and Suez Canal (Table 2). This pattern creates major fluctuations in foreign exchange earnings, especially in combination with that same pattern of concentration in commodity exports of petroleum and agricultural products. Diversification becomes essential in both service and merchandise exports.

III. Assessment of Egypt's Service Trade Openness

As a rough indicator of a country's openness, the trade openness index measures a country's integration in world trade. The most basic openness index equals a country's share of imports and exports combined relative to GDP. Thus, the higher the ratio, the more open the economy. The indicator is not bound by a critical value of one, so that a country may have an openness index greater than one. Table 3 presents Egypt's merchandise and service trade openness indices.[4] Typical of most countries given the present international trade environment, the goods openness index is always higher than the services trade index. The service openness index, however, ranges from 80 percent of the goods index for Egypt to 8 percent of the goods index for Algeria.

Another indicator of openness is the size of Egypt's trade relative to world trade and the relative size of Egypt's GDP to world GDP. If its share in world trade is less than its share in world output, then this is another indication that Egypt's economy is less open than average. Using this indicator, Egypt appears to be more open than an average middle-income economy. When compared to world economies the same conclusion is reached (Table 4). Also for service sub-sectors such as transport and travel, Egypt's share in world trade is larger than its share in world's output. (Table 5).

IV. Egypt's Present GATS Commitments

The number of sectors where Egypt has made commitments is a preliminary indicator of how Egypt is similar to, or different from, other WTO member countries. Notice, however, that these patterns only indicate that commitments have been made in a sector and are not a comprehensive evaluation of the extent of a country's liberalization of services.

Figure 1 shows that countries are more likely to make commitments in sectors such as tourism, travel and other business services. The percentage of WTO countries that made commitments in a sector such as tourism (9) and financial services (7) is 93 and 73 percent, respectively. For sectors such as education (5) and health services (8) that percentage falls to 25 and 27 percent, respectively.

Table 2. Balance of Payments 1992-93-1997-98

US$ millions	1992/93	1993/94	1994/95	1995/96	1996/97	1997/98
Trade Balance	-7003.1	-7309.8	-7853.5	-9498.1	-10219.0	-11770.6
Exports**	3725.1	3337.3	4957.0	4608.5	5345.4	5128.4
Imports**	-110728.2	-10647.1	-12810.5	-14106.6	-15565.0	-16899.0
Services (net)	3561.0	3673.7	4041.8	5791.5	6192.8	4594.5
Receipts	8332.2	8677.3	9555.6	10636.0	11240.9	10443.8
Suez Canal	1941.1	1990.3	2058.4	1884.7	1848.9	1776.5
Tourism	2375.0	1779.3	2298.9	3009.1	3646.3	2940.5
Investment Income	882.9	1197.0	1625.5	1829.4	2052.3	2080.4
Other	3133.2	3710.7	3572.8	3912.8	3693.0	3646.4
Current Account Balance	2295.1	409.9	385.9	-185.4	118.6	-2772.3
Capital & Financial Account	1821.4	2510.9	429.7	1017.3	2040.7	3765.4
Net Errors & Omissions	195.0	814.6	61.4	-261.3	-247.0	-1128.1
Overall Balance	4311.5	2106.2	754.2	570.6	1912.3	-135.0

*Provisional
**Including the exports and imports of Free Zones as from the quarter 1996/97
Source: Ministry of Economy 1999

Table 3. Openness Index for Egypt and Selected Developing Countries

Country	Year	Openness Index Goods	Services	Country	Year	Openness Index Goods	Services
Egypt	1997	0.26	0.21	Bangladesh	1997	0.36	0.06
Indonesia	1997	0.48	0.11	Gambia	1994	0.00	0.00
Malaysia	1997	1.55	0.33	Kuwait	1997	0.73	0.23
Morocco	1997	0.48	0.13	Uganda	1996	0.26	0.13
Pakistan	1997	0.31	0.07	Algeria	1991	0.42	0.03
Tunisia	1997	0.69	0.19	Jordan	1997	0.78	0.46
Turkey	1997	0.42	0.15	Saudi Arabia	1996	0.63	0.20
Bahrain	1995	1.36	0.40				

Source: International Financial Statistics, IMF, January 1999
Note: Openness Index for Goods = Exports +Imports/GDP; Openness Index
for Services = (Services Credit +Services Debit)/GDP

Table 4. Egypt's Share in Output and World Trade, 1996 (%)

	GNP	Service Exports	Service Imports	(Service. X + Serv. M)
As % of middle income economies	3	16	6	10
As % of world	0.22	0.78	0.47	0.63

Source: IFS, January 1999

Table 5. Egypt's Share in Reported World Trade in Services, 1996 (%)

Sector	% of World	Sector	% of World
Transport	1.09	Financial	0.20
Travel	0.71	Computer	0.01
Communication	1.28	Royalties	0.10
Construction	0.00	Other	0.70
Insurance	0.04	Personal	0.02
Total			0.72

Source: WTO, S/C/W/27

When we divide the list into developed and developing countries, the percentage of developing countries making commitments in a sector is consistently lower than the percentage of developed countries making a commitment in the same sector (Figure 2). For sectors such as business (1) and communication services (2), 51 percent and 69 percent of developing countries made commitments. This is significantly lower than the 100 percent for developed countries in both sectors. The drop in percentages is not as significant for tourism (100 percent for developed countries versus 94 percent for developing).

When testing the null hypothesis that the percentage of countries making commitments in a particular sector for a developing country is equal to the percentage of developed countries making commitments in the same sector, we find that the null hypothesis is rejected at the 95 percent confidence level. This supports the finding in Figure 2.

The average number of sectors in which a developed country makes commitments is 9.25, while the average number for a developing country is 5.06 out of the 12 sectors.5 This difference is statistically significant at the 95 percent confidence level. Therefore, while developed and developing countries are more likely to make commitments in particular sectors, developing countries are making commitments in fewer sectors.

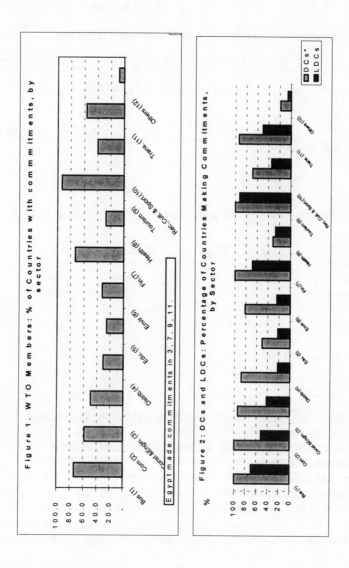

Figure 1. WTO Members: % of Countries with commitments, by sector

Egypt made commitments in 3, 7, 9, 11.

Figure 2: DCs and LDCs: Percentage of Countries Making Commitments, by Sector

In a cross-country comparison, we find that Egypt has made commitments in construction services (3), financial and banking (7), tourism (9) and transport (11). Therefore Egypt's choice of these four sectors is generally consistent with the willingness of countries to offer commitments. There are, however, two sectors where for both developed and developing countries the probability of having commitments is over 50 percent. These are business (1) and communication services (2). Egypt does not have any type of commitment in either of these two sectors.[6]

Two caveats are necessary before we reach the conclusion that Egypt may be less committed to liberalizing its services through GATS. First, whether or not a country makes commitments in a sector does not indicate how many commitments a country made in a specific sector. A country with multiple commitments in a sector will not be distinguishable from a country with a single commitment in the corresponding sector. From Table 6 , for example, we see that the average number of commitments per sector differs widely across countries. Thus, while for countries such as Turkey, Malaysia and Egypt the number of commitments/sector is 8, 7.7, and 7, respectively, the number of commitments/sector for other countries such as Indonesia and Bangladesh is 1.2 and 1 respectively. To complicate this picture further, there are horizontal commitments concerning general market access, national treatment, and most favored nation treatment that cut across all sectors (with occasional exceptions). These are more far reaching than a single commitment for a single sector. Second, the number of sectors where countries have made commitments does not indicate the extent of liberalization coverage that these commitments produce in a sector.

Tables 6 and 7 indicate that, compared to other developing countries, Egypt's number of commitments per sector, its sectoral coverage, etc. are not very different from an average developing country. Egypt is consistently, however, committing less than larger developing countries. This point is especially important given the literature that links trade openness with growth and development.

V. Egypt's Recent Liberalization and Privatization Policies

This section highlights the main developments of the liberalization and privatization policies in five main service sectors: telecommunications; banking and insurance; tourism; maritime services; and air transport. Finally, the last section discusses implications of a general liberalization of services on the whole economy and considers actual and potential linkages between services and the rest of the economy.

Table 6. Service Sectors Covered of Selected Organization for Islamic Countries

Countries	Number of commitments	Number of sectors where commitments were made	Average # of commitments/sector
Turkey	72	9	8.0
Malaysia	69	9	7.7
Kuwait	44	8	5.5
Morocco	41	7	5.9
Pakistan	35	6	5.8
Egypt	28	4	7.0
Tunisia	11	2	5.5
Indonesia	7	6	1.2
Bahrain	4	1	4.0
Bangladesh	1	1	1.0

Sources:http://www.wto.org/services/websum.htm;
http://www.icdt.org/publications.uttyy.htm

Basic and Value-Added Telecommunication

In 1998, Law 19/1998 transformed the National Telecommunications Authority, known as Egypt Telecom (and formerly ARENTO), into a joint-stock company. This law allows private-sector participation in Telecom Egypt. Initially, the state is expected to retain an 80 percent stake in the company. Also in 1998, the Government of Egypt (GOE) signed contracts and awarded licenses to two private sector consortiums to provide mobile telephone services in Egypt. Competition between the two companies has reduced prices and led to wider coverage and better customer service. This experience encouraged the government to offer two consortia franchise licenses to provide public phone service. Each company is allotted 20,000 lines. A regulatory body within the Ministry of Transportation and Telecommunication was established to assign frequencies, rates and interconnection rights and settle disputes.

Studies evaluating countries' experiences with telecom liberalization and deregulation provide powerful evidence of increased efficiency and better allocation of resources.[7] As a result of deregulation of U.S. telecommunications from 1984-87, carriers' average profitability rose in 1984 relative to 1981 and then fell by 1987 due to competition. Productivity of firms increased constantly throughout the period, 1981 to 1987. Competitive pressures from new entrants into the industry induced incumbent firms to reduce their prices between 1984 and 1987 (Majumdar, 1992).

Table 7. Sectoral Coverage of Specific Commitments in Trade in Services (%)

	High Income Countries	Other Countries	Large Developing Countries	Egypt
Market Access				
Average coverage (sectors/ modes listed as a share of total GATS classification, weighted by openness and biding scale factors)	40.6	9.4	17.1	10.48
"No restrictions" as a share of total offer made	56.4	47.3	36.7	47.1
"No restrictions" as a share of total GATS classification	30.5	6.7	10.9	7.9
National Treatment				
Average coverage (sectors/ modes listed as a share of total GATS classification, weighted by openness and binding scale factors)	42.4	10.2	18.8	11.69
"No restrictions" as a share of total offer made	65.1	60.4	49.3	61.5
"No restrictions" as a share of total GATS classification	35.3	8.5	14.6	10.3
Memorandum				
No restrictions on market access and national treatment as a share of total GATS classification	28	6.4	10	7.9

Source: American Chamber of Commerce, Egypt, 1998. Egypt's Financial Liberalization and the General Agreement of Trade in Services (GATS)

Imai (1994) reports similar results for Japan's deregulation of international telecommunication.[8] Deregulation brought about a rapid rise in total factor productivity and a corresponding 22.2 percent fall in Kokusai Denshin Denwa (KDD's) unit cost over the period from 1985 to 1992. Two new carriers entered the market in 1989 and eventually their combined share in the international telephone market reached 29 percent by 1992.

Insurance and Banking

The People's Assembly (Egyptian Parliament) passed Banking Law 155/1998, allowing private-sector entry and privatization of the 'Big Four' state-owned commercial banks.[9] Regulations for transferring a public-sector bank to the private sector, are almost complete. Egypt's commitments for banking, while considered to have the lowest level of restrictions in the Arab world, remain vague and leave many areas unconstrained by either an immediate or a future commitment. Specifically, restrictions are expected to produce a limited impact, except for insurance. The overall commitments account for less than 20 percent of the service sectors, and most of the commitments are not very far from the status quo.

Marshall (1994) argues that the 1983 deregulation of Indonesia's banking sector prompted a dramatic increase in the size of private banks, accounting for most of the growth in total bank assets from 1983 to 1988.[10] Although the 1988 deregulation allowed for a number of new entrants, the growth in assets after 1988 was attributable mainly to the expansion of previously established private banks. By 1992, these banks were about seven times larger than the new entrants were. Increased competition due to the 1988 deregulation induced a decline in bank profits, including those of larger incumbent banks.

In contrast to Egypt, countries such as Indonesia had begun liberalization and were seeing results before the conclusion of the GATS agreement in 1994. But what did Indonesia commit to in GATS regarding its financial sector? After over ten years of major liberalization in the banking sector, Indonesia was more willing to make detailed and specific commitments, which are not necessarily particularly liberal. This raises the issue of why some countries choose to liberalize services without necessarily binding these commitments within GATS.

Egypt's insurance sector is overwhelmingly public with a non-competitive market share, with three insurance companies forming an inefficient state oligopoly with a massive 90 percent market share. Law 156/1998 allows for privatization of these public-sector insurance companies and the privatization of Egypt's sole reinsurance company. The law has also removed all restrictions on majority private ownership (domestic or foreign) of insurance companies. Non-Egyptians may now manage insurance companies based in Egypt, whereas under former laws, all insurance companies operating in Egypt had to have an Egyptian managing director. It also waves the requirement that net profits, after deducting wages, reserves, provisions, and profit sharing for employees, be transferred to the State Treasury. It is reported that over the next two years the GOE will begin privatizing the public sector-dominated insurance industry. But no developments have been announced yet to address the expected privatization.

The absence of an effective anti-trust law in Egypt legally permits non-competitive business practices that can essentially block market entry and thus perpetuate inefficient oligopolies. Therefore, while privatization is important for both insurance and banking, the key to a healthy financial system is demonopolization and promoting of competition. Similar to telecommunications, a complementary regulatory framework for the privatized state-owned firms must be developed for insurance companies.

Other experiences with financial sector liberalization support the argument that caution must be exercised when liberalizing banks especially where a few large (public sector) banks dominate. Bonitsis and Rivera-Solis (1995) analyze the Spanish experience and argue that the entry of foreign banks has not contributed to lowering domestic bank concentration in the long run.[11] Given that domestic bank concentration did not decline significantly after liberalization, they argue that the sector's long-run competitiveness has not improved.

Tourism

Tourism as a service sector is already a major contributor to Egypt's Balance of Payments. It is generally in the private sector and even government-owned hotels are mostly managed by international hotel chains. GATS commitments in tourism, however, are fairly restrictive with many exemptions to market access and national treatment. There are restrictions on the ability of hotels and restaurants to employ foreigners, and there are needs tests and licensing required for the establishment of new hotels, especially in Sinai. Other tourist-related services, such as travel agency, bus services, etc. are either not bound by GATS or are subject to market-needs tests and horizontal commitments related to labor and land ownership. Despite limitations on market access and national treatment, many aspects of the sector are outward-oriented by nature and cannot be protected from international competition, at least in terms of price-quality combinations. Hence, its potential for liberalization.

Maritime Transport

In 1998, the GOE substantially reformed the port and maritime sector to allow private-sector entry. The GOE expects improved and more varied services due to increased private-sector competition. In January 1998, the new Maritime Law 1/1998 was issued modifying Law 12/1964, which gave the state a monopoly in maritime transport. After Law 1/1998 was issued, the Specialized Ports law 1/1996 was amended and new decrees regulating maritime transport works and licensing were issued to facilitate private-sector competition. The Specialized Ports Law 1/1996 was amended by Law 22/1998 on 25 March 1998 which allows concessions to local and foreign investors, at home or abroad, for the establishment of general or specified ports or platforms in existing ports. This law also governs the management, exploitation and maintenance of these ports and regulates fees levied by the GOE for their use.

The inefficient monopolies in ports and airports have long undermined Egyptian competitiveness in international markets. While there are deficiencies in the ports infrastructure and equipment, the main problem is the institutional structure. In the past, Egypt's high port costs have been due largely to public-sector shipping agencies and other government monopolies that control freight unloading, storage facilities and other services for traded commodities into and out of Egypt. Customs clearance is too slow and undertaken by unqualified workers.

Despite Egypt's favorable location, its transport costs to European markets exceed those of Cyprus, Greece and Israel. The government monopoly has led to import and export costs through Egyptian ports that are among the highest in the world and thus lower export competitiveness. Eliminating the government monopolies and introducing private-sector services in a competitive setting would lower the costs of exporting and importing and greatly enhance marketing. According to exporters, there are approximately 20 costly administrative steps, which cannot be justified for the services rendered. In addition, at least 17 percent of the overall costs go to the shipping agents, which is very high compared to ports of competitor countries. The issue of anti-trust and competition policies remains a concern in this sector.

The Holding Company for Maritime Transport and the Holding Company for Inland Transport have privatized fractions of their shares (20 percent and 17 percent respectively). Freight rates are decreasing as a proportion of the value of goods transported—they represented 6.64 percent of value in 1980 and 5.27 percent in 1997. These costs are comparable to other developing countries (8.3 percent) but higher than the corresponding share for developed countries (4.2 percent). More importantly is the implicit added cost of the red tape and lack of transparency. These costs do not even appear in the cost of freight.[12]

Air Transport

Limited progress has occurred in liberalization and privatization of the air transport sector. The government has signed six airport BOOT projects, but no progress has yet been made to offer a BOOT project to build a third terminal at Cairo Airport. The government still maintains its public monopoly at main airports such as Cairo Airport, and Egypt Air continues its monopoly on domestic air transport, with minimal private-sector-charter competition. It does not appear to be a priority sector for liberalization. Whether this situation is a result of concerns about government revenues, protection of Egypt Air and its interests or just a lack of urgency to liberalize the industry is unclear.

Other countries' experiences suggest that there are major gains to be had from liberalization of air transport services. Baltagi et al. (1995) show that the U.S. Airline Deregulation Act of 1978, which ended four decades of Civil Aeronautics Board (CAB) control of the domestic air passenger industry, has resulted in relaxation of price and entry regulations.[13] This led to lower airfares and thus to a significant increase in aggregate output.

Bowen and Leinbach (1996) show that all ASEAN countries partially privatized their state-owned flag carriers.[14] Although four major Southeast Asian carriers (Thai Airways International, Singapore Airlines, Malaysian Airlines and Philippine Airlines) were privatized, the state retained a substantial equity share. The increase in competition from the foreign carriers enhanced the efficiency of flag carriers and other domestic carriers. Domestic reforms increased flexibility in allocating licenses and setting fares and, as in the United Kingdom, allowed for privatization of state-owned companies.

General Liberalization of Services

Underlying the drive towards service liberalization is the fairly well-accepted principle that competition and liberalization of markets (for goods and services) provide the best environment for the allocation of resources. Hoekman (1998) estimates that a free trade agreement (FTA) that eliminates non-tariff barriers (where services usually produce the lion's share of these barriers), adds to welfare one-and-a-half times more than the welfare gain from a 'shallow' FTA that only eliminates tariffs. In other words, even in the context of enhancing benefits from an FTA that targets mostly merchandise trade, service liberalization enhances the benefits from liberalization.

As an example of how failure to liberalize services may dampen or contradict other policies, Galal and Hoekman (1997) show that Egypt's EU partnership agreement, which does not cover liberalization of services, will reverse the effective rates of protection situation prior to the agreement.[15] Prior to the agreement, regulations and different barriers to entry represents a 15 percent protection for services, while average nominal protection for manufacturing is much higher, producing an average effective rate of protection of 51 percent for manufacturing and average ERP of −36 percent for services. Because the Egypt-EU agreement excludes services and part of agriculture from liberalization, when the agreement reaches its final stages after 12 years of signing, the situation is reversed. Manufacturing will become negatively protected (taxed) because of its reliance on a protected service sector, while services will be positively protected because of cheaper manufactured goods.

Preliminary results using Egypt's input/output tables suggest that demand and employment multipliers maybe significantly higher for some types of services (Table 8). Especially with respect to employment creation, services with the potential to compete on international markets such as hotels and restaurants (tourism), insurance and transportation, may have more far-reaching benefits within the economy when compared to other export-oriented sectors in the economy, such chemicals, food production or furniture (Tohamy and Swinscoe, 1999, forthcoming).

VI. Conclusion and Policy Recommendations

Two issues appear to slow down service liberalization in Egypt. First, government monopolies have dominated many service sectors for the past four decades. There is, therefore, legitimate concern that eliminating barriers to allow private sector participation requires strong anti-trust laws and regulatory bodies to govern the newly- privatized sectors.

Table 8. Output and Employment Multipliers in Services for Selected Manufacturing Industries and Services

| | Final Demand Multipliers | | | |
| | Output Multipliers (LE)[1] | | Employment Multipliers (job)[2] | |
Selected Manufacturing Industries	Type I	Type II	Type I	Type II
Food Production	1.4062	1.8918	50.2080	84.8994
Beverages	1.4423	2.1159	38.3131	86.4412
Cotton ginning	2.2087	3.2221	n/a	n/a
Spinning & weaving	1.9374	2.9881	54.8367	129.9152
Ready-made garments & tailoring	1.7675	3.0022	103.4110	191.6257
Shoes	1.8072	3.0263	105.8133	192.9172
Furniture	1.1616	1.5920	75.3021	106.0537
Chemical products excluding refining	1.2266	1.8425	28.5149	72.5216
Porcelain & china	1.5078	2.3450	148.8505	208.6697
Construction & building	1.5389	2.4305	119.9362	183.6426
Services				
Wholesale & retailing	1.1936	1.8214	101.0072	145.8641
Restaurants & hotels	1.7367	2.6634	82.2371	148.4546
Loading & warehousing	1.4103	2.1360	29.3408	81.1937
Transportation	1.1079	1.9112	470.3916	527.7916
Financial institutions	1.1685	3.0938	70.1243	207.6899
Insurance	1.9159	3.4331	149.0635	257.4675
Real estate & housing	1.1944	2.0603	20.3180	82.1872
Social & society services	1.0132	5.6827	232.7136	566.3554
Entertainment & cultural services	1.2822	3.0337	75.3832	200.5317
Personal services	1.4696	2.7332	358.2545	448.5418

Source: The Central Agency For Public Mobilization And Statistics (CAPMAS), Population Census, July 1996. The Central Agency For Public Mobilization And Statistics (CAPMAS), Input-Output Table 1991/92. Multipliers: Tohamy and Swinscoe (1999), forthcoming.

Notes: 1. The final-demand output multiplier of an industry represents the total Egyptian pound change in output that occurs in all industries, for each additional pound change in final demand in the industry.

2. The final-demand employment multiplier of an industry represents the total change in number of jobs in all industries, for each additional 1 million Egyptian pound change in final demand in the industry.

Second, the government's approach appears to see liberalization as a means to achieve other goals such as providing lower prices of services to exporters of commodities, raising saving and investment levels and achieving progress on the program to privatize public sector firms. This emphasis on services as an input in the drive to promote other sectors in the economy, excludes from liberalization service sectors that have a higher growth potential and a smaller risk of market power.

If the commitment to liberalize services is made and the issue is sequencing liberalization, then the obvious place to start is in sectors that are initially private but lack dominant private players. The challenge of these sectors is that further liberalization means openness to foreign participation, and that may be less acceptable to policymakers and interest groups than allowing the domestic private participation through privatization.

If there is a vision for developing Egypt as a service-exporting country, there is a choice to be made: either rely on unilateral liberalization measures to allow for reversal in policies beyond what can be allowed under an international commitment, or lock-in policies through these agreements to enhance their credibility and the risk of reversal. Again quantitative analysis and country experiences suggest that the latter option produces the strongest impact of any change in policy.

Therefore, the decision to liberalize services should not be open for compromise, both by virtue of its role in enhancing the competitiveness of other sectors and by virtue of identifying services as an export-oriented activity. The issue of how to achieve this goal, however, should be allowed to vary from sector to sector and according to how the initial conditions of each sector dictate the choice between simultaneous liberalization and commitment under GATS or liberalization-cum-privatization and then GATS commitment.

Notes

[*] I would like to thank participants at the ERF 'Preparing for the WTO 2000 Negotiations: Mediterranean Interests and Perspectives, July 14-15, 1999 for helpful discussion and comments. I would also like to thank John Suomela, DEPRA, for discussing and providing suggestions to improve the paper. Finally, I am grateful to Malak Reda for excellent research assistance.

[1] Global exports of commercial services totaled $1.29 trillion in 1998, according to the WTO, up from $ 523 billion in 1995.

[2] Commercial services include transport, travel, communication services, insurance, financial services, computer and information, royalties and licenses, other business services, and personal, cultural and recreational services.

[3] Another reason for that pattern is the nature of service reporting, especially in developing countries: production and trade of goods generally lends itself easier to statistical coverage, more than services. For further discussion of data problems in service statistics, refer to WTO S/C/W/27, 'A Review of Statistics on Trade Flows in Services: Note by the Secretariat', (1997).

[4] When oil represents a large share of the country's output and exports, this can create a bias against non-oil producing countries and their level of openness. Therefore, an openness index that excludes oil from production and/or merchandise exports may be a better comparison indicator.

[5] This average applies for the group of 16 developed and 101 developing countries listed in the WTO tables. The list of developed countries is based on the IMF's classification of advanced economies used in *The World Economic Outlook*, May 1998.

[6] This ignores the fact that Egypt may have a comparative advantage in particular sectors justifying liberalization irrespective of other countries' patterns. It should be noted that in analyzing domestic conditions and competitiveness, other countries' patterns of commitments can be used as a proxy of which sectors are more suitable for liberalization.

[7] Majumdar, Sumit K. (1992), "Performance in the US telecommunications services industry: an analysis of the impact of deregulation," *Telecommunications Policy*, No. 4.

[8] Imai, Hiroyuki (1994), "Assessing the gains from deregulation in Japan's international telecommunications industry," *Journal Of Asian Economics*, No.3.

[9] No person or entity will be able to own more than a 10 percent stake in a 'Big Four' bank without Central Bank of Egypt (CBE) approval.

[10] Marshall, Kathryn G. (1994), "Competition and growth: Changes in Indonesia's banking sector since 1988," *Journal of Asian Business*, Volume 10, No. 3.

[11] Bonitsis, Theologos H., and Rivera-Solis, Luis E. (1995), "External liberalization of banking and industrial concentration: the evidence from Spain," *The Journal of Applied Business Research*, Volume 11, No. 3.

[12] See Fawzy (1998) and DEPRA report on constraints facing exporters and how they are estimated to add 15 percent tax on exporters.

[13] Baltagi, Badi H.; Griffin, James M. and Rich, Daniel P. (1995), "Airline Deregulation: The Cost Pieces of the Puzzle," *International Economic Review*, Vol. 36, No.1.

[14] Bowen, John T. and Leinbach, Thomas R. (1996), "Development and liberalization: the airline industry in ASEAN," in G.C. Hufbauer and C. Findlay (eds.), Flying High: Liberalizing Civil Aviation in the Asia Pacific, Institute for International Economics, Washington, D.C.

[15] For details about the expected coverage of the Egypt-EU Partnership Agreement see Galal and Hoekman (1997), several chapters.

References

American Chamber of Commerce in Egypt (1998)."Egypt's Financial Liberalization and The General Agreement of Trade in Services (GATS)."

The Central Agency for Public Mobilization and Statistics (CAP-MAS) (1998). Population Census, 1996. Cairo, Egypt.

The Central Agency for Public Mobilization and Statistics (CAP-MAS) (1992). Input-Output Tables, 1991/92. Cairo, Egypt.

Baltagi, Badi H.: Griffin, James M. and Rich, Daniel P. (1995). "Airline Deregulation: The Cost Pieces of the Puzzle." *International Economic Review*, Vol. 36, No.1.

Bonitsis, Theologos H., and Rivera-Solis, Luis E. (1995). "External liberalization of banking and industrial concentration: The evidence from Spain," *The Journal of Applied Business Research*, Volume 11, No.3.

Bowen, John T. and Leinbach, Thomas R. (1996). "Development and liberalization: The airline industry in ASEAN," in G.C. Hufbauer and C. Findlay (eds.), *Flying High: Liberalizing Civil Aviation in the Asia Pacific*, Institute for International Economics, Washington D.C.

Development Economic Policy Reform Analysis Project, (DEPRA), June 1998. "Enhancing Egypt's Exports."

Fawzy, S. (1998). "The Business Environment in Egypt." ECES, Working Paper No. 34.

Galal, A. and Hoekman, B. (1997). "Egypt and The partnership Agreement with the EU: The Road to Maximum Benefits" in *Regional Partners in Global Markets: Limits and Possibilities of the Euro-Med Agreements*. Cairo, Egypt: CEPR and ECES.

Hoekman, Bernard (1998), An Egypt- US. Free Trade Agreement: Economic Incentives and Effects, Cairo, Egypt: ECES working paper # 22

Imai, Hiroyuki (1994). "Assessing the gains from deregulation in Japan's international telecommunications industry," *Journal Of Asian Economics*, No.3.

IMF (1999). International Financial Statistics, January 1999.

Majumdar, Sumit K. (1992). "Performance in the US telecommunications services industry: an analysis of the impact of deregulation," *Telecommunications Policy*, No.4.

Marshall, Kathryn G. (1994). "Competition and growth: Changes in Indonesia are banking sector since 1988," *Journal of Asian Business*, Volume 10, No.3.

Ministry of Economy, February 1999. Quarterly Economic Digest. Cairo, Egypt.

The World Bank (1999). World Development Indicators (1998).

Tohamy and Swinscoe (1999), The Economic Impact of Tourism in Egypt, Cairo, Egypt: ECES. (forthcoming).

WTO (1997). "A Review of Statistics on Trade Flows in Services: Note by the Secretariat," S/C/W/27.

Web Sites:

http://www.wto.org/services/websum.htm

http://www.icdt.org/publications/uttyy.htm

CHAPTER 13

GATS 2000: As Seen from Senegal

Abdoulaye Ndiaye

I. Senegal's Commitments at the End of the Uruguay Round

The Growing Role of Services in the World Economy

For many years the marginalization of Africa has been the subject of impassioned debate. Sub-Saharan Africa's share of goods exports fell from 3.1 percent of world exports in 1955 to 1.2 percent in 1990.[1] This was due partly to a decline in world demand for the main exported products but also to a marked erosion of the market share of Sub-Saharan Africa. Commercial obstacles do not appear to have played a major role in this decline. It seems, rather, that the policies of the countries of Sub-Saharan Africa with respect to trade and transport heavily penalize exports and make them less competitive on the international markets. While Africa has lost market share in the global trade in goods, it should learn from that experience so as not to miss the rapidly growing trade in services.

Services currently represent over 60 percent of GNP in most of the developed economies and create the majority of jobs in those countries.[2] Service activities are involved in all economic sectors. They play a fundamental role not only in the service industries themselves but also in manufacturing and resource industries. In the United States, for example, 55 to 75 percent of jobs in the manufacturing sector are related to service activities.[3] In trade generally, services are the fastest growing component. Trade in commercial services increased on average by 7.7 percent per year between 1980 and 1993; the increase in the trade in goods was 4.9 percent. The share of commercial services in world trade increased from 17 percent in 1980 to over 22 percent in 1993. The most dynamic component of this category of services comes under the heading "other private services," which includes business services and a variety of other commercial services.

The fall in the cost of information technology offers the developing countries an opportunity to forge ahead with their technological development and to explore new fields of comparative advantage. The countries that will be in a position to exploit these opportunities will find that the internationalization of services helps them to catch up economically with the high-income countries. These opportunities go hand-in-hand with the need to improve the efficiency of the provision of services. This is a precondition not only in order to take advantage of new export opportunities but also because access to efficient services is going to play an increasingly important role in determining competitiveness as the share of services in the production process increases.

It will be essential for developing countries to adopt a liberal trade and investment regime if they wish to derive the maximum advantages from the internationalization of services. It will also be important for them to have an adequate material and human infrastructure, particularly by developing telecommunications and information technology networks and by sharpening the corresponding skills that they will need to benefit from the export opportunities that will open up in the rapidly expanding sector of information-technology-intensive services.

II. Senegal's Strategy with Regard to Commitments

Senegal was quick to realize its potential in the field of services, and it has declared its commitment to become a service-providing country on an international scale. Its attributes include: geographical location, which makes its port a transit point between Europe, Latin America and Africa south of the Sahara; its international airport, which since colonial times has been among the best equipped; and its climate, coastal resorts and culture, which constitute the basis of its tourism potential. Its capital, Dakar, hosts prestigious meetings such as the Francophone summit (1989), the Organization of African Unity summit (1992), and the Education For All conference (2000). Dakar is also the headquarters of a large number of international and subregional organizations. The Dakar International Fair, which takes place every two years and is a meeting place for industrialists, entrepreneurs and businessmen from throughout the world, has done much to shape its image as an international city. Dakar also hosts the biennial arts fair and the biennial African science and technology fair.

In order to play its full role as a service-providing country, Senegal invested early on in modern telecommunications infrastructure (e.g., fiber-optic cables) and undertook reforms to bring about a greater liberalization of the economy by privatizing the water- and electricity-distribution enterprises and the national telecommunication services that play a vital role in the Senegalese economy. In order to enable the private sector to serve as the engine of development and to attract direct foreign investment, the State has set up a wide range of arrangements to promote investment such as the 'one-stop shop' ("*guichet unique*"), which centralizes all the administrative formalities and procedures for approval connected with Senegal's Investment Code. Certain service activities, in particular production-support services, come under the Code.

The conditional offer of Senegal concerning its initial commitments in the field of services submitted in August 1993, on the eve of the closure of the Uruguay Round negotiations, was made subject to the satisfactory conclusion of negotiations to establish the General Agreement on Trade in Services and on securing balanced overall results in the Uruguay Round negotiations. Senegal's commitment depended on a set of balanced results that serve the interests of all the developing countries and which, at the same time, give Senegal good opportunities to export services and to benefit from an inflow of investment and a real transfer of technology.

The Coordinated African Programme of Assistance on Services (CA-PAS),[4] for which this chapter was originally written, has contributed to strengthening Senegalese capacity through an overview study on trade in services and in-depth surveys of four of the seven sectors covered by the Senegalese commitments: telecommunications; tourism and travel; support services for maritime transport; and financial services. The situation for all the seven sectors is summarized below.

Services to Enterprises

The offer by Senegal in the GATS relates to professional services (architecture and medical and dental services) and financial leasing services. In the field of architecture, the profession is well organized through the Council of the Order of Architects that monitors compliance with the rules of professional conduct among its members. Senegal has qualified human resources trained in European and American schools as well as in the University of Dakar, and more specifically, the School of Architecture and Town Planning. This expertise, which has been in existence since the country gained its independence in the early 1960s, made it possible, very early on, to export this service to other countries in the subregion. Thus, Senegalese architects carried out major construction projects (mainly buildings for professional use) in several African countries, often following international calls for tender. The artistic and cultural dimension, which Senegalese architects incorporate in their designs over and above the requirements of modern technical standards, has been highly appreciated by the export market. Architectural design practices have constantly been kept up to date by using the most modern computer tools and specialized software.

In its schedule of specific commitments, Senegal did not bind modes 1, 3 and 4 with respect to limitations on market access. No limitation was set on national treatment except for mode 4 (movement of natural persons) where Senegal retained the status quo. Senegal reserves the possibility to make bolder commitments in the future in the direction of greater liberalization of the sector in conjunction with the Council of the Order of Architects. From the outset, this sector has included foreign architects (in the form of overseas architectural design practices). These practices are members of the Order and enjoy the same prerogatives as national practices.

In the medical field, the faculty of medicine and pharmacy has, since colonial times, trained numerous African doctors and pharmacists, most of whom settled in Dakar after completing their studies. Nationals who are certified by schools of medicine in developed countries tend to return home and to open their own medical practices after having worked for a number of years in hospitals or in a faculty of medicine. However, many of them have taken advantage of post-university scholarship grants to specialize in a state-of-the-art discipline. In this way, the medical services provided by such professionals have become diversified, increasingly specialized, and of a quality equal to that of the developed countries in terms of know-how and technical expertise. These professionals have even acquired distinctive expertise in certain fields such as tropical diseases or the utilization of the traditional pharmacopeia in conjunction with modern medicine. The use of the new information and communication technologies and, more specifically, of telemedicine, bears witness to the immense effort made by the medical sector in order to keep up with technological progress and tailor it to its own situation. Unfortunately, the sector is still subject to the constraints of a developing country; for this reason, there are quite commonly major shortages of basic equipment in the public sector.

At the international level, the health sector is characterized by increasingly sophisticated equipment incorporating the most advanced technologies (computers, laser, digitalization, etc.) and by highly advanced techniques (biotechnology, microsurgery, laser treatment, etc.) which are the product of research laboratories whose budgets are out of all proportion to the resources of the developing countries. Senegal has opted to become a regional center for the provision of medical services. In order to benefit from all these technologies, which are developing at an increasing pace, the best strategy would be to liberalize the sector in order to attract capital, technology and know-how. Already, the success that has been achieved in the creation of a number of clinics with sophisticated equipment (e.g., laser scanners) together with private national and foreign partners, is a sign of what could be achieved through the opening up of the sector.

In its offer on medical and dental services, Senegal's commitments were dictated by prudence. Concerning market access, Senegal did not bind mode 1 while there is no limit for mode 2 (consumption abroad). Senegal thus wished to preserve, on the one hand, the possibility for nationals of the subregion to continue to come to Dakar for treatment and, on the other, the possibility of ensuring medical evacuation for nationals who can afford it to countries that are better equipped or more highly specialized in certain fields. Mode 3 (commercial presence) remains subject to authorization. Mode 4 (presence of natural persons) is not bound, probably because of the fact that the profession is highly organized around the Order of Doctors which safeguards both the interests of the profession and the observance of the rules of professional practice which protect patients.

Communication Services

In the field of postal services, the National Postal Company (*Société Nationale des Postes*), which is a State company with managerial independence, used to have a monopoly. However, with respect to express mail, the State has adopted a flexible and progressive liberalization policy that has attracted the major world-wide express courier companies (DHL, UPS, Federal Express, Airborne Express, and so forth), which have air- and land-transport facilities of their own as well as highly sophisticated international logistics. The presence of these operators encouraged the Senegalese postal service, which had previously been a monopoly, to create its own express courier service (EMS) and, stimulated by the competition thus created, to offer services of higher quality than its other services had traditionally offered.

Senegal has always been at the forefront of investment in the telecommunications sector in Africa. The national telecommunication company (SONATEL) has since 1986 been implementing an investment program to provide all the regions of Senegal with modern infrastructure, including digital telephone exchanges, and to break the isolation of rural localities (rural telephone). Thus, as early as 1988, the extension and modernization of the Dakar network provided a means of meeting the needs of enterprises and offering them a higher quality of service. The implementation of the national-packet data-communication network (SENPAC) offers enterprises and administrations a high-performance, data-transmission tool: access to data banks; and interconnection to the foreign networks of France, Switzerland, Germany, Canada, the United States, Belgium; etc. Between 1986 and 1995, more than 150 villages were provided with modern telecommunication systems which gave them access to the automatic network and to a large range of new services (detailed billing, temporary call forwarding, automatic wake-up, etc.). The *Axe Nord* 11 project, which was designed to extend and modernize the northern regions, introduced digital fiber-optic communication for the first time and launched Senegal into the age of advanced technology that had hitherto been almost unknown in Africa. It also made it possible not only to equip 65 rural localities in inland regions but also to place a reliable high-performance transmission facility at the disposal of industrialists and economic interest groups.

Senegal's offer concerning communication services was made in two phases. The April 1994 schedule had simply retained the status quo in relation to existing regulations. At that time, SONATEL, whose capital was fully owned by the State, had a telecommunications monopoly. In the framework of the reforms of the telecommunications sector, the State announced in 1995 its policy to privatize the national operator. A strategic foreign partner was selected following an international call for tender. The State granted the partner about one third of the capital and kept the same proportion. The remaining shares were distributed among the staff of the enterprise and the public. During this process of privatization, a Telecommunication Code was drafted that took into account the advent of new information and communication technologies and classified the activities of the sector into three categories: those that were a monopoly; those that were subject to authorization; and those that had been liberalized. The State extended the monopoly element of the new structure until to at least 2003, at which time it will consider the possibility of opening up the sector to other operators.

The desire of SONATEL to relinquish part of the operation of the telephone network to private individuals dates back to 1992. A great deal is to be learned from the extraordinary success of the private telecenters, and the information gathered may prove useful in the strategy for disseminating the services. In addition to the telephone service, which is the major feature, some of these communication centers also possess fax machines, Minitel terminals give access to local and international data banks, photocopiers and laptop computers with word-processing software. Increasing numbers of telecenters now offer the opportunity of connection to the Internet. Telecenters were responsible for the creation of over 10,000 jobs between 1992 and 1998 and are widely available in rural areas; their turnover reached CFAF 9,226 million in 1995.[5]

During the same period, as soon as the Uruguay Round ended, WTO member governments agreed to continue negotiations in four areas, including basic telecommunications. They had not offered to make commitments during the Uruguay Round essentially because the privatization of state monopolies had raised complex problems in many countries. Negotiations on basic telecommunications were completed in January 1997, and new national commitments were due to take effect in January 1998.

The schedule of Senegal's specific commitments dates from April 1997. The part of the schedule concerning telecommunication services replaced the initial schedule of 1994. Senegal's schedule took into account the outcome of the reform of the sector that had been institutionalized in the Telecommunication Code. As far as limitations on market access were concerned, Senegal did not make any commitment on the cross-border provision of basic local, intercity, and international services provided in the public telecommunication networks that still came under the monopoly of SONATEL. The same applied to commercial presence. Concerning mobile cellular services, Senegal had announced in its schedule the intention to launch an international call for tender for the selection of one or two operators. A second operator, SENTEL (a subsidiary of the international financial group Millicom), was selected and began its activities in April 1999.

The other telecommunication services may be provided either freely or subject to prior authorization. This applies in particular to value-added services such as Internet service providers, data transmission, radio paging, video conferencing, the engineering of communication systems, inshore communications, and one-way or two-way earth stations.

Distribution Services

Immediately following independence, distribution was in the hands of Lebanese-Syrian enterprises. Senegalese nationals progressively became involved in the sector beginning at the retail level and then wholesale commerce, before embarking on the importation of goods. Better known as the informal sector, they became involved in all types of commerce and finished by dominating the distribution sector. However, during the last 15 years, Senegal has embarked on a policy of liberalization that did away with the majority of the prior authorizations and import licenses. The opening up of the sector made it possible to attract major distribution chains such as Leader Price of the United States, which established a dynamic system of franchises, and the Korean LG (more specialized in the distribution of household electrical goods). Senegal's offer is the confirmation of this desire to liberalize and to attract foreign investors to the distribution sector.

Services Relating to Tourism and Travel

With revenue of CFAF 100.1 billion in 1998,[6] tourism is in second place after fisheries in the export earnings of Senegal, and ahead of groundnuts and phosphates. In 1998, the number of tourists totaled 468,835 as against 419,683 in 1997, a rise of 11.7 percent. Tourism has always played a strategic role in the development of Senegal. The main sources of tourists are France (with 56.6 percent of non-resident visitor-nights), and Africa (14.9 percent), followed by Germany, the Benelux countries and Italy.

Business hotels accounted for one-third of visitor-nights, while holiday villages and hotels accounted for the remainder. The average bed-occupancy rate of tourist establishments was 40 percent in 1998. The spare capacity shows that more effort should be made to attract a larger number of tourists, in particular through the diversification of markets. The potential of the American market is far from having been exploited.

The schedule of Senegal's commitments covers hotels, tourist campsites and other commercial accommodation sites, as one group, and restaurants, bars and canteens as a second group. These commitments are fully in keeping with Senegal's desire to promote direct foreign investment in the sector.

Recreational, Cultural, and Sports Services

Senegal has included recreational fishing under this heading. This activity is directly connected with tourism and travel to the extent that the target market is the same. The sport-fishing club of the multinational company, Air Afrique, has contributed substantially to the promotion of this activity, although a permit is nevertheless required to settle in Senegal for this purpose.

Transport Services

Negotiations on maritime transport were originally to have been completed in June 1996, but the WTO participants were unable to reach agreement on a set of commitments. Discussions will resume with the next round of negotiations on services. Commitments have already been included in the schedules of certain countries covering the three main areas of this sector: access to port facilities; support services; and shipping on the high seas.

The schedule of Senegal's commitments covers maritime-transport-support services, in particular shipping-agency services, handling and transit services, and ship chandlery. In its ninth development plan, Senegal identifies itself as a service-providing country one of whose focal points is the port of Dakar. A recent study (conducted by port management) shows that the port of Dakar remains highly competitive as compared with other ports on the West African coast, in spite of the scope that remains for improvement both with respect to costs and to the quality of services provided.

These sectors, which entail a major outlay of capital investment, were traditionally dominated by branches of foreign firms. Mergers have subsequently taken place between foreign companies, strengthening their dominant position and resulting in an increase in the cost of services. This situation partly accounts for the high cost of services in the handling sector in particular. Handling alone represents 38.7 percent of the cost of a ton of goods passing through the port of Dakar. Local enterprises had difficulty in gaining access to these sectors because of the high level of investment required and the requirement for prior authorization from the Ministry of Finance, which emphasizes good character and solvency checks, in particular in the field of transit and customs clearance. Indeed, many local enterprises that had made a start in the transit and customs-clearance sector and had received a customs waiver from the Ministry of Finance ultimately accumulated substantial debts that they were incapable of repaying because of their poor financial standing.

The opening up of the shipping-services-support sector was to attract other operators from throughout the world and create a competitive environment, resulting in lower costs and enhancing the competitiveness of the port of Dakar. Unfortunately, Senegal's offer has not yet had any effect. There have been few foreign investments. This may be due to the fact that the enterprises that had dominated the sector had been established for a long time (dating back to the colonial period), and so it was difficult for newcomers to compete with them in an unfamiliar country, or because the conditions for a high standard of competitiveness had not yet been met, in particular due to cumbersome administrative procedures. These are questions that must be clarified in order to enable Senegal to receive more direct investment in the maritime sector.

In its schedule for exemption from Article II (MFN), Senegal included coastal trading, as a means of stimulating trade and promoting regional economic integration. Similarly, the desire to comply with the resolutions of the Ministerial Conference of West and Central African States on Maritime

Transport (MCWS) so as to give effect to the UNCTAD arrangement that provides for the sharing of 80 percent of liner trade flows with the national shipping company of the State of destination, induced Senegal to include shipping in its MFN waiver schedule. However, one may question the relevance of such a decision in the light of the fact that most of the attempts to create a national shipping company have failed. Moreover, the high level of investment makes it essential to turn to foreign investors, and that would restore the situation that provided the original motivation for such a decision.

Financial Services

At the end of the Uruguay Round negotiations in 1993, negotiations on financial services, as well as those relating to basic telecommunications and maritime transport, had not been completed. Specific commitments concerning market access and the granting of national treatment for financial services had been made in this sector, but they were not considered adequate to bring the negotiations to a conclusion. There were substantial exemptions to the MFN obligation based on reciprocity. The second annex of the GATS and the Decision on financial services adopted at the end of the Uruguay Round envisaged further negotiations in this sector. The negotiations concluded on December 12, 1997 and the Fifth Protocol, which legally enshrines the outcome of those negotiations, was due to enter into force on March 1, 1999 at the latest.

The schedule of specific commitments by Senegal on financial services covers insurance and related services, and banking and other financial services. It must be noted that the policies relating to the financial sector, which are increasingly tending to be defined on a regional basis, together with the sensitivity of the sector, were among the factors that induced Senegal to invoke the provisions of paragraph 2 (a) of the annex, which provides that countries may take measures for prudential reasons, in particular for the protection of investors, depositors and the holders of insurance policies, and to preserve the integrity and stability of the financial system.

As Senegal is a signatory of the CIMA Code (Inter-African Conference on Insurance Markets), it endeavors to safeguard the preferential treatment granted to signatory States under which insurance contracts applying to persons who have the status of resident or to property located in Senegal, as well as liability insurance, can only be taken out with bodies approved to conduct insurance business in Senegal. As the financial market of West Africa is in the process of being set up, the States justify the preferential treatment on grounds of the need to support the effort to harmonize national policies in the insurance sector with a view to achieving a competitive position world-wide.

At the level of banking services, Senegal is a member of WAMU (West African Monetary Union) and of WAEMU (West African Economic and Monetary Union), which provide the framework governing the monetary policies of the Member States. Senegal's schedule merely reflects the banking regulations that apply uniformly to all the member countries of WAEMU. It relates to the acceptance of deposits and other reimbursable funds from the public, to loans of all types and to all settlement and cash transfer services, including credit cards, charge cards, etc., travelers checks and drafts. Only approved banks and financial establishments can carry out these activities in accordance with procedures that are clearly defined by banking legislation.

III. Service Sectors with Export Potential

Maritime Transport

Senegal has always wished to play a major role in ship repair in West Africa. The Dakar Marine shipyard was created at a time when, for several years, the Suez Canal was closed to maritime traffic, as a result of which ships sailing between Europe, the Far East and Asia had to make a detour passing Dakar and the Cape in South Africa. The state company enjoyed a golden age up to the reopening of the Suez Canal. Thereafter, a difficult period began during which demand was inadequate relative to the oversized capacity of the shipyard. In spite of various rescue attempts (staff cuts, termination or curtailment of certain activities), the enterprise continued to be in difficulty. The State embarked on a process of privatization that was only finally completed in 1999 with Portuguese participation in the capital of the new company, thenceforth named DAKARNAVE. The experience of the Portuguese partners in the field of maritime transport and the increase in the demand for services in this sector, in particular with the Asian financial crisis which included countries traditionally offering this kind of service, were to restore the position of Dakar as a center for the provision of services to foreign shipping.

The West African coast is customarily served by regular shipping conference lines between Europe and Africa that regularly call only at certain ports (Dakar, Abidjan, Lomé, Cotonou, Douala, Libreville). The idea of creating a coastal trading company arose from the need to transport the remaining cargo that was not handled by the major shipping companies. This coastal trading company, which is aimed at a niche market, will initially concentrate its activities on the portion of coastline between the port of Nouadhibou in Mauritania and that of Abidjan in Côte d'Ivoire. This link will subsequently be extended to Togo and Benin if the market survey is positive. The various shippers of the sub-region will be involved, thereby strengthening intra-regional trade.

The reforms of the port of Dakar and the projected investments are designed to make Dakar a hub in the sub-region. Indeed, Dakar could serve neighboring countries such as Mauritania, Mali, the Gambia and Guinea-Bissau on condition that it becomes a highly competitive port with modern equipment (gantry cranes, more advanced computerization) and can offer prompt, high quality services.

Land Transport

In order to enhance its role as a transit country for goods bound for Mali, the Government of Senegal has devised a multi-pronged strategy entailing the building of the Dakar-Bamako trunk road and the relaunching of the Dakar-Bamako railway, as well as the construction of Senegalese warehouses in Mali. Dakar lost its position as the chief city for the transit of Malian cargo to Abidjan, which had more highly developed road links with Mali. However, the development of the Dakar-Bamako trunk road would provide a means of redressing this situation. By adopting the Inter-State Road Transit Convention (ISRT) – which considerably simplifies the formalities for the inspection of goods carried by road to neighboring States – Senegal has confirmed its chosen role as a transit country and as a transshipment terminal.

The Dakar-Bamako railway, which has been in existence since colonial times, has created a trade flow that has become a tradition between Senegal and Mali. Accordingly, there has been a large settled Malian community in Dakar since that time, employed mainly in the railway traffic business, and a similar Senegalese colony in Bamako. Moreover, even if most of the cargo is landed at Dakar and Bamako, there are towns that act as staging posts on either side of the frontier where goods are loaded and unloaded at a steady rate. This activity cannot be replaced by the Abidjan-Bamako link road.

In addition, the Malian warehouse facilities in Dakar, which have been in existence for a very long time, have no equivalent in Bamako. Thus, in order to make the link more profitable, it is necessary to generate traffic in both directions. The construction of the Senegalese warehouses in Mali will contribute to improving the traffic along this link.

Lastly, the decision by the Malian and Senegalese authorities to privatize the railway companies by creating, in particular, a new private company with private Malian and Senegalese capital will enable the link to be managed more rationally and effectively. Bearing in mind the level of investment required to rehabilitate the plant, however, a strategic foreign partner will probably be sought to provide the technology and financing.

Telecommunications

The quality of Senegalese telecommunication infrastructure, the quality of its human resources and the trend toward outsourcing that has been taking place at the international level, open up many possibilities for the country in the field of tele-services: the provision of value-added services, between distinct juridical entities, using the tools of communication. This offers new prospects for job creation in the age of the information society. The following is a short list of a number of tele-service activities:

- Functional tele-services entailing services to enterprises characterized by the remote provision of services: tele-secretarial services; tele-acquisition; tele-translation; tele-management; and tele-counseling

- Tele-informatics—the range of information services provided remotely such as: engineering; software development; installation and maintenance; and backup and archiving
- Tele-management and tele-monitoring of equipment or networks
- Tele-education
- Tele-medicine (medical assistance, diagnosis, transfer of images for therapy, and simulation)
- Tele-services for information, brokerage, computer-based mediation
- Tele-procurement (transaction services)

In view of the export potential of this sector, the Government is considering measures that might promote tele-services in Senegal, including:

- The eligibility of tele-service enterprises to benefit from the regime that applies to duty-free export enterprises and confers fiscal and customs benefits on them. This is a significant advance in the taxation of services that are in the future to be on the same footing as industrial goods.
- Providing the Supreme Council of Industry with the financial and technical resources to facilitate the certification of tele-service enterprises under the standards of ISO 9000.
- Inducing SONATEL (national operator) to set a standard rate for Internet connections on the basis of a rate lower than that in force for local calls. The standard rate would be the same throughout the territory.
- Setting up service incubators.
- Promoting electronic commerce.

Certain recently created private enterprises are already using telematics to export services, in particular through remote capture and the processing of manually drawn architectural plans using architectural design software, and industrial drawings for European clients. As far as the written press is concerned, certain daily newspapers are inputted and formatted every day in Dakar and then sent electronically for printing. Finally, one enterprise is trying to produce cartoons through computer-aided drawings for European clients.

Senegal has computer engineers certified by the world leaders in software engineering and is therefore very well placed to participate in software development for the international market.

Education

Senegal has three universities (two public and one private) and many public and private vocational training establishments. A dozen higher education training institutes have been set up over the past ten years and are far from being able to meet the demand for education from thousands of students and mid-career professionals who apply to them each year. In order to meet this growing demand, Senegal should not only increase the number of training places on offer but also decentralize training activities throughout the sub-region, either through traveling seminars or in partnership with local training facilities in each country.

At the level of general and vocational education, Senegal has since 1972 been a signatory of technical cooperation agreements with Gabon with a view to providing that country with teachers to work in the Gabonese education system, and large numbers of teachers have carried out fairly long missions in Gabon over the past twenty years. Today, 14 teachers occupy teaching posts in that country in the framework of this official cooperation program. But the Gabonese market has also attracted other Senegalese teachers. There are today 250 of them, including 150 with expatriate contracts and 100 with local contracts. Other African countries have followed the example of Gabon, in particular the Central African Republic, the Comoros and Djibouti.

There is also an increasing availability of training opportunities in bilingual (English and French) programs. Private bilingual schools are coming into existence at the primary, secondary and higher levels. There has been a favorable response to such initiatives as shown by the fact that all these schools are operating at full capacity. Senegal might submit a schedule of commitments in this sector in order to attract other investors.

Certain Professional Services

Senegalese accountancy firms and consultants (freelance or established practices) customarily work in other African countries in order to support them in their development process. Accountancy as a profession developed very soon after independence because of the presence of offices representing the major international groups, commonly called "the Big Six" (which later became "the Big Four" because of mergers). Although most of the Senegalese accountants are trained in Europe, training colleges offering courses leading to an accountancy qualification have enabled many managers to join the profession. They have international standing because of the international practices to which they are affiliated and they carry out numerous audit missions commissioned by development agencies in the sub-region. To a lesser extent, non-Senegalese experts have been employed in Senegal, in particular with sub-regional bodies, as either external or internal auditors.

The consulting profession developed early in the 1970s when Senegal, which was then feeling the full impact of the oil crisis, was unable to absorb the personnel graduating from its higher education system. In addition, managers in both the public and the private sector are increasingly tending to leave their employment to become consultants. As a result of their availability, bilateral and multilateral cooperation bodies have begun to seek local expertise to take part in joint missions with international experts. There have also been programs financed by development partners that have helped the national consultants to join together to form professional associations. These bodies have done much to make potential clients (public administrations, donors, private sector) more aware, and above all to upgrade the profession. The quality of the services offered on the international market has prompted the same clients (who, in many cases, are decision-makers in other countries) to involve them in the sub-region.

Increasing numbers of foreign engineering and design offices are now seeking local practices or consultants as partners in missions which the former have to carry out in Senegal or in the sub-region. Certain countries, such as the United States, oblige their consulting firms to associate with local consultants in Africa if they wish to submit offers in response to calls for tender launched by the Government (or one of its agencies) in order to carry out a survey mission in an African country. This arrangement increases the outsourcing opportunities for local practices and even facilitates closer and more balanced participation in the case of partnership where a tender is submitted. Unfortunately, not all countries that support Africa in its development have adopted such arrangements.

In the field of construction, Senegalese manpower has always been much in demand in Africa and the Middle East. Toward the end of the 1960s, Gabon, which was at that time a country fully engaged in construction, called for qualified Senegalese manpower in the building trades and public works. Every year, several hundred Senegalese workers have gone to Gabon on an official basis. Kuwait, in its reconstruction phase after the war, also called on Senegalese workers in various trades. On a more sporadic basis, qualified Senegalese workers are recruited by construction firms working in Saudi Arabia.

As can be seen, the services linked to the expertise of Senegalese human resources have a great deal of export potential. But rather than responding to this world-wide demand on an official but piecemeal basis, or on an unofficial or undeclared basis, Senegal could devise a real strategy for the export of the services of its qualified human resources, for example by means of a data bank on opportunities for appointment abroad that would be widely publicized among Senegalese manpower and among enterprises specializing in the recruitment and placement of qualified workers.

IV. Fields in Which Senegal Might Relax Its Restrictions

Land Transport

Public transport in Dakar and its suburbs used to be provided by a state company, SOTRAC. However, it had managerial problems and difficulties connected with the replacement of its fleet of vehicles and as a result the Government closed the company down. A set of specifications was drawn up with a view to launching an international call for tenders for the management of the new transport structure that was to be created, together with the option of setting up a bus assembly plant. This sector is a classic example of a case in which the lifting of certain constraints, such as the requirement to obtain operating permits, might attract foreign investors with adequate capital and expertise in transport logistics. It is also necessary to emphasize the need to improve the transport environment: to combat the anarchy of black-market carriers; to repair the roads; and to improve road signs and signals, and traffic flow.

Maritim-Transport-Support Services

Certain activities such as the piloting of ships into the harbor of Dakar might be progressively liberalized in order to enable other investors to enter the sector, thus bringing the charges for such services down to a more competitive level. At present, ships arriving at the port have no choice with respect to the tariff charged by the towing company. Moreover, the diversification and increased availability of handling facilities should promote the creation of a more open market and therefore lead to more competitive pricing.

Audiovisual

The progressive liberalization of radio broadcasting has enabled many private stations to establish themselves in Dakar and the regions. RTS (the national company responsible for radio and television production and broadcasting) provides wide radio and television coverage throughout the territory. Five private national FM radio programs compete with it, with varying coverage. Two other international radio stations relay their international frequency modulated signal to Dakar. Although permits still have to be obtained to engage in radio broadcasting activities, the increase in the number of programs available has led to more varied program content, has resulted in more competitive rates and, above all, has made it possible to target the concerns of the public more effectively.

As far as television is concerned, RTS still has a monopoly on certain programs such as news bulletins which are commonly called the "*Journal parlé.*" On the other hand, foreign channels, such as the international channel CANAL+HORIZON (which charges a fee) are authorized to broadcast in Senegalese territory. One private operator (EXCAF TELECOM) operates an MMDS[7] system to broadcast some ten international television channels. After these programs had been broadcast free for several years, the company decided in 1999 to introduce charges.

The lifting of restrictions in the audiovisual field would enable private television channels to emerge with all the attendant advantages of a competitive environment. The establishment of the High Council of Radio and Television, which plays the role of arbitrator when different political parties request access to the state media, has brought greater transparency into their utilization.

Basic Telecommunication Services

The agreement between the State and SONATEL confers on the latter a monopoly over basic telecommunications until 2003. Thereafter, the State may either extend the monopoly or partially open it up. In the spirit of the changes that are taking place internationally, the State might authorize the access of a second operator to the sector, thus enhancing competition and paving the way for a reduction in the charges for local and international telephone communications to international levels. It has been observed throughout the world that the more a country moves toward greater liberalization of basic telecommunications, the more competitive it becomes at the international level, as was the case with Chile. Senegal has all the advantages that would enable it to play the role of a hub in the sub-region and to gain new markets if it were to offer rates closer to those charged on the international scene.

The same reasoning may be applied to mobile telephony. The advent of a second mobile telephone operator has had the immediate result of cutting the cost of communications and multiplying the range of facilities offered by the two competitors, thus giving consumers greater choice. However, the costs of acquiring and using a mobile telephone are still high and it remains the pre-serve of an elite. Senegal might have opted for the broader use of this new technology, for which the cost of extending geographical coverage is much lower than that of a wire-based network. This approach would enable it to be-come a tool of mass communication. Such an extension of the market might attract other operators, a step that would enrich the competitive environment, thus creating a virtuous circle of tariff cuts and increases in the size of the market and in the volume of consumption.

Telecommunication services

The Telecommunication Code defines the services that are subject to prior au-thorization, such as radio messaging and the establishment of radio broadcast-ing stations of all types. The Code provides for the creation of a regulatory agency for telecommunications to monitor all operators, including SONATEL, thus ensuring greater transparency of the rules of competition. No decision has yet been taken to make the agency operational. Thus, SONATEL, which in the past granted authorizations by delegation from the responsible ministry, con-tinues to grant approvals to private enterprises that wish to offer certain tele-communication services. The procedures for the approval of private tele-centers have therefore been entirely defined by SONATEL. The same applies to the requirements to set up as an Internet access provider, in particular with respect to charging.

In signing the Information Technology Agreement (ITA) following the December 1996 WTO Ministerial Conference in Singapore, Senegal took a decisive step toward becoming a country determined to offer value-added ser-vices. By taking progressive measures to liberalize basic telecommunications and by abolishing customs duties on computer equipment as of July 1998 in order to make this type of equipment accessible, Senegal has already taken a step toward establishing an infrastructure for information technology and competitive communication.

V. Fields in Which It Would Be Possible to Develop a Joint Position with the Countries of the Sub-Region

Insurance Services

States can take a joint position on insurance services and related services such as direct life and other types of insurance, reinsurance services, and inter-mediation services such as brokerage and agency services. Indeed, at the regional level, States are signatories to the CIMA (CICARE) agreements and those of the OAU (AFRICARE) which regulate reinsurance companies.

The ideas put forward within CIMA include:

* Repealing legislation obliging any importer of goods to take out an insurance policy with a company established in the country of residence;
* Enabling foreign companies to operate in the African market without being required to establish a branch there; and
* Reviewing certain provisions of the CIMA Code which provide that risks must be insured with a company having its head office in a member country.

Banking Services

The WAEMU Treaty, which was signed in Dakar and entered into force on August 1, 1994, offers the eight member countries opportunities for harmonizing their sectoral policies and their trade relations with third countries. Thus, the member countries adopt the same monetary and exchange policies. In the area of finance, a law regulates banks established in Senegal in accordance with the provisions of the Convention establishing the Banking Committee of WAMU while, at the same time, modernizing legislation to adapt it to the new monetary management arrangements. The member countries of the Union may develop a common position on banking and other financial services such as the acceptance of deposits and other reimbursable funds from the public, loans of all types, including consumer credit, mortgage credit, factoring and the financing of commercial transactions, settlement and cash transfer services (such as credit cards and charge cards), travelers checks and drafts. The member countries may address the question of the best arrangements to make in order to attract banks and financial establishments specializing in the medium- and long-term funding of enterprises.

Maritime Transport Services

The membership of WAEMU includes five coastal countries with a port and three land-locked members, namely Burkina Faso, Mali and Niger. Goods imported by those countries transit mainly through the ports of Dakar, Abidjan, Lomé and Cotonou. In spite of their land-locked position, these countries have set up bodies dealing with maritime transport. The countries of WAEMU are therefore in a position to decide on joint positions which meet their concern to increase the frequency of lines on the West African coast and to reduce freight costs to levels comparable to those found in Asia. The ECOWAS member countries have always said that they were interested in cooperating in the transit of goods. In addition to the WAEMU countries, the membership of ECOWAS comprises Nigeria, Ghana, Liberia, Sierra Leone, Guinea, the Gambia, Cape Verde and Mauritania.

Air-Transport Services

The air-transport sector has been dominated by the multinational company, Air Afrique, which was created by the Yaoundé Convention and by the States of West and Central Africa. The Convention gave the company a monopoly right to engage in air traffic between the member countries other than routes between immediate neighbors. Various difficulties, including the recovery of debts owed by member states, made it possible for national companies, regional private companies and foreign charter operators to occupy a number of niche markets (short inter-State links, the carriage of tourists). In spite of numerous recovery attempts, difficulties remained and the States are now considering the future of the company. However, in a dramatic agreement reached in Yamoussoukro, Côte d'Ivoire in November 1999, they agreed to remove its monopoly rights. In fact, with most other African governments also in attendance, it was agreed to liberalize air transport across Africa – immediately for routes within Africa, and within two years for international routes to other continents. This should help the African members of the WTO reach a joint position and participate in the GATS negotiations with a coordinated and well-developed strategy. It also offers the opportunity for Senegal and the rest of Africa to lock-in this important yet difficult decision and reassure local and foreign investors of its durability.

VI. Conclusion

Senegal became involved very early in the GATT negotiations, and consequently in those of the GATS with the inception of the WTO, and has been able to develop an expertise that is aware of what is at stake in the negotiations and understands the process. This situation created an imbalance with a private sector that had always felt itself to be remote from those negotiations.

The Coordinated African Programme of Assistance on Services (CAPAS) has helped to restore the balance of expertise in the private and public sectors by involving the various actors in a process of preparation based on in-depth sectoral research in the field of services over several years. The program has thus been able to promote a spirit of partnership between the public and private sectors with a view to gaining the best advantage from future negotiations. One key element has been the establishment of a national committee to prepare for the WTO multilateral trade negotiations, comprising the various stakeholders in the public sector (ministries, public bodies) and the private sector (employers' organizations, experts). The committee considers the various service sectors, together with agriculture, with a view to participating more actively in the forthcoming negotiations.

Moreover, coordination with the other countries of the sub-region with a view to finalizing joint positions on issues of regional or sub-regional scope will give greater weight to each member in the negotiations. WAEMU has been able to derive greater benefit from the various integration experiments in Africa and should make it possible for the member countries jointly to address certain important negotiating issues.

Notes

[1] A. Yeats, A. Amjadi, U. Reineke and F. Ng. 1998. "What Caused Sub-Saharan Africa's Marginalization in World Trade?", *Finance and Development*, December:38-41.

[2] M. Kono (ed.). 1997. *WTO in Trade in Services*, Islamic Center for Development of Trade.

[3] World Bank. 1995. *Global Economic Perspectives and the Developing Countries.*

[4] This is a joint program of UNCTAD, UN-DESA, and ITU, funded primarily by the IDRC and the Carnegie Foundation, which started in 1992. The World Bank began collaboration in 1999.

[5] *Conseil Supérieure de l'Industrie - Conseil Interministériel sur les Téléservices -* 1999.

[6] *Ministère du Tourisme et des Transports aériens: Statistiques du tourisme* 1998.

[7] Multipoint Multichannel Distribution System: a signal distribution system which, like cables, enables several television channels to be carried simultaneously on a main carrier wave. It is not interactive.

CHAPTER 14

Kenya's Trade in Services: Should the Country Fully Liberalize?

Gerrishon K. Ikiara, Moses I. Muriira, and Wilfred N. Nyangena

I. Introduction

The forthcoming WTO negotiations provide a good opportunity for developing countries to re-assess their position in various multilateral trade agreements, including the General Agreement on Trade in Services (GATS). Many developing countries had not fully understood the special needs, capacities, obstacles, short-term and long-term interests of their service sectors in the course of the Uruguay Round negotiations. This partly explains why many of these countries have been reluctant, slow and often apprehensive in making decisions on the schedule of service commitments. The intervening period since the conclusion of the Uruguay Round in 1994 has given some of these countries time to have a closer look at their service sectors. A large number of countries have since made commitments with regard to various service activities, giving them a chance to assess the impacts of these on both their short-term and long term needs and interests of their service activities and the overall economy.

This chapter discusses these issues for Kenya's service sector. It begins with an overview of the service sector in the country's economy and a brief description of the main services. The main focus is the identification of the key service sectors and trade strategies that could be of interest to Kenya in the forthcoming GATS 2000 Round. This includes Kenya's service commitments made since the Uruguay round and the rationale for those commitments, identification of the service areas of export interest and areas in which Kenya could profitably improve its position. The question is also posed whether developing countries like Kenya stand to gain or lose from full liberalization of their service markets. Since trade negotiations are a process of give and take, an effort is made to identify the service areas for which Kenya could request new market access and the strategies that Kenya and other developing countries could adopt to strengthen their positions during the services negotiations.

II. Service Sector in Kenya's Economy

The service sector has been a key component of the Kenyan economy in the last three decades, with its share in the GDP rising steadily over time from 46% in 1970 to 54% in 1997 (Table 1). By 1997, the service sector's share of GDP was almost double that of agriculture (29%) and five times that of manufacturing (11%).

The importance of services in Kenya's economy is even more pronounced in its contribution to wage employment. The sector accounted for 50% of the total wage employment, which stood at 319,200 people in 1970. By 1998, about 1,031,800 people were employed in the sector, accounting for almost 62% of the total wage employment in the country (Table 2). The leading service sub-sectors in the country's wage employment are "Community, Social and Personal Services," which accounted for 36% and 43% of total wage employment in 1970 and 1998, respectively, followed by the "Wholesale and Retail Trade, Restaurants and Hotels," with a share of 7% and 9% of the total wage employment in 1980 and 1998, respectively.

The contribution of the services sector in the country's balance-of-payments position has also been highly significant throughout the last three decades. Between 1970 and 1997, services accounted for approximately a third of the total current account outflows and about 50% of inflows. In 1970, outflows related to service imports amounted to K£ 70.1 million, equivalent to 34% of the total current account foreign exchange inflows and 32% of total current account outflows (Table 3). The leading sources of foreign exchange inflows among the service exports in 1970 were transport services (9%), foreign travel (9%), and shipping (5%). The share of services in the current account debits and credits had risen to 37% and 62%, respectively, by 1990, but declined to 27% and 45%, respectively, in 1997 (Table 3).

Export of services has thus continued to be a stabilizing factor in Kenya's balance of payments position with external trade in services especially in travel and communication (Table 4) always enjoying overall net surplus, unlike trade in merchandise which is always in net deficit.

III. Review of Kenya's Key Service Sectors and Trade in Services

This section of the paper reviews Kenya's key service sectors, examining their contribution to the economy, export performance, and the obstacles that hinder faster growth in the production and export of these services.

Table 1. Share of Services in the Kenyan economy, 1970-1997

	1970	1980	1990	1993	1997
I Real GDP, constant 1988 Dollars	3,156	5,306	8,137	8,293	9,443
II Share of GDP, factor cost (%) (millions)					
Agriculture	37	33	32	28	29
Industry	17	21	19	19	17
Services	46	46	49	53	54
III Labor Force Absorbed (%)					
Agriculture	85	81	77	76	80
Industry	6	7	8	9	7
Services	10	12	14	15	14

Source: ADB, *African Development Report*, various issues

Table 2. Wage Employment by Industry in Kenya, 1970-1997

INDUSTRY	1970 Number (000)	1970 %	1980 Number (000)	1980 %	1990 Number (000)	1990 %	1995 Number (000)	1995 %	1997 Number (000)	1997 %
Agriculture and Forestry	204.5	31.7	231.4	23.0	269.7	19.1	294.0	18.9	308.8	18.5
Mining and Quarrying	2.9	0.5	2.3	0.2	4.1	0.3	4.7	0.3	5.0	0.3
Manufacturing	82.3	12.7	141.3	14.0	187.7	13.3	204.8	13.1	216.9	13.0
Electricity and Water	4.8	0.8	10.1	1.0	22.4	1.6	22.9	1.5	23.2	1.3
Building and Construction	30.8	4.7	63.2	6.3	71.4	5.1	76.4	4.9	79.3	4.8
Wholesale and Retail Trade, Restaurants and Hotels	32.5	5.0	70.5	7.0	113.9	8.1	134.9	8.7	150.7	9.1
Transport and Communications	44.9	7.0	55.2	5.5	74.5	5.3	79.1	5.1	85.0	5.1
Finance, Insurance, Real Estate and Business Services	10.0	1.6	39.7	4.0	65.3	4.6	78.0	5.0	84.0	5.05
Community, Social and Personal Services	231.8	36.0	392.1	39.0	600.3	42.6	662.2	42.5	712.1	42.8
Total Wage Employment	644.5	100.0	1005.8	100.0	1409.3	100.0	1557.0	100.0	1664.9	100.0
Total Services	319.2	49.6	557.5	55.4	854.0	60.0	954.2	61.3	1031.8	61.5

Source: Calculated from Republic of Kenya, *Economic Survey*, (various issues)

Table 3 : Kenya's Current Account and the Role of Services, 1970-1997*

	1970 Debits	%	Credits	%	1980 Debits	%	Credits	%	1990 Debits	%	Credits	%
Merchandise	152.5	68.51	102.0	49.73	976.8	85.07	461.0	56.42	2297.61	62.98	1157.75	37.93
Shipment	0.1	0.05	11.1	5.41	0.5	0.04	25.6	3.07	367.83	10.08	58.37	1.91
Other Transportation	9.3	4.18	18.7	9.12	18.3	1.57	128.8	15.42	122.13	3.35	322.83	10.58
Foreign Travel	7.4	3.32	18.5	9.02	8.6	0.74	88.5	10.60	43.86	1.20	533.30	17.47
International Investment Income	25.0	11.23	16.9	8.24	76.0	93.0	16.9	2.07	480.09	13.16	5.30	1.74
Unrequited Transfer	10.1	4.54	19.2	9.36	9.4	0.82	67.2	7.49	64.1	1.76	493.50	16.17
Invisible Balance	70.1	31.49	103.1	50.27	169.3	14.55	367.2	43.97	1350.53	37.02	189.54	62.07
Visible Balance	152.5	68.51	102.0	49.73	994.6	85.45	468.0	56.04	2297.61	62.98	1157.75	37.93
Total Current Account	222.6	100.0	205.1	100.0	1163.9	100.0	835.2	100.0	3648.14	100.0	3052.29	100.00

	1995 Debits	%	Credits	%	1997 Debits	%	Credits	%
Merchandise	6787.22	67.09	4822.4	53.01	8579.18	72.56	5898.75	55.5
Shipment	1086.59	10.74	295.73	3.25	1045.68	8.84	291.77	2.72
Other Transportation	296.38	2.93	635.10	6.98	255.08	2.16	811.61	7.57
Foreign Travel	372.43	3.68	1249.64	13.74	570.73	4.83	1131.82	10.56
International Investment Income	901.38	8.91	65.95	0.73	657.50	5.56	67.50	0.63
Unrequited Transfer	118.1	1.17	1400.9	15.40	0.00	0.00	185.22	7.31
Invisible Balance	3340.33	33.02	4274.27	46.99	3244.80	27.44	4817.35	44.95
Visible Balance	6787.22	67.09	4822.42	53.01	8579.18	72.56	5898.75	55.05
Total Current Account	10116.61	100.0	9096.69	100.0	11823.98	100.0	10716.1	100.0

* Debits and credits are measured in K£ millions

Source: Republic of Kenya, *Economic Survey*, various issues

Table 4: Kenya's Trade In Services, 1997
(US$ Million)

Type of service	Service exports	Service imports
Transport	334	366
Travel	385	194
Communications	24	6
Insurance	15	86
Royalties & License fees	4	39
Other business	2	39
Construction	-	-
Computer and Information	-	2
TOTAL	764	731

Source: WTO (1999)

The services that feature significantly in Kenya's external trade are noted in Table 4 and include: transport; travel; communications; insurance; and royalties and license fees. It is mainly in travel, passenger transport services and other transport services that the country enjoys a surplus in external trade. These are likely to continue to be the country's leading service sectors of export interest in the foreseeable future.

Kenya's services sector has not been strongly export-oriented, although a survey carried out in 1994 shows that about 72% of the firms exported some of their services. Firms engaged in shipping, insurance, air and road transport, and tourism were found to be more export oriented relative to other domestic firms (Ikiara et al., 1994). That survey identified a number of constraints affecting service exports:

- High port tariffs at Mombasa that create a disincentive for ships to dock, leading to loss of business for firms that offer repair services to foreign marine vessels.
- Border insecurity, bureaucracy, convertibility of local currencies, and an underdeveloped road infrastructure, which had adverse effects on passenger and road transport.
- Technological constraints, government controls and political interference and discriminatory legislation in some sectors.
- Weak regional links.

Tourism and Travel Related Services

By the end of 1999, Kenya occupied the fifth position as a tourism destination in Africa, behind South Africa, Morocco, Tunisia, and Mauritius.

Tourism is today Kenya's leading source of export earnings, having surpassed coffee and tea by 1987. Earnings from tourism reached an all time high of K£1,405 million in 1994. Since then, earnings have dropped at an annual average rate of 7.5%, to reach K£875 million in 1998 (Republic of Kenya, 1999a). The largest drop occurred in 1998 when tourism earnings fell by 22.7%. This decline was evident in virtually all indicators, including tourist arrivals and departures, length of stay, hotel bed occupancy, and visitors to parks and game reserves.

By 1998, Kenya's foreign exchange earnings were only 16.9% of those of South Africa. The decline in tourism has had major adverse effects in many sectors of the economy as all enterprises that offer transportation, accommodation, shopping, entertainment, recreation and other personal services depend heavily on sustained tourist flows.

Tour companies are an important component of tourism. In 1994, Kenya was estimated to have had more than 600 tour companies, ranging from small one-man firms to large transnationals (Ikiara et al., 1994). Tour firms in the country estimate that about 80% of tourists visiting Kenya are handled by overseas tour operators based in and outside of the country. The affiliation of some of the overseas tour firms to some major hotels enables them to provide integrated services, including tours, car hire, hotel and lodge bookings, and air ticketing which gives them considerable advantage over local firms.

The tourism sector in Kenya currently faces a number of challenges. First, competition has become stiffer as a result of the increasing number of tourist destinations both within the region and globally. Countries have raised their competitiveness through improved quality of service, diversification of tourist attractions, travel products, and markets. Second, poor infrastructure, inadequate communications and human resources coupled with political and economic instability have become bottlenecks to the development of reliable and sustainable tourist services. Expensive airfares in the regional air routes have further reduced the competitiveness of Kenya and other African countries as tourist markets. Third, on the demand side tourists have become more selective, demanding increasingly higher quality services which many local suppliers are not able to provide.

Financial Services

Kenya's financial sector is dominated by two multinational banks, Barclays Bank and Standard Chartered Bank, and one state controlled bank, the Kenya Commercial Bank (KCB). The three banks control about 60% of the total deposits in the country's banking sector. Foreign and government domination of Kenya's financial sector is, however, gradually changing with the multinational banks and the state owned banks extending minority shareholding to the public through the Nairobi Stock Exchange in the 1990s.

The Kenyan financial sector has remained fairly liberal and competitive. Entry into the country's financial market by foreign investors has been largely unrestricted. One of the few restrictions introduced in 1986 was a requirement for higher minimum paid-up capital for foreign owned banks. To start a new bank, foreign investors were required to have Kshs 150 million as the minimum paid-up capital while local investors needed Kshs 15 million. This discrimination was removed in 1999 when the minimum paid-up capital was made uniform for both locally and foreign owned banks (Republic of Kenya 1999b).

The country's commercial banks have established wide regional and international links with other banks, facilitating considerable trade in financial services. The establishment of the Common Market for Eastern and Southern Africa (COMESA) is deliberately creating the required institutional infrastructure to strengthen regional financial links. Some of the infrastructural facilities already created include: a monetary clearing house; travelers cheques; an insurance scheme; and a regional development bank.

Tapping Kenya's potential in external trade in financial services is, however, hampered by inadequate investments in new technologies, including computerization and electronic banking, to reduce operational costs.

Political and managerial problems have also constrained efforts aimed at enhancing the domestic production capacity and export competitiveness of Kenya's financial services. They include imprudent and unsecured lending, under-capitalization of the financial institutions, over-reliance of indigenous institutions on deposits from large public funds such as the National Social Security Fund (NSSF) and the National Hospital Insurance Fund (NHIF) leading to serious instability, and a weak regulatory role by the Central Bank of Kenya (CBK).

Insurance Services

Kenya's insurance sector has registered high growth rates in the last two decades, particularly in the last five years when the average annual rate of growth was 20%. The country has a fairly well developed insurance industry playing an important role in the mobilization of funds. By the end of 1998, there were 38 insurance companies and 2 re-insurance companies operating in the country, with a large number of other actors.

Kenya's exports and imports of insurance services stood at US$15 million and US$86 million respectively in 1997, creating a deficit of US$71 million (Table 4). Insurance exports are largely in the form of re-insurance business with the Kenya-Re. About 20% of all the re-insurance business generated in Kenya is paid to the three re-insurance firms (Kenya Re, Zep Re, and Africa Re) to which insurance companies are mandatorily required to place 25%, 10% and 5% of their business, respectively.

A number of factors have adversely affected the performance of insurance firms in the country. First, there is restrictive legislation, particularly with regard to the investment of insurance funds. Insurance companies operating in Kenya are required to invest 25% of their funds in government securities and 65% with statutory bodies. Second, poor discipline and supervision of the main actors and firms in the sector have hindered a stable and conducive environment for the growth of the insurance sector. Other constraints include:

shortage of qualified personnel in actuarial and other technical areas; restriction on the range of incentives that insurance firms can offer to clients; impediments associated with limited liability requirements and unrealistic court awards; huge and persistent losses in the motor insurance business occasioned by high rates of vehicle thefts and road accidents; poor infrastructure; and excessive bureaucracy in the office of the commissioner of insurance.

For most of Kenya's post independence period, entry into the insurance sector was fairly liberal, which explains why Kenya's insurance sector has had a highly significant foreign presence. By the mid-1980s, about 45% of the insurance companies in the country had majority shareholding in the hands of foreign investors (Ikiara et al., 1994). However, since the 1980s, a number of amendments to the country's Insurance Act have increased restrictions and regulations for insurance firms operating in the Kenyan market. The entry and operation of foreign insurance companies are, for instance, limited by the requirement that at least one-third of the shareholding as well as board membership must be held by Kenyan citizens. The proportion of the investment funds that can be invested outside the country is also restricted. These market-access limitations were instituted as measures for increasing local ownership and control of the industry. The measures were also aimed at protecting consumers and ensuring that insurance companies retained within the country sufficient funds to meet local statutory requirements and liabilities. Mandatory cessions, totaling 40%, to local and regional reinsurance companies have been another obstacle to the entry of foreign insurance companies into the market.

Transport Services

Transport services constitute another key component of Kenya's service sector, both in their contribution to the country's employment and income generation as well as in their role in the country's external trade, especially at the regional level. The main transport services include road transport, rail transport, maritime transport, and air transport. The most important category of transport services on the basis of output is road transport, with its share of total output of the transport sector standing at 34% in 1998. This share is followed by air transport (25%) and water transport (16%).

With the Mombasa port and its strategic location in relation to the neighboring countries, Kenya has benefited from relatively dynamic and important domestic and external trade in transport services over the years in all six modes of transport services in the country.

The main transport services exported from Kenya include: freight insurance; port services such as fuel and ships' stores; port handling; repairs and servicing of foreign ships; and repairs and servicing of foreign aircraft. While the country generally records deficits in some of its external trade in services, it usually enjoys a significant surplus in its current account records for passenger transport services.

The demand for transport services in the region is significant and is expected to rise with the growing regional economic co-operation among the three East African countries, including the Common Market for Eastern and Southern African countries. Existing regional arrangements that promote transportation in the Eastern and Southern African region include: the Northern Corridor Transit Agreement (NCTA) that unifies transportation rates and regulations in Kenya, Uganda, Rwanda and Burundi; and the Preferential Trade Area (PTA) Communications Development Program that tries to strengthen the regional transport network and collaboration. Some of the concrete steps taken in this direction include: the identification of centers for aircraft maintenance and training (engine maintenance in Ethiopia and Zimbabwe); avionics in Zambia and Tanzania; small aircraft maintenance in Kenya; and personnel training in Ethiopia, Kenya, Uganda and Zambia; and the opening up of the Kenya-Uganda border to allow free movement of trains in 1993.

Road transportation has been adversely affected by the high cost of imported spare parts, tires, diesel oil, licenses, insurance premium, and other costs that have eroded the sector's profit margins. The dilapidated nature of most of the Kenyan roads, including the Nairobi-Mombasa highway, has compounded the problem.

The significance of rail transport in the country's transportation sector has been on a decline in the last two decades. In 1975, for instance, rail transport accounted for 17% of the total output from Kenya's transport sector but the share dropped to 7% by 1998 (Table 5). Kenya Railways Corporation, a public corporation that is privatizing some of its services, has a 2,050km-long metric-gauge single track with connections to Uganda and Northern Tanzania. In addition to being a major channel for Kenya's commodity exports and imports, Kenya Railways (KR) exports some services to Uganda and other landlocked countries in the region. KR also carries out considerable repair and maintenance services for some foreign transporters.

Technical, managerial and financial bottlenecks and increasing competition from other modes of transportation have contributed to the declining output from rail transport. Ongoing plans to restructure the operations of the KR include: tariff adjustments; commercialization of services; privatization of some services; award of locomotive maintenance contract to the U.S. General Electric Corporation; and termination of unprofitable services. Staff reductions and aggressive marketing are expected to increase KR's capacity to produce quality services for local consumption and for export to the COMESA region.

The port of Mombasa handles transit cargo for Uganda, Tanzania, Rwanda, Burundi, Zaire, Zambia and Sudan. Since 1982, the volume of cargo handled and the number of cargo vessels calling at the port of Mombasa have fluctuated, with a general declining trend that may be attributed to: the diversion of cargo from Uganda, Rwanda and Burundi to the port of Dar es Salaam due to: inefficiency and corruption at Mombasa; long delays in loading and off-loading; higher tariffs at Mombasa relative to Dar; border conflicts between Uganda and Kenya; declining transit cargo resulting from political and economic instability in the region; inadequate facilities at the port of Mombasa; and planning difficulties associated with uncertain demand for services from the neighboring countries. High port tariffs at Mombasa relative to other regional ports have adversely affected their business as an increasing number of ships avoid Mombasa. Frequent congestion at the port has increased vessel turn-around time and forced shipping lines to impose surcharges on exporters and importers. Inefficiency in road and rail transport often translates into congestion and delays at the port, reflecting the extent of interdependency of various forms of transport services and underscoring the need for an integrated approach to the management of these services in the country.

Virtually all shipping lines operating at the port of Mombasa are foreign owned. The Kenya National Shipping Line (KNSL), a government owned line established in 1990, is the only locally owned shipping line but without its own ships.

Air transport is the second most important category of transport services in Kenya in terms of its share of total value of output from the transport service sector, which was 25% by 1998 (Table 5). The country's aviation industry is highly competitive, but heavily dominated by foreign investors.

Kenya Airways (KA), originally wholly government owned, has been privatized, with KLM acquiring 26% of the shares and the public getting a significant proportion through the Nairobi Stock Exchange market. Before its privatization, KA had experienced persistent financial losses associated with overstaffing, operation of old and fuel-inefficient aircrafts, escalating costs of operation, poor management and lack of skilled manpower, operation in unprofitable routes, and political interference with commercialization of services. These costs, coupled with inadequate quality of service and poor marketing, high insurance premiums, and slow technological adaptation had constrained the growth of services provided by KA.

The privatization of KA and contracting of its management to a British firm remarkably turned the airline around. The airline has experienced considerable improvement in the quality of its services, leading to increased flights and larger profits under the partnership with KLM. The airline's control of the domestic and regional market is increasing rapidly, and export of air travel services is expected to be of much greater importance for Kenya in the coming years.

**Table 5. Structure of Kenya's Transport Service Sector, 1975-1997*

Type of Transport Services	1975 Output	%	1980 OutPut	%	1985 Output	%	1990 Output	%	1995 Output	%	1997 Output	%
Road Transport	35.8	24.4	92.3	33.1	248.8	45.1	476.9	44.3	810.7	36.3	870.7	33.7
Railway Transport	25.4	17.3	32.9	11.8	57.7	10.5	94.5	8.8	225.0	10.1	187.4	7.3
Water Transport	34.5	23.6	62.7	22.5	89.2	16.2	134.2	12.5	372.3	16.7	408.6	15.8
Air Transport	39.9	27.2	41.6	14.9	86.8	15.8	268.2	24.9	471.1	21.1	650.5	25.2
Services Incidental	10.9	7.4	31.2	11.2	45.2	8.2	72.7	6.7	153.8	6.9	186.7	7.2
Pipeline Transport	-	-	18.6	6.7	23.4	4.2	31.1	2.9	197.8	8.9	278.0	10.8
Total	146.5	99.9	279.3	100.0	551.1	100.0	1077.6	100.1	2230.7	100.0	2581.9	100.0

Source: Republic of Kenya, *Economic Survey*, various years
*Output is measured in millions of Kenyan pounds. The percentage figures refer to the share of each transport service in the total transport sector's output.

Some of the factors that have adversely affected the performance of the aviation sector include: shortage of trained personnel; high duty and VAT on aircraft and spare parts; inadequate facilities at airports; depreciation of the Kenyan shilling and high inflation rates that have made tickets costly, reducing demand for air transport; and high operational costs resulting from high jet fuel prices and landing costs. Despite these bottlenecks, however, KA's performance has been impressive, placing it in a position where it can expand its share of the regional and international air transport industry. Partnerships and regional agreements that could enhance the country's capacity to export air transport services and the removal of obstacles that stand in the way of provision of more competitive services are some of the measures needed to facilitate faster growth of the country's air transport.

Telecommunication Services

The low level of development of telecommunication services remains a major constraint in the provision of various services both in terms of high costs as well as limited accessibility to the country's population. By 1999, the country had only 290,000 telephone lines to serve a population of about 30 million people. Only about 1% of this population was served with fixed telephone lines. There were only about 9,000 mobile telephones in the country due to relatively high installation and running costs. Kenya's teledensity (telephone lines per 1000 people) in the second half of the 1990s was lower than the sub-Saharan African average (World Bank, 1999a).

As a result of KPTC's monopoly over a long period of time, there is currently low foreign presence in Kenya's telecommunications services subsector. The KPTC, however, has two antennae that provide direct links between Kenya and the rest of the world, enabling the country to export services via cross-border and consumption abroad modes. The monopoly status of the KPTC was dismantled in 1999, allowing restructuring of the corporation and opening up postal and telecommunication services to foreign competitors.

The ongoing reforms of the telecommunication sector are expected to make the sector more efficient and competitive and help to expand the level of export of telecommunication services. The ongoing liberalization of the telecommunications sector is also expected to have a positive impact in strengthening the country's information technology.

IV. To Liberalize or Not to Liberalize

As the GATS 2000 negotiations approach, debate is mounting on the issue of whether sub-Saharan African countries like Kenya are ready for a fully liberalized environment for trade in services. This is partly why the number of service sectors committed by African countries within the GATS agreement is still relatively small.

The level of competitiveness of developing country service suppliers in the world market is the main determinant of the net benefit that these countries can receive from liberalizing their service sectors, as it would shape their comparative advantage. While comparative advantage derives from natural factors for trade in goods, in the case of services trade such factors hardly play any role, except in tourism where cultural and geographical factors afford some developing countries comparative advantage.

Comparative advantage, in the case of service trade, derives largely from the level and pattern of a country's development (Gibbs and Hayashi, 1989). It is this development that determines how factor and institutional-rich a country is and therefore, its comparative advantage. Factor-related comparative advantage emanates from:

- Endowment in knowhow and skills
- Amount (and quality) of existing physical infrastructure such as the stock of fixed capital, including high technology equipment
- Information capital, that is checked information and the ability to apply technological innovations.
- Institutional-related comparative advantage emanates from:
- The size of suppliers and the size of market, which determine the capacity to exploit economies of scale and build knowhow
- Economies of specialization and accumulation of specific knowhow and information
- The role of state regulation in enhancing scale economies

With more of the factor and institutional-related advantages, developed countries are likely to be more competitive than developing countries in most services (OECD, 1989). Developed country firms, moreover, are better able to build competitiveness. The major factors responsible for building competitiveness among service suppliers include:

- Financial capacity. This is a key requirement for competitiveness in most service sectors, particularly in banking, securities, trading, insurance, air transport, and information services. Asymmetries in the distribution of financial resources have posed an enormous barrier to the quest by developing countries to increase their share in world services markets. Developing countries will have to find effective solutions to their financial and debt problems for them to be more competitive.
- Ability to make effective use of telecommunication and information technologies. These technologies are very important given the intangible and information-intensive nature of services.
- Accumulated knowledge, skills, and reputation. These human resources are essential, especially for the knowledge-intensive professional services. Developing country firms have serious difficulties competing with developed country firms that have already established international reputations.
- Networking ability.

- Established relationships between suppliers and buyers. This explains why foreign service producers in the Kenyan market, for instance, may have a competitive edge over local service firms especially with respect to locally based subsidiaries of multinationals.
- Presence in major markets. This presence helps firms to obtain precise information on the potential customer and competitors and facilitates human-skills development and product innovation when the market has intense competition and pressing demands. In the case of computer software service, for instance, Srivastava (undated) reports that the presence of developing firms' staff in the most sophisticated developed country markets has been found to be essential for improving firms' competitiveness.
- Ability to offer a package of services. This ability improves a firm's competitiveness as it affords customers more convenience, greater choice, and cost saving. It is important in many service sectors, such as banking, tourism and the media, and is a function of human and financial resources and advanced information technology.
- The size of the domestic market. This is crucial for service industries that target "mass" consumers, such as audio-visual and transport services, where the size of the market is important. One role that a large domestic market can play is to enable cross subsidization from the domestic market to foreign operations (Christopherson and Ball, 1989). Regulations and other factors could protect domestic markets for the local firms as a way of facilitating their ability to compete internationally.
- Government incentives. Protection of domestic markets and incentives are necessary to develop competitiveness in certain services, particularly in developing countries. An example of an effective incentive is government procurement policy that favors domestic service suppliers.

Developing countries score poorly in all the above variables as a consequence of which their service firms are weak competitors in the world market. This competitive weakness appears to be a general phenomenon in all service sectors (Noyelle, 1989), with concentration of market power in the hands of developed-country enterprises being a major hindrance to developing-country firms' quest for building competitiveness. Gibbs and Hayashi (1989), indeed, note that any developing-country "strengths" as far as trade in services is concerned would seem to arise from the ability to move persons across borders, international trade regulatory frameworks that secure a minimum market share for developing countries' unique cultural and geographical factors, and an ability to link lower-cost skills to information. If liberalization of trade in services is to benefit developing countries, their firms have to acquire the factors discussed above and international regulatory frameworks together with compensatory actions that can help to secure a share of the world services market for these countries.

Government policy for services in developing countries, including the critical issue of which services to liberalize and the pace at which marketing opening should be granted, should take cognizance of all these important factors and strive to enhance them. Trade liberalization should also concentrate more on free movement of developing-country personnel to developed country markets to supply services and access to information networks and distribution channels.

Kenya's Commitments

By the end of 1999, Kenya had committed a small number of service sectors under the GATS. Out of the 12 main categories of services defined by the GATS, Kenya had committed five: financial services including insurance; communication services; tourism and travel-related services; transport services; and 'other' services.

One of the sectors in which the country made early commitment was financial services. The details of the specific financial services commitment and the limitations on market access and on national treatment for each mode of supply are contained in Kenya's "Schedule of specific commitments" (supplement 1) GATS/SC/47/suppl.1, dated 26 February 1998. The specific services committed by early 1998 were:

1. Banking and other financial services (excluding insurance) sector:
- acceptance of deposits and other repayable funds from the public
- lending of all types, including consumer credit, mortgage credit, factoring and financing of commercial transactions
- all payments and money transmission services
- guarantees and commitments
- participation in issues of all kinds of securities and provision of services related to such issues except underwriting
- asset management except pension fund management
- advisory and other auxiliary financial services

2. Transport Services
- aircraft repair and maintenance
- sale and marketing of aircraft transport services
- road transport with regard to passenger transportation, freight transportation, rental of commercial vehicles, maintenance and repair of road transport equipment, and support services for road transport services

3. Insurance services sector
- life insurance
- non-life insurance
- brokering

- agency services
- auxiliary services, assessors, intermediaries and loss adjusters
- re-insurance and retrocession

4. Communication Services

5. Tourism and Travel Related Services
- hotels and restaurants services
- travel agencies and tour operators
- tourist guide services

6. Other Services
- meteorological data/information

Modal market access has different limitations for each of the financial and insurance services. In general, however, there are horizontal restrictions in the case of mode 4 (movement of natural persons). The limitations on this mode of supply apply to all service sectors committed. The specific limitations with regard to this mode are that entry is allowed only for intra-corporate personnel and to areas of the economy in which skills are needed. In the case of cross-border supply, there are no market access limitations except with regard to:
- participation in issues of securities where securities issued in a foreign jurisdiction are not allowed to be traded or offered in the Kenyan market
- life insurance, where this mode of supply is unbound
- non-life insurance, where it is unbound except for aviation, marine and engineering services
- brokering, where it is unbound
- agency services, where it is unbound except for re-insurance services
- re-insurance and retrocession, where market access for mode 1 is granted on condition that mandatory cessions are placed as follows: 25% with Kenya Re; 10% with Zep Re and 5% with Africa Re

Market access for consumption abroad (mode 2) is also generally unrestricted with the exception of: life insurance services where it is unbound; non-life insurance services where it is unbound except for aviation, marine and engineering services; brokering services where approval of the commissioner of insurance is required before Kenyan business can be placed with an insurer who is not registered under the Kenya Insurance Act; agency services where access is unbound; and re-insurance and retrocession services where mandatory cessions must be placed with Kenya Re, Zep Re and Africa Re (in the proportions indicated above) as a condition for market access.

Market access with regard to commercial presence (mode 3 of services supply) is also limited in several of the financial services committed by Kenya. In most of the limitations for this mode of supply, foreign service suppliers seeking to establish commercial presence in Kenya are required to have a specified minimum capital controlled by Kenyan nationals. In other words, commercial presence is restricted to fixed equity limits. Thus, to be allowed to establish commercial presence with the objective of accepting deposits and other repayable funds foreign firms must be approved as banks according to Kenya's Banking Act. For this recognition, some of the capital must be controlled by Kenyan nationals. Moreover, foreign-owned banks face minimum capital requirements ten times larger than locally-owned banks. Foreigners seeking to establish commercial presence in Kenya in order to supply asset-management services can only do so if 30% of the firm's paid-up capital is held by Kenyan nationals. The limitation of commercial presence through fixed equity limits is also reflected in the ongoing liberalization of the telecommunications sector. Foreign firms recently short-listed for possible licensing to supply mobile phone services were required to have at least 60% local shareholding.

Commercial presence in the re-insurance and retrocession services is allowed on condition that mandatory cessions have to be placed with the Kenya Re, Zep Re and Africa Re in the same proportions indicated above. Foreign companies wishing to set up in Kenya for the purpose of participating in issues of securities are restricted in that foreign investors can hold a maximum of only 40% of the shareholding of any locally listed company and can take a maximum of 40% of the shares floated to the public by any listed company.

Offering qualified market access is regarded as a measure that allows the country to retain some control in crucial service sectors, while also enhancing scope for negotiations.

In comparative terms, national treatment limitations are more serious than market access limitations in Kenya, indicating that a considerable level of discrimination exists against foreign-controlled service providers. This, however, may not be the reality on the ground given that public procurement is often in favor of the large multinational service providers as a result of the perception that the quality of their services is superior.

There are also horizontal limitations on the movement of natural persons. With regard to cross-border supply, national treatment is unbound for all the financial and insurance services committed except: lending; payments and money transmission; advisory and other auxiliary financial services; agency services; auxiliary services, assessors, intermediaries and loss adjusters; and re-insurance and retrocession services. In all these services there are limitations to national treatment.

There are no national treatment limitations in the case of consumption abroad in almost all of the services committed by Kenya. Notable exceptions are life insurance, non-life insurance and agency services. The opposite picture emerges in the case of commercial presence, which is unbound in most of the services committed. It is only in the following services where commercial presence is not limited: life insurance; brokering, auxiliary insurance services and re-insurance and retrocession services.

Tourism and travel-related services constitute a service sector with the highest number of GATS commitments due to its popularity with developing countries (Honeck, 1999). By September 1998, a total of 112 WTO member countries had committed at least one sub-sector of tourism and travel-related services even though the number of sub-sectors committed and the modal market access and national treatment restrictions listed varied across these countries.

The rationale for Kenya's commitments in the tourism services sector is, to a considerable degree, based on the fact that the sector is one of the country's leading foreign exchange earners and that capacity to have the infrastructure required to meet international standards in tourism services is inadequate locally. In addition, the country has found it easier to make commitments on tourism because the sector had been largely liberalized even before GATS.

V. Prospects and Strategies for further Commitment within GATS Framework

The level and nature of service imports are indicators of sectors that can be profitably committed. For Kenya, the existing structure of imports and exports suggests that the country could bind transport, travel, insurance and several other services without adverse repercussions. In the case of services that are not being produced in the country, it is better to liberalize their market because competition would stimulate efficiency and higher quality. It is necessary for Kenya to commit sectors but retain some of the restrictions allowed under GATS to enable the country to take advantage of prevailing opportunities. Some of the restrictions could include: employment criteria; local content criteria; export performance conditions; transfer of technology and training conditions. GATS also allows developing countries to liberalize in a gradual and piecemeal fashion and to seek special and differential arrangements with other trading partners. Kenya and other East African countries have not utilized these provisions effectively.

One of the service areas that Kenya has offered for liberalization is telecommunication. The country has committed voice-telephone services and a few other services. There are a number of reasons for Kenya's willingness to liberalize telecommunications services. First, the sector is already going through major restructuring towards liberalization, largely as a result of pressure from donors pushing for economic reforms under the Structural Adjustment Programme. Secondly, it is widely recognized that the only way to enhance the country's telecommunications infrastructure and raise the efficiency with which other services are provided and increase their quality, is by attracting foreign suppliers and investors into the sector. There is accordingly increased pressure for technological developments in telecommunications, internet and electronic commerce to stimulate the country's cross-border trade in various services. Services such as accountancy, architectural, engineering, and consultancy are increasingly supplied electronically, further underscoring the importance of an efficient, competitive, and sophisticated telecommunication network.

Promising developments occurred around 1999 in the East African regional telecommunications system. First, both Uganda and Kenya committed certain communication services that were expected to attract foreign service suppliers and investors especially through the establishment of commercial presence, with consequent improvement in efficiency and competitiveness not only of telecommunication services but also other services as well, especially those whose principal mode of supply is cross-border. This was also expected to stimulate technological transfer. For the purpose of projecting East Africa as a single market to attract more foreign direct investment, it was increasingly felt that the three countries ought to adopt a common strategy and coordinate their commitments. Secondly, East African countries have started regional initiatives to enhance regional telecommunications infrastructure. The planned setting up of a digital telecommunication transmission system in East Africa is expected to transform information and communications technology in the region and raise the attractiveness of this East African region to both local and foreign investors.

Thirdly, Kenya has embarked on serious privatization of its telecommunications service sector. These privatization measures are likely to expand the existing infrastructure, raise efficiency, and reduce service prices. The British Company, Vodafon, has acquired 49% of Safaricom's stake recently. In addition, another mobile telephone company (with at most 40% foreign shareholding) has been licensed although it is yet to start supplying its services in the Kenyan market.

Other sub-sectors of communications in which Kenya could easily make binding commitments are information, computer, and internet services. The country is already implementing measures aimed at stimulating the growth of information technology. One significant example of these measures is the recent reduction of the tax rate on imported computer equipment. These measures are, however, inadequate and need to be strengthened. One way in which this could be done under the GATS is to commit computer software and computer services. By opening its market for computer software and computer services to the United States, Kenya could request reciprocal market access in other services in which it has comparative advantage. An immediate advantage to Kenya from such an arrangement would be transfer of computer services knowhow more cheaply with consequent improvement in the efficiency of supply and export of other services.

Rather than liberalizing only cross-border (Mode1) trade in these software and computer services, Kenya could obtain greater benefits by committing mode 3 (commercial presence). The benefits would include creation of employment for Kenyans, faster and greater transfer of technology and knowhow, and reduced foreign exchange payment for imported services. To ensure that these benefits accompany the liberalization process, Kenya could try to provide qualified access, with specified benefits to the country as conditions for access.

In the maritime transport service sub-sector, Kenya does not have comparative advantage in actual shipping but has advantage in various auxiliary port facilities. To create business opportunity for the port of Mombasa and the road and rail transporters, it is more advantageous for Kenya to commit shipping services. This would ensure greater competition and lead to more efficient and competitive services. To be able to effectively negotiate for and acquire greater market access into the sub-regional and continental markets, which absorb an important proportion of the country's service exports, Kenya could grant preferential treatment in the area of shipping services to African countries that have export capacity. Another rationale for Kenya to commit shipping services is that foreign-owned shipping lines already dominate the sub-sector. The sub-sector could, therefore, be committed without significantly changing the actual access situation from what it is currently.

That Kenya Airways has acquired a reasonable level of international competitiveness, that the country's aviation industry is already heavily dominated by foreign investors, and that efficient and competitive air travel services are crucial for the growth of tourism, make a strong case for Kenya to commit this sub-sector. Commercial presence and movement of natural persons should be particularly encouraged in this sub-sector, but these should be conditional on such requirements as transfer of technical and managerial knowhow and restriction of the entry of foreigners for the benefit of certain labor cadres for the benefit of the nationals

Since negotiations require give and take, Kenya could reduce market access and national treatment limitation in the five service sectors in which it has made commitments in addition to committing new sectors. To ensure that new commitments and further liberalization of committed services are beneficial to the country, mechanisms and structures for consultation, evaluation, discussion, and decision making will, however, need to be put in place.

VI. Summary and Conclusion

Services constitute the most important sector of the Kenyan economy today, with its share of national gross domestic product and employment larger than the combined share of agriculture and industry. The sector, with an overall net surplus in the current account, also plays a crucial role in the country's balance of payments position. The ongoing process of liberalization of trade in services within the World Trade Organization framework will have an immense impact on virtually all aspects of the Kenyan service sector.

At the time the GATS was launched at the end of the Uruguay Round multilateral trade negotiations in 1994, there was limited understanding of the services sector in many countries. This explains why Kenya and other developing countries were rather cautious in their schedule of commitments with regard to liberalization of trade in services. So far Kenya has made commitments in a limited number of service sectors, viz., banking and other

ments in a limited number of service sectors, viz., banking and other financial services, insurance services, tourism and travel related services, transport services, communication services and 'other' services. Discussions with stakeholders in various service sectors show that there is still considerable fear arising from uncertainty about the impact of immediate and full liberalization of trade in services in spite of the fact that for most of the post-independence period, the country has had a rather liberal policy on trade in most services. Some of the restrictions that exist against foreign suppliers of services or foreign investors are relatively recent, with many of them having been introduced in the 1980s. Thus, the impressive growth and performance of various service sectors in Kenya in the last three decades took place in a largely competitive environment.

The most important service sectors for Kenya today, in terms of external trade, are tourism which has been a key foreign exchange earner in the 1990s, and transport, especially road, air, pipeline transport and other services related to port and shipping activities. These two service sectors play an important role in the country's current-account balance, with net surpluses in most years. Communication, computer, information and other services are emerging as important new export sectors for Kenya. On the other hand, the most important service imports for Kenya are shipping and insurance services.

In the context of the ongoing GATS negotiations, Kenya's interests in international trade in services will be largely in foreign travel (tourism), transport, insurance, professional services, communication services and information technology in the foreseeable future. Some of the specific issues which the country could pursue in order to maximize its interests in international trade in services include:

- **Binding** those services that already enjoy little or no protection and pushing for reciprocal actions from other WTO members.
- **Liberalizing** and making commitments on those sectors where the country stands to benefit from transfer of technology for the **benefit of** consumers and producers, through lowering of the costs of supplying the services. A good example is the country's telecommunication and information technology where domestic competitiveness is currently weak. Opening up and making firm commitments through the GATS framework would facilitate inflow of required foreign investments to allow these services to enjoy modern technology.

There are, however, service areas that will require some restrictions on foreign suppliers and investors in order to allow domestic firms to restructure and prepare themselves to face global competition. This will be the case especially in those sectors where there is a considerable number of domestic firms already involved in the supply of certain services. Some of the sectors that are likely to benefit from such restricted access include financial, insurance, and transport services. Some of the conditions could be in terms of the cadres of the labor force that should be confined to nationals, proportional shares that can be held by foreign investors in joint ventures for a given period of time, and parts of the country for the exclusive operation of local suppliers. A good example of the latter is restricting the provincial and district air-transport market to local firms that is already being implemented in the country.

There are a number of areas in which Kenya could request more market access, both at the regional and international levels. These are:

- increased mobility of professional, skilled, semi-skilled and unskilled labor force across national boundaries. The country could benefit much more given its large pool of well trained manpower (relative to the economy's absorptive capacity) after three decades of intensified investments in education and training, both at the national and individual levels.
- recognition of local qualifications in areas such as accounting, auditing, and other professional fields would allow the country to export some of the existing surplus of its well-trained labor force.

In order to have an impact on the GATS negotiations, there is a need for a co-ordinated regional approach in the negotiations, especially in the case of services where there are broad common interests among the member states.

Member states belonging to regional and sub-regional groups will need to consider granting preferential market access and national treatment in services to each other as a way of facilitating the development of national services production capacities. For the same purpose, member states should consider pooling resources for the joint provision of such services as shipping, air transport, tourism and other services where economies of scale could benefit these countries' economies.

References

ADB, *African Development Report*, various years.

Christopherson, S. and S. Ball (1989). "Media Services: Considerations Relevant to Multilateral Trade Negotiations", in *Trade in Services: Sectoral Issues*, United Nations Publication, UNCTAD/ITP/26, New York, 1989.

Honeck, D.B. (1999). "The General Agreement on Trade in Services", *The Courier*, No.175, May-June 1999.

Gibbs, M. and M. Hayashi (1989). "Sectoral Issues and the Multilateral Framework for Trade in Services: An Overview", in *Trade in Services: Sectoral Issues*, United Nations Publication, UNCTAD/ITP/26, New York, 1989.

Ikiara, G.K., W. N. Nyangena and M. I. Muriira (1994). "Services in Kenya" UNCTAD/CAPAS Report, August 1994.

Noyelle, Thierry (1989). "Business Services and the Uruguay Round Negotiations on Trade in Services", in *Trade in Services: Sectoral Issues*, United Nations Publication, UNCTAD/ITP/26, New York, 1989.

OECD (1989). *Trade in Services and Developing Countries*, Paris, OECD.

Republic of Kenya (1999a). *Economic Survey, 1999*, Government Printer, Nairobi.

Republic of Kenya (1999b). "Budget Speech for the Fiscal Year 1999/2000 (1st July –
    30th June)".
Republic of Kenya, *Economic Survey,* various issues.
Republic of Kenya, *Statistical Abstract,* various issues.
Srivastava, S. "Computer Software and Data Processing Export Potential", in *Services
    and Development Potential: The Indian Context*, United Nations Publication,
    UNCTAD/ITP/22.
UNDP (1999). *Human Development Report* 1999, Oxford University Press.
World Bank (1999a). *African Development Indicators 1998/99*, Oxford University
    press.
World Bank (1999b). *World Development Report 1998/99*, Oxford University press.
World Bank (1997). *World Development Report 1997*, Oxford University press.
WTO (1999). "Recent Developments in Services Trade – Overview and Assessment",
    Background Note prepared by the Council for Trade in Services, February
    1999. S/C/W/94.

CHAPTER 15

Examining The Potential Benefits of Services Liberalization in a Developing Country: The Case of South Africa

James W. Hodge

I. Introduction

Comprehensive negotiations on services liberalization are a mandatory part of the next round of trade talks under the WTO. The Uruguay Round bought about little liberalization by developing countries, but in this Round there will be considerable pressure on countries like South Africa to give greater market access to foreign providers. While many industrial countries argue that service liberalization can only bring about net benefits for developing countries, there remains some skepticism in the developing countries themselves. This skepticism is less about the benefits of pro-competitive regulatory reform—a necessary step on the way to liberalization and a process already started in most countries—but more about the additional benefits that will stem from granting greater market access.

This chapter attempts to unpack some of the costs and benefits of reforms and the granting of further market access for South Africa in the producer services sectors. For this purpose, it draws on a number of recent sectoral studies of service liberalization in South Africa.[1] The chapter begins with an overview of how the economy may benefit from implementing pro-competitive reforms, irrespective of conceding market access. This is followed by a discussion of the additional benefits and costs that may come from granting greater market access on top of regulatory reforms. These results are tempered by an exploration of how economic environmental factors may limit or possibly extend the benefits of reform. The chapter then moves towards an analysis of the case of South Africa. It begins with a brief overview of the current state of producer services in South Africa before moving onto an assessment of how completed reform has impacted on the sectors. Finally, some comments are made on how developing countries like South Africa might proceed with liberalization demands.

II. Costs/Benefits From Pro-Competitive Regulatory Reform

Liberalization of trade in service sectors characterized by network economies[2] requires that these sectors are first opened to competition through a variety of pro-competitive regulatory reforms. It is for this reason that much of the focus of trade negotiations in services has revolved around moving countries down this path and establishing clear regulatory principles for opening network industries in a non-discriminatory and competitive fashion.[3]

The general principle behind such reforms is to separate the market for network infrastructure from the market for services provided over that network. As the network component usually retains monopolistic features, some form of license auction combined with price-capping and non-discriminatory access requirements are used to effectively regulate this part of the industry. The service provision component is then opened to full competition without need for much regulatory oversight.

All countries have benefited from the demonstration effects of a select group of industrial countries that have pursued such reforms to date. This has served to reduce the regulatory risks of opening these markets and has shown that there are enormous benefits for the countries involved without significant adjustment costs. It is for this reason that countries like South Africa have already been moving down this path without significant prodding from the international trading system. Delays in implementation usually stem from the political economy difficulties faced by any reform process.

The potential direct benefits for the national economy stem from the following sources:

- Reduction of price-cost margins—the introduction of competition limits the market power of industry players, thereby limiting the extent to which they can restrict output to raise prices and maximize profits. Regulatory reform should see a shift to marginal cost pricing and hence lower mark-ups of prices over costs coupled with output expansion. Of course, amongst price-regulated network providers, it is the regulator and not competition that must bring about reductions in these margins.
- Static efficiency gains—the introduction of competition should see a reduction in the level of X-inefficiency in the market as firms adopt *domestic* best practice and inefficient producers are squeezed out. This contributes to further price reductions and output expansion.
- Scale efficiency gains[4]—the expansion of the market through price reductions will impact positively on scale and result in efficiency gains if scope for further scale economies exists.
- Dynamic innovation gains[5]—the introduction of competition in components of the sector should result in a higher rate of process and product innovation as firms strive to gain market share. Process innovation

will reduce costs through efficiency gains while product innovation will expand market demand.

- Potential trade gains—regulatory reform will result in opportunities for domestic entrepreneurs to establish a presence in the industry and make the incumbent parastatal a commercial concern. If the country develops a competitive advantage in the sector, then commercial firms are likely to pursue export or foreign investment opportunities resulting in trade gains. The incentive stems not only from the pursuit of earnings growth, but also to reap greater scale economies in production (of services and knowledge) and to stabilize earnings through market diversification. These benefit the local country along with the potential supply of investment and production inputs as well as foreign exchange earnings from the repatriation of profits.

The adjustment cost of this efficiency drive is potential employment loss in the reforming sector. The loss from productivity improvements will be offset to some extent by output expansion but this is rarely sufficient in the short-run. In addition, the drive for productivity improvements will alter the structure of employment. The result will be a shift in demand towards higher skilled workers, leaving lower-skilled workers to bear the brunt of job losses.[6]

A further concern for many countries is the potential social loss from reform. This may arise from low income households losing access to necessary services once cross-subsidization is removed and commercial concerns focus on profitable segments of the market. However, subsidization of such groups can still occur under a reformed regulatory regime but through different mechanisms, such as a non-discriminatory levy on all providers in the industry that is distributed directly to the households requiring assistance. Regulatory reform provides the additional benefit of facilitating price reductions that allow more low income households to demand such services and raises the real income of those households that are already making use of the services.[7]

Within-sector analysis constitutes only a portion of the impact of reform. The downstream effects of price reductions and new product development, combined with upstream intermediate demand effects, constitute a large part of the impact of pro-competitive regulatory reform. In fact, many commentators feel that these are the real economic benefits from reform and more than offset the cost of potential employment loss.[8] These benefits include the following:

- Expansion of demand for investment goods—the reforming sector will demand greater investment goods not only to bring about improvements in efficiency, but also to expand production capacity as price reductions stimulate demand and new entrants establish a presence.
- Expansion of demand for intermediates—higher output volumes in the reforming sector will lead to a permanent increase in the level of intermediate input demand.

- Intermediate price reduction—price reductions in the reforming sector feed through to lower production costs in all other sectors of the economy, including private households. These permit price reductions and consequent output expansion in downstream industries, while increasing real income and demand amongst households.
- Innovation effects—product innovation and quality improvements in the reforming sector can have a significant effect on productivity and business practices in downstream industries that make use of these products. These in turn can lead to price reductions, product innovation and output expansion in the downstream sectors.
- Trade gains—the reduction of prices and efficiency gains in downstream industries should impact positively on their trade performance, whether they are import-competing or exporters.

These effects will feed back into the system resulting in further iterations. Further, the additional payments to households in the form of wages or returns to capital that result from the process will be a source of further demand stimulation to the economy. Equally important, these downstream effects should have a significant and positive effect on employment which can offset potential losses in the reforming sector.

III. Costs/Benefits From Granting Market Access to Foreign Providers

Once network-based service markets have undergone pro-competitive regulatory reform, they are in a position to grant market access to foreign providers along with the other service sectors without this characteristic.[9] Market access in service industries can take four forms: cross-border supply; consumption abroad; commercial presence; and presence of natural persons. The level of substitutability between these different modes of supply will be imperfect, and in fact some options may be technically infeasible for delivery of many services.

The costs and benefits of opening market access to foreign providers, regardless of mode of supply, can be drawn from the standard industrial organization and trade literature. The benefits can be broadly summarized as follows:

- Sharpening of competition—market access to foreign providers sharpens competition in the domestic sector. This results in less market power and thus lower price-cost margins, a further reduction of X-inefficiency and greater incentives for firm-level innovation.
- Transfer of technology—trading provides enhanced access to foreign technology. For domestic firms this access should accelerate learning and innovation, while also providing for the elimination of duplicative research. It will bring about as well the introduction of new service products benefiting other final goods producers.
- Broadening of the market—trade broadens the market available to a service provider. This has the effect of: (1) allowing scope for greater

exploitation of scale economies and by implication a larger product variety available to each country; (2) increasing the returns to R&D, leading to an acceleration in the innovative efforts of firms; and (3) allow for greater specialization within a service industry resulting in improvements in the quality of services.

- Resource allocation—trade leads to greater specialization across countries resulting in more efficient allocation of domestic and world resources. This offers a once-off efficiency gain.
- Enhanced downstream benefits—the forces above will lower prices, improve quality, increase product variety and accelerate innovation. These will have a positive impact on downstream users in the same vein as pro-competitive reform.
- Potential trade gains—reciprocal market opening could lead to increasing exports if the country has a comparative advantage in the sector concerned. In addition, competitive pressure may force domestic firms to seek opportunities in other markets to prevent loss of scale efficiency as they lose market share in their own markets.

The potential adjustment costs to an economy from granting market access can be summarized as:

- Output and employment loss—if the economy is producing services for which it has no comparative advantage, then these sectors may experience a decline, leading to a short-term structural adjustment where output and employment may be lost. This can be compensated for by opening markets in which the country holds some advantage.
- Loss of future growth opportunities[10]—specialization along comparative advantage can lock a country out of sectors where there is scope for rapid learning and productivity improvements or for future trade growth. This will impact on future growth opportunities.

However, different modes of supply and the pace of market opening will influence the extent to which each benefit and cost is realized by the liberalizing economy. There are also additional costs and benefits peculiar to each mode of supply which may counter-balance some of the impacts discussed. By implication also, the experience of opening different service markets to foreign access will differ depending on whether they favor one mode of supply over another.

Commercial Presence

Opening market access through commercial presence represents one of the least risky paths that can be taken by a liberalizing economy as it combines many of the benefits without much of the costs. Almost all services can be traded by commercial presence and it is the preferred option for many due to the gains from market proximity. The exceptions are those services that are by definition cross-border activities (such as international air and maritime transport). Some services can only be traded by commercial presence, specifically those that require the provision or use of physical infrastructure located in the market. These include local and long-distance telephony, domestic transportation and local energy distribution.

- The advantage of trade via commercial presence is that production must take place in the host country, which means that there are no domestic output and employment losses from trade—only a transfer of ownership. The country still gains from technology transfer and a sharpening of competitive forces. In fact, technology transfer may well be enhanced via spillovers through local supplier use and employee turnover. Further, the demonstration effect of using new technology and management techniques could also improve their uptake amongst domestic firms.

- The additional benefit of commercial presence is that it involves foreign investment, freeing local capital to pursue other opportunities in the domestic market and raising the overall level of investment in an economy. In addition, trade and domestic output gains may be enhanced if the country establishes itself as a regional center for supply of a particular service by multinationals.

- The limitations of only opening commercial presence is that many of the potential benefits will be reduced, especially if the local market size is small. In particular, competitive forces will be lower if the market can only sustain a few entrants, and there will be lower levels of specialization and exploitation of scale economies. This may be partially overcome through regulatory price-capping or the active promotion of greater competition either through facilitating greater competition between different modes of supply or opening other channels of domestic supply.[11] Of course, for services that can only be provided by commercial presence, these approaches are entirely necessary as opening other modes of supply are not an available cure.

- Further, foreign ownership may well restrict trade from the host country that competes with subsidiaries held in other countries or which accrues to the home country office. A portion of profits and returns to capital will also leak from the host country over time. This may be handled to an extent through limitations on foreign ownership, which is an approach that many developing countries have adopted.

Cross-border

Cross-border supply is becoming more viable in many service sectors due to the advancements in information/communications technology. This electronic commerce has either created the possibility of cross-border trade for some services where it was not possible before or greatly enhanced trade that was already taking place, making it more substitutable with other modes of supply.

For services such as international transport, cross-border supply has always been dominant, yet highly distorted by bilateral supply-sharing agreements. In this case, opening cross-border trade would involve removing such trade distortions.

Opening cross-border market access exposes the country to the potential loss of output and employment. However, it also exposes the domestic economy to greater levels of competition, a larger variety of technologies and products, and a broader market for exploiting scale economies. These benefits to downstream users could well offset any losses in the competing service sector.

The extent to which each of these costs/benefits occur depends crucially on a number of factors, namely the degree of substitutability between cross-border and other modes of supply, the relative competitiveness of the domestic sector, and the extent to which the local market size restricts competition, scale and specialization. Of course, if market access is reciprocal, then there is also the potential for trade gains if any one of the local service sectors has an established comparative advantage. Finally, countries need to be aware that restricting access to cross-border electronic commerce may prove impossible except through means such as exchange controls.

Presence of Natural Persons

Opening market access to trade in services via the presence of natural persons concentrates on the temporary movement of persons to a country for the purpose of providing a service. In essence, such trade provides direct competition to labor services in the host country. Although this differs from commercial presence as it is the individual and not the corporation competing, the two are linked in that foreign corporations usually require the movement of key personnel for at least an initial establishment period.

The cost/benefit of such market access can be seen as a combination of the impacts experienced with the cross-border and commercial-presence modes of supply. Firstly, similar to cross-border, some returns to labor services are shifted to foreign labor, away from local labor. However, as production still takes place domestically, the returns to other factors and any positive spillovers remain in the domestic economy. These spillovers include a portion of income demand and the technological spillovers from interaction with the rest of the economy.

Secondly, similar to commercial presence, the temporary movement of labor provides an inflow of capital, in this case human capital. In the case where human capital is a scarce resource, trade will not only lower the cost of such services but remove any restriction that it has on growth. Further, there will be only a very small displacement effect on domestic labor services and it will rather act as a complement to domestic skills. In the alternative case where the person moving to provide the service has little human capital, the impact is concentrated on the price of labor services and the displacement of domestic labor services. In both cases, downstream benefits flow from the lowering of input prices and in the case of skilled persons, a greater range of 'products.'[12] It is for this reason that countries currently restrict the temporary movement of labor to include needed skills only.

Consumption Abroad

Consumption abroad requires the movement of the consumer to the country where the producer resides. This commonly includes tourism, education and health services. This mode of supply is mostly out of the control of any country and so has largely remained unrestricted. The main barriers include items such as exchange controls, visas, the recognition of foreign qualifications and the portability of health insurance.

In contrast to other modes of supply, opening of one's own market provides a stimulus for exports and domestic production with all the benefits associated with this such as market broadening and exchange earnings. Opening other markets provides potential domestic output loss but is countered with the benefits of offering the consumer a greater product variety and a degree of competition for similar domestic services. Variety enhances utility and competition acts as a pricing constraint on domestic services.

IV. Developing Country Characteristics that Limit or Enhance the Benefits of Reform

To what extent a country benefits from liberalization and pro-competitive reform is determined to a large extent by other factors in their economy. Developing countries in particular have numerous structural deficiencies which may well limit some of the potential benefits. That said, reform of the service industries may well assist in removing some of the other constraints on growth and so have unexpected benefits for the country.

The potentially limiting factors mostly concern service sectors where *commercial presence* is the dominant form of production due to physical restrictions. The limitations include:

- Low average incomes—low incomes limit market size, which limits the level of potential competition and scale economies that can be achieved in a liberalized sector. This will result in lower productivity and price reduction benefits than in the more industrial economies. Opening other modes of supply if possible will of course relieve this problem.
- Importers of capital goods—much of the demand created for investment goods will leak to industrial countries. Balance of payments constraints may also limit the rate of purchase and hence the pace of reform and its benefits.
- Market risk and return—higher risk and (in the case of African countries) lower returns may either see a lack of interest in establishing a

commercial presence in a country or see establishment with retention of high price-cost margins. This may favor trade through other modes such as cross-border, where the potential benefits to the receiving country are lower. High risk premiums on interest rates will also limit domestic investment expansion in response to demand stimulus in the reforming sector.

- Regulatory and competition policy capacity—network-based services that undergo pro-competitive regulatory reform require close supervision afterwards to ensure that anti-competitive practices do not occur in the service component and that price-capping is sufficiently binding in the network component. Weak regulatory and competition-policy capacity in developing countries may therefore result in higher than necessary pricing and so limited benefits from reform.

- Human capital constraint—growth stimulus from regulatory reform may be limited by the human capital constraint. Even though foreign companies may enter the domestic market, employment is still likely to be dominated by local labor. Human capital constraints can limit both the level of investment growth and the potential for productivity improvements. In addition, the demands placed by the reforming sector may crowd out access to human capital by other sectors while raising the costs of skilled persons.

For *cross-border supply* of final demand services, a lack of confidence in the regulatory and legal systems in developing country may limit the extent of imports by industrial consumers, fearful of fraud and the lack of recourse to legal action.[13] This would result in a large trade imbalance in this mode of supply. These problems would probably not exist for intermediate demand, and this may in fact favor some developing countries. This potential of unidirectional trade is probably less of a concern with opening *the presence of natural persons* mode of supply even if restricted to skilled workers. This is because developing country professionals are lower priced and already export their services to a large extent.

A further concern regardless of the mode of supply is the level of competition in other parts of the economy. Weak competition in downstream industries will result in much of the price reductions in intermediate services being absorbed by profits and not reflected in price reductions in these sectors. This will limit the demand and employment expansion in these sectors, which would usually offset the costs of employment loss in the reforming sector.

Reform has the potential to remove some of the constraints on growth. Again these are concentrated in the commercial-presence mode of supply and can be divided into the influx of foreign capital and influx of foreign technology. Foreign capital inflows provide a higher savings rate and so the potential for a higher investment rate as domestic funds can be diverted to other opportunities. Inflows of foreign capital also lower the balance of payments constraint on growth and allow lower real interest rates. This, and the boost to short-term growth rates, crowds in greater domestic investment. As foreign entrants will employ significant numbers of the local workforce, this process should result in a period of sustained development of the human capital of the local labor force involved.

Finally, many services make use of common inputs. Thus, a reform package that liberalizes a few sectors at once may well see the emergence of a sufficient critical mass to develop an intermediate industry. Of particular interest in this case is the information-technology industry, which is a crucial input to all services and fundamental in bringing about productivity improvements and new product development.

V. A Brief Overview of the South African Producer Services Sector

South Africa (SA) has a modern economy that is reflected in a relatively sophisticated producer services sector. This is also a sector that still contains numerous government monopolies and limited international market access. However, reforms are being introduced that are gradually altering the economic landscape in the country.

The telecommunications industry has progressed considerably in the last five years with the licensing of two mobile telephony providers, the corporatization and partial equity sale in the fixed line monopoly (Telkom) and the opening of the VANS sector. The networks are modern and high growth has left SA with the largest GSM market outside of Europe and amongst the top 20 Internet users in the world. However, productivity is low, quality of service lags behind world leaders and prices are relatively high across the board. Teledensity remains low and large inequalities in access persist.

To address rollout in under-serviced areas and upgrade the competitiveness of the state incumbent (Telkom), it was decided that the national monopoly in local, long-distance and international telephony would be extended until 2003. In addition, VANS service providers were restricted to using Telkom's network infrastructure. Foreign access to the market exists through minority shareholdings in all parts of the market, but with holdings in the mobile and fixed line networks restricted to 30%. The sophistication of the SA industry relative to the region has meant an outward flow of investment especially in cellular network provision. This complements South Africa's role as a regional routing hub for international calls.

The transport sector has moved more sluggishly down the road of privatization and reform. The sector is dominated by the state-owned Transnet group, which has control of all major ports, airports and rail infrastructure. The road and domestic air transport sectors were deregulated in the mid-eighties while maritime and international air transport have always been open to numerous international carriers under bilateral agreement restrictions. More recently, airports were unbundled from the Transnet group and a minority shareholding sold, and public-private partnerships are being sought for road infrastructure development. Dominant problems in the system include a backlog of infrastructure spending, low productivity/high costs and a lack of inter-modal integration. Although there is intent to introduce further pro-competitive regulatory reform, the task of unbundling the debt-ridden Transnet remains an obstacle. As South Africa is the hub of trade in the region, there is a strong trade in port and land transport services regionally.

The financial sector in South Africa is a well-regulated and sophisticated industry. The soundness of the financial system was reflected in its resilience during the Asian financial crisis. The industry's technology, infrastructure and supervision are seen to compare favorably with industrial countries. Foreign entry to the industry was once again welcomed in 1994 and has been rapid in brokerage, short-term insurance and investment banking. The remaining sectors are dominated by a handful of local institutions. There is generally no discrimination amongst SA-registered entities (foreign-owned or not), but foreign-registered entities are constrained in numerous ways. These include the need to be locally capitalized and the exclusion from retail banking and long-term insurance markets. Exchange controls persist and act as a discriminatory factor against cross-border supply but not amongst commercial-presence suppliers. Despite these restrictions, many foreign financial services firms are using South Africa as a springboard into Southern Africa, following the established SA banks and insurance companies. This has led to the growth of SA as a regional financial center.

Business services in South Africa are open and competitive. The sector offers a full range of specialized services and includes significant numbers of foreign-affiliated local partnerships in most fields. Employment in the industry is dominated by local professionals due to a large local pool of skilled labor and various restrictions on foreign entry such as some limitations on the recognition of foreign professional qualifications and a lack of transparency in the domestic regulations governing the temporary movement of persons. Overall, the sector is relatively competitive on an international level and has also begun to branch out to service the region in support of domestic firms investing in these economies.

VI. How Has Reform Impacted on the South African Economy to Date

Telecommunications[14]

The partial opening of the telecommunications industry has brought significant benefits for the South African economy already. The licensing of new products—specifically cellular and VANS—has added a few percentage points to GDP and created large numbers of jobs. Many of these jobs have been lower-skilled because they were created in the retail sector.[15] In fixed line telephony there has been an improvement in productivity, service quality and a rebalancing of tariffs which has reduced international call rates but increased local call rates. Part of this can be ascribed to increasing competition from the cellular industry as it began before an equity partner was found, and some can be ascribed to the transfer of technology from the foreign equity partners. This has had a cost in terms of employment loss, but this is dwarfed relative to the expansion of jobs in cellular and VANS. Further, there has been a growing investment in human capital since foreign entry. It has also provided necessary capital for network expansion, aiming to double the teledensity of the country in eight years. A slight macroeconomic downturn following the Asian crisis has impeded expansion slightly.

For downstream industries, much of the investment demand created by these new investments leaked from the economy as expected. These purchases of equipment and services did place some pressure on the balance of payments initially as cellular network infrastructure was rolled out. However, this has been mostly offset by capital inflows as foreign investments in telecommunications have accounted for roughly 25% of all FDI since 1994. There appears to be a sizable impact on downstream productivity, though no estimates are available. There has also been outward investment by most operators. One cellular company has established itself in five other markets, while the other has been less ambitious to prevent competing for license bids with its major foreign shareholder.

However, current reform has also had major limitations, mostly relating to competition and regulatory policy issues. The extension of the fixed line monopoly has prevented competition from reducing price-cost margins and accelerating productivity growth to the point where significant inroads are made into the productivity gap with leading providers internationally. Price-capping has not provided an alternative disciplining effect because it has been set at a non-binding level. While there has been some competition from the cellular market, this has focused on service rather than price. A significant reason for this is the cross-holding in one of the two providers by the fixed line monopolist. The result is that South Africa is estimated to have one of the highest cellular call rates internationally,[16] and fixed line prices have not seen the dramatic drops that characterized liberalization in other countries. This has limited any downstream effects on other industry to impacts stemming from new products and improvements in quality, with no significant price effects. Finally, the incumbent has shown anti-competitive tendencies by using the courts to disrupt the competition in both the ISP and VANS markets.

Financial Services[17]

There has always been some foreign participation in SA financial services, but the end of apartheid and the relaxation of exchange controls have provided impetus for greater foreign entry.[18] However, the current regime prevents cross-border transactions and so market opening has been characterized by commercial presence only.

In banking, foreign entrants have secured 5% of the market but concentrated on commercial/syndicated loans, corporate finance advisory services, foreign exchange dealings, trade finance and securities trading. They have pioneered the introduction of new products that help firms to manage risk and lower the cost of capital. They have improved industry regulation through strong support for initiatives from the regulatory authority[19] and provided easier access to international capital.

In the insurance industry, foreign participation has focused on individual and corporate short-term insurance, creditor insurance and reinsurance. They have secured a 38% market share in short-term insurance and 100% of the reinsurance market. Their entry has resulted in increased price competition, forcing local companies to respond. New products have been introduced, such as alternative risk transfer, which have helped corporates manage risk better.

Securities trading was deregulated in a 'big bang' in 1995 and introduced negotiated commissions, corporate ownership and principal trading. This opened the market to foreign brokerages which have subsequently acquired between 30-40% of the market. However, the market has expanded equally rapidly, ensuring little loss for local players. For instance, in the bond exchange, turnover has increased three-fold and liquidity doubled. Commission rates have also come down while the quality of research has improved. Foreign entrants offer better analysis of international markets while bringing new techniques and competitive pressure to local research. They also bring new products, such as customized derivative products, which lower the costs of capital and help manage risk.

Market expansion in all financial services has expanded employment in South Africa significantly. In addition, foreign entrants across all segments of the market have played an important part in promoting SA as a regional financial center. This has developed partly because of their use of SA as a regional base, but also because their entry has improved the competitiveness of the financial services market through cutting prices, expanding the range of products and improving service.

However, all this success has had some adjustment costs too. Dramatic market expansion has encountered a human-capital constraint resulting in very large increases in salaries in the domestic industry and high turnover of staff. Where reform itself has failed is that certain markets have remained protected through discriminatory legislation. In these markets, particularly retail banking and long-term insurance, there has not been the same extent of changes in prices, products and service. In fact, there has been growing dissatisfaction with what is alleged over-charging by retail banks. It is here where other modes of competition, such as cross-border or internet banks may well pressure the markets to reform to the extent of other financial services.

Transportation[20]

Transport has not seen significant reform as yet. Deregulation of the air and road sectors has had important impacts on price and service through competition. This has impacted on other modes of supply, especially rail where competition from road transport has lowered rail's share of freight transport to 20%. In airports, the foreign equity sale has provided a much needed capital injection that has raised airport efficiency through facilities expansion. Despite protection, some parts of the transport system remain internationally competitive due to heavy investments in them to bolster specific commodity exports.[21]

The deregulation that has already occurred has also not been without problems. In particular, the domestic air transport sector has seen a number of local carriers exit the market soon after establishment. The allegations are that aggressive and anti-competitive price wars by the dominant carrier are being used to force competitors out of the market. Foreign buy-ins have provided some stability to the remaining local competitors. Current reform also does not go far enough as large parts of the transport sector are inefficient and overpriced.

Business Services

Business services have always been relatively open in South Africa, and political constraints rather than regulation have been a force preventing foreign entry. The main regulatory restrictions have been, and still remain, the temporary movement of natural persons and the recognition of qualifications. Since 1994 there has been a rapid expansion in the commercial presence of foreign providers, accounting for around 7% of all FDI inflows since then. Cross-border trade has also been growing rapidly and now accounts for over 1% of exports and 1% of imports.

The entry of foreign firms has shaken up the local industry, raising the quality of local business services and introducing new products. Although market share has been taken away from local firms, employment has been created locally due to the preference for commercial presence. The competition has also forced local firms to restructure and become more internationally competitive, providing scope for them to go global themselves. This has particularly been the case with the information-technology services where a number of firms have grown to the status of powerful international players.

The dominant problem with reform has been the pressure on the labor market. Foreign firms entering the market were initially highly restricted by the tight market for skills locally. This gave local firms some breathing space to respond to competition, but also resulted in high staff turnover and rapidly increasing salaries. A further problem is that temporary immigration regulation is in practice obstructionist and untransparent and offers limited relief from a tight labor market in the short term.

VII. How South Africa Might Approach Further Liberalization of Services

The experience from existing reform and liberalization in South Africa has shown that although pro-competitive regulatory reform and liberalization bring numerous benefits, the process needs to be managed properly so that adjustment costs are limited and benefits maximized. The lessons from theory and experience suggest that the reform process needs to be aware of the following issues:

1. *Importance of pro-competitive reform*—a large portion of the benefits to the economy stem from having effective competition in a sector, regardless of whether or not trade in that sector is liberalized. It is also feasible that uncompetitive conditions remain after foreign entry, restricting the flow of benefits and allowing foreign capital to reap monopoly rents. Therefore countries need to tighten competition policy and even consider opening multiple modes of supply simultaneously to ensure adequate competitive pressure.

2. *Importance of foreign technology access*—access to foreign technology is most important when the innovation rate in a sector is high, as in telecommunications and finance. In these cases, the introduction of new products not only expands the market sufficiently to offset potential employment and market share losses, but also offers the most benefits to downstream final goods producers.

3. *Regional comparative advantages*—a country needs to consider its role in both the regional and international trading system. The case of South Africa shows that a country may have a regional comparative advantage that differs from its international comparative advantage. This difference allows scope for a developing country to benefit more significantly from liberalization than expected as regional exports may offset international imports. It also, however, raises the question of whether it is better for a country to liberalize services more rapidly in the region before committing to multilateral liberalization.

4. *Human-capital constraint*—the human capital constraint can be considerable in a developing country undergoing a rapid reform process. This can slow down investment and see a large portion of the gains accruing to skilled labor, to the detriment of downstream users. Addressing this constraint may require a more liberal stance on the temporary movement of persons or a slower pace of reform until the gradual upgrading of domestic human capital has caught up.

5. *Package of reforms*—the package of reforms within a single sector and between a number of sectors is important to determining the distribution of gains. The trade-offs may be over modes of supply, for instance, reform on commercial presence without a liberal position on the presence of natural persons may introduce the human-capital constraint. They may be inter-sectoral, that is, opening the portability of health insurance may harm the domestic insurance industry but benefit domestic health tourism. And they may be in the extent to which liberalization occurs. For example, it seems that foreign entry without competition in telecommunications brings few benefits.

6. *Extent of market opening*—it is not clear whether full liberalization is required to reap the benefits of reform. It would seem that many of these benefits can accrue while still retaining some limitations (such as limits on foreign holdings) that would enable development goals to be achieved too.

7. *Benefits for industrial countries*—there are large benefits for industrial countries from developing country liberalization that are reflected in returns to investment, export growth and demand for investment goods. This affords developing countries some bargaining power to ensure that development of domestic industry and human capital occurs.

Notes

[1] In particular, Butterworth and Malherbe (1999), Eisenburg (1999), Hodge (1999) and Naude (1999).

[2] The main sectors that fall into this category are communications, rail transport, electricity, and to a lesser extent air and maritime transport.

[3] The Reference Paper of the WTO Agreement on Basic Telecommunications is the first to provide regulatory guidelines to signatories of the agreement

[4] See Tybout et al. (1991).

[5] Grossman and Helpman (1991).

[6] See Bhorat and Hodge (1999).

[7] Hodge (1999).

[8] The OECD (1997) study finds that downstream employment creation offsets sectoral employment losses under certain reasonable assumptions regarding the flexibility of the labor market.

[9] It is common that limited foreign access is provided prior to the completion of pro-competitive regulatory reform in order to inject capital and know-how into incumbent national monopolies.

[10] Lucas (1988).

[11] For example, allowing different types of financial institutions to enter each other's markets and opening the market to outsiders like retailers.

[12] The mix of skill and experience contained in the human capital can be seen as a new product variety and so offers similar benefits to downstream users as discussed previously.

[13] In the cross-border trade of financial services, final consumers may perceive the exchange risks of developing countries as unmanageable and again limit trade to one direction.

[14] See Hodge (1999) for a more detailed analysis.

[15] Retailers selling air-time, phones, computing equipment and software.

[16] This is based on purchasing power parity.

[17] See Butterworth and Malherbe (1999) for a more detailed analysis.

[18] Roughly half of the current market participants have established a presence since the establishment of a democratic government in 1994.

[19] For example, more stringent money-laundering regulation.

[20] See Naude (1999) for a more detailed analysis.

[21] The main coal and steel bulk port has one of the most efficient bulk ports in the world.

References

Bhorat, H. and J. Hodge. 1999. "Decomposing Shifts in Labor Demand in South Africa," *South African Journal of Economics*, September.

Butterworth, B. and S. Malherbe. 1999. *The South African Financial Sector: Background Research for the Seattle Round*, TIPS Working Paper, July.

Eisenburg, G. 1999. *Study into Policy Instruments Affecting Labor Movement to South Africa and the General Agreement on Trade in Services*, TIPS Working Paper, August.

Grossman, G. and E. Helpman. 1991 *Innovation and Growth in the World Economy*. Cambridge, MA: MIT Press.

Hodge, J. 1998. *Developing a Trade and Industry Policy Agenda for Service Sectors in South Africa*, TIPS Working Paper, September.

Hodge, J. 1999. *The State of the Telecommunications Industry in South Africa and the Potential Costs/Benefits of Further Liberalization*, TIPS Working Paper, August.

Lucas, R. 1988. "On the Mechanics of Economic Development," *Journal of Monetary Economics* 22:3-42.

Naude, W. 1999. *Trade in Transport Services: South Africa and the General Agreement on Trade in Services*, TIPS Working Paper, August.

OECD. 1997. *The OECD Report on Regulatory Reform*, vols. 1 & 2. Paris: OECD.

Tybout, J., J. de Melo, and V. Corbo. 1991. "The Effects of Trade Policy on Scale and Technical Efficiency: New Evidence from Chile," *Journal of International Economics* 31:231-50.

Part 3. Negotiating Options and Issues

CHAPTER 16

Implementing Telecommunications Liberalization in Developing Countries after the WTO Agreement on Basic Telecommunications Services[*]

Peter F. Cowhey and Mikhail M. Klimenko

I. Introduction

Many countries have drastically changed their policies for the telecommunications services industry in the past 15 years. Yet developing and transition economies were choosing significantly different approaches to competition and privatization than OECD countries. Rapid and diverse change created an impetus for finding some new common ground in the global market. In 1997, a new framework emerged through the World Trade Organization (WTO) Agreement on Basic Telecommunications Services. This agreement combined binding commitments on market access that included the cross-border supply of telecommunications services and capital, the hallmarks of every market in high technology. Moreover, most countries listed a set of "pro-competitive regulatory principles" as additional market access commitments. These principles have rapidly come to define the policy revolution under way in this market.

   This chapter analyzes two of the Agreement's consequences and the lessons for economic reform. First, the Agreement changed expectations about the supply, pricing, and demand growth of communications services. It forged clear and credible information about future market changes in key developing countries that change expectations of all economic agents. In particular, it has speeded up a major shift in the market for cross-border services, like international telephony, although many countries limited market access in ways designed to blunt the change. The pricing shift in turn forces a reevaluation of other market arrangements. Second, contrary to the advice of critics of WTO regulatory codes, a common code for regulation (the "Reference Paper") on the model of competitive policy in the United States and Europe has narrowed the range of risks for all investors, domestic and foreign, by strengthening the position of domestic advocates of market reform. This effect is similar to the process of "gaiatsu" that is familiar to all students of trade negotiations between the United States and Japan. While there is considerable uncertainty about the agenda for future WTO talks on telecommunications, the process will increase the number of countries adhering to the 1997 Agreement and improve the quality of market-access commitments.

II. The Global Market Revolution

In 1984 the United States forced the divestiture of AT&T and created competition in the market for long-distance services. Only a few countries (the United Kingdom, Japan, Australia, New Zealand, and Canada) followed the American lead on phone services in the next few years. Only a few governments were ready to begin discussing liberalization of basic telecommunications at the start of the Uruguay Round. Unsurprisingly, the Round's major agreement on services—the General Agreement on Trade in Services (GATS) signed at the conclusion of the Uruguay Round in 1994—narrowed its attention to value-added telecommunications services such as data networking which then constituted about five percent of the world telecommunications market.

During the Round, the digital information technology revolution began to change the market very fundamentally. An inefficient market for telecommunications services threatened competitiveness in the computer, software, and information industry markets. As a result, the U.S. extended competition to local phone services (and, thus, the hardest element of the communications network to duplicate—local termination and origination of services). Meanwhile, in its effort to stimulate the information industry and unify its internal market the European Union (EU) decided to introduce general competition in telecommunications services in 1998.

As competition began in the major industrial countries, their phone companies looked to foreign markets to create new business opportunities. Yet all phone companies faced major limits on foreign market access, and once in a foreign market they confronted serious regulatory uncertainties about how they would be treated. Suspicion among industrial countries ran deep. The OECD countries were impatient to secure their mutual rights to market access in basic telecommunications services (including telephony), and the WTO was a convenient forum for achieving this goal.

One of the Annexes in the GATS (the Annex on Negotiations on Basic Telecommunications) outlined a legal framework for reopening negotiations on basic telecom services under the auspice of the WTO. However, the multilateral features of the WTO (particularly the Most-Favored-Nation [MFN] and National Treatment obligations) meant that mutual opening among OECD countries automatically conferred benefits on telephone carriers of developing countries. The industrial countries feared a two-tier market would emerge—general competition in industrial countries and a blend of privatization and very limited competition in developing countries. This would sabotage hopes of creating truly global competitive networks. Thus, the fate of the WTO telecom talks became joined to the spread of competition in basic telecommunications services to developing countries (see Cowhey and Richards, 2000).

The trade talks could not have forced the developing countries to adopt unacceptable reforms. But the political effort generated by the negotiations induced leaders among the newly industrializing countries (NICs) to make deeper and faster market changes that binding trade commitments would make irrevocable. (The NICs were especially important in the trade process because competition would surely not become common in developing countries if the NICs did not soon move to general competition.) The timing was right even though reform posed a dilemma. On the one hand, traditional state-owned monopoly suppliers had largely failed to provide low-cost, efficient, or even widely available services in many countries while increased volumes of trade and factor mobility at both regional and global levels had intensified reliance of business users and households on telecommunications services. Households were demanding even more sophisticated services at lower prices. Moreover, the pricing, quality and flexibility of telecommunications services were becoming a larger factor in production. The NICs especially saw advanced networking as an important infrastructure attraction for foreign business investment, especially in high value-added industries. On the other hand, the incumbent phone companies were very significant features in their national stock markets (and, usually, a major holding for the finance ministry). And the profits from international phone services permitted governments to keep prices for local phone services below costs. Therefore, the NICs both saw advantages in general network competition and feared its financial fallout at least during a prolonged period of adjustment.

III. The WTO: The Creation of a New "International Regime"

The WTO agreement featured specific commitments on market access from an impressive number of signatories: 67 of 69 participating governments made significant liberalization commitments.[1] The poorest participation was from Africa and the smallest developing countries. Participation from the NICs was strong. The commitments on market access typically included all forms of basic communications services (from cellular through land-line), were technology neutral (made no distinction, for example, between satellite and terrestrial services), and included the right to ownership by foreign investment.[2] The obligations went into effect on January 1, 1998. (The date deliberately coincided with the introduction of competition in the European Union.)

One way to capture the extent of the agreement's impact is to look at its effect on markets. The U.S. government has calculated that approximately 85 percent of the world market, measured by revenues, is covered by strong market-access commitments in the negotiations. With a few specific exceptions on particular issues or market segments, all the OECD nations essentially were bound to unconditional market access on January 1, 1998. A review of the major industrializing countries shows very significant commitments on market access that increased very rapidly over a period of a few years (typically after transition periods ranging from two to five years).[3] There cannot be a fundamentally new way of doing business, including regulating business, in 85 percent of the world market that will not spill over to the rest of the global market.

The changes embodied in the WTO pact will accelerate. For example, some governments used the WTO Agreement on Basic Telecommunications to accelerate policy reforms and bind intended future liberalization of basic telecommunications. Other governments bound only the existing policy regimes or even made WTO commitments that were below existing levels. However, even if a government could not, for political reasons, bind the existing levels of liberalization, the commitments were still valuable. For example, commitments binding at less than the current limit on equity to any foreign investor will be " ratcheted up" after even one investor exceeds them because of the MFN clause (see Low and Mattoo, 1997).

More importantly, the agreement is a fundamental change in the international regime. The concept of a "regime" captures the principles, norms, and rules expected of participants in major fields of governance in the world economy. In other words, it captures expectations about how the market and governments will interact that go beyond strict legal agreements.[4] This regime change has at least three major implications.

First, for countries that are not yet members of the WTO, the WTO telecommunications agreement will influence the terms of their accession. Their commitments on telecommunications will have to be significant, as evidenced by China's telecom concessions as part of its entry to the WTO.

Second, the agreement has changed the expectations of all economic agents, including governments. The NICs were vital to these talks, and their binding commitments on introducing general market competition provided credible and easily summarized evidence (the opposite of "cheap talk") to all other developing countries that competition was coming. This influences the financial markets. Lucrative international traffic is to some extent subject to rerouting and arbitrage, for example, so that a move to general competition in a major regional traffic center undermines the high profits earned on international services in less competitive markets in the region.[5] Moreover, investors become skeptical about the viability of continued monopolies in the region. Countries with less regulatory transparency and little competition are considered riskier, because markets suspect that traditional monopolies are not sustainable beyond some carefully defined period of transition.

Third, any dominant set of regulatory arrangements creates its own set of supportive political coalitions (see Baron, 1995). The WTO agreement will create interest coalitions that will promote further market opening in economies where open competition has not yet taken root. These coalitions will use consensus building among experts, trade negotiations, transnational political lobbying, and market activities to expand the realm of competition. For example, OECD governments and firms persuaded the World Bank and the International Telecommunications Union to provide technical assistance on how to introduce competition by committing to the WTO regulatory principles. This campaign successfully advanced the proposition that network economics were similar enough across countries for any nation to embrace competition confidently. Since the 1997 agreement, key NICs have quickened the pace of introducing competition. For example, in 1999 Argentina, Peru, and Brazil introduced competition in long distance services that went beyond their WTO commitments. This in turn has turned their former monopolists into companies interested in expanding new services and entering the markets of neighboring countries.[6]

The WTO agreement's global scope also made it easier to create new trans-border services. For example, new entrants with innovative business models and new technological approaches, such as Level Three (a wholesale carrier) are building a fiber-optic network that covers the United States and large parts of Europe and Asia. The network serves only other carriers, not retail customers. Global Crossing is creating a worldwide undersea cable system that caters to the needs of new carriers in the retail business by offering them specialized credit and service plans. Its first cable, Atlantic Crossing 1, accounted for about half of all transatlantic capacity in 1999.

The new ways of providing global telecommunication services are reshaping the economics for services within and among countries. This price revolution will be a fundamental consequence of the new telecom regime.

IV. International Services and Rate Rebalancing: Changing the Market Equilibrium

Pricing will change because the old market structure for international telecommunications services is in deep trouble. The old regime supported the "joint supply" of international phone services using settlement rates. Under this system each carrier theoretically contributed half the international phone or fax service—for example, taking the international call from a hypothetical midpoint in the ocean and terminating the call to a local household in its country. Presumably the supply of an international call depended on each national carrier providing half of the facilities for the call. For contributing this capability the national carrier received a fee called the "settlement rate (which is the price negotiated between the two national carriers for one minute of a traditional circuit-switched call).[7] Jointly provided services allowed one party to block production and control the total cost of production through unilateral decisions about the pricing of its services.

Given the problems with pricing in most developing countries, there was enormous pressure to cover shortfalls on local services by inflating rates for international services. All countries suffered from inflated rates for international services. But the situation was far worse in developing country than in industrial countries. International services in Asia were typically 30 to 60 percent of total revenues even though international traffic was a small percentage of total traffic (see Irvine, 1998). In larger South American countries prices for international services in 1998 were still typically four to six times higher than for domestic long distance (see Davis et al., 1998). Demand is elastic and these pricing practices effectively turned communications into a lower volume luxury good in these countries.

At the same time, the developing countries found it particularly attractive to extract rents from carriers in industrial countries by inflating settlement rates.[8] The U.S. carriers paid over $5 billion in net settlement payments to foreign carriers in 1996, mostly to developing countries. (This is a remarkable sum in a world market for international telecommunications services amounting to a little over $50 billion in 1996.) The FCC estimated that at least 80 percent of this total was purely an economic rent (see Cowhey, 1999). Moreover, in the era of monopoly, companies relied primarily on national public financing to build the network. Profits from settlement rates were thus an important source of the convertible currency needed to finance purchases of foreign telecommunications equipment.

Joint supply is becoming anachronistic in a world economy where companies run sophisticated global production and distribution networks with complex integrated communications system to support them. Moreover, the gradual integration of all forms of services over the Internet, a packet-switched network whose transmission is not even measured in minutes of use, is just beginning to provide price limits on many international services. (Internet services can substitute for faxes readily and for voice at some price to quality.) Using the surge in transmission capacity, new entrants are catering to the growth of hybrid Internet Protocol network mixtures of voice, fax and data services that defy traditional market categorizations and pricing (see Staple 1998).

In theory, the WTO agreement did not demand radical changes in the settlement rate system.[9] Competition could add more carriers but not change the fundamental structure of jointly provided services or discourage cozy oligopolistic pricing of international services. But, in fact, by 2000 the ability to enter markets freely across national borders and to own and lease facilities for services on nondiscriminatory terms will force major change.[10] Carriers in competitive industrial markets who wanted to move traffic under the traditional system of jointly provided services have already lowered settlement rates to levels in line with the costs of owning and running a global network. As a result, settlement rates among industrial countries have plummeted since the WTO agreement. Figure 1 and panels A, B and C in the Appendix represent the dynamics of the U.S. accounting rates with a group of selected countries in U.S. Dollars. (Typically, the settlement rate is one-half of the accounting rate.)

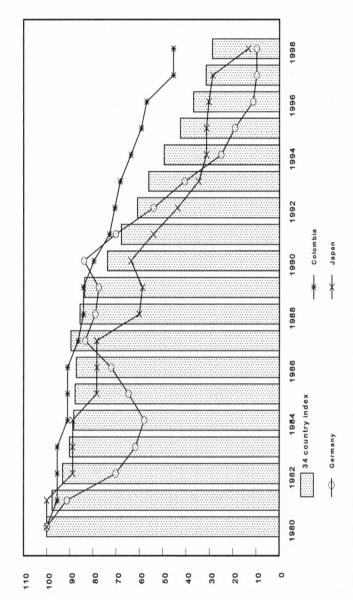

Figure 1. Decline in the U.S. Accounting Rates*

*34 country index is the Fisher ideal index for the U.S. accounting rates with the countries in Table 1 plus Australia, Canada, France, Germany, Greece, Israel, Italy, Japan, Netherlands, Spain, Switzerland, United Kingdom.

Source: Blake and Lande (1999).

Panel A provides data on WTO countries making full market access commitments effective in 1998; Panel B provides data from countries with lesser commitments; Panel C contains data on WTO countries that did not make any commitments and selected non-member countries.

As seen from Figure 1 and the Appendix, the U.S. accounting rates have been declining on average by 16% every year since 1997. This is a much faster rate than the annual average decline by 6.2% in 1992-1997. For a number of countries the rate of decline of the accounting rates has significantly accelerated after 1997. The data suggest that accounting rates with countries making full-market-access commitments declined by 22% since 1997. These countries account for more than a third of total U.S. settlement payments to WTO countries. Accounting rates with carriers from WTO countries making lesser commitments have declined 14% since 1997. Accounting rates with carriers from all WTO countries making commitments declined by 15% since 1997. Carriers from a group of 29 countries managed to reach settlement rates that are below the "benchmark" levels established by the FCC in 1997.

But a more significant story (as of 2000) can be summarized by four points. First, no industrial country with full commitments had a settlement rate above 15 cents and many were heading to eight cents. This was the bulk of the world's traffic. Second, every industrial country had introduced "international simple resale," ISR, the right of a carrier to lease plain transmission facilities and route traffic on an end-to-end basis between two countries without the use of any settlement rate. Many dominant incumbents tried to keep margins up on international voice and data traffic by maintaining high prices for international leased circuits. (This tactic has the added advantage of raising margins on Internet traffic which now dominates international routes but is priced much more cheaply than voice traffic.) However, an explosion in backbone long-haul infrastructure will eventually undermine high rates for ISR.[11] Third, no NIC was likely to have a settlement rate above 19 cents by the end of 2000, and some were matching the rates of industrial countries. For example, a number of East European countries with aspirations to join the EU (such as Croatia, Estonia and Lithuania) managed to reach very low settlement rates even without the WTO commitments. Fourth, with only a few exceptions (such as Hong Kong and South Korea) most developing countries drafted their WTO obligations so that they could avoid ISR.[12] They desired a slower decline in international rates than industrial countries while acknowledging that the settlement rates will decline steeply and likely disappear in the long-term.

The rapid changes in the settlement rates opened numerous opportunities for arbitrage in delivering traffic to developing countries. Settlement rates were extremely inconsistent; the United States typically had the lowest settlement rates in the world. Moreover, most settlement rates were kept secret (only the United States fully disclosed them).[13] Inconsistency and secrecy created a vigorous arbitrage market for rerouting bilateral traffic through third parties who enjoy lower settlement rates. In addition, many carriers were offering volume discounts that they denied officially in order to discourage arbitrage. Larger flows of traffic outside of traditional settlement rates made it harder to enforce bilateral pricing and route arrangements designed to reinforce high prices. All that said, settlement rates still remained high and end prices for international services higher yet. Our point is that the WTO created a regime where market expectations are that change (i.e., much lower margins and prices on international services) is inevitable in the medium-term, and players are beginning to adjust in anticipation of that predicted equilibrium.

In short, the trade agreement accelerated changes that will transform pricing and supply options for the world market. Even countries that made no commitments on telecommunications services at the WTO face significantly different market economics and politics.

Declining margins on international services force rate rebalancing (because domestic services must cover more of their own costs) and expansion of new services (to create new revenue streams). These shifts favor more competition because a major deterrent to competition was the protection of cross-subsidies and high margins on some services. For example, the tradition of keeping local rates below costs to encourage universal service discouraged investment in building out the local network.[14] Meanwhile, incumbent operators have a powerful political weapon to use against introducing competition: the argument that new entrants are likely to serve only urban areas (thus "skimming the cream" from the market).[15]

What is being done? There is a significant movement to cost-based rates for all services by rebalancing rates across classes of services and much less averaging of rates. The cost of local service prices may rise (at least in some regions of a country), but many other prices will decline and tap significant demand elasticity.

The good news about rebalancing is that while it is politically controversial, even dramatic needs for rebalancing can occur without any net loss of universal service. The Philippines was especially dependent on revenues from international services from the United States. As those rates declined, the Philippines undertook significant rate rebalancing. (As of 1998, households paid about US$20 per month for basic local service.) Lower prices for long distance services, along with the belated rapid expansion of cellular services, have also generated more domestic long distance traffic and income (Merrill Lynch, 1997; National Telecommunications Commission, 1997). The Philippines was typical in that the take-off of mobile services opened major new streams of revenue for most operators.[16] At the same time, somewhat fortuitously, the Internet explosion in data traffic provided new revenues, but at the cost of accommodating services that will ultimately subvert high price structures. More generally, modern financial techniques allowed for effective commercial financing to handle many cash-flow issues during rebalancing. When these techniques could not suffice, international financial institutions like the World Bank could assist (Braga et al., 1999).

V. The Value of the Reference Paper

Another major achievement of the WTO negotiation was the creation of the "Reference Paper" on pro-competitive regulatory principles, which was accepted as an additional commitment by 67 of the countries (Arena, 1997). Most remarkably, the parties agreed on what constituted the heart of sound regulation in the market.[17] The obligations of governments to create effective interconnection rules and the need to separate the regulator from the operator are at the core of the principles (Box 1).

Box 1. The WTO Reference Paper

- What does the WTO Reference Paper say to the telecommunications industry? It makes six major points, which we summarize below. The General Agreement on Tariffs and Trade in Services (GATS) contains additional rules, because the telecommunications agreement operates as an industry-specific code within the GATS framework.

- The Paper sets out rules for governments on regulating "major suppliers" of telecommunications services. A major supplier controls "essential facilities for the public network" that cannot reasonably be duplicated either for economic or technical reasons, or both.

- It requires governments to take measures to ensure that major suppliers do not engage in anticompetitive practices such as cross-subsidies, use information obtained from competitors, or withhold needed technical information from competitors.

- It states that governments will assure interconnection with a major supplier for competitors at any technically feasible point in the network. The terms, conditions, and quality must be nondiscriminatory (that is, no less favorable to the competitor than to the major supplier). Interconnection must be timely, and rates must be reasonable and transparent, taking into account economic feasibility. Services must be unbundled so that suppliers are not paying for network components or facilities they do not need. The terms for interconnection must be publicly available and enforceable on a timely basis.

- It allows governments to maintain policy measures that are designed to achieve universal service. However, these measures must be administered in a transparent, nondiscriminatory, and competitively neutral way. They should not be more burdensome than is necessary to achieve universal service.

- It stipulates that the regulatory body be separate from the actual suppliers, and that it employ procedures ensuring impartiality for all market participants.

- It requires governments to use procedures for the allocation and use of scare resources (including frequencies) that are timely, objective, transparent, and nondiscriminatory.

Requirements for interconnection with the network of the dominant incumbent go to the heart of competition, so vigorous disputes over its precise terms are predictable. But a consensus exists in industrial countries. Interconnection policy sets pricing for interconnection based on long-run incremental costs. It requires the timely provision of leased circuit capacity, some unbundling of the network elements available for interconnection, nondiscriminatory access to rights of way, and portability for telephone numbers when subscribers decide to switch carriers. And it features direct negotiations among commercial parties and a timely dispute resolution that allows the regulator, relying on existing guidelines to settle matters that cannot be resolved during the commercial negotiations (European Commission, 1998).

A standard question is, "how will a WTO dispute-resolution panel interpret the principles on interconnection or other regulatory principles?" But a better question is: "how will the WTO dispute-resolution process foster compliance with the principles?" The principles are important because they remove a fundamental barrier to timely intervention by foreign governments to oppose poor regulatory practices. This means that valuable time and diplomatic capital are not wasted on establishing the political right to have a negotiation. Instead, there is a common set of principles that form the basis for coalitions of countries to oppose anticompetitive practices. As is well known in WTO circles, most disputes do not end up before a panel. The political process of negotiation often leads to a compromise. And, in the case of telecommunications, the combination of diplomatic pressure and litigation risk before a WTO panel strengthens the position of regulatory authorities (and their domestic allies) who favor more competition. This process is very akin to the process of *gaiatsu* that have fuelled many economic reforms in Japan. While such tactics are far from certain, they have the great virtue of legitimizing external international pressure and creating a focal point for the negotiation.[18]

If there is a panel, then one approach may be to see if national practice appears to be significantly inconsistent with international "best practices." Disputes over interconnection pricing in industrial countries, for example, may focus on whether the basic form of interconnection between two local networks should add up to $0.01 or $0.03 per call. However, despite these heated disputes the estimates of costs in industrial countries do not vary wildly. Indeed, the process of building an expert consensus globally has produced many studies of network economics by regulators in NICs that can inform WTO dispute panels about how low "cost-based" rates should be.

A telling example of the implementation issue involves the revisions of interconnection charges and practices in the Philippines and Mexico. Both countries were leaders in introducing competition in telecommunications services. Both have independent regulatory commissions but relatively weak judicial and administrative processes. Both have dominant carriers that have had significant build-out programs but still lag behind network build-out levels of the leading Asian NICs. Both rely heavily on revenues earned from settlement rates from the United States to compensate the dominant carrier for local services. Both undertook a significant rebalancing of rates. Yet in terms of pricing interconnection, the two countries could not be further apart. The 1998 reforms in the Philippines lowered interconnection charges from about US$0.28 per minute to US$0.19 cents. The reforms in Mexico announced in December 1998 lowered the base charges to US$0.026 per minute. In the Philippines the high costs of immediately eroded the confidence of new entrants while the Mexico's lower per-minute cost boosted the hopes of competitors.

A major difference in reforming interconnection fees was the difference in their WTO obligations. The Philippines had modified the Reference Paper on regulatory principles in its commitments so as to give it considerable leeway on interconnection. Mexico had committed itself to the Reference Paper as adopted by most countries. Thus, Mexico knew that its high rates were certain to draw a serious challenge at the WTO so, while keeping rates above cost, it sharply lowered them to a level easier to defend at the WTO.[19] In contrast, there was more uncertainty about when a WTO panel would rule that a country is at fault for failing to maintain transparent procedures and enforce reasonable rules quickly enough.[20] Delay in implementing competition rules favors the dominant incumbent because it controls essential network facilities. This became such a contentious problem in Mexico that the United States Government made it into one of the centerpieces in a WTO complaint brought against Mexico in August 2000. The outcome of this dispute may clarify how the WTO pact will influence the administrative and judicial processes of countries.[21]

The story of interconnection policy and the WTO Reference Paper is also important for a broader debate over the best direction for trade policy. The WTO treats regulatory policies as the legitimate domain of each national government. But the negotiating parties did not settle for a minimalist solution to the issue of market barriers created by regulatory conduct. They included the regulatory principles in the WTO agreement precisely because they put proponents of competition policy squarely into the process of implementing trade policy. The WTO deal was a vehicle for promoting the creation of independent regulatory authorities whose professional competence, administrative authority, and bureaucratic political interests were essential to making a trade pact on telecommunications policy viable. In short, negotiators looked ahead to the difficulties of implementing a trade pact by using the negotiation to influence who would have to be involved in its implementation.

VI. Next Challenges

Despite the failure of the "Seattle Round," there is already an agreement to reopen the negotiations on services. But there is no agreement on the agenda for telecommunications services. However, one can expect several possibilities.

First, at a minimum, the industrial countries will press for broader geographic coverage in the agreement. The majority of WTO members have yet to make any commitments. The OECD nations also will argue for fewer restrictions on market access. They are particularly keen to remove loopholes in regard to international services. And, in a complementary move, they will look for ways to broaden the list of network terminal equipment that is exempt from tariffs while broadening the coverage of "mutual recognition agreements" that simplify the licensing of new terminal equipment (that is often vital for providing new global services).

Second, the OECD countries will selectively advance some cases to dispute resolution at the WTO in order to "test" the range and power of the principles. Challenges were not that practical until the EU and Japan had put in place more of their regulatory reforms. It would be hard to bring certain challenges to practices of developing countries if industrial countries were not implementing the Reference Paper in particular ways. Moreover, there are disagreements among the industrial capitols about the full import of the WTO obligations on such matters as spectrum licensing.

Third, developing countries may try for some reverse leverage on issues tied to international settlement rates. In particular, they may seek some diplomatic understanding about the decline of settlement rates before entering into agreements favored by industrial countries in regard to electronic commerce and the Internet. This is likely to be a quixotic quest but it could complicate the negotiation.

Fourth, there is great uncertainty about what to do in regard to issues concerning the Internet and "convergence" (the growing intersection of telecommunications and broadcast service made possible, inter alia, by the Internet). So far, the United States has demurred on this issue. But the questions couldn't be clearer. For example, does a combination of the market-access commitments on "packet switched networks" made by many countries in 1997 and "value-added services" (made in the Uruguay Round) mean that countries have obligations in regard to the Internet? None of the major questions will be addressed, however, unless there is a consensus in industrial nations that it is worth trying to do so. For reasons of their own domestic politics, they may decline to do so.

Irrespective of what happens in the prospective negotiation, telecommunications policy in developing countries has changed fundamentally as a result of the WTO. The creation of new market expectations through a change in the international regime means that the debate over the merits of monopoly versus competition that seemed so vivid even in the mid-1990s has ended. The WTO agreement of 1997 is as close to a roadmap of market reform as political life can produce, and the key industrializing countries have already accepted it. The rest of the developing world will follow.

Notes

* This paper draws materially on a report prepared for the World Bank. We thank the Bank for its support but the conclusions are solely the responsibility of the authors.

[1] The number of signatories is especially significant, because most WTO agreements emerge from multi-sector and multi-issue negotiations where tradeoffs can occur over many industries and items. The telecommunications agreement broke this pattern (see Hoekman, 1996).

[2] Countries could, and did, schedule limits on market access. These might include limits on total foreign ownership of a common carrier, limits on the total number of phone companies in the market, or a phase-in schedule for obligations on market access. The full schedule of all commitments can be found on the web site of the WTO.

[3] The U.S. Government scoring system on market-access commitments for Asia, for example, rated the Korea, Singapore and Hong Kong offers as strong; the Philippine and Malaysian offers as good; and the offers of India, Indonesia and Thailand as ranging from poor to fair. (Based on USG materials made available to the authors.)

[4] In terms of economic theory a close analogy would be a "focal point" in a bargaining game—a point in the continuum of options that comes to dominate expectations and thus shapes the initial strategies of actors (see Keohane, 1984 and Cowhey, 1990).

[5] Callback services are the most familiar version of this arbitrage but it takes many other forms.

[6] Embratel, the former long distance monopoly in Brazil, plans to enter local phone service and to focus on the data services market, which is growing at over 30 percent annually in Brazil, while expanding into other South American countries (Molinski, 1999).

[7] Carriers conduct the negotiations and conclude a commercial contract to establish the accounting rate. (Technically, the settlement rate is a subset of the accounting rate. We discuss only the settlement rate because it is the economically relevant concept.) The settlement rate is not the end price to consumers. National carriers mark up the price still further for originating an international call. But the costs created by settlement rates influence the minimum price for the service. The key cost for a national carrier is the net settlement payment (the settlement rate multiplied by its net surplus or deficit of minutes of traffic with another country). Large traffic imbalances and high settlement rates soon balloon the size of net settlement payments.

[8] It was so attractive that finance ministries routinely diverted the monies to cover other budgetary needs.

[9] The WTO negotiation carefully finessed the issue of whether the settlement rate system has features that make it incompatible with trade obligations. The agreement included a "standstill agreement" that practically exempted all countries from a WTO challenge to settlement rate policies until January 1, 2000 (see Arena, 1997).

[10] The United States believed that the WTO agreement created the political opportunity (and competition policy necessity) to further speed the change. The Federal Communications Commission (FCC) created an international uproar when, in August 1997, it introduced the equivalent of price caps on the settlement rates that American carriers may pay to foreign carriers. Whether or not the FCC ever drops its "benchmarks," the initiative contributed mightily to the expectation that the settlement rate system will change fundamentally (see Cowhey, 1999).

[11] For an account of the EU Commission's concerns, see Telecom Report International, 1999.

[12] For an analysis of how countries in the Americas limited ISR in their WTO commitments, see the presentation of Maria Cruz Alonso Antolin to the World Services Congress, Atlanta, Georgia, November 1999, which is available at www.ahciet.es.

[13] The settlement rate to Hong Kong from the United States is very low. So, Hong Kong may be used to reroute traffic from the United States in order to reach other Asian countries where Hong Kong enjoys a favorable settlement rate.

[14] Using revenues from long distance services to subsidize universal service (as is done in the United States) is also a bad idea because it distorts pricing and economic incentives for network development.

[15] A geographically averaged rate, which inflates prices for urban areas, makes entry into urban areas quite profitable. See Cowhey and Klimenko (1999) for suggestions on how to address universal service issues more efficiently.

[16] Mobile services had 1998 world revenues of $154 billion, as opposed to $429 billion in fixed-line revenues. Over 160 countries have mobile networks (see The Economist, 1999).

[17] The regulatory principles allow for diverse national rules and practices but are sufficiently specific to hold governments accountable for the fundamentals of market-oriented regulation. Negotiators spent considerable time on "what if" examples to understand how various practices might fit, or contradict, the principles.

[18] The IMF packages for economic reform also have featured these combinations of domestic reformers and external international pressure. Their record is mixed. However, the IMF lacks a similar set of voluntarily accepted codes of binding conduct created independent of the IMF negotiation. See Kahler (1993).

[19] The basic Mexican rates were at the high end of the OECD range but were consistent with the rates Argentina had announced (since reduced) and that Chile already had. (See FCC, 1998, for a list of rates.) Mexico tried to add further revenues to the incumbent by allowing it to impose surcharges for special network modifications (bring the total up to $0.046/minute frequently). This formula tried to finesse the WTO requirement for cost-based rates. To further understand the impact of WTO commitments, Mexico phrased its market access commitment on ISR in an ambiguous manner that has permitted it to dodge questions about how quickly it should reform the policy. See OECD (1999).

[20] An example of problematic compliance by the incumbent to interconnection obligations surfaced in 1999 when the Philippine President had to intervene personally to get the dominant carrier to provide physical interconnection to a rival mobile carrier. "PLDT and Globe Telecom Agree to Settle Interconnection Problems," Reuters News staff, Total Telecom, 16 November 1999 (www.totaltele.com) Moreover, as of early 2000 it has yet to be proved that the Mexican regulatory authority has sufficient authority to force timely compliance, as opposed to lip service, to its interconnection rules. This led to a WTO dispute with the US.

[21] Cowhey and Klimenko (1999) also point out that the regulatory principles ease the problem of "regulatory regret"—the desire of a regulator to change the terms of regulation for foreign investors because the initial rules usually unduly delay substantial competition. Adherence to the WTO principles sends a powerful message that a shift in the rules is not anti-market or anti-foreign investment.

References

Arena, Alex. 1997. "The WTO Telecommunications Agreement: Some Personal Reflections." In TeleGeography 1997. Washington, D.C.: Telegeography.

Bagwell, K. and Staiger, R. 1999. "Domestic Policies, National Sovereignty and International Economic Institutions." NBER Working Paper No. 7293, August 1999.

Baron, David P. 1995. "The Economics and Politics of Regulation: Perspectives, Agenda and Approaches." In Jeffrey S. Banks and Eric A. Hanushek, eds., Modern Political Economy. New York: Cambridge University Press.

Bhagwati, Jagdish. 1994. "Fair Trade, Reciprocity and Harmonization: The New Challenge to the Theory and Policy of Free Trade." In A. Deardorff and R. Stern, eds., Analytical and Negotiating Issues in the Global Trading System. Ann Arbor: University of Michigan Press.

Blake, Linda and Jim Lande 1999. Trends in the U.S. International Telecommunications Industry. Washington, D.C.: FCC, Common Carrier Bureau's Industry Analysis Division. http://www.fcc.gov/Bureaus/Common_Carrier/Reports/FCC-State_Link/Intl/itltrd99.zip

Braga, Carlos A. Prinzo, Emmanuel Forestier, and Peter A. Stern. 1999. "Developing Countries and the Accounting Rate Regime." Private Sector: Viewpoint 167. Washington, D.C.: World Bank. Online at www.worldbank.org/html/fpd/notes.

Brennan, T., and J. Boyd. 1997. "Stranded Costs, Takings, and the Law and Economics of Implicit Contracts." Journal of Regulatory Economics 11: 41–54.

Cowhey, Peter F. 1990 "The International Telecommunications Regime: The Political Roots of High Technology Regimes." International Organization 44 (Spring):169–99.

Cowhey, Peter F. 1999. "FCC Benchmarks and the Reform of the International Telecommunications Market." Telecommunications Policy 22(11):899–911.

Cowhey, Peter F. and Mikhail Klimenko. 1999. The WTO Agreement and Telecommunication Policy Reforms. Washington, D.C.: World Bank.

Cowhey, Peter F., and J. Richards. 2000,"Dialing for Dollars: The Revolution in Communications Markets." In Jeffrey Hart and Akheem Prasash, eds., Coping with Globalization (New York: Routledge).

Davies, G., S. Carter, S. McIntosh, and Dan Stefanescu. 1995. "Technology and Policy Options for the Telecommunications Sector." Telecommunications Policy 20(2):101–123.

Davis, Myles, Luisz Carvalho, and Josh Milberg, 1998, "International Long Distance in Latin America," Telegeography, 1998, Washington, D.C.: Telegeography.

Economist, 1999, "Telecommunications Survey: The World in Your Pocket" October 9.

European Commission. 1998. Fourth Report on the Implementation of the Telecommunications Regulatory Package. Brussels.

FCC International Bureau, "Report on International Telecommunications Markets, 1997–1998." Prepared for Senator Ernest F. Hollings, Committee on Commerce, Science and Transportation, United States Senate, December 7, 1998.

Gilligan, Michael. 1997. Empowering Exporters: Reciprocity, Delegation, and Collective Action in American Trade Policy. Ann Arbor: The University of Michigan Press.

Grossman, G. and Helpman, E. 1994. "Protection for Sale." American Economic Review 84: 833-50.

Haggard, Stephan and Mathew McCubbins. Forthcoming. Presidents, Parliaments and Policy, New York: Cambridge University Press)

Hoekman, Bernard. 1996. "Assessing the General Agreement on Trade in Services." In Will Martin and Alan Winters, eds., The Uruguay Round and the Developing Economies. New York: Cambridge University Press.

Hoski, H. 1998, "Liberalisation, Regulation and Universal Service Provision in the European Telecommunications Markets." Helsinki: Research Institute of the Finnish Economy (ETLA). Mimeo.

Irvine, Craig, 1998, "International Telephony and Asian Network Expansion," Telegeography, 1998, Washington D.C.: Telegeography.

Kahler, Miles, 1993, "Bargaining with the IMF: Two-Level Strategies and Developing Countries," 363-94, in Peter B. Evans, Harold K. Jacobson, and Robert D. Putnam (eds.), Double-Edged Diplomacy-International Bargaining and Domestic Politics. Berkeley: University of California Press.

Keohane, Robert. 1984. After Hegemony: Cooperation and Discord in the International System. Princeton, N.J.: Princeton University Press.

Levy, B., and P. Spiller. 1994. "The Institutional Foundations of Regulatory Commitment: A Comparative Analysis of Telecommunications Regulation." Journal of Law, Economics and Organization 10:201–45.

Low, P., and A. Mattoo. 1997. "Reform in Basic Telecommunications and the WTO Negotiations: The Asian Experience." Staff Working Paper, Research and Analysis Division. Geneva: World Trade Organization.

Madden, G., and S. Savage. 1998. "CEE Telecommunications Investment and Economic Growth." Information Economics & Policy 10:173–95

Merrill Lynch. 1997. The Asia-Pacific Phone Book, First Quarter Review. New York, pp. 103–4.

Molinski, Michael. 1999. "Brazil's Embratel to focus on Data Transmission, New Markets," Bloomberg News, September 8, found at www.Totatele.com/view/asp?ArticleID=23770&Pub=tt

National Telecommunications Commission, Department of Transportation and Communications, Philippine Long Distance Telephone Company, Inc. 1997. CCC Case No. 97-039 (Re: Application for Rate Rebalancing with a Further Request for the Immediate Issuance of a Provisional Authority). November 10.

Ordover, J., R. Pittman and P. Clyde. 1994. "Competition Policy for Natural Monopolies in a Developing Market Economy." Economics of Transition 2:317–43.

Organization for Economic Co-operation and Development (OECD). 1999. Regulatory Reform in Mexico. Paris: OECD.

Staple, Gregory. 1998. "Introduction." TeleGeography 1998. Washington, D.C.: Telegeography, pp. 20-21.

Svensson, J. 1998. "Investment, Property Rights and Political Instability: Theory and Evidence." European Economic Review 42:1317–43.

Telecom Report International. 1999. "Eurocrats Investigate High Leased-Line Prices," p. 14, October 29, 1999, Vol. 10, No. 20.

Appendix
Accounting Rates of the United States, 1995-1999*
December 1, 1999
(A) Countries with Full Market Access Commitments Effective 1998

COUNTRY	1995	1996	1997	1998	1999	Benchmark Settlement Rate	Effective Date
Australia	$0.59	$0.45	$0.42	$0.30	$0.30	$0.15	1/1/99
Austria	$0.67	$0.43	$0.41	$0.26	$0.27	$0.15	1/1/99
Belgium	$0.71	$0.56	$0.37	$0.28	$0.27	$0.15	1/1/99
Canada	$0.22	$0.18	$0.16	$0.16	$0.16	$0.15	1/1/99
Chile	$1.10	$1.00	$1.00	$0.70	$0.70	$0.19	1/1/00
Denmark	$0.74	$0.29	$0.27	$0.22	$0.22	$0.15	1/1/99
Dominican Republic	$0.90	$0.90	$0.70	$0.60	$0.38	$0.19	1/1/01
El Salvador	$1.20	$1.10	$0.88	$0.77	$0.60	$0.19	1/1/01
Finland	$0.59	$0.51	$0.41	$0.32	$0.27	$0.15	1/1/99
France	$0.54	$0.35	$0.26	$0.21	$0.21	$0.15	1/1/99
Germany, Federal Rep.	$0.39	$0.23	$0.20	$0.21	$0.21	$0.15	1/1/99
Guatemala	$1.18	$1.00	$0.90	$0.77	$0.64	$0.19	1/1/01
Iceland	$1.04	$0.94	$0.75	$0.48	$0.27	$0.15	1/1/99
Italy	$0.71	$0.52	$0.33	$0.22	$0.22	$0.15	1/1/99
Japan	$0.94	$0.91	$0.86	$0.29	$0.29	$0.15	1/1/99
Korea, Republic of	$1.26	$1.23	$0.98	$0.85	$0.71	$0.19	1/1/00
Luxembourg	$0.74	$0.58	$0.27	$0.28	$0.27	$0.15	1/1/99
Malaysia	$0.70	$0.89	$0.79	$0.79	$0.38	$0.19	1/1/00
Mexico	$0.67	$0.68	$0.70	$0.74	$0.38	$0.19	1/1/00
Netherlands	$0.37	$0.36	$0.27	$0.19	$0.14	$0.15	1/1/99
New Zealand	$0.59	$0.43	$0.27	$0.26	$0.27	$0.15	1/1/99
Norway	$0.45	$0.29	$0.22	$0.17	$0.16	$0.15	1/1/99
Philippines	$1.23	$1.00	$1.00	$0.72	$0.57	$0.19	1/1/01
Spain	$1.20	$0.64	$0.48	$0.26	$0.27	$0.15	1/1/99
Sweden	$0.37	$0.17	$0.12	$0.12	$0.12	$0.15	1/1/99
Switzerland	$0.52	$0.51	$0.34	$0.28	$0.27	$0.15	1/1/99
United Kingdom	$0.37	$0.29	$0.17	$0.17	$0.17	$0.15	1/1/99

(B) Countries without Full Market Access Commitments Effective 1998

COUNTRY	1995	1996	1997	1998	1999	Benchmark Settlement Rate	Effective Date
Antigua	$1.00	$1.00	$0.91	$0.81	$0.73	$0.19	1/1/00
Argentina	$1.43	$1.43	$0.85	$0.70	$0.56	$0.19	1/1/00
Bangladesh	$2.00	$2.00	$1.60	$1.60	$1.37	$0.23	1/1/03
Belize	$1.46	$1.42	$1.20	$0.95	$0.75	$0.19	1/1/01
Bolivia	$1.50	$1.25	$1.10	$0.92	$0.74	$0.19	1/1/01
Brazil	$1.14	$1.03	$0.85	$0.65	$0.60	$0.19	1/1/00
Brunei	$1.80	$1.45	$0.95	$0.62	$0.30	$0.15	1/1/99
Bulgaria	$1.20	$1.00	$0.90	$0.70	$0.60	$0.19	1/1/01
Colombia	$2.97	$2.90	$2.73	$2.76	$2.74	$0.19	1/1/01
Cote d'Ivoire	$2.77	----	----	----	$1.65	$0.23	1/1/03
Czech Republic	$1.19	$0.72	$0.61	$0.55	$0.37	$0.19	1/1/00
Dominica	$1.00	$1.00	$0.91	$0.81	$0.81	$0.19	1/1/01
Ecuador	$1.39	$1.10	$1.00	$1.00	$1.00	$0.19	1/1/01
Ghana	$1.10	$1.00	$1.00	$1.00	$0.75	$0.23	1/1/03
Greece	$1.26	$1.01	$0.86	$0.55	$0.34	$0.19	1/1/00
Grenada	$1.00	$1.00	$0.91	$0.81	$0.81	$0.19	1/1/01
Hong Kong	$1.00	$0.94	$0.79	$0.72	$0.14	$0.15	1/1/99
Hungary	$1.34	$1.01	$0.61	$0.55	$0.38	$0.19	1/1/00
India	$1.80	$1.60	$1.42	$1.28	$1.28	$0.23	1/1/02
Indonesia	$1.58	$1.40	$1.30	$1.05	$0.85	$0.19	1/1/01
Ireland	$0.67	$0.35	$0.33	$0.22	$0.21	$0.15	1/1/99
Israel	$1.58	$1.18	$0.70	$0.59	$0.30	$0.15	1/1/99
Jamaica	$1.40	$1.30	$1.25	$1.25	$1.05	$0.19	1/1/01
Mauritius	$1.50	$1.50	$1.50	$1.50	$1.50	$0.19	1/1/00
Morocco	$1.78	$1.45	$1.09	$0.83	$0.82	$0.19	1/1/01
Pakistan	$2.30	$1.80	$1.60	$1.20	$1.20	$0.23	1/1/02
Papua New Guinea 8/	$1.63	$1.59	$1.23	$1.04	$1.03	$0.19	1/1/01
Peru	$1.30	$1.23	$1.00	$0.85	$0.66	$0.19	1/1/01
Poland	$1.15	$0.95	$0.70	$0.55	$0.38	$0.19	1/1/01
Portugal	$0.97	$0.83	$0.60	$0.43	$0.30	$0.15	1/1/99
Romania	$1.72	$1.51	$1.23	$1.05	$0.69	$0.19	1/1/01
Senegal	$2.20	$2.20	$2.20	$1.38	$1.18	$0.23	1/1/03
Singapore	$0.92	$0.90	$0.85	$0.52	----	$0.15	1/1/99
Slovak Republic	$1.34	$1.30	$0.68	$0.58	$0.41	$0.19	1/1/01
South Africa	$1.20	$1.00	$1.00	$0.80	$0.70	$0.19	1/1/00
Sri Lanka	$2.00	$2.00	$2.00	$1.60	$1.20	$0.23	1/1/02
Thailand	$1.55	$1.50	$1.20	$0.90	$0.70	$0.19	1/1/01
Trinidad & Tobago	$1.40	$1.30	$1.15	$1.00	$0.83	$0.19	1/1/00
Tunisia	$1.59	$1.55	$0.94	$0.97	$0.88	$0.19	1/1/01

(C) WTO member countries without commitments and selected non-member countries

COUNTRY	1995	1996	1997	1998	1999
Angola	$1.95	$1.45	$0.00	$1.38	$0.55
Central African Rep.	$2.97	$2.90	$2.18	$2.21	$2.19
Chad	$5.10	$4.97	$2.67	$2.71	$2.69
China	$2.67	$2.13	$1.69	$1.40	$1.01
Costa Rica	$1.17	$1.15	$0.80	$0.70	$0.56
Croatia	$1.04	$1.01	$0.68	$0.55	$0.11
Egypt	$1.40	$1.40	$1.30	$1.30	$1.10
Estonia	$1.19	$1.01	$0.75	$0.62	$0.11
Haiti	$1.20	$1.20	$1.20	$1.20	$1.00
Honduras	$1.50	$1.30	$1.10	$0.97	$0.97
Kenya	$1.40	$1.40	$1.30	$1.10	$1.10
Kuwait	$1.71	$1.67	$1.57	$1.59	$0.30
Latvia	$1.93	$1.88	$0.82	$0.83	$0.82
Liberia	$1.00	$1.00	$1.00	$1.00	$1.00
Lithuania	$1.74	$1.74	$1.40	$0.85	$0.55
Mozambique	$1.62	$1.58	$1.49	$2.38	$1.10
Namibia	$2.00	$1.40	$1.40	$1.40	$1.40
Nicaragua	$1.25	$1.30	$1.00	$0.86	$0.86
Nigeria	$1.50	$1.50	$1.50	$1.40	$1.15
Panama	$1.30	$1.25	$1.20	$0.95	$0.69
Paraguay	$1.70	$1.45	$1.20	$1.00	$0.79
Russia, Republic of	$2.60	$2.12	$1.60	$0.80	$0.60
Saudi Arabia	$2.20	$2.20	$2.03	$1.73	$1.37
Slovenia	$1.11	$0.72	$0.68	$0.69	$0.69
Taiwan	$1.20	$1.20	$1.14	$0.45	$0.30
Tanzania	$1.50	$1.50	$1.20	$1.10	$0.75
Uganda	$1.50	$1.20	$1.00	$0.50	$0.50
Ukraine	$1.50	$1.40	$1.20	$1.00	$0.44
United Arab Emirates	$1.65	$1.65	$1.65	$1.65	$1.65
Uruguay	$1.40	$1.27	$1.10	$0.86	$0.62
Uzbekistan	$1.80	$1.70	$1.60	$1.40	$0.90
Venezuela	$1.15	$1.07	$0.98	$0.80	$0.64
Yemen Arab Republic	$1.50	$1.50	$1.50	$1.50	$1.50
Zambia	$1.50	$1.20	$1.10	$1.10	$0.80
Zimbabwe	$1.50	$1.50	$1.30	$0.80	$0.70
Average Accounting Rate	$0.81	$0.73	$0.63	$0.52	$0.41

* Settlement rates are traditionally one-half of the accounting rate. These tables present the accounting rates for countries and the target for the settlement rate set by the FCC by a given date. The information contained in this Appendix is based on the IMTS accounting rates published by the International Bureau of the FCC. See http://www.fcc.gov/ib/td/pf/account.html

CHAPTER 17

Domestic/International Regulation and Trade in Insurance Services: Implications for the Services 2000 Negotiations

R. Brian Woodrow

As the Services 2000 round of multilateral trade negotiations commences, Domestic Regulation and International Cooperation are at the very center of those negotiations as far as insurance services are concerned. At first glance, these two concepts would appear relatively uncontroversial and essentially compatible with one another, given that no one would dispute the authority of legitimate governments appropriately to regulate activities within their borders or to work in concordance with counterpart governments in other countries on common problems. The apparently non-threatening, even facile appearance of these two concepts, however, can be deceptive because neither is as settled as each might appear and when combined together could pose interesting substantive public policy and negotiating challenges in the years ahead. This chapter argues that domestic regulation among WTO member countries in the insurance field—and increasingly a range of international regulatory activities as well—will need to come under serious scrutiny, and that this could possibly result in countries agreeing to additional and perhaps innovative disciplines on trade in services in this area.

I. Domestic Regulation and International Cooperation—A Tale of Two Concepts

One of the important systemic changes of the past two decades has been the steady erosion of boundaries between the domestic and international realms of activity in virtually all countries. Essentially domestic political, economic and cultural activities have given way increasingly to extensive cross-border activities, both international and global in character, and to exogenous influences that now routinely impinge on the separateness and integrity of the "domestic domain."[1] National policy-making and regulation more and more take place on the interface between the domestic political and economic realm, particularly where matters of industry structure are at issue, and an external international realm of negotiation and dispute settlement among countries shaped increasingly by the forces of globalization. What some have called a "new sovereignty"[2] is being fashioned especially in the area of international trade and regulatory agreements. This "new sovereignty" focuses neither on the constant vigilance against external treats nor the jealous protection of internal decision-making power that has so often characterized country action in the past. Rather, it is based on the recognition that a nation state's domestic actions must be closely calibrated to international regulatory agreements that it seeks to negotiate and in which it participates voluntarily but often on the basis of binding obligations. As a further important corollary, this collapsing of the domestic and international realms is at the same time opening nation-states to more intense outside scrutiny of their domestic practices. As well, it tends to afford considerably greater scope for private-sector activity, both domestically within countries and transnationally, and for the possibility of an expanded scope for private authority within the international political economy.[3]

Despite assertions of its gradual demise, government regulation—in all its myriad and varied forms—remains one of the constant, though certainly not unchanging, features of nation-state activity across most services sectors worldwide. Several years ago, the OECD issued a rather odd-sounding monograph entitled *Insurance and Other Financial Services: Structural Trends*. It detailed the pervasive way in which regulation in myriad forms and fashions— through market segmentation among line of insurance, through product differentiation and distribution by different financial entities, through supervisory activities at the national and increasingly the international level—pervades the insurance industry worldwide, probably more so than is the case either for banking or securities. Differences among developed countries in the role and functions of regulation in insurance proved to be extensive, although a process of "convergence" was clearly at work, both at the regulatory level and at the industry/corporate level as well.[4] Subsequent analyses have shown that regulation of insurance services is also becoming a more prominent feature in developing countries and transition economies, often premised on the assumption that regulatory structures and "best practices" from the developed countries should be diffused to developing countries and transitional economies. Specifically with regard to insurance as one key financial services sub-sector, the roles and functions of regulation then are both extensive and quite diverse even among OECD countries, let alone between OECD and other countries.

Regulation is a concept with deep and varied institutional roots in most countries as well as internationally in the area of insurance, clearly much deeper and longstanding than the competitive pressures currently at work domestically within the industry or internationally. The supervisory role of the state in overseeing—and sometimes even guaranteeing—the solvency and soundness of insurance companies allowed to do business within their boundaries is widely recognized in life and non-life insurance, even while market mechanisms, primarily on an international scale, have often been predominant in reinsurance and various specialized types of insurance.[5] National regulation of insurance in most countries can involve an eclectic mix of different types of regulation: economic regulation of entry and operations that establishes industry boundaries and prudential practices; various forms of social regulation that govern the relationship between the public and private insurance spheres within the country or ensure consumer protection; and perhaps even a modicum of self-regulation as regards competitive relations among companies or professional standards within the industry. Regulation of insurance within any one country then is not cut from a single piece of cloth but is more a patchwork of different types of regulation subject to significant national variations.

Moreover, it is not only a question of the types of regulation that may differ but also the essentially different functions that regulation serves within the national and increasingly an international context. In the first instance, one can readily see that regulation in insurance often serves primarily a policing function: ensuring safety and soundness of insurance companies; protecting the interests of consumers; and distinguishing good industry practices from bad. Additionally, regulation in insurance can and often is used for promotional purposes: to establish (or eliminate) boundaries between banks and traditional insurance companies; to advantage (or disadvantage) mutual insurance companies vis-à-vis public share companies; and to promote particular social insurance schemes rather than leave these areas open to the private market. And finally, though with less and less frequency, regulation in insurance has been used by countries as an explicit planning tool: to separate insurance and other financial services into segmented markets or to accumulate savings in the hands of state companies. For any developed country[6], one could easily produce a rich profile of the ways in which the different types and functions of regulation have been utilized over the years and how the institutional role of insurance is currently changing.

Up to now, we have been exploring regulation in insurance primarily within a national context, but that is clearly not the immediate reality as we enter the new millenium. Increasingly, the international and even the global character of insurance activities and their regulation overlays must be subsumed with the concept of domestic regulation. Internationally, while international cooperation in banking and securities regulation has been evolving since the 1970s,[7] only during the 1990s have there been efforts at cooperation among national insurance regulators and even some embryonic attempts at global regulation across the financial services sector more broadly. Additionally, however, efforts at international cooperation in insurance and cross-sectorally among other financial services sectors must also be viewed in the context of ongoing pressures towards globalization affecting the world insurance industry. Such globalization takes many forms, most notably wave upon wave of merger and acquisition activity across a variety of different sectors but involving many other forms as well. In the view of many, globally managed competition—more so than complex interdependence among nation-states—has become the logic on which global capitalism currently operates.[8] Globalization, it should be made clear, is primarily a private-sector driven phenomenon quite different from and often, though not always, potentially at odds with the kind of international cooperation on which this chapter focuses.

What then, in a general sense, would constitute effective international cooperation among insurance regulators and how might this relate to trade in insurance services?[9] Effective international cooperation in insurance can be achieved by several different means, and no single means need necessarily predominate. Explicit harmonization of national laws and regulations relating to insurance would of course be one sure route to effective international cooperation. But this is clearly not possible except perhaps among very small numbers of countries and then only within very limited areas and with great difficulty. A second route to effective international cooperation might be to invest a global regulatory authority with supranational powers to oversee particularly dangerous regulatory problems. But countries are of course extremely wary about ceding sovereignty to international bodies over which they may lose control and influence. Carefully negotiated international regulatory agreements are the obvious third way to achieve effective international cooperation, allowing countries and affected industry actors to bargain towards acceptable disciplines that can be enshrined in domestic law and regulation or, in some instances, rendered into international law. In the insurance field, as we will see, there is relatively little in the way of international authorities or agreements that at present constitute a public international regime for insurance. In this context, the WTO and particularly its GATS agreement, may increasingly provide a convenient "nest" for such an emerging public international regime.

Before moving on, let us attempt to situate international cooperation among insurance regulators within the broad context we have outlined. Moving counter-clockwise from the left box, figure 1 provides a possible key:

In the first instance, supervisory regulation of insurance companies and markets takes place routinely at the domestic level in most countries for solvency, consumer protection and other purposes while, internationally, a number of cross-border and sometimes cross-sectoral issues like accounting standards and licensing and accreditation increasingly draw attention. In addition, however, insurance and other financial services may also raise macroeconomic and cross-sectoral public policy issues domestically and internationally while, with increasing frequency, the development of global public policies may be required to deal with crucial cross-border and systemic issues. In this last regard, strategic management of financial crises and systemic risk, regulation of the increasing number and complexity of financial conglomerates, the treatment of derivative instruments, offshore financial centers and taxation issues all raise global public policy concerns where international regulatory cooperation is being pushed to the limit. From being primarily domestic and narrowly supervisory, insurance regulation is moving quickly towards enhanced international regulatory cooperation and the new challenges of global public policy.

The rest of this chapter now proceeds to examine the changing role and functions of regulation within the insurance field, both domestically in major countries and on the international level, and how domestic/international regu-

Figure 1. Evolution of Domestic/International Insurance Regulation/ Supervision

	REGULATION/ SUPERVISION	PUBLIC POLICY CONCERNS
DOMESTIC LEVEL SUPERVISION	National/Sub-National Regulation of Sectoral & Cross-sectoral Activities	National Macroeconomic Policy/ International Policy Coordination
INTERNATIONAL LEVEL SUPERVISORY ACTIVITIES	International Cooperation Among Domestic Regulators	Global Public Policies To Deal with Cross-Border Issues

lation might come to be treated in the upcoming international services trade negotiations. Three dimensions of this evolving relationship will be briefly investigated:

1. how domestic regulation of insurance services within selected countries is itself changing and has implications for the treatment of regulation in the upcoming services trade negotiations;
2. how international regulatory coordination and standards-setting and other activities in insurance are growing in importance and likewise have implications for the upcoming services trade negotiations;
3. how the sensitive role and functions of regulation in insurance and other financial services might be negotiated in Services 2000.

II. The Changing Face of Domestic Regulation/Supervision of Insurance

The insurance industry worldwide is changing rapidly just as is the world of insurance regulation/supervision, domestic and international, but it has become an accepted truism that trends in regulation always lag well behind what's happening in business and technology. This is true because regulation by its very nature is designed primarily to respond to the current conditions and behavioral expectations. In addition, however, domestic regulation/supervision of insurance also varies considerably from country to country, even among the major developed countries let alone between developed and developing countries, but distinct patterns and trends can be identified. By way of summarizing the changes currently taking place, let me advance SIX propositions about current and future patterns and trends in domestic insurance regulation/supervision that draw upon our earlier conceptual discussion. Only the basic circumstantial evidence for each proposition can be provided here, leaving more detailed testing and reasoned proofs for another time.

FIRST, commitment to liberalization of the supply and use of insurance products and services as a primary goal both within domestic markets and through enhanced foreign competition will continue and intensify in virtually all countries.

Liberalized insurance markets—rather than segmented, protected and narrow supply and use of insurance products and services—are clearly the industry trend and public policy and regulation/supervision in most countries are moving to reinforce that trend. A recent OECD study of cross-border trade and establishment of foreign branches confirms this trend as far as the major developed countries are concerned, showing that national treatment for establishment purposes is the norm but that cross-border trade remains problematic.[10] Developing countries and transition economies are, of course, continually under pressure to commit to liberalization of insurance and to build or enhance their insurance regulatory systems. Their record in committing to liberalization norms remains uneven but the capacity is often there, ironically in part because their markets and regulatory systems are weakly developed.[11]

Liberalization in the insurance field usually has at least three subcomponents: increased competition among insurance service providers in domestic markets; greater market access and guarantees of national treatment for foreign service suppliers seeking to operate in domestic markets; and more consumer choice and effective consumer protection for all parties involved in domestic markets. In North America, the European Union and increasingly in Japan, these three liberalization sub-components have now been readily accepted, with only minor deviations from these norms allowed.[12] Developing countries that are currently lagging behind in their commitment to liberalization of insurance services often lag behind in different areas. For example, India which has failed utterly to reform its monopoly structures in life insurance or Malaysia or Brazil which continue to restrict foreign ownership.

Re-regulation within the domestic insurance market and selective privatization measures where appropriate—more so than wholesale deregulation—have become the key instruments for achieving these liberalization norms. Fully open and unfettered markets for insurance services are both unattainable and probably undesirable, with the closest approximation to this standard probably being the offshore financial centers that have sprung up around the world and increasingly pose a global public-policy problem. What is more acceptable and desirable in most countries as ways and means to achieve liberalization norms is privatization—i.e., eliminating state ownership and control and enhancing private sector activities – combined with re-regulation—i.e., regulatory activity designed to reinforce liberalization norms where previously it had been used primarily to promote monopolies or oligopolies. Indeed, the lesson should be clear that liberalization of the supply and use of insurance services typically requires more effective regulation/supervision activities, domestic as well as international, in order to meet its goals.

SECOND, the policing function of insurance regulation/supervision will remain primary—at the same time moving from narrowly sectoral, case by case, often ex post facto assessment of the safety and soundness of insurance companies more towards consumer protection and broader systemic risk considerations; meanwhile, other traditional roles and functions for regulation such as promotion and planning fall increasingly by the wayside under market and globalization pressures.

Once upon a time, countries could and did use regulation deliberately for promotional and planning purposes but those days are behind us.[13] In the past, restrictive business practices and market-access restrictions were utilized even in relatively liberal countries to structure domestic markets and to penalize prospective foreign insurance providers. With the possible exception of the UK, one need look no further than European insurance markets prior to the Single Market exercise of the late 1980s to see how the promotional and planning functions of regulation were used extensively by national governments and how these have now largely been curbed.[14] Furthermore, in developing countries, the promotional and planning functions of regulation were also used deliberately, for example, to benefit particular local companies or to inhibit access to international reinsurance markets. Both in developed and developing countries, however, these expansive uses of regulation beyond its primary policing function have been brought into disrepute and countries are pulling back from their use, not least of all because of the transparency and liberalizing provisions of international trade agreements like GATS.

Today, the policing function of regulation remains in the forefront, although the ways and means whereby that function is being carried out are changing. Supervision of insurance companies and markets by independent regulatory authorities has traditionally been at the core of that policing function and ensuring the solvency of individual insurance companies the main though not its only task within the domestic domain.[15] Insurance supervision, however, is moving beyond narrow economic regulation of an industry sector towards social regulation and cooperation among self-regulatory authorities within a global context. Consumer protection issues and cross-border activities are more and more the focus of most insurance supervisory authorities in most countries, particularly as a result of growing liberalization and globalization trends. Likewise, insurance supervision requires sophisticated accounting and risk management techniques to ensure safety and soundness, whether such regulation remains entity-based or of broader scope, and is shadowed increasingly by the growing power and influence of private rating agencies.[16] Like analogous policing systems, insurance supervision is being challenged to move from the realm of the fingerprint into that of sophisticated DNA testing.

THIRD, there is a definite trend toward more integrated regulation/supervision across the financial services field, usually involving the establishment of a single regulatory authority, though this has sometimes been confounded by domestic jurisdictional considerations and political/bureaucratic infighting in various countries.

The establishment in 1998 of the Financial Services Authority in the UK, bringing together nine separate regulators including the former Insurance Directorate within Treasury within a single consolidated agency, took integration of domestic financial supervisory authorities to an unprecedented level.[17] Previously, other countries like Canada or Australia had created supervisory agencies that partially integrated their financial services authorities but always without certain sectors included or with derogations to sub-national jurisdiction exempted. The UK FSA, however, is the most comprehensive supervisory authority to date and is serving as a model for Japan and Asian countries that are seeking to strengthen their financial regulatory systems in the wake of the 1997 Asian financial crisis. Integration of banking, securities insurance and other financial supervisory authorities—premised upon shared problems and common approaches across the sub-sectors—has led to an informal new club of "integrated financial services regulators," distinct from the "segmented regulators" who continue to supervise separate financial services sub-sectors in most countries and which numbered 12 countries when a first meeting of this select group took place in 1998.[18]

Notable by its absence from this club is the United States which continues to adhere to segmented regulation of its various financial services sectors, including the Treasury and Comptroller of the Currency in banking and the SEC in securities, while insurance as well as savings and loan regulation/supervision takes place primarily at the state level. This "separate pillars" approach to financial services regulation has its institutional roots in American federalism and governmental responses to financial crisis during the 1930s. In insurance, federal jurisdiction has largely been given over to the states. This has meant that separate state-level regulation/supervision in all fifty states is the rule, although the National Association of Insurance Commissioners (NAIC) has acted in recent years to promote harmonization of standards and to press cooperation among the states.[19] While greater federal involvement in insurance regulation is viewed by some as necessary and desirable, Congress has failed consistently to pass such legislation over the objections both of industry and state legislators. Segmented regulation in the United States, however, remains intact for insurance and other financial services but is very much under siege, and continued pressures for greater integration across both jurisdictional and bureaucratic lines are likely in the future.

In a rather different way, the European Union has pursued integration of its regulatory/supervisory structure through Commission-driven single market and other directives to member countries as well as DG XV action to oversee and coordinate member-state regulation/supervision of insurance and other financial services. Subsidiarity has meant that EU countries continue to exercise direct regulatory/supervisory authority and may choose to be more or less integrated domestically while mutual recognition ensured coordination among member states and served as a kind of internal MFN principle. Still, EU financial integration continues to be characterized by a "battle of the systems" with countries like the United Kingdom pursuing somewhat different strategies than others like France or Germany.[20] Integrated regulation/supervision of financial services, and particularly the single regulatory authority being pioneered by the United Kingdom, is trend-setting, not only in that it responds very much to the mergers and networking activities going on within the financial services field and the spillover problems across different sub-sectors but because it speaks to the need for a more generic approach to regulation/supervision issues.

FOURTH, "financial convergence" is proceeding apace across the financial services field, both on a cross-sectoral and cross-border scale, raising difficult regulatory issues that go well beyond normal domestic regulatory capabilities and will require new forms of international regulatory cooperation.

Atchinson and Krohm have recently painted a stark picture of the competition between marketplace and regulatory convergence in the insurance field in the years to come:[21]

> "It's 2005. Twelve insurance-financial service conglomerates sell 80 percent of the world's commercial insurance, and are after the same dominance of personal lines. These giants integrate a full complement of life, health, property, casualty, retirement, and investment products—eradicating the distinctions between insurance, banking and investments. New products emerge previously not thought of as 'insurance,' such as hedges against currency fluctuation, commodity price movements, and other speculative risks. This scenario exaggerates to make a point: consolidation, innovation, and globalization are happening at an unprecedented pace. Today's regulatory systems are ill suited to the world described in the above sketch."

In other words, domestic insurance regulators in every country—however integrated they may be or not—face the challenge of applying policing regulation techniques to an increasingly cross-sectoral and cross-border marketplace.

The cross-sectoral dimension of the task is exemplified at the industry/firm level by attempting to determine what exactly constitutes an insurance company any more. To be sure, it is not only those traditional firms that over the past 300 years provide guarantees in the future against presently anticipated risks and have operated narrowly within their own sub-sector of the financial services field. Insurance, even in countries that maintain segmented regulatory policy and regulation, can be supplied by a variety of enterprises: banks that offer insurance allied to their banking activities;[22] financial market providers who collectively guarantee their members through self-insurance schemes; non-financial companies that insure themselves through affiliated insurance subsidiaries; mortgagors and mortgagees who guarantee their asset in case of the death of the principal; and investors who seek to balance off risk by building insurance as well as diversification into their portfolios. Insurance needs to be seen as a function rather than a set of discrete products, in much the same way that intermediation is the primary service function of banking or exchange is the primary service function of stock markets.[23] Increasingly, marketplace convergence brings acknowledgement of insurance as a function rather than a product, although recognition of the need for functional regulation of insurance domestically and within a global marketplace lags further behind.

The cross-border dimensions of policing regulation are also gaining increased recognition among domestic policy-makers and regulators. It is well known that failures among insurance companies in one country can have effects not only domestically within that country but also, because these companies may operate subsidiaries and write business in other countries, those effects can spread readily across borders, though only rarely in a systemic fashion.[24] As well, the recent spate of mergers and acquisitions among insurance and other financial services companies raises not only domestic regulatory considerations, but each merger within one country may well have spillover effects for regulation in other countries where one or other party operates.[25] More generally, the electronic commerce world in which insurance and other financial services will be supplied and used in the future raises as yet largely unknown problems of a cross-border character as regards insurance services. "Financial convergence"[26] in all its manifestations promises to further challenge both domestic regulatory capacity as well as international regulatory cooperation.

FIFTH, developing countries and transition economies, though by no means these countries alone, face important challenges in building regulatory capacity—both institutional and in terms of 'best practices'—whereby they can cope with the kind of marketplace and regulatory issues they will face.

Much of the emphasis on building regulatory capacity in insurance and other financial services realms is directed at developing countries and transition economies. The effort is to induce these countries to establish proper regulatory institutions and 'best practices' along developed country lines. It is being pressed very much by international organizations and by international business groups that view this capacity-building as an essential infrastructure for further liberalization affecting insurance. Foreign insurers operating in developing countries and transition economies continue to face numerous and varied obstacles to establishment and operation within many of those countries, despite the GATS and other trade and regulatory agreements.[27] Building regulatory capacity in developing countries and transitional economies is viewed as essential in combating protectionism and pressing liberalization within these countries.

While efforts are directed primarily at developing countries and emerging economies, domestic regulatory institutions and practices in developed countries cannot be left exempt from scrutiny. The need for regulatory reform in insurance regulation/supervision in developed countries is very much to the point. Reform of segmented regulatory structures needs to be considered in many countries, and efforts within the U.S. Congress to pass financial modernization legislation—which has now been on the congressional agenda for some 10 years without any version being passed into law—comes immediately to mind.[28] Regulatory reform in developed countries, however, needs to go beyond structural issues related to jurisdiction and interagency coordination and confront the public sector/private sector dimension. Public regulation of private sector activities in insurance continues to be accepted but exactly how intrusive that regulation should be and what regulatory instruments are most appropriate. The OECD, as the established locus for developed country opinion, has endorsed a principle and standards of "effective regulation" to be applied against the wide scope of regulatory activities currently undertaken within insurance and other financial services.

Developing countries and transition economies face quite a different task. In many cases, their current insurance regulatory/supervisory systems are weak or non-existent and capacity building rather than regulatory reform needs to be the order of the day. The OECD has established a set of guidelines for developing countries and transition economies for establishing and operating insurance regulatory/supervisory systems, but such guidelines are not always easy for a country to follow. Just as among developed countries, developing countries have established economic interests and long-standing practices that may work against full commitment to liberalization and easy adoption of 'best practices'. The countries of Central and Eastern Europe are a case in point. Non-life insurance markets, and to a much lesser extent life markets, are growing rapidly as the result of decreased dominance of former state monopolies and market access on the part of foreign insurance providers. Regulation/supervision is typically undertaken by Ministries of Finance that license domestic insurance companies and establish rules and conditions for foreign insurance companies entering and operating within their countries. Monitoring and reporting requirements, technical requirements and solvency margins, and other legal requirements are gradually being put in place but progress is slow.[29] It should be noted, however, that the countries that are most advanced within this group—Hungary, the Czech Republic and Poland—are building regulatory capacity not primarily for that purpose alone, but in order to respond to opportunities for membership in the European Union or meet commitments made during WTO negotiations.

SIXTH, improving regulation/supervision of insurance may be a desirable goal in its own right, but the impetus for domestic regulatory reform in devel-

oped countries and capacity-building in developing countries and transition economies is coming increasingly from the international trade and regulatory arenas.

The "domestic domain" wherein insurance regulation/supervision has traditionally been set is being influenced very much by the approach of a new round of multilateral trade negotiations and developments related to the new global financial architecture. As one author has recently argued, "it is impossible to separate domestic insurance regulation from international trade issues"[30] and a similar argument could equally be made for the linkage between reform of the international financial system and domestic insurance regulation. The crux of the matter is that domestic regulation/supervision in insurance is no longer purely domestic in conception or implementation but must be closely calibrated to international trade and regulatory agreements affecting the field. This interaction of the international realm with domestic regulation/supervision in insurance has never been greater and promises to become even more pronounced in the years to come.

It is important, however, to draw out the different processes that the multilateral trade negotiations and the international financial architecture entail. Reform of the international financial architecture is primarily a matter of coordination and cooperation among governments and regulators seeking to redesign institutional mechanisms and improve current practices affecting the regulation and surveillance of world's financial system. It is taking place almost exclusively among high-level governmental officials of the G-7 countries—recently expanded by invitation to extend to a group of G-20 countries—and largely without much domestic political involvement or direct participation by affected interests. Where insurance regulation/supervision fits in is as one component within an overall cooperative intergovernmental strategy for responding to threats of systemic failure.

By contrast, multilateral trade negotiations are two-level processes of negotiation among countries at the international level as well as bargaining with affected interests on the domestic level. Domestic/international regulation of insurance is becoming an issue to be negotiated and bargained over during these negotiations, with the outcome determined by much more broadly-based political processes. Players find themselves caught up in a "two-level game"—a "double-edged diplomacy" involving negotiation among governments on the international level as well as bargaining between governments and affected interests on the domestic level.[31] It is in this context that transnational efforts by internationally-oriented insurance industry associations and firms are pressing hard to have pro-competitive regulatory principles adopted as part of any future multilateral services trade negotiations.[32] How successful these insurance industry representations will be in the "double-edged diplomacy" of the Services 2000 trade negotiations remains unclear.

III. Emergent International Regulation/Supervision of Insurance

Returning to figure 1 on the evolution of domestic/international regulation/supervision in insurance, it should be abundantly clear that during the 1990s the international dimensions of insurance regulation/supervision have received unprecedented attention. In previous years, insurance regulation/supervision within developed countries was predominantly domestic in character, taking place primarily within nation-states and focusing on policing activities vis-à-vis private sector actors. That domestic dimension remains predominant but insurance regulation/supervision has increasingly "gone international" in a number of respects. In addition to institutional development in this area, important developments have taken place in the areas of international policy coordination, international cooperation among regulators and global public policies affecting the insurance industry worldwide. Once again, only the basic circumstantial evidence for each of these FOUR propositions can be provided here, leaving more detailed testing and reasoned proofs for another time.

FIRST, insurance regulation/supervision concerns have come to be "nested" in a number of different international institutions—both in Basle and elsewhere—all of which are involved to varying degrees in attempting to reform the "international financial architecture."

Reform of the "international financial architecture"[33] came to the forefront in the wake of the 1997 Asian financial crisis, but many of the building blocks for that initiative had begun to be put in place earlier. The three main lines of this reform are: (1) enhancing transparency and accountability; (2) strengthening financial systems; and (3) managing financial crises.[34] The world's major governments, international organizations, and private sector groups are all involved in furthering these efforts. Among international organizations, the "Basle Group" of the main financial regulation/supervision authorities have key roles to play, along with the IMF and World Bank, as well as regional bodies like OECD and UNCTAD and more specialized sectoral organizations like the International Accounting Standards Council. How and to what extent insurance regulation/supervision issues will fit into the mix is difficult to judge, but indications are that these may be substantial.

For purposes of administration and coordination, the "Basle Group" is located institutionally within the Bank for International Settlements (BIS), which has served after World War II as the primary international coordinating mechanism for the major central banks worldwide. Within BIS, the Basle Committee on Banking Supervision has since 1974 brought together national banking regulators from key countries to cooperate in establishing standards and principles that give guidance to national regulators and the banking industry.[35] In 1986, IOSCO was established as the counterpart body among securities regulators and, in 1994, the IAIS for insurance regulators. Each of these sectoral cooperative authorities establishes its own membership and operates separately but, increasingly, has found it necessary to work together on common problems. The work of the Joint Forum on Financial Conglomerates over the past five years is a highly successful case in point of cross-sectoral international regulatory cooperation.[36] In many respects, Basle has become the international hub for financial supervision, in much the same way that Geneva is for international trade and Washington is for international economic and monetary affairs.

SECOND, the International Association of Insurance Supervisors (IAIS) is gradually moving to consolidate its role as the world's insurance regulatory/supervisory authority, following very much along the path of international regulatory cooperation set earlier by its sister organization.

Prior to its establishment in 1994, the IAIS began informally as a grouping within the National Association of Insurance Commissioners in the United States. NAIC is an association of state insurance commissioners from all 50 states that attempt to coordinate their separate intrastate supervisory activities and, where appropriate, to harmonize interstate practices. By the late 1980s, their efforts at regulatory cooperation on a nationwide basis began to spill over into the international realm. Since IAIS was established in 1994, it has expanded to more than 70 members and, since 1998, has moved to Basle and established a small secretariat.[37] Its modus operandi is much like its sister organizations: elaborating principles and standards to guide insurance regulators/supervisors worldwide (not only their members) in dealing with sectoral issues; and cooperating cross-sectorally with other financial regulators and with other economic and monetary authorities.[38] Its initial work on principles and standards has been carried out by working groups drawn from member regulatory/supervisory authorities and, as with others in the "Basle Group," these can then be adopted or not on a voluntary basis by members or non-members alike, depending upon the sovereign decision of their governments.

In this regard the primary work of the IAIS fits within our typology as "international cooperation among domestic regulators." International cooperation among domestic regulators—whether sectoral or cross-sectoral—works primarily on the technical supervisory level and does not normally extend to broader public policy concerns. It seeks to coordinate and harmonize in favor of existing 'best practices' rather than grapple with emergent problems and new issues. It works within a specified field of expertise on problems whose scale and scope are carefully delimited rather than surveying the horizon to identify and anticipate potential problems and mobilize resources to deal with them. As regulators from different countries work together within the IAIS, they confront common issues and learn how their counterparts deal with similar problems, gradually building levels of trust and confidence in their fellow regulators which is critical when cross-border cooperation is required.[39]

THIRD, an important recent development at the international level has been the establishment, at the request of the Group of Seven governments, of a Financial Stability Forum bringing together all the major countries and institutional stakeholders to meet on a regular basis to monitor developments within the international financial system as yet another matter of international policy coordination.

The creation of the Financial Stability Forum is both a response to threats of systemic instabilities within the international financial system and to the perceived need for improved international policy coordination in this area. International policy coordination is dramatically different from international cooperation among domestic regulators. Growing directly from the high-level, broad-based coordination achieved over the past 30 years among heads of government meeting now as the Group of Seven countries, international policy coordination is directed at specific areas and particular issues mandated by heads of government as being particularly important for government officials to examine and assess. Until the Financial Stability Forum was established in April 1999, these mandates had been given on an ad hoc basis. The Financial Stability Forum is significant because it brings together representatives of all the major countries and institutional stakeholders in the financial field—though specifically not private sector interests—and constitutes this group of 37 officials as a permanent, high-level public monitoring body.

The idea behind such a new body flowed easily from the work of the three groups set up to examine reform of the "international financial architecture" as a consequence of the 1997 Asian financial crisis. After these groups reported in October 1998, it was decided that further work should be done and an eminent person report prepared on "international cooperation and coordination in the area of financial market supervision and surveillance." That report by Hans Tietmeyer of the German Bundesbank made specific provision for a Financial Stability Forum as follows:

"... Such a Forum should meet regularly to assess issues and vulnerabilities affecting the global financial system and to identify and oversee actions needed to address them. The Forum would report to the G-7 Ministers and Central Bank Governors. It would replace the series of ad hoc groups that have been convened over the past years with a view to strengthening the international financial system....Given the need for the Forum to have a manageable size, national representation would be limited to three members [typically high-level representatives G-7 Finance ministries, central banks and senior supervisory authorities]; the International Financial Institutions (IMF and World Bank) would be represented by two participants each, the other international organizations (BIS and OECD) by one member each; the international regulatory groupings (the Basle

Committee, IOSCO and IAIS) would be represented by two members each, and [by one member each from central bank experts on the payments system and market functioning]. Participation could over time be extended to include representatives from a small number of additional[i.e., non G-7] national authorities that could contribute substantially to the process, or to invite them to attend meetings as guests...."[40]

After the G-7 ministers quickly accepted this recommendation, the Financial Stability Forum was established and met for the first time in April 1999.

This new type of international policy coordination mechanism will bear close attention, not only in terms of the specific actions it takes but also the quality of international policy coordination it provides. Among its first actions has been the creation of three working groups to examine current threats to the stability of the international financial system: one to look at highly-leveraged institutions whose demise might cause systemic risk; a second dealing with short-term capital flows; and a third on the problems of offshore financial centers. Insurance figures prominently in this last area because of the high concentration of captive and other insurers domiciled in offshore financial centers around the world. As well, when the Financial Stability Forum held its first working meeting in September, it was reported that questions were raised about vulnerabilities in the world reinsurance market and the IAIS has been asked to conduct a special study and report its findings back to the Forum within six months. Whether this new body will be able to provide the kind of anticipatory international policy coordination on these kind of issues—an early warning radar network if you will—remains to be seen.

FOURTH, there have already been embryonic, and thus far largely unsuccessful, attempts at global public policies which deal with the global financial problems, but further attempts along these lines are definitely to be anticipated.

"Global public policies," which deal particularly with the problems that recent globalization pressures have spawned, are cases where international level actors seek solutions to international level problems, even though the actors, the problems and often the solutions arise and must be determined primarily within the "domestic domain." What is being attempted is "governance without government" because countries for the most part remain unwilling to surrender custody of their sovereign decision-making authority to supranational bodies. Such governance goes beyond international cooperation among regulators or even international policy coordination among governments to engage private authority with governments and regulators in the resolution of cross-sectoral, cross-border issues.

The evolution of the Basle Committee's capital adequacy requirements represents a case in point of embryonic global public policy. When originally put in place in 1987, they represented an attempt largely organized by the

United States and United Kingdom to impose narrow, compulsory standards of financial probity on countries and their regulators/supervisors worldwide. By 1996, when these standards were substantially revised, there had been acceptance on the part of most countries that capital adequacy standards represented a legitimate form of global public policy but significant changes were introduced in how these standards were to be arrived at and put in place. For better or worse, more flexible standards to accommodate the wider range of financial instruments involved and greater reliance on private sector involvement in their implementation became features of an embryonic global public policy, in this area. Insurers are now included under these requirements but held to a lower capital adequacy requirement than are banking operations, both of which are determined according to appropriate private as well as public risk-based capital measures.[41] Other areas where global public policies might evolve in the future include financial crisis management where systemic risk is involved or common approaches to dealing with corruption and money-laundering on the international level.

IV. Treatment of Domestic/International Regulation and Implications for the Services 2000 Round

In the context of the Services 2000 round of multilateral trade negotiations, it can be anticipated that domestic/international regulatory/supervisory arrangements in insurance will come very much into play. Country trade negotiators will want to establish whether domestic/international regulation inappropriately inhibits trade in insurance services and whether new disciplines need to be put in place to further liberalization in this and other services fields. The starting point for any such initiatives must be the current situation with regard to domestic/international regulation under provisions of the GATS as well as the scheduled specific commitments made by countries on insurance services as of the completion of the 1997 extended negotiations.

Liberalization of trade in financial services must clearly be a long-term goal, to be achieved in stages, over several years and many rounds of negotiation, and without the expectation that there will probably ever be full uniformity among all participants.[42] In December 1993, all countries agreeing to the Final Act which ended the Uruguay Round accepted overall the GATS, including its framework of principles, rules and decision-making arrangements regarding financial services, but were unable to agree on any complete and mutually-acceptable set of binding country commitments in banking, securities and insurance, even though a total of 84 countries (71 in insurance) did register at least some commitments in financial services. In July 1995, extended negotiations on financial services achieved an "Interim Agreement," among a smaller group of those countries led by the EU and involving improved country commitments from 29 participants who agreed to hold to those improved commitments through the end of 1997, though most notably not including the United States which decided for the time being not to participate and actually extended its MFN exemption to cover insurance services. When the 1997 financial services negotiation finally concluded, the outcome was not only a broader, though still not yet comprehensive, set of improved country commitments among developed and key developing countries, but also U.S. participation based upon wide-ranging, MFN-based commitments across all financial services sub-sectors.

Before commenting on specific features of the GATS in more detail, it is perhaps more useful first to focus on the underlying philosophy behind its treatment of Domestic Regulation. Summarizing his analysis of domestic regulation under GATS, Roger Kampf makes a significant point in this regard:

> It can be stated that the GATS' ultimate objective is neither to achieve harmonization of national regulations nor to establish supervisory cooperation in the field of financial services; but to ensure that basic principles are respected and that the exercise of domestic regulatory autonomy does not constitute a barrier to trade. One might say that GATS aims at establishing a level playing field with equally competitive opportunities both for foreign and local financial institutions within a country; what it does not aim to do is to create a level playing field that would be more or less identical in all WTO member countries.[43]

If countries or industry actors wish to pursue broader and deeper deregulatory or harmonization objectives, that is quite appropriate but will require them to push beyond existing GATS disciplines and levels of country commitments.

In terms of existing general commitments, Article VI of the GATS on Domestic Regulation, accepted by all WTO members as part of the 1994 Final Act, expresses the obligation of countries to prevent unjustifiable barriers to trade in services arising from domestic laws and regulations, specifically that "all matters of general application relating to trade in services be administered in a reasonable, objective and impartial manner." In addition, Article VII obliges countries, pending implementation of agreed upon sectoral disciplines, to accept what is effectively a 'standstill' on licensing/qualification requirements and technical standards that might affect the quality of country commitments and to utilize where possible any international requirements/standards established by international organizations as relevant for monitoring enforcement. While insurance industry groups will definitely press broadly for a full range of pro-competitive regulatory principles for a sector like insurance, it may well be that these objectives will have to be scaled down to focus more on transparency of policy and regulation and elaboration of a "necessity test" before moving on to matters of equivalency and acceptance of international standards.[44] In particular, an appropriate "necessity test" for domestic/international regulation in insurance would have to take account of the particular functions which regulatory action serves as well as the objectives pursued through government policies.

Most importantly, the GATS Annex on Financial Services, also accepted in 1994, provides for what are essentially derogations from general obligations where specific financial services are supplied "in the exercise of governmental authority" (monetary and exchange rate policy or social security); or in matters of prudential regulation, where "a Member shall not be prevented from taking measures for prudential reasons, including for the protection of investors, depositors, policy-holders or persons to whom a fiduciary duty is owed by a financial services supplier, or to ensure the integrity and stability of the financial system." While little needs to be done on the first derogation, the scope of the existing "prudential carve-out" as well as how and when it might be invoked remains unclear and may require further clarification in light of ongoing trade liberalization and reforms to the international financial architecture.[45]

In addition, the Understanding on Financial Services, also accepted in 1994, outlines an alternative scheduling method and formula approach to liberalization that could be subject to further elaboration. That alternative liberalization formula, which countries are free to adopt instead of the positive list approach set out in the Annex on Financial Services, focuses primarily on commercial presence while largely excluding cross-border and consumption abroad modes of delivery and applies only to the already more internationalized sectors of insurance such as reinsurance and MAT. Progress might be possible on expanding the scope of the Understanding, particularly into cross-border and consumption abroad.[46] The formula approach holds considerable attraction and now 31 countries, including a handful of developing countries, have adopted its use, where originally only OECD countries had used it.

While the extended negotiations on financial services did not lead explicitly to any further elaboration of regulatory principles and rules in this sector, it is noteworthy that, in the 1997 Financial Services Accord, the major developed countries, first Japan, and then the EU and the United States, followed the practice of several developing countries in registering Additional Commitments involving specified future changes to their domestic/international regulatory arrangements in banking and insurance. Japan effectively multilateralized its earlier bilateral insurance agreements with the United States while the United States and EU each undertook commitments to make its "best efforts" to harmonize state-level and member-state regulation, respectively. These additional commitments are particularly interesting because, in each case, they go somewhat beyond a country's trade-discriminating behavior and begin to delve more deeply into domestic regulation. Since Additional Commitments are arguably just as binding in GATS terms as other specific commitments, then these might provide an opening for pressure and accountability relating to major country government actions to reform their domestic regulatory arrangements.

Finally, in non-financial services sectors that might serve as guides to further development in the financial services field, WTO members moved in subsequent negotiations concluded in 1997 to adopt a "regulatory reference paper" as a common understanding about the appropriate scope and operation of domestic/international regulation in basic telecommunications services and, in December 1999, to agree to at least minimal disciplines on licensing and accreditation in the accountancy sector. In the insurance field, the "regulatory reference paper" has considerable appeal and underlies some of the current efforts to develop and adopt a set of pro-competitive regulatory principles and rules that would serve as a separate sectoral agreement on insurance.[47] On the other hand, the non-binding principles and rules adopted for accountancy are what many believe must be avoided because they do not offer enough real liberalization in the field. While disciplines on domestic/international regulation of insurance services are appealing to the industry as a way of binding both developing as well as developed countries to common pro-competitive rules, governments are not so likely to espouse the harmonization of policy and regulation which this implies and are more likely to pursue looser negotiated international regulatory agreements.

By way of conclusion, it is clear that financial services trade liberalization remains an "incomplete game." More remains to be achieved in the way of improved country commitments on insurance services, particularly in the area of cross-border and consumption abroad not to mention the largely untouched area of temporary presence of natural persons. The "rules of the game" have now basically been set with the adherence to the GATS framework by now 133 member-states and with several more, including major countries like China and Russia, moving towards accession. Modest changes to the rules are possible and, in some cases desirable, during Services 2000, but fundamental changes to the "rules of the game" are unlikely. Going back to an earlier analogy, further efforts to "level the playing field" are to be encouraged but, on the evidence of our earlier survey of trends in domestic/international regulation of insurance, it would be unrealistic to expect "a level playing field that is more or less identical in all WTO countries." As any soccer devotee knows, playing at home is always different than playing away, despite the fact that the pitch and the rules are the same for both teams.

Notes

[1] It would be wrong to suggest that any particular observers discovered this trend but, in the trade policy context, Sylvia Ostry began to identify this trend towards the collapsing of the separate domestic and international realms of activities and coined the term "domestic domain" in this regard. See Sylvia Ostry, *The Post-Cold War Trading System* (Chicago: University of Chicago Press, 1997).

[2] Abram and Antonia Chayes outline just such a "new sovereignty" emerging as countries of all sizes and status find it increasingly in their interest to carefully negotiate and then subsequently comply with broad-based international regulatory agreements—of which the WTO trade regime and agreements are but one example. See Abram and Antonia Handler Chayes, *The New Sovereignty: Compliance with International Regulatory Agreements* (Cambridge: Harvard University Press, 1995).

[3] The late Susan Strange was one of several acute observers who sees the growing importance of different kinds of private authority in the international political economy as a consequence of what she referred to carefully as "the retreat of the state"—most definitely not its erosion or demise. Interestingly, she includes a chapter specifically on international insurance as one of those areas where private authority is now well established. See Susan Strange, *The Retreat of the State* (Cambridge: Cambridge University Press, 1997.

[4] Referring to the early 1990s, the OECD authors conclude that "For the time being, ['convergence'] concerns only a sub-set of financial products, activities and firms—but it clearly exists and it can be expected to develop further, in line with the progressive interpenetration of markets and reduced segmentation of activities. It is certainly not a question of full and integral desegmentation; there will still remain important barriers and structural forms of separation between market compartments but important new channels and linkages have developed at the economic and regulatory level. True, insurance, banking and other financial activities retain their specificities. As in the past, the various forms of financial services continue to embody specific, and in many instances unique, features; nonetheless, further advances in the 'convergence' process will provide scope for a more complementary and integrated approach to management and marketing of services across a wider section of the financial market." OECD, *Insurance and Other Financial Services: Structural Trends* (Paris, 1992), p. 15.

[5] At present, there is no definitive treatment of the historic role of regulation in structuring life and non-life insurance markets worldwide, possibly because of the myriad differences among domestic regulatory arrangements and the dizzying changes taking place among market participants. On the development of a "private international regime" among major market players in the area of insuring large risks, see Virginia Hauffler, *Dangerous Commerce* (Ithaca: Cornell University Press, 1997).

[6] This typology of the policing, promoting and planning functions of regulation draws upon Richard Schultz and Alan Alexandroff, *Economic Regulation and the Federal System* (Toronto: University of Toronto Press, 1985). It was applied specifically to Canada and did not cover insurance but the possibilities of interpolation to other countries and the insurance sector are clear.

[7] These developments have been examined and assessed often in harsh terms in a number of recent books, including Tony Porter, *States, Markets and Regimes in Global Finance* (New York: St Martin's Press, 1993); Ethan B. Kapstein, *Governing the Global Economy* (Cambridge: Harvard University Press, 1994); and Louis W. Pauly, *Who Elected the Bankers?* (Ithaca: Cornell University Press, 1997).

[8] Recent books which highlight the increasing scope for private sector activity worldwide and the move towards managed competition are William Greider, *Only One World: The Manic Logic of Global Capitalism* (New York: Simon & Schuster, 1997) and Daniel Yergin and Joseph Stanislaw, *The Commanding Heights: The Battle Between Government and the Marketplace that is Remaking the Modern World* (Simon & Schuster, 1997).

[9] For a discussion of this issue in the abstract, see Scott Jacobs, "Regulatory Cooperation for an Interdependent World: Issues for Government," in OECD, *Regulatory Cooperation in an Interdependent World* (Paris, 1995), pp. 18-46.

[10] See, in particular, the study recently released by its Insurance Committee, OECD, *International Insurance Operations - Cross-Border Trade and Establishment of Foreign Branches* (Paris, 1999).

[11] For an examination of market and regulatory developments in the Eastern European transition economies, see Yoshihiro Kawai, "Insurance Markets in Central and Eastern Europe," paper presented at the 15th PROGRES Seminar on Regulation in Financial Services, Geneva, September 16-17, 1999.

[12] Japan is the most recent convert to these norms. The 1994 and 1996 U.S.-Japan Bilateral Agreements on Insurance, subsequently multilateralized through its commitments in the 1997 WTO Accord on Financial Services, contain increased domestic competition, greater market access, and insurance regulatory system elements. See Wook Jean Kwon and Harold D. Skipper, "Regulatory Changes in the Japanese Insurance Market," *Journal of Insurance Regulation*, (Winter, 1997), pp. 151-69.

[13] Prevailing theories of regulation, such as capture theory and rent-seeking, hinge very much on the promotional and planning functions of regulation. Renewed emphasis on its policing function shifts attention back to the public interest rationale for regulation. For an application of this kind of analysis, see M. B. Abrams and G. D. Tower, "Theories of Regulation: Some Reflections on the Statutory Supervision of Insurance Companies in Anglo-American Countries," *The Geneva Papers on Risk and Insurance* (April 1994), pp. 156-77.

[14] See Frank L. Fine, "Recent Developments in EU Insurance Law," *Journal of Insurance Regulation* (Winter, 1997), pp. 125-50.

[15] On solvency as the primary task of insurance supervision, see the seminal paper by Gerry Dickinson in OECD, *Policy Issues in Insurance* (Paris, 1996); also, his presentation on "Insurance Regulatory Issues: Safety and Soundness," 15th PROGRES Seminar on Regulation in Financial Services, Geneva, September 16-17, 1999.

[16] On risk-based capital measures as one technique, see Robert W. Klein, "Insurance Regulation in Transition," *Journal of Risk and Insurance* (1995), pp. 363-404. This technique has been pioneered by the National Association of Insurance Commissioners in the United States.

[17] The surprise creation of the UK FSA was one of two major initiatives of the new Labour government, along with the separation of the Bank of England from the Treasury. On the thinking behind this bold move and its implications for insurance, see Martin Roberts, Speech to the 25th General Assembly of the Geneva Association, June 25, 1998.

[18] Canada's Office of the Superintendent of Financial Institutions was created in the late 1980s and brings together banking and insurance at the federal level, but not securities which is under provincial jurisdiction.

[19] The NAIC model is to encourage harmonization through commonly-accepted standards and model laws rather than through direction.

[20] On continental European style insurance supervision, see Alain Tossetti, "Insurance Regulatory Issues: Ensuring Safety and Soundness," 15th PROGRES Seminar on Regulation in Financial Services, Geneva, September 16-17, 1999. For an excellent

treatment of this "battle of the systems," see Jonathan Story and Ingo Walter, *Political Economy of Financial Integration in Europe* (Cambridge: MIT Press, 1997).

[21] These are from the introductory remarks by Brian Atchinson and Gregory Krohm, "International Regulatory Developments: A Symposium," *Journal of Insurance Regulation* (Winter, 1997), p. 117.

[22] The linkage between banking and insurance is perhaps the most elementary of these cross-sectoral dimensions. On how this affects marketplace convergence in two countries, see Glenn Morgan et al., "Bancassurance in Britain and France: Innovating Strategies in Financial Services," *Geneva Papers on Risk and Insurance* (April, 1994), pp. 178-95.

[23] On insurance within the broad spectrum of risk management, see the Geneva Association Lecture delivered by Peter L. Bernstein in Paris, May 1998. This lecture elaborates upon the perspective he has laid out in his magisterial work *Against the Gods: The Remarkable Story of Risk* (New York: Wiley, 1997).

[24] The failure of Confederation Life in Canada in 1994—the largest insurance failure in North America—had ripple effects in many U.S. states where that company had operated. Likewise, another Canadian life insurer recently had to increase its capital reserves in the UK to meet UK regulatory requirements, because its risk-based capital adequacy requirements had deteriorated. These ripple effects of normal cross-border activities should be distinguished from systemic failures where multiple companies and multiple countries are typically involved.

[25] The recent Citicorp/Travelers merger in the United States raises just such issues. Not only is such a banking/insurance merger of concern to federal banking supervisors, and state insurance supervisors but it may well draw the attention of banking and insurance supervisory authorities in the many countries in which these two companies currently operate.

[26] The term "financial convergence" is coming to be used to signify the industry/firm level phenomenon whereby traditional boundaries between and within companies are breaking down at the same time that, as a result of liberalization, insurance and other financial services companies seek operate routinely across national and sub-national borders. Drawing in part on the experience of the Dutch company ING, Lutgard van den Berghe used this term to describe the current marketplace and regulatory challenge at the 15th PROGRES Seminar on Regulation in Financial Services, Geneva, September 15-16, 1999.

[27] See Harold D. Skipper, Jr, *Foreign Insurers in Emerging Markets: Issues and Concerns* (Washington: International Insurance Foundation, 1997).

[28] Even as recently as the fall of 1999, Kevin Cronin of the International Insurance Federation indicated at the PROGRES seminar that the prospects for passage of this legislation were not good. Not only did proposed legislation face objections from Congress but also from state legislators and insurance regulators as well as from some insurance industry interests. Somewhat unexpectedly, the Financial Modernization did pass both the House of Representatives and Senate in the spring of 2000. This reform will serve to strengthen the federal role in insurance regulation/supervision and start to break down some of the segmented regulatory practice associated with the Glass-Steagall and McFadden Acts.

[29] For a survey, see Yosihiro Kawai, "National Regulatory Developments in Insurance in Central and Eastern European Countries," at 15th PROGRES Seminar on Regulation in Financial Services, Geneva, September 16-17, 1999.

[30] See Harold D. Skipper, Jr, "The Impossibility of Separating Domestic Regulation in Insurance from International Trade Issues," 15th PROGRES Seminar on Regulation in Financial Services, Geneva, September 16-17, 1999.

[31] Robert Putnam pioneered this concept and international trade negotiations are "two-level games" in the sense that not only must countries agree among themselves but, individually, they must also deal with the various bureaucratic and private sector interests affected by any agreement. See Robert Putnam, "Diplomacy and Domestic Politics: The Logic of Two-Level Games," *International Organization*, (Summer, 1988), p. 427.

[32] The recent release of a joint statement on "pro-competitive regulatory principles" by eight international insurance industry associations in August 1999 is a case in point. The full set of regulatory principles proposed would strongly reinforce and substantially extend the existing GATS disciplines across a wide range including right of establishment and foreign equity issues, treatment of remaining state monopolies, access to reinsurance markets, financial and taxation issues as well as governmental regulatory practices. See Financial Leaders Group, Insurance Evaluating Team, "Pro-Competitive Regulatory Principles in Insurance," July 1, 1999.

[33] The term "architecture" is an interesting choice of terminology. In contrast to possible alternatives such as "system" or "regime," it connotes neither a concern with all the technical detail nor the essential principles underlying international public finance, but rather a concern with the conceptual issues and design questions.

[34] The main report was prepared and issued by the Group of Seven Finance Ministers and central bank governors as three separate but interrelated reports at the end of October 1998. See Group of Seven, "Reports on the International Financial Architecture," October 1998.

[35] Perhaps the two main endeavors that the Basle Committee has been involved with are the capital adequacy requirements for banks issued first in 1988 and amended in 1996 and the core principles for banking supervision issued in 1996. It must be stressed that the Basle Committee has no authority to compel countries to adopt its initiatives but must rely on voluntary compliance.

[36] On the work of the Joint Forum, see Johanne C. Prevost, "The Supervision of Financial Conglomerates," 15th PROGRES Seminar on Regulation in Financial Services, Geneva, September 16-17, 1999.

[37] The U.S. presence in IAIS remains strong and NAIC collectively maintains 13 memberships on behalf of its state regulators within an organization with more than 70 members in total.

[38] The evolution of IAIS requires further attention. On its founding and early years, see George Pooley, "The IAIS: A Progress Report and Some Thoughts for the Future," *Journal of Insurance Regulation* (Winter, 1997), pp. 170-78; also, by its first Secretary-General, Knut Hohlfeld, "Global Cooperation Among Financial Market Regulators," 15th PROGRES Seminar on Regulation in Financial Services, Geneva, September 16-17. 1999.

[39] This theme of trust and confidence is a prominent feature of regulators' perceptions of the benefits of international regulatory cooperation.

[40] Report by Hans Tietmeyer to the G-7 Finance Ministers and Central Bank Governors, February, 1999.

[41] There differences of opinion among authors as to the significance and effectiveness of these capital adequacy measures. Reinecke sees them as a good first approximation of global public policy; Strange viewed them as further evident of the 'retreat of the state' and the growing importance of private authority in international relations.

[42] For further treatment of earlier episodes, see R. Brian Woodrow, "Insurance Services in the Uruguay Round Services Negotiations: An Overview and Assessment of the Final Agreement" and "The World Trade Organization and Liberalisation of Trade in Insurance Services: Impact and Implications of the 1995 Protocol on Financial Services," both in *The Geneva Papers on Risk and Insurance*, July 1995, pp. 57-73 and July 1997, pp. 400-13. Also, "The 1997 World Trade Organization Accord on Financial Services: Impact on and Implications for the World Insurance Industry," *The Geneva Papers on Risk and Insurance* (January, 2000), pp. 78-103.

[43] For an assessment of domestic regulation under GATS and the increasing importance of the international dimension, see Roger Kampf, "Liberalization of Financial Services in the GATS and Domestic Regulation," *International Trade Law and Regulation* (1997), pp.155-66.

[44] This point was made in the context of the current Working Group on Domestic Regulation that has found that, given the diversity of country views, it must move sequentially and cautiously on difficult and contentious issues rather than promote any overly ambitious plan.

[45] Sydney Key has recently examined prudential regulation in the context both of trade liberalization and ongoing financial system reforms and finds relatively little need for greater precision about the scope of the existing "prudential carve-out". Sydney Key, "Trade Liberalization and Prudential Liberalization: The International Framework for Financial Services", *International Affairs*, 75 (1999), pp 61-75.

[46] For an argument along these lines, see Masa Kono, "The WTO Understanding on Financial Services: Questions and Issues for the Next Round," 15th PROGRES Seminar on Regulation in Financial Services, Geneva, September 16-17, 1999.

[47] It should be noted, however, that this may represent a misunderstanding of the status of the "regulatory reference paper" developed during the basic telecommunications negotiations. This was developed essentially as a set of guidelines for countries making commitments rather than as a set of binding principles and rules and has no status within the GATS on a stand-alone basis.

CHAPTER 18

Canadian Magazine Policy: International Conflict and Domestic Stagnation

Keith Acheson and Christopher Maule

I. Introduction

The World Trade Organization (WTO) panel decision on periodicals drew attention to a dispute between Canada and the United States that had been brewing for a number of years. It arose from the interaction between domestic policies and international trade obligations.

Canadian magazine policy has been based on five pillars: postal subsidies and pricing to aid the distribution of Canadian periodicals; screening of foreign investment in Canadian periodicals; tax treatment of advertising expenditures by Canadian advertisers so as to discourage use of regional editions or split-runs of foreign magazines; tariff measures to prevent the shipment of foreign split-runs into Canada; and measures to tax or prohibit the publication of split-runs. The fifth pillar was addressed in 1995 by an excise tax (Bill C-103) on split-runs. After the United States successfully challenged the legislation in the WTO, it was withdrawn and replaced by Bill C-55, the *Foreign Publishers Advertising Services Act*, a prohibition on foreign publishers selling advertising aimed primarily at the Canadian market.[1] Modifications to Bill C-55 and the tax treatment of advertising expenditures in split-runs were negotiated between Canada and the United States in an agreement announced in June of 1999.

Of the five policies, three—the postal subsidy, the tariff measures and the excise tax—were addressed in the ruling of the WTO dispute panel and appellate body—see Exhibit 1.[2] Canada argued that the tariff measures were necessary to sustain the purpose of the income-tax policies, and pointed to policies that had permitted certain long-time foreign publishers to continue producing split-runs. The negotiations leading to the final outcome surrounding Bill C-55 were conditioned by the obligations of trade agreements (the North American Free Trade Agreement [NAFTA] and the WTO), but have not been the object of any formal dispute procedures.

Exhibit 1. Recent Changes to Canadian Magazine Policies

Measures	Sources of Modification	Canadian Action
Postal subsidy	WTO ruling: disallowed	Rates restructured. Subsidy paid directly to publishers.
Investment screening	Negotiated agreement with the United States of 1999	Authority transferred from Industry Canada to Canadian Heritage.
Tax deductibility	Negotiated agreement with the United States of 1999	Amendment of Bill C-55
Tariff item	WTO ruling: disallowed	Withdrawn
Excise tax	WTO ruling: disallowed	Withdrawn. Bill C-55 introduced prohibiting advertising in split-runs.

The mix of policies has evolved over four decades to address objectives that successive Canadian governments have supported. Until recently, no political party in Canada has voiced any significant opposition to the underlying rationale for the policies expressed in the 1961 report of a Royal Commission inquiry into publications:[3]

> ...communications are the thread which binds together the fibers of our nation. They can protect a nation's values and encourage their practice. They can make democratic government possible and better government probable.... it is largely left to our periodical press, to our magazines big and little to make a conscious appeal to the nation, to try to interpret Canada to all Canadians, to bring a sense of oneness to our scattered communities....Only a truly Canadian printing press, one with the feel of Canada and directly responsible to Canada can give us the critical analysis, the informed discourse and dialogue which are indispensable in a sovereign society.

Ten years later a Canadian Senate report echoed this view:[4]

> Magazines are special.... Magazines, in a different way from any other medium, can help foster in Canadians a sense of themselves. In terms of cultural survival. Magazines could potentially be as important as railroads, airlines, national broadcasting networks, and the national hockey leagues.

And recently, in a government sponsored task force report, the 1961 Royal Commission's theme is reiterated:[5]

Free speech would lose much of its potency if there were no magazines. Without the means to express a distinctive voice speaking to a Canadian audience, cultural expression, social cohesion and a sense of national destiny would be impaired, if not irrevocably damaged.

Writing in 1994, at a time before publishers had begun to make extensive use of the Internet to distribute editorial and advertising content, the task force did not foresee that new technology might provide a means for individuals to communicate with each other locally, nationally and internationally that would complement and supplement the traditional media.

We begin by briefly noting the organizational and contractual arrangements that have conditioned the evolution of policy and provide a chronology of that evolution. A more detailed examination of each of the five pillars follows. We argue that at least some pillars were more illusion than reality. A failure to enforce critical measures and the prevalence of "black box" discretionary decisions, which often appear inconsistent based on the little evidence available, made actual policy differ from nominal. As the international challenges to Canada's policies have their counterparts in disputes affecting other countries, we conclude that there is a pressing need to integrate the cultural industries into the WTO and to reorient domestic policies away from their protectionist history.

II. Organizational Features

Canadian policies have made it more expensive for Canadian readers to purchase foreign as opposed to domestic magazines and have discouraged or prevented foreign, especially American, split-runs from being distributed in Canada. Periodicals consist of two components, editorial content (news, stories, letters and pictures) and advertising. Revenues accrue to publishers from the sale of space to advertisers and the sale of magazines through newsstands or subscriptions delivered by mail. A third source of revenue results from government subsidies especially for literary and other specialized publications which have difficulty in attracting either paid circulation or advertising. Some periodicals, known as controlled circulation magazines, depend entirely on advertising and are made available at no charge. At the other extreme are magazines, such as scholarly publications, which depend almost completely on subscription revenue, perhaps with some subsidy. In between are a large number of periodicals that rely on different combinations of advertising and circulation revenue.

The commercial viability of a magazine can be enhanced by product differentiation whereby publishers offer different mixes of advertising and editorial content to different audiences. In the parlance of the magazine industry, publishers offer regional editions or split-runs of magazines. In a split-run, all or substantially all the editorial content is the same in all editions, but the advertising differs by edition. Thus the copies of the magazine sold on the west coast contain different advertising from the copies sold in the central and eastern parts of the country. Some regionally specific content may be added and the ordering of the common content may be changed. The term *split* refers to the separation of the editorial from the advertising content. The optimal number of editions of a magazine depends on the trade-off between scale economies of offering fewer variants and the added value to readers of differentiated content and advertising. Technology is altering this trade-off as consumers are able to select content of individual interest and have it delivered electronically. The challenge for publishers will be to find a way to finance this ultimate degree of customization.

Split-runs are used in domestic as well as foreign markets, although Canadian policy has been aimed primarily at the latter. In 1999, the Canadian news magazine *Maclean's* had fifteen split-runs in Canada. *Time* has a number of regional editions in the United States as well as split-runs in Canada and other countries. Time Canada describes its foreign involvement as follows:[6]

> The ability to sell advertising—without restrictions—exists in every one of the nearly 200 countries in which we circulate. Significant local advertising appears regularly in France, Germany, Hong Kong, Australia, Pakistan, India, South Africa, Brazil, Mexico etc. In many of these countries we publish split-run editions, combining editorial material for the U.S. with that produced locally, and selling advertising space to local advertisers.

Similar marketing techniques and modifications of the basic product to broaden the market are found in other segments of the print media. Newspapers have regional editions where some of the advertising will differ by market, and books are published so as to appeal to different linguistic and cultural audiences. The incentive for the print publisher, as for the owner of rights to a film, television program or sound recording is to spread the up-front costs of production as widely as possible. Because these products have high fixed and low incremental costs, the concept of dumping is not easily applied. One of the arguments has been that United States publishers engage in unfair competition by dumping editorial content through distributing split-runs in Canada.[7] In the GATS unlike the GATT, there is no procedure for dealing with dumping.

Foreign magazines, such as the *New Yorker*, reach Canada as overflow circulation, that is with the same editorial and advertising content that appears in the foreign market. Others such as *Time* and the *New England Journal of Medicine* publish split-runs for the Canadian market. Split-runs can enter Canada in one of two ways. The editorial content can be imported, combined with advertisements and printed in Canada; or the editorial and advertising content can be printed in the United States and the finished periodical shipped to Canada. Each of the magazine policy measures addresses either overflow or split-run distribution of foreign magazines.

III. Five Pillars

The policies have evolved over time to address the objectives of Canadian policy in the light of the economic imperatives of magazine publishing. We present in the appendix below a chronology of the major events in the postwar period noting a number of special inquiries detailing the state of the industry and the policies that were introduced. Prior to that, and dating back to before the turn of the century, there had been concerns expressed in parliamentary debate and elsewhere both about the desirability of assisting the widespread distribution of all publications throughout the country, and about the overflow of unsuitable material especially from the United States.[8]

Postal Subsidy

A postal subsidy to Canadian publishers dates from the turn of the century. Its original purposes were to provide Canadian readers with magazines at reasonable prices, especially those living in rural areas and unable to make newsstand purchases, to support Canadian magazine publishers, and to encourage American publishers to use the Canadian rather than the United States postal service.[9] In the postwar years, a series of rates have been used for different types of periodicals. Major rate revisions took place in 1968-69 subsequent to legislation that aimed at addressing a growing deficit experienced by the post office.[10] For example: paid for periodicals have been charged a lower rate than controlled circulation periodicals; domestic periodicals paid less than foreign periodicals; but foreign periodicals printed in Canada such as *Time* and *Reader's Digest* paid the same rate as domestic periodicals. The special status granted the publishers of these two magazines under the last element of postal pricing policy was later withdrawn.

In 1998-99, the postal subsidy for periodicals absorbed C$37.4 million of the C$47.3 million per year allocated to the new Publications Assistance Program. The allocation for postal subsidies has declined from over C$200 million per year in the 1980s as part of the government's program of fiscal restraint. It is paid by the Department of Canadian Heritage directly to the deposit accounts of Canadian magazines held by Canada Post to reduce their net mailing costs. Published rates for foreign and domestic magazines are identical, but as a result of the subsidy the net cost to mail a copy of *Maclean's* in Canada is C8.2 cents compared to C30 cents for *Time*.[11] *Reader's Digest*, due to a ruling by the tax department, is considered a Canadian magazine and receives the subsidy and treatment similar to *Maclean's*.

The subsidy reduces the subscription price to Canadians of Canadian as compared to foreign magazines. A further consequence is that the newsstand spread between the price of a foreign and a Canadian magazine is narrower than that facing a subscriber, resulting in relatively more purchases of foreign magazines at the newsstand. Other factors such as demand conditions and linkages between advertising and subscription revenue also affect the pricing of subscriptions to different editions and of newsstand sales. In 1999, an annual subscription to *Maclean's* in Canada was C$43.96 plus taxes, compared to C$77.40 for the Canadian edition of *Time*. A similar differential existed for the *New Yorker*, while the *Atlantic Monthly* was about 80% higher in Canada. The *Economist* sold a North American edition with separate advertising. The annual subscription in U.S. dollars was higher for the edition sold in the U.K. (US$180) than for that sold in North America. For the latter the subscription price was US$125 in the United States and US$118 in Canada, despite the Canadian postal pricing discrimination.[12]

The WTO panels addressed the postal rate structure and the associated subsidy. They treated magazines as a good and ruled against the differential postal rates for domestic and foreign magazines. The subsidy was disallowed because it was paid indirectly through Canada Post rather than directly to the Canadian publishers.[13] The Canadian government conformed to the panel ruling by charging the same rates to foreign and domestic periodicals and altering the way in which the subsidy was received by domestic publishers.

The importance of the postal subsidy to the Canadian periodical industry is evidenced by the strong lobbying that has accompanied any planned reduction of the subsidy.[14] Subsidies have been an issue in recent discussions surrounding Bill C-55. Trade policy specialists advised that a subsidy for the industry was less likely to be challenged under the WTO than a measure that discriminated against foreign split-runs. Canadian magazine publishers argued against dependence on a new subsidy mindful of the evaporating postal subsidy and its dependence on renewal each year in the government's budget. The publishers also disliked the visibility of a subsidy.

Foreign Ownership

As with other cultural industries such as broadcasting, the Investment Canada Act[15] (formerly the Foreign Investment Review Act) has been flexibly interpreted or modified to limit the expansion of existing and restrict the establishment of new foreign owned periodicals as a way of ensuring that Canadian owned periodicals continue to receive the bulk of advertising revenue aimed at Canadian consumers.

An example of how this policy has been adapted in the past is illustrated by the entry of the split-run edition of *Sports Illustrated*. At the time of proposed entry, Time Canada was publishing a split-run edition of *Time* in Canada. Under the related business guidelines of the Investment Canada Act, Time Canada was given approval to publish *Sports Illustrated* as an expansion of its existing business. The government considered the *Sports Illustrated* initiative to expose a loophole in its anti split-run policy and the guidelines were changed in 1993 so that existing foreign publishers would require permission to expand in the same line of business.

The process of administering and enforcing the Investment Canada provisions for the cultural industries is opaque. There is no public documentation of the arguments supporting decisions in the review process. This lack of transparency is also characteristic of the income tax policies discussed in the next section. The Canadian government publishes no listing of existing foreign split-runs and claims not to have that information. After years of administering policies that discriminate between existing and new split-runs, this lack of pertinent information is surprising.

From an economic viewpoint, the investment policies make little sense. They assume that a Canadian owned publication is more likely to publish some desired but undefined Canadian content rather than commercial content that sells. Evidence from both film exhibition and broadcasting tell another story. When Cineplex-Odeon, Canada's largest chain of cinemas, was Canadian owned, the national content of films shown in their theaters did not change noticeably from when it was foreign owned. Similarly, the Canadian content rules for Canadian broadcasters are enforced because the required Canadian ownership does not ensure that culturally benign content is voluntarily chosen. Even the government owned Canadian Broadcasting Corporation has had to be cajoled into broadcasting more Canadian content. Despite the contradictory evidence, the "Canadian ownership ensures Canadian content" mantra is used as a rationale for ownership policies.

The investment guidelines were not at issue in the WTO magazine decision although their administration affects the ability of foreign firms to service the Canadian market with split-runs. As administered to date they have affected trade in goods, the hard copies of magazines, and would be subject to GATT obligations. However increasingly magazines are distributed as a service via the Internet which would make GATS applicable. The boundary between magazines as a good and service became an issue in the WTO ruling regarding the excise tax (Bill C-103) discussed below. The latest measures contained in Bill C-55 do not relate to magazines distributed electronically, probably because it was unclear how to deal with this form of delivery.[16]

Tax Deductibility of Advertising

Section 19 of the Income Tax Act which disallows advertising by Canadians in foreign periodicals to be deducted from taxable income is aimed at discouraging the publication and distribution of foreign split-runs. It was not challenged in the complaint referred to the WTO. There are two reasons. First, countries including the United States have tax codes that are riddled with preferences for domestic firms and there is little enthusiasm to drag these into a process as public as the WTO. Second, it may have become increasingly difficult to enforce section 19 so that it has become an ineffective deterrent to Canadian firms advertising in foreign split-runs.

The evolving enforcement problem is noted in the Task Force Report which states:[17]

These provisions have been in place since 1965. Over the years, section 19 has played an important role in strengthening the Canadian periodical industry. The Task Force heard from many sources over the course of its deliberations that the provisions of section 19, for a variety of reasons, have gradually been more honored in the breach than in the observance.

The Report recommends that the Department of National Revenue publish a list of split-run periodicals and issue an information bulletin to ensure that the industry is aware of the provisions of section 19. This supports the view noted previously that for the three decades since the passage of section 19 in 1965, and especially since Bill C-58 in 1976, the Canadian authorities have had a less than substantive grasp on which magazines qualified for tax deductibility treatment under section 19 and on whether advertisers were claiming the deductions or not in accordance with the policy. Revenue Canada ruled that it is up to advertisers to determine the status of a publisher for section 19 purposes. Our inquiries at Revenue Canada failed to elicit a list of known split-run magazines or examples of the auditing process.

Indications of the difficulty of enforcement were noted in 1983 in an article on the then current success of *Time* seven years after the removal of its exemption from the section 19 provisions in 1976. At first revenues fell to $3.7 million from $10.2 million, but by 1981 they had risen to $12.4 million. Avoidance of the tax-deductibility problem was alleged to have been achieved by placing the advertisements through offshore companies, with *Time* advising advertisers on how to structure their expenditures.[18]

If section 19 became less of a deterrent to advertisers over time, one would expect to see an initial decline in advertising rates charged by *Time*, followed by rising rates and a closing of the gap between *Time's* rates and those of the competing Canadian news magazine, *Maclean's*. The data confirm this sequence of events. The rates for a one page black and white insertion for the eastern edition of the two magazines are shown in Table 1.

Prior to Bill C-58, advertising rates for the two magazines were on a par around C$5000. The *Time* rate then fell to one third and has since risen to 75% of *Maclean's* rate. A more meaningful comparison adjusts for circulation by comparing the cost per thousand (cpm). Throughout this period, on a total circulation basis, *Maclean's* has had a larger circulation than *Time*—40% larger in 1976 and 60% larger in 1999. Assuming that this proportional difference applies to the rates for the eastern edition shown above, *Time* had a higher cpm before the introduction of Bill C-58. It fell to about half *Maclean's* cpm in July 1976 after tax deductibility was removed and has since risen so that it is now higher than *Maclean's* cpm even though advertising expenditures are supposed not to be tax deductible.[19]

Table 1. Comparison of Advertising Rates and Cost per Thousand (cpm),
***Time* and *Maclean's* 1976 to 1999, selected years**

(1) Date	(2) *Time* Cost of Ad. C$	(3) *Maclean's* Cost of Ad. C$	(4) (2) as % (3)	(5) cpm: *Time* as % of *Maclean's*
Jan. 1976	5160	5185	0.99	1.4
July 1976	1880	5608	0.34	0.49
July 1981	3180	7325	0.43	0.85
July 1986	5060	10385	0.49	0.94
July 1991	10448	14920	0.7	1.18
July 1996	11770	17130	0.69	1.07
Jan. 1999	13690	18320	0.75	1.2

Source: Canadian Advertising Rates and Data, various months 1976 to 1999.

The contracting procedure for placing advertisements also suggests why it may have been difficult to enforce section 19. Many clients contract with an agency to place a bundle of advertisements in different print and other media. A price will be quoted for the package. In order to conform to section 19, it would be necessary to identify those expenditures relating to one or more periodicals that do not qualify for tax deductibility and not claim them as expenses.

Based on these facts, it appears that either *Time* is such an attractive vehicle for advertisers that it can charge rates similar to or higher than *Maclean's* and still compete even though advertising in *Time* is not tax deductible, or advertisers can avoid the constraints of section 19. The latter in our view is the more likely case. If so it raises the question of why other foreign publishers did not copy the *Time* format and introduce split-runs into Canada. The only other barrier to new entry was the foreign investment guidelines. We comment on this question below.

In sum, it appears that one of the main policy instruments aimed at advertising services has not worked effectively for a number of years, and this may continue to be the case in the absence of any official list of foreign split-runs. The recent enactment of Bill C-55 puts another twist on this policy. It permits Canadian advertisers to deduct 50% of their expenditures on advertising in foreign publications as long as the publication does not contain more than 18% of advertisements aimed primarily at the Canadian market—the 18% exemption is phased in over three years. One interpretation of this change would see it as a concession to foreign publishers because the limit was previously 5%. But if the constraint was previously not binding, there may now be greater attention given to identifying and monitoring advertising which qualifies for the exemption. Even though a 50% tax deduction is now permitted for a higher level of advertising in foreign publications, a larger amount of tax may be collected than under the previous policy with lax enforcement. In part the outcome will depend on how the tax authorities interpret "aimed primarily at the Canadian market."

Tariff Measures and Excise Tax

Along with section 19 of the Income Tax Act (previously section 12a), Tariff Code 9958 was introduced in 1965. Its aim was to deter the importation into Canada of physical copies of split-runs. There were also procedures in place to prevent the entry of subsequent copies of a magazine if some ineligible copies crossed the border. Such errors were likely because of the difficulty of making a split-run determination, which depends on the wording of advertisements, at the border. Many foreign magazines, e.g., *National Geographic*, *Paris Match* and the *Economist*, enter Canada legally by way of overflow circulation. They may contain advertising for firms and products such as Kodak, Givenchy or British Airways whose goods or services are available in Canada as well as other countries. According to a trade publication, the practice has been that if the advertisement contains a location of specific availability in Canada, such as a Canadian city, street address, telephone number or postal code, it is considered aimed at the Canadian market. A message of general availability is deemed not to be primarily addressed to a Canadian audience unless it appears only in a Canadian edition.[20]

The tariff item dealt with the importation of a good, the physical copy of a magazine. It surfaced as a service issue in 1993 when Time Canada, after receiving approval from Investment Canada in 1990, shipped electronically from the United States the editorial content for a Canadian edition of *Sports Illustrated* to a printing plant in Canada. Because the tariff measure applied only to physical goods, Time Canada was advised by the Department of National Revenue that its actions were not contrary to any existing Canadian policy.[21]

This led to the formation of the Task Force on the Canadian Magazine Industry which concluded that, because of the crossborder electronic transmission of page proofs "the customs tariff, by itself, can no longer implement Canada's long standing policy on split-runs."[22] It proposed the imposition of an 80% excise tax on advertising in foreign split-runs. Recognizing that it could no longer stop this form of periodical at the border, the government accepted this proposal for what was in effect a prohibitive tax (Bill C-103). The fate of this tax was decided by the WTO panel decision which concluded that although it was levied on advertising services, the tax affected a good, periodicals. The measure was withdrawn and the government introduced Bill C-55. It was by no means clear that a WTO panel, if asked, would have ruled differently on Bill C-55 than Bill C-103. Both affected the shipment of goods even if the latter is explicitly directed at advertising services for which Canada has made no GATS commitments. For the moment the legality under the WTO of Bill C-103 will not be tested because of the negotiated settlement between Canada and the United States, unless another WTO member makes a challenge.

The Phantom Loophole and Prospective Split-Run Invasion

There are two puzzles about the rationales for recent Canadian policy measures. The first is the assumption that the *Sports Illustrated* split-run revealed a new loophole in Canadian legislation by avoiding the tariff through transferring content electronically across the border. The second is the widespread presumption that there were a large number of American publications about to exploit this loophole.

Since 1976, when Time Canada closed its Canadian editorial office, it has been publishing a split-run in Canada using editorial material shipped in from the United States, at first on microfilm and since 1986 electronically to the printing plant of Quebecor Inc. in Ontario.[23] Time Canada was never grandfathered with respect to the tariff and its actions have not been challenged for over two decades, during which time there was speculation about other firms entering Canada by imitating *Time's* way of doing business.[24] In 1984, *Newsweek* did so and published a number of Canadian split-run issues before ceasing publication for economic reasons.[25]

Elsewhere, we have speculated on why successive Canadian governments and the domestic periodical industry failed to draw *Time's* evasion of the tariff to the attention of the customs authorities.[26] One reason is that, like *Newsweek,* most other publications have not found a Canadian split-run to be an attractive proposition even with ineffective enforcement of the tariff and the income tax provision. Perhaps, the threat that significant entry would result in more effective Canadian enforcement of existing law deterred entry, but there is no evidence that enforcement became more vigilant after *Newsweek*, a significant player in the magazine industry, entered.

The assumed magnitude of the threat of split-run entry originates in a background study for the 1994 Task Force Report suggesting that any foreign magazine with an overflow circulation in Canada of 50,000 copies is a candidate for a split-run. This conclusion is repeated in a 1998 study for the Department of Canadian Heritage.[27] Our analysis of past entry and the nature of the Canadian industry indicate that this is an overestimate. The latest Periodical Publishing Survey produced by Statistics Canada lists 1166 publishers with 1552 publications. Many appeal to specialized segments of the market some of which have a unique Canadian focus such as *Quebec Home and School News* and *Lethbridge Living.* Some consumer magazines might be attracted to initiating a Canadian split-run, particularly now that attention has been drawn to the issue by the WTO decision and fallout, but, we repeat, they could have done this at any time since 1976. The authors consider the Internet a more significant challenge to and opportunity for the Canadian magazine industry than that posed by a "sucking noise" created by a northward flow of split-runs.

The 1998 study also notes that the Canadian magazine industry is underdeveloped relative to other countries because of the "lack of advertiser available titles and little or no coverage for many editorial segments."[28] We have argued elsewhere that the protection of culture has frequently fostered a dysfunctional culture of protectionism in the cultural industries.[29] Although we believe that to be generally true, the response of different sectors has varied. Those which have looked to external markets have prospered relative to those that have not. For example, Canadian film, video, and audiovisual production and exports grew at a rate of 8% and 32% respectively from 1990-91 to 1995-96. In 1995-96, exports were valued at C$321 million representing 37% of the value of production.[30] In contrast, the magazine industry has been stagnant in Canada. The value of output of newspapers and magazines declined at an annual rate of 2.7 percent between 1990 and 1995.[31] We have no figures for exports of magazines but they are generally considered to be negligible and industry spokespersons claim that exporting is virtually impossible.

Television producers still promote protection of the domestic market despite their growing dependence on international sales, but they do so less stridently. They have much to lose from being restricted to selling only in the Canadian market as a result of foreign retaliation. On the other hand, spokespersons representing magazine publishers continue to see the United States as a source of unfair competition through split-runs. If retaliation occurs, it will affect other sectors as the Canadian magazine industry has no significant hostage interests abroad. That there is another side to an open policy—the opportunity created to access a market for split-runs of Canadian originated magazines that is significantly larger than the domestic market—is seldom mentioned in the domestic policy discourse. It should be. The economies of scale from distributing content over a wider audience are significant in publishing. The financial commitments and managerial sophistication required to market a magazine abroad are not more demanding than for television programs and films.

IV. Conclusion

What implications follow from recent challenges and modifications to Canadian policy?

1. Domestic policies differ across the cultural industries depending on the configuration of economic coordination problems faced by the industry and the contractual and organizational arrangements that have evolved to cope with them. Where "black-box" administrative discretion is prevalent and enforcement is inconsistent, as has been documented for Canadian magazine policy in the past, real constraints as compared to nominal ones are difficult to determine. This opaqueness and the vagueness of the cultural imperative make policy assessment extremely difficult.

2. Magazine publishing typically involves both trade in goods and services. The fuzzy boundary between the significantly different obligations of GATT and GATS creates uncertainty about legal obligations and difficulties in establishing a consistent case law. The position of the boundary may change if electronic distribution becomes more important, but the overlap of regimes is

unlikely to disappear. Reducing the regime differences and clarifying the boundary will have a high payoff.

3. The Agreement between Canada and the United States of June 4, 1999 allows foreign publishers of periodicals to invest in Canada subject to the project generating net benefits. Net benefit requires, *inter alia*, a majority of original editorial content, either authored by Canadians or unique to the Canadian edition. The *alia* include hiring a resident editorial and support staff, establishing a business presence in Canada, and locating editing, typesetting, and printing in Canada. The Foreign Publishers Advertising Services Act will be amended to comply with the changed foreign investment rules and to allow foreign publications some leeway for carrying Canadian oriented advertisements. Canadian firms placing advertisements in foreign periodicals containing prescribed levels of original editorial will also be able to deduct a proportion, scaled to the amount of unique editorial content, of the expense for income tax purposes. The two countries have agreed to discuss any problems arising from implementation of the agreement with twenty days notice. Canada has introduced a subsidy program, the Canadian Magazine Fund, to compensate for the relaxation of the protective measures. C$150 million will be provided to the industry over the first three years of this program.

4. Whether the terms of the agreement coupled with the subsidy represent a net liberalization of current policy is moot. These changes occurred because of reactions and threatened responses by the U.S. Government to Canadian policies. The agreement may represent another square in the complex patchwork quilt of protective initiatives, grudging compromises, and special arrangements that have characterized the governance of the magazine trade in Canada. Perhaps they mark a long overdue turning point. Despite decades of protective policy attention, the Canadian periodical publishing industry is not entrepreneurial and has had little success in export markets. This is in contrast to the international successes achieved by Canadian individuals, organizations, and companies in other cultural industries.

5. Successive use of an informal political bargaining process to address foreign challenges to domestic policies is one way of proceeding. In our view it creates uncertainty for the industry players, in this case magazine publishers. Elsewhere we have proposed that consideration should be given to the negotiation of a sectoral agreement on the cultural industries similar to the approach taken for telecommunications and financial services.[32] Its architects will have to address many difficult measurement issues such as those documented above for the magazine industry—the nationality of content, to whom advertisements are addressed, and who controls firms.

Chronology of
Canadian Magazine Publishing Policies

1951   The Royal Commission on National Development in the Arts, Let-
        ters and Sciences notes that Canadian magazines did not request any
        protective measures but recommends lower tariffs on paper imported
        for publishing purposes.[33]

1961   The Royal Commission on Publications makes two substantive rec-
and   ommendations: Canadian advertisers should not be allowed to deduct
1965   for tax purposes advertising in foreign periodicals directed at the Ca-
        nadian market; and foreign periodicals containing advertising di-
        rected at the Canadian market should be stopped at the border.[34] In
        1965, these two recommendations are implemented as section 12a,
        now 19, of the Income Tax Act and item 9958 of the tariff schedule.
        Time and *Reader's Digest* are exempted from the discriminatory
        provisions of section 19 but not from the prohibitive tariff.

1970   A Canadian Senate committee on the mass media observes that *Time*
and   and *Reader's Digest* have increased their share of Canadian periodi-
1976   cal revenue from 43% in 1958 to 56% in 1969 and advocates cancel-
        ing the exemptions.[35] In 1976, Bill C-58 amends section 19 of the
        Income Tax Act eliminating the grandfathering of *Time* and
        Reader's Digest.[36] *Reader's Digest* establishes a Canadian Founda-
        tion that is licensed by the parent company to publish and sell adver-
        tising in Canada and is ruled to be a Canadian magazine.[37] *Time*
        closes its Canadian editorial offices but continues to publish a Cana-
        dian edition and sell advertising to Canadian companies. Editorial
        content is imported on microfilm into Canada.

1984   *Newsweek* publishes a number of split-runs in Canada but ceases
        publication in 1988. *National Geographic* considers but refrains
        from publishing a Canadian split-run.

1985   The Investment Canada Act requires a review of foreign investments
        in the cultural industries over $5 million for a direct acquisition and
        over $50 million for an indirect acquisition. A reviewable investment
        can only proceed if it generates a "net benefit."[38]

1986	*Time* begins importing editorial content for its Canadian split-run over telephone lines.
1989	The Canada-United States Free Trade Agreement exempts the cultural industries with four exceptions. Of these, three affect the magazine industry: the removal of Canadian tariffs for goods that are inputs to the cultural industries, an assurance by Canada of fair market compensation to foreign companies required to divest because of foreign ownership restrictions, and a removal by Canada of a restriction that magazines must be typeset and printed in Canada for a Canadian advertiser to be able to deduct advertising as a business expense.
1993 to 1995	Investment Canada rules that Time Canada may publish a Canadian edition of *Sports Illustrated.* The Canadian government establishes a Task Force on the Magazine Industry to address *inter alia* the development of more effective means of preventing foreign split-runs. Based on a recommendation in its interim report, the government bars further expansion of offerings by foreign magazine publishers operating in Canada under the Investment Canada Act. The Final Report of the Task Force contains eleven recommendations, one of which is levying an 80 percent excise tax per issue on the value of advertising of magazines distributed in Canada in foreign split-runs including those published by Canadian firms.[39] In 1995, the government enacts Bill C-103, levying an 80% tax on the total gross fees collected by the publisher for all advertisements in the Canadian edition of a split-run. *Time* and *Reader's Digest* are exempted but not *Sports Illustrated.*
1996 and 1997	In response to a 1996 request by Time Warner, the U.S. Government consults with Canada over its magazine policy and subsequently initiates the establishment of a panel under the WTO dispute settlement process over the excise tax, tariff, and the postal rates and subsidy. In 1997, both sides appeal different parts of the dispute panel's ruling. The original decision as amended by the Appellate Body rules against Canada on the excise tax, the tariff item, the preferential postal rates and the indirect manner in which the postal subsidy is paid.[40]

1998   Canada repeals the tariff and excise tax. Bill C-55, *The Foreign Pub-*
and   *lishers Advertising Services Act*, which prohibits foreign publishers
1999   from selling advertising aimed primarily at the Canadian market, is
passed and comes into force on July 1st, 1999. After protests from
the U.S. government over its contents, an agreement is negotiated.
The U.S. commits not to take any trade action with respect to Bill C-
55 under the WTO, NAFTA, or Section 301 of the U.S. Trade Act.
Canada agrees to amend Bill C-55 to allow foreign publishers to
publish up to 12% of advertisements aimed primarily at the Canadian
market with the percentage to rise to 15% in 18 months and to 18%
in 36 months time and to allow 50% of the normal deduction for
these advertisements. Canada will allow a new foreign publisher to
publish in Canada providing the magazine contains 80% original or
Canadian content and will grant Canadian advertisers 100% deduction for tax purposes on advertising in these publications. Canada
also shifts the administration of investment reviews for all the cultural industries including periodicals from Industry Canada to the
Minister of Canadian Heritage. The Canadian industry is promised a
subsidy package.[41]

Notes

[1]See *Statutes of Canada*, 1st session, 36th Parliament, Chapter 23; and News release,
Canada and United States Sign Agreement on Periodicals, Canadian Heritage, Ottawa,
June 4, 1999.

[2]See World Trade Organization, Report of Panel *Canada—Certain Measures Concerning Periodicals*, WT/DS31/R, 1997a; and Report of the Appellate Body, *Canada—
Certain Measures Concerning Periodicals*, WT/DS31/AB/R, 1997b.

[3]See Canada, *Report of the Royal Commission on Periodicals*. Ottawa: Queen's Printer,
1961, 4-7.

[4]See Canada, *Report of the Senate Committee on the Mass Media*. Ottawa: Queen's
Printer, 1970, Vol.1, 153.

[5]See Canada, *Report of the Task Force on the Canadian Magazine Industry, A Question
of Balance,* Ottawa, Minister of Supply and Services, 1994, 63.

[6]See Time Canada, Brief to the House of Commons Standing Committee on Transport
and Communications, Ottawa, April 29, 1999, 10.

[7]Developing predation benchmarks is particularly difficult with respect to subscription
prices and advertising rates. Advertising rates, for example, vary with circulation, characteristics of subscribers/readers and inter- and intra-media competition. More detailed
discussion of dumping issues is contained in our paper delivered to the 26th Annual
Conference of the Society for Historians of American Foreign Relations, June, 2000,
Toronto. Please contact the authors for a revised copy of the paper, now entitled, "No
bite, no bark: the mystery of magazine policy."

[8]See I. A. Litvak and C. J. Maule, *Cultural Sovereignty: The Time and Reader's Digest Case in Canada*, New York, Praeger, 1974, 14-39.

[9]American magazines shipped to Canada were mailed in the United States for delivery in Canada. Under the revenue-sharing arrangements between the two postal services, Canada carried most of the costs but collected few of the revenues. In 1981 new arrangements were negotiated so that the American postal service increased by 450% the terminal dues paid to Canada for mail originating in the United States, at which point there was less incentive to offer foreign periodicals lower rates to mail copies in Canada—see *Quill & Quire*, May 1983, 24.

[10]See Canada, *supra* note 4, at 453-66.

[11]See Time, *supra* note 6, at 11.

[12]Subscription information obtained from websites and subscription departments of periodicals.

[13]Direct subsidies paid exclusively to domestic producers are permitted under Article III.8(b) of the GATT. A specific subsidy that injured another WTO member's magazine industry or seriously prejudiced Canada's balance of WTO concessions and obligations is actionable under the Agreement on Subsidies and Countervailing Measures.

[14]See, for example, *Quill & Quire*, December 1984, 24-25.

[15]Revised Statutes of Canada, 1985, c. 28 (1st supp.).

[16]In testimony before a Canadian senate committee, a representative of an association representing Canadian magazine publishers stated that Internet magazines were not likely to be a significant competitive factor in the industry. Later it was noted that *Maclean's* a Canadian consumer magazine with a circulation in excess of 500,000 copies is available to subscribers on the Internet prior to hard copies being received. Many other magazines are also experimenting with different approaches to distributing material through their websites. See proceedings of the Standing Senate Committee on Transport and Communications, May 6, 1999.

[17]See Canada, *supra* note 5, at 66-7.

[18]Some years earlier in testimony to the Senate committee, a Canadian publisher pointed out the difficulty of administering the proposed changes to the income tax provisions- see Canada *supra* note 4, at Vol. 1, 161; and *Canadian Business*, February, 1983, 13-14.

[19]Other comparisons use Print Measurement Bureau data that measure readership rather than circulation. Using these data and various demographic subsets of audiences, it is probably possible to develop better comparisons, but the overall conclusion drawn seems to be a reasonable assessment of the situation.

[20]See *Quill & Quire*, December 1984, 24.

[21]Letter from Pierre Gravelle of Revenue Canada to the Managing Director of Time Canada Ltd. April 8, 1993.

[22]See Canada *supra* note 5, at 4.

[23]See Time *supra* note 6, at 7.

[24]See I. A. Litvak and C. J. Maule, "Bill C-58 and the regulation of periodicals in Canada," *International Journal,* 36(1), Winter 1980-1, 79; and *Quill & Quire*, May 1983, 24.

[25]A telephone interview with a former executive of *Newsweek* confirms that a number of issues were published in Canada between 1984 and 1988 containing both Canadian and American content. Printing took place in Owen Sound, Ontario. Some advertisers felt that they effectively reached the Canadian audience in the advertising paid for in the edition of *Newsweek* that reached Canada by way of overflow circulation.

[26]See Keith Acheson and Christopher Maule, *Much Ado about Culture, North American Trade Disputes*, Ann Arbor, University of Michigan Press, 1999, 199-200.

[27]The study undertaken for the Task Force is "The Canadian Periodical Publishing Industry: An Overview," prepared by Infometrica Ltd, Ottawa, February 10, 1994. It suggests that there are 44 consumer magazines with circulations of at least 50,000 copies per issue and another 65 with circulations between 20,000 and 50,000. The study estimates that about 53 American consumer magazines are potential entrants to the Canadian advertising market (pp. 6-2). The study by Harrison, Young, Personen and Newell (January 15, 1998) for the Department of Canadian Heritage picks up the 50,000 figure from the Infometrica study and undertakes an analysis on the impact on advertising expenditures in the magazine industry in Canada (pp.19-21).

[28]See Harrison study *supra* note 27, at 22.

[29]See Keith Acheson and Christopher Maule, "The Culture of Protection and the Protection of Culture—A Canadian Perspective in 1998", Paper presented at the Cultural Policies Symposium, Center for the Study of Western Hemispheric Trade University of Texas, Austin, February 2nd, 1998. An earlier version is available as Working Paper CIORU 98-01, Department of Economics, Carleton University, Ottawa, Canada, February 1998.

[30]The information is based on a survey designed to cover all firms in the industry. The revenue figure includes sales of assets. The figures for 1990-91 are from Statistics Canada 87F0010XPE, faxed to the authors by Statistics Canada. The 1995-96 data are from Statistics Canada, *The Daily* of March 27, 1998.

[31]Series D665376 of CANSIM matrix 5502. There is no series published solely for magazines. Canadian newspaper publishers have actively expanded abroad through production. Canadian magazine publishers have not.

[32]See Acheson and Maule, *supra* note 26, at Chapter 18. A 1999 report, *New Strategies for Culture and Trade*, by an advisory committee to the Minister of International Trade has proposed a new international instrument to address cultural diversity. It leaves open the question of whether it should be inside or outside the WTO.

[33]See Canada, *Report of the Royal Commission on National Development in the Arts, Letters, and Sciences*. Ottawa: King's Printer, 1951.

[34]Canada, *supra* note 3.

[35]Canada, *supra* note 4.

[36]In order for advertisers to be able to claim full deductibility for their advertisements in foreign periodicals, the publisher has to be 75% Canadian owned and the publication to contain content that is not substantially the same as the issue of the periodical that was printed, edited or published outside Canada.

[37]The details of the organizational changes are set out in the submission of Reader's Digest Magazines Limited to the House of Commons Standing Committee on Canadian Heritage, Ottawa, November 10, 1998.

[38]The definition of cultural industries in the act includes the publication, distribution and sale (including by a corner store) of magazines, see Investment Canada Act, *Revised Statutes of Canada*, 1985, c.28 (1st supp.), section 14.6(b).

[39]See Canada, *supra* note 5, at vi-vii

[40] See World Trade Organization, *supra* note 2.

[41]See News Release, *supra* note 1.

CHAPTER 19

Chile and Australia
GATS 2000: Towards Effective Liberalization of Trade in Services—Proposals for Action

Francisco Javier Prieto and Alison Burrows

I. Introduction

This chapter attempts to identify issues which, in our view, call for a special and decided effort to make significant progress towards the liberalization of trade in services in a new round of multilateral trade negotiations. These issues essentially refer to five major categories of problems in the agreement and ten weaknesses in the provisions currently in force, which we need to address in order to achieve fully the GATS goals.

1. Substantially reduce the discriminatory treatment among participating countries (Article II "Most-Favored-Nation Treatment"). Due account should be taken of justified exceptions falling under Article V "Economic Integration."

2. Improve provisions on transparency in order to guarantee compliance with this requirement (Article III "Transparency").

3. Improve the general disciplines to reduce and, ideally, avoid the impairment or nullification of specific commitments. Such impairments probably arise from deficiencies in the implementation of procedures, especially domestic regulations (Article VI "Domestic Regulation") and also practices that may impair the effectiveness of markets in conditions of full competition (Article VIII "Monopolies and Exclusive Service Suppliers" and Article IX "Business Practices").

4. Improve the effectiveness of provisions related to the adoption of Specific Commitments so that they may contribute more effectively to the purposes of transparency and progressive liberalization. These goals should be based on mutual advantage, and should achieve an overall balance of rights and obligations (Article XVI "Market Access" and Article XVII "National Treatment").

5. Improve provisions related to the application of Article IV "Increasing Participation of Developing Countries," especially to enhance the effectiveness of Article IV subparagraph 1.c) with regard to "liberalization of market access in sectors and modes of supply of export interest to them" and to the "Annex on Movement of Natural Persons Supplying Services Under the Agreement."

In light of these five major categories, we believe that the current state of the institutional framework regulating services is deficient and inadequate. Traditional issues of trade in goods have been solved to some extent in the different multilateral and regional arrangements.

Deeper integration of the world's economy seems unlikely, however, without substantial liberalization in a sector that is dominant in terms of its contribution to the world's GDP and employment. It is also an essential supplement—and the critical backbone—that will help secure the benefits arising from open and competitive global markets. The lack of substantial progress in trade in services may end up by weakening, and possibly even diluting, the dynamism shown by international trade in the past fifty years.

Reforms and improvements of the weaknesses affecting the GATS should, ideally, be addressed within the multilateral framework on which it is based, i.e., the WTO. Initiatives within regional or subregional agreements also offer a "second best" option to improve the insufficiencies of the multilateral institutional framework.

II. The Chilean and Australian Agendas for GATS 2000

Chile

The performance of Chilean services abroad has encouraged the Chilean Government to increase the liberalization of trade in services by entering into bilateral and regional Free Trade Agreements intended precisely to bring in strong disciplines in services with a view to developing a larger market for Chilean exports.

Chile has therefore signed Agreements on Trade in Services with Mexico and Canada. It is promoting similar initiatives with other Latin American and extra-regional partners—such as Mercosur and Central America—and furthering the process to create the Free Trade Area of the Americas (FTAA), and free trade agreements with the European Union and Korea. Chile is also participating actively in efforts to liberalize services in the APEC framework.

Chile continues to favor, as in the past, progress towards full integration of its economy to the world economy. Because Chile firmly believes that the multilateral system is the best route to make full use of the advantages of foreign trade, it wishes to advance towards making its bilateral and regional commitments multilateral ones. This is a sure way to open up markets around the world, make better use of its competitive advantages, benefit from efficient, less costly, imported services and, consequently improve the global competitiveness of the Chilean economy and the well being of its population.

Therefore, just as Chile has been willing to open up its markets to the world and has clearly benefited from this process, we also would like the world to open up to Chilean services and to share with us most of the advantages that this new scenario has to offer. We strongly believe that, in order to achieve this goal, GATS 94 needs to be subjected to significant reforms.

Australia

Australia's services sector creates more than 8 out of every 10 jobs in Australia and accounts for more than two thirds of GDP. Services also comprise almost a quarter of Australia's total exports. Since the end of the Uruguay Round, services exports have increased so they are roughly equivalent to imports. Operating within an open and extremely competitive regime, service providers across the range of service sectors, particularly education, tourism, telecommunications, banking and insurance, professional and business services, have significantly improved their capacity to compete with overseas service providers in any market. Equally importantly, they have enabled cost savings and productivity gains across the range of Australia's primary and secondary sectors.

Because of the substantial scope for productivity improvements in the services sector, liberalization would be expected to result in big gains. Modeling commissioned by the Australian Government[1] has indicated a substantial annual gain in world welfare of US$250 billion if global distortions in the provisions of services were reduced by 50 per cent. The biggest winners in dollar terms would be the biggest economies. All economies would stand to gain, however, and, in proportion to the size of GDP, the gains would be spread fairly evenly.

For these reasons, Australia is closely committed to the WTO services negotiations and wants to see results both in terms of market access and national treatment, and in terms of transparent, stable and predictable trading regimes.

III. Main Weaknesses of the GATS: Ten Challenges For Negotiators

The weaknesses affecting the current GATS architecture are being increasingly acknowledged by its Members. The Agreement needs to advance further in the liberalization of trade in services. There is a general feeling that the commitments undertaken are limited in terms of sectoral coverage, as well as in respect of the modes of supply. Furthermore, the measures listed in the schedules either reflect, at best, a *status quo,* or else they establish conditions and limitations that fail to reflect the real level of the liberalization of domestic service industries.

Another fact that precludes assessing the commercial significance of the commitments included in the National Schedules is the lack of adequate provisions covering various issues. This leaves ample space for ambiguity and lack of transparency, a fact that has given rise to references to the Agreement as "what you see is not what you get." This section will attempt to summarize the main weaknesses that, in our view, characterize the current architecture of the WTO General Agreement on Trade in Services (GATS)[2].

1. GATS Classification Systems and Coverage

The relative newness of the international dimension of services partly accounts for the preliminary nature of the existing service classification systems. Full clarity in this regard is essential to advance in the process of liberalization, particularly in terms of clearly defining the scope of the commitments involved.

Classification systems are a key factor in providing clear and precise terminology, with mutually excluding components, that enable an unequivocal definition of the set of activities falling under the specific disciplines of the trade agreement. The heterogeneous nature of services and the constant emergence of new services also make work complex.

There are two main sources used by GATS Members to specify their commitments on trade in services. First, the Central Product Classification (CPC) system—prepared provisionally by the United Nations, which is still under review. Second, on that same basis, a summarized list prepared by the former GATT Secretariat, known as the Services Sectoral Classification List[3].

Both classification systems are clearly insufficient since they provide incomplete coverage and ambiguous definitions. Thus, for example, the NAFTA countries have developed their own classification system for all industrial activities included in the agreement through the so-called NAICS (North American Industrial Classification System). The WTO Secretariat itself has pointed out the problems created by these deficiencies, and the OECD has drawn up different proposals to supplement and expand the sub-categories of services in areas such as Environmental Services. These documents show how deficiencies in the classification systems can give rise to major trade divergences when it comes to specifying and interpreting the scope and depth of the commitments undertaken by the parties.[4]

In this regard, it is important for the disciplines to be fully comprehensive and applicable to all services. For example, air transport is increasingly important for the internationalization of many other services (such as professional services, tourism, etc.) and also as a supplement to trade in goods (perishable goods such as fruits and flowers). Expanding the coverage of air transport will be a priority for the new round of services negotiations and, in the long term, fully incorporating air transport to the Agreement would be desirable.

The question of electronic commerce also needs to be addressed. We support the WTO work program's premise that e-commerce is simply another means of transacting commerce. WTO commitments relating to trade—for instance, regarding national treatment, protection of intellectual property or market access in services—apply regardless of whether trade is conducted electronically or otherwise. In a practical sense, the advent of e-commerce exemplifies and accentuates the general trend towards borderless commercial exchanges and the facilitation of access to world markets that are essential elements of the background to the WTO. Digital technology and the growth of digital networks provide an unprecedented means for taking advantage of the market opportunities created by the WTO trade regime. In particular, they offer opportunities for SMEs and enterprises in developing countries to improve their access to international markets.

It follows that e-commerce should be subject to the principles of free and fair trade that apply to conventional commerce, as conducted within the existing framework of the WTO's binding commitments, with appropriate clarifications and adaptations if necessary. We should maintain a clear separation between the nature of services supplied and the means of supply ("content" and "carriage," respectively). It would then be possible to view the components of an electronic transaction, such as financial services transactions and use of telecommunications infrastructure, as already covered by different aspects of the GATS.

Goods ordered and delivered electronically should continue to enter tariff-free. We therefore support the indefinite extension of the May 1998 Ministerial decision not to impose customs duties on electronic transmissions. It would clearly be a retrograde step to respond to the advent of e-commerce as a significant factor in economic growth by introducing a new category of tariffs.

The expected benefits of the growth of e-commerce will only be fully realized if there is widespread and equitable access to the infrastructure supporting electronic transactions. Effective access entails, at least, the technical means for interconnection, the establishment of a reliable and widespread telecommunications infrastructure capable of supporting high bandwidth traffic, and low-cost and equitable pricing of telecommunications and Internet-related services.

A pragmatic approach should be followed on classification issues, recognizing that, on the whole, the challenges thrown up by e-commerce are simply accentuated forms of existing trends in international trade in goods and services. This observation applies to a specific issue that will arise in this context: whether things ordered and delivered electronically are properly characterized as "goods" or "services," and the consequent implications for the application of the relevant WTO rules. It is probably mistaken to seek a definitive determination of this question, which may, in the end, be resolved according to the nature of the specific transaction. The classification process should aim for the maximum separation between the nature of services supplied and the means of supply.[5]

Challenges in terms of classification are not limited to simply improving the coverage provided by the classification. As we shall see below, organizing service industries into clusters of interconnected services may prove essential in order to improve the negotiating modalities currently used by the GATS.

The effectiveness and efficiency of the internationalization of specific services usually depends on the possibility of articulating bundles or clusters of related services. A cluster may thus be defined as a service node around which several interconnected services are articulated and which allow the main service to operate efficiently. Identifying services to be included in a cluster could be done in close consultation with industry.

Multimodal transport is a precedent for this work. During the maritime services negotiations, model schedules were prepared for multimodal transport. The schedules were designed to cover various regulatory regimes and services, subsectors and transactions going beyond the maritime transport sector.

Electronic commerce provides another clear example. E-commerce acquires the features of a service node which, in order to operate efficiently, needs a cluster of services such as courier services, air cargo transportation, customs agents, distribution services, etc.

Careful consideration should also be given to cluster negotiations on environmental services. The cluster could include all services that are necessary for environmental management and protection: sewage and refuse disposal; sanitation and other environmental protection services; installation and construction services; wholesale and retail trade services; professional, scientific and technical services; production services; and maintenance and repair services.[6]

Energy is not classified as a sector at all in terms of the sectoral classification list. There is further work to be done in identifying the cluster of subsectors that make up energy services without changing the mutually-exclusive structure of the services sectoral list.

For example, making full use of professional services commitments may be impaired or nullified by the lack of commitments related to air transport. Likewise, within a given professional service, commitments undertaken with regard to legal services may prove less attractive if they are not accompanied by similar commitments in accountancy and auditing.

Similarly, the marketing of many services (including education, business and transportation services) may be seriously affected by the lack of commitments in the liberalization of distribution services or information networks. The conclusion to the above is that it may be interesting to explore the possibility of identifying clusters of services that need cumulative binding to make them operative and render them commercially significant.[7]

The adoption of a liberalization scheme based on clusters could allow for more coherent and effective procedures. Member countries could thus establish their commitments based on a list of clusters that reflects their specific trade interests and that, furthermore, adequately protects their aspirations in terms of exchanging concessions. At the same time, the parties could reserve the existing measures that do not conform with Market Access and National Treatment obligations. Countries could then undertake commitments in clusters of their choice (Positive List with respect to the clusters) and at the same time maintain the existing non-conforming measures they intend to keep (Negative List with respect to the treatment of non-conforming measures).

2. Defining Trade on the Basis of Modes of Supply

A commonly accepted fact is that the internationalization of services differs considerably from the internationalization of goods. Two forms of internationalizing services are usually identified: the first involves cross-border transactions while the second involves establishing a *commercial presence*. Cross-border trade is similar to trade in goods since it involves trade between residents of different countries. Commercial presence, however, involves transactions between residents of the same country. Equating this last mode with traditional "foreign trade" relations has been more difficult to grasp.

Cross-border trade involves—among others—using transportation based on telecommunication systems (telephones, fax, e-mail, e-commerce for consultancy services, databases, sale of software, music CDs, books, etc.) in a manner quite similar to the methods used by trade in goods when air, land and maritime transport is used. Cross-border trade also takes place when the transactions involve the temporary movement of consumers to the country of residence of the supplier (e.g., tourism, health care, education) or the temporary movement of the supplier to the country of residence of the consumer (e.g., professional, technical and specialized services, entertainment and promotional services).

Commercial presence, on the other hand, requires the "permanent" movement of the factors of production, including capital and human resources. It is primarily used in services that require direct and sustained contact between suppliers and consumers. Such is the case with many financial services (customer banking); distribution services (large department stores, supermarkets and the like); domestic transport services (urban and interurban, air, land and maritime transport); chains of movie houses, fast-food outlets, hotels and restaurants. Commercial presence may vary substantially depending on the type of legal entity authorized as well as on requirements of international capital movements. Thus, commercial presence may range from franchising, to establishing representative offices, opening up branch offices, establishing affiliates or purchasing an existing company.

The mutually-exclusive definition of the four modes of supply as in the current architecture of the GATS has led to numerous ambiguities. In many industries it is difficult—and perhaps even impossible—to distinguish a single adequate mode of supply to conduct trade operations. Governments may find it equally difficult to identify the measures that affect only one specific mode of supply, and may therefore be forced not to make binding commitments for related measures. Consequently, this arbitrary separation renders ambiguous the true commercial significance of the measures listed by the member countries in their National Schedules.

Furthermore, the inclusion of commercial presence as a mode of supply has tended to produce a serious imbalance in the outcome of the agreement. The current use of four modes of supply introduces a bias against the undertaking of commitments in "cross-border trade in services" and favors the adoption of commitments under Mode Three "Commercial Presence."[8] Indeed, a significant number of countries have felt more inclined to undertake commitments under this mode of supply. Commitments in the other modes of supply tend to be functional to Mode Three.

In fact, a comparative analysis of the frequency of commitments of each of the four modes of supply shows Commercial Presence as the mode with the lowest percentage of unbound activities.[9] Moreover, in a number of sectors, e.g., financial, construction and engineering, commitments under other modes of supply are usually designed to give effect to the Commercial Presence commitments. In other words, most commitments under Mode Four (Natural Persons) essentially serve to make effective commercial presence commitments since they usually involve intra-firm movement of personnel—e.g. top-level executives, members of the board and professional staff linked to commercial presence. A similar situation is apparent with regard to Mode One (Cross-Border Supply).[10]

The above gives rise to considerable confusion among trade diplomats as well as among individuals who should benefit from its results, i.e., service industries and consumers.

There are some sectors, however, where commercial presence has never been the dominant mode of supply—e.g., telecoms. We will also need to take account of the growing use of the Internet—commercial presence may no longer be required when services can be provided over the Internet—this is particularly relevant to services involving design, telemedicine and audiovisual services.

3. Provisions on Transparency

The heterogeneous nature of measures affecting trade in services underscores the importance of improving the transparency of such measures. This is a key element to make a user friendly GATS for the business community. Current provisions on transparency in Article III are quite limited in this respect. Requirements are confined to the gradual establishment of inquiry points and to notification requirements that are limited to amendments in measures listed in the National Schedules. These obligations are clearly insufficient to provide greater transparency with respect to measures affecting trade in services.

That said, we need to be clear on the fact that the idea is not to impose a long, complicated and costly procedure on Members that would translate into exhaustive notification procedures of encyclopedic proportions. This process would be impossible for the countries to undertake and it would also offer no operational advantages to the users of such information. Measures that may affect trade in services—particularly non-conforming in terms of the obligations established by the agreement—are numerous and varied. Not all these measures have the same capability to obstruct trade in services, however, and different measures have a different impact depending on the services involved. Some ideas are proposed under item 5 for the development of formulas that could rank approaches on the basis of their relative impact on trade in services.

Model schedules would assist in making schedules more transparent and user friendly, but other methods are needed. In sectoral negotiations, we want to see more readily available information on regulatory measures to help us assess whether a measure is the least trade-restrictive necessary to achieve a policy objective. We do not want to see all regulatory measures listed in schedules. That would appear to legitimize unduly trade-restrictive measures, and would require frequent updating in some cases. We need direct links between sectoral schedules and inquiry points, or electronic schedules linked to websites on the full range of domestic regulation, maintained by individual Members.

The disciplines on domestic regulation could, however, be strengthened by additional requirements: a prior consultation obligation, such as the one envisaged in the accountancy disciplines; and an obligation to explain the policy rationale of a measure—especially of a new measure—on request.[11]

We will also need to consider how to build on the examples of model schedules and of the Reference Paper developed during the telecoms negotiations. The telecoms model delivered transparency—the schedules for basic telecoms are more consistent and more user friendly than the original schedules, and mis-scheduling was avoided. The model schedule also gave a framework for binding the important principles of the Reference Paper, especially competitive safeguards and separation of regulatory and operational functions. It is a flexible approach, which allows Members to make commitments consistent with the level of development of their economy. The Reference Paper is obviously sector specific, but it would be possible to create other such papers for particular sectors, using its principles on competitive safeguards, transparency and access to other individual sectors. Its provisions on universal obligations would also have application to some sectors.

4. Discrimination among Members: Exemptions to the Most-Favored-Nation Clause

Most-Favored-Nation Treatment has been defined as the cornerstone of the multilateral trade system and the key piece in all the WTO agreements. Unconditional adherence to this obligation is perceived as the best protection to prevent undue use of economic and political pressures among Members, and also as the fastest and most efficient way to multilateralize the commitments exchanged by Members.

The Annex on Exemptions to the obligations of Article II sets forth "the conditions under which a Member, at the entry into force of this agreement, is exempted from its obligations under paragraph 1 of Article II." Likewise, paragraph 2 establishes that "Any new exemptions applied for after the date of entry into force of the WTO Agreement shall be dealt with under paragraph 3 of Article IX of that Agreement."

Although the Annex establishes that: "In principle, such exemptions should not exceed a period of ten years...," both the number of exemptions listed—especially by developed countries—and the numerous cases in which exemptions involve an indefinite duration period raise a point of concern with regard to the full implementation of the MFN obligation. If we take too long in meeting this obligation, we will weaken the main purpose of the multilateral trade system and its credibility among countries adversely affected by exemptions will also be reduced.

5. Limiting "Free Riders" and Negotiating Modalities

Notwithstanding the assertions in the preceding paragraph, aspects of the Agreement that induce all Members to assume substantive commitments on liberalizing services evidently need to be strengthened. Accordingly, a scheme should be sought to prevent having a significant number of Members benefit from commitments exchanged by some Members without making significant contributions to the efforts of the international community to advance in the nondiscriminatory liberalization of services.

Maximizing the benefits of free trade requires considerable contributions by all Members of the Agreement. Other regional or sub-regional trade agreements seem to have dealt with this issue more satisfactorily. One possible alternative is to modify the structure of the existing agreement so as to have Market Access (Article XVI), National Treatment (Article XVII) and Additional Commitments (Article XVIII) become part of the General Obligations of the Agreement.

This may be facilitated by the adoption of commitments on the basis of clusters of related services. In many cases, undertaking commitments in a specific service activity may be totally ineffective and commercially insignificant, if the commitment is not accompanied by commitments adopted in other activities that supplement the service in question. This situation, which is slightly clearer in the case of telecommunications services where the same activity simultaneously involves a service and a means of distribution and transportation, may be less evident than in other service categories where important linkages occur for business opportunities to materialize.

A third aspect of the negotiating scheme is related to the provisions of Article XIX "Progressive Liberalization." Article XIX establishes that progressive liberalization shall be achieved by means of successive rounds of negotiations, the first of which should take place five years after the date of entry into force of the Agreement, and periodically thereafter. The weakness of this provision is that it does not contemplate methods for further liberalization in the periods between negotiating rounds. An approach similar to the "ratchet effect" included in other trade agreements would allow for progress in binding measures subject to liberalization in the time between one round and the next.[12]

More immediately, in the 2000 negotiations, we will have to find a pragmatic means of giving Members credit for autonomous liberalization. This issue closely affects a number of developing countries, and/or countries that have been affected by the East Asian crisis. A relatively simple mechanism would be to allow countries that have undertaken substantial liberalization since the Uruguay Round to trade off binding those measures against new offers from other Members in the request-offer process.

But the possibilities of making progress in this sphere would require some amendments to the current wording of GATS Articles XVI and XVII. In particular, such amendments should contemplate the inclusion of mandatory provisions setting forth the limitations and conditions that the Members may wish to establish regarding the application of said articles. The obligations suggested should be based on existing measures.

The fourth concern in this respect is linked to the issue of transparency. As opposed to trade in goods—where legitimate, clear and transparent instruments are available to regulate trade flows, i.e., customs tariffs—trade in services is affected by a complex mixture of non-tariff measures that make it difficult to determine the degree of liberalization for a given service market. Furthermore, the multilateral system has been able to deal effectively with the main non-tariff barriers affecting trade in goods.

Several efforts are under way to categorize and even quantify the commercial impact of measures affecting trade in services. The World Bank and the Australian Government's Productivity Commission[13] are leading these efforts.[14] In light of such work, methods could probably be developed to establish a set of measures, for each category of services, grouping these with the biggest impact on trade flows in each of the identifiable categories or subcategories of services. The WTO Secretariat has provided effective support for the exercise of identifying measures affecting trade in services. The material collected in twenty-two sectors and the documents distributed by several member countries in these same sectors may be a highly valuable source to make progress in this respect.[15]

6. "Loopholes" that Impair Commitments: "What You See Is Not What You Get"

Trade in services underscores, in a very particular way, the significance of special considerations on issues as important as consumer protection, market stability, level of specialization, technical proficiency and professional responsibility of service providers, national security, health protection, protection of law and order and the prevention of fraudulent practices.[16] Some of these concerns are reflected in Article VI (Domestic Regulation), Article XIV (General Exceptions) and Article XIV Bis (Security Exceptions).

The current wording of Article VI, however, still leaves room for arbitrariness and discrimination in establishing the requirements and procedures for certification, technical standards and licensing requirements, especially in the rendering of professional, technical and specialized services.[17] Given that these requirements and procedures do not fall within the scope of Article XVI (Market Access) and Article XVII (National Treatment), frequently the commercial significance of a commitment that includes the term "None" in both columns may be totally impaired due to the lack of transparent, appropriate, nondiscriminatory mechanisms with respect to the requirements and procedures regarding qualification requirements, technical standards and licensing requirements.[18]

Nevertheless, cause for concern arises from the unfinished tasks and the slowness in working to make effective the provisions of GATS Article VI.4 establishing that the Council for Trade in Services shall, through appropriate bodies it may establish, develop any necessary disciplines to ensure that measures relating to qualification requirements, technical standards and licensing requirements do not constitute unnecessary barriers to trade in services.

The current wording of this article makes the final goal of this provision ambiguous. On the one hand, it is part of the General Obligations of the Agreement since it establishes the objective of advancing towards achieving harmonized systems for accreditation, licensing requirements and technical standards. On the other hand, and especially with regard to Article VI.5, it sets forth a more restricted interpretation of this objective. This last point establishes the obligation that measures relating to qualification requirements, technical standards and licensing requirements do not create unnecessary barriers to trade in services, but this is limited exclusively to sectors subject to specific commitments.[19]

The development of an effective necessity test, according to the provisions of Article VI.4, would be an important contribution to the results of the next round of services negotiations. The necessity test would be used to determine whether measures to implement a policy objective are the least trade-restrictive available. It should be developed so it is consistent with other WTO Agreements. For example, the following definition of the necessity test in the SPS Agreement could be revised so that it applied to services: "a measure is not more trade-restrictive than required unless there is another measure, reasonably available taking into account technical and economic feasibility, that achieves the appropriate level of sanitary or phytosanitary protection and is significantly less restrictive to trade" (SPS Article 5, footnote). For "the appropriate level of sanitary or phytosanitary protection," Members could consider substituting "a legitimate policy objective."[20]

Domestic regulation disciplines should also take into account the work performed by the Working Group on Accountancy Services (particularly the adoption of "Disciplines on Domestic Regulation Applicable to Accountancy Services"),[21] the regulatory disciplines contained in the GATS Annex on Telecommunications, the "Reference Paper" on regulatory principles[22] for Basic Telecommunications prepared by the pertinent negotiating group, the Annex on Financial Services in the paragraphs referring to prudential issues (point 4), and the recognition agreements (point 5). This path would ensure an acceptable degree of nondiscriminatory liberalization and would adequately safeguard issues linked to consumer protection, market stability, technical proficiency and the professional responsibility of service providers.[23]

The numerous instances in which nationality or permanent residence requirements are established for service suppliers is another situation that, in practice, completely closes access to certain markets. Members should encourage the elimination of nationality or permanent residence requirements as a precondition to meet qualification requirements, technical standards and licensing requirements. The establishment of no local presence requirement is also a desirable goal.

7. Defending Fair and Loyal Market Competition

As progress is made in introducing free market policies, making regulatory systems more flexible, and advancing in exposing domestic economic activities to international competition while confining the State to purely subsidiary activities, the need to improve institutional schemes to ensure markets function efficiently becomes even more essential.

This reality is particularly significant with regard to services, where natural monopolies continue to operate in large sectors. Some of the problems that make it imperative to have regulations to stimulate competitive conditions in markets where these do not arise spontaneously, include the use of restrictive trade practices, the relative imbalance involving big companies vis-à-vis poorly organized consumer groups—such as the users of many services—and the inefficiencies that may result from difficulties in identifying critical links in the complex network of interconnected services.

GATS provisions are clearly insufficient in this respect. One particular cause for concern is the status of Article IX "Business Practices." Although the Article acknowledges that "certain business practices (...) may restrain competition and thereby restrict trade in services," it merely calls for member countries to enter into consultation with a view to eliminating such practices and to establishing that Members should examine these matters with "sympathetic consideration." We should examine the feasibility of drawing up multilateral and mandatory disciplines, using as a precedent the principles already agreed to by a number of Members in the Financial Services Understanding (FSU). The FSU goes significantly beyond Article VIII on treatment on monopoly rights, by requiring that Members list all existing monopoly rights in its schedule, and endeavour to eliminate them or reduce their scope.

8. Meager Progress in Terms of the Movement of Natural Persons

As briefly mentioned in point 2 above, commitments achieved in services provided through the temporary presence of natural persons are extremely limited. This has been a determining factor in reducing the attraction of the Agreement, especially for developing countries. Differences in the financial capability of countries—where direct foreign investment is concentrated among a reduced number of developed countries—makes Mode Three (Commercial Presence) less attractive and feasible as a mode of supplying services to a large number of GATS member countries.

From this perspective, the commercial value of the abundant concessions and commitments undertaken under this mode are scarcely interesting to a large number of participants. Most member countries have little likelihood of making use of international markets if they can only do so by exporting their meager capital that, potentially, has multiple alternative allocations in their own economies. This serious imbalance may make it impossible to convince a large group of countries of the opportunities and benefits offered by the multilateral trading system.

Big opportunities are opening up for countries with ample supplies of qualified human resources, ready to render low cost services thanks to increasingly lower costs in international transport, improved controls for supervising foreign citizens in the countries, enhanced fluency in world communications and a growing and homogeneous demand for standardized and massive goods and services from different markets.

Unfortunately, this is not the case with the results achieved through the GATS to date. The limited commitments available in this field are restricted to intra-company personnel movements and to top-level executives, with little progress in the field of professional services and much less—if not none at all—in the case of suppliers of technical and specialized services in less sophisticated jobs.

Once more, the experience of regional arrangements might throw some light on how to approach needed reforms in this field. Undoubtedly, such agreements have known how to protect justified concerns on how to preserve the stability of their own labor markets and their independence to implement their own migration policies and regulations. But nothing has stopped them from creating the necessary conditions to facilitate the international movement of service suppliers to their mutual benefit.

The limitations of the current "Annex on Movement of Natural Persons Supplying Services Under the Agreement" and the difficulties that the WTO Working Group has encountered in making progress on this subject should not discourage the search for efficient solutions in this important matter. The current asymmetry between the provisions and the rigorousness of regulations governing obligations in terms of commercial presence should point the way to a balance on the temporary entry of service suppliers. We should develop measures that will facilitate their movement and not threaten the natural prerogatives of the countries with regard to their migration policies. Possibilities include adoption of speedy business visa systems, clear definitions of who is deemed to be an international service provider, facilitation of the movement of intracorporate transferees etc. As patterns of services trade evolve, e.g., greater use of the Internet and employment of highly-skilled local employees rather than expatriate staff, business mobility will become even more important.

Australia and Chile have already demonstrated their interest in facilitation of travel for business people. Both Australia and Chile, as well as Malaysia, Hong Kong, Korea, New Zealand, and the Philippines have joined the APEC Business Travel Card scheme. The APEC Business Travel Card is an Australian initiative based on an innovative pre-clearance process allowing business people applying to their home government to receive short-term entry to participating APEC countries. The APEC Business Travel Card not only simplifies pre-travel arrangements but also streamlines the entry and exit of cardholders through special lanes at major international airports in participating countries.

9. Imprecisions and Deficiencies in Provisions on "Economic Integration"

One of the basic principles of the Multilateral Trade System, since its beginnings, has been to allow pairs or groups of member countries to advance faster in enhancing their mutual economic integration than what multilateral agreements allow. The rationale underlying this approach is the expectation that these more advanced integration agreements will eventually converge towards a deeper global integration system. The inclusion of Article XXIV of the GATT in the original text of said Agreement is proof of this fact.
Implementing these requirements has not been easy. The last Round of Multilateral Trade Negotiations (Uruguay Round) had to address this issue once more, and improve the provisions established in the original articles, by means of an "Understanding on the Interpretation of Article XXIV of the General Agreement on Tariffs and Trade of 1994."[24]

The subject has caused concern among several Members of the WTO, who underscored the need to supplement and improve GATS Article V on Economic Integration,[25] together with the provisions related to Article XXVII "Denial of Benefits." Both are fundamental aspects when it comes to determining legitimate spaces for granting mutual preferences, and guaranteeing that benefits instituted in economic integration agreements will not allow the concessions exchanged to spill over and benefit third countries.

Australia has proposed two bodies of work to cover issues of importance to WTO Members, to be completed within three years, in line with the time-frame agreed for key negotiations on agriculture and services. This would ensure that outcomes of these negotiations are not undermined by even greater derogation from MFN obligations as regional trading arrangements (RTAs) continue to be established. One body of work would examine the systemic issues associated with RTAs. The relationship between RTAs and the multilateral trading system should be scrutinized, leading to clarification of the legal rights and obligations of WTO Members when negotiating RTAs. The other body of work would relate to improving the procedures for the WTO's work on RTAs.[26]

10. Weak Provisions on "Increasing Participation of Developing Countries"

GATS Article IV on "Increasing Participation of Developing Countries" includes some provisions intended to facilitate their participation "... *inter alia*, through access to technology on a commercial basis..." and "...the improvement of their access to distribution channels and information networks." In most cases, however, developing countries have been unable to take advantage of the possibilities apparently offered by these provisions. This calls for a major effort, in terms of imagination and practical measures. Possibly, some of the solutions are linked to the themes developed in *paragraph 5 above* on the need to identify service clusters to give real commercial meaning to commitments and also to what is described in *paragraph 8* on the Annex on the Movement of Natural Persons. Credit for autonomous liberalization will also be relevant.

IV. Proposals for Action

We believe that addressing all these ten issues simultaneously in the multilateral arena is, undoubtedly, the ideal route. The potential of regional agreements, however, appears to be a *second best* option of undeniable value. Insofar as regional spaces permit like-minded economies to come closer, they also allow reforms to cut deeper and permit enhanced trade liberalization aimed at full economic integration. Likewise, by making such regional spaces larger, contradictions with the multilateral system will diminish while the possibility of generating trade will increase and the potential effects of trade distortion and deviation will decrease.

The Australia–New Zealand Closer Economic Relations (CER) Protocol on Trade in Services is a benchmark for liberalization of services trade internationally. In contrast with the positive list approach used in many free trade agreements, the CER Services Protocol adopts a negative list approach. The few sectors excluded from the obligations of the Protocol are listed, in the form of inscriptions. The Protocol is broad in terms of sectoral coverage, and the inscriptions are regularly reviewed.

These benefits of regional agreements are clear and feasible in the case of Western Hemisphere countries. The process set in motion by the Santiago Summit in April 1999 to negotiate a Free Trade Area of the Americas (FTAA) guarantees this. This process offers a unique opportunity for the countries of the hemisphere to place themselves at the vanguard of the reform process of the Multilateral System by developing disciplines that effectively comply with the requirement of being GATS plus in terms of services and of creating the conditions to give new impulse and vigor to intra-hemisphere trade and, consequently, to the wealth and well-being of its population.

In 1994, FTAA member countries attained 23.5% of the total world exports in services and 22.8% of world exports in goods. Although the average hemispheric ratio of services to goods is similar to the worldwide average (27% for FTAA countries versus a 26% world average), the ratio changes considerably among FTAA countries.[27] Twelve out of the 34 participating countries export services at least at double the rate of their export earnings in goods (including one, Antigua and Barbuda, with a seven-fold ratio) while 6 other countries export services at rates ranging from 34 % to 97% of their export earnings in goods.

These are some of the reasons for developing a series of hemispheric disciplines related to services that may, eventually, converge towards the multilateral system, particularly in fields in which it is not possible to initiate reforms in that respect during the forthcoming Round of Multilateral Trade Negotiations.

V. Urgent Priorities

1. Promote expanded commitments in *all* service sectors and modes of supply.

2. Develop a negotiating modality based on the adoption of commitments organized, *wherever possible* around *clusters*, allowing for reservations on non-conforming measures regarding the Market Access and National Treatment obligations.

3. Develop a methodology to enhance greater transparency of the commercial significance of reservations that affect Market Access and National Treatment, selecting and weighting the protection effect of measures on specific *clusters*.

4. Develop a domestic regulation necessity test to prevent qualification requirements and procedures, technical standards and licensing requirements from turning into unnecessary barriers to trade in services.

5. Facilitate, by means of special disciplines, the temporary entry of service suppliers to the markets of member countries.

6. Improve foreign and domestic institutional schemes to ensure the adequate functioning of the markets. The existence of natural monopolies, asymmetries in the size of competitors, and the need to protect the interests and well-being of users call for developing standards that permit simulating highly competitive conditions in markets where these do not occur spontaneously.

Notes

[1] "Global Trade Reform: Maintaining Momentum," Australian Department of Foreign Affairs and Trade, 1999. Canberra, Australia.

[2] See especially, "Recent Developments in Services Trade -Overview and Assessment" Background Note by the Secretariat. Doc. S/C/W/94 9 February 1999. WTO.

[3] See also: UN Central Product Classification Revision 1 1998 United Nations Statistical Division (UNSD); Lista de Clasificación de los Sectores de Servicios. Doc. MTN.GNS/W/120. GATT Secretariat; Íssues Paper No 6: Services Classification, March 1994, p.2 Bureau of Economic Analysis, US Government; IMF Balance of Payments Manual rev. 5, International Monetary Fund; "A system of health accounts for international data collection, Part I: Principles and methods. Doc. STD/NA/RD(98)4 OECD Statistical Directorate.

[4] See "Preparing for the GATS 2000 Negotiations" Communication from Switzerland. Doc. S/C/W103 23 March 1999, WTO.

[5] "Work Program on Electronic Commerce," Communication from Australia. S/C/W/108. WTO 18 May 1999.

[6] APEC EVSL Experts' Group document, 1999.

[7] See especially the Notes prepared by the WTO Secretariat to the Council on Trade in Services with regard to: Accountancy Services (S/C/W/73); Advertising Services S/C/W/47; Air Transport Services (S/C/W/59; Architectural and Engineering Services (S/C/W/44); Audiovisual Services (S/C/W/40); Computer and Related Services (S/C/W/45); Construction and Related Engineering Services (S/C/W/38; Distribution Services (S/C/W/37); Education Services (S/C/W/49); Energy Services (S/C/W/49); Energy Services (S/C/W/52); Environmental Services (S/C/W/46); Financial Services (S/C/W/72); Health and Social Services (S/C/W/50); Land and Transport Services Part 1 (S/C/W/60); Land and Transport Services Part 2 (S/C/W/61); Legal Services (S/C/W/43); Maritime Transport Services (S/C/W/62); Postal and Courier Services (S/C/W/39); Telecommunication Services (S/C/W/74); Tourism Services (S/C/W/51).

[8] So much so, that a document of the WTO Secretariat describes the Agreement on Services as "Rules for Growth and Investment."

[9] "Structure of Commitments for Modes One, Two, and Three" Note by the Secretariat. Doc. S/C/W99 and "Presence of Natural Persons (Mode Four)" Doc. S/C/W/75. WTO 3 March 1999 and 8 December 1998, respectively.

[10] Op. Cit.

[11] Communication from Australia on domestic regulation. S/WPDR/W/1. WTO, 19 July 1999.

[12] See Chapter XII of the North America Free Trade Agreement.

[13] "Australia's Restrictions on Trade in Financial Services" Greg McGuire, Staff Research Paper, Productivity Commission, November 1998. Canberra, Australia.

[14] "Internationalization of Financial Services in Asia," Claessens, S. and Glaessner, T. 1998, World Bank, Washington D.C.

[15] See especially Survey of Measures Affecting Trade in Professional Services in the OECD Area. Doc. S/WPPS/W/4. OECD.

[16] See especially the "Background Notes by the Secretariat" on different professional services. S/C/W 73 (Accounting); S/C/W/44 (Architecture and Engineering); S/C/W/43 (Legal Services); S/C/W/49 (Educational Services)

[17] "International Regulatory Initiatives in Services" Note by the Secretariat. WTO S/C/W/97. 1 March 1999.

[18] See also "Preparing for the GATS 2000 Negotiations" Communication by Switzerland Doc. S/C/W/103, 22 March 1999, WTO.

[19] "Article VI:4 of the GATS: Disciplines on Domestic Regulation Applicable to All Services" Note by the Secretariat Doc. S/C/W/96 1 March 1999, WTO.

[20] Communication from Australia on domestic regulation. S/WPDR/W/1. WTO, 19 July 1999.

[21] "Document WTO S/L/64, 14 October, 1998.

[22] Adopted on 24 April 1996.

[23] On this subject, see also the provisions of the Agreement "Closer Economic Relations" between Australia and New Zealand.

[24] "Los Resultados de la Uruguay Round" WTO pp32-35.

[25] "Systemic Issues Arising from Article V of the GATS" Communication from Hong Kong-China. Doc. WT/REG/W/34. 19 February 1999 WTO.

[26] "Preparations for the 1999 Ministerial Conference: Proposal on Regional Trading Agreements," Communication from Australia. WT/GC/W/183. WTO, 19 May 1999.

[27] "Regional Liberalization of Trade in Services by Countries of the Western Hemisphere" Francisco J. Prieto and Sherry M. Stephenson. Paper prepared for the Conference "Multilateral and Regional Trade Issues" sponsored by Georgetown University and the OAS, Washington, D.C. May 26-27, 1998.

CHAPTER 20

Inter-State Bargaining Coalitions in Services Negotiations: Interests of Developing Countries

Amrita Narlikar

I. Introduction

Services entered onto the Uruguay Round with a bang. The first casualty of that explosion was the grand alliance of the South in the GATT, and the bloc-type diplomacy that accompanied it. The big bang however, also created a new universe of coalitions.[1] Two trends typified this universe and continue to do so today. First, a proliferation of coalitions along diverse axes has replaced the pattern of North-South bloc-type confrontation of former years. Second, the substitution has been a poor one. Most of the new coalitions reveal short life spans, almost all involve members with conflicting allegiances, and the few that have survived have proved long-lasting in little else but name.

This chapter proceeds in six steps. It begins by describing the riot of services coalitions that have emerged and considers the implications of these new trends. It then analyzes attempts by developing countries to form a new coalition type with a sectoral focus, but within former Southern boundaries.[2] Both the successes and limitations of these attempts also point to alternatives. The next section deals with sub-sectoral coalitions that transcend North-South boundaries. This coalition type is found to be a viable alternative for some developing countries. This is followed by an examination of coalitions formed along the Cairns Group lines, and reasons for their failure in the services sector are explained. Regionalism as a basis to bargaining coalitions in trade are then discussed. This final coalition type emerges as a suitable alternative, under unique conditions that are specified. Accompanying the descriptive and analytical content of this chapter is also a prescriptive one. The ad hoc coalition experiments of developing countries are utilized to find formulae for more stable coalitions that would allow their members greater certainty as well as bargaining power in further negotiations on trade in services.

II. Post-South Coalitions in Services

The services sector occupies a historic position in GATT negotiations. This position derives only partly from the newness of the issue, and the fact that international legislation in the area implied an unprecedented encroachment on domestic economic policy. From the perspective of coalition formation, the significance of the services sector lies in the fact that it was the issue immediately responsible for the final fissure within the Informal Group of developing countries in the GATT.[3] It is noteworthy that the Informal Group collapsed when it was at its most formalized i.e. in its G-10 incarnation. The G-10 had brought together the traditional leadership of the Informal Group i.e. Argentina, Brazil, Egypt, India and Yugoslavia, plus Cuba, Nigeria, Nicaragua, Tanzania and Peru. The hard-line towed by the G-10 and its bloc-type diplomacy, however, yielded few concrete results. By the time of the launch of the Uruguay Round, most of the developing countries of the Informal Group had joined the Jaramillo track, that evolved into the G-20[4] and subsequently the Café au Lait bringing together developed and developing countries.[5] It was the draft of the Café au Lait (and not the G-10's) that provided the blueprint for the Punta del Este declaration. By precipitating the fissure within the Informal Group and the alternative, issue-based diplomacy typified by the Café au Lait, the introduction of services proved to be a dramatic catalyst in the coalition activity of developing countries in the GATT. The direct association of the services issue with subsequent coalition types and the search for an effective and long-lasting model coalition-type, makes it an area that demands attention.

The immediate fallout of the collapse of the Informal Group and the GATT was, and continues to be (over a decade later), the greatly diminished leverage of developing countries in subsequent multilateral negotiations. The failure to create a more effective substitute for the South is surprising, especially in light of the significant effort that has been expended in combining the lessons of the G-10/ G-20 episode and subsequent coalition patterns. The only coalition pattern that has emerged so far, is that of 'shifting coalitions'[6]—a pattern defined best by its lack of pattern and a multiplicity of ad hoc coalitions. This multiplicity of shifting coalitions is particularly dominant in the services sector.

Learning a bitter lesson from the G-10 episode, subsequent coalitions involving developing countries have focused on the structural needs of their members rather than indulge simply in grand bloc-based rhetoric.[7] This has involved construction of coalitions around an identified collective goal. The easiest to construct along these lines are coalitions with a single issue-area focus. Such a focus is relatively new to developing countries and owes its origins to the successes of the G-20. Its manifestations are not restricted to services, and include the Cairns Group on agriculture, the W-74 Food Importers Group, several agenda-setting coalitions on natural resources,[8] the International Textiles and Clothing Bureau over the MFA, the broader Hotel de la Paix group with the agenda of preventing a breakdown of talks in the Uruguay Round, and the Beau Rivage group formed along similar lines with developed-developing countries. Some of these coalitions draw on old South loyalties, others disregard the North-South divide and focus on very particular sub-sectoral matters, and still others derive from regional affiliations.

Within the services sector, the network of coalitions is even more complex. A sample of the cross-cutting, overlapping loyalties among developing countries is illustrated in Annex 1. These diverse coalitions can be classified into four analytical types. In continuation with old habits, which die hard, the first type includes attempts at coalition building within former South boundaries but with a services focus. Type two includes North-South coalitions with a sub-sectoral focus, e.g., like-minded, similarly endowed countries pushing for an inclusion of the labor mode of supply within GATS. The third type involves North-South coalitions with a sector-wide agenda, e.g., Friends of Services group. Finally, some coalitions utilize regionalism as a springboard for bargaining, e.g., ASEAN. A simplified illustration of these analytical categories appears in Annex 2. Simultaneous membership of these coalition types and varying degrees of longevity of each group have produced crosscutting overlapping networks, across space and time. Each type has yielded varying degrees of successes. None has generated a model that can be universally adopted by developing countries to build a stable coalition.

The failure to build any long-lasting, influential coalition, in spite of the demand for it and concerted attempts directed towards achieving it, requires explanation. The answers become even more important, given the costs generated by the continuous search for new allies and defections from old alliances—costs that most developing countries are ill equipped to meet. For the former leaders of the South, these costs have involved a dramatic reduction of their domestic and international credibility, besides the transaction costs of striking new bargains according to the particular issue area. For smaller countries, the costs have come in the form of greater uncertainty. Unfruitful attempts to establish certainty through short-term bandwagoning with the developed countries on a sub-sectoral basis have undermined their bargaining power further. Balances with their more developed counterparts have generated additional costs of reducing the credibility of the former coalition type. In general, the effect has been to undermine whatever little unified market power that developing countries might have had, and to detract from their ability to exchange sub-sectoral concessions and gain superior package deals.

This pattern of quicksilver coalitions, nevertheless, has invited the enthusiastic support of observers who had long been dismayed by the North-South stalemate. The new pattern has also been seen as a method by which developing countries may improve their bargaining position. Hence writings like, '...from the point of view of the proverbial hard-nosed trade negotiator, promotion of national or group interests—is best conducted in the context of shifting and eclectic coalitions of countries and/or interests.'[9] Other practitioners of trade diplomacy in the WTO, noting the willingness of developing countries to undertake unilateral liberalization, have questioned the purpose of building coalitions at all today. Both reasons for optimism are questionable for reasons described below.

Dealing with the second viewpoint first, the willingness of developing countries to agree to unilateral liberalization is frequently an attempt by the weak to make a virtue of necessity. In the absence of any bargaining alternatives, and in the face of bilateral and organizational pressures (such as from the Bretton Woods institutions on structural adjustment), developing countries have frequently opened up certain sectors to international competition at a pace that even free traders would caution against.[10] This 'willingness' to undertake unilateral and competitive liberalization is as much a product of the absence of viable coalition possibilities as a cause of them. In the absence of the bargaining power derived from collective action, developing countries are compelled to make unilateral concessions, which in turn, further deters the operation of joint platforms.

The utility of the shifting coalitions model in terms of allowing greater maneuver to developing countries is also very questionable. From a systemic point of view, it is true that an absence of a North-South stalemate is most conducive to the rapid progress of the multilateral negotiations. For weak states however, continuously shifting, ad hoc coalitions mean renewed transaction costs for each new alliance. These costs include the loss of bargaining chips in striking intra-coalition deals among potential partners, but also involve time costs. The desperate search for new allies to assist agenda-setting and bargaining, when groupings of developed countries come well equipped with carefully researched proposals, is not an attractive option for developing countries. The time and diplomatic effort lost in such a search is especially expensive for developing countries, given their minimal presence in Geneva and limited technical expertise.[11] The co-existence of divided loyalties further detracts from commitment to any single negotiating platform, and hence also its credibility. For the weak in international relations, stability of allies is an enormous source of strength. That strength has been destroyed with the new trend of shifting coalitions. The strategy of forming shifting coalitions has been a white elephant for most members of the Informal Group.

III. Sectorally Resurrecting the South: Grand Alliance on Services

The critical lesson of the G-10/G-20 episode was simple. The concrete give-and-take across issue areas had of necessity produced a disaggregation of the ideational and rhetorical stance of the Informal Group into individual member structural interests.[12] One of the first post-South coalition types, working within these parameters, attempted to resurrect the South in services.

The effort to construct a new coalition with a sectoral focus, within Southern boundaries, does not come as a complete surprise. Developing countries as a group, and most of them individually, run deficits in trade in services (with the exception of tourism and services delivered through the movement of labor, though the latter are often categorized as 'labor remittances' than 'other services'). In traded services, nine of the top ten exporters and importers in 1982 were developed countries. Despite the higher export earnings that developing countries record through labor remittances, the position of the developed countries on the credit side becomes overwhelmingly dominant through the export of services through FDI. At the disaggregated level too, some similarities among developing countries have been noted. For instance, most developing countries reveal a deficit in 'other services'—the category in which critical producer services are included.

There were also some qualitative similarities in the services component of the GDP profiles of developing countries. First, in many developing countries, services patterns are significantly influenced by colonial links—railways for instance, in the case of India. Pre- and post-colonial political considerations have been important especially in Africa. Inadequate intra-South networks in transport services have been a major deterrent to intra-South trade. Second, contrary to the predictions of the product-cycle model or the historical experience of the North, an important segment of labor has moved directly from the primary sector into services in developing countries, without the intermediate manufacturing stage. This employment, however, has usually not been in services jobs demanding a skilled output. Third, in the developed countries, producer services occupy close to 20% of GDP. This figure is limited to 5% in low-income, developing countries, 7.5% in middle income developing countries, and 10.5% in the upper income developing countries. As services with the highest international tradability and creation of the highest value-added, the weakness of the producer services sector is a deterrent to their international competitiveness.

In spite of the G-10 'debacle,'[13] attempts to develop a broad Southern position continued, being founded on the qualitative and quantitative similarities described above. In the early phases particularly, the critical infrastructural role and political sensitivity of some services sector were cited for a cautious application of conventional trade theory to services. It was also noted that the inclusion of services within GATT auspices would unleash unprecedented international encroachments into the authority of the state.[14] These common concerns were used to build a grand alliance on services on the ruins of the South.

This coalition type, in spite of its formidable precedents in the Informal Group in the GATT, was a non-starter. The process of experimentation continued, often striving to overcome its weaknesses. The chief deterrents to the longevity and success of this coalition type were twofold. First, and particularly in the case of developing countries, the services sector proved especially prone to disaggregation, thereby defeating any attempts at the construction of broad, sectoral alliances. The sub-sectoral disaggregation, which precipitated the failure of this coalition type, also produced a network of narrower interest alignments. This network of interest alignments is described in some detail below. Second, even at the sectoral level, it was found that certain countries revealed a positive position on services. This commonality of position often revealed a regional bias. The possibility of exploiting this regional bias as a springboard for bargaining is also discussed below.

IV. North-South Alignments with Sub-Sectoral Focus

The transience and frailty of attempted grand alliances on services resulted significantly from a sub-sectoral disaggregation of the sector. Three sources of division may be found. The first is a resource-based division that results in the dominance of labor-intensive services in some countries, technology-intensive in some, and services based on geographic/strategic/cultural advantage in others. The second source of division is located in the actual vs. potential advantage that the country sees for itself in the services sector. This, in turn, has depended on factors such as the size and nature of the domestic market, fixed costs already invested in services, and the infrastructural context. Third, developing countries find their interests in services differentiated according to the extent of specialization in one sector vs. diversification of the economy (disallowing a concentration of diplomatic resources in one sub-sectoral category in the case of diversified economies). This tripartite division of interests created a problem that was the opposite of the one that had afflicted the broad bloc-type approach to services. Attention to sub-sectoral considerations based on resource endowment and actual vs. potential advantage resulted in the proliferation of coalitions with a very narrow sub-sectoral focus and crosscutting memberships.

Beginning with the first source of sub-sectoral differentiation, differential resource endowments and infrastructure levels allow countries to develop a competitive advantage in certain sub-sectors. For instance, a common advantage in labor-intensive services led to the successful initiative by like-minded countries (Argentina, Colombia, Cuba, Egypt, India, Mexico, Pakistan and Peru) on an inclusion of the Annex on Movement of Natural Persons in the GATS. A notable absentee from this developing country coalition was Brazil. Through their culture and labor-intensive audio-visual industry, India and Pakistan have found unlikely allies such as the United States in the developed world. Bhagwati cites the example of the advantage that Singapore or Japan Airlines enjoy over others such as Pan Am or TWA due to the effusive onboard treatment by the former. While the ASEAN example is discussed in greater detail below, it is noteworthy that the well-coordinated ASEAN position on telecommunications, financial services and air transport derives in part from a similarity of infrastructural endowment and culture.

Just as fascinating are alignments that have not materialized, despite the prevalence of common interests in the sub-sector. The failure of certain sub-sectoral coalitions to form may be attributed to the differentiation of interests along the two other lines described above. To cite an example of such a non-emergence, many developing countries share a competitive advantage in professional services, based on the resource endowment of knowledge, culture and labor. Disembodied professional services facilitated by telecommunication technology have greatly expanded the export potential of developing countries, even without the temporary relocation of labor. Further, even with economic needs tests and other barriers to the movement of professionals especially from developing to developed countries, the potential of developing countries in this area is significant.[15] The recent hire of nurses from the Philippines to meet the shortfall in Britain provides one example of the use of this advantage. Tunisia similarly exports professionals throughout French-speaking Africa and the Middle East. The export opportunity is founded in a domestic surplus of highly educated nationals (covering a wide range of professionals including engineers, doctors, qualified security guards), capable of speaking French and Arabic, and replacing European practitioners for one-half to one-third of their cost.[16] India has the third largest pool of scientific and technological manpower in the world, and the second largest reservoir of such expertise that is English-speaking. Despite these common advantages, a coalition of developing countries on professional services has still not emerged.

Another sub-sector in which developing countries share a competitive advantage as exporters, is that of Construction and Engineering Design (CED).[17] Admittedly, this advantage is at different levels and has different sources. It thrives best in countries that have founded it on low wages, foreign collaboration and subsequent indigenization. The Indian CED advantage has hence proved longer lasting than the Korean and Brazilian examples. Yet even with these differing sources and degrees of advantage, several coalitions are still possible. India and Brazil continue to dominate disembodied technical and consultancy exports—another issue that brings the former leaders of the South together. The labor component of CED gives India an incentive to continue with former coalitions such as the group of like-minded countries on the inclusion of the mode of supply through the movement of natural persons. The coalition could be expanded to include other low wage economies of Asia like the Philippines, Sri Lanka and other labor-exporting economies of West Asia, i.e., economies which have traditionally maintained their relative surplus in services through labor remittances (though they may also be trying to build upon the skills of returning service workers to develop an export-oriented service industry).[18]

The bargaining strength of at least some developing countries in subsectors of services, lies not only in their role as suppliers of services but also as significant importers. Irrespective of the differences in current figures of the growth of the CED sector in developing countries, the largest potential market for these services exists in the developing world. This dependence on CED services could be transmogrified into a bargaining strength, not unlike the attempt to use their severe indebtedness by developing countries to form a debtors' cartel.

In telecommunications, except for the coordinated positions from the ASEAN group (in support of the majority Northern position), the general stance of developing countries was that of resistance. In this sector too, developing countries wield considerable market power. Admittedly, some successes

were had in expressing resistance—the attempt in the Telecom annex to strike
a balance between the needs of the users for fair terms of access and the needs
of the regulators and public telecommunications operators to maintain a system that functions and fulfils public policy objectives—was a result of the two
submissions by India, Egypt, Cameroon and Nigeria. But all blocking attempts, especially at the December 1996 Ministerial on Information Technology, proved unfruitful.[19]

Certain sub-sectors showed promise of combining a similarity of interests
of most developing countries. One such issue was that of financial services.
With rare exceptions like Singapore, Hong Kong and Chile, most developing
countries recognized that their financial firms had not reached the size and efficiency that could make them competitive in developed country markets. The
implications that financial services liberalization might have for domestic financial stability made it an issue on which few trade-offs could be made. This
remained true of some of the most developed among the developing countries,
until as late as 1996.[20] Nevertheless, financial services were included in an annex of the GATS, and the agreement was finally signed in 1997.

Financial services was seen as an area especially by the UNCTAD as one
of lost opportunity,[21] where common material interests among developing
countries had existed and yet a coalition had failed to materialize. Common interests had emerged across various lines in banking and financial services. A
large number of LDCs provided centers for offshore banking. Some 20% of
euromarket activity is accounted for by LDC offshore centers in the UAE, Ba-
hamas, Cayman Islands, Bahrain, Netherlands Antilles, Panama, Singapore,
Philippines and Hong Kong.[22] Yet no attempt was made by these countries to
develop a joint position. As a huge potential market for financial services and
with a well developed national sub-sector and potential export advantage (already in 1984, Indian commercial banks had 141 branches operating in 25
countries; by 1989, international operations that had been confined to financing India's foreign trade were increased to include raising funds in money and
capital markets abroad), there were several ways in which India could have
chosen to combine its bargaining prowess with that of other countries seeking
a slower financial liberalization. But no such attempt was made.

Each of these weak attempts at resource-based sub-sectoral coalitions, as
well untrodden sub-sectoral paths, were in some ways a product of conditions
unique to each sub-sector. Discussion on the financial services sector came to
the fore in a milieu of financial liberalization, accompanied by the carrots offered to countries, which embarked on such a process by the Bretton Woods
institutions. These carrots included not merely loans from the IMF, but also
the stamp of approval from the WTO that serves as a critical signaling device
in attracting investors. These various benefits were timely sustenance for governments, which had, since the mid-1980s, encountered balance-of-payments
crises of several types. Attempts towards a more cautioned liberalization
would find few partners. As developing countries fell over each other in the
rush to liberalization, it was gradually recognized that liberalization within the

multilateral framework of the GATS might yield alternative concessions, rather than the unilateral liberalization that had been taken on hitherto. Even though the separate annex on financial services legally precludes cross-sectoral linkages and retaliation, such deals are implicit and commonplace in the bargaining among states, especially when the approval of international organizations like the IMF is involved. Also, united pressures from the European Union and the United States were unprecedented.

Underlying failed and attempted coalitions, despite a convergence of sub-sectoral interests, however, have been several factors common to most sub-sectors. Guiding the resource-based disaggregation of services into sub-sectors have been the two aforementioned considerations of levels of realized advantage and the specialization principle.

Interest and commitment to a particular sub-sectoral coalition derives from the level of advantage achieved in the sub-sector, in relation to the rest of the economy. In the context of interests and coalitions in services negotiations, three groups may be noted. Group I comprised a small number of developing countries that had acquired a well-developed material advantage in the particular sub-sector. Most such countries found it easiest to build alignments with each other and also to form direct alliances or through indirect linkages with the North. The East Asian NICs feature most frequently in this group, though memberships vary according to sub-sector. Group II comprised those that had a developing advantage in the sub-sector concerned. These economies had already incurred a form of 'fixed costs' in the particular sub-sector, and expected returns from them to materialize within the short/medium run. For these countries, the opportunity costs of yielding domestic markets to foreign competition was the highest. Group III included some of the smallest and poorest of the developing countries. The high proportion of the services imports of these countries makes arguments of efficiency gains from liberalization particularly important to them; their resource base and level of development offer them little opportunity of building their competitive advantage in the area. Trade-offs and linkages with the North offered cheaper access to services imports, as well as perhaps an inclusion of items on their agenda. Countries from Groups I and III would have a greater propensity to bandwagon with the North, depending on the position of each sub-sector. The possibility of forming a blocking or agenda-setting coalition was much higher with Group II countries.

The survival of a sub-sectoral coalition also depends on the extent of diversification of the economy and the role played by the particular sub-sector within it. The international political economy implications of this specialization principle are simple. Specialization of an economy allows a concentration of diplomatic effort and commitment in selective coalitions, dissuading conflicting loyalties or crosscutting issue linkages. Such a specialization was indeed characteristic of small island economies. These countries have higher than average export intensities in all services categories, but are clearly most specialized in tourism. The relative importance of tourism receipts was about twice the world average in 1980, rising to over 3 times in 1992.[23] The categorical export advantage in the tourism sub-sector is complemented by an absence of national economies of scale in the production of several essential services such as telecommunications. These countries must devote larger shares of their resource base for the provision of basic infrastructure services than larger countries.[24] For small countries, very close to the continent or to each other, the costs of this provision may be reduced through scale economies of trade. But the case of services and its inclusion in the MTN provided these small economies with a bargaining chip. As exporters of tourism services, they could extract better terms by including the sub-sector on the agenda. As small economies hugely reliant on services imports from the developed countries, they would gain from the assured supply that would come from an inclusion of services onto the GATT agenda. Most countries of the Caribbean fell into this pattern of behavior, and Jamaica's leading role in the G-20 may be traced to imperatives just described.

Multilateral measures that promote travel services, for instance, far outweigh any gains that small countries of the Caribbean could make through cross-sub-sectoral compensatory arrangements (hypothetically, for example in shipping with other developing countries). Similarly, gains in professional services for selective countries would be far greater than costs of liberalization of even critical sectors such as telecommunications.

Many developing countries do not have such unambiguously defined interests. This is specially the case for the bigger and more advanced of the developing economies, with large markets that allow for the possibility of exploiting economies of scale. Here, interests in sub-sectors are divided, and no sub-sector is dominant enough to allow concentrated loyalty and attention to one coalition. Large markets and already expended costs for potential economies of scale render losses from concessions particularly expensive. India presents a classic example of Group II countries with diversified and huge potential advantages in services. The diversification yields a mayhem of conflicting loyalties, and India has found itself enmeshed in several competing coalitions. Its interest in promoting the labor mode of supply has brought it into a coalition with Argentina, Colombia, and Peru—countries that had gone along the Jaramillo/ G-20 path, and had expressed a consistent preference for concessions on services for returns on other sectors. Its former alliance with Brazil as a leader of the South has been retained with their joint lobbying in the telecommunications sector. Unprecedented, de facto commonality of interest emerged with the United States over audio-visual services.

That leadership in coalition formation has been largely unforthcoming in the case of the bigger developing countries, is hence, on closer inspection, unsurprising. The diversified interests of these economies produce crosscutting loyalties and memberships. Resulting linkages and concessions adversely affect the efficacy of most sub-sectoral coalitions involving these countries. A weak and diversified interest in the services sector is the burden of the richer developing countries. Note that this diversification works differently in the

Northern economies, where irrespective of diversified production and trade in different sub-sectors, the primacy of the services sector (i.e., a strong and expansive interest) as a whole renders broad sectoral coalitions and sub-sectoral linkages possible.[25]

Based on the operation of the three sources of divisions, the larger of the developing economies would find the opportunity costs of yielding to pressures to open their markets and bandwagoning with the North to be particularly high. Such has indeed been the case with the former leaders of the South. For smaller economies, either with one dominant services sub-sector in total exports, or with a great dependence on services imports, the choice has been simpler. Once the particular sub-sector was brought under consideration, all other sub-sectoral memberships became superfluous; alternatively, concessions across sub-sectors only benefited the heavily, import-dependent small economies. The interests in the particular sub-sector, however could only be met through bandwagons formed through linkages. This is because the smallness of these economies meant that their combined market influence would still be limited (e.g., the Caribbean interests in tourism exports and cheaper transport imports), irrespective of level of commitment. The bandwagons with other developing countries with less focused interests, however, adulterated the sub-sectoral agenda and expanded it to crosscutting issues.

Already, some policy prescriptions became evident. For small economies that could afford to maintain a sub-sectoral focus, more suitable bandwagons would be with countries whose interests are less diversified, so that the coalition is not distracted by cross-sectoral linkages. These bandwagons could combine exporters, or importers and exporters with similar sub-sectoral interests (e.g., small economies heavily reliant on transport imports, would do well to bandwagon with exporters of transport services). These bandwagons would work best with Northern economies. This is because, irrespective of their diversification, the sub-sectoral shares of these economies in the particular issue-interest would be large enough to allow the coalition adequate structural strength, while the smaller countries with greater stakes in the sub-sector (because of its predominance in the economy) could provide diplomatic momentum to the coalition. Depending on the other members of the coalition, cross-sectoral linkages and concessions in areas where these small economies enjoy an export advantage may be obtained—to allow greater political feasibility to the coalition.

The question of coalition strategies for Group II countries is a much harder one to answer. The interests of these countries are indeed sub-sectorally diversified, and their large markets and services potential (in the services sector as a whole) too great to be unilaterally surrendered or bartered away for concessions in some issue area of lesser growth potential. Disaggregation at the sub-sectoral level produces conflicting loyalties in these cases. The services sector as a whole is also not dominant enough to allow coalitions with a broad sectoral focus with a Southern base, especially as it involves the differing priorities of smaller developing countries. Two alternatives however, remain—explored in the next two sections.

V. Emulating the Cairns Group: Friends of Services

Except for some of the smallest developing countries, sub-sectoral coalitions were found to be too narrow in their focus to provide a viable alternative for more diversified developing economies. The same strategy, i.e., an issue area focus and a combination of developed and developing countries, may be used at the sectoral level. Considerable energy has been expended in the construction of such a coalition, particularly as it is founded on an attempt to emulate the successes of the Cairns Group (CG) of Fair Trading Nations on agriculture. This section argues for the exceptionality of the Cairns Group and thereby its unsuitability for serving as a 'model' coalition for services. It compares the CG with the Friends of Services Group (the most long-lasting if somewhat ineffective services coalition formed along CG lines) to illustrate this unsuitability. Developing countries need to search elsewhere for their model coalition pattern.

This author has argued elsewhere, that the CG *should* not be seen as a model coalition. The grounds for this argument are that the goals of the coalition were limited; its achievements, moreover, did not live up to even its limited goals.[26] The uniqueness of the objective and subjective conditions specific to the CG is demonstrated through a comparison with the Food Importers Group (FIG—working within the same issue area as the CG) and the Friends of Services Group.[27] For limitations of space, it is not possible to present this comparative study here. This chapter limits itself to answering the critical question of why developing countries *could* not replicate the Cairns model in services.

The CG was a product of a unique set of objective and subjective peculiarities. The most critical of these objective conditions was the subsidies war between the European Community and the United States, which transformed agriculture into a transatlantic issue. Further, in its agenda of liberalization, the CG enjoyed hegemonic support.[28]

A crisis of similar proportions was certainly not visible in the new issues, including services, precisely because they were new. They still had to be understood epistemically, and also achieve their production potential especially in developing countries. Hence most coalitions on services involving a strong developing country component remained little more than 'chat groups', at the very most, involved in a preliminary exploration of where their interests lay.[29]

The successful operation of developing countries in the CG, was also conditioned by the comparative advantage of members in agriculture. This comparative advantage determined the intra-group dynamic and subjective considerations of participation. In most other issues, developing countries occupy a minuscule segment of the international market as suppliers or consumers. Agriculture, in contrast occupies a significant portion of discrete production profiles of developing countries, giving them an interest and commitment in the coalition. The contribution of some developing countries to international trade in agriculture as exporters, is also significant, which gives them considerable bargaining power. This gave developing countries a voice in the CG, and the CG a voice in international negotiations, which was unmatched in other issue areas where developing countries lacked such market shares. Such was the case with the developed country members of the CG too, in terms of the importance of agriculture in national shares as well as world shares. Subjectively, this made participation in the CG worthwhile, but objectively too, it necessitated a serious consideration of its activities by the European Community (EC), Japan, and the United States.

This comparative advantage in the sector was a product of interest aggregation patterns that were unique to agriculture. As soon as agricultural reform came up for discussion on the GATT agenda, the commodity-specific approach was abandoned in favor of the sector-wide one.[30] Note that this situation was the very opposite of the services sector, with its tendency towards sub-sectoral disaggregation.

The Cairns Group thus emerged in the unique political space that was allowed to it by the sumo-style diplomacy of the EC and the United States and the support of American hegemony. The sector-wide approach necessary for the preservation of subjective member interests was sustained by the nature of agriculture itself, and the large shares that sub-sectors occupied in national economies (making sub-sectoral trade-offs feasible).

Contrast the Cairns Group with the membership of the Friends of Services Group. The Friends' Group was founded on the core of the G-20. The successes of the CG were seen as a reaffirmation of the methods demonstrated by the G-20, i.e., mediation between the extremes of developed-developing country memberships and issue-area focus. After the launch of the Round, the G-20 took various avatars. The Friends' Group was one of these avatars, with an undefined membership and a limited agenda of facilitating liberalization in services. The group continued into the late 1990s, but has to date, never been more than a chat group for an exchange of views. No coordinated positions emerged, nor did the forum give rise to offshoots, which operated as functional coalitions in services. The few sub-sectoral coalitions that emerged seldom owed parentage to the Friends' Group.

The reasons for the minimal influence of the Friends' Group reside foremost in the configuration of individual state interests in the services sector. Like agriculture, the services sector was a large and diversified one. The disaggregation of the services issue, however, opened a Pandora's box of conflicting interests, generating loyalties and allowing few constructive intrasectoral linkages or trade-offs. The three-fold sources of these conflicting allegiances were described in the previous section. This divergence was intrinsic to the nature of the services sector in developing countries, rendering any attempt to operate at the sectoral level, as attempted by the Friends' Group, doomed to failure. Admittedly, smaller economies with a clearly expressed interest in services liberalization, largely in conformity with the U.S. position, were natural members of the group. But the larger part of the varying and fluid membership of the coalition lacked this clarity of interest, and the agenda of the group to this day remains unspecified and vague.

These economic conditions were accompanied by an international political scenario markedly different from that dominated by the transatlantic polarization, which had provided the prelude to the CG activity. In fact, irrespective of differences within the Quad in certain sub-sectors (e.g., U.S.-EC differences over audio-visuals), on balance, a divided South faced a fairly unified North.[31] The unity of the North derived from diversified interests in services, which constituted the greater part of individual country exports and GDPs, as well as through trade-offs. The EC-U.S. differences over audio-visuals, for instance, were well balanced by a similar pro-liberalization stance on financial services. In the absence of a counter-coalition from which to enhance self-definition, coalitions involving developing countries in the services sector were weakened even further. The CG had provided the means for compromise for the great powers; actors within the Quad were not involved in a similar search in services. Undergirding these external conditions was the internal characteristic of the services sector, which made aggregation of sub-sectors along CG lines impossible. The exceptional conditions internal and external to the CG could not be reproduced; a coalition based on the unique model of the CG unsurprisingly failed. For the middle powers from the developing world, coalitions in services lie in another direction.

VI. Regionalism: A Springboard for Bargaining?

In the two unsuccessful coalition types, i.e., sectoral coalitions with a Southern base and North-South sectoral coalitions, there is an underlying theme that is appropriate to highlight now. Attempts at sectoral coalitions within the South dissolve not only at sub-sectoral levels, but also disaggregate into regional aggregations.[32] Potential divisions in the Cairns Group appear most frequently along regional lines.[33] While I have earlier demonstrated the viability of sub-sectoral North-South coalitions for some smaller developing countries, this section utilizes the regional undercurrents in the two failed coalition types to suggest an alternative for coalition building among the larger countries.

Attempts at using the regional platform for bargaining in multilateral negotiations are not new. Most such attempts were founded on regional integration arrangements, even if they had an explicit bargaining purpose since the inception of the arrangement. Some of the well-institutionalized examples include the SELA in Latin America and the many joint positions produced under its auspices in the pre-Uruguay Round phases. Efforts at joint bargaining positions have persisted even in the second phase of regionalism, for instance through the MERCOSUR and the G-3. The Abjua Treaty Establishing the African Economic Community mandates members to 'adopt common positions within the Community on issues relating to international negotiations in order to promote and safeguard the interests of Africa.'[34] But few of these attempts – in the old regionalism or the new, have hitherto yielded any visible influence in the GATT. The lackluster performance of region-based coalitions requires explanation, given especially the long history of institutionalization and multiplicity of such attempts. To this history of failures, there is moreover, one exception—the ASEAN. The cross-sectoral presence and successes of the ASEAN, as a bargaining coalition in the GATT/WTO, is as much an intellectual challenge, as is the failure of its other regional counterparts.

I would argue that there are two pathways to building coalitions with regional foundations. First, coalitions may be launched on the strength of prior efforts at regional liberalization. The alternative route requires the establishment of a bargaining coalition among countries of a region, with limited pre-existing aims, as opposed to elaborate schemes of liberalization. Attempts at building regional coalitions usually adopted the former path; in most instances involving developing countries, they were unsuccessful. Some perverse correlations emerge—in the absence of economic institutionalization, regionalism provides a workable base to coalition formation and maintenance.

The explanation of these perverse correlations is simple. Developing countries, which sought to build bargaining coalitions from regional integration arrangements, began the enterprise on a flawed base. In most developing country regions, geographical proximity was not accompanied by more trade. Apart from historical reasons and consumer preferences, which favored extra-regional trade, similarity in resource endowments, skills and comparative advantage among developing countries further limited trade within the region.[35] The most significant deterrent to the success of regional integration arrangements was the nature of their trade.[36] As opposed to the intra-industry trade, which has undergirded the successful regionalism in the developed world, inter-industry trade dominated in developing regions. Traditional inter-industry rather than intra-industry trade among LDCs meant that their economies had not reached the interdependence that had bought developed countries together. Attempts at regional integration only heightened the competition among these already competitive, rather than complementary economies, and further reduced the likelihood of using these regional arrangements as a springboard for bargaining in multilateral negotiations.

This fatal flaw persists in the 'new regionalism'.[37] For all its tantalizing benefits,[38] some authors have noted the dubious utility of sub-regional/ regional integration of the services sector for developing countries.[39] The argument here is taken a step further. Accepting that most theories of goods are applicable to the services sector, developing countries continue to suffer from the problem of inter-industry trade.[40] The problem is especially manifest in the services sector, where destabilization of potential or actual, crucial sub-sectors due to competitive inter-industry trade, greatly exacerbates inter-regional antagonism. Indian Telecom expansion into Pakistani telecommunications under a hypothetical SAARC led liberalization would not be welcomed by Pakistan. Promotion of services trade within the region through regional integration is more likely to heighten regional antagonism through intra-regional competitive displacement of services production, and make the development of a common bargaining platform even more difficult.

Expectations of limited successes of such regional arrangements for bargaining purposes are borne out in recent negotiations. Based on a SELA type coordination, though not within its auspices, eleven Latin American countries presented a joint position on services. The position differed radically from the SELA position that had been adopted six years, in now 'recognizing the need for a multilateral framework of principles and rules for trade in services and negotiations thereof, aimed at expansion of such trade under conditions of transparency and progressive liberalization as means of promoting economic growth of all trading partners and the development of developing countries....'[41] The communication included the demand for relative reciprocity for developing countries, a priority to the liberalization of sectors and modes of delivery of interest to developing countries, special clauses of technical cooperation to assist developing countries, and so forth.

But some Latin American members had jointly proposed the draft on the temporary movement of services personnel. The lack of support of this position from other SELA or MERCOSUR members has been striking.

A part of the reason for these crosscutting loyalties is, once again, the configuration of interests in services. No amount of regional institutionalization can reconcile these differential interests, and hence the confusion of coalition loyalties that has resulted from a superimposition of regional alignments on these structural interests. Further, we find that attempts at regional integration, at best, have little impact on reconciling these differences; at worst, they exacerbate competition and differences and produce a flurry of counter-balancing activity.[42]

The same pattern is evident in other attempted regional coalitions involving developing countries. Hence while several regional organizations participated as observers in the second ministerial conference of the WTO, in May 1998, few among them had histories of joint bargaining.[43] Their member countries would often present their independent stance that bore little relation to the 'common' regional position. Nor did the WTO accord them the recognition that it accorded to the EU (which is a negotiating party in the trade negotiations), or even a coalition status similar to the Cairns Group. To all these cases, there is on exception—the ASEAN.

The ASEAN adopted the second route to formation of a bargaining coalition with a regional base. Instead of constructing a coalition based on incompatible regional integration measures as attempted by most developing countries, the ASEAN utilized competitive member interests emerging from a similarity of production patterns to develop a common bargaining position. ASEAN joint positions pre-date the launch of the Uruguay Round, when the region began to strike a path that showed some independence from the traditional South position. In the WTO, ASEAN members have spoken through one negotiator who is selected on a rotation basis from member countries. It is the only developing-country coalition that is accorded full recognition by the WTO. In the realm of services, the common platform has been even more firmly cemented.[44] Among all developing-country coalitions operational today, the ASEAN is perhaps the most functional in its defined membership, clear distinction from other coalitions, and unambiguous loyalties.

It is ironic to note that as a scheme of regional integration, the ASEAN may be rated as only marginally successful, Yet it has uniquely used its regional institutions as a springboard to form one of the most effective and stable bargaining coalitions in trade today. ASEAN regional aims and strategies are far removed from the elaborate mechanisms of regional integration that have been devised in other parts of the developing world—mechanisms which have proved inadequate in allowing these countries any bargaining power in multilateral trade negotiations. The contrast is telling. In some instances, a second-best or even failed attempt at regional integration provides a more effective bargaining base than a far more successfully integrated region. Of course, success is dependent on exploitation of conducive structural conditions—in the ASEAN case, competing interests have been successfully hijacked to give the region a common agenda.

The ASEAN-type solution may provide a viable basis to coalition formation among many developing countries. Such coalition types must be built on non-RI institutions, and may be harder to construct where regional animosities have already been ignited due to RI generated competition. In most instances, therefore, it might be useful to wipe the slate clean and begin regionalism anew along the second ASEAN-type route.

VII. Conclusion

The purpose of this inquiry has been to find a viable coalition pattern for developing countries, to enable them to enhance their bargaining leeway in services negotiations. Despite the mixed performance of a large number of such coalitions, the chapter affirms the utility of certain alignments for bargaining purposes. I have explored and highlighted the lessons of history, to suggest directions in which the most effective alliances might lie. To the madness of alliance formation in trade in services, this chapter offers a method.

Two ingredients are critical to the success of any coalition. First, membership of the coalition must fulfill the discrete, structural interests of participants. The situation is ideal if these discrete structural interests are shared, i.e., form the collective interest. Second, coalitions must be endowed with a collective bargaining strength. An immediate reason for the short life spans of many coalitions in sub-sectors of services was their lack of the latter ingredient. Attempts at quantification of this collective weight are unlikely to be useful. This is because political presence, regional prestige, alternative alliances, the importance of the sub-sector/sector to the individual economy, and the latter's place in the international economy all contribute to this collective weight.

These two ingredients still leave considerable scope for expensive trial and error with bandwagons and balances. Drawing on the post-South experience of developing country coalitions in services, four pathways were examined and two of these alternatives were found to be relatively ineffective. Grand coalitions continuing with former North vs. South alignments but with a focus on services were discovered to be inadequate, owing to the vast differentiation within the group of developing countries. Alternative North-South alignments with an issue area focus along Cairns Group lines were found to be irreproducible in the services sector. The unique objective and subjective conditions and accompanying hegemonic support were highlighted. It was argued that the proneness of the services sector to disaggregation along regional, resource-based and sub-sectoral lines would render any sectoral South-South/ North-South coalitions futile.

The two remaining alternatives, however, retain much promise. First, bandwagoning with the developed countries along sub-sectoral lines, was found to be the best strategy for the small economies. This policy prescription includes the two extremes in small economies. Highly specialized economies with a well-developed competitive advantage in one or a small number of services sectors would have an interest in services liberalization. In terms of conformity of agenda and commitment, these economies would derive the greatest strength by bandwagoning with the developed economies. Economies dependent on commodity exports and generating their greatest deficits through services imports would also derive significant benefits by bandwagoning. The gains would include assured services imports and other trade-offs and concessions in areas of export interest to these economies.

Second, for the bigger developing countries with more diversified economies and larger markets, a different alternative is prescribed. Coalitions with a sub-sectoral focus are the bane of such economies, as cross-cutting and conflicting loyalties result due to the equal importance that various sub-sectors carry for these countries. Bandwagoning is also not a preferred option, as their markets and levels of development allow them a potential export advantage in services, which requires some cultivation still. Sectoral balances represent the obvious answer. However, when built with other random, large-sized developing countries, a disaggregation of the services sector follows and the house of sub-sectoral cards comes tumbling down. The best option for such economies is formation of coalitions based on regional affinities.

Coalitions based on regional alignments enjoy a broad similarity of structural interests due to a common resource-base as well as local markets among members. The strengths of a region-based coalition lie in the similarity of the structural interests of members; the same similarities are however also the source of inter-industry trade and increasing competitiveness when regional liberalization is attempted. Hence a strategy of developing common positions on services on a regional basis, without attempting intra-regional liberalization, along ASEAN lines, is urged.

Both these strategies should allow increased bargaining power and also greater certainty of alliance partners to developing countries.

A prescription of two divergent strategies is admittedly based on the rejection of bloc-based strategies that developing countries had pursued as members of the Third World, or the Informal Group avatar of it in the GATT. The impact of these alternative strategies on the concept of the Third World, however, can only be judged over time. It is true that an extension of these two strategies to other sub-sectors, and their consistent pursuit may result in divisions within the bloc. But as of now, in terms of representing instruments for the weak, both resulting bandwagons and balances reinforce the concept of the Third World. The dominoes of proliferating coalitions and counter coalitions resulting from regional balances, and as a reaction to developed country alignments like the Quad, are as likely to exacerbate North-South differences as annul them.

Notes

[1] The term coalition is used here to refer to 'any group of decision-makers participating in... a negotiation and who agree to act in concert to achieve a common end.' (Colleen Hamilton and John Whalley, Coalitions in the Uruguay Round, *Weltwirtschaftliches Archiv*, vol. 125, no. 3, 1989, p. 547). While the term can be loosely interpreted to include even momentary cooperative action, I restrict its usage to concerted action among state actors, sustained over a fairly long period of time, aimed at achieving a well-defined, shared interest. This restricted interpretation allows a distinction to be maintained between coalition activity and ad hoc, incidental, policy convergence among state actors, or long term harmonic games. The element of conscious coordination is necessary; a coalition exists only when its members are aware of acting in such a collectivity. (This point is drawn from Barbara Hinckley, *Coalitions and Politics*, New York: Harcourt Brace Jovanovich, 1981, who draws on William Gamson. Coalition actors consciously join resources, work in a mixed motive situation and apply power to determine outcomes; and they assume that the other actors are similarly aware.) For further classifications of coalition types, see Amrita Narlikar, *Bargaining Together in Trade: Developing Countries in Coalitions*, D. Phil. Thesis, International Relations, University of Oxford, August 2000.

[2] It is true that the category of developing countries is somewhat problematic, given the high level of diversity among developing economies. The small island economies of the Caribbean, for instance, face very different threats and opportunities from the smaller African economies. Brazil and India, despite their comparable economic size, differ significantly in their historical legacies and threats from within the neighborhood. The contrasts across regions are wider still. At first glance there appears little in common between the rich East Asian NICS and the LDCs of Sub-Saharan Africa. In spite of these differences, however, it is possible to identify two features that bring these diverse countries together into one category and reduce their bargaining power. First, developing countries are characterized by peripherality (Chris Clapham, Third World Politics, London: Croom Helm, 1985). The concept of peripherality can be taken further than is envisaged by dependency theory. It relates to the inability of developing countries to emerge as full players in the international system despite the post-war

egalitarianism. The sources of this inability may be found at the domestic, regional and international levels. For details, see Robert Jackson, *Quasi-States: Sovereignty, International Relations and the Third World*, London: Croom Helm, 1990, and Mohammed Ayoob, *The Third World Security Predicament: State-Making, Regional Conflict and the International System*, Boulder: Lynne Rienner, 1995. Different vulnerabilities produce a common result i.e. developing countries have still not been able to emerge as agenda-setters in an international system designed by the developed countries. Resulting peripheralization of developing countries is as true of the least developed among them and the poorest, as the rich oil-exporting economies. The recognition of this peripheralization was the chief force that underlay the creation of the 'Third World'. But it also created and reinforced a second feature common to developing countries, which has been succinctly termed, 'Third World Schizophrenia' (Mohammed Ayoob, The Third World in the System of States: Acute Schizophrenia or Growing Pains, *International Studies Quarterly*, Vol. 33, No. 1, 1989, pp. 67-79). As the intruder majority in a system of states that was not built to suit their advantage, developing countries have sought to divest the developed world of its control and power in international institutions by calling for systemic change. But the vulnerabilities of these states give them a vested interest in the preservation of predictable norms of state behavior. Systemic change would destabilize their weak state structures and possibly undermine their newly achieved international recognition. While peripherality adversely affects the bargaining skill of developing countries, schizophrenia impairs their will.

[3]The Informal Group was an avatar of the South in the GATT, which operated as a weak coalition for over thirty years. The possibility of inclusion of services in the new round, in 1982, mobilized the group into a much more formalized and vocal coalition—the G-10. For a detailed account of the Informal Group, the G-10, its counter-coalition the G-20, and the broadening of the latter into the G-48, see Narlikar, Bargaining Together in Trade. Also, Rajiv Kumar, "The Walk Away from Leadership: India," in Diana Tussie and David Glover (eds.), *The Developing Countries in World Trade: Policies and Bargaining Strategies*, Boulder: Lynne Rienner, 1993, and Narlikar, *Divided They Fell: The South in Trade Negotiations*, M.Phil. Thesis, International Relations, University of Oxford, 1998.

[4] The G-20 included Bangladesh, Chile, Colombia, Hong Kong, Indonesia, Ivory Coast, Jamaica, Malaysia, Mexico, Pakistan, Philippines, Rumania, Singapore, Sri Lanka, South Korea, Thailand, Turkey, Uruguay, Zambia and Zaire.

[5] The Café au Lait was so named after its co-chairmen—Colombia and Switzerland. The group was a product of the alliance between the G-20 and the group of developed countries that had come to be known as the 'Dirty Dozen.' For further details, see Alan Oxley, The Challenge of Free Trade, New York: Harvester Wheatsheaf, 1990 and Narlikar, Bargaining Together in Coalitions.

[6]The term has been borrowed from Rohinton Medhora, "Emerging Issues in International Trade Relations: Some Research Directions," *IDRC: Research Programs: TEC*, http://www.idrc.ca/tec.emerging.html. For a summary of initial developing country positions on services, see Bernard M. Hoekman, *Developing Countries and the Uruguay Round on Services*, No. 822, Discussion Paper Series, Centre for Economic Policy Research. October 1993.

[7] On the uniqueness of the cement that bound the Informal Group and also made it a weak coalition of diversified, log-rolled interests, see Narlikar, Bargaining Together in Trade.

[8] E.g., the group of four African countries comprising Senegal, Cameroon, Côte d'Ivoire and Zaire, which emphasized liberalization especially in processed and semi-processed products, as noted in Hamilton and Whalley, "Coalitions in the Uruguay Round," p. 554.

[9] Rohinton Medhora, "Emerging Issues in International Trade Relations."

[10] An only slightly disputable and very important example of such liberalization is the Korean financial liberalization in an attempt to gain OECD membership. Similar strategies are noticeable even with the erstwhile leaders of the South—the reticence of Brazil, Egypt and India to coordinate any position opposing the Washington consensus—was revealing. Related to this, see Amrita Narlikar, "Implications of the Asian Financial Crisis: Developing Countries in Bargaining Coalitions," paper presented at the *Annual Workshop of the International Political Economy Group (IPEG), British International Studies Association (BISA)*, March 13, 1999 (Forthcoming in S.D. Lee ed., The Asian Financial Crisis: Causes and Consequences, Boulder: Lynne Rienner, expected December 2000).

[11] On some of the logistical difficulties affecting the participation of weaker countries, see Richard Blackhurst, Bill Lyakurwa, and Ademola Oyejode, "Improving African Participation in the WTO," paper commissioned by the World Bank. 1999.

[12] For the qualitative difference in strategies of developing countries as members of the Informal Group (a version of the South) and as members of subsequent coalitions, and on the differing composition of the cement which bound the Informal Group together into a coalition as opposed to post-South groupings, see Narlikar, Bargaining Together in Trade.

[13] The G-10 yielded some important lessons for subsequent coalition formations, and also decelerated the process of services liberalization, in accordance with its aims. But the new round was launched, services were included, and an alternative coalition type emerged that brought an issue-area focus into coalition formation and challenged the nature and workings of the Informal Group and the G-10. Hence the G-10 is generally viewed as a failure.

[14] A summary of developing country positions may be found in Jagdish Bhagwati, "International Trade in Services and its Relevance for Economic Development," in Orio Giarini (ed.), *The Emerging Service Economy*, Oxford: Pergamon, 1987, pp. 3-25.

[15] For details on barriers to trade in professional services, see Murray Gibbs and Mina Mashayekhi, "Services: Unfinished Business and Built-In Future Agenda," Third World Network, Seminar on the WTO and Developing Countries, Geneva, 10-11 September, 1996.

[16] *Trade in Services and Developing Countries*, Paris: OECD, 1989.

[17] Kenneth Heydon, "Developing Country Perspectives" in Messerlin and Sauvant (eds.), *The Uruguay Round: Services in the World Economy*, Washington: World Bank and UNCTC, 1990, pp. 159-196; Carlos Alberto Primo Braga, "Brazil," in Messerlin and Sauvant (eds.); Sanjaya Lall, "Exports of Technology by Newly Industrializing Countries: An Overview," *World Development*, Vol. 12, No. 5/6, pp. 471-80.

[18]There is a striking regional complementarity among the economies of West Asia, reflected in the imports of manpower services including: domestic services; contracting and consultancy; and shipping and travel, by the petroleum exporting countries of the Gulf Cooperation Council (Bahrain, Kuwait, Oman, Qatar, Saudi Arabia, and United Arab Emirates) from other countries of the region such as Tunisia. For charts displaying this complementarity and also a case study of Tunisia, see UNCTAD, *Trade and Development Report, 1988*, Geneva: UNCTAD.

[19]The Ministerial was repeatedly cited by UNCTAD officials as the prime example of developing countries' blocking strategies gone wrong. On possible explanations on why any non-ASEAN developing country coalition remained a non-starter, see Narlikar, Bargaining Together in Trade.

[20]In 1996, the Financial Leaders Group (FLG), comprising American and European financial firms, noted that offers of South Korea, Thailand, Malaysia, India and Chile were deficient. See Wendy Dobson and Pierre Jacquet, *Financial Services Liberalization in the WTO*, Washington: Institute of International Economics, 1998, p. 84.

[21]Interviews, UNCTAD officials, summer 1997.

[22]"Trade in Services and Developing Countries," p. 17.

[23] Bernard M. Hoekman, "Assessing the General Agreement on Trade in Services," in Will Martin and Alan Winters (eds.), *The Uruguay Round and the Developing Countries*, Cambridge: Cambridge University Press, 1986.

[24]*Services and the Development Process*, TD/B/1008/ Rev.1, UNCTAD: Geneva, 1985.

[25]For a description of divisions within the North and their impact on coalition formations of developing countries, Narlikar, "Bargaining Together in Trade."

[26]*Ibid.*

[27]The comparative study was useful in isolating factors that were unique to the CG, even within the issue area of agriculture, and which thereby were key to the successes of the group. While both the FIG and the CG faced similar objective conditions of a transatlantic showdown and special characteristics of agriculture, two factors were critical to the failure of the FIG: (1) varied structural interests of members that deterred the operation of CG type intra-group dynamics; and (2) the absence of hegemonic support for the group's agenda. For evidence, details of argument and references, see Narlikar, "Bargaining Together in Trade."

[28]*Ibid.*, for the interplay between the agenda of the United States and the CG, and responsiveness of the CG to U.S. pressures.

[29]Interview with Ambassador Zutshi (Indian representative at the GATT), 22 March 1999.

[30]Bernard M. Hoekman, *The Uruguay Round of Multilateral Trade Negotiations: Investigating the Scope for Agreement on Safeguards, Services and Agriculture*, Ph.D. thesis, University of Michigan.

[31] The attempt to exploit a potential rift between the EC and United States on services, in the pre-negotiation phase of the Uruguay Round, was attempted only with limited success by the G-10. For an account of this attempt, see S.P. Shukla, "The Emerging International Trading Order," in G. S. Bhalla and Manmohan Agarwal, eds., *World Economy in Transition: An Indian Perspective*, Delhi: Har-Anand Publications, issued under the auspices of Indian Institute of Advanced Study, Simla, 1994, pp. 95-120.

[32]A threefold classification emerges even at the broad sectoral level. The first category comprises exporters of minerals and commodities, i.e., economies that have deficits in services trade and surpluses in merchandise trade. Most countries of Latin America and Africa belong to this category. In the second category fall countries whose earnings from labor and travel compensate for their negative positions on trade in goods and other services categories. Sometimes, then, these countries record a surplus in the general category of trade in services. Sri Lanka is characteristic of this category, as also are the small island economies of the Caribbean that generate a huge surplus in tourism but have considerable dependence on merchandise and services imports. South Asia with its exports of labor services fits into this category. The third and much smaller category in the ASEAN countries, i.e., countries whose characteristic surplus in services has historically offset merchandise deficits, though in recent years, they have cultivated their competitive advantage in exports of manufactured goods (TDR, 1988).

[33]Among the various rifts that threatened the cohesion of the Cairns Group, the regional one was important. The Latin American members of the group particularly utilized this regional dimension to threaten/actually stage walkouts, when their middle power counterparts suggested compromise. On other rifts within the Cairns Group, see Diana Tussie, "Holding the Balance: the Cairns Group in the Uruguay Round," in Tussie and Glover eds., *Developing Countries in World Trade*; and Narlikar, "Bargaining Together in Trade."

[34] For details of some of these recent attempts, see Blackhurst et al.

[35]For more on the coordination problems within regions, see Rajiv Kumar, "The Coordination Problem," in *Towards Regional Cooperation in South Asia*, ADB/EWC Symposium on Regional Cooperation in South Asia, 9-11 March 1987, Manila (Manila: Asian Development Bank, February 1988), pp. 99-119.

[36]On inter- vs. intra-industry trade and its impact on regionalism, see Diana Tussie, *The Less Developed Countries and the World Trading System: A Challenge to the GATT*, London: Frances Pinter, Studies in International Political Economy, 1987.

[37]The new regionalism involves conscious attempts to incorporate services in processes of economic integration at the regional and sub-regional levels. Not only is this focus new (former regional efforts had included the occasional project of joint construction of roads/facilitation of regional transportation and communications, but never the effort to promote 'trade in services' within the region, as well as through the region for export purposes), but its basis differs from the former inward-looking bias that had sought self-sufficiency for the region. Despite this new rationalization for regional integration in services, the utility of such efforts in themselves and for bargaining purposes remain debatable.

[38]For recommendations supportive of the trend towards the regionalization of services among developing countries, see Luis Abugattas, "Services as an Element of Cooperation and Integration among Developing Countries: Implications for the Uruguay Round of Multilateral Trade Negotiations," in *Trade in Services: Sectoral Issues*, UNCTAD/UNDP Projects of Technical Assistance to Developing Countries for Multilateral Trade Negotiations, UNCTAD/ ITP/ 26, Geneva: UNCTAD, 1989.

[39]"From an economic point of view, sub-regional liberalization of services may make little sense, if the members of an integration grouping are all developing economies at roughly the same level of development, and all net service importers for most services

(with the exception of tourism). In such situations these countries would benefit the most from an opening of their service markets on a wider basis, in order to attract needed foreign direct investment from the most efficient service suppliers (most often based in developed economies). Also, the trade-offs needed for a real liberalization to take place in the services area are less obvious at the sub-regional level among more similar economies, than at a broader level among more diversified economies." Sherry M. Stephenson, *Approaches to Liberalising Services*, Policy Research Working Paper 2107, Development Research Group, World Bank, Washington: World Bank, May 1999, p. 73-74.

[40]"Conventional trade theory applies not only to goods but also to services...," André Sapir, "Trade in Services: Trade Policy Issues for the Eighties," *Columbia Journal of World Business*, 1982—quoted in André Sapir and Chantal Winter, "Services Trade," in David Greenaway and L. Alan Winters (eds.), *Surveys in International Trade*, Oxford: Basil Blackwell, 1994, p. 283. A detailed examination of the application of the theory of intra- vs. inter-industry trade to sub-sectors of services would require an inquiry that lies beyond the purview of this chapter and is clearly a challenge for the future.

Note however, that most efforts at services liberalization at the regional level have been founded on pre-existing institutions of regional integration or ones that undertake a simultaneous liberalization in other sectors. If it were found that the services sector is less subject to the extreme results of the intra-industry vs. inter-industry trade, the regional antagonisms rooted in alternative sectors would persist. These antagonisms would be further carried over into the services sector, due to the operation of services liberalization within the same regional institution.

[41]Preamble, MTN.GNS/W/95, "Communication from Brazil, Chile, Colombia, Cuba, Honduras, Jamaica, Nicaragua, Mexico, Peru, Trinidad and Tobago, and Uruguay," GATT Secretariat, Group of Negotiations on Services, 26 February 1990.

[42]For details on the exacerbation of differences through regional institutionalization, *Bargaining Together in Trade*.

[43]Regional bodies that presented a position at the Ministerial included the ASEAN (WT/MIN(98)/ST/108), the SAARC (WT/MIN (98)/ST/49), the Common Market for Eastern and Southern Africa (WT/MIN/ (98)/ST/74), the OAU/African Economic Community (WT/MIN(98)/ST/72), and the South Centre (WT/MIN(98)/ST/20).

[44]For an account of the joint positions of the ASEAN in the GATT, particularly in the pre-Uruguay phase, see Special United Nations Service, *SUNS* (published everyday in Geneva and Rome, by the IFDA, in cooperation with IPS Third World News Agency). For an analysis of joint positions, see Mohamed Ariff and Tan Loong–Hoe eds., *ASEAN Trade Policy Options*, Singapore, ASEAN Economic Research Unit, Institute of Southeast Asian Studies, 1988); Sherry Stephenson, "ASEAN and the Multilateral Trading System," *Law and Policy in International Business*, Georgetown University Law Center. vol. 25. no. 2. 1994.

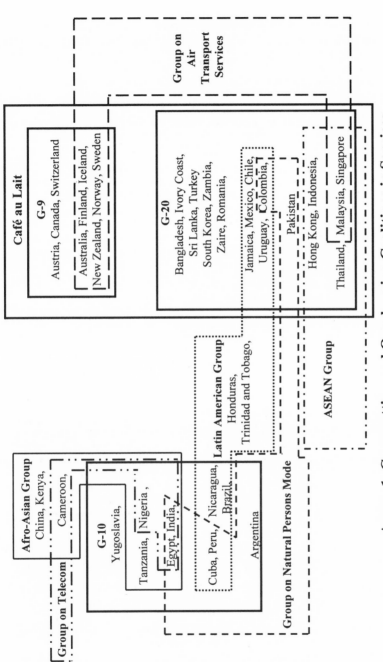

Annex 1. Crosscutting and Overlapping Coalitions in Services

Annex 2

Types of Coalitions:
Analytical Categories and Linkages

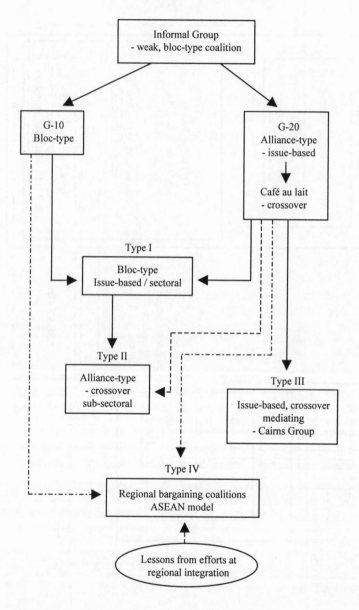

Recommendations of the Global Services Network and Business Policy Forums for Services 2000 Trade Negotiations

World Services Congress 1999
November 1-3, 1999
Atlanta, Georgia, USA

Contents

Expanding Business Opportunities: China on the Brink of WTO (BOF3)
Establishing Pro-Competitive Regulatory Regimes Through Services
Negotiations (A15)

Introduction

Following are the recommendations agreed by the Global Services Network
(GSN) and the Business Policy Forums that convened at the World Services
Congress in Atlanta on November 1-3, 1999. The Congress drew over 800
participants from more than 50 countries. Participants included representatives
of the business, government, and academic communities concerned with
liberalization of trade in services and issues relating to the services economy.

The recommendations were developed by the participants in the panel
discussions based on drafts prepared and in most cases circulated by Forum
chairs and rapporteurs to panelists and others prior to the Congress. These
recommendations were then subject to discussion and debate among the
panelists, scholars who prepared papers for a given panel, and the audience
attending each forum.

These recommendations encompass some important sectors that have not
previously received concentrated attention by services trade negotiators. These
include: air cargo; energy; legal services; aspects of financial services like
pensions; mobility of business personnel; and pro-competitive regulatory
reform.

The recommendations reflect the viewpoints of the private sector, not
governments, though many representatives of governments were present at,
and contributed their ideas to, the panel discussions.

In addition to recommendations of the Business Policy Forums, the
Business Opportunity Forum on China also made recommendations, as did the
Academic Track Panel on Pro-Competitive Regulation. Also note that the
members of the Global Services Network (GSN) met on Sunday afternoon,
October 31, to arrive at agreement on a position paper expressing their views
on a number of cross-sectoral issues affecting the services negotiations.

Global Services Network (GSN)

Statement on WTO Negotiations on Services

The Global Services Network (GSN) is an informal, private sector-led, forum
which gathers the global services community of business people, government
officials, academics, and others who are committed to increased trade and
investment in services, and a rules-based, multilateral trading system. The
Network's participants are dedicated to build global support for the
liberalization of international services trade through multilateral negotiations
under the auspices of the World Trade Organisation (WTO).

Services underpin all forms of international trade and all aspects of global economic activity. The broad range and diversity of the service sector includes services such as accountancy, audio-visual, distribution, energy, engineering & construction, environmental, express delivery, financial services, health care, information technology, legal, telecommunications, transportation, travel and tourism, and professional and business services. The liberalization of services markets enhances economic growth, and helps provide developing countries with essential infrastructure to speed their modernization. It provides increased choice and opportunities for consumers of the broadest range of products and services at the lowest cost.

Negotiations on services in the WTO present governments with the opportunity to liberalize trade in services by committing themselves to reducing barriers to market entry in all modes of supply, and to reform domestic regulations that hinder fair and open markets. The WTO negotiations on services should be used to achieve a contestable, competitive market in every services sector in every WTO member country.

To accomplish this, WTO member governments are encouraged to:

- Implement and enforce all GATS commitments and in particular the services agreements already negotiated. All WTO members should strive to undertake and implement commitments to open markets for the supply of telecommunication services and adopt the regulatory principles of the reference paper. All signatories of the Financial Services Agreement should ratify and implement their commitments under that agreement.

- Secure binding commitments in as many sectors as possible for market access and national treatment.

- Give priority to reviewing MFN exemptions to exclude only the most sensitive issues from liberalization, and ensure that exemptions are precise, transparent, temporary, and limited to the minimum required for their purpose.

- Recognize that liberalization of services markets in both developing and developed countries is critical to their economies to strengthen domestic services capacity, its efficiency, and competitiveness. Governments should extend technical assistance to developing countries to ensure their full preparation and participation in the negotiations on services.

- On a sector-by-sector basis where appropriate, develop pro competitive regulatory principles that promote open and efficient markets. Such regulation will foster clear and reliable information about sector-specific laws and practices.

- Improve the transparency and openness of the World Trade Organization. To engender confidence in the WTO, proceedings, access to documents and decisions should be improved and made available to the public on a timely basis.

- Under Article VI of the GATS, develop horizontal disciplines for domestic regulation that result in transparent and predictable regulatory institutions and outcomes, and the imposition of the least burdensome or least trade restrictive rules based on objective criteria, so as to promote freer trade and equitable competition and to encourage cooperation between independent sectoral regulators.
- Reformulate the classification of services whenever necessary to accurately describe the structure of services industries.
- Make all possible efforts to progressively eliminate barriers to the free movement of key business personnel.
- Agree on transparent procedures in public procurement, with the long-term objective of a single binding WTO multilateral set of rules on procurement.
- Advance electronic commerce by removing unnecessary restrictions to cross-border services to encourage trade without requiring establishment. Seek to remove unnecessary restrictions on the ability of foreign firms established in a market to supply services electronically within their territory, under both existing and future commitments on commercial presence.
- Continue the WTO Work Program on Electronic Commerce to clarify outstanding issues, and extend the WTO moratorium on customs duties on electronic transmissions.
- Use innovative and time-saving negotiating methods to obtain market-opening commitments, including horizontal, formulaic, and sectoral negotiating approaches.
- Conclude the negotiations on services in three years.

The negotiations on services represent an important opportunity to achieve greater liberalization in all service industry sectors. Opening markets for all services will promote economic growth in WTO member economies.

BPF1

Effective Strategies for Insurance Providers in the Global Market Place: Goals and Objectives for Negotiations

The insurance industry provides benefits for WTO member economies, workers and citizens in a very broad and beneficial manner through promotion of trade, risk financing, internal capital-market development, life insurance and retirement products, and individual consumer protection through individual and group products. In the 1997 financial services negotiations, efforts were made to establish a structure of commitments to provide increased and assured market access and non-discriminatory treatment in insurance markets around the world. Some 70 countries undertook insurance-related obligations at that time. While many simply codified existing practices, some new liberalization was achieved as well.

During the upcoming WTO negotiations, the insurance industry believes it is important build on these achievements through broader and deeper commitments by a wider range of countries, and should be done based on the approach embodied in the "Understanding on Commitments on Financial Services". Significant restrictions remain in many important markets, including nationalized markets in several key instances. In addition, it is critical for the WTO to address issues that relate to the restrictive nature of insurance regulation in many markets. Insurers do not dispute the necessary role of regulation. Our focus is on encouraging the development and implementation of regulation which promotes competition as well as consumer protection.

Over the last several months insurance industry representatives in North America and Europe have worked to develop a set of guidelines that seek to provide a basis for further negotiations in this area. (Joint US-European Working Document on "Pro-Competitive Regulatory Principles in Insurance") These "pro-competitive regulatory principles" enjoy a broad range of support from insurance underwriters, intermediaries, reinsurance providers and others in the insurance industry. The critical elements of these principles can be summarized as follows.

- Full market access and freedom of form of establishment and operation;
- Non-discriminatory treatment for foreign insurance providers and intermediaries in foreign markets;
- Development of transparent legal, administrative and regulatory environments based on "best-practices" and international standards;
- Regulatory focus on solvency and prudential standards, not micro-management of price and form;
- Freedom to introduce new products and services;
- Standstill on new restrictions and protection of existing investments;
- Permit cross-border trade and free access to international reinsurance markets.

Ultimately, the international insurance industry will determine its support for future WTO insurance commitments based on a simple but essential bottom line criterion — the commercial value of the commitments.

Recommendation:

- World Services Congress (WSC) insurance industry representatives recommend that governments pursue full market access and national treatment commitments from all WTO members, according to the Understanding on Financial Services, as well as additional commitments that result in a pro-competitive market environment for foreign insurers in those markets.

BPF2

Freeing Up Cross-Border Trade in Financial Services: Considering the Electronic Dimension

Financial services play a fundamental role in most countries' economies: financial services facilitate virtually every other economic activity. Trade in financial services has grown rapidly in recent years as the countries of Latin America, Asia, and Central and Eastern Europe have become more integrated to world financial markets.

Liberalization of trade in financial services is good for both developing and developed countries. For developing countries, free trade in financial services usually means greater competition. This competition increases efficiency, leading to cheaper and better financial services. It also leads to better allocation of capital, more investment opportunities, and greater ability to manage risks and withstand shocks. Studies show that developing countries that open their financial markets generally experience faster economic growth than those with closed financial markets. As competition produces better returns for investors, savings increases and this in turn increases economic growth.

Electronic commerce has the potential to expand the benefits of trade in financial services even further. Electronic delivery of financial services can create even greater efficiencies, reduce costs further, and facilitate new markets and products. Buyers and sellers need not be physically present to conduct business. In addition, the electronic marketplace is currently free from explicit trade barriers.

Although a good first step, the 1997 Financial Services Annex to GATS did not eliminate all barriers to international trade in financial services. While some countries opened access to their markets completely, others opened access only to certain sectors or only to limited degrees. Certain countries took exemptions from national treatment in the Financial Services Agreement. The following recommendations are intended to ensure that consumers reap the maximum benefit from electronic cross-border trade in financial services and financial information.

Recommendations:

- More countries need to make commitments in financial services and financial information. WTO members should expand existing commitments to cover more services and more modes of supply and to reduce existing exemptions. Existing exceptions to the flow of financial information should be eliminated.

- In telecommunications, existing commitments need to be implemented, more countries need to make commitments, and discriminatory tariffs should be eliminated. Additional commitments to greater unbundling by communication providers should be made. There should be more specificity on reasonable rates for leased lines, and specific commitments on Internet access. Internet providers should not be regulated as common carriers.

- WTO members should reaffirm that existing commitments are technology-neutral and that financial service providers may use any protocol, including the Internet, to supply a service. Explicit barriers to the electronic marketplace must be avoided. The customs moratorium on electronic transmissions should be made permanent. A technological infrastructure of connectivity between the Internet "backbone", Internet service providers, and end users is also necessary to ensure that financial services can make the most of the "electronic dimension." A legal "infrastructure" of certification, disclosure, payment and privacy standards is also important. Tariffs on end-user devices, such as PCs, should be reduced.

- In addition, WTO members should recognize that national-based regulation of items such as safety and soundness and consumer protection can pose a barrier to cross-border provision of financial services. Review of best practices, harmonization of regulatory standards, mutual recognition of regulatory regimes, and recognition of the greater sophistication of whole-sale customers as compared to retail customers would do much to reduce that barrier. WTO members should evaluate how well their regulation of financial services providers is advancing the goals of fairness and transparency.

If WTO members follow these recommendations, the electronic dimension of financial services will promote economic growth and financial stability. The OECD estimates that general liberalization of services around the world could raise the pace of global growth by over 1.5% per year. Electronic commerce promises the greatest gains for developing countries, where services are least efficient and transaction costs are highest. WTO members should seize the opportunity offered by the new round to unleash the positive force of electronic delivery of financial services.

BPF3

How the Energy Services Industry Can Use Trade Negotiations to Secure and Expand Markets

Energy services comprise an array of service activities related to the development, extraction, production, marketing, consumption and management of energy products, including coal, electricity, gas, nuclear, oil and renewable energy resources.

Energy services provide the critical linkages in ensuring continued access to adequate energy supplies at reasonable prices.

A thriving energy services sector is critical to economic well-being and improved living standards, especially with its potential to serve the 2 billion people who today do not have access to commercial energy.

A growing energy services sector helps protect the environment by promoting efficient energy management and energy resource use.

Recommendations:

- WTO Ministers are urged to increase substantially global market access opportunities for energy services providers through all appropriate modalities in the new round of WTO services negotiations.
- The application of existing GATS commitments to certain energy services must be clarified; existing GATS commitments should be extend-ed to other energy services; and new disciplines should be developed (as necessary) to ensure meaningful market access commitments, including an open regulatory environment that covers such areas as interconnection guarantees and transparent, non-discriminatory licensing procedures.

BPF4

Moving Business Personnel: An Agenda for WTO Action

We recommend that the temporary movement of key business personnel between WTO member states should be placed, as a matter of priority, on the agenda of the 2000 round of WTO negotiations. The objective of this recommendation is the reduction of government measures which impede or prevent key business personnel from timely movement between, and temporary presence in, WTO member states.

The panel agreed that liberalization in this area is a "win-win" situation for developing, as well as industrialized countries, as the seamless and consistent provision of services assists with infrastructure development and creation of employment opportunities.

We are seeking a harmonized set of rules, which will bring certainty, transparency and speed to the issue of mobility of key business personnel. We look to the new round of GATS negotiations to place the following items on its agenda.

Recommendations:

- Agreement on common definitions of key business personnel.
  Commitments as to the fourth mode of supply often include definitions and terms of key business personnel which are neither clear nor consistent from one member to another. As a result they are often subject to arbitrary and discriminatory application by regulatory authorities. In the future, a precise definition or cross-referencing of key business personnel should be agreed by the WTO.
- Agreement on transparent process.
  The process of movement of key business personnel would be aided by each signatory preparing a simple explanation of visa and work permit requirements and the publication on an annual basis of statistics relating to the numbers of temporary working visas granted.
- Provision for the short-term movement of key business personnel.
  Of utmost importance is the establishment of an expedited procedure for strictly defined short-term transfers. Certain criteria could be established to allow eligible employers to apply for program certification with the local immigration department. Upon certification, the individual applications could be self-administered by employers and adjudicated at the consulate/embassy of the host country.

BPF5

Airing Differences: What Business Needs in a New Agreement on Air Cargo Services

Air transport is one of the world's fastest growing industries, making a vital contribution to the development of international trade, travel and tourism. Although "air transport" primarily conjures up images of passengers traveling, the majority of commercial aircraft are carrying cargo in some form or other. While in terms of weight only 2% of all cargo moves by air worldwide, the OECD estimates that air freight transport now accounts for well over a third of the value of the world trade in merchandise.

The new services provided by the air cargo industry—in particular the development of fully integrated express delivery services on a worldwide basis—have positioned cargo operators as key players in ensuring business ability to attain and maintain global competitiveness. Integrated carriers allow businesses to streamline their supply chains leading to reduced delivery lead-times, faster responses to market needs (including after-sales service), reduced inventory and savings in warehousing. Using air cargo services, manufacturers can acquire components and materials in the best value markets, locate facilities where labor and skills are available at competitive rates and market their products globally.

Air Transport Services

Air-transport services should continue to be treated separately under the Aviation Annex. The required review of the Annex should focus on the best way to liberalize that sector. There is a disagreement among the panel members as to whether hard traffic rights should be included under the GATS. One panelist strongly believes that hard traffic rights should continue under a separate aviation agreement, either bilateral or multilateral, but not under GATS. The other panelists believe that hard traffic rights should be included in the GATS.

Undoubtedly, cargo-service providers and shippers worldwide would benefit from an open international air-cargo market, and also an open regime for express-delivery services.

Regulatory Constraints on Integrated Express Delivery Services

The panel noted a clear distinction between air transport services and express-delivery services. Because express-delivery services must integrate many different services together to provide a true express service, any regulatory constraints on any part of the chain creates a barrier to express services. The panelists take the view that all services that make up an express service, with the exception of air-transport services should be treated as a separate new sector under GATS.

Recommendations

- The globalization of the manufacturing process and the growth of e-commerce have created a need for a globally integrated air-cargo network. Further multilateral liberalization in the air-cargo sector, and particularly with respect to the services provided by integrated cargo carriers, is urgently needed and should be a priority of governments.
- Air-transport services should continue to be treated separately under the Aviation Annex. The required review of the Annex should focus on the best way to liberalize that sector.

BPF6

The Basic Telecom Agreement: Securing the Gains & Framing the Services 2000 Agenda

The panel strongly supports the trade liberalization objectives of the WTO. The 1999 Seattle Ministerial provides an opportunity to move towards the objective set in the GATS of progressive liberalization of trade. The panel was evenly divided and was unable to agree on a recommendation on the issue of internet access charging.

We urge Trade Ministers to address the following issues in negotiations on telecommunications services.

Recommendations

- Countries that have committed to full liberalization in the WTO should implement those commitments in their entirety, including the terms of the Reference Paper.
- Countries that have committed to partial liberalization should expand their commitments to include full liberalization and adoption of the pro-competitive principles contained in the Reference Paper, and accelerate implementation if prior commitments are for future implementation.
- Countries that are WTO Members but have not made commitments under the Basic Telecommunications Agreement should schedule full commitments by a date certain in the near future.
- Standardized scheduling.
- Special consideration of developing countries.
- Clarification of the Reference Paper including definitions of terms, strengthening the role of the regulator and domestic regulation (one member expressed a dissenting opinion that clarification could serve to weaken existing commitments).

BPF 7

Services in the Asia-Pacific Region

The panel discussion noted that several of the once booming economies of the Asia-Pacific were drawn into a whirlpool of business failures and havoc following the flotation of the Thai Baht in July 1997. The consequent collapse of asset prices and currency depreciation in several East Asian economies revealed important structural weaknesses that eventually triggered the economic slump now referred to as the Asian financial crisis.

To deal with the crisis, many experts concluded that structural reforms of government, business, and the financial sector had to be undertaken rapidly. In light of the need for decisive action to stop the downward swing of the financial crisis and set the affected countries back on the road to recovery and future prosperity, several governments undertook reform programs.

In the session, each panelist spoke on services in the region from their respective country perspectives, and commented on how services trade can provide economic stabilization and growth in the region in the wake of the Asian financial crisis. The panelists also emphasized the need for improvements in the recording and use of services statistics for more accurate reflection of the impact and value of services trade. The panelists agreed that progress in the APEC process can strengthen the region's participation and influence in the WTO negotiations, and highlighted the need for regional organizations like APEC and ASEAN to put forward solid positions that reflect the experience and needs of those regions.

Recommendations

- APEC countries fully implement structural reform programs that reflect the private-sector consensus on actions to be taken in supporting services liberalization;
- APEC countries work together to strengthen the region's participation and influence in the WTO negotiations;
- APEC countries allow the private sector to play a more involved and constructive role in the policy-formulation and implementation process;
- The WTO facilitate and assist in the development of institutions and relevant associations and bodies, and through these groups help with the development of regulatory frameworks that advance the internationalization of the global services markets.
- The WTO assist with capacity-building efforts to facilitate structural reforms and the full implementation of reform measures.

BPF8

Creating an Open Market for Accountancy: Its Essential Role in Economic Modernization, Capital Mobilization and Stable Financial Markets

Recommendations

- Improving the movement of people, knowledge and skills is at the heart of the forum's recommendations.
- In the short term, spreading knowledge and best practice comes through the deployment of people. Ministers should therefore agree to the elimination or reduction of government measures which prevent or impede key business personnel from timely movement between, and temporary presence in, WTO Member countries.
- In the long term, the movement of people will be helped by the recognition of professional qualifications. Ministers should therefore increase the number of bilateral mutual recognition agreements between WTO Members (following the *Guidelines for Mutual Recognition Agreements or Arrangements in the Accountancy Sector*)
- Knowledge should not be crowded out by restrictions on market access. Ministers should therefore urge more WTO Members to make commitments for accountancy services and further develop the

Disciplines on Domestic Regulation in the Accountancy Sector (in accordance with the requirements of GATS Article VI:4).

- In these ways, accountancy will become the genuinely global profession, as it needs to be, to serve the world's capital markets and to support economic development.

BPF9

Creating a Global Marketplace in Legal Services: A Roundtable Discussion

Description of the Issue: Trade in legal services is growing in response to the increasing demands of legal-service consumers. However, the continued growth of this trade faces multiple challenges in the form of national laws, regulations and professional rules of governance limiting the extent to which non-nationals may offer their services. While rules of governance for the legal profession are important in all jurisdictions to ensure the competence of lawyers, protect consumers and preserve the independence of judgment of lawyers, the development and implementation of these rules need not, and must not, serve as barriers to trade which restrict the consumers' ability to obtain the services they desire. Any multilateral rules governing trade in legal services will have to allow legal-service consumers freedom of choice while maintaining the professional standards with which legal services will be provided.

Status of the Issue: Governments have devoted relatively little attention to addressing the barriers restricting trade in legal services. The WTO covers legal services under the GATS, but thus far the treatment of legal services under the GATS has been limited to certain signatory countries submitting an initial schedule of commitments, and preliminary work in the WTO Working Party on Trade in Professional Services. At the regional level, treatment of cross-border trade in legal services has been sporadic.

The European Union regulates the provision of legal services among Member States, but this regulation has not been extended to legal service providers from non-Member States. Under the NAFTA, certain aspects of a Joint Recommendation and Model Rule issued in 1998 were rejected by significant state-bar associations in the United States as being too restrictive, and these objections now have been raised at the governmental level. Trade in legal services also is covered by some bilateral trade agreements, as well as agreements between private-sector professional bodies.

Recommendations

Multilateral rules governing trade in legal services should allow consumers to obtain the services they need on a non-discriminatory basis. The multilateral rules also should establish a framework within which the national regulation of the legal profession continues without unduly restricting the ability of non-national legal service providers to offer their services. To achieve such an agreement, negotiators should focus their efforts on the identification and evaluation of the barriers that currently exist. Specifically, negotiators should address:

- Existing national restrictions relating to the ability of non-national legal service providers to offer their services in a host country, and the rules relating to the scope of the legal services they may provide
- Existing national restrictions relating to the form of association between national and non-national legal service providers
- Nationality requirements which restrict the manner in which non-national legal service providers operate (issues of "management" and "control")
- Nationality requirements on local licensing, registration, and bar membership
- Restrictions on the name under which the legal service providers may offer their services
- The transparency of national rules and regulations. By framing future negotiations around these issues, progress can be made in liberalizing trade in legal services without compromising the standards of the profession.

BPF10

After The Freight Hits The Dock: Achieving New Efficiencies in Rail, Transit, Trucking, and Air Freight

This panel discussed issues that impact the services involved in moving goods in international commerce. Because of the importance of express services in today's trade environment, this panel focuses on that sector. The panel recommends that the elimination and reduction of trade impediments and other measures restricting the express-delivery services should be a primary objective in the next round of WTO negotiations. Specifically, the panel recommends the following issues as negotiating priorities: sector specific negotiations for express delivery services; trade facilitation measures; and electronic commerce.

Express-delivery services are one of the major infrastructures for trade. The major characteristics of the express delivery services sector are: time-definite, door-to-door shipments of all weights and sizes; integration of a wide array of services; end to end control of each shipment and extensive use of advanced information technologies.

As the world advances into the 21st century, more and more of world trade will be comprised of the kind of high value/high-tech goods transported by express delivery trade in goods and services that is growing faster than the aggregate world GDP. Express-delivery services bring together distant sellers and purchasers, as well as bridge the geography of global supply chains. Through their global networks, express-delivery service providers have become a part of a major revolution in manufacturing: fast-cycle logistics and just-in-time manufacturing and processing.

Because of the integrated nature of express-delivery services, any governmental measure adversely impacting any portion of the service impedes the entire service. The governmental measures applied to express-delivery services are diverse and numerous. To provide its service, the sector integrates, i.e., performs, a large number and variety of services including pick-up of the item, ground and air transport, delivery, warehousing, distribution, customs brokerage and customs clearance, and the completion of all types of required administrative, commercial, and customs procedures. Effective trade liberalization for the sector necessarily involves the reduction or elimination of all trade restrictions and trade-distorting measures applied to all of these services. The removal of trade barriers and other impediments to the efficient operation of express-delivery services will stimulate trade expansion and have a dynamic effect on all international-business sectors.

Meaningful liberalization for the express-delivery-services sector can be achieved only through a sector-specific approach. Express-delivery services are not adequately classified within any sector or subsector contained in the sector classification list in the Uruguay Round negotiations. A sector-specific approach would require that all express-delivery services currently scattered throughout the GATS be addressed in a single classification and sector-specific rules and principles be developed. Because air-traffic rights are specifically excluded from GATS, those services would not be part of the negotiations for express-delivery services. Discussions on liberalization for air services would take place in other fora.

Customs-related measures often adversely affect the provision of express-delivery-services and place a burden on international trade. The negotiations can most easily address these issues under the umbrella of "trade facilitation". Without trade-facilitation advances, market-access gains may be diluted if trade is otherwise frustrated by non-tariff barriers. Given the role of the express-delivery-services sector as a trade facilitator, the adoption and implementation of guidelines on express shipments would enhance export promotion and facilitate the cross-border movement of all goods and services.

A chief element of express-delivery services is heavy reliance upon advanced information technologies, the Internet, and e-commerce. The governing principle in the negotiations should be that the imposition of customs duties, where such duties do not currently exist, is contrary to trade expansion. WTO Members should formally recognize that such duties constitute barriers to trade in services and have the potential to dilute the trade-promotion and facilitation benefits of electronic commerce. The GATS most-favored-nation and national treatment principles should have unconditional application to the provision of Internet access and to other forms of electronic commerce. WTO Members should ensure that all measures affecting electronic commerce are administered in a reasonable, objective, and impartial manner. The trend towards applying internationally recognized and accepted commercial legal standards to electronic commerce should continue, and strong disciplines must be developed to prevent domestic service suppliers from adopting or engaging in practices relative to electronic commerce which would reduce the competitiveness of foreign-service suppliers.

Recommendations

- Express-delivery services are one of the major infrastructures for global trade and are particularly critical to the explosive growth in electronic commerce. Express-delivery services have become not only an important facilitator but also a key creator of world trade.
- Because of the integrated nature of express-delivery services, any governmental measure impacting any portion of the service impedes the entire service. The governmental measures applied to express delivery services are numerous and diverse, including restriction on ownership of trucking operations and burdensome and archaic custom-clearance procedures.
- Express-delivery services are not adequately classified within any single sector or subsector contained in the sector-classification list used in the Uruguay Round negotiations.
- Meaningful liberalization for express-delivery services can be achieved only through a sector-specific approach.
- The panel recommends that the express-delivery services sector be a negotiating priority for the next round of WTO negotiations.

BPF11

Barriers to Electronic Commerce: The Agenda for WTO Negotiations

To advance electronic commerce, the overarching objective of the global business community in the coming WTO Services 2000 negotiations is to broaden and deepen countries' GATS liberalization commitments in all sectors. Those service industries that use electronic commerce need market access and national treatment to extend the benefits of international electronic commerce.

Recommendations

- Make permanent the WTO's moratorium on Customs Duties on Electronic Transmissions to codify the duty-free treatment of electronic transmissions.

- Adopt and fully implement the WTO Agreement on Basic Telecommunications as well as the Reference Paper on an accelerated basis as a fundamental step to expand the benefits of electronic commerce.
- Recognize that the expansion of electronic commerce in WTO member economies will require substantial commitments in cross-border and consumption abroad of services where most electronic transactions take place.
- Refrain from enacting trade-related measures that would impede electronic commerce, even if enactment of such measures would not otherwise violate existing international legal obligations.
- Recognize the role of electronic commerce in promoting and facilitating international trade and reaffirm that current WTO obligations, rules, disciplines and commitments, namely the GATT, GATS and TRIPS agreements, are technology and application neutral.
- Assess the degree to which national measures now affecting electronic commerce promote or hinder that medium, and seek to eliminate or modify existing regulations that unnecessarily impede electronic commerce.
- Agree that Article VI of the GATS should not be weakened by introducing exceptions or carve outs.
- Seek to strengthen Articles III & VI of the GATS to ensure transparent and least burdensome rules in the application of domestic regulations.
- Continue the WTO Work Program on Electronic Commerce inter alia to identify, reduce and eliminate barriers to international electronic commerce.
- Agree to extend technical assistance to developing countries to ensure their full preparation and participation in the Services 2000 negotiations.

The Services 2000 negotiations represent an important opportunity to move beyond the status quo and achieve greater liberalization in all service industry sectors. Opening markets for all services will open the market for electronic commerce.

BPF12

Achieving Regulatory Transparency and Pro-Competitive Regulatory Reform Through Trade Negotiations

The GATS has developed disciplines on domestic regulation as part of the 1994 Marrakesh agreements. One of the key issues of the "Millennium" round for WTO Members will be to respect these disciplines but also to go further and establish pro-competitive regulatory principles.

Services are regulated by governments to ensure consumer protection and guarantee the supply of services to consumers. Regulation is enacted to ensure the integrity of the market and therefore protect the system itself (e.g., in financial services). It is essential that domestic regulation is kept strong and transparent. However, domestic regulation should not affect international trade in services, should not discriminate between foreigners or between nationals and foreigners, and should not limit product availability.

A good example of what can be done in the area of "pro-competitive regulatory principles" is the Reference Paper adopted by many countries in the WTO negotiations on Basic Telecommunications in 1997. It provides an obligation to promote competition as well as imposing transparency in the regulation. General principles on pro-competitive regulation can probably be defined at the horizontal level. However, concrete progress will not be made unless each sector conducts its own in-depth analysis of the specific meaning and implications of these principles.

Basic principles of domestic regulation

Failures to encourage competition among domestic suppliers weaken the integrity of the markets and even encourage corruption or monopolistic behavior, to the detriment of the customers. The aim should be promoting competition among all suppliers, national and foreigners, under the same regulatory conditions.

In addition to the provisions on National Treatment and Market Access, the GATS establishes, in Article VI, basic principles on domestic regulation. Domestic regulations which apply to foreign service suppliers in Member countries must be reasonable, objective and impartial. Pro-competitive regulatory principles should be based on the same objectives.

Importance of transparency

Transparency is an essential element of all regulatory principles. In accordance with their obligation in Article III of the GATS, governments should be transparent in their decision processes in order to identify new (or existing) restrictions, to avoid protectionist decisions, to adopt the least trade-restrictive option in their new regulation, when necessary, and to achieve market liberalization.

Recommendations

The industry representatives participating in the World Services Congress:
- Call on the WTO members to develop pro-competitive regulatory principles, while strengthening regulatory frameworks. Domestic

regulation should find the right balance between competition and stability. In financial services, stability of the industry is important, while in industries like telecommunications or postal services competition is paramount. They encourage the trade negotiators to involve the regulators in their discussion so as to ensure that the benefits of competition are reflected in regulatory principals.

- Invite the WTO members to analyze the possible transferability of the approach adopted in the Basic Telecommunications Reference Paper to other services domains and to proceed to a necessity test of any new regulation. Equal treatment should be ensured between public- and private-sector suppliers,
- Encourage the WTO members to work on the notion of capacity building, in order to help the developing countries to correctly regulate their service sectors in a competition friendly framework.

BPF13

Globalization of Entertainment and the Media: A Roundtable on Creating New Freedoms and Markets

Background: The rules of the GATS apply to the audiovisual industry in the same manner as they apply to all other services. Currently, 19 countries have made market access commitments in audiovisual services, including, the Dominican Republic, Hong Kong, India, Japan, Korea, Malaysia, Mexico, New Zealand, Panama, Singapore, the United States and others.

Status: Several issues have affected countries' willingness to make market-access commitments in this sector. A number of industry representatives have expressed concern that the services classification list itself is an impediment to countries taking meaningful commitments. The classification list either completely omits, or badly describes, key services, including cable system operators, channel operators (also know as programmers), satellite television service providers, and cinema operators. Some have expressed the belief that countries should have unimpeded flexibility to retain current measures and to adopt new measures to promote and protect their domestic film industries, whether or not those measures are discriminatory or limit market access. Others have noted that countries already have accepted trade commitments on audiovisual products pursuant to the GATT.

Recommendations

- Negotiators should revise the services classification list to better describe the range of services industries that are relevant to trade in audiovisual services.

- As part of the built-in agenda's mandate to address trade rules affecting services subsidies, negotiators should be mindful of the special role that subsidies play in many countries in promoting production of a diverse range of film and television products and services.
- Negotiators should seek to ensure that this highly trade-intensive service industry enjoys the benefits of world-trade rules, both with regard to traditional audiovisual services and to new media, while respecting the importance of promoting and preserving cultural diversity. Given the very constructive discussion at the World Services Congress, participants agreed that discussions should continue on how to secure the benefits of trade rules while maintaining diversity and quality of audiovisual services worldwide.
- Negotiators should extend the WTO standstill agreement on duty-free treatment for electron-ic transactions.
- WTO members should fully implement TRIPS to ensure that audiovisual works of all nations are protected from piracy. Negotiators should avoid weakening, reopening or delaying implementation of TRIPS.

BPF14

Aging Populations and How the WTO Can Help

Over the next half century, most WTO member nations will experience dramatic demographic transitions resulting in larger retiree populations and shrinking numbers of active workers supporting traditional pay-as-you-go social security systems. This fact and the inevitable economic pressures placed on citizens, economies, and governments should be of concern to the WTO trade ministers in Seattle as they launch the 2000 round of negotiations.

Private-sector, financial-service providers strongly support the development of a WTO agenda to address the issue of aging populations and trade mechanisms to increase the stability of the global trade economy and the financial security of member governments and their citizens

Recommendations

- The WTO classifications should be improved to cover the provision of pension products and services as well as the management of pension assets. In addition, we call for the development of a WTO mechanism to strongly encourage global pension reform based on free market principles, with sound regulation and tax mechanisms that encourage citizens to offset the forecasted large gaps in public expenditures through either group or individual forms of savings and benefits.

- Member governments should commit to maintain current liberal practices. Within a reasonable time frame and by a specified date, they also should schedule phase-in plans and market-access improvements consistent with the pension-reform recommendations of the World Bank and Organization for Economic Cooperation and Development. These schedules should not only include commitments in the provision (underwriting, sales, servicing) of pension and related services, but also commitments to liberalize investment restrictions. Any reservations under WTO regulatory carve-outs should be narrow and clear so as to avoid inappropriate and unjustified restrictions on the management of retirement funds.

The global problem of aging populations will be a major challenge to WTO member governments in the next century. The private sector believes it can play a constructive role in helping meet this challenge if WTO mechanisms to protect market-based retirement systems are implemented as part of the outcome of the 2000 round. We call on WTO member governments to recognize the urgent nature of these issues and hope to work with them to find solutions to our common problems.

BOF3

Expanding Business Opportunities: China on the Brink of WTO

The World Services Congress panel on China and the WTO discussed both the economics and politics of China's bid to join that organization. The panel also reviewed the role that the private sector can play to support China's economic reform efforts and to spur governments to conclude the WTO negotiations, which have now lasted for over a decade.

On the economic issues, the panel agreed that China's domestic reforms, while incomplete, are on track and are, in fact, irreversible. Whether China joins the WTO, the panel expressed confidence that China's leaders will move forward with plans to adopt more market-oriented policies.

The panel also agreed that the pace of economic reform would be governed by China's need to ensure stability. In this regard, services industries, especially financial services companies, can make a significant contribution to stability by creating jobs and mobilizing long-term capital. The panel believed that WTO membership would accelerate this process by embedding the rule of law into the Chinese economy.

On the political side, the panel noted that the window of opportunity for Chinese membership is closing. Domestic political considerations in China, the United States, and Europe may be overriding the economic rationale for Chinese membership and making it difficult for China to participate at the Seattle ministerial in other than an observer capacity. This will diminish the legitimacy of the WTO, will raise the price tag for eventual Chinese membership and will expose the fragility of, in particular, the U.S.-China bilateral relationship.

The panel believed that the task of pressing the case for China's WTO bid may well fall to the international private sector. The panel concluded it is critical for international business to press all governments to avoid drawing out the negotiations and to act quickly to make China a part of the drafting of the next generation of trade rules.

A15

Establishing Pro-Competitive Regulatory Regimes Through Services Negotiations

The importance of competitiveness and productivity in the Services Sector, because of its size and growing contribution to global trade, is key. Investment, as much as trade, is now the driving force of integration of the global economy. Labor mobility, the so-called "movement of natural persons," is a priority area for liberalization in the WTO round. Considering these three crosscutting issues, the panel put forward the recommendations below:

The WTO should in the Round:
- Adopt and strengthen pro-competitive reform measures
- Recognize the need for a balance between:
  - ➤ competition and social and economic stability
  - ➤ the interests of developing and developed countries with an emphasis on capacity building in developing countries
- Involve regulators in dialogue on the trade negotiations to a much greater degree than in the past
- Consider the sector-by-sector approach against the benefits of horizontal and more innovative approaches, looking in particular at the relevance and transferability of approaches such as the Telecoms Reference Paper approach
- Renew the mandate of the WTO Working Group on Trade and Investment
- Address investment liberalization forcefully in the GATS negotiations
- Seek a more structured dialogue between immigration, labor market and trade officials on the issue of regulation of labor mobility
- Promote a broader and more structured information exchange on immigration, labor market and trade strategies
- Seek to produce clearer and more relevant classification systems relevant to temporary entry (with reference to the ILO classification system)

APPENDIX 2

First World Services Congress: Business, Government, and Academic Sessions
November 1-3, Atlanta, Georgia

Opening Plenary Session

Services and the World Economy in the Next Millennium

Welcoming Remarks
Dean R. O'Hare, Chairman and Chief Executive Officer, The Chubb Corporation and Chair, World Services Congress
Greetings
Paul Coverdell, United States Senator, Georgia
Special Welcoming Message on "The Importance of Services on the Eve of the Millennium"
Renato Ruggiero, Former Director General, World Trade Organization
Conveyed by:
Michael Duffy, Consultant, Mallesons Stephen, Jaques, and Former Minister of Communications and Trade Negotiations, Australia

Main Address
- Richard W. Fisher, Deputy United States Trade Representative
- Fidel Ramos, Former President, the Philippines
- Ambassador Arima, Special Representative of the Minister of Foreign Affairs, Japan

Concurrent Sessions

BOF 1: Ripe Opportunities: Modernizing the Services Infrastructure in Latin America and the Caribbean
Recent reforms in Latin America create vast opportunities for growth in the service industries. How should local corporations reevaluate their place and options in a global marketplace? How have Latin American services companies prepared to open up to a world of opportunities through foreign direct investment, joint ventures and/or strategic alliances?
Panelists:
- Jorge Alberto Jimenez, Vice President, Bavaria and Inversiones Bavaria, Colombia
- Javier Aguirre Noguez, President of CTC Comunicaciones, Chile

BOF 2: Creating Your Global Electronic Business: Pitfalls and Opportunities

Whether you want to set up a one-man international business over the Internet or build a conglomerate, you can avoid costly mistakes and benefit from the experience of others. This session will provide a road map around the obstacles and a guide to the best solutions.

Chair: Michio Naruto, Vice Chairman, Fujitsu, Tokyo, Japan
Panelists:

- Pinkard A. "Pinky" Brand, Director, idNames Division, Network Solutions, Washington D.C.
- Reinaldo Gonzalez, Executive Vice-President, Visualcom, Miami, Florida
- David Moxam, President, Global Strategy & Marketing, E-Solutions, EDS, Plano, TX
- Andrès Felipe Rodriguez, Partner, CybeRegulation Consulting Group, Washington, D.C.
- Todd Tweedy, Chief Marketing Officer, NetComOne.com, Washington, D.C.

BPF 1: Effective Strategies for Insurance Providers in the Global Marketplace: Goals and Objectives for Negotiations

Insurance providers increasingly see their markets as global and look to governments to help them break down barriers to establish cross border trade. Regulatory barriers—in advanced as well as emerging markets – have come under scrutiny as major barriers to entry. How can trade negotiations be used to secure a fairer, more open playing field for insurance providers? Part of the answer is in understanding the key role insurance plays in mobilizing capital and creating economic growth.

Chair: L. Oakley Johnson, Senior Vice President, Corporate & International Affairs, American International Group Inc., Washington, D.C.

Panelists:

- Gérard de la Martinière, Senior Executive Vice President and Chief Financial Officer, AXA Group, Paris, France
- Thomas Hess, Chief Economist, Swiss Re, Zurich, Switzerland
- Patrick Liedtke, Deputy Secretary General, The Geneva Association, Geneva, Switzerland

Background Papers/Resources:

- Harold D. Skipper, Jr., Professor of Risk Management & Insurance, Georgia State University, Atlanta, GA, "Insurance in the General Agreement on Trade in Services: Successes and Prospects."
- R. Brian Woodrow, Professor, Political Science, University of Guelph, Guelph, Canada, and Julian Arkell, Consultant, International

Trade & Services Policy, Menorca, Spain, "Trade In Insurance Services: Implications For the Services 2000 Negotiations."

BPF 2: Freeing Up Cross-Border Trade in Financial Services: Considering the Electronic Dimension

Considerable progress has been made in securing rights to establish brick and mortar commercial presence in many key emerging markets. But increasingly, the business plans of global businesses call for serving markets by doing business across borders, and doing that business electronically. What does business need from governments in the next WTO round on financial services? Are governments up to the job?

Chair: Toru Kusukawa, Chairman of the Board of Counselors, Fuji Research Institute Corporation, Tokyo, Japan

Panelists:

- Juan Domingo Cavallo, Presidente, Fundación Mediterranea, and former Finance Minister, Argentina
- Mitchell Feuer, Vice President for Government and Regulatory Affairs, Reuters International, Washington, D.C.
- Charles S. Levy, Partner, Wilmer, Cutler & Pickering, Washington, D.C.
- John Pattison, Senior Vice President for Regulatory and Corporate Affairs, CIBC, Toronto, Canada
- Hernan Sommerville Senn, Asociación de Bancos e Instituciones Financieras, Chile

Special Guest:

- Meg Lundsager, Deputy Assistant Secretary for International Affairs, U. S. Department of the Treasury, Washington, D.C.

BPF 3: How the Energy Services Industry Can Use Trade Negotiations to Secure and Expand Markets

Energy services are for the first time being considered subject to multilateral trade negotiations both in the US and EU. But issues of definition need to be resolved: which services and products should be defined as "energy services?" What are the most important goals for energy services companies and energy producing countries?

Chair: Terence H. Thorn, Executive Vice President, International Government Relations & Environmental Affairs, Enron International, Houston, TX

Panelists:

- John J. Easton, Jr., Vice-President, International Programs, Edison Electric Institute, Washington, D.C.
- Ian Miller, President, EDS Global Energy Business, Plano, TX
- Tim Richards, Senior Manager, International & Government Affairs, General Electric, Washington, D.C.

Background Papers/Resources:

- Dennis Jay O'Brien, Director, Institute for Energy & Economics Policy, University of Oklahoma, Norman, OK, "GATS 2000 and Sectoral Liberalization: Energy."
- Rachel Thompson, Administrator, Trade Directorate, OECD, Paris), France "Environmental Services."

BPF 4: Moving Business Personnel: An Agenda for WTO Action

Capital moves across borders swiftly. But movement of business personnel is impeded by visa and other restrictions, adding substantial costs to the operation of knowledge intensive global business. How can these issues be addressed in the WTO services 2000 negotiations?

Chair: Jerker Torngren, Director, European Public Telecom Network Operators' Association-ETNO and Chairman, Policy Committee, European Services Network, Brussels, Belgium

Panelists:

- Jeremy Seddon, Director General, British Invisibles, London, UK
- Des Shaw, Managing Director, Global Facilitation Center, PricewaterhouseCoopers, Washington, D.C.

G1: Getting What You Pay For: Maximizing Your Use of Procurement Dollars

Governments are often faced with a wide range of service providers offering a number of service quality and price-points. Learn from major consulting practitioners how to align value and price when awarding these major service contracts. Of interest to state and local procurement officials and the vendors who work with them.

Panelists:

- Steven Rohleder, Andersen Consulting, Washington, D.C.

G2: Managing the Procurement Process: Lessons from Canada

Canadian procurement officials and leading vendors have come together to produce a set of guidelines that redefine the procurement process in that nation. Learn what they did and how you can replicate their success. Of interest to all government procurement officials and the vendors who work with them.

Panelists:

- The Honorable Dan Baker, IBM Canada, and Former Deputy Minister, Alberta Health, Edmonton, Alberta, Canada
- Howard Grant, President, Partnering & Procurement Inc., Ottawa, Canada
- Ray Hession, Chairman, HLB Decision Economics, and former Deputy Minister, Canadian Department of Supply and Services, Ottawa. Canada.

- Alan Hurd, Executive Vice President, EDS Canada Ltd., Toronto, Canada
- Linda Lizotte-MacPherson, Chief Information Officer, Treasury Board of Canada, Secretariat, Government of Canada, Ottawa, Canada
-

G3: Cutting-Edge Municipal Finance: Bringing Local Government Assets to Market
Governments often have substantial unrealized assets. The country's most sophisticated municipal finance advisors give you the inside track on securing funds by securitizing your local government's assets.
Panelists:
- Eugene Duffy, Executive Vice President, Paradigm Asset Management Company, Atlanta, GA
- Ernest Green, Managing Director, Lehman Brothers, and Chair, National Association of Security Professionals.
- Micah Green, President, the Bond Market Association, Washington, D. C.
- Daniel Heimowitz, Managing Director, Lehman Brothers, New York, NY
- William Hayden, Senior Managing Director, Bear, Sterns & Company, New York, NY
- Lenda Washington, GRW Capital Corporation, Washington, D.C.
- LoRita Wallace, Program Director, NASP, Washington, D.C.

A 2: Recent Developments in Measuring Services Productivity
Services do not readily lend themselves to quantitative measurement in the same ways as goods, which makes it difficult to determine how services productivity should be measured. Nonetheless, it may be possible to devise useful methods for measuring productivity in various services sectors.
Panelist:
- Jack Triplett, The Brookings Institution, Washington, D.C., "Measurement of Services Productivity."

Luncheon

The Value of the WTO Services 2000 Agenda in a Fast Changing World Economy.

Introductory Remarks and Luncheon Chairman
Michio Naruto, Vice Chairman, Fujitsu Ltd., Tokyo, Japan.

Luncheon Address
- William M. Daley, Secretary of Commerce, United States

- Herminio Blanco Mendoza, Secretary for Commerce and Industrial Development, Mexico

Concurrent Sessions

BPF 5: Airing Differences: What Business Needs in a New Agreement on Air Cargo Services

Air freight has become an essential service for efficient world business operations. Air freight services are constrained by a wide range of impediments, including landing rights and custom and clearing procedures. Multilateralizing the current bilateral landing rights procedures could lead to new efficiencies.

Chair: Thomas W. Weidemeyer, President, Air Operations, United Parcel Service, Atlanta, GA

Panelists:

- Rush O'Keefe, Vice President Regulatory Affairs, Federal Express Corporation, Memphis, TN
- Jeffrey Shane, Partner, Wilmer, Cutler and Pickering, Washington, D.C.

Background Paper/Resource:

- Tendal Gregan, Economist, Market Operations, NEMMCO, Sydney, Australia "Modeling the Effects of Liberalized International Air Service Agreements."

BPF 6: The Basic Telecom Agreement: Securing the Gains and Framing the Services 2000 Agenda

Trade agreements are only as good as their implementation. The 1997 WTO Telecommunications Agreement was widely heralded as a breakthrough, but its implementation by signatories is incomplete. What lessons from the 1997 agreement's implementation should inform the 2000 negotiation? What are the priorities for securing new liberalization?

Chair: Michael Duffy, Consultant, Mallesons Stephen Jaques, and Former Minister of Communications and Trade Negotiations, Melbourne, Australia

Panelists:

- David Dorman, CEO, AT&T/BT Global Venture, Atlanta, GA
- Francisco Gomez Alamillo, Secretary-General, AHCIET, Madrid, Spain
- Laura Sherman, Counsel, Commercial, Paul, Weiss, Rifkind, Wharton & Garrison, Washington, DC

Background Papers/Resources:

- Meriel V. M. Bradford, Vice-President, Teleglobe, Ottawa, Canada, "From Monopoly to Global Telecommunications Enterprise: The Teleglobe Case

- Peter F. Cowhey, Director, and Mikhail Klimenko, Institute on Global Conflict and Cooperation, University of California at San Diego, San Diego, CA, "Implementing Telecommunications Liberalization in the Developing Countries after the WTO Agreement on Basic Telecommunications Services"
- Stephen McDowell, Assistant Professor, Department of Communication, Florida State University, Tallahassee, FL., Ana Luz Ruelas Monjardin, Facultad de Historia de la Universidad Autonoma de Sinaloa, Culiacan, Sinaloa, Mexico, and Martin Dowding, Information Studies, University of Toronto, Toronto, Canada, "Telecommunications Services: NAFTA and National Legislation."

BPF 8: Creating an Open Global Market for Accountancy: Its Essential Role in Economic Modernization, Capital Mobilization, and Stable Financial Markets

Freedom to practice the accounting profession is constrained in many countries in many ways. The WTO has made a weak initial effort to progress toward more freedom to practice. Is it possible to achieve liberalization in the multilateral WTO forum? If so, what should industry ask, and expect, of government in the next round of negotiations?

Chair: Peter Smith, Global Industries Leader, PricewaterhouseCoopers, London, UK

Panelist:

- John Hegarty, Regional Financial Management Advisor, Europe and Central Asia Region, The World Bank, Washington, D.C.

Background Paper/Resource:

- Lawrence J. White, Arthur E. Imperator Professor of Economics, Stern School of Business, New York University, "GATS 2000 and Sectoral Liberalization: Accounting."

BPF 9: Creating a Global Marketplace in Legal Services: A Roundtable Discussion

Bringing Legal Services in Tune with the 21st Century Marketplace—Although international law is becoming increasingly harmonized, including through the effect of WTO Agreements, national barriers to legal services remains widespread. Many countries restrict foreign lawyers, regardless of whether they are advising on national or home jurisdictions. As cross-border activities increase, such as global mergers and acquisitions, it is all the more necessary to reduce regulations on legal services to reflect the 21st century marketplace.

Chair: Greg Spak, Partner, White and Case, Washington, D.C.

Panelists:

- José Rafael Bustamante, Partner, Bustamante & Bustamante, Quito, Ecuador

- Ernesto Cavalier, Partner, Parra, Rodriguez & Cavalier, Bogota, Colombia
- Peter Morrison, Head, World Trade Group, Clifford Chance, London, UK
- Sydney M. Cone, III, Counsel, Cleary, Gottlieb, Steen & Hamilton and C.V. Starr Professor of Law, New York School of Law, New York, NY
- Steven C. Nelson, Partner, Dorsey & Whitney, LLP, Minneapolis, MN

BPF 14: Aging Populations and How the WTO Can Help
An expert panel reviewing the global problem of aging populations, with reviews of international efforts to quantify and minimize negative economic impacts for workers and dependents in emerging and developed markets. Panelists from government, international organizations, academia, and the global pension industry will discuss how WTO 2000 Negotiations can complement, rather than impede, efforts to encourage retirement saving and strengthen world pension systems.
Chair: Cathy Heron, Assistant General Counsel, The Capital Group Companies, Inc., Los Angeles, CA
Panelists:
- George N. Curuby, President, Curuby & Company, Tokyo, Japan
- David Harris, Consultant, Research & Information Center, Watson Wyatt Worldwide, Bethesda, MD
- Alan Shortell, Vice President, Asset Management, New York Life, Parsipanny, N.J.

Special Guests:
- Everette James, Deputy Assistant Secretary for Service Industries & Finance, U.S. Department of Commerce, Washington, D.C.
- Gerard de Graaf, First Secretary (Trade), European Commission Delegation, Washington, D.C.

G4: The Challenge of the Desktop: How Business and Government Manage their Computing Environments
Every organization—both public and private—must face the challenge of managing the desktop-computing environment. How can they learn from each other's experiences? Of interest to any organization rising to the desktop revolution.
Panelists:
- Charles A. Self, Assistant Commissioner, General Services Administration/FTS Office of IT Integration, Falls Church, VA
- Jeff DePasquale, Federal Program Manager, Cisco Systems
- Bill Piatt, Chief Information Officer, General Services Administration

- Chris Wren, Director, Special Projects and New Product Development, Office of Information Technology Integration

G6: Managing Public-Private Partnerships

How can a state or local government and technically sophisticated service providers work together without one being captured by the other? Learn how to develop procedures and measures that allow both sides to share the risks when negotiating service contracts. Of interest to all government procurement officials and the vendors who work with them.

Panelists:

- Bonnie Ewart, Assistant Deputy Minister and Director, Business Transformation Project, Ministry of Community and Social Services (MCSS), Toronto, Canada
- Anthony Grant, Partner and Project Manager for the MCSS Business Transformation Project, Andersen Consulting, Toronto, Canada
- Raymond V. Hession, Chairman, HLB Decision Economics, Ottawa, Canada
- David Lewis, President, HLB Decision Economics, Ottawa, Canada
- Stephen Uhlig, Director, Infrastructure Finance, Deutsche Bank AG, London, UK

A 3: Achieving Market Access Through Mutual Recognition Agreements

One very effective way to reduce barriers to trade and foreign direct investment in services may be to negotiate so-called mutual recognition agreements that provide for the harmonization of product and technical standards and other pertinent aspects of services.

Panelists:

- Americo Beviglia Zampetti, Directorate-General 1 (US Desk), European Commission, Brussels, Belgium "Market Access Through Mutual Recognition: The Promise and Limits of GATS Article VII (Recognition)."
- Kalypso Nicolaïdis, Associate Professor, Harvard University, Cambridge, MA, and University Lecturer, Oxford University, Oxford, UK, and Joel P. Trachtman, Professor of International Law and Academic Dean, The Fletcher School of Law and Diplomacy, Tufts University, Medford, MA, " From Policed Domestic Regulation to Mutual Recognition: Assessing the Boundary Between GATS Articles VI (Domestic Regulation) and VII (Recognition)."

A 4: Services Contributions to Economic Growth: Country Experiences

In order to enhance the understanding of how the production and trade of services and foreign direct investment have evolved, much can be learned from case studies of the experiences of individual countries.

Chair: Harinder Kohli, President and Chief Executive Officer, Centennial Group, Washington, D.C.

Panelists:

- Wolfgang Grassl, Department of Economics & Business, Hillsdale College, Hillsdale, MI, "Growth of Service Sector and Development: Is There a Dutch Disease?"
- Oksana K. Mont, Research Associate, Lund University, Lund, Sweden, "Strategic Alliance Between Products and Services."
- Nanno Mulder, Economist, CEPII, Paris, France, "The Economic Performance of the Service Sector in Brazil, Mexico, and the USA."
- Jose L. Pereyra, Economic Researcher, Central Reserve Bank of Peru, Lima, Peru, The Trade of Services In Peru: Analysis and Empirical Evidence 1990-1994."
- Genevieve H. Plank, Attorney-at-Law, Oakville, Canada, "Double Taxation: Riding on the Backs of Filipino Export Labor."
- Frederico Rocha, Professor, IE/UFRJ, Rio de Janeiro, Brazil, "Service Sector Growth in Brazil."
- Morshidi B. Sirat, Associate Professor, University Sains Malaysia, Penang, Malaysia "Exporting of Professional Services: Issues and Challenges for Malaysia."
- Chibuike U. Uche, Senior Lecturer, Department of Banking & Finance, University of Nigeria, "Banking Regulation in an Era of Structural Adjustment: The Case of Nigeria."

A 6: Services 2000: Is there a Better Way?

There is concern that only a limited degree of liberalization of services was accomplished in the Uruguay Round GATS negotiations. The issue then is to consider different modes for achieving more meaningful liberalization in the WTO-2000 service negotiations.

Chair: Jun Yokota, Deputy Director General, Economic Affairs Bureau, Ministry of Foreign Affairs, Tokyo, Japan

Panelists:

- Peter Collins, Deputy Assistant, U. S. Trade Representative Services & Investment, Office of the U. S. Trade Representative, Washington, D.C.
- Giles Gauthier, Chief, Trade in Services and Investment, International Trade Policy Division, in collaboration with Erin O'Brien and Susan Spencer, Department of Finance, Government of Canada, Ottawa, Canada, "Contingent Protection for Services: Distilling the Debate on Subsidies and Safeguards."
- Bernard Hoekman, Principal Trade Economist, Development Research Group, The World Bank, Washington, D.C., and Patrick Messerlin, Director, Groupe d'Economie Mondiale (GEM), Paris,

France, "Liberalizing Trade in Services: Harnessing Reciprocal Negotiations to Regulatory Reform."
- Aaditya Mattoo, Senior Economist, The World Bank, Washington, D.C., and Patrick Low, Director, Economic Research & Analysis, World Trade Organization), "Is There a Better Way? Alternative Approaches to Liberalization under the GATS."
- Michel Servoz, Head of Unit for Services, Directorate General I, The European Commission, Brussels, Belgium
- Rachel Thompson, Administrator, OECD Trade Directorate, Paris, France, "Formula Approaches to Improving GATS Commitments: Some Options for Negotiators."

Concurrent Sessions

BOF 3: Expanding Business Opportunities: China on the Brink of the WTO

As China prepares for possible entry into the WTO, what are the best strategies for gaining the right to do business there? How quickly can the rules change in case of WTO accession? How does China now see the role of the foreign investor in furthering its own economic modernization interests?
Chair: Cynthia Y. Valko, Executive Vice President, New York Life International, Philadelphia, Pennsylvania
Panelists:
- Philippe Brahin, Director for European and International Affairs, Fédération Français des Sociétiés d'Assurances, Paris, France
- Long Yongtu, Vice Minister, Ministry of Foreign Trade and Economic Cooperation, Beijing, PRC
- Gary Tooker, Vice Chairman of the Board, Motorola, Schaumburg, IL
- Ira Wolf, Senior Policy Advisor, Senator Max Baucus, Washington, D.C.

Background Papers/Resources:
- Wai-Kwan Chan, Secretary General, and Thinex Shek, Hong Kong Coalition of Service Industries and Hong Kong General Chamber of Commerce, Hong Kong, "China's Liberalisation of Trade in Services and Accession to the WTO."

BPF 10: After the Freight Hits the Dock: Achieving New Efficiencies in Rail, Transit, Trucking and Air Freight

The vast expansion in international trade owes much to a revolution in the business of moving freight. Logistics and supply chain management are expanding to include information services. Express companies are the physical reflection of the Internet's ability to provide major infrastructure to trade in the next century. Customs and clearance operations are an integral part of increasingly widespread "on-time" delivery of packages and freight. How can liberalization in these domains reinforce these trends?

Chair: David Roussain, Vice President, ECCS Marketing, Federal Express Corporation, Collierville, TN

Panelists:

- Alan Amling, Director, Electronic Commerce, United Parcel Service, Atlanta, GA
- Michael Canon, Country Manager, DHL Worldwide Express, Sao Paulo, Brazil
- Dr. John D. Kasarda, Director, Kenan Institute of Private Enterprise, The Kenan Center, The University of North Carolina at Chapel Hill, Chapel Hill, NC
- Anthony Pellegrini, Director, Transportation, Water and Urban Development, The World Bank, Washington, D.C

Background Papers/Resources:

- Wayne Cottrell, Research Assistant Professor, Department of Civil & Environmental Engineering, University of Utah, Salt Lake City, UT, "Automated Transit as an Indicator of National Economic Status."
- Brian Hindley, London School of Economics & Political Science, London, UK, and Principal, Legg Inc., London, UK, and Daniel M. Kasper, Managing Director, Law and Economics Consulting Group (LECG), Cambridge, MA, "Air Transport and the GATS."
- Isabelle Rabaud, Economist, University of Angers, CEPII, Paris, France "Export Performance of Industrialized Countries in Transport."

BPF 11: Barriers to Electronic Commerce: The Agenda for WTO Negotiations

The WTO has conducted an extensive work program on electronic commerce issues. What issues have now arisen to the top of the agenda requiring decisions by Trade Ministers and action in the coming negotiations? Will these decisions lead to more open trade?

Panelists:

- Robert D. Kramer, Vice President International Government Relations,
- Bank of America, Washington D.C.
- Catherine L. Mann, Senior Fellow, Institute for International Economics, Washington, D.C.
- Michel Servoz, Head of Unit for Services, Directorate General I, The European Commission, Brussels, Belgium
- Rachel Thompson, Administrator, Trade Directorate, OECD, Paris, France

Background Papers/Resources:

- Claude E. Barfield, Resident Scholar and Director of Trade and Science and Technology Policy Studies, The American Enterprise Institute, Washington, D.C., and Mark Groombridge, Research Fellow, Center for Trade Policy Studies, Cato Institute, Washington, D.C., "Breaking Down Barriers in Electronic Commerce."
- Jason Cruz, Law Student, University of Washington, Seattle, WA, "Are You the Master of Your Domain: Cybersquatters, Dilution, and the Private Side of Domain Names."
- William M. Drake, Senior Associate and Director of the Project on the Information Revolution & World Politics, Carnegie Endowment for International Peace, Washington, D.C., and Kalypso Nicolaïdis, Associate Professor, Harvard University, Cambridge, MA, and University Lecturer, Oxford University, Oxford, UK. "Global Electronic Commerce and the General Agreement on Trade in Services: The "Millennium Round.""
- Catherine L. Mann, Senior Fellow, Institute for International Economics, Washington, D.C., "Electronic Commerce and the Developing Countries: A Complementary Strategy for Domestic Policy and WTO Negotiations."
- Sandip Soli, Law Student, University of Washington, Seattle, WA, "Governing Electronic Commerce: Choice of Law, Consumer Protection, and the Role of the WTO."
- Rachel Thompson, Administrator, Trade Directorate, OECD, Paris, France "Services Liberalization to Support Electronic Commerce."

BPF 12: Achieving Regulatory Transparency and Pro-Competitive Regulatory Reform Through Trade Negotiations

As gains are made in securing more open markets for services trade, it becomes increasingly apparent that domestic regulation can block competition. Are trade negotiations a means of achieving regulatory reform that is "pro-competitive?" What are the most effective strategies for influencing domestic regulators to adopt pro-competitive policies? Are commitments to improve regulatory transparency a substitute for pro-competitive reform?

Chair: Andrew Buxton, Chairman, Board of Directors, Barclays PLC Bank, and Chairman, European Services Leaders Group, London, UK

Panelists:

- Jeff Lang, Attorney, Wilmer, Cutler & Pickering, Washington, D.C.
- W. Kenneth Lindhorst, International Vice President, AT&T, Basking Ridge, New Jersey
- Kevin Mulvey, Director–International Government Relations, American International Group, Inc., Washington, D.C.
- Anton van der Lande, Vice President, Public Affairs International, United Parcel Service, Brussels, Belgium

Special Guest:
- Hideichiro Hamanaka, Deputy Commissioner, Financial Supervisory Agency, Tokyo, Japan

Background Papers Resources/Resources
- Geza Feketekuty, Director, Center for Trade & Commercial Diplomacy, Monterey Institute of International Studies, Monterey, CA, and Claude E. Barfield, Resident Scholar and Director of Trade and Science and Technology Policy Studies, The American Enterprise Institute, Washington, D.C., "Regulatory Reform and Trade Liberalization in Services."
- Malcolm McKinnon, Head of Trade in Services Unit, U.K. Department of Trade and Industry, London, UK, "Negotiating 'Pro-Competitive' Regulatory Systems."
- Mark A. A. Warner, Legal Counsel, Division of Policy Inter-Relations Trade Directorate, OECD Trade Directorate, Paris, France, "Exploring the GATS Implications of Integrating Competition Policy into the WTO."

BPF 13: Globalization of Entertainment and the Media: A Roundtable on Creating New Freedoms and Markets

Technology is enhancing "trade", or global consumption, of all forms of entertainment, news and advertising. New distribution channels are creating new opportunities and new partnerships for bringing films and music from all countries to worldwide audiences. Is there a role for the World Trade Organization in removing barriers to cultural interchange while respecting national cultural promotion objectives? What avenues are there for making progress in the multilateral forum?

Panelists:
- Karen Flischel, Managing Director, Nickelodeon International, New York, NY
- Preston Padden, Executive Vice President, Walt Disney Company, Washington, D.C.
- Ricardo Salina Pliego, Presidente, Television Azteca, Mexico DF, Mexico
- C. K. Poon, Managing Director, Golden Harvest, Hong Kong
- Kunal Dasgupta, Chief Executive Officer, Set India, Ltd.

Background Papers/Resources:
- Keith Acheson, and Christopher J. Maule, Professors of Economics, Carleton University, Ottawa, Canada, "Canadian Magazine Policy: International Conflict and Domestic Stagnation."
- Patrick Messerlin, Director, and Emmanuel Cocq, Groupe d'Economie Mondiale (GEM), Paris, France, "Preparing Negotiations in Services: EC Audiovisuals in the Millenium Round."

- Steve Siwek, Principal, Economists, Inc., Washington, D.C. and Patrick Messerlin, Director, Groupe d'Economie Mondiale (GEM), Paris, France, "GATS 2000 and Sectoral Liberalization: Entertainment and Cultural Industries."

G8: No Money Down: Share-in-Savings Government Contracting
How governments use "share in savings" contracting to procure vital services by giving service providers a share of the cost savings they create: examples will be drawn from both computing and energy / environmental services. Of interest to state and local procurement officials and the vendors who work with them.
Panelists:
- Ken Buck, General Services Administration, Washington, D.C.
- Ed Burke, Andersen Consulting
- Roger Dower, SYCOM Enterprises
- Steve Kelman, John F. Kennedy School of Government, Harvard University, Cambridge, MA
- Chip Mather, Acquisition Solutions

G9: Information Please: What Government Data Can Tell You About Your Industry and Location
How to get your hands on government data on industries, markets, localities, trade patterns, demographics, and everything else you need to know to make business decisions.
Panelists:
- Carole A. Ambler, Chief Services Division, U. S. Department of Commerce, Bureau of the Census, Washington, D.C.
- Hugh Knox, Associate Director, Bureau of Economic Analysis, Washington, D.C.
- Armando Lopez, Economist, STAT-USA, U.S. Department of Commerce, Washington, D.C.
- Obie G. Whichard, Assistant Chief, International Investment Division, Bureau of Economic Analysis, U.S. Department of Commerce, Washington, D.C.

A9: How to Measure Barriers to Services Trade and FDI
Because many services do not cross national boundaries in the same way as goods and because of the need for proximity between producers and consumers, it is often very difficult to determine how existing barriers to trade and foreign direct investment affect services prices and quantities. Nonetheless, information of this kind is needed as the basis for negotiating reductions in services barriers and the economic effects involved.
Chair: Josephine Ludolph, Director, Office of Service Industries, U.S. Department of Commerce, Washington, D.C.

Panelists:

- James W. Hodge, Senior Researcher, Development Policy Research Unit, Atlanta, GA, "The Real Cost of Services Protection in a Developing Country: The Case of South Africa."
- Wing Fai Leung, Assistant Professor, Department of Economics & Finance; Anming Zhang, Head; Steve Ching and Clement Wong, Assistant Professors, City University of Hong Kong, Hong Kong, and Victor Hung, Principal Consultant, Apogee Consultants, Kowloon, Hong Kong, "Effects of Administrative Barriers to Trade on Cross-Border Flow of Services."
- Neela Mukherjee, Consultant, New Delhi, India, " Producer Subsidy Equivalent (PSE) Approach—An Alternative Policy Estimate for Negotiations: A Case Study of U.S. Shipping Services."
- Christopher Findlay, Adelaide University, Department of Economics, Adelaide, Australia and Tony Warren, Research Fellow, Australian National University, Asia Pacific School of Economics & Management, Canberra, Australia, "Measuring Impediments to Trade in Services."

A13: Education & Training: Supporting Global Services Industries

Worker education and training are key factors in promoting efficient services sectors. What are the key considerations that need to be taken into account? What can be learned from individual country experiences in promoting the education and training of workers?

Chair: Gunnel Mohme, Director, Federation of Swedish Industries, Stockholm, Sweden

Panelists:

- Shivganesh Bhargava, Associate Professor, Department of Humanities & Social Sciences, Indian Institute of Technology, Bombay, India "Are Public Enterprises of the Developing Nations at the Crossroads: Role of Human Resources Management in Transformation."
- Kamel Esseghairi, General Secretary, Afro-Mediterranean Movement for Sustainable Development, Bardo, Tunisia, "Privatizing University in Tunisia: Contribution to Implementing Structural Adjustment Reforms and Adapting Training to Employment in the Context of Globalization."
- Shangquan Gao, Ph.D. Supervisor, Professor, Peking University, Beijing, PRC, "China's Unemployment Situation and Policy Recommendation."
- Yuko Harayama, Assistant Professor, University of Geneva, Geneva, Switzerland, "The Relationship Between Stanford University and Silicon Valley Industry."

- Stefan O. Lagrosen, Senior Lecturer, School of Management & Economics, Vaxjo University, Kronoberg, Sweden, "Introducing TQM in Schools."
- Tate Miller, President and CEO, Asia Industrial Group, Inc, Beijing, PRC, "China: Workforce Development in a Transition Economy."
- Jennifer R. Moll, Assistant Director, Global Alliance for Transnational, Washington, D.C., "Barriers to Trade in Education Services."
- Allan Charles Sensicle, Consultant (Strategic Planning, Auditing and Quality Management), Vocational Training Council, Hong Kong, "The Development and the Role of the Vocational Training Council During a Period of Rapid Social and Economic Change."
- Enoch Young and John A. Cribbin, Senior Administrator, School of Professional and Continuing Education, University of Hong Kong, Hong Kong, "Servicing the Service Economy: Lifelong Learning In Human Capital Development In Hong Kong."

Reception Hosted by the Hong Kong Special Administrative Region of the People's Republic of China
Stuart Harbinson, Permanent Representative of the Hong Kong Special Administrative Region of China to the World Trade Organization and Chairman, World Trade Organization Council on Trade in Services

Tuesday November 2

Business to Government Dialogue: Recommendations for the WTO Ministerial and the "Services 2000" Negotiations
Business leaders present the recommendations of the Congress Business Policy Forums for discussion with government officials.
Session Chair:
Lord Hurd of Westwell, Deputy Chairman, NatWest Bank and Chairman, British Invisibles
Private Sector Representatives

- Cynthia Valko, Executive Vice President, New York Life International
- Toru Kusukawa, Chairman of the Board of Counselors, Fuji Research Institute Corporation, Tokyo, Japan
- Terence Thorn, Executive Vice President, International Government Relations and Environmental Affairs, Enron International
- Jerker Torngren, Director, European Public Telecom Network Operators' Association (ETNO) and Chairman, Policy Committee, European Services Network

- Thomas Weidemeyer, President, Air Operations, United Parcel Service
- Michael Duffy, Consultant, Mallesons Stephen Jaques, and Former Minister of Communications and Trade Negotiations, Australia
- Peter Smith, Global Industries Leader, PricewaterhouseCoopers
- Greg Spak, Partner, White and Case
- David Roussain, Vice President, ECCS Marketing, Federal Express Corporation
- Andrew Buxton, Chairman, European Services Leaders Group
- Catherine Heron, Assistant General Counsel, The Capital Group Companies, Inc.

Government Remarks
- Stuart Harbinson, Permanent Representative of Hong Kong to the World Trade Organization and Chairman of the World Trade Organization Council on Trade in Services
- Patricia Kelly, Division Head for Services and Emerging Industries, the Australian Department of Industry, Science and Resources
- Katsuhiro Nakagawa, Special Advisor, Ministry of Trade and Industry, Japan
- John Mogg, Director-General, European Commission, Directorate General XV, Internal Market & Financial Services
- Diego Molano, President, Comisión Nacional de Regulación de las Telecomunicaciones, Colombia
- Joseph S. Papovich, Assistant United States Trade Representative, Services, Investment and Intellectual Property

Concurrent Sessions

BOF 4: New Business Opportunities and Alliances in Emerging Markets: What Key Factors Should You Consider?
Senior business and government experts will share their insights and experiences on entering new markets, establishing critical linkages to local power structures, and doing business on the same terms as a national or local company.
Chair: Joseph Sutton, Chairman and CEO, Enron International, Houston, TX
Panelists:
- Nicholas Brooke, Chairman, Brooke International, Hong Kong
- Rolf Passow, Vice President, European Federation of Investment Funds and Companies and Member of the Board, Deutscher Investment Trust, Frankfurt, Germany

Background Papers/Resources:
- Nicholas Brooke, Chairman, Brooke International, Hong Kong, "The Challenge Facing a Service Provider in Immature and Emerging Markets: A Practitioner's Perspective."

- Cristiana T. Cristureanu, Professor, Faculty of International Business & Economics, Academy of Economic Studies, Bucharest, Romania, "Services In Romania: FDI Opportunities (Case Study: Insurance Market)"
- Agnes F. Ghibutiu, Head of Department, Institute of World Economy, Bucharest, Romania, "Considering the Contribution of Services to Economic Growth and Development in Emerging Market Economies: The Case of Romania."
- Sergey B. Shlikhter, Principal Researcher, Institute of Geography, Munich, Germany, "Tertiary Sector as a Basis of Transition in the Post-Industrial Era."

BOF 5: Japan on the Rebound: A Roundtable on New Opportunities for Service Industries
Experts, business leaders and key officials present informed opinions on Japan's business environment, recent regulatory reforms, and competitiveness in the global services market. Will Japan turn the corner toward new growth? Has there been any real change in the climate for foreign investment?
Panelists:
- Toru Kusukawa, Chairman of the Board of Counselors, Fuji Research Institute Corporation
- Minoru Makihara, Chairman, Mitsubishi Corporation, Tokyo, Japan
- Tadashi Omiya, Executive Vice President, Japan External Trade Organization (JETRO), Tokyo, Japan
- Jeremy Seddon, Director General, British Invisibles, London, UK

G11: Getting Local Governments Ready for E-Commerce
Electronic commerce is the future: is your state or local government ready? Find out how to assess your preparedness and how to take the next steps to make your agencies e- commerce proficient.
Panelists:
- Ken Kay, Computer Systems Policy Project, Infotech Strategies, LLC, Washington, D.C.
- Edmund Perry, Director, Government Relations and Growth Projects, IBM Corporation, Washington, D.C.
- Pari Sabety, Director, Technology Policy, Ohio Supercomputer Project, Columbus, OH

G12: Pioneering Public-Private Partnerships: Counties Partner for Savings and Success
Many counties today are facing crises in their service provision. How do they meet the growing demand for quality services without increasing taxes? Many counties are investigating cost savings and better service delivery and as a result more and more are looking toward private sector companies. Quorum,

the largest hospital management firm in the United States, is a company that has worked closely with county governments and their programs. This company will present a case study of two county governments that saved significant amounts of money and improved service provision and performance as a result of this partnering.

Session Objectives

- Describe the process of identifying a private sector company to help provide county services and how to avoid the pitfalls
- Provide sample requests for proposals and contracts for private sector partnerships
- Measure the cost effectiveness of private sector partnering versus county service provision
- Describe how counties gain citizen support for partnering with the private sector
- Demonstrate successful partnering
- Respond to questions from attendees on specific areas of private sector partnering

Moderators:

- Ron Holifield, Principal, Governmental Relations Specialists, Quorum Health Resources, Inc., DeSoto, TX
- Roy Orr, Principal, Governmental Relations Specialists, Quorum Health Resources, Inc., DeSoto, TX

Panelists:

- Bob Green, Division Sr. Vice President, President, Quorum Health Resources, Inc., Brentwood, TN
- Don Stapley, Maricopa County Supervisor and Board Chairman of Maricopa Intergrated Health System, Maricopa County, AZ
- Mark Hillard, CEO of Maricopa Intergrated Health System, Maricopa, AZ
- Judge Van Knight, County Judge, Cheatam County, KY

G 13: Achieving Dial Tone: New Approaches to Procuring Local Phone Service

Governments have already learned how to procure long-distance services at dramatically lower cost—can the same be said about local service as well? Learn about new contracting arrangements that will get you there.

Panelists:

- Larry Irving, U.S. Department of Commerce, Washington, D.C.
- Dennis Fischer, General Services Administration, Fairfax, VA.
- Christina A. Polley, Deputy Director, Telecommunications Division, Department of General Services, State of California, Sacramento, CA
- John Doherty, Vice President for Government Markets, AT&T, Washington, DC
- Bailey Hartmeyer, Director, Federal Systems Group, Pacific Bell

G 14: Trends in the Global Health Care Industry
What will determine the size and character of the international health care services market in the years ahead? Find out from leading providers in each segment of the global industry.
Chair: Ronnie L. Goldberg, Senior Vice-President Policy & Program, U.S. Council for International Business, New York, NY
Panelists:
- Charles Bouchard, Executive Director, External Affairs, and Director, Center for European Government Affairs, Merck Sharp & Dohme, Brussels, Belgium
- Bruce Fried, Shaw Pittman Potts & Trowbridge, Washington, D.C.
- Jay H. Sanders, M.D., F.A.C.P., President and CEO, The Global Telemedicine Group, McLean, VA

A5: Classification Systems and Data Collection Methods
In order to keep track of trade and foreign direct investment in services and to provide the basis for designing priorities for the WTO-2000 negotiations, it is imperative that the collection and reporting of services data be improved. This is a matter both of devising acceptable international classification systems and improving ways in which the data are to be collected and published in both the industrialized and developing countries.
Chair: Harry Freeman, President, The Mark Twain Institute, Chevy Chase, MD
Panelists:
- Julian Arkell, Consultant, International Trade & Services Policy, Menorca, Spain, "The Draft Manual on Statistics of International Trade in Services."
- Guy Karsenty, Head, Trade in Services Section, Statistics Division, World Trade Organization, Geneva, Switzerland, "Just How Big Are the Stakes? An Assessment of Trade in Services by Mode of Supply."
- Hugo P. Lueders, Attorney-at-Law, Brussels, Belgium, "Service Classification Schemes: What Role for Manufacturing Services?"
- Chi M. Luk, Assistant Commissioner, Census & Statistics Department, The Government of the Hong Kong Special Administrative Region, Hong Kong, "Statistics on Service Industries in Hong Kong."
- Shaila Nijhowne, Director, Standards Division, Statistics Canada, Ottawa, Canada, and David Usher, Trade Policy Analyst, Department of Foreign Affairs and International Trade, Government of Canada, Ottawa, Canada, "Classification and the Measurement of Production and International Trade in Services."
- Obie Whichard, Assistant Chief, International Investment Division, Bureau of Economic Analysis, U.S. Department of Commerce,

Washington, D.C., "Measurement and Classification of Service Sector Activity: Data Needs for GATS 2000."

A8: Globalization and The City: Location of Services Activities
What are the factors that influence the location of services in particular countries and regions, and how do multinational corporations organize their production structures and decide on outsourcing of parts of these structures?
Chair: Wai-Kwan Chan, Secretary General, and Thinex Shek, Hong Kong Coalition of Service Industries and Hong Kong General Chamber of Commerce, Hong Kong
Panelists:

- Peter W. Daniels, Professor of Geography, Birmingham University, Birmingham, UK, "Globalization Producer Services, and the City: Is Asia a Special Case?"
- Alan V. Deardorff, Professor, Department of Economics, University of Michigan, Ann Arbor, MI, "Fragmentation and Outsourcing: Implications for the Location of Services Activities."

A11: Structuring Services 2000 for More Effective Results
There are several different options to be considered in structuring the WTO-2000 negotiations to help achieve a greater degree of liberalization than was accomplished in the Uruguay Round.
Chair: Joseph S. Papovich, Assistant United States Trade Representative, Services, Investment and Intellectual Property, Washington, D.C.
Panelists:

- Alison Burrows, Director, Services Trade & Negotiations, Department of Foreign Affairs & Trade, Government of Australia, Barton, Australia, and Francisco Javier Prieto, General Directorate for International Economic Affairs, Ministry of Foreign Affairs, Republic of Chile, "Chile and Australia GATS 2OOO: Towards Effective Liberalization of Trade In Services, Proposals For Action."
- Simon J. Evenett, Rutgers University, The Brookings Institution and CEPR, and Bernard M. Hoekman, Principal Trade Economist, Development Research Group, The World Bank, Washington, D.C., "Government Procurement of Services: Assessing the Case for Multilateral Disciplines."
- M. Teresa Fernández, Associate Professor, and Miguel A. Díaz Mier, Professor of Institutional Economics, University of Alcalá and Servilab, Madrid, Spain, "Foreign Direct Investment in Services is Demanding a Multilateral Agreement"
- Stuart Harbinson, Permanent Representative of the Hong Kong Special Administrative Region of China to the World Trade Organization and Chairman, World Trade Organization Council on

Trade in Services, "Focus and Priorities of New Round of Services Negotiations."
- Pascal P. Kerneis, Managing Director, European Services Network (ESN), for Tillman E. Prinz, Legal Advisor, Bund Deutscher Architekten BDA, Berlin, Germany, "GATS 2000 and Public Procurement."
- Allison Marie Young, Dalhousie University, Canadian Department of Foreign Affairs and International Trade, Ottawa, Canada, "Labor Mobility and the GATS. Where Next?"

A15: Establishing Pro-Competitive Regulatory Regimes Through Services Negotiations

Trade and foreign direct investment in services are subject to a variety of border and especially domestic regulations that inhibit these transactions. It is therefore crucial to consider how regulatory regimes can be adapted to achieve liberalization objectives.

Panelists:
- Byung-il Choi, Ewha Woman's University, Seoul, Republic of Korea, "Making the GATS More Pro-Competitive."
- Pierre Sauvé, John F. Kennedy School of Government, Harvard University, Cambridge, MA, and Christopher Wilkie, Administrator, Directorate for Financial, Fiscal and Enterprise Affairs, OECD, Paris, France, "Exploring Approaches to Investment Liberalization in the GATS."

The Services Marketplace in the Next Millennium.

Luncheon Chair

David Hunter, Worldwide Managing Partner, Global Marketing Unit, Andersen Consulting

Luncheon Address

Frederick W. Smith, Chairman and Chief Executive Officer, FDX Corporation

Concurrent Sessions

BOF 7: Creating the Infrastructure for Your Global Electronic Business: Establishing the Telecommunications and Platform Infrastructure

Even in advanced markets sophisticated telecommunications and platform services are an essential component of doing business electronically. What do you need to know and where do you turn for advice and solutions? How can you best work with established and new providers? What is the role of the newer companies offering innovative, enhanced services?

Chair: Jack Pellicci, Vice President, Oracle Service Industries. Reston. VA

Panelists:
- Oscar A. Bazoberry, Founder & President, World Data, Inc.
- Vineet Nayyar, Chief Executive Officer, HCL International, India
- Richard Simpson, Director General, Industry Canada, Ottawa, Canada

Background Papers/Resources:
- W. Kenneth Lindhorst, International Vice President, AT&T, Basking Ridge, NJ "Infrastructure: Setting the Groundwork for Electronic Commerce."
- Richard Simpson, Director General, Industry Canada, Ottawa, Canada, "Infrastructure Requirements for Electronic Commerce."

BOF 8: Hong Kong: Headquartering Your Services Business in "Asia's Service Center"

What are the advantages and disadvantages of establishing your regional operations in Hong Kong? Hong Kong's recent efforts and policies to transform itself into Asia's services hub.

Chair: Stanley Ko, Chairman, Hong Kong Coalition of Service Industries, and Director, Jardine Pacific Limited, Hong Kong

Panelists:
- Richard Pyvis, Chief Operating Officer, Credit Lyonnais Securities (Asia) Ltd., Hong Kong
- Alan Wong, Director, Services Promotion, Hong Kong Trade Development Council, Hong Kong.

Background Papers/Resources
- Richard Pyvis, Chief Operating Officer, Credit Lyonnais Securities (Asia) Ltd., Hong Kong, "Asian Recovery and Public Sector Privatization: Hong Kong's Role as Financial Service Centre."
- Alan Wong, Director, Services Promotion, Hong Kong Trade Development Council, Hong Kong, "Hong Kong At Your Service."
- Robin Wong, Center Director, MDC, Hong Kong, "Setting Up a Business Start-Up Centre in Hong Kong."

G16: Local Government Contracting: Banding Together to Create New Market Power

Local governments around the country are banding together to create contracts that are national in scale, with all the attendant benefits for both sides. Of interest to all government procurement officials and the vendors who work with them.

Panelists:
- Monica Luechtefeld, Vice President, Contract Marketing & Sales Administration Office Depot Business Services, Delray Beach, FL
- Duane Meek, President, Nationwide Retirement Solutions, Inc., Columbus. OH

- Steven Swendiman, Managing Director, NACo Financial Services Center, Washington, D.C.
- Chrys Varnes, Director, Product Marketing, Commerce One, Walnut Creek CA

G17: Restructuring Structures: New Approaches to Procuring Architects and Engineers

Architects, consulting engineers, and construction companies are reorganizing themselves to integrate their services into complete packages, allowing governments to determine how they wish to manage construction projects. Learn what these firms now offer and how to work with these service providers most effectively.

Panelists:

- Fred Berger, Vice-President, Louis Berger and Associates, Washington, D.C
- Felix L. Martinez, Director, Procurement and Federal Markets, American Consulting Engineers Council (ACEC), Washington, DC
- John Miller, Massachusetts Institute of Technology, Department of Civil and Environmental Engineering, Cambridge, MA
- Donald R. Trim, Chairman, Wade-Trim Group, Taylor, MI

G18: Heroes of Reinvention: People Who Have Made a Difference

The personal experiences success stories in Government Reinvention. Award-winning men and women discuss their successes in reinventing key government programs.

Panelists:

- Patricia McGinnis, President & CEO, Center for Excellence in Government, Washington, D.C.
- Nancy Bienia, Special Assistant for Systems, Division of Program Operations, Office of Child Support Enforcement, Washington, D.C.

G 19: Promoting Service Exports: How Government Can Help

Building competitive advantages in services. What do governments need to do? These are the successful stories.

Chair: Lloyd Downey, Manager, National Services Export, Australian Trade Commission (Austrade), Sydney, Australia

Panelists:

- Rodolfo Martinez, President, Union Argentina de Entidades de Servicios (UDES), Buenos Aires, Argentina
- Awilda Marquez, Assistant Secretary & Director General, U.S. & Foreign Commercial Service, U.S. Department of Commerce, Washington, D.C.

A7: Regional Service Sector Negotiations: Impact on the GATS
Services negotiations undertaken in the context of regional trade agreements
may have accomplished considerably more liberalization of trade and foreign
direct investment in services as compared to the GATS multilateral process.
The question then is how the regional negotiations may inform and improve
the conduct and results of the WTO-2000 services negotiations.
Chair: John Richardson, Deputy Head of Mission, Delegation of the
           European Commission, Washington, D.C.
Panelists:
- Jeffrey H. Bergstrand, Associate Professor, College of Business,
  University of Notre Dame, Notre Dame, IN, "International Trade in
  Goods and Services and Regional Free Trade Agreements."
- Sherry M. Stephenson, Principal Trade Specialist, Organization of
  American States Trade Unit, Washington, D.C., "Regional
  Agreements on Services and Multilateral Disciplines: Interpreting and
  Applying GATS Article V."
- Francisco Javier Prieto, Former Chair, FTAA Working Group on
  Services, and Consultant, Ministry of Foreign Affairs, Chile, and
  Sherry M. Stephenson, Principal Trade Specialist, Organization of
  American States Trade Unit, Washington, D.C., "Multilateral and
  Regional Liberalization of Trade in Services"
- Julio César Canamasas, Adviser, Office of Strategic Projects, Cabinet
  of Ministers, and Permanent Secretary, Board of Architecture,
  Agronomy, Geology and Engineering Professional Entities for
  Mercosur Integration (CIAM); Eduardo Volman, Architect,
  (Argentina), Maria Teresa Pino, Engineer (Paraguay), Henrique
  Ludovice, Engineer (Brazil), Marcos Bigatti, Engineer (Uruguay),
  Members of the Executive Committe of the Board of Architecture,
  Agronomy, Geology and Engineering Professional Entities for
  Mercosur Integration (CIAM), Buenos Aires, Argentina,
  "Harmonization of Requirements in the Architecture, Engineering
  and Agronomic Services Sector in Mercosur Region (GATS's
  Articles VI and VII)."

A12: Negotiating Priorities: The Stakes for Developing Countries
Most developing countries made limited concessions to reduce services
barriers in the Uruguay Round GATS negotiations. It is important to identify
what liberalization benefits the developing countries may realize in the WTO-
2000, and the problems that they may encounter in devising effective
negotiating strategies.

Chair: Gautam S. Kaji, Chairman, The Centennial Group, Washington, D.C., and former Managing Director, The World Bank, Washington, D.C.

Panelists:

- Rudolph Adlung, Economic Counselor, Trade in Services Division, World Trade Organization, Geneva, Switzerland, "The Political Economy of Adjusting to Services Trade Liberalization: Developed and Developing Country Perspectives."
- Ann Main, Director, Services Trade Negotiations, Office of the U.S. Trade Representative, Washington, D.C.
- Amrita Narlikar, Balliol College, Oxford University, Oxford, UK, "Negotiating Priorities for Developing Countries: Identifying State Interests and Possible Coalition Alignments."

A14: Forecasting Trade in Services: New Approaches

It is essential in planning business strategies and in formulating economic policies to devise systems to track services trade and make forecasts of future values of this trade. This can be done for both services exports and imports in the aggregate as well as for the major disaggregated services categories.

Chair: Harry Freeman, President, The Mark Twain Institute, Chevy Chase, MD

Panelist:

- Alan V. Deardorff, Saul H. Hymans, Robert M. Stern, and Chong Xiang, Professors, Department of Economics, University of Michigan, Ann Arbor, MI, "Forecasting U.S. Trade in Services."

Reception and Congress Dinner

The World Trade Organization: Shaping the Services Global Marketplace

Dinner Chair

Dean R. O'Hare, Chair, World Services Congress

Video Address

Michael Moore, Director-General, World Trade Organization

Concluding Remarks

David Hartridge, Director, Trade in Services Division, World Trade Organization

Wednesday November 3

BOF 10: India After the Elections: A Roundtable Discussion on Implications and Opportunities for Global Services Providers
Emerging in the autumn from another round of changes in political leadership, what realistic expectations are there for renewed emphasis and action on privatization, competition, and open markets? Leaders from India's private and government sectors will provide timely insights and guidance to the 'new' business climate in the world's second largest market.
Panelists:
- Michael Clark, Executive Director, U.S.-India Business Council, Washington, D.C.
- Vineet Nayyar, Chief Executive Officer, HCL International, India

Background Papers/Resources:
- Rajesh Chadha, Advisor, National Council of Applied Economic Research, New Delhi, India, "GATS and Developing Countries: A Case Study of India."
- K. Elumalai Kuppan, Professor, Vaikunth Mehta National Institute of Cooperative Management, Pune, India, "Impact of Financial Sector Reforms – The Indian Experience Case Study."

BOF 11: The Promise of Electronic Commerce for Developing Countries and Small and Medium Size Companies: A Roundtable Discussion
Electronic Commerce creates a level playing field for small and medium size corporations and developing countries. Electronic commerce reduces market entry barriers and increases access to markets previously unpenetrated. Professionals from developing countries can sell services in developed markets, while manufacturing industries and farmers can export with lower distribution costs. With e-commerce small and medium size companies can also develop economies of scale!
Chair: Claudio Garcia, Vice President, Banco, and Director, Santiago Chamber of Commerce, Santiago, Chile
Panelists:
- Edward Alexander, Director, Management Information Systems, Grace, Kennedy & Co. Ltd., Kingston, Jamaica
- Rodolfo Martinez, President, Union of Service Companies, Buenos Aires, Argentina
- Allen Miller, Executive Director Global Government Affairs, EDS, Washington D.C.
- Luigi Nese, President, Federated Services of the State of San Paulo, Brazil
- Robert Shagawat, Director of E-Commerce, Atlantic Duncans International (India), Chantilly, VA

- Thomas Tang, Executive Director, Hong Kong Productivity Council, Hong Kong, "E-Commerce for Business Excellence in Hong Kong and China."
- Vijay Thadni, President, NIIT Ltd., (India)
- Nicole Williams, Senior Consultant, Services-Growth Consultants, Canada

BOF 13: Building Consumer Confidence On-line and How to Protect Free Flows of Critical Business Information

What confidence building practices should your firm adopt to attract and retain on-line consumers? Review of the most advanced technological solutions and business practices to protect data privacy and build consumer confidence on-line.

Chair: Bill N. Poulos, Director, Electronic Commerce Policy, Office of Government Affairs, EDS, Washington, D.C.

Panelists:

- Madhu Ankarath, Vice President, SRA Systems Ltd., Atlanta, GA
- Joseph Griffin, Partner, PricewaterhouseCoopers for WebTrust, Atlanta, GA
- Robert Lewin, Executive Director, TRUSTe, Cupertino, CA
- Patrick Taylor, Vice President Risk Assessment, Internet Security Systems, Atlanta, Georgia
- Reid Watts, Vice President, Research & Advanced Technology, NCR, Inc., Washington, D.C.

BPF 7: Services in the Asia Pacific Basin

Services markets in East Asia and the Pacific Basin have been shaken by the economic crisis in the region. How can the efforts in APEC and the WTO 2000 Negotiations help overcome obstacles to the development of services markets in the region?

Chair: Roberto de Ocampo, Senior Advisor, SGV & Company/Arthur Andersen, Manila, The Philippines

Panelists:

- Koichi Danno, Executive Vice President, Mitsibishi Research Institute, Tokyo, Japan
- Brant Free, Senior Vice President of International External Affairs, The Chubb Corporation, Washington, D. C.
- Judith King, Chief Executive Officer, Australian Services Network, Melbourne, Australia
- Kwok-Chuen Kwok, Chief Economist NE Asia, Standard Chartered Bank, Hong Kong

G20: Reinventing State Government Through Technology

Adventurous state governments are using new disciplines to reorganize the way they procure and deploy information technology. Of vital interest to state and local procurement officials and the vendors who work with them in this crucial area.

Panelists:

- John B. Thomasian, Director, NGA Center for Best Practices, National Governors' Association, Washington, D.C.
- Martin I. Cole, Managing Partner, Americas State Government, Andersen Consulting, Hartford, CT

G 21: Building a National Strategy for Health Services Exports: What Governments Must Do

How can the health services industry work with government to improve its penetration of world markets?

Chair: Ernest Plock, Ph.D., International Trade Specialist for Health Care, Office of Service Industries, U.S. Department of Commerce, Washington, D.C.

Panelists:

- J. Michael Fitzmaurice, Ph.D., Senior Science Advisor, Agency for Health Care Policy & Research, U. S. Department of Health and Human Services, Rockville, MD
- Paul Maiden, Ph.D., Associate Professor, University of Central Florida, Orlando, FL
-

G 22: Sustainability and Local Government Participation in the New World Economy

In the new era of economic competitiveness, local governments can no longer afford to be spectators. As advances in technology and communications have accelerated, the characteristics that businesses and investors are seeking from their host communities have changed. In this era, rapid growth and expansion are not necessarily viewed as positive characteristics either to potential business investors, or to the citizens of a given community. Today, quality of life issues dominate the landscape, and those communities which can best demonstrate that they posses the characteristics which ensure that higher quality of life hold the competitive advantage.

In this session county leaders will discuss opportunities and challenges to local competitiveness in new economy. In particular, they will discuss how the development of *sustainable communities*, which promote economic development, social stability, and environmental stewardship as equal partners, is a vital component to assuring a high quality of life for its citizens and the long-term health of a region.

During this session, panelist will provide answers and insights on the following subjects:

- Why creating sustainable communities that reflect a balanced commitment to economic prosperity, environmental stewardship, and social stability enhance a region's attractiveness and competitiveness in the new economy.
- How developing City/County, and regional partnerships strengthen communities in a range of areas, from increasing global competitiveness, to mitigating the effects of disasters
- Why the redevelopment of brownfields is a high priority as a means of community revitalization, and curbing unwanted sprawl; and
- What some of the challenges and obstacles are that communities face in strengthening their position in the new economy, and what can be done to overcome them.

Chair: Nick Keller, Co-Director, Joint Center for Sustainable Communities, National Association of Counties, Washington, D.C.
Panelists:
- Michael Hightower, County Commissioner, Fulton County, GA, and Past President, National Association of Counties
- Jean Jacobson, County Executive, Racine County, WI
- Chris Hart, County Commissioner, Hillsborough County, FL
- Robert Dowling, County Commissioner, Calhoun County, AL

G 23 Building a Web Enabled Government
Governments at all levels are using technology, specifically web technologies, to reorganize the way they do business, from web-enabled procurement to web-enabled public service delivery. Understanding the changes involved in this crucial area is key to success in working with IT and procurement officials and the vendors who work with them.
Chair: J. Thomas Hennessey, Jr., Ph.D., Mason Enterprise Center, George Mason University, Fairfax, VA.

A 1: Assessing the GATS: Has it Worked? What are the Flaws?
The negotiation of the GATS during the Uruguay Round was a milestone in recognizing the importance of services issues in the multilateral trading system. This session will address the successes and failures of the implementation of the GATS and provide insights into issues to be addressed in the WTO-2000 services negotiations.
Chair: David Hartridge, Director Service Division, World Trade Organization, Geneva, Switzerland

Panelists:

- Geza Feketekuty, Director, Center for Trade & Commercial Diplomacy, Monterey Institute of International Studies, Monterey, CA, "Market Structure and GATS-Based Liberalization"
- Joseph Francois, Professor, Erasmus University, Rotterdam, The Netherlands, and Ian Wooton, Glasgow University, Department of Economics, Glasgow, Scotland, "Implementation and Surveillance of the GATS Agreements."
- Neela Mukherjee, Consultant, New Delhi, India, "Market Access Commitments under GATS in the WTO: An Analysis of Horizontal Commitments from Developing Countries' Perspective."
- Christopher F. Thornberg, Assistant Professor, and Frances L. Edwards, Economics Department, Clemson University, Clemson, SC, "Determinants of Services Trade Liberalization: A Study of the GATS Negotiations."
- Sahar Tohamy, Egyptian Centre for Economic Studies, Cairo, Egypt, "Case Study of Egypt's Regulatory and Other Services Barriers and Implementation of the GATS Agreements."

A 16: Services Contributions to Economic Growth: Country Experiences

This session deals with case studies of the role of services in the growth and development of a variety of countries.

Chair: Vince FitzGerald, Executive Director, The Allen Consulting Group, Melbourne, Australia

Panelists:

- Gianni A. Carbonaro, Senior Economist, European Investment Bank, Kirchberg, Luxembourg, "Providing Infrastructure Services Through Efficient Risk Sharing: Insights From European Experiences."
- Fuad Cassim, Senior Lecturer, University of Witwatersrand, Department of Economics, Johannesburg, South Africa "Labor and Services in South Africa."
- Alexandra Fenzl, and Robert L. Goldman, Aspect Development, Basingstoke, Hampshire, UK, "Moving from Strategic Planning to Contingency Planning"
- Meelis Kitsing, Consultant, Mercuri International, Estonia, "Service Sector's Contribution to the City of Tallinn."
- Hildegun K. Nordas, Research Director, Michelsen Institute, Bergen, Norway, "How Liberalization of Trade in Services May Help Conserve Natural Resources."
- Joal Teitelbaum, Civil Engineer, EEJT/CCIBC-RS, Porto Alegre, Brazil, "Services: Public-Private Co-Operation at a World in Transition."
- Konstantin N. Todradze, Senior Researcher, Technion-Israel Institute of Technology, Haifa, Israel, "The Urgent Need to Restore Scientific

Activities in the Republic of Georgia as a Lever for Its Socioeconomic Development."

A 17: Modeling the Economic Effects of Barriers to Services Trade and FDI

Using available data on trade and foreign direct investment in services for the major industrializing and developing countries together with estimates of the barriers that exist, it is possible to devise numerical models that will provide estimates of how services liberalization will affect national and global economic welfare as well as sectoral production, trade, and the movement of capital and labor in individual countries.

Panelists:

- Drusilla K. Brown, Associate Professor, Department of Economics, Tufts University, Medford, MA, and Robert M. Stern, Professor, Department of Economics & School of Public Policy, University of Michigan, Ann Arbor, MI, "Modeling the Economic Effects of Trade and Investment Barriers in Services
- Philippa S. Dee, Assistant Commissioner, and Kevin Hanslow, Productivity Commission, Government of Australia, Belconnen, Australia, "Multilateral Liberalization of Services Trade."

Plenary Session

The Role of Government in the Age of Knowledge

Experts and business leaders discuss what governments can do and how they can do it better: from lessons in privatization and outsourcing to new regulatory and institutional developments and new technologies that are shaping the role of government in the information age.

Introductory Remarks

Everett Ehrlich, President, ESC Co., and Former United States Under Secretary of Commerce for Economic Affairs

Public and Private Sector Partnerships—New Models of Service Delivery in the Age of Knowledge.

David Hunter, Worldwide Managing Partner, Global Marketing Unit, Andersen Consulting

Comments

- David Barran, Administrator, General Services Administration, United States of America
- Steve Kelman, John F. Kennedy School of Government, Harvard University

Different Perspectives on the Future of Government
- Maynard Jackson, Chairman Emeritus, National Association of Security Professionals, and Chairman of the Board, Jackson Securities.

Closing Remarks
Dean R. O'Hare, Chair, World Services Congress

Contributors

Keith Acheson

Keith Acheson is Professor of Economics at Carleton University in Ottawa. His research has addressed organizational and policy issues of central-bank operations, government-purchasing arrangements, alcoholic-beverage distribution, international and regional economic governance, and the retail and wholesale industries. For the past decade, he and Christopher Maule have published a number of articles and a book, *Much Ado about Culture,* which deals with North American trade disputes concerning the economic organization and policies related to the cultural industries.

Scott L. Baier

Scott L. Baier is an Assistant Professor of Finance and Business Economics at the University of Notre Dame where he has taught since 1996. He received his Ph.D. in economics in 1996 from Michigan State University. His research interests include growth and development, international trade, international monetary policy coordination, and fiscal policy's effect on growth and welfare. At Notre Dame, he teaches business conditions analysis and international finance.

Jeffrey H. Bergstrand

Jeffrey H. Bergstrand is Associate Professor of Finance and Business Economics at the University of Notre Dame. He received his B.A. in Economics and Political Science from Northwestern University in 1974, and his Ph.D. in Economics from the University of Wisconsin at Madison in 1981. From 1981-86, he was an economist at the Federal Reserve Bank of Boston. In 1986, he joined the faculty of the College of Business Administration at Notre Dame. His research on exchange rates, international trade flows, international finance, and open-economy macroeconomics has been published in leading journals and conference volumes. Since 1996, he has been a coeditor of the *Review of International Economics.*

Barry Bosworth

Barry Bosworth has been a Senior Fellow in the Economic Studies Program at The Brookings Institution in Washington, D.C. since 1979 and served as Research Associate from 1971-77. He was Director of the President's Council on Wage and Price Stability,1977-79; Visiting Lecturer at the University of California, Berkeley, 1974-75; and Assistant Processor, Harvard University, 1969-71. He received his Ph.D. from the University of Michigan in 1969. His research has concentrated on issues of capital formation and saving behavior. His current projects include a study of the Social Security system and an examination of capital flows to developing countries.

Alison Burrows

Alison Burrows is the Director of the Services Trade and Negotiations Section in the Australian Department of Foreign Affairs and Trade (DFAT). She was educated at the University of Sydney. She has worked in a number of trade policy areas in DFAT. Her most recent posting was to Manila to work on APEC. Her other postings have been to Suva, where she covered South Pacific Forum issues and managed an aid program, and to Rome, where she analyzed EU developments. She has also worked in the Australian Department of the Prime Minister and Cabinet.

Rajesh Chadha

Rajesh Chadha is Reader in the Department of Economics, Hindu College, University of Delhi, and Honorary Advisor to the National Council of Applied Economic Research, New Delhi. He obtained his M.A. in Business Economics from the University of Delhi in 1976 and Ph.D. in Industrial Economics and Modeling from the Indian Institute of Technology, New Delhi, in 1984. His current interests include issues relating to international trade and CGE modeling. Since 1993, he has collaborated with Robert M. Stern and Alan V. Deardorff of the Michigan Department of Economics on research analyzing the impact of unilateral and multilateral trade policy reforms on the Indian economy.

Peter F. Cowhey

Peter Cowhey is Professor at the Graduate School of International Relations and Pacific Studies at the University of California, San Diego. He is also Director of the University of California's Institute on Global Conflict and Cooperation. He is the author of numerous works on international trade and on the global communications industry. He is former Chief of the International Bureau of the Federal Communications Commission and a member of the U.S. negotiating team for the WTO Agreement on Basic Telecommunications Services.

Peter W. Daniels

Peter W. Daniels is Professor of Geography and Director, Service Sector Research Unit, School of Geography and Environmental Sciences, The University of Birmingham, UK. He has published articles and books on the location and development of office activities and on the emergence of service industries as key agents in metropolitan and regional restructuring at the national and international scale. His books include *Services and Metropolitan Development* (1991), *Service Industries in the World Economy* (1993), *The Global Economy in Transition* (with B. Lever, 1996), *Services in the Global Economy, Vols. I and II* (with J. R. Bryson, 1998). A book on *Services in the New Economy* (with J. R. Bryson and B. Ward, 2002) is in progress. He was recently President of the European Research Network on Services and Space (RESER).

Alan V. Deardorff

Alan V. Deardorff is John W. Sweetland Professor of International Economics and Professor of Public Policy at the University of Michigan. He received his Ph.D. in economics from Cornell University in 1971 and has been on the faculty at the University of Michigan since 1970. He served as Chair of the Department of Economics from 1991 to 1995. He has also served as a consultant to many government agencies and is currently on the editorial boards of the journals *World Economy, Journal of International Economics*, the *International Trade Journal*, and the *Journal of International Economic Law*. He is co-author, with Robert M. Stern, of *The Michigan Model of World Production and Trade* and *Computational Analysis of Global Trading Arrangements*. He has published numerous articles on various aspects of international trade theory and policy. His current research interests include: the interactions between trade patterns and economic growth, the causes and effects of fragmentation, and the appropriate use of trade policies for issues of economic inequality, including labor standards and child labor.

Philippa Dee

Philippa Dee has been Assistant Commissioner at the Productivity Commission (formerly Industry Commission) since 1991. There she has worked on a wide range of economic-policy issues, from evaluating Australia's greenhouse gas, R&D, telecommunications and competition policies to evaluating the effects of multilateral Uruguay and APEC trade liberalization. Her research contribution to this volume was the result of a three year collaborative project with the Australian National University and the University of Adelaide designed to measure and evaluate barriers to services trade. She has also been a Senior Research Fellow at the Australian National University and research economist at the Kiel Institute of World Economics. She was educated at Victoria and Canterbury Universities in New Zealand and at Simon Fraser University in Canada.

Joseph F. Francois

Joseph F. Francois is a professor of economics at the Erasmus University in Rotterdam, where he holds a chair in political economy and international development. He is also a research fellow of the Tinbergen Institute and the Centre for Economic Policy Research, and the director of the European Trade Study Group. He was a research economist with the WTO/GATT during the close of the Uruguay Round, and was also past chief of research and acting director of economics with the U.S. International Trade Commission. He has published extensively in academic journals and books on international trade, international economic policy, global and regional integration, and their links to growth and development.

Kevin Hanslow

Kevin Hanslow studied mathematics at the University of New South Wales and the University of Sydney, and economics at the Australian National University. His recent work has included developing the Productivity Commission's FTAP model for analyzing the liberalization of trade in services. Previous projects include the development of ABARE's MEGABARE (now GTEM) model for the analysis of greenhouse issues. He has an interest in incorporating policy relevant, non-standard features in CGE models, and has examined such extensions as game theoretic effects, induced innovations, and labor-market adjustment costs.

James Hodge

James Hodge is currently a Lecturer in the School of Economics at the University of Cape Town, South Africa. He has previously worked for Andersen Consulting and the Development Policy Research Unit (University of Cape Town). He has been co-ordinating research in South Africa aimed at preparing the Department of Trade and Industry for future WTO trade negotiations on services. This research has focused on both the broad trade and development impact of service liberalization, and also on the particular issues facing specific sectors. Other areas of research include the dynamics of economic growth and services development, services in the context of regional integration, and regulation in a globalized economy.

Saul H. Hymans

Saul H. Hymans is Professor of Economics and Statistics and Director of the Research Seminar in Quantitative Economics (RSQE) at the University of Michigan. He has been at Michigan since 1964. He holds a Ph.D. in economics and an M.A. in statistics from the University of California, Berkeley. He served as senior staff economist on the President's Council of Economic Advisors in 1967-68 and has been a member of a number of government advisory panels and consultant to several business enterprises. He is the author of numerous journal articles, chapters, and research papers dealing with macroeconometric forecasting and a variety of other topics.

Gerrishon K. Ikiara

Gerrishon K. Ikiara is a Senior Lecturer in Economics at the University of Nairobi where he has taught in both the Department of Economics and the Institute of Diplomacy and International Studies (IDIS). He has researched and published widely on the Kenyan and African economies with special focus on industrialization, international development cooperation, international trade and services. He has served as the coordinator of Kenya's Coordinated African Programme of Assistance on Services (CAPAS) study team since 1992.

Mikhail Klimenko

Mikhail Klimenko joined the faculty of the Graduate School of International Relations and Pacific Studies at UCSD in 1996. He has master's degrees from Brown University and Stanford University and a Ph.D. in business from Stanford University's Graduate School of Business. He specializes in international trade, high technology, the telecommunications industry, and the economics of transition in East Europe and Russia.

Catherine L. Mann

Catherine L. Mann is a Senior Fellow at the Institute for International Economics. She published in July 2000, *Global Electronic Commerce: A Policy Primer*, co-authored with Sue E. Eckert and Sarah Cleeland Knight. The Primer examines the economic and policy prerequisites for and implications of the Internet and electronic commerce. Her last book, published in September 1999, was *Is the U.S. Trade Deficit Sustainable?* Previous to the Institute, she held several posts at the Federal Reserve Board of Governors, was on the staff of the President's Council of Economic Advisors, and worked for the Chief Economist of the World Bank. She received her Ph.D. in Economics from the Massachusetts Institute of Technology and her undergraduate degree is from Harvard University.

Christopher Maule

Christopher Maule is Research Professor of Economics and International Affairs at Carleton University in Ottawa. His research has addressed issues of industrial organization, foreign investment and international trade. Past publications have dealt with competition policy and with multinational corporations and government policies. For the past decade, he has collaborated with Keith Acheson in research on the economic organization of the cultural industries with particular attention to trade, investment and intellectual-property-rights policies.

Nanno Mulder

Nanno Mulder was educated in economics at the University of Groningen (M.A. and Ph.D.) and joined the CEPII (Centre for International Economics, French Planning Agency) in Paris in 1996. Most of his research deals with international comparisons of productivity in the service sector and economic growth: until 1996 as part of the ICOP-research programme at the Groningen Growth and Development Centre and presently as part of CEPII. Mulder's previous work focused mostly on Latin America, but at present he also works on European countries. He has been a consultant to the Economic Commission for Latin America and the Caribbean (ECLAC), the European Commission, and the French Ministry of Transport. Currently Mulder is also responsible for a global database on GDP, services trade and balance of payments (CHELEM).

Moses Muriira

Moses Muriira is a lecturer in the School of Environmental Studies (SES), Moi University, Kenya. He obtained his Ph.D. in Environmental and Natural Resource Economics at the University of Amsterdam, in 1999. Previously, he had obtained a Bsc. in Agriculture and M.A. in Economics from the University of Nairobi. He has been a member of the Kenyan CAPAS study team since 1992. His research interests include fisheries management, environmental/natural resource problems, trade in services, and tourism.

Amrita Narlikar

Amrita Narlikar is a Junior Research Fellow in International Relations at St. John's College, Oxford. She obtained her M.A. degree from the School of International Studies, Jawaharlal Nehru University (1994-96), and M.Phil. in International Relations from Balliol College, Oxford (1996-98). She has recently completed her doctoral dissertation at Oxford. Her current interests pertain to issues of international political economy and the international relations of developing countries.

Abdoulaye Ndiaye

Abdoulaye Ndiaye is an international consultant and researcher in Entrepreneurship, Management, Private Sector Development and ITC in Western, Eastern and Central Africa. He has performed many research, training and consulting activities in ITC, E-commerce and GATS throughout African countries. After his post-graduate degree in Banking (DESS) at the University of Paris Rene Descartes in 1980, he became General Manager in a group of SMEs in Senegal for three years. He later joined a Regional Management training institution (CESAG) based in Dakar as a Professor of International Trade and Director of Research, Consulting and Entrepreneurship. As a Research Team Leader, he has conducted many surveys in GATS through the Coordinated African Programme of Assistance on Services (CAPAS) sponsored by the UNDP. Since 1992, he has been consultant, trainer and researcher for the World Bank in many African countries in the field of telecommunications reforms and policy, privatization, and has worked with the World Bank Institute in disseminating research results in WTO negotiations.

Wilfred Nyangena

Wilfred Nyangena is a Lecturer in Economics at the University of Nairobi, Kenya, where he received both B.A. and M.A. degrees. Currently, he is a doctoral candidate at Gothenburg University, Sweden, and a member of the CAPAS (Kenya) study team. His research interests include environment, growth and development issues.

Francisco Javier Prieto

Francisco Javier Prieto did his undergraduate studies in Business Administration at the Catholic University of Valparaíso-Chile, and later did graduate work in economics at Indiana University. He has held positions at the OAS and ECLAC and been a consultant on services issues to international organizations and governments. He has published several works on issues of services and economic development as well as trade in services. He is currently Professor of Economics and former Director of the Graduate School at the Institute for International Studies, University of Chile, Santiago.

Robert M. Stern

Robert M. Stern is Professor of Economics and Public Policy (Emeritus) at the University of Michigan. He received his Ph.D. in economics from Columbia University in 1958. He was a Fulbright scholar in the Netherlands in 1958-59, taught at Columbia University for two years, and joined the faculty at the University of Michigan in 1961. He has been an active contributor to international economic research and policy for more than four decades. He has published numerous papers and books on a wide variety of topics, including international commodity problems, export-led growth, quantitative international economics, the determinants of comparative advantage, price behavior in international trade, balance-of-payments policies, the computer modeling of international trade and trade policies, trade and labor standards, and services liberalization. He has been a consultant to and done research under the auspices of several U.S. Government agencies and international and regional organizations. He is currently working with Drusilla Brown (Tufts University) and Alan Deardorff on the computational modeling and analysis of multilateral and regional trade liberalization, assessment of the post-1991 liberalization of economic policies in India, issues in U.S.-Japan international economic relations, and issues of child labor and international labor standards.

Sahar Tohamy

Sahar Tohamy is currently an Associate Principal Economist at the Egyptian Center for Economic Studies (ECES), which she first joined as a Senior Economist in 1997, after receiving her Ph.D. in Economics from Emory University. With ECES, she has designed and implemented economic research on a wide range of topics including public finance, privatization, development economics, and public choice. Foremost among her most recent undertakings is a project in collaboration with the Egyptian Ministries of Economy and Tourism and the Federation of Chambers of Tourism that aims to define tourism's contributions to Egypt's GDP.

Jack Triplett

Jack Triplett is a Visiting Fellow at the Brookings Institution, in Washington, D.C. His current research concerns productivity in health, finance and other services industries, with a focus on developing improved measures of output for these notably difficult to measure sectors of the economy. He serves as a consultant to international organizations and to the statistical agencies of a number of countries on issues of economic measurement and economic statistics. From 1985 to 1997, he was Chief Economist, U.S. Bureau of Economic Analysis. From 1971 to 1985, he held positions at the U.S. Bureau of Labor Statistics. In 1979, he was Assistant Director for Price Monitoring at the

Council on Wage and Price Stability. Before his government positions, he taught economics at Washington University (St. Louis) and the University of Oregon. He has written extensively on problems of economic measurement, including price indexes, national accounts, capital stock and labor input, and productivity and technical change. He holds A.B., M.A., and Ph.D. degrees from the University of California, Berkeley.

Obie G. Whichard

Obie G. Whichard is Assistant Chief of the International Investment Division of the Bureau of Economic Analysis (BEA), U.S Department of Commerce. Since the mid-1980s, he has been involved in BEA's program to improve and expand U.S. Government data on international trade and investment in ser-vices. He has participated in several OECD meetings on trade-in-services sta-tistics and has consulted with the Task Force on Statistics of International Trade in Services on its project to produce an international manual on trade-in-services statistics. He holds a Ph.D. in economics from the University of North Carolina, and prior to joining BEA, he was on the economics faculty of the University of Georgia.

R. Brian Woodrow

R. Brian Woodrow is Professor of Political Science at the University of Guelph in Ontario, Canada. Holding a Ph.D in Political Economy from the University of Toronto, he has focused his research and teaching primarily on topics related to international trade, telecommunications and insurance issues and on Canadian government and public policy. Since the late 1980s, he has been associated with the Geneva Association, and particularly the Applied Services Economic Centre, a group of researchers who have monitored and analyzed developments across the services industries. He has written specifi-cally on various issues of relevance to the world insurance services industry, including information technology, regulatory, and trade in services issues, and has published articles in the *Geneva Papers on Risk and Insurance* and other journals and edited collections.

Ian Wooton

Ian Wooton has been the Bonar-Macfie Professor of Economics at the Univer-sity of Glasgow since 1995, having previously been an Associate Professor at the University of Western Ontario. He is also a Research Fellow of the Centre for Economic Policy Research, and a director of the European Trade Study Group. His major interests in international trade are: the theory of preferential trading, economic integration and the European Union; international factor mobility, foreign direct investment and the location of economic activity; environment policies and international trade. He has published in a wide range of academic journals and edited volumes and serves as an Associate Editor of the *Journal of International Economics*.

Chong Xiang

Chong Xiang is currently pursuing a Ph.D. degree in economics at the University of Michigan, Ann Arbor.